AMERICAN LEGAL REALISM AND

EMPIRICAL SOCIAL SCIENCE

STUDIES IN LEGAL HISTORY

Published by the University of North Carolina Press

in association with the American Society for Legal History

Thomas A. Green and Hendrik Hartog, editors

JOHN HENRY SCHLEGEL

AMERICAN LEGAL REALISM AND

EMPIRICAL SOCIAL SCIENCE

University of North Carolina Press / Chapel Hill & London

© 1995 The University of North Carolina Press
All rights reserved
Manufactured in the United States of America

The paper in this book meets the guidelines for
permanence and durability of the Committee on
Production Guidelines for Book Longevity of the
Council on Library Resources.

Library of Congress Cataloging-in-Publication Data
Schlegel, John Henry.
American legal realism and empirical social science /
by John Henry Schlegel.
p. cm. — (Studies in legal history) Includes
bibliographical references and index.
ISBN 0-8078-2179-9 (cloth : alk. paper)
1. Jurisprudence — Research — United States —
History. 2. Jurisprudence — United States —
Methodology. 3. Law — United States — Methodol-
ogy. 4. Social sciences — Research — United States —
History. I. Title. II. Series.
KF380.S34 1995 349.73′01 — dc20
[347.3001] 94-17950 CIP

99 98 97 96 95   5 4 3 2 1

FOR HENRY,

whose absence grows
more noticeable with time,

AND EMILY

CONTENTS

Preface   ix

Introduction: Whys and Wherefores   1

Prologue: As the Story Is Usually Told   15

CHAPTER 1
Legal Science, Social Science,
and Professional Identity   23

CHAPTER 2
Empirical Legal Research at Yale:
Charles E. Clark and William O. Douglas   81

CHAPTER 3
Empirical Legal Research at Yale:
The Singular Case of Underhill Moore   115

CHAPTER 4
Empirical Legal Research at Johns Hopkins:
Walter Wheeler Cook and His Friends   147

CHAPTER 5
Empirical Legal Research since World War II:
The Reinvention of the Square Wheel   211

Afterword: On the History of Intellectuals,
Including Lawyers   259

Biographical Appendix   263

Notes   271

Bibliography   377

Index   403

Way back when I began this project, some year B.C. (before children), I explained to my then colleague L. Thorne McCarthy that I wished to write about the reception of the twentieth-century notion of science into law. I was startled when he quipped: "Schlegel, that's not history; that's futurology." Over time I have come to appreciate the truth of his statement. Similarly when beginning this book I conceived of it as part of an attempt to counter some mistaken notions about American Legal Realism first put forth by William Twining. Over time I have come to realize that, in a real sense, this book is nothing but an attempt to answer some of the questions that he posed when he asked:

> A thorough and informed post mortem, comparable to Currie's articles on the Columbia experiment, is still awaited. Among the points awaiting clarification are the following: how far can the espousal of "the scientific analogy" by Cook and Moore be treated as valid in the light of modern developments in the philosophy of science? Were Moore's methodological postulates sound? What were the differences in conception and method between the Johns Hopkins studies in judicial administration and other studies in the area, contemporaneous and subsequent? What are the grounds for maintaining that the Johns Hopkins studies were in some sense inferior? To what extent, if at all, can the "failure" of these studies, if they were a failure, be attributed to defective basic conceptions and faulty planning as opposed to poor execution and chance factors such as the economic situation and the personalities of the participants? Was the Johns Hopkins "failure" relative not only to inflated expectations of a quick breakthrough but also to a more sober assessment of what might reasonably have been expected of a pioneering effort? All of these questions are to some extent matters of opinion: nevertheless, it would be instructive to set the detached appraisal of an informed expert armed with the wisdom of hindsight against the impressionistic and heated judgments of the Scientists' contemporaries.[1]

I will let the reader judge whether in both cases my initial conception or my later understanding is the more accurate.

As is the case with any project that has taken this long to complete there is an enormous long list of individuals to whom I am indebted for their assistance. First on that list is Felice Levine and the National Science Foundation program in Law and the Social Sciences [NSF Grant #SES 870-6687] who funded a sabbatical in a scruffy little beach town near Barcelona where I beat this manuscript into some sense of order. Other funds have come from the Research Foundation of the State University of New York through its Faculty Research Fellowship and Grant-in-Aid Program and a Baldy Summer Research Fellowship from the State University of New York at Buffalo School of Law.

Support of a different kind has come from numerous archivists who seriously tried to make their collections accessible to me. I remember, in alphabetical order, Albert Tanler of the University Archives, Regenstein Library, University of Chicago; the staff of the Rare Book and Manuscript Library, Butler Library, Columbia University; Robert Colasaco, Sharon Laist, and Kyle Reis, of the Ford Foundation Archives; Erika Chadbourn, archivist, Harvard Law Library, Harvard University; Kathern Jacob, Julia Morgan, Cynthia H. Requuard, and James Stimpert, archivists, Milton S. Eisenhower Library, Johns Hopkins University; John M. Nugent, university archivist, Kenneth Spencer Research Library, University of Kansas; Susan Czaky and D. J. Wade, archivists, University of Missouri Library; Joseph Svoboda, archivist, University of Kansas Library; J. William Hess, assistant director, Rockefeller Archive Center; Donald Marks and Steve Masar, archivists, Memorial Library, University of Wisconsin; Eugene M. Gressley, director, and Emmett Chisum, archivist, American Heritage Center, University of Wyoming; the staff of the Beinecke Library, Yale University; Judith Schiff and Patricia Bodak, archivists, Sterling Memorial Library, Yale University; and Arthur Charpentier, director, Yale Law Library. Emma Corstvet Llewellyn and Stewart Macaulay made personal records available to me; Jane Moore gave me access to the papers of her father, Underhill Moore; George D. Vale, associate secretary, the Yale Corporation, allowed me access to the corporation's records; Harry Wellington, as dean, Yale Law School, allowed me to use the faculty's minutes of its meetings, and W. Willard Wirtz made available to me the surviving papers of Walter Wheeler Cook. Betty Walf, interlibrary loan librarian here at Buffalo, managed to find what I needed no matter how obscure.

Dozens of individuals helped with this project. Those who gave of their time for interviews include Paul H. Douglass, the late Leon Green, the late Robert Maynard Hutchins, Fleming James, Jr., David Kammerman, Ida Klaus, the late Emma Corstvet Llewellyn, the late Mark May, Jane Moore, Sylvia Samenow, the late Donald Slesinger, Richard Joyce Smith, the late Dorothy Swaine Thomas, and W. Willard Wirtz. Gilbert Sussman, Esq., supplied extensive taped recollections.

Others who answered my written inquiries include Alan Axelrod, Saul Richard Gamer, the late Grant Gilmore, the late Frederick Kessler, Aaron Nassau, Paul O. Ritter, Hon. J. Joseph Smith. Especially helpful were George Jaffin, who provided reams of first-hand information about the Institute of Law at Johns Hopkins University, and Samuel Howard, the real, unacknowledged author of the history of the Columbia Law School.

Friends gave of their time in other ways. Two deserve to be mentioned first, Miss Janet, who told me to stop doing what I was doing and instead to do what was more fun, and Fred, who was always there with a citation, a red pencil and, most important, an idea and an ear. Bob, Tom, and Ted were all helpful in the final stages of writing. Others who contributed in diverse ways include Bob, Guyora, Barry, Bliss, David, Alan, Tom, David, Joan, Jack, Al, Duncan, Thorne, Betty, Frank, Tom, and Rob. Ellen taught me much about writing when she edited an earlier version of Chapter 2. Ron and Brian at the Press were the patient, careful, and unobtrusive editors one always wishes for. Roseann was the most burdened of a long series of devoted secretaries; Darlene and Joyce completed the work Roseann had to leave behind when she sensibly chose love over Realism. Constantine and Tamsin helped with the last details. Joanne nagged at appropriate times but at all others endured, if not always stoically. Liz and Steve surely came to see the project much like the height chart on the wall, a measure of their growing up. Five friends contributed paw prints: Ginger, Munchen, Ritz, Tammy, and Missy.

Assistance of still another kind must be publicly acknowledged as well. Three significant pieces of scholarship are largely uncited in the footnotes and not because I have ignored them. William Twining's biography of Karl Llewellyn[2] and Robert Stevens's history of the American law school[3] were available long before I began this project. I have read them, reread them, and stolen shamelessly from their footnotes. The work of William and Robert informs every page of what follows and so citations would be numbing. Laura Kalman's history of the Yale Law School in the twenties, thirties, forties, and fifties[4] was published after some of this book was out in article form and after nearly all the research was completed, but while I wrestled, how successfully the reader will have to judge, with the ideas in Chapters 1 and 5. I have sung my song for Laura's efforts in another place.[5] Her work was an excellent check on my own research and has obviously informed my thinking on both chapters at dozens of points. Here too, I have chosen not to multiply citations. Rather, to all three I offer simply a public, general "thanks for making my work easier." A fourth body of work needs also be mentioned, that of Simon Verdun-Jones.[6] This work on which, to my knowledge, I have not drawn directly because it is much more an example of the traditional intellectual history that I have attempted to avoid than of the history of intellectuals that I have worked to present, ten years later seems to me to be rather helpful. I would not be surprised if someone were to conclude that some of his ideas had slid unnoticed into mine. The same should be said of the work of Ed Purcell[7] which I reviewed fifteen years after I first read it when preparing the following introduction. And then there is Neil Duxbury, another Brit who has noticeably enriched our understanding of Realism.[8]

I surely have forgotten some individuals who should have been named. To them, my apologies. I doubt there will be a second edition, so that is the best I can do.

Buffalo, N.Y.
September 1993

AMERICAN LEGAL REALISM AND

EMPIRICAL SOCIAL SCIENCE

IN THE SPRING of 1974 I chanced on some old files that once belonged to Charles E. Clark while looking for a way of killing time when in New Haven on weekends seeing my wife, who was finishing a degree at Yale. In those files I discovered a story worth telling. As I worked on that story, I discovered a problem in the history of American legal education that seemed to me to be significant. The problem can be stated briefly. Why did law not become a scientific study, in the twentieth-century sense of science as an empirical inquiry into a world "out there," as did all the other disciplines in American academic life that formed in the late nineteenth and early twentieth centuries?

Unfortunately, it is difficult to answer that question directly. While all of the other disciplines that formed between, say, 1875 and 1910 — anthropology, economics, history, psychology, and sociology — sought a guarantee of "objectivity" in the embrace of an empirical science,[1] law already saw itself as practicing a science, "legal science." Now, looked at critically, legal science, as nineteenth-century lawyers and academics understood that term, is a species of rational ordering. However, during the years on either side of the turn of the century the academic practitioners of legal science passed law off as a species of empirical study by making the thoroughly misleading, but intensely revealing, assertion that the law library was the law professor's laboratory and by arguing for the politically neutral, and so "objective," results of the appropriate juridical method. As a result, the question of whether legal science was in fact empirical in any relevant sense was elided. Indeed, as best as anyone can tell, at the relevant time no one suggested that law needed to become an empirical science. Thus it was not until the 1920s that more than an isolated soul would claim that legal science was unscientific[2] and so elicit clues as to why that was, and still is, the case. The group of scholars that made this claim and so brought the notion of science as an empirical inquiry if not into, then at least up against, law was the American Legal Realists. And so this book is largely a book about American Legal Realism.

Even to make that statement is, however, to enter shaky ground. The questions of who were the Realists and what was Realism are not trivial and are still contested. In large measure the "openness" of these questions is a result of the fact that as a coherent intellectual force in American legal thought American Legal Realism simply ran itself into the sand.[3] Why that is so — largely a matter of a change in the interests and activities of the major participants that accompanied a change in political sensibility as this country followed the European states in their slow slide into World War II — is a long story for another time.[4] That it is so can be confirmed by asking a group of law school faculty members what Realism was and what it accomplished. If one gets any but the most cursory of responses, the answers will center on "a movement of jurisprudence that quickly played itself out because it really had no technical competence and little to say" and "a group of scholars who did much to destroy the 19th Century doctrinal universe but left nothing in its place."[5] Both of these answers are wrong. The Realists' jurisprudential activities gave out when, faced with the implications of their own constructions, the protagonists lost their nerve; and their destruction of the nineteenth-century doctrinal universe left behind enduring achievements in commercial law, corporations, and procedure that point toward the largely legislative legal universe in which we live. Yet, more important than the errors embedded in the common understanding of Realism is the fact that each is invariably accompanied by the implicit, fatherly assertion, "We are all realists now; don't worry about these questions." While one may speak prose without knowing it, and similarly put forth ideas without knowing their lineage, it is more difficult to have learned a lesson — to no longer be that young and foolish, but rather to have grown up, as it were — without having a rudimentary understanding of the something about which the lesson was learned. And so this book is part of an attempt to understand what Realism was by looking at one of the things that the Realists did that never figured in the common understanding, at least until I began to write about it — empirical legal research.

Again, to make that statement is, however, not to exit from shaky ground but to remain resolutely on it. To suggest that Realism is best understood as something that the Realists did is to break with a substantial, traditional approach to the subject. Both the common understanding of Realism and the fatherly assertion of our having absorbed the lessons taught by Realism are founded on the understanding that Realism *is* a jurisprudence rather than that the Realists *had* (or shared, not the same thing) a jurisprudence.[6] Such has been the assumption since the 1930s, indeed since the famous Llewellyn-Pound exchange about Realism. Here Llewellyn made the first misstep, at least for someone who believed that Realism was a "technology" and not a "philosophy."[7] His famous essay, "A Realistic Jurisprudence: The Next Step," began with an ancient problem in jurisprudence, defining "law," a topic not too terribly surprising for a paper presented at a session on "Current Trends in Political and Legal Thought" at the annual meeting of the American Association of Political Science, but nonetheless hardly a question of technology. Pound responded in kind, suggesting that Llewellyn's emphasis on securing facts about law was not new in jurisprudence and that among the facts that are most important are the ideals expressed by judges in the course of judicial opinions.[8] It was only after Pound made his reply that Llewellyn seems to have dimly understood the mistake that he had made and so responded to Pound by emphasizing the disparate positions taken by various individuals that he thought ought to be seen as comprising the Realists.[9] That would have been fine, except that thereafter Llewellyn further confused matters by taking the position that almost none of the individuals in question believed the horrible things that Pound had accused the group of and followed that assertion with a list of "common points of departure" that they all shared. He thus managed to reinforce the idea that it was a jurisprudence that held the group together in the process of denying that fact.

Thereafter, it was all downhill. The great and not so great (often, the really awful) and the serious and not so serious (often, the really frivolous) criticism of Realism saw its job as commenting on a school of jurisprudence. John Dickinson emphasized the importance of traditional notions of legal rules as authoritative pronouncements and not as predictions of official action.[10] Lon Fuller criticized the group for its "positivistic and behavioristic ethical philosophy."[11] Philip Mechem complained that Realists viewed "society and its most important institutions" as a "great joke."[12] Walter B. Kennedy saw and objected to the "cumulative effect of the constantly widening attack upon law, order (in the sense of regularity), principles and rules."[13] Father Lucey saw Realism as leading "from the thesis of Democracy and reason to the antithesis" of the "Absolute State."[14]

Realism's defenders did no better. Myres McDougal sought to intervene in the dispute between Fuller and the Realists.[15] Unfortunately, he only made matters worse by taking seriously — well, semiseriously — Fuller's identification of the flaws in Realism by pointing out jurisprudential mistakes in Fuller's own preferred "natural law" jurisprudence. Edwin N. Garlan not only accepted the common understanding of Realism as a philosophy, he attempted to shore up that philosophy by providing a more complete understanding of what justice would be for a Realist.[16]

So, by the time that the jurisprudence treatise writers got to the problem, recovering the ground that Llewellyn had started from was impossible. Edwin W. Patterson, for example, one of the individuals on Llewellyn's list of Realists, somehow duplicated Llewellyn's mistake as well. Though recognizing that "the legal realists sought reality in human behavior, in judicial and other official conduct, in concrete operations rather than in essences," Patterson followed this observation with an examination of how "[t]his trend is exemplified in their conceptions of law."[17] Karl Bodenheimer saw in Realism "a tendency to minimize the normative or prescriptive element in law. Law appears to the realist as a body of facts rather than a system of rules, a going institution rather than a set of norms."[18] Predictably what followed was a subtle criticism of this definition of law. Substantially less subtle, but no less critical, Harold G. Reuschlein found the essence of Realism to be "the emphasis on what the judge does in contrast to what he says," and the proposition that "order and coherence in the legal system are a sad illusion."[19] Only Wolfgang Friedmann managed to avoid this view of Realism and he had the advantage of being both a foreign lawyer and at Columbia, where he knew Llewellyn.[20] And so for three generations now Realism has usually equaled jurisprudence and discussion has centered on the ideas that make up that jurisprudence.

I suppose that there is nothing wrong with jurisprudes discussing Realism as jurisprudence, timeless answers to what are taken as timeless questions. For historians, though, it is a matter of some consequence whether Realism is seen as a jurisprudence rather than Realists, as having or sharing a jurisprudence. Under the former conception the central question to be answered is what is Realism, a matter of philosophical essence, and so scholarly work proceeds by first identifying and explicating the classic texts. Membership in the group seen as comprising "*the* Realists" is thus derivative of the selection of texts seen as classic by a given scholar; *the* Realists are the individuals who have written *the* classic texts. There is a problem with such a procedure beyond the likelihood that a scholar's understanding of what Realism "must be" will heavily influence the choice of texts seen as the classic ones. Texts, like all objects of human culture, do not offer up their meaning transparently. Rather, texts take their meaning from their context, that which is "without" the text but necessarily, intentionally, or accidentally joined with it. Thus, to understand a text as an artifact of a past time, one needs to understand the full context of that past time.

It is for this reason and others that I believe that intellectual history, as traditionally understood as a history of ideas embodied in texts, is an essentially empty exercise,[21] though intelligible as the practice of a group of historians who participate in a professional identity that sees history as a largely autonomous enterprise of academics responding to other academics. Rather than a history of ideas, intellectual history needs to be the history of intellectuals, people who do things with ideas — in this case in an academic setting. The academic setting is important because, whatever may have been the case in earlier times, since the rise of the university and the establishment of academic disciplines and disciplinary organizations, for any text that might be seen as the product of a school or movement,[22] that context is the activities — educational, scholarly, economic, and political — of the author of the text and of the individuals with whom the author regularly interacted, for it is within this group that the text, as a human activity, had meaning. Thus, the context of a text cannot sensibly be limited to the classic texts with which it is temporally associated but must be situated in the manifold of activities of its author and others at the time and place of its creation.

The result of not attending to this understanding of the historian's task can be seen in historian's attempts, each excellent in its own way, to write about Realism over the past twenty-five years. In the earliest of these attempts, Wilfred E. Rumble, Jr., chose to order his discussion of Realism by focusing on Jerome Frank's distinction between fact and rule skepticism and on the issue of prediction of legal decisions and its mirror image, judicial method.[23] Given these topics, he not surprisingly centered his discussion on Frank and Llewellyn — indeed, in large measure, his book is a tug of war between the two gentlemen. Whether the choice of topics dictated the choice of scholars to focus on or whether the choice of scholars dictated the topics to focus on, the result was the same. Individuals like Thurman Arnold, Charles E. Clark, Walter Wheeler Cook, William O. Douglas, Underhill Moore, Herman Oliphant, and Wesley Sturges were seen as bit players and all of the Realists' efforts at empirical legal research, work that was central to the lives of several of these individuals, became nothing more than a largely unsuccessful attempt to do the work promised by Pound's sociological jurisprudence and so evidence for the continuity between the two jurisprudences.

Edward Purcell's excellent, if briefer, look at Realism, part of a discussion of political and social thought between the wars, likewise centered on Llewellyn and Frank.[24] However, because he saw the growth of empirical studies across disciplines as part of a general shift in the direction of what he called "scientific naturalism," Purcell saw the Realists' empirical work as more integral to Realism than had Rumble. Thus, Purcell found a place in Realism for more scholars and scholarship. Still, since he viewed Realism as predominantly a jurisprudence, he failed to question the appropriateness of seeing as central to the movement two individuals who were not particularly good friends, who worked together but once, whose careers were anything but parallel, and whose intellectual styles were quite disparate. Moreover, his focus on jurisprudence led Purcell to pay particular attention to a group of catholic critics of Realism whose actions were so far out of the mainstream of American legal education as to be essentially irrelevant to the debate over Realism, such as it was, and so to fail to see as problematic the association with these critics of scholars such as Morris Cohen, Dickinson, Fuller, and Pound, itself a curious network and, as such, worthy of serious attention.

William Twining was, of course, limited by his choice to write an intellectual biography of Llewellyn.[25] Since Llewellyn's major interests were jurisprudence and commercial law, that biography could not have given a central place to empirical research by the Realists because Llewellyn never really engaged in any. Still, it was Twining's avowed attempt to link Llewellyn to "the Realist Movement," and that objective ought to be the basis on which criticism of his work proceeds. With Llewellyn as the center of that movement, jurisprudence would have to be the center of the movement as well. And so Twining focused on Llewellyn's work, largely as an excursus into jurisprudence. At the same time, Twining had the good sense to realize that Llewellyn's work had a specific context and so focused his discussion of Realism on the work of individuals at Yale, where Llewellyn was first a student and then a faculty member, and at Columbia, where Llewellyn moved from Yale. Doing so allowed Twining to see Cook, Moore, and Oliphant as central to Realism and so to advert to Realism and science. Still, focus on place alone meant that Corbin and, of all strange things, Hohfeld were seen as equally central to Realism and that Twining could suggest that "[a]fter 1928 the realist movement lost such coherence as it ever had."[26] Moreover, it allowed Twining to miss the importance, for understanding Realism, of the fact that it was Llewellyn who was left behind at Columbia when that faculty split up. Llewellyn was never asked to leave Columbia and join the others, largely because he was on the social fringe of the group. So, while the choice to see his work as central to Realism made coherent the choice to see dominant influences on his thinking—Corbin and Hohfeld—as central to Realism, it hid the possibility of recognizing that Llewellyn's view of Realism was really the view from the margin and so questionable evidence of what the movement was and of whom the movement consisted.

Robert Stevens's history of American legal education had the salutary effect of focusing attention on the roots of Realism in, and the results of Realism for, legal education.[27] Such an approach, taken to a sensible conclusion, would suggest that discussion might follow Twining's lead and so focus on groups of law professors at individual law schools. Laura Kalman took up that suggestion in her study of the Yale Law School from the 1920s through the 1950s.[28] Yet, despite the sensible delimitation of her topic and the many excellencies of that book, she found it necessary to outline Realism as a jurisprudence and in so doing failed to follow her central insight. Instead, she lumped together isolated works by all sorts of varied individuals that together yielded such a generalized picture of Realism that it provided no check on the scope of her topic. Thus, it was not Realism at Yale that she ended up talking about, but legal education and legal educators at Yale. And so she missed the way that the intellectual core of her subject changed as the generations changed at that school and missed the significance of those generational shifts.

The most recent major treatment of Realism is by Morton Horwitz.[29] This work, rooted in the history-of-ideas tradition, is a return in approach to that of Rumble and Purcell. Horwitz wished to tell the story of the shift in legal thought from nineteenth-century "formalism" to something he first called "instrumentalism" but later slipped into calling "realism." The generality of these conceptions and their rootedness in the idea that what he was attempting to describe is a jurisprudence allowed Horwitz, like Kalman, to assemble a quite diverse group of scholars and permitted him to assert that they belonged together. But, unlike Kalman or Purcell, Horwitz used this freedom to assemble a cast that included not only all of the suspects usually seen as Realists, but also such unusual suspects as A. A. Berle, Francis Bohlen, James Bonbright, Morris R. Cohen!, John Dawson, Lon Fuller!!, Louis Jaffe!!!, James Landis, and Warren Seavey!!!! — indeed, almost any legal academic vaguely related to legal reform between 1920 and 1960, except for Pound and Felix Frankfurter.

Horwitz's cast of characters was not the random assemblage it might otherwise appear to be. It included all individuals who could be counted as having critiqued any of the conceptual keystones of nineteenth-century formalism and so exemplified the critical legal studies view of Realism as embodying that critique. From this perspective empirical legal research by the Realists was essentially irrelevant to that movement — indeed, Horwitz argued that such research was sterile and sapped the Realists' energy for reform. Whether that assertion is correct is largely unimportant. What is important is to see that Horwitz's failure to attend to social relationships between scholars as a delimiting factor in understanding what Realism was and who the Realists were blinded him to what I think is a significant observation that might have been derived from his work — namely, that there were two groups that worked for legal reform in the interwar years, one of which was largely centered in the usual group of Realists and another, centered around Pound and Frankfurter. A significant part of the criticism of Realism in the 1930s was offered by this second group, criticism that Purcell could only present as the work of isolated, seemingly unrelated individuals, but that Horwitz might have seen as somewhat unified. If seen as unified, this criticism might represent objections to substantive positions that were felt to undermine reform or objections to a new and noisy claimant to the title of "progressive," depending on one's perspective, and in either case might offer clues to the origins of the so-called "legal process" school of the postwar generation.

This book has been written largely in response to the choices of Rumble, Purcell, Twining, Kalman, and Horwitz either to see Realism as a jurisprudence or not to follow through on alternative understandings of Realism. In contrast, I have proceeded from the proposition that Realism is what various Realists have done.[30] One of those doings is my narrow topic, the attempts of some of the Realists to do empirical social science. In accordance with what I have said earlier, I have tried to place this part of the story of Realism into as full a personal, social, and institutional context as I am capable of doing without so slavishly imitating Braudel as to turn a merely long book into a grotesquely long one. By the choice of my topic I do not wish to be seen as arguing that Realists did not "do" jurisprudence. Of course they did. But they did other things as well, most notably attempt to do some empirical legal research and to turn their policy preferences into law in such areas as civil procedure, commercial law, and securities law. To understand Realism one needs to understand all of what the Realists did and not just that part of their activities that Llewellyn intentionally or unintentionally called attention to sixty years ago.

I begin my story of the Realists' attempts to do empirical legal research with a discussion of the early careers of two of those individuals, Walter Wheeler Cook and Underhill Moore. Each began his academic career at a time when Langdellian legal science was being brought from Cambridge out into the provinces as part of the spread of the new profession of law teaching. Chapter 1 examines the way that Cook's scholarship changed as it began to challenge the received understandings of Langdellian legal science, first as a result of his commitment to the analytic jurisprudence of Wesley N. Hohfeld and thereafter as result of both his and Moore's exposure to John Dewey's assertion that law was best seen as an empirical science. This chapter, which is most like traditional intellectual history because of the limited nature of the available archival material, identifies two ways that a scholar might have responded to Dewey's message: see Dewey's exhortations as Cook did, as implying that the old tasks of doctrinal analysis must be done more scientifically and that they should be accompanied with empirical studies of "how the law worked," or see those exhortations as Moore did, as implying that the old tasks of doctrinal analysis were meaningless and should be supplanted by empirical studies.

The next chapter presents empirical legal research done by Charles E. Clark and William O. Douglas at Yale. These individuals did not respond directly to Dewey's exhortations, but responded more generally to a sense that they were gathering the facts that would be needed to fuel reform, an idea that Dewey nevertheless would have understood. Clark's work centered in studies of civil procedure in Connecticut and in civil and criminal procedure in the federal courts, the latter study undertaken on behalf of the Wickersham Commission. But he also did some work on the losses by, and recoveries of, victims of auto accidents. Douglas's work was with the bankruptcy laws. Both Clark and Douglas had the help of real social scientists — Emma Corstvet and Dorothy Swaine Thomas — and so each was exposed directly to the understandings of empirical method that were then growing in the social sciences. Both had difficulty accommodating the desire of law professors to do empirical legal research with the norms of the social scientists about how such work was to be done. Douglas ignored those norms and simply abandoned his research when it became irrelevant to the course of bankruptcy reform. Clark, in contrast, was more torn between the exigencies of the cause of reform and its adherents and the norms for doing empirical work brought by the social scientists. He persisted in the face of reformer critics of his enterprise and completed his research, but soon thereafter he turned to other, more interesting pursuits, such as reforming the rules of federal civil procedure. The actions of both suggest why the social scientists were not much interested in working with the lawyers on empirical projects over any long haul.

Chapter 3 looks at the work of Underhill Moore, the Realist who most thoroughly attempted to develop a purely empirical science of law. Moore's work centered on two topics: the law and practice of commercial banking and the behavior of citizens in response to parking and traffic rules and regulations. In this work he too had the assistance of Thomas and Corstvet. Unlike Clark and Douglas, however, he was under no illusion that his work was a response to a felt need for reform or even vaguely relevant to such causes. But, though Moore considered himself to be a social scientist, other social scientists, particularly those at Yale's Institute of Human Relations from which much of the funding for his research came, did not treat him as if he were a social scientist. And so, in the end, Moore's work gave out just as did Clark's and Douglas's.

The fourth chapter returns to the career of Walter Wheeler Cook. It chronicles Cook's work at Johns Hopkins University where he was joined by three exiles from the breakup of the Columbia Law School faculty: Herman Oliphant, Leon Marshall, and Hessel Yntema. These four individuals formed the Institute of Law, designed to be a community of scholars engaged not in the professional training of lawyers, but in the full time study of law as Cook had seen that pursuit after his exposure to Dewey's thought. This is a story of the search for a topic or topics of research and the search for permanent funding by four individuals so unlike each other that it is hard to conceive of them agreeing on a single approach to anything. Ultimately Marshall and Yntema focused their attention on presenting a statistical picture of the court systems of Ohio and Maryland and Oliphant, on efforts to gather data to support the reform of trial court procedure in New York City. Cook, in contrast, continued to write about legal method and to criticize the conflict of laws "scientifically" and so raised, if only indirectly, the question of whether it made sense to understand Dewey's message as he had done. Curiously, however, nothing turned on the plausibility of Cook's understanding of Dewey or on the quality of the work in Ohio, Maryland, and New York. Without answering those questions, the Institute was closed because of animosity to its members on the part of the arts and sciences faculty at Hopkins and that institution's President, all of whom saw the group at the Institute as an overpaid distraction from the central part of a university that was under severe financial strain as a result of the Depression.

The last chapter picks up the story of empirical legal research in the law schools after the World War II, that is after the Realists had left the scene. It looks first at the so-called Jury Project, really a collection of projects, at the University of Chicago. Then it looks at the activities of the Walter E. Meyer Research Foundation that funded empirical research starting in the late 1950s and at the work of the Russell Sage Foundation that funded law and social science programs at several major law schools during the 1960s. Examination of all three efforts shows some notable successes but, at the same time, a pattern of overall failures like that disclosed in the previous three chapters. Good empirical work can be done in a law school, but it seems incapable of institutionalizing itself in such a way that, when funding shifts or is withdrawn altogether, empirical research continues; instead such research dies out and the researchers go on to some other pursuit. This chapter concludes with the argument that the reason for this pattern of activity is located in the professional identity of the law professor.

While the story I have just outlined is intended primarily as a contribution to our understanding of American Legal Realism as a historical phenomenon, I would hope that it would be seen as well as a contribution to our understanding of two broader topics. First, there is the history of American legal education, which, at least since the turn of this century, is the history of the American law school. The law school, conceived of as a place for instructing students and other legal professionals by identifying and justifying, in the broad sense of both approving and constructively criticizing, norms, is a very durable institution. While the content of the dialogue of justification that is the law school class and the scholarly legal article has changed much in the past one hundred years, its structure has changed little and its centrality to legal education, none. The story of the Realists' attempts to engage in empirical legal research shows the resilience of the law school as an institution in which teaching and scholarship of a particular kind are done, in the face of challenges of other possible institutional forms and of other possible scholarly attitudes.

Second, there is the study of legal academics. Little work has focused directly on this topic and, in a real sense, it is perverse to attempt to delineate the nature of what it was (and is) to be a law professor by looking at individuals who, through their work, challenged accepted understandings of professional role. Still, it would be a mistake to ignore the brooding omnipresence of those traditional legal academics who, in the background of this story, quietly, but firmly, maintain a notion of professional role and thus of appropriate activities. To follow Cook and Moore as they work their way back east is to watch the first slow and then faster growth of differently deviant notions of what it is to be a law professor, the emergence of a figure that defines the ground. It is that ground of individuals, committed to the understanding that legal education is focused solely on norms, against which the Realists engaged in empirical research reacted — indeed, against which the Realists defined themselves and so define themselves for us. Seeing that ground, if only in negative outline, begins to show the contours of the legal academy then and, realistically, now.

What follows, however, is by no means as straightforward an enterprise as might be suggested by this obligatory preview of coming attractions and contributions to the literature. Instead, I have taken what my wonderfully tolerant series editor has not improperly seen as a doubly idiosyncratic approach to the presentation of these materials. It is idiosyncratic first because, believing in the need to place the ideas that I treat in their full personal, social, and institutional context, I therefore must knowingly run the risk of presenting "ideas and people hopelessly intermingled," in the words of my good friend, Fred Konefsky. I do this because, in my experience, ideas and people are usually hopelessly intermingled. While I make no pretext of trying to do a *von Ranke*, I do think it important that I try to let my reader sample that hopeless intermixture. Thus, I have tried to give a sense of what it was to teach in the early years of this century in "the West," as it was called then, which was a matter of both doing and thinking and of how that doing and thinking changed as (at least) two young law professors moved progressively east and not coincidentally began to challenge the received wisdom of their elders. Similarly, I have tried to give a sense of what it was to do empirical research in law in the late 1920s and 1930s, a matter of doing and thinking in which the doing seemed to overwhelm the thinking and, thus, in which the actual results, the traditional "stuff" of intellectual history, were far less important than one might otherwise expect. So, while I have worked to make my presentation reasonably clear, some hopeless intermingling is an integral part of my story, hopefully not so much that my readers despair and move on.

My presentation is idiosyncratic in a second way as well. Each of the first four chapters begins with a story, often one told at great length, and concludes with some discussion and analysis of a select few of the factors that might be said to "explain" that story and that story alone. It is not until the beginning of the fifth chapter that I attempt to draw all four stories together and so attempt to "explain" their commonalities, to explain the aspect of Realism that I have chosen to focus this book on. And the balance of the fifth chapter recapitulates my form — story, explanation — as it brings the narrative about empirical research in law schools down to the early 1970s. I have made this choice for three reasons.

First, as I have suggested earlier in this introduction, I believe that intellectual history as presently practiced is generally wrongheaded. Intellectual history is not the history of ideas; it is the history of the intellectuals or other thinkers and writers who made those cultural products we call "thought." To emphasize this point I put the narrative, the story of my intellectuals in their time and place, first.

Second, I dislike the heavy hand of the contemporary historian/explainer. I find that this person is constantly getting in the way of "my" understanding. So, though I am anything but an unintrusive narrator, I have chosen to tell my story first and let my readers form their own opinions of meaning before I start down that road. In doing so I have no illusions, as do some narrative theorists, that my narrative is more direct, more unmediated, less controlled than would be the case were I to adopt a more argumentative form of presentation. Indeed, it is possible that an author exerts more control through narrative than through a more obviously argumentative form. This is because, less constrained by cultural notions of what a rational argument is, the author of a narrative can better fashion the argument being made by trimming here, filling there, and diverting attention by pointing somewhere else. In so saying, I wish to concede a reasonably obvious, but often hidden, when not denied, point of theory. Both the narrative and the explicitly argumentative form of the intrusive analytic historian are arguments, accepted or rejected because of their persuasiveness as to the truth of the matter stated, their verisimilitude as it were. Each draws on cultural and thus limited and limiting understandings of what might have happened and how that "what" might be understood as part of its claim to truth. So, by choosing to put narrative first, I am not choosing unmediated truth. All that said, to put the reader to the job of rooting through an entire book or article for the pieces that might make possible the telling of other stories, the making of other arguments, seems to me to ask too much of the reader. I prefer to make my critics' tasks easier, not harder.

Third, I love stories and I am better at narrative than analytic history. Any writer ought to be indulged when leading with the strongest suit available.

But enough of this. The point of this book is the stories. However, before I turn to them, I should offer my readers a capsule summary of *the* story of Realism as it is usually told, lest those readers lose their way in my story. What follows as a prologue is such a summary.

prologue

EVERYONE KNOWS some story that is *the* story of Realism. Of course, all of these *the* stories are not the same and they bear, I would argue, only a modest resemblance to what it was like to be a Realist in the 1920s and 1930s. But, if I am to help my reader understand what follows, I need set forth some version of *the* story that most knowledgeable readers will recognize, so that all can have a sense of where my story fits into the known terrain and thus make connections such as, "Oh, Cook did this at the same time that . . ." Thus, what follows should be taken for what it is, an attempt to situate the story that I shall tell into a narrative that everyone knows. While there is no need to begin with, "Once upon a time in a land not so far away . . . ," there is reason to be cautious of this tale. Some of these things may not have happened this way.[1]

IN THE YEARS after the World War I a group of law professors at Columbia were dissatisfied with American law and legal education. These individuals, Walter Wheeler Cook, Underhill Moore, and Thomas Reed Powell, joined together to educate their dean, Harlan Fiske Stone, in these matters. As this group began to drift away from Columbia, Nicholas Murray Butler, the University's President who had feuded with Stone for years, attacked legal education overtly and publicly. In his annual report issued in spring 1922 Butler criticized legal education for being too narrow and technical in approach and for failing to cultivate the relations between law, ethics, and social science. In response to Butler's criticism, in the following fall Stone appointed a curriculum committee. On it he placed Moore and Herman Oliphant, first a student, then a colleague of both Cook and Moore, who had just joined the Columbia faculty. Oliphant began attempting to sell the committee and indirectly the faculty on plans for the reorganization of the Columbia curriculum along "functional" lines roughly paralleling the organization of the curriculum at the University of Chicago's College of Commerce, where he had briefly taught before joining the Law School faculty there.

Exactly what Oliphant meant by "functional" was anything but clear, but a functional organization of the curriculum was seen, in opposition to the then current organization in terms of "legal technicality," as emphasizing the social situation out of which a legal problem grew and as roughly paralleling divisions among three social sciences — economics, sociology, and political science — in an effort to make easier the integration of those bodies of knowledge into law, seen as comprised of business relations, family relations, and government relations. Oliphant's ideas reasonably impressed both Butler and Stone, Butler to the extent that he apparently hinted that if Oliphant were patient he would eventually become Dean.

A chance to test that supposition came quickly, for in spring 1923 Stone chose to resign. A fight then broke out over who should be his replacement, Oliphant or Young B. Smith, a traditional but not hidebound teacher of torts, who was a relatively new faculty member too. When the faculty was unable to agree on a candidate, Butler chose to appoint neither Oliphant nor Smith, but rather Huger W. Jervey, a former partner of Stone's. Oliphant seemed not to be particularly upset by this turn of events or by the fact that his efforts seemed to have moved curriculum reform in no particular direction. He continued to hector the faculty on the subject and in fall 1924 joined with James C. Bonbright of the Columbia Business School to offer a year-long seminar in business organization. This seminar was intended to be an example of what Oliphant's proposed functionally organized curriculum might look like and so to keep the project of curriculum reform alive. Participants in it included Moore, Karl Llewellyn, who had moved from Yale where he had begun teaching after completing his law degree, and Robert L. Hale, a young economist-lawyer who had achieved some notice at the Law School with an article suggesting that the power to withhold goods from another who wished them, a power that was made possible by the law's definition of contract and property rights, was an example of state-sanctioned coercion exercised by "private" individuals and not state officials. The seminar was enough of a success that the following year Bonbright and Oliphant joined again to offer a similar seminar, this time on corporate finance.

When, in spring 1926, the Harvard Law School announced an endowment drive, in part to provide for research professorships, Columbia responded by accepting Oliphant's entreaties and beginning a mammoth study of the potential for reorganizing the curriculum along functional lines. Leon C. Marshall, Oliphant's Dean when he taught at the College of Commerce and a great advocate of the functionally organized business school curriculum, was brought to Columbia to lead the faculty's seminar on the curriculum that continued for eighteen months starting in spring 1927. The Great Curriculum Debate that ensued was probably the most searching review of the law school curriculum ever undertaken. In the course of the effort, a basic difference of opinion emerged between those, surely including Smith, who wished simply to create a better school for the training of practicing lawyers and those, surely including Moore and Oliphant, who wished to create a school aimed at scientific research in law. This disagreement was successfully papered over in the course of the seminar with the engaging assertion that both could be done successfully and simultaneously. However, this basic cleavage reappeared when in spring 1928, just as the curriculum study was drawing to a close, Jervey, who was in bad health, decided to resign the deanship. Predictably, the unresolved conflict from five years before again pitted Smith against Oliphant and, just as predictably, the faculty deadlocked. This time, however, Butler, probably acting to preserve the income that Columbia derived from its horde of law students, chose Smith as Dean. In the resulting brouhaha William O. Douglas, a recently hired faculty member, resigned without first securing another teaching post and other faculty began to look elsewhere.

While the Columbia faculty was having all of this fun with its curriculum, the Yale Law School was slowly emerging from a comfortable, if lethargic, existence. Its Dean, Thomas W. Swan, had built a strong, if not necessarily exciting, faculty that included Arthur Corbin, Charles E. Clark, and Cook, who had left Columbia in 1922. The excitement level was, however, raised noticeably, when, in fall 1925, the faculty added to its staff a recent graduate, Robert Maynard Hutchins. A confidant of Yale's President, Hutchins immediately teamed up with Clark to offer proposals for the reform of legal education at Yale. One of them, to begin empirical research in the field of civil procedure, was offered in response to Harvard's endowment drive as well. Though adopted, it was left unfunded, a fate similar to many of the other Hutchins-Clark proposals, which were usually adopted after being watered down. Then, in December 1926, Dean Swan was appointed to the Second Circuit Court of Appeals, and Yale had a chance to follow (or lead, depending on your time frame) Columbia with a deanship fight of its own. When the faculty was unable to reach a consensus, Corbin suggested that Hutchins be appointed Acting Dean, a choice that became real Dean six months later when consensus still eluded the faculty. The whirlwind of activity that was thereupon released included, as its first turn, securing funds for the study of procedure proposed fifteen months earlier.

In a very small, third ring Walter Wheeler Cook, who had left Yale in spring 1926 just as everything was heating up everywhere, struggled to get the Johns Hopkins University to fund a law school or a research and graduate teaching institute or something that would allow him to stay there on a permanent basis and so continue his research into two topics: scientific method and the conflict of laws. His break came when the Columbia faculty engaged in its deanship fight, freeing the most disaffected to leave. Hopkins quickly snapped up Oliphant, Marshall, and Hessel Yntema, a young faculty member, all of whom joined Cook as the originating faculty of the Institute of Law, conceived of as a research institute. Hutchins fished in the same pond and landed Douglas and Moore, then almost immediately took a job as President of the University of Chicago.

During the next two years Clark, who succeeded Hutchins as Dean, Douglas, and Moore turned their attention to empirical research, the crew at Hopkins tried to decide what their institute would be and then slid into topics for empirical research, and the individuals left behind at Columbia attempted to complete the casebooks promised in the curriculum study. Others worked at more traditional projects with the result that, in 1930, a torrent of significant publications appeared. Jerome Frank published *Law and the Modern Mind* in which he argued that legal thinking is suffused with a craving for certainty that reflects a failure to give up dependency on the father and so a failure to become truly adult. Leon Green published *Judge and Jury* in which he argued that the law asked the wrong question of juries in negligence cases and concomitantly controlled them too much. And Llewellyn published *The Bramble Bush* in which he suggested that law could be reduced to official behavior and nothing more. Thereafter Green published a torts casebook that completely eschewed a doctrinal organization and substituted an organization in terms of the factual circumstances — railroad accident, auto accident, farm machinery accident, and the like — and Llewellyn published a sales casebook that all but ignored the concept of "title" that had been central to the subject for over fifty years. Llewellyn followed this with an article that denominated an agglomeration of activities and arguments by his friends and colleagues as "Realism," analyzed commonalities among its adherents, and suggested appropriate "Next Steps."

A predictable reaction then occurred. First was the eruption of the so-called Realist Controversy. In 1931 Roscoe Pound, apparently feeling slighted because his work in developing "sociological jurisprudence" was disparaged in Frank's book, chose to respond quite negatively to Llewellyn's "Call for a Realist Jurisprudence." Llewellyn felt obliged to reply in an article in which he chose to examine the work of a sample of Realists to see whether Pound's rather amorphous charges held up. Not surprisingly, Llewellyn found that they did not (and, in the process of naming a list of "Realists," guaranteed that thereafter there would be constant fights over who the Realists really were). At that same time, Mortimer Adler and Morris R. Cohen, real philosophers with some knowledge of law, argued that the work of Llewellyn, Frank, and others ignored the rational science of law in the pursuit of meaningless empirical knowledge, and John Dickinson, a law professor soon to become Secretary of Commerce in the Roosevelt administration, argued that the group's theories of judicial decision making simply did not square with what lawyers understood legal method to be.

All of the noise in the journals was, I suspect, good for book sales and generated much other excitement. Whether it was good for empirical research was another matter. By 1931, most of Clark and Douglas's empirical work was completed, though not necessarily published. The work at Hopkins would continue for two more years before the participants would go their own ways. Only Underhill Moore would mount a major research project after 1933. But there were other things to do, for that year brought the Roosevelt administration to Washington. The list of Realists who served, sometimes only for summers that somehow stretched into fall, sometimes for years, in the administration's emergency and permanent bureaucracy includes Thurman Arnold, who came to Yale early in Clark's deanship; Douglas; Abe Fortas, who barely had a chance to teach at his law school before heading off; Frank; Walton H. Hamilton, an economist hired by Hutchins; Oliphant; and Wesley Sturges. And somehow, amid all of the running back and forth and all of the excitement, scholarship got done, most notably Arnold's *Symbols of Government* and *Law and the Lawyers* by Edward S. Robinson, a psychologist at Yale and Arnold's collaborator in a legendary seminar called "The Cave of the Winds." Arnold's work emphasized the irrationality of the symbols like law or Congress or the Supreme Court that we as citizens treat as meaningful in political discourse, while Robinson attacked the legal profession for its obsession with rules and certainty.

These works and others that attacked the doctrinal structure of both common law and constitutional law and emphasized law as the prediction of outcomes in individual cases brought forth still more predictable reaction. This time the tone was more socially and politically conservative than the time before and participated more fully in a general reaction to interwar social science that saw all of it as undermining the institutions of American society from within while the rise of fascism and the growth of godless communism undermined them from without. The truth of these charges is doubtful but irrelevant, for, by 1939, when Clark joined the Second Circuit and Douglas, the Supreme Court, Realism had generally run its course. Arnold and Fortas were in Washington permanently, and Frank, who had never really taught law anywhere, had embarked on a public service career that eventually led to the Second Circuit as well. Oliphant had been in Washington for six years and Sturges and Hamilton were spending much time trying to get there. In one generation the noise was over. By the time World War II had ended Cook was dead, Moore had stopped publishing with the completion of his second research project, and Hamilton had retired, become a lawyer by act of the Georgia legislature, and joined Arnold in practice. Only Llewellyn (and Sturges) remained to argue authoritatively about what Realism was.

THERE ARE, of course, other stories about Realism that might be told. The most prominent[2] starts with "formalism," "conceptualism" or "classical legal thought," seen as a way of thinking about law in terms of broad principles that entailed whole edifices of legal doctrine, which in turn compelled results in individual cases. For this story formalism, identified with Christopher Columbus Langdell and his disciples, was utilized by a conservative judiciary to undermine, where it could not invalidate, progressive social legislation designed to alleviate the social consequences of the industrial expansion that followed the Civil War. Formalism or "mechanical jurisprudence" was attacked by pre–World War I progressives, such as Louis Brandeis, Robert Corwin, and Roscoe Pound, who argued the need for reform of the law; by anything but progressives, like Oliver Wendell Holmes, Jr., who argued for the importance of allowing legislative majorities to have the final say even when wrong; and by just good lawyers like John Chipman Gray and Benjamin N. Cardozo, who asserted that judges did not find but made law. Realism then built on the work of these individuals through a sustained and withering critique that over and over demonstrated that law did not work as the formalists said, that the principles entailed no particular doctrine and the doctrine compelled no results in individual cases.

For this story individuals such as A. A. Berle, Felix Cohen, his father Morris, Fuller, Hale, James Landis, and even Felix Frankfurter are Realists, for all participated in one way or another in destroying the plausibility of formalism at the doctrinal level. I shall not quibble about names. It is clear that all of these scholars and the individuals who were featured in the longer story of Realism knew each other more or less during the interwar years. They corresponded; they assisted in each other's scholarly and more political projects at times; they may even have been guests in each other's homes. But if one looks carefully there is more than a modest antagonism, sometimes in print and sometimes in private, between the individuals featured in the longer story and the individuals who would need to be added to make the enlarged group of Realists. While the narrower group of Realists did not lack for disharmony among themselves, they kept their sniping in private until well after World War II and, at least in certain subgroupings, were much more likely to be found together socially than they were likely to be found with the additional Realists. So, I am comfortable setting forth as *the* story of Realism, the story I have offered at length. Given our interest in the past as lesson and progenitor, we may now see the larger grouping as the more important one. Things are likely to have been seen differently in those inter-war years.

A WORD NEEDS be said about a vexing topic, if only to invite discord in the attempt to forestall (though not to engross or regrate) it. Throughout this book I have used the phrase "empirical legal research" or its cognates with what I believe is a consistent meaning. By that term I mean to encompass what Charles E. Clark called "fact" or "field," as distinguished from "library," research. Such research was usually, but not exclusively, seen as research into present social, economic, or legal conditions or practices and as attempting to quantify relationships, though not to require hypothesis formulation and testing. Thus, history was not a favored social science, and casual inquiry, such as calling up an expert to learn how a particular transaction was carried out, was disfavored as well. I know that there are other, broader meanings to the term, indeed other, broader understandings were at least available, if not known to any of the Realists except possibly Llewellyn, in the interwar years. I know that there were other, narrower meanings to the term equally available at that time. I have chosen this meaning because I believe that it generally captures the meaning that the individuals about whom I write would have understood. Would they have insisted on its use in precisely that sense? Surely not! But in an attempt to maintain consistency I have.

Now you have *the* story; on to my story.

LEGAL SCIENCE, SOCIAL SCIENCE,

AND PROFESSIONAL IDENTITY

BY ANY MEASURE, the time immediately after World War I was a quite extraordinary one at the Columbia Law School. Years later, T. R. Powell remembered the "cooperative intellectual interchange" and "the full joy of sympathetic co-operation with fellow faculty members" that yielded results for the Law School and the individuals "that we all saw to be good."[1] This brief instant began in the fall of 1919 when Walter Wheeler Cook joined Powell and Underhill Moore, peaked with Herman Oliphant's arrival from Chicago in the summer of 1921, broke with Cook's departure for Yale at the end of the summer of 1922, and then died with Harlan Fiske Stone's resignation as Dean, the ensuing fight over his replacement, and Powell's departure in 1923.[2] For four years these men were a hearty, heady band who joined together to educate their Dean and each other about law. Their expansiveness was understandable. All were in their intellectual prime; all but Stone were, or at least considered themselves to be, politically left; and all were anticipating the near, optimistic future of the Law School, which was about to experience the retirement of its entire, conservative, old guard save only Stone's law partner. They, as the middle-aged heart and effective head of that faculty, were, for all practical purposes, in control.

As part of the act of asserting control, of both showing and giving meaning to that control, they convinced Stone to have the Law School offer a series of "Special Conferences in Jurisprudence" as part of the summer session in 1922. Now, a great deal should not be read into this choice. This was the assertion of control, not of revolution. The courses were designed for a select audience of "members of the bar, teachers of law, and advanced students of law"; this was not a movement toward jurisprudence for every first-year law student by any means.[3] Nor was the idea particularly new. For over ten years the Boston Book Company had been churning out volumes in the Modern

Legal Philosophy Series, sponsored and overseen by a committee of the Association of American Law Schools (AALS), which was designed to make contemporary European legal philosophy available in translation to the American academic legal community.[4] But talk of legal theory and its importance
had seldom reached the omnipresent law reviews, so in that sense the idea
was adventuresome. The ambiguity of doing something new but not so new
was reflected also in the speakers. The first was Roscoe Pound, talking on the
ever popular "Sociological Jurisprudence," apparently a repeat of a seminar,
"Problems in Social Philosophy," he had given the year before at Harvard,
and a topic he had been pushing for over ten years.[5] He was an obvious
choice, in ways that the other two speakers were not. One was a big name,
John Dewey, *the* professor of philosophy at Columbia who was to speak on
"Some Problems in the Logic and Ethics of Law," billed as "an attempt to
apply the method of contemporary pragmatic logic and a social theory of
ethics to some of the more fundamental questions relating to legislation and
the procedure of the courts." The other was a comparatively small name,
Cook, who was to speak on "Some Problems in Legal Analysis," an exercise
in the analytical jurisprudence of such concepts as "right; ownership; title;
'void' and 'voidable'; possession; capacity; intent and motive; legal personality; etc." developed along the lines laid out by the then late Wesley N.
Hohfeld, once Cook's colleague at Yale.[6]

The conferences were said to be "a success," though "Dewey did not have
as much legal material as would be desirable" and Pound said "nothing
new."[7] Yet, if one looks at the speakers, there was something paradoxical
underneath the entire event. Each of the three subjects was a lively, contemporary topic, at least if one overlooks the purely academic legal reputation of
Hohfeld. Dewey's pragmatic philosophy was a centerpiece of the general
intellectual consciousness of the time. Pound's jurisprudence with its similar
emphasis on experimental, social engineering was likewise highly topical, at
least in legal circles, and exhibited clear resonances with Dewey's method,
both in its antiformalism and in its emphasis on securing practical solutions
to current problems. And Hohfeld's analysis was in some ways all the rage.
Yet, if one looks carefully, it would be hard to find two more antithetical or at
least skew topics than Dewey's pragmatism and Hohfeld's analytics.

Dewey's was an antiformalism; Hohfeld's a high formalism. One looked
toward use in everyday affairs; the other, toward nothing more than clear
thinking about what was called "jural" — that is, legal and equitable — relations. So when Cook, who went to all of Dewey's lectures, pronounced them
to be "one of the most helpful things I have ever had" and announced that

when he gave his course again he planned "to include the bulk of Dewey's,"[8] somewhere, somehow the scoreboard should have lit up TILT. But it did not. Indeed, Cook soon took up the role of cheerleader for science in the law schools and yet spent the rest of his career doing the conflict of laws, the least scientific of subjects.

Such is the central paradox in Cook's life and, in a parallel way, of American Legal Realism. Realism too was an antiformalism that preached, and occasionally delivered evidence of, the importance of an empirical understanding of the workings of the legal system and yet somehow Realism always returned to case law analysis. That this paradox was by no means a necessary one can be seen from the career of another member of that hearty band at Columbia. Underhill Moore in all likelihood sat with Cook in the audience at Dewey's lectures, and was enough taken by Dewey's message to have soon after told a friend, "There is no God and Dewey is his prophet."[9] But, in contrast to Cook, soon after 1922 Moore simply abandoned case law analysis and took up empirical work; he even began to recast his major courses to reflect his interest in empirical understandings of law.[10] Thus there was a tolerably clear choice, as is almost always the case, as to how to understand Dewey's message for law. But for most people the choice was obvious, as can be seen from the fact that Moore's colleagues and fellow Realists thought him a bit mad in his single-minded pursuit of science. To understand why that choice was obvious, why it was somehow easier to live with the paradox and at best work at ways to elide it, is to understand the peculiar way that the twentieth-century notion of science was received into American legal thought. In order to begin to gain that understanding one has to begin with a look at the world of the American law professor at around the turn of the century.

Becoming a Law Professor in the West

Langdell's revolution in legal education — the shift from teaching the "principles" of law by means of text, lecture, and recitation to "deriving" those principles solely from the examination of cases in large-class, question-and-answer format — can only be understood as the aperçu of one possessed.[11] Had this revolution been begun anywhere else than Harvard[12] and lacked the assistance of James Barr Ames,[13] in all likelihood it would have sunk beneath the waves as John Norton Pomeroy's similar innovation had.[14] Indeed, twenty years after Langdell began his revolution, he had but one major convert, Keener's Columbia,[15] and the merits and demerits of the innovation were still quite seriously being discussed in the pages of the second university-based law review, that of Yale.[16] But, accompanying Keener's victory at Columbia, a succession of individuals, of whom John Henry Wigmore and Nathan Abbott are among the most notable, effectively conquered the law schools west of the Appalachians in the name of Langdell and his system.[17] The lucky ones like Abbott returned to the East Coast; the others, for example Harry Richards, longtime dean at Wisconsin, learned, or chose, to live in the provinces.[18] But for all it was an exciting enterprise, at least at the start.[19] The work of conquest done, there then came the problem of populating these law schools with law teachers devoted to Langdell's system. The problem was not unprecedented; the English civil service had met it as the British colonial empire expanded, and there are earlier Roman precedents. But peopling colonial law schools is a different problem from that of claiming territory in the name of Langdell.

While there were several ways of solving the problem of populating the law schools with Langdellian case law teachers, one seems to have been chosen. Promising young aspirants for teaching posts at major law schools like Harvard and Columbia were sent to, or placed in, provincial law schools, most notably in the Midwest, with the expectation that they would learn their craft and, in effect, work their way back east.[20] There were obvious exceptions to this pattern of advancement; indeed, careful examination of the growth of the Harvard and Columbia faculties shows that, by and large, service in the provinces was not the most likely way to a major teaching appointment.[21] Nevertheless, career patterns of early twentieth-century law professors suggest that the idea of working one's way up through a kind of "colonial" service was at least widespread, if not well founded, and wholly new for this group of academics that had traditionally been recruited from local practitioners, often locally educated practitioners.[22]

Individuals were not, however, simply thrown to the wolves that quite literally still were to be found in the West, as it was called at the time, and told to teach law for the greater glory of Christopher Columbus Langdell. Rather, several different kinds of support were provided for these young law teachers. First, and most obvious was personal support and encouragement in correspondence from the folks back home. Beyond this the case method itself provided a common identity in academic endeavors as well as a link to the past that helped to justify colonial life. Similarly, common hazards and the camaraderie often engendered in the course of meeting them created a network of friends whose help could be called on when advancement was sought.[23] However, at least as important as these forms of support was the notion of professional role that received its early definition by Dean Ames and substantial affirmation at almost every meeting of the visible focus of the profession, the new Association of American Law Schools.[24]

When Ames, drawing on ideas of Thayer[25] and, to a lesser extent, Langdell,[26] posited the "threefold vocation of the law professor — teacher, writer, expert counselor in legislation" — and adverted to the "strenuous" nature of these tasks, as well as their importance for "the maintenance and wise administration" of the law, he created an appealing vision of the academic lawyer's role in society. Central to that vision was its scholarly aspect; Ames expected the "full-time" law professor to create "a high order of treatises on all the important branches of the law, exhibiting the historical development of the subject and containing sound conclusions based on scientific analysis."[27]

For the first twenty years of the century, if not longer, Ames's vision of professional role, embroidered in dozens of slightly different variations, but almost always emphasizing an ideal of detailed, systematic, sustained, and comprehensive works of scholarship on the German grand scale, formed the core of the identity of the professional law teacher.[28] It was instantiated by the scholarly landmarks of the time, Williston's and Wigmore's treatises, and the more monumental of the early casebooks, of which Gray's six-volume work on property is surely the most extraordinary. For the harried, underpaid young law professor who found himself in Columbia, Lawrence, or Lincoln with many students and many courses but few colleagues and precious little in the way of library resources,[29] it provided at least rhetorical support for enduring those teaching responsibilities and, at the same time, it resonated with the idea of advancement through colonial service in such a way as to hold out the possibility that better conditions at better schools would bring better chances for writing and legislative drafting.[30]

The twin notions of advancement through colonial service and of a serious commitment to legal scholarship that provided a systematic presentation of a properly bounded particular branch of law by and large defined much of the world of aspiration for the pre–World War I law professor.[31] It was into this world that Walter Wheeler Cook and Underhill Moore came as young law teachers. How much they knew about this world is not clear. Cook's background was the more academic and he had actually lived in the Midwest for a while. He was said to be descended from "early Pilgrim stock," the son of a high school principal who, at the time of Cook's birth in Columbus, Ohio, ran a school that "admitted Negroes on the basis of full equality" and who later ran the preparatory schools associated with Potsdam State Normal School and Rutgers College and finally was superintendent of the Flushing,

New York, school system.[32] Moore's background was more professional. His father was a Park Avenue ophthalmologist and there were lawyers among his family, most notably his grandfather, Abraham Underhill and his grand uncle, Thomas S. Moore.[33] Both Cook and Moore were graduates of Columbia College and both completed the course work for degrees in both the Law School, at that time at the peak of its early development,[34] and in the School of Political Science, the premier department in the country.[35] Indeed, they were in all likelihood at least nodding acquaintances, though not good friends, while at Columbia. But for a while, at least, their paths diverged.

Moore completed his masters in political science in 1901 and law degree in 1902. He then entered practice in New York City doing "probate, the construction of wills and trusts, the 'disentangling' of statutes and the law of property."[36] Cook on the other hand immediately headed west in pursuit of what appeared to be a career as a political scientist. That was not surprising for he had come at law quite obliquely. As an undergraduate his strengths were in mathematics and physics.[37] Apparently he initially decided to pursue a career in the physical sciences, for upon graduation in 1894 he took an instructorship in mathematics and a year later he headed off to Germany on a two-year fellowship in physics. Inexplicably, while in Germany he studied not just the sciences but also philosophy and law under Paulsen and psychology under Wundt.[38] This deviation did not seem to bother the Department of Mathematics, which, on his return in late fall 1897, hired him as an assistant for two more years, even though he had enrolled in both the Law School and the School of Political Science.[39] After a year of full-time study of law, Cook, seemingly not much captivated by the subject, increased his course load in the School of Political Science, completing a masters degree there in 1899 with an essay on "Citizenship in the U.S.A. under the XIV Amendment to the Constitution."[40] He thereafter enrolled in the department's Ph.D. program and announced his intention to complete not his LL.B., but the joint law and political science LL.M. that had been introduced eight years before. For this latter degree, awarded in spring of 1901, Cook completed his undergraduate law courses as well as work in political science in political economy, history, public law, and administrative law.[41] Then, like so many other Ph.D. candidates, course work completed but thesis only in his mind's eye — or, as they say, "A.B.D." — Cook left for Lincoln, Nebraska, and the Department of American History and Jurisprudence at the University of Nebraska, where he was hired to teach courses on state and local history, constitutional history of the United States, and administrative law.[42]

What Cook made of the West, or it of him, is unrecorded. The University was barely thirty years old; the town, only slightly older.[43] And though the University's reach was great, nothing less than bringing civilization to the prairies, its grasp was small. The entire faculty was well under one hundred and the student body under 2,500.[44] But it was a time of optimism at the University. A year before, E. Benjamin Andrews, a well-known historian and economist, had come to Lincoln as Chancellor after spending nearly a decade as President of Brown University, enlarging and strengthening that tiny university until forced out because of his support for bimetallism.[45] He immediately set to work expanding and strengthening his new university. In his short tenure this program was remarkably successful, though in many ways a curious counterpoint in a university where some of its students were not even graduates of high school and where the dominant student culture was shifting from that of an approved, indeed encouraged, vocational school toward that of a tolerated, if not encouraged, fraternity-centered finishing school.[46]

In these respects Nebraska was hardly unique. Kansas, where Moore began his teaching career in 1906, though a few years older than its northern neighbor, was even smaller, boasting a faculty of eighty-nine but only 1,300 students. It too was optimistic about its future under its new chancellor, Frank Strong, formerly the President of the University of Oregon, who was dedicated to advancing the University's fortunes through service to the state.[47] Even Missouri, a far older school where Cook took his second job, had but two thousand students. Located off the main lines of the east-west railroads in a very small town that only recently had acquired a dependable water supply and a sewage system, the University endured the existence of enough saloons to make difficult the enforcement of its ban on drinking. It too was said to be under the direction of an able president, and had grown markedly in the previous fifteen years, especially in the quality of its faculty, despite the fact that its financial situation was often very precarious.[48] Football was the major passion of most students; social life was centered around fraternities and sororities, in part because they provided cheap housing at a time when university dormitories were essentially unknown.

Now, all prewar midwestern university presidents were not great leaders; indeed, much of the growth of their universities would surely have taken place under any kind of leadership, so great was the economic expansion of the middle class during this time. But the sense of small islands of academic culture amid vast seas of a largely otherwise indifferent populace and of a student body more interested in social than intellectual matters is not out of place, and in large measure adequately describes the law schools of the period as well.

Kansas, for example, where Moore began, was a school of about 175 students and faculty of four, newly enlarged by Moore's appearance. It was an integral part of the undergraduate culture as its only, and recently imposed, requirement for admission, a high school education, was the same as that of the College of Liberal Arts and Sciences. It was "the hottest hot bed of support for winning [football] teams" and its Dean was known as "the patron saint of K.U. football"[49] in part because his school was the "dumping ground" for athletes.[50] Faculty course load was high and teaching was largely by means of textbooks and recitations, though Moore brought case method teaching with him when he arrived.[51]

The situation at Missouri was largely identical when Cook got there. The school had an enrollment of about two hundred, and had largely "modernized" itself as most classes were taught from casebooks by Socratic dialogue rather than by the older text and lecture method. Yet, it was still effectively an undergraduate school, requiring of its entering students but two years of high school education, and thus produced the usual undergraduate high jinx, in this case a running feud with the engineering undergraduates. And the faculty was small. Cook was brought there as part of an increase of the full-time faculty from three to four necessitated by an extension in the program of instruction from two to three years undertaken some two years earlier.[52] Course loads were correspondingly heavy.

In such an environment scholarship was surely not encouraged, but it was not impossible, at least once one had one's courses firmly under control. For example, at that time Missouri was headed by a prolific, if somewhat ordinary, scholar and onetime law review editor, John D. Lawson,[53] and William L. Burdick at Kansas was a serious, if less regularly prolific, scholar.[54] Yet teaching six diverse courses, as Moore did at Kansas,[55] or eight, as Cook did at Missouri,[56] was surely a drain on one's energy. Thus it is not surprising that while at Kansas Moore only managed to republish his A.M. thesis.[57] Cook, though, published much more. Indeed, from the start he demonstrated that steady productivity that was one of the hallmark's of his academic career.

Representative of Cook's early efforts was a piece in the *Columbia Law Review* called "Agency by Estoppel." The topic was a classic one. What were the "true principles" that established the liability of a principal for contracts entered into by an agent beyond his express, but within what we now call his apparent, authority? The point was simple enough. On a will theory of contracts, of individuation of contract, acts of an agent in entering into contracts in excess of actual authority (i.e., at a lower price or for the sale of other goods) were "not willed" by the principal and thus ought not be binding on him for there was no "meeting of minds." Yet, for over three hundred years courts had imposed liability in cases such as these where agents nevertheless somehow seemed to have sufficient authority. The standard explanation for this "un-willed" contractual liability, given by a leading expert on the subject, a Canadian practitioner who had written a treatise on "Estoppel by Misrepresentation,"[58] and by several English judges, was that by clothing the agent with the indicia of authority the principal misrepresented the agent's actual authority and would be estopped from denying his representations. It was a sensible theory that in many ways fit the action of the principal perfectly. But Cook did not like it. Instead he argued, "the principal is bound because according to all sound principles he has entered into a contact with the third party."[59]

Cook's argument on the point was clever. Working with the so-called objective theory of contract popularized by Holmes, Cook observed, following *Adams v. Lindsell*[60] (the mailbox rule) and other cases, that it was "by his manifested intention, i.e., by his intention as manifested to the other party" and not his real, subjective intention that any contracting party was bound. He then added the idea that one may manifest intention through the act of another, so that "the principal is bound by his intention as manifested through his mouthpiece, his agent, to the third party, the latter having accepted the offer thus made." He thus came out with a "true contractual liability," a liability that, as he went to great pains to point out, was imposed in cases of a wholly unexecuted contract where liability based on estoppel theory with its requirement of action in reliance would not be imposed.[61]

The point of the entire exercise may seem more than a little obscure. Yet, the question was theoretically a quite important one. Cook was working within that system of legal discourse variously called "formalism," "conceptualism," or more neutrally "classical legal thought."[62] Classical legal thought was a way of organizing and thus of understanding the world of common and constitutional law in terms of hierarchically ordered, binary categories, such as agent/independent contractor, negligence/intent, tort/contract, and public/private. Because these were not just binary but also oppositional categories, the central question for the solution of a legal problem was one of classification, treated not as a matter of shading or "line drawing," but as a matter of essential character. Aid in deciding such classificatory questions was normally found not explicitly in the purpose of the classification in question, but from the higher-order binary oppositions, explained, if necessary, in terms of the ideas underlying late nineteenth-century political economy or in terms of the history of doctrine. The activity of making these decisions about classification was seen as a large part of "legal science," a distinct branch of knowledge in the academic universe of the time.

In examining the question of the true basis of a principal's liability for acts of an agent outside the scope of authority, Cook was attempting one of these exercises in classification typical of the legal science of his day. The universe of classical legal thought was built in part on the basis of protection of a sphere of individual action free from government regulation. This was the world of contract, of freely willed liability. To impose liability in the absence of will, as the cases on the apparent authority of agents had done, was to mix tort principles, unwilled liability imposed by the state, with contract principles and thus to undermine the notion that there was a sphere of individual action free from government regulation — that is, to undermine the notion that there was a "private" sphere of law. At some level, if only an intuitive one, Cook knew this, as did the authors he opposed. The advocate of the estoppel solution chose to push the problem out of contract and via misrepresentation and reliance into tort at the cost of some small slice of liability. Cook simply recast the problem to turn it back into contract via the notion of manifest intention as evidence of will.

Who was right as a matter of true principles is irrelevant. What is important is to notice that such debates about classification were the grist of the intellectual life of the pre–World War I law professor practicing legal science as two other pieces of Cook's scholarship show. The earlier piece was on the vexing question of whether to govern the empire acquired as a result of the Spanish-American War, in particular, the Philippines, through a governor appointed by the president or by means of a tripartite government patterned after the national one.[63] The question and related ones had obvious racial overtones, the ability of non-Aryans to govern themselves, and had been debated extensively by Langdell, Thayer, and others two years earlier,[64] but the constitutional details of the obvious answer had yet to be fully worked out. Here Cook chose to respond to a prominent New York lawyer[65] who argued that one supposed constitutional barrier to the use of a governor appointed by the president — the doctrine of separation of powers, in its guise of the prohibition on delegation of legislative power to the president — while recognized by the Supreme Court, "is not practical, has never been applied by the court, . . . has been to a great extent departed from in certain decisions of that court, and would perhaps not be invoked by the court to nullify" a grant of legislative power in these circumstances. Here again Cook attempted to develop an argument that was not based "on wrong premises."[66]

His argument was straightforward. Separation of powers has no application to the governance of territory, he asserted, for in governing a territory Congress is exercising local and not national law-making power. Congress therefore may set up any form of local government organization that it wishes, including one that vests all authority in a single person, and could designate the president as that person.[67] Again to dismiss Cook's argument as nothing more than technical noodling, a tempting alternative given that the substitution of "right" principles brought no change in result, is to miss the point of the exercise. The separation of powers was an important part of the constitutional manifold for keeping public power within its appropriate sphere. To counsel that the doctrine was ultimately either impractical or nonexistent was directly to undermine the constitutional theory that held classical legal thought in place. So, Cook simply moved to push the pieces back into their proper order by invoking better premises, or at least different ones.

Cook's third piece of scholarship was also designed to set categories right. This time the problem was that of the nature and extent of the "police power" of a government. Unfortunately, the existence and extent of the police power did not fit very well into constitutional theory. Indeed, it seemed to work as a wild card upholding governmental action in circumstances where it would otherwise seem to violate a specific constitutional provision, most notably the due process clause. Ernest Freund, then a young, but ultimately extremely influential, scholar, who was part of the faculty of the University of Chicago in both the Law School and the Department of Political Science, had argued that the police power was nothing more or less than a power for "the promotion of the public welfare" and that both the states and the federal government had such power.[68] Cook rejected Freund's argument on the grounds that although so identifying the police power may be "useful . . . for the student of political science . . . our problem is to find a definition of the power which will both square with the usage of the courts and also prove of help in solving constitutional problems."[69]

Cook began with a wholly conventional analysis of "the distribution of governmental power in the American constitutional system." Proceeding from the notion of the federal government as one of exclusive or, where not exclusive but exercised, paramount powers, he identified "an indefinite, though clearly not an unlimited residuum of governmental power" in the states, and analytically divided that residuum of state power into the powers to maintain its existence, to maintain right or justice, and to promote the public welfare. This third class of the objects of government he then asserted was both "the residuum of governmental power left after subtracting from the sum total of the State's residuary powers of government," that is, the first two classes, and the police power, "the unclassified, residuary power of government vested by the constitution of the United States in the respective States." To thus support his assertion that Freund was wrong in asserting that the federal government possessed any police power, Cook used the example of "a law regulating the shipment of diseased cattle from State to State," which "the constitutional lawyer in classifying this law [if] passed by Congress would put it in the pigeon-hole labeled 'Regulations of inter-state commerce' and not that labeled 'The police power'" but "should a State pass a similar law . . . we should now . . . discuss it as a police law. . . ." "The determination of the apparent power of Congress to pass the law under discussion as a valid exercise of its power to regulate inter-state commerce tells us very little concerning the solution of the problem as to the power of the state to pass its law."[70]

Here, of course, the classificatory exercise is apparent right on the surface, even to Cook, who apologized for what was "perhaps after all very largely a quarrel over words." He could defend his part of the quarrel only with the observation, amusing in the context, that to say "that the national government has a police power . . . represents a result rather than a reason" and with an elaborate argument for the greater efficiency of organizing treatises according to the traditional classification.[71] But what was at issue, in fact, was the scope of national and state power to promote the public welfare.

Freund's reorganization of the traditional classification permitted one to argue in favor of state or federal regulation by saying in effect, "Why, of course, it's constitutional; the states (or the federal government) can do it in the exercise of their police power, so why can't we?" That Cook vaguely understood the point of Freund's argument is apparent, for he felt it necessary to observe that his preference for following legal categories in discussing the subject "should not lead . . . to any narrow view of the powers of the States to promote the general welfare or — what amounts to the same thing — any undue widening of the scope of the constitutional limitations" and to emphasize that the states "are the bodies vested with power and authority to meet the changing needs of society . . . by appropriate change in the law."[72] Yet, direct references to the necessity of what would later be called restraint when reviewing legislation, especially when passing on claims of denial of due process, were somehow left vaguely hanging, as if Cook were aware of, but reticent in talking about, the constitutional debates (crisis is surely too strong a word) swirling around.[73] And even this concern was tempered with the observation that "occasional lapses" by courts from the desirable standard "are sooner or later, if not expressly, least in effect overruled."[74]

Yet, something was still more curious than Cook's unease at talking about the real issues that animated the constitutional debates of the time. Freund's analytic point, that the federal government, like the states, had and exercised a police power, a power of promoting the general welfare, was both accurate and important. Cook's criticism of that point for what amounted to a failure to follow accepted legal categories was strange coming from a man who was a trained political scientist. Somehow Cook had come to accept the professional world view of the law professor.

Why Cook came to see himself as a law professor and not as the political scientist he came to Nebraska seemingly prepared to become is lost to us. I suspect that somehow, in some way that can no longer be demonstrated, the agent of change was Roscoe Pound, who was the jurisprudence part of the Department of American History and Jurisprudence.[75] But the course of his rather quick transformation is clearly recorded. In his second year at Nebraska, Cook added to his departmental course list the courses on constitutional law and comparative government and at the same time in the Law School offered the courses on domestic relations, wills, and federal jurisdiction.[76] By his third year, the outgoing Dean of the Law School was recommending that Cook's title be changed to Professor of Law[77] and Cook was increasing his teaching for the incoming Dean, Pound, by adding courses on equity, corporations, and constitutional law, while reducing his teaching in the Department of American History and Jurisprudence to constitutional history.[78] And then, at the end of that year, the new Professor of Law, faced with a call, "entirely unsolicited," which offered "many inducements, financial and otherwise," left Nebraska for Missouri and a full-time place in the Law School.[79] He would teach courses on agency, bills and notes, constitutional law, criminal law, equity, partnership, torts, and wills, a load that left little ambiguity as to his professional identity.[80]

How much actual psychic sustenance was provided by Ames's vision of a law professor's vocation and the related notion of working up through colonial service it is hard to say. Conditions in the West left much to be desired. The undergraduates surely had many other things on their minds than the refinements in tort, contract, and constitutional theory that emanated from the law reviews. And the corps of old practitioner teachers that often dominated these schools could have provided little support, even when they were not actively hostile. Moreover, the places were surely anything but idyllic.

Western winters in uninsulated frame houses that lacked central heating could be bitter and summers beastly hot; every outpost was miles away from nowhere, and every university community insular (and thus intolerant) as a defense against all that open space and the natives. Yet some people, like Cook and Moore, stuck it out. Which is not to say they loved it. Moore, about whom more is known, complained regularly about his low pay, lack of rapid advancement, and the awfulness of the places he was at. And at one point he even quit teaching.[81] But somehow he stayed anyway.

Some of the staying power on which Cook and Moore drew was in the mutual support network that all colonial officers develop. For example, each regularly tried to help the other to get and develop opportunities to teach at better schools and provided other support and encouragement. Other staying power was provided by mentors who offered necessary support and simultaneously reinforced the colonial and vocational perspectives.[82] But external support was by no means enough. Internalization of the professional norms implicit in the notion of a law professor's vocation was equally important. One can see examples of the internalization in Cook's early writings, most obviously in his rejection of Freund's argument. But it is clear as well in Moore's early work. First, he criticized a damages casebook for giving only a "half-hearted" rather than "thorough-going" application of the inductive method by lumping together tort and contract cases rather than separately working out the development of each form of action.[83] Later, he picked Williston as the model against which to measure "true scholarly instincts."[84] This was Ames's vocation written out.

The development of the norms of a scholarly vocation is, however, but a part of the process of creating a professional discipline. Another important part of that process is the identification and delineation of a field of knowledge that would be peculiar to, and the exclusive preserve of, the nascent legal academics. For numerous reasons, the field chosen by these law professors was the doctrinal world of largely private law that Langdell and his colleagues institutionalized at Harvard in the last third of the nineteenth century.[85] Scholarship was to be directed toward the task of rationalizing this doctrinal universe and keeping it free of poachers. The basic cleavage in the doctrinal system was the separation of the public from the private, of tort from contract. In confronting the question of the proper understanding of the basis for liability on contracts made by agents without their actual, but within their apparent, authority, Cook worked to keep the base of professional knowledge clean and well ordered. This was also one of the points of his arguing that the doctrine of separation of powers was not at all relevant to the question of how to govern the Philippines. But there was another point as well. To argue, as had Cook's antagonist, that the doctrine of separation of powers was irrelevant because the Supreme Court would never apply it was to undermine directly the key notion in the Langdellian universe — that law, the subject matter of legal science, the special field of knowledge of the academic lawyer, was a matter of principles and their invariable doctrinal application. If law was not invariably applied then legal science was not about anything, or at least anything that was distinct from what other individuals in the academy studied. It is here then that the real point of Cook's criticism of Freund's work on the police power is buried. To admit that there was a power in the federal government to advance the general welfare was not only to muck up the categories of constitutional law — though that was bad enough — it was also to muck up the boundary between law and political science. And it was on that boundary that the professional identity of the law professor depended. Freund's work may have been "useful . . . for the student of political science"[86] but it was dangerous for the student of law. And so Cook proceeded to give reasons, the lameness of which he all but admitted, why lawyers should ignore Freund's work and go about their business as usual.

Such was legal science in the first years of the twentieth century, boundary maintenance both inside and out attached to the notion, central to classical legal thought, that the proper subject of law was principles routinely applied by their terms — a vision of the rule of law such as Dicey would have approved of. The subject matter was not difficult, nor was the technique. It was, however, sufficiently academic to stake a plausible claim to membership in the university community, given that many other disciplines were no more rigorous or technically difficult. Besides, virtually all the disciplines outside of classics and the hard sciences were similarly professionalizing at this time, adopting a distinctive subject matter and a distinctive technique, and so were similarly vulnerable to claims that they did not really belong in a university.[87]

Yet that fact makes Cook's behavior, if not Moore's, all the more intriguing. Cook had available to him two potential professional identities — political scientist and academic lawyer. In some sense, by turning down the J.D. and instead pursuing the LL.M. and Ph.D. degrees as well as an initial appointment teaching political science, he had already chosen one identity. And yet somehow that choice was altered. But, however obscure the factors influencing that decision may be, one should not forget that there was a choice available, a choice to view law relatively more broadly or relatively more narrowly, political science or legal science. Cook went for the more narrow vision. That decision was not without its consequences.

Taking a Professional Identity Seriously: The Practice of Analytic Jurisprudence

After two years at Missouri, in 1906 Cook moved on to Wisconsin where two years later he was joined by Moore, who was surely glad to be anywhere but Kansas where the Dean had tried, and almost succeeded, to fire him after his first year of teaching.[88] Then, in 1910 Cook moved to the University of Chicago and four years later Moore followed him there. Wisconsin was a clear step up the law school pecking order from the schools at which each had been and Chicago a step up from Wisconsin, though in truth it is hard to see any significant difference between either school or university other than in the social class of the students. Wisconsin was at the beginning of its major growth. With the appointment a few years earlier of President Charles R. Van Hise, an intimate of progressive Governor LaFollette, the University began a period of active involvement in service to the state and people of Wisconsin, the so-called Wisconsin Idea. Enrollment in the University was large and growing at an unprecedented rate; the College of Letters and Science doubled in size from 1,300 to 2,600 students in the years between 1903 and 1917 and the entire University doubled in size from 2,000 to 4,000 between 1900 and 1910 and then almost doubled again in the next ten years. Like other midwestern universities, fraternities were growing in importance as was football, but, unlike others, the University already had a distinguished faculty, including Frederick Jackson Turner in history, John Commons and Richard T. Ely in economics, Edward A. Ross in sociology, and F. C. Sharp in philosophy. And this was a faculty deeply involved in creating the ideal of academic freedom as it participated in the political and intellectual controversies of the day in a state highly polarized between "stalwart" Republican, conservative, commercial and industrial interests and LaFollette's progressive supporters.[89]

Chicago was growing less and was less notable for its stands on academic freedom than for its intolerance of faculty sexual transgressions, as the cases of Thorstein Veblen and W. I. Thomas indicate, but was otherwise intellectually similar. Led by its dynamic, if academically rapacious President, William Rainey Harper, the school was a hotbed of the progressive reform movement in Chicago, fulfilling a role in "state service" for the "outs" in local politics that Van Hise's school did for LaFollette's progressives when they were the "ins."[90] Similarly, the faculty was quite distinguished—Albion Small and Thomas in sociology, George Herbert Mead and John Dewey in philosophy, Charles E. Merriam in political science, and James R. Angell in psychology and, at least briefly, Veblen in economics.

The law schools were equally similar. The Wisconsin law faculty was less notable intellectually than the University as a whole, but was still quite strong, and significantly better than that at places like Kansas, Nebraska, or Missouri. Its Dean, Harry S. Richards, was Harvard-trained and an active participant in the activities of the Association of American Law Schools. It was a smallish school, about 165 students, only recently turned over to the case method of instruction, but it required that its students have two years of college in order to enter, more than most schools.[91] Its faculty was relatively large so that teaching loads were relatively lighter than the more western schools.[92] While hardly elite, it had, on its faculty, in addition to the Dean, at least two strong and vaguely productive scholars.[93] Cook was the fourth and Moore was the fifth and thus completed the dominance of the faculty by instructors committed to case method legal education.

Chicago had started as a clone of Harvard and so was a largely case method school from the beginning.[94] It was a relatively small school as well, with a student body of about four hundred and a faculty of seven.[95] But a still lower teaching load than at Wisconsin and substantially higher salaries made it quite an attractive place to teach.[96] James Parker Hall, its Dean, was, like Richards, a Harvard product, active in AALS affairs, and a moderately competent scholar. Overall the school had two other reasonably competent scholars[97] and one first-rate one, Ernst Freund. Here too Cook and Moore provided depth.

There was a third law school in the area. Northwestern, located in downtown Chicago, a full ten miles away from its parent University and thus more than a little detached from it, was overall probably as good as Wisconsin or Chicago. It was run by the only truly distinguished scholar in the area, John Henry Wigmore, with the help of a few full-time faculty and a corps of devoted part-time practitioner teachers, some of whom were quite serious scholars.[98] Unfortunately, whatever their distinction, these part-time teachers gave the place a bad name in academic legal circles in which it was more important for professional standing to have all, or almost all, full-time faculty than any practitioner, however distinguished.

The three schools were physically close enough to break down some of the social and intellectual isolation that characterized life in the West and to foster some local interchange. The main site for the intellectual interchange was the Chicago summer session;[99] for the social, treks around and about Madison's two beautiful lakes and time in Chicago's beer gardens.[100] It was in this environment that Cook and Moore developed their professional vocation, where they practiced legal science.

Of the two, Moore's work was the less interesting. It included a jointly authored casebook on negotiable instruments,[101] a new edition of a standard student/practitioner's treatise on the subject,[102] and a short article,[103] all of which work was generally expository and notable primarily for the copiousness of its footnotes. It was but a species of encyclopedism like much of the work of Wigmore and Williston but of substantially less distinction. Cook's work on the other hand was more unusual and illuminating. To understand it, however, one needs to pick up on a peculiar intellectual cross current in Cook's life — Wesley N. Hohfeld.

In 1911, when Cook was on the faculty at Chicago, he met Hohfeld who was a young associate professor from the Stanford Law School and who was there spending part of his sabbatical teaching a course on evidence. The two became "companions-in-law." Hohfeld was very impressed by Cook whom he found to have "a very genuine enthusiasm for the deeper analysis of legal problems commonly dealt with in works on 'analytical jurisprudence.' "[104] Just what this enthusiasm was for is hard to state clearly. But an event that followed Cook's semester of teaching with Hohfeld provides an example from which to work and a clue as to the more important question, What difference does it make?

Roscoe Pound, who was President of the Association of American Law Schools for the year 1912 and who had made Hohfeld's acquaintance when both taught in the Chicago summer session in 1910,[105] asked Hohfeld to be the principal substantive speaker at the Association's annual meeting, then held in the summer.[106] The idea was a quite obvious attempt to advance the career of a friend who had published little and that little on an obscure point about the proper way of treating the contingent personal liability of the shareholders of California corporations in the conflict of laws.[107] In response, Hohfeld, who could not attend without upsetting his plans for a trip to Europe during the second half of his sabbatical, made a suggestion in much the same spirit. Why not have Cook, whose views were in "full sympathy" with his own, deliver the address?[108] Pound agreed and Cook took up the task with great seriousness.

The speech Cook produced was entitled "The Place of Equity in Our Legal System," though the real issue was the plausibility of continuing the separate course on equity. Cook asserted that the continuation of such a separate course, as an example of which he had the bad taste to use Hohfeld's own course description from the Stanford catalog, was "belated and reactionary, because it is unscientific both from the point of view of analysis and from that of educational expediency." He then briefly controverted Ames's justification of the separateness of equity on the ground that "equity acts upon the person" with an observation — "Procedure in personam may be, and frequently is used to protect and enforce rights in rem, as well as rights in personam, and the nature of equitable rights is not necessarily different from that of legal rights because a different remedy for their actual or threatened violation is offered" — before turning to the business at hand, a detailed review of the content of the equity course. His conclusions are hardly startling to modern readers. He approved of the separate course in trusts and advocated the inclusion of equitable remedies for tortious conduct with the torts course, equitable remedies for breach of contract with the contracts course, and restitution with the course in quasi-contracts, contracts implied in law. That any other course of action was "not a scientific procedure" seemed to Cook "obvious, and not to require further discussion." The distribution of materials proposed, while admittedly "of no small difficulty" and one requiring "the best thoughts and efforts of at least a whole faculty working in cooperation for a considerable period," would, however, Cook asserted, "by the constant contrasting of the two systems [law and equity] principle by principle rule by rule — the less ethical view of the common law . . . with the more ethical view of the court of equity . . ." — serve to emphasize "the special nature of equity," the "discretionary element," " 'the balance of convenience.' "[109]

By no means did all of Cook's listeners see the matter as obvious. At least the principal commentator on Cook's paper, Henry Schofield, a quite conservative specialist in constitutional law and equity at Northwestern,[110] thought Cook's idea to be less than good. Relying heavily on the existence of the separate course in damages for his starting point, he did not find it "unscientific" to distinguish substance and procedure and therefore to study separately the law "regulating the application, operation and effect of the remedy of compulsion and coercion, as distinguished from the remedy of damages to redress torts and breaches of contract."[111] Moreover, in contrast to Cook's call, really an echo of Pound's, for a reinvigoration of equity,[112] Schofield felt it important both to remind Cook that such a call needed to bear in mind "our indispensable and just rule of precedent and the constitutional prerogatives of the Legislature" and to call for a reinvigoration of damages, "giving lawyers and judges more freedom to fuse the liberal and daring, but consistent and coherent spirit of equity into the administration of the remedy of damages, exploring and expanding the fountains of the law in the best feelings, manners, creations, and traditions of the people, and giving less attention to the rivulets."[113]

Hohfeld, who had believed that Cook's address would track, not attack, the syllabus of his own course, was not happy when he found that Cook had made that course into an object lesson in what not to do. So Hohfeld felt obliged to try "twitting" Cook a bit for holding his course up to scrutiny.[114] The result was a piece that combined a defense of his syllabus with a presentation of "an analytic synopsis and a diagrammatic sketch" that Hohfeld distributed to students to get across the points that Cook made about the relationship between law and equity and a sharp attack on the proposition, advanced by Maitland, Ames, and Langdell, that equity and law do not conflict. The last was clearly the point to be made: "There is . . . a very marked and constantly recurring conflict between equitable and legal rules relating to various jural relations; and whenever such conflict occurs, the equitable rule is, in the last analysis, paramount and determinative." Yet, Hohfeld made clear that his purpose was less pedagogical, as Cook's had been, than purely analytical. He noted that other courses such as damages, persons, and the conflict of laws mix substantive legal categories and that whether to do so or instead to follow Cook's plan "has generally been determined primarily by convenience or accident." And in keeping with this observation, he suggested that the only solution to giving a student "an appreciation of the common law as a coordinated system" was to institute "a solid and comprehensive course in . . . analytical jurisprudence."[115]

Analytical jurisprudence, there is that name again. Two years later Hohfeld asserted that from its name "there would be fairly general agreement as to what it should include" and so went on to show that its purposes were "to gain an accurate . . . understanding of the fundamental working conceptions of all legal reasoning" in order "to ascertain the exact relations . . . between the larger parts of our jural system" and "to understand, to explain and to improve, when necessary, the leading divisions and subdivisions of the whole field of law considered as an integral, harmonious and symmetrical body of doctrine."[116] Yet all of these words somehow obscure more than they illuminate. For example, all of Cook's early scholarship was analytical in an important sense. It relied on the analysis of basic legal concepts — assent and agency, the police power, and separation of powers — to establish and maintain "the leading divisions and subdivisions of the whole field of law considered as an integral, harmonious and symmetrical body of doctrine." And in this sense much of pre–World War I legal scholarship was analytical and thus Cook's "genuine enthusiasm" unremarkable. Yet, there is a difference between the implicit boundary maintenance that was Cook's early scholarship and the explicit discussion of boundaries that was Cook's and Hohfeld's work on law and equity. Still, I doubt whether explicitness makes jurisprudence analytical.

Hohfeld tried an implicit definition of analytical jurisprudence when he distinguished it from "historical or genetic jurisprudence"; "comparative or eclectic jurisprudence"; "critical, or teleological, jurisprudence," "the *systematic* testing or critique of our principles and rules of law according to considerations *extrinsic* or *external* to the principles and rules as such, that is, according to the psychological, ethical, political, social and economic bases of the various doctrines and the respective purposes or ends sought to be achieved thereby"; "legislative, or constructive jurisprudence," "the constructive science and art of legislation in all its phases"; and "functional, or dynamic, jurisprudence," "the systematic and empirical study of the actual functioning of the various rules of law."[117] In this context analytical jurisprudence is not historical, comparative, critical, legislative, or empirical — that is, it deals with present, domestic, judge-made law in ways that ignore both its purposes and effects. All of which leaves only "*intrinsic* or *internal* considerations of logical consistency and system," which brings one back to Cook's early scholarship, which is absolutely unremarkable, taken as a type.

But, if one ignores Hohfeld's words and looks at his own scholarship, analytic jurisprudence differs quite markedly from normal boundary maintenance. His next two articles expounded in great detail "Some Fundamental Legal Conceptions As Applied in Judicial Reasoning," a system for classification of jural relations. The system, which was by no means novel to Hohfeld, was designed to provide a basis for distinguishing and discriminating various legal terms such as "right," "duty," and "liberty." The details of the system are unimportant. Like any system for defining legal terms, it had its own elements of arbitrariness, yet, unlike other systems of definitional analysis, for a brief instant it was all the rage, and in subsequent years it has been rediscovered with amazing frequency.[118] Its most notable characteristic was that it pushed the task of classification to an Austinian level of abstraction, something not difficult, I suppose, for one who had a heavily annotated copy of Austin's *Province of Jurisprudence Determined*, which had been in his possession since his days as an undergraduate.[119] This rise in the level of abstraction can be seen in Cook's shift from talking about agency by estoppel or governing the Philippines, matters of doctrine, to the relationship between law and equity, a matter higher up on the hierarchical totem pole, and so from using those abstractions to maintain the edifice of classical legal thought to explicating those abstractions. But to identify analytical jurisprudence with work within the system, but at a high level of abstraction, does not explain why Cook — or anyone else, for that matter — cared about this or any other set of formal relations, of interrelated definitions.

The answer to this question can be seen by considering again Cook's and Hohfeld's work on equity. This work seems both to strike a new note in scholarship and to be more than a bit audacious. The new note is easy to describe but more than a little ephemeral. There is a sense in both pieces of driving through, of analytic exercises pushed more for the purpose of getting "it" right than for doing anything with "it." That can be seen negatively in Hohfeld's criticism of Cook's curricular suggestions, as well as positively in Hohfeld's point about the conflict of law and equity. Hohfeld's analysis made no practical difference in the outcome of cases and thus might be called an "academic exercise" in ways that Cook's proposal about the necessity to reflect the substantive role of equity in curriculum design could not. Now, of course, Cook and others had engaged in academic exercises before; the entire piece on governing the Philippines was admittedly an academic exercise. But, once one notices the audacity of the arguments, the academicism takes on a different light.

If there were grand legal boundaries to the legal system, then the boundary of law and equity was up there on a par with that of tort and contract, just below public and private. And, if there were real heroes in the academic pantheon, they included Langdell, Ames, and Maitland. So to suggest that the grand divisions of law and equity, rule and discretion, the carrying out of private agreement through the assessment of damages and the imposition of public force could be dispensed with in the interest of substantive wholeness or that the real heroes got the basic proposition wrong — indeed, that public force overrode private agreement — was not a matter of keeping the boundaries in good order, but of undermining those boundaries, as Henry Schofield in his encomium for damage law, at least intuitively understood. Cook and Hohfeld were asserting that not only was law two systems of rules and not one system of rules — "Equity follows the law" — with two sets of remedies, but also that, as a result, law was less a matter of the invariable application of norms, as classical legal thought would have had it, and more a matter of equitable, and thus variable, discretion on the part of officials of the state.

Not only was there a substantive challenge in what the two men had said, but also this substantive challenge was accompanied by a change in the use of simple analytic tools in addition to the obvious shift in the level of the abstraction of the analysis — a sense of grand purpose and of power. The source of this sense of grand purpose is the continuing development of the professional identity of the law professor. The grandness can be seen in numerous places. The 1914 meeting of the Association of American Law Schools brought forth three of them. First, there was Henry Bates's presidential address in which he noted that "not since the time when Langdell and Ames proved that there is a science of justice principles and that law may best be taught, not as dogma or a trade, but as a science and a profession, have law teachers occupied a position of equal strength for helping to direct social movements towards a more nearly perfect justice."[120] The old guard in the person of Joseph Beale noted that the current generation of law professors was "called" not only to carry on "the work of the former generation" by improving "the art of teaching law" and continuing "to study the separate branches of our science," but also "to a more modern task: to bring the law into closer relation with the needs of contemporary life."[121] Finally, came Hohfeld who put forward a grand plan for establishing a "Vital School of Law and Jurisprudence," as "not a mere matter of juridical ornament or intellectual delight," but of "economic and social value" that "would be difficult to overestimate."[122]

Grand is perhaps not even a strong enough word for this school. First, it would engage in "the professional or vocational study of the Anglo-American legal system" so as to turn out "ordinary practicing lawyers," albeit ordinary practicing lawyers who would have prescribed courses in legal history and general jurisprudence as well as in office practice. Second, it would engage in the civic and cultural study of legal institutions by "non-professional college students" lest "the lay leaders of public opinion" be "inadequately or misleadingly informed both as to the foundation principles of our system of justice according to law and as to the most elementary requirements for its successful operation." Third, and most important, it would engage in "the systematic and developmental study of legal institutions," that is, of the six branches of general jurisprudence previously enumerated, by "professorial jurists" who would use such training to "influence . . . the development and amelioration of law and its administration . . . through teaching others," as well as through the writing of "constructive books, magazine discussions and proposals, appearances before legislative committees and commissions, and occasionally through actual membership in constitutional, legislative or administrative commissions and associations, 'uniform act' commissions, etc." Such training would even be for "those who are in charge of the ordinary professional courses" as well as for legal authors, legislative draftsmen, members of administrative commissions, and legislators.[123]

That hindsight suggests the futility of such a grand scheme should not be allowed to obscure its contextual significance. The search for a vocation is always a part of forging a professional identity.[124] And, as noted before, the attempt to articulate that identity was already twenty years old when Bates, Beale, and Hohfeld wrote. Thus, the important thing to note is the great optimism that underlay Hohfeld's grand scheme and the sense of potential power to influence the development of law. The American academic lawyers were going to follow the path of the German academic lawyers who drafted the German Civil Code.[125] What was called for was to provide training for these academics at a suitably elevated and specialized institution, a school not just of law but of jurisprudence as well, indeed a school where jurisprudence was given pride of place. The younger generation, of which Hohfeld was a prime example, stuck, as he was, out at Stanford (a third-rate law school, which like most in the West taught undergraduates),[126] had absorbed the professional identity articulated by Ames and others and was not only comfortable with it but also was eager to push it onward.

It was, I suggest, this eagerness to push the academic enterprise on that Hohfeld identified as a "genuine enthusiasm" in Cook for "analytic jurisprudence." Analytic work had been Cook's metier since the beginning. Hohfeld offered a system for that analytic work, it is true, but, more important, he offered a vision of why that analytic work was significant. The work was a necessary prerequisite to the task of improving, "when necessary, the leading divisions and subdivisions of the whole field of law." It was the linchpin of the grand vocation for the law professor. And so Cook took up Hohfeld's system and ran with it.

Or more accurately plodded, for the question that Cook chose to explore for nearly eighty pages of the *Columbia Law Review*[127] was the viability of the old aphorism "Equity acts *in personam*, Law, *in rem*." The details of the argument are, in fact, unimportant.[128] The conclusion Cook drew from his analysis was that while actions and judgments have a necessary relationship, actions *in rem* (or *in personam*) always yield judgments *in rem* (or *in personam*), "there is . . . no necessary connection between the character of the . . . right and the character of the action and judgment"[129] or with the procedure that enforces it.[130]

This conclusion was supported with examples, often argued at length, designed to show that equity sometimes acts *in rem* and law *in personam*, generally by demonstrating the similarity of the remedial procedure used in both courts. Cook's leading example was the enforcement of a judgment or decree for the payment of money. Here he followed out the common law writs of *capias ad satisfaciendum, fieri facias, levari facias,* and *elegit* and the equity proceedings for contempt and sequestration. Here his conclusion was, "if the common law did not at times act *in personam* in enforcing money judgments, it is hard to say what *in personam* means; and if the chancellor did not at times act *in rem* in enforcing decrees for money, he gave so good an imitation of it that it can with difficulty be distinguished from the genuine article."[131]

Throughout the entire exercise the dominant notes were two, the same two that were to be found in Cook's speech to the AALS and in Hohfeld's reply. First was the audacious attack on revered elders, in this case Langdell, whose "A Brief Survey of the Equity Jurisdiction"[132] was the then baseline of learning on the subject, and second was that of "seeing through" the mass of legal rules to get at "the real object of the action," of getting past form and to substance.[133]

The obvious change in attitude from that which underlay Cook's earlier articles is here significant. For example, in the article on the police power, form was seen as more important than substance and the seeing through that Freund engaged in when concluding that the federal government had a police power was roundly rejected. Now, Cook himself was seeing through form and emphasizing substance. But there is another aspect of the article that merits recognition: the slow creeping into the analysis of Hohfeld's recognition that rights in a *res* are not unitary things but are both "the physical object and congeries of legal rights, privileges and other jural relations which go to make up title or ownership." Thus, although the analytic task was always seen as reaching "the proper classification," that task of classification became considerably more complicated when this insight about the nature of rights in a *res* became transformed into the assertion that "a legal right *in personam*" was *res.*[134]

The point of these analytic shenanigans was, of course, not particularly clear, though there is a recurrent note of concern about matters of the appropriate scope of the practice of securing jurisdiction through publication and of seeing that "the superior ethical character of equity" not be hampered by adherence to outmoded understandings more "suitable to the time of Coke" than to "modern courts of equity, as they exist, both in the absence of statutes and under typical modern statutes."[135] But, in a real sense, no point was necessary. The point was getting it right, just as it had been when Cook wrote fifteen years earlier. Now, however, it was the traditional understandings about law that were under attack rather than being defended.[136]

Further shift in this classificatory enterprise can be seen in a dispute Cook engaged with the venerable Samuel Williston in the pages of the *Harvard Law Review*. The subject was the alienability of choses in action and Cook's point was short and sweet. Ames had said that choses in action (debts, contract rights, etc.) were not assignable, alienable, or transferable or, more conservatively stated, that the transfer of a chose in action created only an equitable title and not a legal title. Cook, drawing heavily this time on Hohfeld's "Fundamental Legal Conceptions," especially the notions of "power," "privilege," and "immunity," notions that "some of us, especially those who are engaged in the teaching of law" are coming to use, proceeded to show that while at one time the rights of the assignee were recognized only in courts of chancery, under "modern" law, really eighteenth- and early nineteenth-century law, courts of law had come to recognize the same rights in the assignee as had chancery courts, except for the right of the transferee to sue on the obligation in its own name. Even that limit had evaporated with the adoption of the various "real party in interest" statutes. Thus, Cook suggested, "The old bottles are filled with entirely new wine and it is time to change the label" and say that the assignee is the legal owner of the chose.[137] Again the dominant notes were the audaciousness of the target, Ames, and of seeing through the mass of legal rules to learn what was really going on.

The analysis seems essentially flawless today, to the extent anyone would care. Professor Williston, however, did not see matters this way. He suggested that the conclusion that the assignee "should be regarded as having a legal rather than an equitable right" was undesirable because of the effect it would have on three classical cases, for, given that "the methods by which . . . results are obtained at law and in equity are fundamentally different," the risk that courts would apply the legal rule in these three cases if it were seen that ownership was legal was great enough that no change in the classification of the right of the assignee ought to be made.[138]

It was a nice little article; indeed, Williston's reasons for preferring the equitable rather than the legal rule in all three classes of cases seem persuasive. Even Cook was perhaps persuaded of the correctness of the results in all three classes of cases; at least he did not dispute them. Nevertheless, he felt obliged to reply and with big guns. Characterizing Williston's argument, perhaps a bit, though not wholly, unfairly, as one based on the " 'fundamental' or 'essential characteristics' of legal and equitable 'rights' " and of the "necessary or logical connection" of "jural effects" with the "legal or equitable character of the ownership of the assignee," Cook attempted to demonstrate that Williston had "failed to follow the essential features of the analysis presented . . . and so . . . failed to understand" what Cook's conclusions were.[139]

Most of Williston's failures were relatively trivial.[140] However, Cook thumped Williston hard for believing in the existence of any fundamental or essential characteristic of equitable rights, "aside from the fact that they are recognized and sanctioned by courts of equity,"[141] and also attacked the notion that necessary consequences would attach to a right from being labeled legal. Here Cook noted again and again that "there is no *inherent* reason why the chancellor should change his views as to . . . [the scope of rights] or why the law court, recognizing their historical origin, may not give them precisely the same limitations they previously had when exclusively equitable." Finally, Cook, sounding more like Bentham and Holmes than Hohfeld, triumphantly concluded that the justification for any rule "is ultimately in principles of fairness, of public policy . . . rather than in the supposed requirements of logic."[142]

The tone throughout Cook's reply was one of a teacher's impatience with a slow learner, but there was also a sense of young men impatient with their elders, especially in the call for "men adequately trained to analyze with accuracy the fundamental concepts which lie at the basis of our legal system in a terminology that will not mislead" in order to aid the attempt "at the present time not only to adapt our law to modern social and industrial conditions, but also to restate much of it in the form of codes of uniform state laws."[143] Williston, who was obviously bewildered by the vehemence of Cook's reply could only note in his own defense that his usage was that of "many distinguished judges and lawyers." But his reliance on "established principle," "a legal possibility for a court bound by the system of Anglo-American common law," and the "natural and necessary consequences of the essential characteristics of personal rights," an observation much like that made by Henry Schofield six years earlier, suggested that there was more of a disagreement between the two men than Williston would recognize. Curiously there was more agreement as well, for, although Williston could not see it, the horrible results he was trying to avoid, judicial action "not because of any consideration of teleological fitness, but mechanical reasoning,"[144] was precisely what Cook was seeking through his advocacy of "scientific" terminology. Such was analytic jurisprudence before World War I — Austin (deriv-atively through Hohfeld), a hint of Benthan and Holmes, but mostly exercises in classification understandable as participating in classical legal thought. It was legal science and not social science by any stretch of the imagination.

Bringing a Professional Identity Back East: Changes in the Practice of Analytic Jurisprudence

Within eighteen months of arriving at Chicago, Moore got the call that all colonial officers long for. He was offered a post at Columbia. Though he negotiated diffidently,[145] he clearly wanted the post. This was the big time. Not only was Columbia historically the first major convert to Langdell's case method, but it was a big school with over five hundred students and fourteen full-time faculty.[146] The school was growing in reputation under the leadership of Harlan F. Stone after a relative decline, starting around the time that both Cook and Moore left law school, as a result of both ineffective leadership and weak faculty appointments.[147] The University was perhaps at the peak of its eminence, especially in the social sciences. In addition to the still excellent political science department, there were James Harvey Robinson and Charles Beard in history, Thorstein Veblen[148] and Wesley C. Mitchell in economics, Franz Boas in anthropology, E. L. Thorndike in educational psychology, William F. Ogburn in sociology, and, of course, John Dewey. And so Moore quickly came to terms and accepted Stone's offer.

Even before leaving Chicago, Moore began trying to bring friends with him.[149] His efforts were at least temporarily unsuccessful and so in the same year Cook went to Yale instead. Why Cook made this switch is a bit of a puzzle. Though a post at New Haven was a return to the East for a colonial officer, Yale was definitely not the big time. The University was at best an overgrown college, not particularly happy at having become such, and other than William Graham Summer in sociology, a man hardly at the cutting edge of that new discipline, its eminence in the social sciences was nonexistent.[150] The student body was "old blue," which meant that social status and the "gentleman's C" were much in evidence in the selection and education, respectively, of its students. The Law School was for all practical purposes moribund. Its student body was small; its dean, Henry Wade Rogers, a recent appointee to the Second Circuit Court of Appeals, was a part-time teacher who did not want to retire, and its faculty, but for two members, were thoroughly undistinguished, if not better described as unknown.[151] One of those two known members was a respected contracts scholar, Arthur L. Corbin; the other, a relative newcomer to the faculty, Wesley Hohfeld. Hoh-

feld had moved to Yale two years earlier. In 1913 when he had submitted his
piece on the fundamental legal conceptions in response to an invitation from
the *Yale Law Journal*,[152] Arthur Corbin had read it and liked it so much that
he convinced Hohfeld to join the Yale faculty.[153] Thereafter Corbin recruited
Thomas W. Swan, a Yale College graduate and *Harvard Law Review* Editor
in Chief, then in practice in Chicago, to replace Rogers as Dean.[154] Swan and
Hohfeld seem to have together recruited Cook,[155] whom the Yale student
newspaper called "one of the foremost teachers of Law in this country."[156]

Though some may have thought it surprising that Cook should have left
Chicago, "about as desirable a place as there was in the country,"[157] in truth
the place was a bit "close and stuffy."[158] Yale, in contrast, where much of its
faculty was aging, offered, with the coming of a new dean, a certain optimism
and the exciting sense of starting over. And then there was Hohfeld's presence. Cook had clearly been taken with Hohfeld's work since the two had
first met in Chicago. And Hohfeld clearly enjoyed Cook's companionship.[159]
So it is not surprising, though hardly necessary, that the two should have
contrived to teach together on a more permanent basis.

And at the start it was exciting. Cook said later that he had seen the job
as offering a chance "to build up a school along broader lines than law
schools generally have been built upon" and as presenting the chance to
"have greater influence in carrying out the ideals . . . [he had] for law school
education."[160] Not surprisingly, Hohfeld too found his heart solely centered
on "the development of . . . [Yale] along larger lines of effort."[161] And the new
Dean, described by one of his students as "susceptible to the influence of
people who did have the vision of the grail,"[162] apparently did too. At least
Cook and Hohfeld, obviously with the encouragement, support, and assistance of Corbin, were able to convince Swan to announce a drive to increase
the school's endowment by $2.5 million in order to turn Yale Law School
into the "Yale School of Law and Jurisprudence" with a proposal that bore
an uncanny resemblance to the institution described in Hohfeld's "Vital
School."[163]

The echo of Hohfeld in the proposed title for the school was but the
smallest part of the resemblance. Courses such as "Historical Jurisprudence,"
"Comparative Jurisprudence," "Analytic Jurisprudence," "Teleological and
Functional Jurisprudence," and the "Science and Art of Legislation" were
straight out of Hohfeld's article. So was the tripartite division of its activities
into programs of "professional education," "civic and cultural education of
non-professional college men," and "scientific and constructive" instruction
of "jurists broadly trained for service in many fields of useful and far reaching

activity" who would study "law and its evolution, historically, comparatively, analytically and critically, with the purpose of directing its development in the future, improving its administration and perfecting its methods of
legislation."[164]

Optimism surely ran high over the proposal.[165] Such optimism was stimu-
lated in part by the receipt two years previously of the income from an
endowment of over one-third of a million dollars.[166] Hohfeld looked forward
to "a friendly institutional competition" between Harvard and Yale, so that
Yale's "own ambitions and efforts" would spur Harvard to "yet greater efforts and bigger achievements"[167] and confessed that he had "never been
more interested in or more cheerful as to the outlook for things in the future."[168] Cook, more mercurial, negotiated for a job at Columbia up until the
minute the Yale Corporation gave its blessing to the plan[169] and then abruptly
shifted to recruiting his friends to come to Yale.[170] But, quite suddenly, everything changed. During the winter of 1918 Hohfeld fell ill, first with the
"grippe" and then with a bacterial infection resulting from a dead tooth.[171]
Hospitalized for several months, he felt that he was "steadily improving" so
that "by fall" he would be "on hand as of old."[172] Although that expectation
continued into September,[173] Hohfeld never returned to teaching and died
from complications of an acute inflammation of the lining of the heart in mid-
October of that year.[174]

Cook found Hohfeld's death a "sad and irreparable loss"[175] and noted that
it would "be impossible to fill his place with a man of equal analytical ability."[176] Condolences from Cook's friends came directly.[177] Pound who had
"known him longer than most of you" suggested organizing a festschrift "as a
monument worthy of his achievements and his promise," "a memorial to a
true, thorough-going legal scholar."[178] Instead, Yale planned to reprint Hohfeld's articles with "a suitable memoir of him" by Cook as he "had known
him as long and intimately as anyone in the country and at the time of his
death was probably more fully acquainted with his plans and ideas than
anyone else."[179]

Cook's memoir, initially published in the *Yale Law Journal*, is remarkably
flat.[180] Indeed, Llewellyn's student appreciation of the man is far more moving.[181] Cook ignored the idea of a memoir and chose merely to preface a
simplified restatement of Hohfeld's "Fundamental Conceptions" and "Relations between Law and Equity," with a tribute to the practical value of
analytic jurisprudence, which, like any branch of "pure science," is an "aid to
the correct solution of legal problems" so that they are "not only easier but
more certain." He then appended to the whole a plug for Yale as the embodi-

ment of Hohfeld's program for a "Vital School" that would train "men, not merely for the business of earning a living by 'practicing law,' but also for the larger duties of the profession . . . in so shaping and adjusting our law that it will be a living, vital thing, growing with society and adjusting itself to the *mores* of the times."[182]

There is something more than a trifle ironic in these closing lines, for Hohfeld was dead barely six months before Cook was actively attempting to move elsewhere, seeking a place at which "the greatest progress is to be hoped for in really doing constructive things during the next twenty years."[183] The choice he made was to rejoin Underhill Moore who, much to his surprise, had been quite happy at Columbia since his arrival in 1916.[184] Cook was trumpeted as "a teacher of wide reputation."[185] That he was paid $10,000 per year, the highest salary of any law teacher in the country, and at least $2,500 more than his Yale salary three years earlier,[186] could not have hurt, but to suggest purely mercenary reasons for this move or for the disappointing memorial to Hohfeld is surely inappropriate. For Cook's published work over the previous three years and over the subsequent three years showed better than words ever could Hohfeld's influence on Cook and thus Cook's debt to Hohfeld.

A good deal of this scholarship is in the form of case notes written to keep the *Yale Law Journal* publishing during the enormous decline in its enrollment caused by drafting law students after the American entry into World War I. For the most part these articles build on Cook's earlier work on equity. They use Hohfeld's analytic tools, often merely to suggest that a case, otherwise correct, had been poorly reasoned.[187] Thus, the dominant note in these pieces is, not surprisingly, the same as elsewhere. Better analytic techniques would disabuse people of implausible notions and thus make solving problems easier. But two new notes need to be recognized. The first is purely substantive, the appearance of material on the conflict of laws.[188] This interest too can be ascribed to Hohfeld who had taught the course both at Stanford and Yale[189] and who left Cook all of his notes on the subject in his will.[190] The second is the continuation of the note briefly sounded at the end of the reply to Williston: social policy.

The problem of pure analytic jurisprudence was, as both its critics and defenders recognized, that it led nowhere. Accurate statement and clean analysis that showed exactly what was at issue in a case left one wondering what to do about the precise issue identified. Here Cook often stuffed in Pound and sociological jurisprudence. For example, commercial questions were to be determined as a matter of "sound business policy."[191] But, understanding the relationship between analytic jurisprudence and social policy is more complicated than simply noting that the latter gets stuffed in where the former left off. This relationship can best be seen free of the obscure details of early twentieth-century business law by focusing on cases concerning labor injunctions that caught Cook's eye during these years.

The most famous of these pieces and a sensible example to work with is the one on *Hitchman Coal and Coke v. Mitchell*.[192] *Hitchman* was an action by the owner of a nonunion coal mine to enjoin the United Mine Workers from attempting to organize its mine. All the workers at the mine were employed "at will" and each had "agreed" that he would work as a nonunion miner. Mr. Justice Pitney, one of Cook's goats,[193] held that the injunction was appropriately issued even in the absence of acts or threats of picketing or of physical violence. He began from the premise that the mineowner was acting within its rights in running a nonunion mine and in agreeing with its employees that they would be employed only as long as they were not union members. He then concluded that a court could issue an injunction to protect that agreement from the harm to it resulting from the organizing activities of the mine workers union, especially since the union was, on the most charitable construction of its activities, attempting to persuade the employees to leave their employer.

Using Hohfeld's categories, Cook first established that the mineowner had not a "right" but a "privilege" to employ nonunion labor, noting however that that statement "tells us nothing about the *rights*" of the mineowner since "a privilege may exist without an accompanying right." Cook next recognized the right "in the strict sense" to the benefit of lawful agreements and thereafter recast the constitutional "right" to make nonunion membership a condition of employment into an "immunity" from governmental power, so that governments "are under legal (constitutional) *disabilities* (lack legal power) to make laws which will deprive employers of the *privilege*" of running a nonunion mine. He then summarized, "Clearly from propositions concerning any one of these [three legal relationships — privilege, right, immunity], no inferences can be drawn concerning the others by any logical process which is *merely deductive*." Thus, to the extent the Court "meant to say that the *right* of the plaintiff to protection *necessarily* followed as a matter of mere logical inference from the *privilege* to make the agreements . . . [with his employees], the reasoning is clearly fallacious." If, on the other hand, it meant to say "that good policy demands that such a right to protection be given, it is clear that . . . nothing has been proved and that we are at last face to face with the real question at issue: 'Against what kinds of acts ought protection as a matter of policy be given?'" And then he concluded, "[N]either by the citation of binding precedents and the logical application of settled rules of law, nor by an adequate discussion of the social and economic problem involved, is any real progress made [by Justice Pitney] toward the solution of the question at issue."[194]

Cook never went on to work out the proper solution to the question beyond offering the observation that "the minority [Holmes, Brandeis, and Clarke] are more nearly right upon most points than the majority."[195] But the thrust and structure of the argument are clear. Analytic jurisprudence could be used to expose for discussion questions that classical legal theory had managed to hide within its categorical structure. By subdividing or narrowing and thus isolating the question posed by the court, one could escape that monolithic categorical structure and attack issues piecemeal in the light of assumably good social and economic policy.

Whether Hohfeld ever contemplated this use of his grand analytic engine is doubtful; at least his published work nowhere suggests that he did.[196] But plainly Cook had figured out that analytic jurisprudence had this potential, for other arguments with the same structure abound, for example in his discussion of union boycotts of nonunion goods where he quickly stripped the question of the "rights" of the union down to the question of its "privilege" to engage in such a boycott,[197] and in his discussion of an injunction given in the 1922 railway strike in which he subdivided the issue into several different questions only to find that on none of these is there any "'well settled law'" by which he "meant law settled by decision of the Supreme Court of the United States in cases directly in point, rather than by quotations culled from opinions in cases only more or less analogous."[198]

In these two comments Cook did not work out a resolution of "the economic and social problems involved" any more than he had in his discussion of *Hitchman*. Instead, over and over he hammered at a single point: the importance for judges to recognize that, as Cook put it in reviewing a labor case where the union was victorious, "where there is no precedent precisely in point, in the last analysis the court is legislating, and in doing so is legalizing the act of the union because on the whole, it believes that the interests of society are better served by permitting the union to carry on 'the free struggle for life' in this way."[199] Or as he put it another time, "the case presented . . . was one which required the making of new law; that is, it involved the exercise of power to legislate, to establish law for the case in hand."[200] Curiously, he was by no means optimistic that, once judges like Mr. Justice Pitney understood the precise policy question involved, they would come up with a different judgment. He noted, "Whether our courts will show themselves competent to settle rightly the questions of policy involved is perhaps doubtful. If not, we have our legislative bodies to fall back on."[201] But at the same time there was to Cook's writing a sense that change would come, that "the reshaping by judicial legislation of our law governing the relations of capital and labor goes steadily on," and that the development of nationwide labor unions "is bound to take place and that any attempt on the part of our courts to prevent its attainment by peaceful methods . . . will in the end prove ineffective."[202]

The ultimate intellectual source of all of these ideas in Cook's work are three. The first is, of course, Pound either directly,[203] through their long, though distant association,[204] or, more likely, indirectly through Hohfeld. Hohfeld had always, almost fawningly,[205] supported Pound's work and his call for teleological jurisprudence in a "Vital School" is pure Pound. Cook's reference to "social engineering" in one of his pieces from these years,[206] and his failure, identical to Pound's, to specify what "sound economic and so-cial policy" or appropriate labor policy might be, are dead giveaways. But, Pound seldom talked so directly or matter of factly about judicial legislation and, though everything in his work had a formative period, followed by a period of strict law, then, of equity, and finally a modern synthesis, he spoke little in terms of evolution. Rather, emphasis on law making, evolution, and the mores of the time comes from Corbin whom Cook met for the first time in 1916 and who three years before in "The Law and the Judges," a paper written in opposition to the movement for recall of judicial decisions, empha-sized both topics. Corbin argued that judges make law in individual cases and that this law making should be done in accordance with the *Sittlichkeit*, the prevailing sense of justice or mores of the community. But he noted:

> [T]he growth of the law is an evolutionary process. Its principles consist of such generalizations as may tentatively be made from a vast number of individual instances. The instances change as man and society change, with the climate, with the growth of population, with the progress of invention, with social selection. And as the instances change, so must our generalizations change. So must our idea of justice change.[207]

An editorial in the *Yale Law Journal* summed the matter up this way:

> [L]aw forms but a part of our ever changing social *mores* . . . it is the function of lawyers, of jurists and of law schools to cause the statement and application of our legal rules to be in harmony with the *mores* of the present instead of those of an outgrown past.[208]

One should also note echoes of Holmes in all of this, echoes that Cook was quite a bit more willing to acknowledge[209] than he was the influence of either Pound or Corbin. It is the Holmes not of *The Common Law* but of "a proposition of policy of rather a delicate nature" from "Privilege, Malice and Intent"[210] and of the "free struggle for life," from *Vegelahn v. Guntner.*[211] In addition the patient reader would notice echoes of Williston's estimate of "what the law . . . ought to be" in his reply to Cook, where he emphasized what was "socially desirable," and protection of what was of "commercial importance."[212] But for present purposes origins are not an important point. What is important is that what made Cook's work unusual and interesting is that in it he had pushed analytic jurisprudence a bit out of its Hohfeldian mold and into a mold of discourse vaguely recognizable to the late twentieth-century legal mind, especially when he noted in a subsequent book review that resolution of a problem involved "our attempt to balance the conflicting demands of capital and labor."[213] That is where matters rested when, despite the addition of Oliphant, whom both Cook and Moore had known at Chicago, to the crew at Columbia, Cook changed his mind about where the greatest progress in legal education would be made in the next twenty years, chose to return to Yale and another salary increase, this time to $12,000 per year,[214] and with his friend Moore stopped to listen to John Dewey.

Assault on Professional Identity: John Dewey, Empirical Social Science, and Law

Why what John Dewey had to say made such an impression on Cook and Moore will never be known.[215] What Dewey had to say is reasonably clear, however, for Cook's notes on those lectures survive.[216] These notes disclose a sprawling, poorly organized, though not uninteresting, tramp over terrain that could vaguely be described by the course description's assertion of a focus on "contemporary pragmatic logic and a social theory of ethics." The argument, to the extent there was an argument, might be presented as follows.

To dispose of the easiest matter at the outset, Dewey offered no coherent social theory of ethics at all. He did offer three things: a quite interesting demonstration of the centrality of the many-faceted concept of nature or naturalness in ethical theory; the suggestion that there were two kinds of ethical theories, those emphasizing right or correct behavior and those emphasizing good consequences; and a list of the interests to be taken into account in any consequentialist ethics, plainly the one he was selling. This was the last third of the course. The balance of the course only dealt with contemporary pragmatic logic in the interstices of a sustained criticism of Aristotelian deductive, and interestingly, J. S. Mills's inductive, logic. Central to this criticism was the assertion that people reason in response to the need to decide something, to deal with some trouble, and that in these circumstances people look not for rules to govern the case or instance at hand, but for solutions that will dispose of the matter to be decided, fix the trouble. The point of reasoning is thus to do or learn something. Doing or learning something new was, however, impossible under the formal logic of the syllogism, which could at most demonstrate the interrelatedness of propositions, or even through inductive logic, which smuggled in its conclusions with the assumption that the events being studied were similar. Deductive logic was so limited because it assumed the truth or obviousness of its premises when the question at issue in reasoning to a conclusion was the appropriateness and truth of the premises; inductive logic, because it assumed the question of similarity or difference that was central to reaching a conclusion of what to do since that question was rooted in our knowledge of what had worked to solve problems before.

This rendering of Dewey's argument is, in fact, charitable; the entire presentation was disorganized and repetitive. Indeed, the careful listener might have noticed that all the law that Dewey knew could be found in a few issues of the *Harvard Law Review* and *Columbia Law Review*, citations that looked remarkably like reprints from students, friends, and admirers, and the popular press.[217] It was his all-purpose lecture, doctored a bit for his audience. Yet one particular point stands out. Dewey emphasized that in the process of "solving" a problem one simultaneously adjusts both the "rule" one intends to apply and the facts that one chooses to draw from the welter of events. In the course of making such adjustments deductive logic was good for checking one's conclusions, but that was all.[218] For reasoning it was pointless, since in all cases the relevant questions for reaching a conclusion were what are the available premises, what facts does each premise imply, and what facts can be drawn out of this event that might fit with any of the available premises to yield a solution. It was all that simple.

OF THE TWO listeners Moore was the first to react. Returning from a sabbatical spent in Europe, he produced an extraordinarily vicious review of a rather commonplace book of essays edited by John Henry Wigmore and his philosophical sidekick, Albert Kocourek, called *Rational Basis of Legal Institutions* and published as part of the Modern Legal Philosophy Series. Wigmore's book was intended to be a representative compendium of post hoc justifications by various scholars of existing legal "institutions" — liberty, property, succession, the family, and punishment.[219] Although the collection was a useful one at this time when many parts of the legal profession thought that mere existence was a sufficient justification for a legal rule, the volume itself was of limited import. The essays were largely Anglo-American and no more than twenty years old. As such the book was a monument to the relative poverty of recent jurisprudential thinking. It was an example of rational thought about legal institutions only in the sense that any product of sustained thought without extensive regard to the plausibility of its factual premises was rational.

In reviewing the book at length, Moore perversely ignored its manifest content but took its title at face value. He thus observed that legal institutions were only patterns of habitual human behavior, the rationality of which depended on the ends to which the behavior was a means. Quickly disposing of historical inquiry into ends as largely valueless and of a more philosophical inquiry into ends based on "human nature" as flimsy speculation, he suggested that the rationality of legal institutions was an unsolvable, nonproblem. What was a problem to Moore was, "What are means to legal institutions and to what proximate ends are legal institutions means? Concretely, of what facts are group habits consequences and what are the consequences of group habits?" He then reasoned that the solution to this problem would lie in "the direction of detailed observation and systematic experiment" into the psychology of "habit formation, stabilization, modification, and obliteration," the limitations on habitual behavior resulting from biological and social inheritance, and the impact on habitual behavior of changes in material and nonmaterial culture. He also suggested the importance of examining "the available means of experimentation" in the modification of group habits, that is, "the legislative power of the government," and "current experiments," such as collective bargaining, public utility rate regulation, and minimum wages for women, in the exercise of that power. Finding in Wigmore's book few examples of the inquiry he proposed, Moore then proceeded bitterly to slash at what was presented for missing the point, only to give up before reaching the end in a "spirit of weariness" with the entire enterprise that he was criticizing.[220] These propositions, emanating from the pen of a man who had almost never before published a word outside the bounds of the law of negotiable instruments, were, in context, a trifle astonishing.

Cook's reaction was more delayed. In fall 1924 he published one of the truly great pieces of scholarship in the conflict of laws: "The Logical and

Legal Bases of the Conflict of Laws."[221] Beginning with head note quotes from Ernest Mach and Henri Poincare to the effect that it was important for progress, and thus a joyful occasion, to give up old modes of thought, Cook used a then recent book by Dewey[222] to make the point that:

> [In] the field of the physical sciences . . . the purely deductive method of ascertaining the "truth" about nature has given way to what is called . . . the inductive method of modern science, in which the so called "laws of nature" are reached by collecting data, i.e., by observing concrete phenomena, and then forming, by a process of "trial and error," generalizations which are useful tools by means of which we describe in verbal shorthand as wide a range as possible of the observed physical phenomenon, choosing that form of description which on the whole works most simply in the way of enabling us to describe past observations and to predict future observations.[223]

Cook then renamed this "method of modern science" the "experimental" method,[224] again citing Dewey,[225] and asserted that the shift from the deductive to the experimental method was going on in the social sciences as well. Shifting to law, Cook noted that Dicey had isolated two ways — the theoretical method and the positive method — of working in the conflict of laws that roughly corresponded to the deductive and experimental methods and that, "So far as the theoretical method has influenced Anglo-American writers, it has done so chiefly in the form of 'territorial' theories about law and legal rights." He then boldly disassociated himself from any such procedure and instead announced, "In the present discussion it is proposed to adopt the procedure which has proved so fruitful in other fields of science, viz. to place the emphasis upon the observation of concrete phenomena."[226]

What followed, however, was case law analysis utterly impossible to distinguish from some of Cook's earlier work; indeed, in one of the parts of "The Powers of Courts of Equity" he had chosen to "re-examine" the question of the *res judicata* effect of equity decrees "in the light of the modern cases, with special reference to the American authorities" and so to attempt to settle the question "by the decisions in the cases."[227] Moreover, such observation of the phenomena as Cook did was largely limited to the use of famous cases as illustrative of the problems he wished to discuss and to one assertion of fact, undoubtedly true, that in conflict of laws cases courts do not make detailed investigation of how a foreign court would decide the exact case in question were that exact case brought before it for decision. That assertion, however, was made without any discussion of the actual cases, the phenomena in question, at all. Moreover, that assertion was crucial to the argument that Cook made when attacking the theory that in conflicts cases courts enforce foreign law because, under the territorial theory, they lack the power or jurisdiction to apply any of their law. So, it is hardly obvious what part, if any, the experimental method had made to Cook's conclusion.

Though Cook asserted that other conclusions were "the results of inadequate observation" and emphasized the need to "examine carefully into judicial phenomena" because what a given court did "is . . . purely a question of fact, to be ascertained, like any other fact by observation," he did precious little observation of anything. Rather, he largely kept to exposing the inadequacies of various judicial statements of conflict of laws doctrine. Cook then tied Hohfeld's categories, specifically the category of "right," to Holmes prediction theory of law and closed with a long, unacknowledged recounting of Dewey's argument from the lectures that human reasoning was not deductive but in any "new situation," in any "situation of doubt," consisted in the comparison of the new facts with facts in prior cases. In such comparison, consideration of "the policy involved in the prior decisions and . . . the effects which those decisions have produced" led to the "re-defining of the middle term of the major and minor premises of the syllogism; that is *the construction or creation of premises* for the case in hand, which premises did not pre-exist."[228]

Exactly what Dewey contributed to the effort of either Moore or Cook is by no means clear, though in different ways. On the one hand, Moore's piece is through-composed; references to Dewey are only a part of a piece that contains no obvious Dewey-inspired passages.[229] On the other hand, Cook's piece seems more pasted together. The opening and closing are pure, if garbled, Dewey, but the middle has much about it that is reminiscent of Cook's earlier work. The tone throughout was that of a junior high teacher lecturing to a particularly recalcitrant class, a tone Cook had adopted earlier.[230] And the notes prominent in this piece of attacking great authorities—Holmes, Cardozo, and Story were the major named targets—and of seeing through what courts have said to what they have done[231] were present in earlier, equally high-toned work as well.[232] The only explicit tie of this middle section to Dewey was the assertion that:

[W]e as lawyers, like the physical scientists, are engaged in the study of objective physical phenomena. Instead of the behavior of electrons, atoms or planets, however, we are dealing with the behavior of human beings. As practicing lawyers we are interested in knowing how certain officials of society—judges, legislators, and others—have behaved in the past, in order that we may make a prediction of their probable behavior in the future.[233]

And even there it is not at all clear that—but for the scientific analogy, and that too could have been found in Langdell—Dewey, as opposed to Holmes, contributed anything to the conclusion.

After his explosion at poor Colonel Wigmore, Moore fell silent. He did little beyond collect materials on the operation of commercial checking accounts and loan mechanisms[234] as he had done for several years, and even this effort was halfhearted. Moore was unhappy over the present condition and future prospects of his Law School as a result of what he thought was a bad deanship appointment following Stone's elevation to, first, the attorney generalship and, then, the Supreme Court. And so Moore sulked.[235] Three years later, when the Great Curriculum Debate at Columbia[236] led to a revival of his optimism, he began work on a book on banking law and practice along the lines he had outlined in his review of Wigmore's book.[237] The method behind the research was notably eclectic. Moore used secondary sources extensively, but to these he added direct inquiries to bankers about bank practice[238] and questionnaire surveys designed to show some representativeness in their findings, though hardly any sophistication in design.[239] The immediate result of this renewed activity was an article by Moore and his research assistant about the practice of giving interest on the balances of checking accounts.[240] That article, however, showed only exhaustive case law research and comprehensive knowledge of the secondary banking literature both in the United States and in the British Empire. Moore's optimism was short-lived, however, as another deanship fight brought forth another unacceptable Dean.[241] But this time his unhappiness did not stop him from continuing work. Moore's work produced an article setting forth a method quite obviously designed to test the ideas first put forth over five years earlier at the expense of Colonel Wigmore.[242]

Moore began with the assertion, not made in the earlier piece but implicit in it and current in Moore's thought at that time,[243] that "[t]he central problem of the lawyer is the prediction of judicial and administrative decisions of government officers."[244] Then, ignoring entirely the possibility that legal rules might provide an adequate basis for making such a prediction, he quickly dispatched as "not . . . verified in experience" the new notion, prominently associated with Oliphant[245] and Llewellyn,[246] that "study of the relation between decisions and 'the facts' of recorded cases" might provide such a basis. Moore's explanation for not verifying the newer technique was that the facts of a case were only one element in a situation the balance of which was not possible to control for "in the actual behavior situations of everyday life." Although thus admitting that perfect prediction was impossible because of the singularity of the phenomenon to be explained, Moore nevertheless proposed, in line with his argument in the Wigmore review, to examine the relation between the "facts" in a given case and the "institutional (frequent, repeated, usual) ways of behaving" in the relevant community in the hope that, "if such relation be found to be significant, a step towards more reliable prediction will have been made."[247]

In the abstract, Moore's proposal to investigate the relationship between what is classically known as law and custom was hardly novel, especially coming from a teacher of negotiable instruments;[248] the question had a long history in both the general jurisprudential literature as well as that more narrowly limited to commercial law. But, in the context of the traditional discussion of the question, Moore's "institutional method" for going about the enterprise was nothing less than astonishing. He began with the idea of an institution, a set of practices routinely engaged in by individuals in a trade, popularized by Commons, Veblen, and the other institutional economists. He proposed to compare institutional practices, the routine practices of individuals who participated in the institution, with the actions of parties in reported cases. But, instead of proceeding as the institutional economists had, by means of casual observation, expert participant inquiry, and an examination of the secondary literature, as he had done in the piece on interest-bearing checking accounts, Moore proceeded to work within the framework of a generalized behaviorist psychology, still a controversial thing to do at the time. Thus, he subdivided the "facts" of a case, as lawyers would know them, into "terms," which when aggregated serially made up "transactions," which when aggregated serially made up a "transaction-series." Grouping transactions by their descriptive similarity yielded a group of "sequences"; similarly grouping transaction-series yielded a "sequence-series," also known as "institutional sequences."[249]

All of this apparatus was then assembled for "comparing with comparable sequence-series actual transaction-series followed by judicial behavior" or, more simply, comparing customary behavior, habit, with the parties' behavior in cases later litigated. Methods were also described for establishing comparability of transactions-series when one of the transactions, implicitly assumed to be a part of the series litigated, was "deviational," which is to say not "institutional," not in the relation "frequently following — frequently pre-ceding," and for evaluating the degree of deviation — "slight" or "gross" — according to the efficiency, certainty, familiarity, and riskiness of the devia-tional as against the institutional transaction. The entire procedure was pre-sented with the expectation that "after the method has been applied to large numbers of cases in many fields it may be possible to state 'law' for some fields in terms of" the correlation between "the decision and the measured degree of deviation between 'the facts' and the institution," a correlation with "appar-ent" utility in the prediction of decisions.[250]

If the apparatus was not enough to intimidate all but the most determined lovers of social science jargon,[251] the examples Moore gave of the process of comparison, complete with symbolic notation, were. Each was a common banking transaction in which the bank had breached an agreement, explicit or implicit, made with a customer, for example, by refusing to discount a note tendered under a loan agreement or by dishonoring an overdraft despite the existence of an overdraft agreement. Yet, in the process of an analysis designed to isolate exactly in which ways the bank had acted contrary to expected behavior, Moore managed to deform each into something queerly unrecognizable, for example, by turning the overdraft agreement into a note offered for discount and the overdraft into a draft for the balance of the account.[252] Any reader who was both undeterred by the jargon and willing to fight through the seeming disorientation of the examples might have noticed that there were problems with the relationship between the concepts of cau-sality and institutional relation,[253] that the surface impression of a complex-ity unnecessary for the simplicity of the inquiry was indeed accurate,[254] and that the complexity was potentially misleading.[255] Unfortunately careful ex-amination by outsiders, although sought, was not forthcoming,[256] so what-ever deficiencies there were in the method remained. But, at least it was a method, a start toward research, and, when he moved to Yale in 1929, Moore began that research never to look back at case law analysis again.[257] He would do three of these "institutional" banking studies and then a large study of parking and traffic behavior in the next fifteen years.[258]

While Moore sulked at Columbia, Cook kept busy at Yale finishing up his three-volume casebook on equity,[259] working on the Restatement of the Con-flict of Laws, of which he was an advisor, or more accurately fighting battles with Joseph Beale of Harvard and losing them all,[260] and making the per-sonal connections that in 1926 brought him to Johns Hopkins as a visiting professor where he was expected to work on a book on conflict of laws, on a book on legal method, and on plans for a school of jurisprudence.[261]

In his first year at Hopkins, Cook had a chance to set out the details of his theories about law offered briefly in the earlier piece on the conflict of laws, just as Moore had done with his description of his institutional method. In the address, "Scientific Method and the Law," Cook began by noting that the generations of Langdell and Ames had asserted that the case method of studying law was "truly scientific," "the equivalent of the laboratory method in the physical sciences." Expressing "doubt" as to the truth of that assertion, Cook then suggested that we can "discover at least some of the causes of our legal difficulties and do something to remedy them" by "the application of truly scientific methods to the study of legal phenomena." And what were truly scientific methods? Here Cook began historically with the suggestion that eighteenth- and early nineteenth-century science was based on the assumed validity of Aristotelian logic, by which he meant the assumption that there exist certain factually true propositions, either general or particular, that when combined together in the proper way can yield new truths "by deduction, without observation." This assumption was undermined, he said, by the development of Mill's inductive logic, of the non-Euclidean geometries of Bolyai, Lobachevski, and Riemann, and of the evolutionary theory of Darwin, the latter two of which made it clear that, "as applied to the physical world, a given arithmetical formula is in the abstract neither true nor false" but "useful for some purposes and not for others" and that no classification of organic things was objectively valid but only a matter of "convenience for the purpose in view." These developments, when taken with the new phenomena discovered in physics and chemistry, led to the recognition that the world had entered an "era of relativity" founded on the recognition that "all our thinking is based on underlying postulates of which we are frequently unaware," that the universe cannot be "fully described or explained in terms of matter in motion" and that there are "limitations of the process of deductive and inductive logic" since the world "does not present itself to us in classes" and thus cannot be handled "merely by a class logic."[262]

For Cook the last point — the limits of deductive and inductive logic — was the important one, for he elaborated it at length. He began by asserting that the basis of any "classification will vary with our purpose and must be relevant to it" so that "any grouping . . . appears as at most a working hypothesis" and is thus "to be tested by its results and altered if those results were not satisfactory." Thus, "[w]hen confronted with a new situation," "[o]ur real task is to determine whether the differences involved which make us think of it as new, are as a practical matter . . . important for the end in view; and so whether or not we can safely enlarge our class so that when we have finished our thinking it will include the new situation." Then, after a gibe at inductive logic and a good word for the use of deductive logic for working out the consequences of rival hypotheses and arranging knowledge in an orderly way, Cook proceeded to assert, using quotations from, among others, Beale, that in law and law teaching most individuals still hold "the naive belief that men think in syllogisms and new truth about the world can be deduced from general laws arrived at by induction." Technique based on such an assumption was "grotesquely inadequate" for "the problems which confront the lawyer and the judge," which are respectively "to forecast future events" and to "give . . . meaning" to rules rather than to "find the pre-existing but previously hidden meaning" in them. For the judge this task will require "choice . . . based upon consideration of social or economic policy" for which a judge "will need to know two things: (1) what social consequences or results are to be aimed at; and (2) how a decision one way or another will affect the attainment of those results," questions that will require the judge "to call upon the other social sciences."[263]

All of this out of the way, Cook then turned to the scientific study of law for which there was "one fundamental postulate":

> that human laws are devices, tools which society uses as one of its methods to regulate human conduct and to promote those types of it which are regarded as desirable. If so, it follows that the worth or value of a given rule of law can be determined only by finding out how it works, that is, by ascertaining . . . whether it promotes or retards the attainment of desired ends. If this is to be done, quite clearly we must know what at any given period these ends are and also whether the means selected, the given rules of law, are indeed adapted to securing them.

And so he proposed establishing "a university school of law or jurisprudence" organized as "a community of scholars" to obtain knowledge without direct reference to its professional use, devoted to "the scientific study of law as a social institution." This school was to emphasize "an entirely new and different approach to legal problems," which would consist of, first, "a clear conception of what the scientific study of anything involves and of the available tools for pursuing it in the legal field"; second, "observation and study of the actual structure and functioning of modern social, economic and political life"; third, knowledge of "the existing rules of law," which will demand "a careful analysis of the prevailing concepts and terminology now in use by the legal profession, and a restatement of existing law in a simpler and more accurate terminology"; and fourth, studies in the "actual operation of our law."[264]

In concluding, Cook asserted that the time was "ripe" to establish such a school.[265] The year following his speech he worked at Hopkins to turn those plans into a reality. When, in spring 1928, Hopkins was ready to move, he brought with him two friends, Oliphant and Leon C. Marshall, to become part of the founding staff. The Johns Hopkins Institute of Law devoted most of its resources to the empirical study of the operation of civil courts in Ohio, Maryland, and New York. Though Cook headed one of those studies, that of Maryland, his name never appeared on a piece of empirical research. Instead, for the five years that the Institute survived, he worked on legal method and the conflict of laws, tasks he continued until his death.[266]

Professional Identity and the Individual
Law Professor: Cook and Moore Compared

There are good theoretical reasons for the proposition that no two readers will, except by the sheerest of accident, read a substantial text in exactly the same way. For these reasons, it is not at all surprising that Cook and Moore read Dewey's text in such different ways that one could devote his life to empirical research and the other, to the conflict of laws. But, before looking at what in Dewey's text and in the lives of the two men may account for two such divergent readings, it is important to remember what in the lives of these two men might have led one to expect, if not identical, at least similar, readings.

Though by no means identical twins, the parallels in their lives are astonishing. Only three years apart in age, both came from professional backgrounds, went to the same college and law school, took degrees from the same political science department, began teaching in the West and worked their way back through colonial service. They taught together for a total of seven years at Wisconsin, Chicago, and Columbia and thus knew many of the same people. Their initial scholarship was within the same narrow range of acceptable work by young men and, as shown by their steady advancement in a world where teaching was important, their teaching was clearly at the upper end of the norm. They lived in the same dignified university ghetto at Chicago, a block apart in the same pleasant suburb in New Jersey while at Columbia (and so, often shared the same ferry ride), and in quite elegant neighborhoods in New Haven while at Yale.[267] Indeed, each lived quite well once he had made it and, when not teaching, hid from the world in a rural summer home.[268] They even both came back east as part of an attempt to improve the quality of a law school, though here Cook was in on the ground floor; Moore, one of the middle floors. And both were essentially shy individuals who made up for that shyness with a kind of sustained bluster, a fierceness that kept the world at a comfortable distance.[269]

Differences there were, of course. Moore's family was clearly wealthier; Cook's early training was in science and included study in Europe; and only Moore practiced law, though this absence in Cook's career has been sadly misunderstood. It is also significant, I think, that Cook made it east to Yale, while Moore landed at Columbia, and that Cook knew, and was influenced by, Hohfeld and Pound. Still, the similarities could have overwhelmed the differences. Why didn't they then? To get at that question one needs to look at what Cook drew out of Dewey and what Moore did with the same message.

Taken at face value, Dewey's lectures offered nothing more — or, I might add, less — than an understanding of, as he once entitled a book, *How We Think*, or as Cook put it later and more formally, a logic of inquiry,[270] coupled with some good liberal rhetoric about the civil war between capital and labor. Dewey's primary assertion, the factual rock on which his argument was built, was simply — some would say, though I think wrongly, "simplistically" — that people do not think axiomatically in syllogisms but, rather, with an end or problem in view, and so adjust both the theoretical and the factual premises with which they work until these premises fit together, make sense, or seem coherent. By emphasizing that sense of fit, or coherence, was decided in terms of the end in view or what works in practice, I am not at all sure that Dewey advanced questions of method one iota, but, from my experience over many years of trying to make intelligible to another human being the careers of Cook and Moore, I am convinced that Dewey adequately described what I hope I have done. By its terms, however, Dewey's insight said absolutely nothing about what to think about and, indeed, in its generality, it suggested that one might think pragmatically about anything at all. Pragmatic logic was the universal solvent.

The similarity of that sense of general usefulness to the claims made about the Aristotelian logic that Dewey sought to discredit is, of course, overwhelming, ironically so, but that does not mean that Dewey did not leave clues about what needed to be thought about and thus, where to apply his logic. Pragmatic logic was to be used anywhere that Aristotelian logic was thought to hold forth, that is, anywhere that modern empirical science did not hold sway. Whether, in 1920, there was in fact any such field of knowledge is another matter, but in law, at least, some people talked as if the process of decision was that assumed by classical legal thought, of judges applying established premises to previously unknown, but self-evident, facts to reach new conclusions. So law was a perfect place to apply pragmatic logic. Which meant doing what? Well, examining the ends in view and seeing whether the means used were adapted to the ends in view or whether some other ends or means had to be adopted. Which meant doing what?

If one looked at Dewey's examples, the answer was quite simple. One was being adjured to engage in empirical social science, for that was the enterprise closest to the examples from the physical and biological sciences that Dewey used. And that is the conclusion Moore drew from Dewey and acted upon for the rest of his scholarly life. But, at the same time, this was in no sense a necessary conclusion. Dewey had at one time written quite scathing attacks on British empiricism. His continual reliance on examples from the physical and biological sciences when illustrating his points and his failure to rely on examples from the nascent quantitative studies in the social sciences suggest a certain lack of sympathy with the latter enterprise. So, one could conclude, as Cook did, that one could apply pragmatic logic to determine what the rules of law were, to identify what formulaic expression best described the legal phenomena — what the courts did in fact — and so to isolate, in Llewellyn's words, "the true rule," at least, if that was the end one had in view. Such an enterprise did not necessarily imply that even the most accurate statements of what the courts did, the truest of rules, identified efficacious means for accomplishing the social ends in view — that is, efficacious means of social control — though at times Cook seemed to assume that rules were in fact efficacious.[271] Efficacy was another separate matter, itself a question to which pragmatic logic might be applied, presumably with methods closer to those of empirical social science.

Cook made just such an assertion of separateness when he stated as a fundamental postulate, identified as such, that "laws are devices, tools which society uses as one of its methods to regulate human conduct" and, consequently, that law is a "social institution." Based on that statement, he planned a community of scholars devoted to the nonprofessional study of that institution, which had for two of its objectives the observation and study of "modern social, economic, and political life" and of the "actual operation of our law," issues related to efficacy and topics for empirical research, if ever there were any, and seen as such. Yet he still included in that community individuals who would ascertain just what are the "existing rules of law."[272] He was thus not being "illogical" in following out Dewey's premises. But, at the same time, in doing so he was being more than a bit perverse. To get at the reason for his perversity one needs to go back to Cook and Moore out in the West.

There is something mildly amusing about the fact that writers upon Realism usually remark upon Cook's undergraduate and graduate training in the physical sciences and his failure to practice as somehow contributing to our explaining his academicism or interest in science,[273] but that no one notices that Moore, who never focused on the physical sciences while in school and seems to have had a successful practice experience, in fact jumped the intellectual traces completely while Cook kept on analyzing doctrine. In understanding this paradoxical relationship between these two men, one should remember that for any individual one becomes a professional in the same way one puts on boots, by the straps. Professionalization is literally the magic of self-help. The forms and habits are "out there" in some strange sense, but one must put them on oneself; a dresser will not do. At the same time the forms and habits are only part of this bootstrapping. Another part of professionalization is what I have earlier, and quite crudely, called the internalization of professional norms and practices.[274] I say crudely, because "internalization" smacks too much of swallowing something out there, the cognate to putting on a coat. Rather, the process is much more like an adult's growing into a job, where sometimes the growing is not just into a thing, but somehow the growing, subtly, and at times not so subtly, alters the thing grown into. The process of "internalization" thus is the coming to believe in the naturalness of an otherwise socially constructed set of practices, so that, as is the case for the wearer of a wedding ring — a strange and foreign object that one puts on — one ultimately comes to "feel naked without it."

This "individual" — I hesitate to say "internal" for obvious reasons — view of professionalization should be compared with the earlier discussion of aspects of the professionalization of a "group." For any academic group taken as a whole, the forging of a professional identity is a relatively unproblematic enterprise. Pick a distinctive subject matter, fight to gain exclusive control over that subject matter, come up with a vocation to justify that control, and work to see that new entrants into the profession share the definition of the field.[275] Of course, careful research shows that what seems unproblematic at a distance is less obviously so close up. Development is never smooth; fights about subject matter leave casualties and about control, redefinitions of turf; vocations are never quite settled and youngsters have a habit of wanting to do things their own way, which leads to redefinitions, new fights, adjustments in vocation, and new recalcitrant youngsters. Looked at still closer up, as the individual, the trivial case, the forging of a professional identity is still more deeply problematic in that the records of any department or school are littered with the names of individuals who disappeared physically, or only metaphorically, the relevant professional identity never having taken, or who stayed but adopted some deviant professional identity — no scholarship, only teaching; no scholarship, but consulting. Occasionally there is even to be found the name of an individual of whom it can be said "the place would be less without," who somehow showed a slightly different way to be a professor "in" the field. Thus, whether looking at great populations or at individual cases, there is both a putting on and a growing into that is a part of professionalization. Looked at as a matter of putting on professional identity, the way I have looked so far, Cook and Moore look much the same. Yet, looked at as a matter of growing into, as a matter of naturalness, the absence of which makes for nakedness, there is reason to believe there was a difference.

There is a sense of restlessness to the life of Walter Wheeler Cook that cannot be explained, as it has been, solely as a search for the highest salary available[276] or "the best place" to do "constructive work." The longest he stayed at any school was his eight years until retirement at Northwestern. Granted, he would have been pleased to have stayed at Hopkins had that been possible, but he did not sulk over opportunities lost. Instead, he turned, seemingly eagerly, to educating students and faculty at Northwestern as soon as he got there.[277] It is both a physical and an intellectual restless, for it begins back as early as his time at Columbia where in five years he sampled from mathematics, physics, psychology, law, and political science and seemingly could not make up his mind which of the latter to do, even into his first job. And yet, at the same time, there was in Cook a strong desire to be, and be seen as, settled, as at home. Both Charles Clark and Homer Carey in obituaries and other friends in interviews note the settled, peaceful vitality of his homelife.[278] A strange memoir of the little colony where Cook had inherited a summer home, a place with the improbable name of Hollywood, New York, confirms this impression, with a view of that home, a real Adirondack lodge with hardwood walls and ceilings, worth clearly twice what anyone else's in the encampment was, as the center of community gatherings.[279] And even in his mid-forties Cook was seriously concerned about his pension, that emblem of the ultimate settlement that can be retirement.[280]

The source of this restlessness is unclear, though the temptation to attribute it to the financial insecurity of a schoolmaster's son ought to be resisted, if for no other reason than for lack of evidence, as Cook seemed from the beginning more overextended than innately poor. But this restlessness should be contrasted with Moore's more phlegmatic existence. He seems to have been headed toward law from the beginning, using the Columbia School of Political Science as a way to get the public law instruction that a young liberal would feel necessary, but which was generally unavailable in law schools, even Columbia's, at the time. He may have only stayed at Kansas for a short while, for obvious reasons, and he was clearly happy to get quickly out of Chicago,[281] but he stayed at Wisconsin for six years, and not for lack of offers to go elsewhere, and settled in at both Columbia and Yale. His scholarship, but for the Wigmore review, is all matter of fact in tone, even when, at the end of his career he had reason to feel embattled. And his life away from school seems to have had that same solid matter of factness of the late-Edwardian gentleman to it; one has a hard time seeing Moore crawling around on the floor with his children as Cook did.[282]

One can see the contrast between the two men in other ways as well. When one is given descriptions of Moore's mind at work one has the vision of an enormous, black steam locomotive — difficult to get up to speed but nearly impossible to stop once gotten up to speed.[283] While it would be implausible to describe Cook's mind with words like "quicksilver" because of his ability to pick a course and stick with it, that mind was surely much more like a fancy sports car — extraordinary pickup, easily maneuverable — than a steam locomotive.[284] Their pictures show the same characteristics. Moore looks stolid and a bit overweight; Cook, excited and lean.

The contrast continues into their response to professionalization. Sliding into his professional identity more than adopting it, Moore could put it on rather directly and put little effort or reflection toward the growing into. One can almost hear him say, "Oh this is what I'm supposed to wear." In contrast Cook at Nebraska made a choice, a choice to become a law professor. In making that choice he grabbed the professional identity of the law professor in ways, and with an intensity, that Moore never knew. Let there be no question, it was a peculiarly academic identity. His first foray into casebook construction was that almost purely academic subject, common-law pleading,[285] and as soon as he could, he began to participate in the affairs of the Association of American Law Schools, serving as its Secretary from 1912 until 1916 and its President in 1916–17. In the latter role Cook, in his presidential address, began the second push toward engineering American Bar Association support for limiting the number of law schools and raising the standards for admission by suggesting a line of attack that had been taken by the American Medical Association in the years after the turn of the century.[286] And he helped found the Order of the Coif, an organization that amalgamated several local law school honor societies, and that was designed to rival Phi Beta Kappa because "its standards will be the highest of any of the honorary societies."[287]

All of which is not to say that Cook was entirely happy with the professional identity he assumed. He worked and struggled as he grew into it. Here the shift in his scholarship after meeting Hohfeld is important. By adopting Hohfeld's terminology Cook hoped to make his own work more scientific, as that word was understood by law professors whose scholarship participated in classical legal thought, that is, more careful, more precise, more rational. Such was an objective squarely within the received understanding of the law professor's vocation. But, it is important to notice the way he chose to alter that vocation, as evidenced by the force of the attacks on ancient heroes in Cook's scholarship of the time. It was these heroes who had set the vocational norm and then not stuck to it. Here too the new notes in Cook's scholarship of the period — seeing through and boundary questioning — are examples of trying to move the norm of professional vocation away from the cataloging that dominated prewar scholarship, including Moore's, and toward that higher order of work, the dogmatic literature, that Thayer and Ames had always held out as the ultimate objective of study, but that Cook and Hohfeld felt they had not achieved. Likewise, the choice to embrace Hohfeld's grand vision of the university school of law and jurisprudence was both an acceptance of the basic professional vocation and participation in an effort to shape and embroider that vocation as well. Thus, by the time Cook had finished his years at Chicago, he had invested much in putting on and shaping his professional identity, an identity that suited him, that fit him as obviously and unconsciously as an old wedding band and that, since he had never practiced, was the only identity he had ever known.

Moore, on the other hand, spent the same years doing the patient cataloging of cases that was squarely within the received understanding of professional vocation. He did not venture into the AALS forum until he reached Chicago. He had not chosen his identity as a *law* professor (indeed he had experienced an earlier identity as a practicing lawyer), much less actively worked to reshape it. Instead he had simply accepted that identity. So, for Moore it was "just there" in ways that Cook's identity could never be.

Then, in 1916, both men left Chicago and the West for the East and attempted to improve the quality of their new law schools. The significance of this move cannot be underestimated. Take Moore first. When he got to Columbia he had made it, and he knew it. He worked to build his "power and influence" in many ways. He increased his activities in the AALS by taking on the chairmanship of the round table on commercial law for two years[288] and by actively participating in floor debate on proposals to classify law schools.[289] He increased his efforts at scholarly productivity by acquiring a student research assistant to aid in "briefing, examination of law and collection of authorities" on the grand negotiable instruments project.[290] He even planned a casebook on suretyship.[291] In short, he acted as if he believed in scholarship on the grand scale and was in every way fully committed to the "strenuous" career of the law teacher.[292] Yet almost as soon as Moore's position at Columbia was established, somewhat curious things began to take place. First his research, once urgently up to date,[293] began to fall behind.[294] Then he stopped participating in AALS affairs.[295] Instead he began to read Dewey on education,[296] and various authors on psychoanalysis.[297] He made friends with members of Columbia's sociology department, already the most quantitatively inclined in the country,[298] and helped raise money for a "detailed inquiry into several lines of productive industry and business enterprise" to be run by Thorstein Veblen.[299]

Of course, this shift in Moore's interests was gradual. During this same time he published two bits of case law research notable largely for the copious footnotes,[300] and completed a previously contracted for revision of his jointly authored casebook.[301] But, however gradual in cumulative effect, the change was well enough known in the New York intellectual community that when Morris R. Cohen, a prominent City College professor of philosophy who was interested in legal topics, chose to take a swipe at the critics of Colonel Wigmore's book as "marxians, positivists, behaviorists, and psychoanalysts . . . united in the dogma that the reasons we give for any legal institution cannot possible have any effective influence on its growth or administration," a position he characterized as "a snap judgment" unsupported by "any serious evidence from the realm of law,"[302] T. R. Powell, one of the hearty crew of those years, considered this criticism a "slap" directed squarely at Moore.[303]

How did Moore come to head off in this direction? The key to understanding his activities is one of the ideas that held together the notions of advancement through colonial service and of professorial vocation: the university law school. This idea was first formulated by Thayer, who affirmed that "law must be studied and taught as other great sciences" at the universities, "as deeply, by like methods, and with as thorough a concentration and life-long devotion of all the powers of a learned and studious faculty" and then relegated the "difficult main work of teaching" to an "of course."[304] It was then reformulated by Ames[305] and others and embroidered by Hohfeld in his

"Vital School." As these leaders of the profession saw the matter, it was in the true university law school where one advanced and in which one could most fully practice one's scholarly vocation. In support of this goal, they identified as one of the reasons for the superiority of the university-affiliated law school the advantage to be derived from the manifold resources of the other departments of the university.[306]

Looked at critically the idea of a university law school was partially a device whereby academic lawyers attempted to differentiate themselves from their inferiors in the proprietary schools. At the same time, it was an idea that could be acted upon, just as the notion of a professional "vocation," in part a plea for higher salaries, could be.[307] Moore quite obviously acted on the notion of a professional vocation as he did his colonial service. Likewise, he acted as if he believed in the idea of the university law school. And, with his move to Columbia, Moore reached the university law school par excellence. Columbia, unlike almost any other major law school, had had a constant, if rocky, relationship with studies in political science for nearly sixty years.[308] The school was thus, in theory at least, more open to the resources of the university than were most law schools at the time. When Moore arrived, he started to explore just what he had been told would be his reward for successful advancement up the ladder of colonial service — the resources of a major university, the same resources he had begun to explore in a very tentative way during his last semester at Wisconsin.[309] What Moore found was a vibrant intellectual community.[310] And again Moore did just what he was expected to do, or at least what the idea of a university law school purported to expect; he attempted to learn what this exciting atmosphere had to offer for the study of law.

Part of what Moore in fact learned in this atmosphere is easy to isolate. As the citations in the Wigmore review indicate, he gained a basic grounding in social science as it was taught in the years around World War I with a decidedly quantitative bias, as would be expected at a school with E. L. Thorndike in psychology, Frank Giddings in sociology, and Wesley Mitchell in economics, pioneer quantifiers all.[311] But specific knowledge is not all that Moore acquired in these six years. A more important, though less tangible, acquisition was an understanding of the modern concept of science as an empirical or experimental activity,[312] the concept underlying the Dewey lectures and the Wigmore review.

Contrast Cook's experience. When reaching Yale, he did not find a great university; he barely found a university at all.[313] The social sciences, where not nonexistent, were moribund; sociology was dominated by the shade of

William Graham Sumner, in the person of his disciple A. G. Keller, a duo that refused any move toward empirical studies; psychology was still a part of the philosophy department and the Dura-Europos excavations were years away. Indeed, the university in general, and empirical social science in particular, were stronger at both of Cook's previous schools — Chicago and Wisconsin — than at Yale. Thus, had Cook come to explore the university as a part of the university law school as Moore did, there would have been little to explore.

But, of course, Cook came to Yale less to explore the University than to be with Hohfeld and to rejuvenate that Law School. Looking at the University was unnecessary because Hohfeld had already confronted the social sciences in his "Vital School." They were carefully consigned to their appropriate box, as "functional or dynamic jurisprudence," studying the actual operation of the law, handmaidens to the main job of analyzing the law and then, in the light of social and economic policy, improving it. Under this scheme, the twentieth-century notion of science was not something that one might discover as a new way of thinking about familiar problems, not that, given his undergraduate training, Cook need discover it. This notion of science would not cause one to rethink one's activities because empirical science was already there in the grand scheme, in its proper place, after the "and" in "law and." Thus, Hohfeld did for empirical studies what Pound had done for policy studies a few years earlier in his sociological jurisprudence articles.[314] By first recognizing social and economic policy and the needs of business and then putting them in their place, as Pound had, one did not have to talk much about the subject and could stick with law. Cook could thus criticize Pound's praise of the "traditional and known technique of the common law"[315] as "grossly inadequate"[316] and simply substitute for it another method of case analysis. Pragmatic logic required nothing more.

The precise relationship of science and law under this set of ideas that Cook took from Hohfeld can easily be seen from two short pieces Cook did for the New Republic right around the time of Dewey's lecture. The first, a review of the Pound-Frankfurter Cleveland Crime Survey,[317] began by noting that, "No genuine scientific and thoroughgoing study of our substantive law of crimes or of criminal procedure with a view to their simplification and modernization has yet been undertaken by the legal profession." Cook then laid out what would be "[a]n adequate study of our system of criminal justice," starting with an analysis of "substantive criminal law" and "the details of criminal procedure" and only then turned to "the machinery for the enforcement of the law," of which the Survey was an example, a matter not for lawyers but for "men who were experts in the fields involved."[318] The second, an announcement of the formation of the American Law Institute, emphasized the job of the Institute in alleviating the "state of legal chaos" where "it's becoming increasingly difficult for both courts and attorneys to find their way through the maze of conflicting decisions and statutes." Then, after going through the Institute's plan for generating an authoritative statement of "the 'best' rule" where legal analysis had identified conflicting rules, Cook observed that choosing the best rule would involve in many cases "a knowledge of economic facts which the legal experts will not have." Rather, one would need "the cooperation of real economic experts," people who are "trained in getting at and in interpreting the meaning of the facts relating to our industrial and financial organization."[319]

Of course, the procedure advocated in these two pieces would have been an advance on the traditional way lawyers had dealt with economic and social questions — as inarticulate premises and so predicates for silent consequentialist reasoning. Still, even with this advance, the lawyers might have gone about their business pretty much as before, turning to the experts only for the facts that would answer the nonlegal puzzle of the "bestness" of a choice of rules or of the "efficiency" of the machinery of justice. Thus, when Cook actually got to a law school in a real university, when he moved to Columbia and heard Dewey lecture on law, he could easily "include the bulk of Dewey's" course in his own for there were already places for it. The material on the syllogism went into the box labeled analytic jurisprudence, where it would supplement and eventually dwarf Hohfeld's categories, and the limited examples of scientific method, into the box labeled "functional or dynamic jurisprudence." There was even a place for Dewey's summations on the social ethics of law; it was the box, designed by Pound and named by Hohfeld as "critical or teleological jurisprudence," "the *systematic* testing or critique of our principles and rules of law according to considerations *extrinsic or external* to the principles and rules as such, that is, according to the psychological, ethical, political, social and economic bases of the various doctrines and the respective purposes or ends sought to be achieved thereby."[320] The key phrase, of course, is "extrinsic or external," just as the key to understanding the role of fact gathering was that this work was to be done by "experts in the field involved" and not lawyers. A "Vital School" might be a broader school, but that breadth would stay at a distance, quite clear of the statement and analysis of law, the business of the lawyers and law professors.

It should be remembered that it was just this division of function that Moore criticized in his Wigmore review. The Colonel's little book was a classic example of teleological jurisprudence, and as such was, as far as Moore was concerned, an example of an unsolvable nonproblem. Similarly, Dewey's argument with respect to the interrelationship between the "facts" we find and the rules we construct completely undermined the neat division between the fact-finding job of experts and the analysis of the law, even the best law. But Cook did not seem to notice.[321]

Moore may not have noticed either; at least, his criticism of the Hopkins proposal when it was made to him was not of the theoretical merits of Cook's scheme, but of the likelihood that Cook and Oliphant would carry it out.[322] But somehow he learned something else. Though he said "There is no God and Dewey is his prophet,"[323] most likely Dewey was not the only source. Indeed, Moore once named James Harvey Robinson and Thorstein Veblen, together with Dewey, as the men who during the "first years of enthusiasm at Columbia . . . made me over."[324] Notably all three shared and were known for their thorough commitment to the modern notion of science and their equally thorough opposition to the more ancient notion of science as a rational activity, specifically, as an Aristotelian rationalistic activity.[325] But, whomever the source, what Moore learned, or at least came to understand, was that science could not be combined with law in the way Cook chose to do it. Despite all of the talk about law's being an inductive enterprise, legal science, even in Cook's hands, was precisely the kind of science Dewey, Robinson, and Veblen had attacked. Concerned with the formal interrelationship of rules and the principles from which they were supposedly derived, legal science assumed the efficacy of the rules and ignored their origins, except as readily disclosed in old English cases or as produced out of an ill-defined custom or a hypothesized sovereignty, as well as their action in the world. It thus purported to describe and understand a human activity without putting that activity into its social context and then subjecting that complex of conceptual artifact and social context to empirical, especially causal, scrutiny.[326] Therefore, legal science was open, first, to the charge that it had ignored its ostensible subject matter and, second, to the prescription that direct examination of that subject matter in a detached, empirical attitude would improve understanding of the activity or institution far more than further formal elaboration. And thus Moore gave up the legal science that Cook was content to follow in its narrow cabin.

Why each took a different view of the matter is, of course, a deeply personal mixture of experience and psyche. Previously I have identified a literal-mindedness in Moore and the relationship of empirical social science to progressive politics as contributing factors.[327] A different list could be made for Cook. Cook was by all accounts extraordinarily good at legal analytics. All biographical sources agree in this assessment and, having read the entire corpus, I have to add my vote as well.[328] He could make a legal concept stand up, salute, and whistle Dixie backward, to amend a phrase. It is surely hard to adopt an intellectual position that makes such a skill, a skill that quickly brought him fame, if not fortune, in that fine English phrase, redundant. At the same time legal analytics afforded an outlet for the basic combativeness of Cook's personality. Whether that combativeness was only a defense born of shyness, or whether it was somehow deeper in his being, Cook clearly loved an argument. In two of his first three pieces he picked arguments; when Williston happened on the scene, Cook could not resist participating in another one; for the last twenty years of his life he was consumed in an argument with Beale and the Restaters and, while at Northwestern, he and Leon Green carried on a daily luncheon argument for the benefit of the young faculty that clearly was something to behold.[329] But it seems to me that there is something more important that helps explain this choice.

Cook spent a long time and much effort growing into a scholarly vocation in his chosen field. Moore spent none. It is surely not insignificant that on Cook's understanding of Dewey the professional identity of the law professor was still intact. True, a bit of the world had been ceded to experts, experts in facts and in social policy, but this part had never before been seriously claimed by the law professors and social policy would be quickly reclaimed in any case. So, with thanks to Chuck Berry, for all one heard about a new way of talkin' and a new way of walkin', after Cook and Hohfeld had rearranged the subject matter of the law professor's enterprise, it was still much the same as that of the law professors who had created the world of classical legal thought that Cook had started out with earlier. The subject was rules and their interrelationships. Questions of efficacy, previously ignored, had been given over to others to consider, and so might just as well have been ignored. Law professors were to discuss whether the duty to mitigate damages was really a duty or only a privilege and whether courts enforced foreign law or a local law modeled after the foreign domestic rule, but those questions were really not very different from whether the liability of the principal was in tort via misrepresentation or in contract or whether the United States had a police power or only one to regulate interstate commerce. On either view of the subject matter of law, the lawyers had possession of their little piece of the intellectual world all to themselves.

For Cook, who, unlike Moore, had only an academic identity, who could never say "Oh, hell, let's chuck this and go back to practicing law," and who had toyed with another available professional identity, political science, maintenance of professional identity was important. It was the home, the stability he had made for himself in his restlessness. It was himself so deeply that at the end of his career he could still write, nearly twenty years after the slight, that the assertion that his position was "that one cannot draw any generalizations" was "absurd" and "unfounded."[330] Rules were the center of the law professor's enterprise and Cook's task that of freeing "the intellectual garden" of "rank weeds" so that "useful vegetables" might "grow."[331]

Contrast Moore in the Wigmore review. The job set forth there, "detailed observation and systematic experiment" with respect to the formation and modification of "group habits,"[332] suggested that there was absolutely nothing to distinguish the law professor from two or three kinds of social scientists. In such a situation the law professors could not possibly have kept their professional identity, their place in the academic division of labor. That fact seems not to have bothered Moore, though in his piece on interest-bearing checking accounts he quite obviously tried to find a halfway house between law and some kinds of social science. More secure than Cook, less reflective, having already available a nonacademic identity and above all with less of himself invested in the conclusion, Moore simply gave up being a law professor. He recognized that he had been asking the wrong questions, that in the words of the largely apocryphal Moore throwing out his research notes, "It's my life work . . . and it's all wrong."[333] He had been seeking an understanding of law by asking questions about doctrine when all the other social sciences had been asking questions about society and individuals in society. And so, perversely, since the lack of activity about the resources of the university suggests the rhetoric was not intended to be taken seriously, Moore started off to acquire a social understanding of law, while Cook tried to bring Hohfeld's dream of a "Vital School of Law and Jurisprudence," or at least a part of it, to reality.

AT THE SAME TIME Charles E. Clark and William O. Douglas tried to put their own less grand, more occasional understandings of the place of social science in law into operation. It is to their activities that we now turn to see what happened to the twentieth-century notion of science when mixed with, not ideas about law and law professors, but real laws and real law professors.

EMPIRICAL LEGAL RESEARCH AT YALE:

CHARLES E. CLARK AND WILLIAM O. DOUGLAS

THE MOST LIKELY place for a law professor to meet the twentieth-century notion of science was not listening to John Dewey lecture on law at the Columbia Law School. At least if one was politically liberal, one was more likely to meet this notion as part of some "progressive reform" project. Progressive reform was a style of politics that in America dated back through Brandeis's brief in *Muller v. Oregon*[1] at least as far as the Sanitary Commission's investigations during the Civil War.[2] It was a capacious house of only vaguely allied projects that included such enterprises as Jane Addams and the American Settlement House Association,[3] Florence Kelley and the New York Industrial Commission,[4] and Charles Frances Adams and the Sunshine Commission[5] and journals of opinion such as the *Nation* and the *New Republic*. What all these projects and journals shared, beyond a vaguely left, reformist, though seldom socialist, politics was a commitment to what might be called a methodology of reform. That methodology, based essentially on an "all men of goodwill" ethics, postulated that if the facts about social conditions were known, improvement of those conditions — that is, reform — would follow. Lawyers had always participated in these reform projects. Often their interests were narrowly professional as can be seen from Pound's estimate of "The Causes of Popular Dissatisfaction with the Administration of Justice," a call to action that effectively ignored the possibility that substantive law might be a major cause of such dissatisfaction. But, perhaps as often, lawyers participated, generally as counsel, in efforts at reform of broader social significance, for example, Brandeis in fights over hours of employment;[6] Pound, in child labor;[7] Charles Evans Hughes, in abuses by public utilities;[8] and Hughes and Horace Deming, Moore's employer, in more general attacks on corruption in state and local government.[9] Since it was assumed that knowledge of the facts would bring about improvement in social and political conditions, the staple of these reform movements was the social survey, sometimes in the form of the legislative or commission hearings or a grand jury investigation, sometimes, the findings of fact collected and presented by the relevant reform organization.

Over time these social surveys became more elaborate and real social scientists, drawn to their discipline because of an interest in reform and the lingering association of their discipline with philanthropy and social work, began participating. On the legal side as well, a certain amount of interest in such investigations came with the spread of Pound's preachings about sociological jurisprudence,[10] which implied that knowledge of social conditions was necessary to wise judicial (and legislative) decision making. And though in some aspects quite narrowly focused in the world of the reform of legal procedure, the Pound-Frankfurter survey, *Criminal Justice in Cleveland*, the best of many such surveys,[11] suggested that some version of the social survey was appropriate for lawyers' concerns as well. What the lawyers who wished to use the social survey model for collecting information for law reform projects would make of the social scientists' concerns should the two ever try to work together was unclear, just as it was unclear how the lawyers interested in the traditional project of reforming procedure would react to the concerns of lawyers who would use social survey methods to push such reforms. But since joint projects of this kind, however potentially plausible, were untried, no one thought about such questions. And plausible they must have been, for the idea managed to penetrate even the sleepy Yale Law School.

Studies in Procedure:
The Law Professors Meet Reform

Dean Thomas W. Swan's appointments policy had been generally to hire established teachers with good reputations.[12] In following out that policy over Arthur Corbin's opposition,[13] he created a good but hardly exciting faculty. When, in the second half of that deanship, the policy was effectively reversed and Yale began hiring the more promising of its recent graduates,[14] these youngsters worked at trying to make the school both better and more exciting with the aid of a few vaguely senior faculty, most prominently Charles E. Clark, a Yale College and Yale Law School graduate who, after six years in practice in New Haven, had begun to teach property at the Law School in 1919.[15] Prime instigator in this activity was Robert Maynard Hutchins, then Secretary to the Yale Corporation, who began teaching right out of law school.[16] Most of his exploits, which ultimately led to his brief deanship and which resulted in making Yale quite a lively place, are not important for present purposes. But one is.

In 1926, Hutchins and Clark proposed that the Law School "perform distinguished public service by assisting in the solution of the most pressing problem in the law by scientific study of all procedure in its functional, comparative, and historical aspects."[17] When they found it necessary to justify their proposal, they began by lamenting the low estate to which the administration of the law had fallen, harking back to the criticisms of Bentham and Dickens as well as noting similar complaints of contemporary leaders of the bar. Then, after recounting the unsuccessful efforts at procedural reform and detailing contemporary efforts, including those of the American Law Institute, they concluded: "The reformers have failed, we believe, because the necessary basic research has been lacking. . . . We regard facts as the prerequisite of reform." Their prescription followed directly from their diagnosis: "We believe that the way to escape from the morass into which law administration has fallen lies through study. This study should be directed to discovering the working in practice of our present rules. It should be correlated with the study of allied subjects outside the law."[18] To carry out the necessary studies they proposed to establish an Institute of Procedure, which would examine civil and criminal procedure and evidence.[19]

The source of these ideas of Hutchins and Clark is unclear.[20] Karl Llewellyn, once at Yale, but then teaching at Columbia while still dabbling in Yale Law School politics, probably had his hand in their formulation,[21] but that fact only broadens the question to include his sources also. In one sense the ideas are too commonplace to have clear roots, as the reference to Bentham and Dickens might suggest. At least since the nineteenth century, liberal intellectuals, and especially liberal intellectual lawyers, have focused their efforts at reform around two central ideas: first, that the common law was in chaos and thus in need of restatement and simplification and, second, that procedure was too technical and complicated and, as a result, allowed lawyers imbued with "the sporting theory of justice" to avoid decisions on the merits of claims by playing procedural games. These ideas were literally everywhere. They can be found in legal magazines, law reviews, speeches of the presidents of the Association of American Law Schools, bar association publications, and almost under any mossy rock. In their shorthand form these ideas yielded the assertion that the delays and uncertainties in litigation are an evil crucially in need of reform. The lineage of this proposition can easily be traced, as it was by Hutchins and Clark,[22] through such events as the various English and American pleading and practice reforms — the Hilary rules and the Field Code, for example; Roscoe Pound's St. Paul speech to the American Bar Association;[23] and the founding of various legal "reform" organizations, such as the American Judicature Society, the American Law Institute (ALI), and the National Crime Commission.

The plausibility of this proposition about the importance of procedural reform and its equation with law reform generally is beside the point;[24] it was at hand and easily available to teachers of evidence and procedure such as Hutchins and Clark. Yet their explicit criticism of the practice of progressive law reform for centering its attention "on the presentation and adequacy of an ideal system" rather than on "the working in practice of our present rules" and on "progress in allied fields" is a distinct variation on prescriptions for progressive law reform of which the proposal was a quite self-conscious part.[25] Here, where roots are an important matter, the proposal offers no insight. Of course, there are echoes of Deweyan ethics, of the investigative commissions that were a part of the strategy of countless progressive reform movements of the 1910s and earlier, and of a general interest in, and perhaps even wonderment at,[26] the scholarly resources of the new university in which the two men found themselves; but evidence of a conscious drawing on any of these sources is lacking. Apparently the sources, such as they were, were "in the air,"[27] and the two men just grabbed them.[28]

Although the faculty adopted the proposal,[29] funding for it was not to be had.[30] As a result the idea languished until a year later when Hutchins was elected dean. On that day he, with the assistance of two new faculty members, secured money for Clark to hire four research assistants and thus begin the work of the projected institute.[31] That work was to follow generally from the Pound-Frankfurter Cleveland Crime Survey, adapting the techniques first developed there — largely a census of a year or more's case load — to civil suits in state trial courts.[32] At the time, Hutchins described the endeavor with remarkable candor and without the sense of excitement one might have expected at the outset of such a new enterprise:

> The distinction between law in action and law on the books, and the great relative importance of the former, have frequently been emphasized. Little work has been done, however, which gives any indication of how practicable investigation into operation of legal rules may be. An experiment in this type of research has therefore been initiated.[33]

The actual project description, probably written by Clark, was more positive when it proposed "to take the field in Connecticut in the effort to discover

how the administration of justice is working. . . . The actual effect of procedural devices on the progress of litigation will be studied in detail."[34]

Clark must have "taken" to the field with some relish, or at least put his
research assistants right to work and worked them hard, for in July 1928,
less than a year after the assistants were hired, he published his initial findings, based on but five months of work.[35] The scope of the research on which
the article was based was comparatively small — one or two years of cases in
the upper trial courts of the three largest counties in the state and three years
of federal district court cases, a total of about 9,300 cases — but the amount
of effort must have been prodigious. No sampling techniques were used, and
all the counting was done by hand.[36] Considering the relatively primitive
technique, it is not surprising that the results were not elaborate.

Following the Cleveland model, Clark created a simple table showing
disposition by type of action and also took a stab at determining the frequency of the use of jury trial, prejudgment attachment, and various dilatory
pleas. He was somewhat tentative in his interpretation of the data. Examination of the data suggested that, given the preponderance of uncontested
divorces and foreclosures, settled automotive negligence claims, and simple
debt collections, the largely administrative nature of state court civil litigation had already emerged in urban Connecticut by 1925. But, rather than
announce this somewhat surprising discovery, Clark was content to state the
findings specifically and wonder about the appropriateness of using complex
judicial machinery to resolve such apparently simple disputes.[37] He also presented evidence that jury trials were infrequent,[38] that prejudgment attachment, especially of large sums, was an effective way to promote settlement of
contract disputes, and that most often motions directed at the pleadings in a
case were effective only as a delaying tactic, but all without much comment.
However, he was less cautious in describing his understanding of the value of
his enterprise:

> It is believed, and experience so far shows, that this, although almost a
> virgin field to the social scientist, is one of the most fruitful for this type
> of investigation. . . .
>   These records are capable of use for at least two important purposes.
> They may be used to illustrate and to test the efficacy of our rules of
> procedure and our general methods of administering justice. And they
> may be used, second, as starting points for the further detailed investiga-
> tion of social problems of many and varied kinds.[39]

And his conclusion was enthusiastic:

It is felt that the limits of possible investigation of this kind are only set by the capacities of the investigators. Thus it may be possible eventually to go behind the court records and to trace somewhat the potential law suits which never come to court.[40]

Apparently, a rush job with simple results and a glorious vision was exactly what was called for, for as soon as results were available, the Laura Spelman Rockefeller Foundation made a grant of $55,000 to extend the study for five more years.[41] Thus fortified, Clark set his research assistants upon the necessary but time-consuming and hardly glamorous job of refining their questionnaires and expanding the scope of their study to include more years, different states' courts, and criminal cases.[42]

While Clark and his assistants worked away largely unnoticed, America elected a new president—Herbert Hoover. When Hoover took office, he indicated not only his support for the Eighteenth Amendment but also his near outrage at the nationwide failure to enforce Prohibition.[43] Since the liquor problem and its near twin, the crime problem, had been issues in the preceding campaign, the President's position was not much of a surprise. Nor was that of Congress which, in response to a request made in his inaugural address, on the same day appropriated monies for a "thorough inquiry into the problem of enforcement of prohibition under the provisions of the Eighteenth Amendment . . . together with the enforcement of other laws."[44] And thus was spawned the National Commission on Law Observance and Enforcement, a prestigious body headed by George W. Wickersham, former Attorney General of the United States, and including Ada Comstock, President of Radcliffe College, and Roscoe Pound.[45]

Despite the existence of the Wickersham Commission, as the National Commission on Law Observance and Enforcement became known, President Hoover was not without "volunteers" who offered to help with investigations of the problem of the administration of justice. Among them were Robert Hutchins and Charles Clark who, but two weeks after the inauguration, met with Hoover and other federal officials to propose a $250,000 study of the operation of the federal courts patterned on the Connecticut courts study.[46] Hoover's response to the proposal is not recorded, but eight months later Wickersham asked Clark, who was by then dean, to meet with him about conducting one of the Commission's studies of law enforcement.[47] The meeting was successful; Wickersham liked the old Hutchins-Clark proposal. So after he conferred with the two members in charge of the Commission's inquiry into the courts[48] and with potential members of an advisory committee to be set up to aid the project,[49] Clark was hired in January 1930 as a consultant to the Commission.[50]

Clark, who had been told that only $3,000 to $4,000 was available for the preliminary organization of his study and that it might be difficult for the Commission to obtain any future appropriations from a Congress generally uninterested in any of the Commission's work other than on Prohibition,[51] began work immediately. Or, more accurately, William O. Douglas did, for he was to design the forms on which the research assistants were to record their data.[52] In this task he had the help of Charles Ulysses Samenow, Clark's primary research assistant on the Connecticut courts study, who was to occupy the same position with respect to this project.[53] Working at a feverish pace, the two men began by creating the forms for collecting data on criminal cases, since those cases were the ones the Commission was most interested in, as well as the ones with which the Connecticut courts study had had the least experience. Once the forms were ready they were pretested and then re-worked, and then pretested again and again revised, each time after consultation with the advisory committee.[54] Simultaneously, Douglas and Samenow developed and pretested a form covering civil cases.[55] Meanwhile, Clark began to assemble a collection of law school deans and faculty members who were to participate in the study by securing and nominally supervising local research assistants.[56]

When in May 1930 Clark and Douglas paused to help the Commission obtain further funds by explaining exactly the purpose of their research, they suggested that they wished to "collect concrete factual, statistical information" in order to "illustrate and test the efficiency of our rules of procedure and our general methods of administering justice" in the federal courts. They intended to secure "actual figures bearing on congestion," on the "types of business" in the federal courts, and on "bargain days" and other aspects of the so-called breakdowns in the systems.[57] All were quite topical, practical inquiries, given that President Hoover had asserted that these "problems" were leading to a general lawlessness of which the lack of enforcement of Prohibition was only a single example.

Time for thought about purposes was, however, limited.[58] As soon as the Commission's appropriation was renewed, Clark finished lining up law schools to help with the research.[59] As fast as Clark lined up law schools, Douglas and Samenow set to work what was soon to be a small army of fieldworkers whose task was enormous. In each of the thirteen districts to be studied, all civil cases and all criminal cases terminated in the five years ending June 30, 1930 (except for Prohibition violations), were to be examined and coded; for Prohibition cases, a 10 percent sample was to be taken in the seven most populous districts, while all cases were to be examined and coded in the less populous districts.[60]

At the outset it was estimated that it would take two years to gather and process the data Clark sought.[61] Why such a vast project was planned when funding was known to be precarious is unclear,[62] but soon problems with the original timetable appeared. The civil forms proved to need more pretesting than expected and the examination and coding of cases went very slowly.[63] Some change in plans was surely indicated. Exactly how serious a change did not become apparent until early January 1931 when the Commission filed its Prohibition report. That report satisfied neither wets nor drys because it both supported Prohibition and suggested that, if more vigorous enforcement of existing criminal statutes proved to be unsuccessful in reducing the general prevalence of violations, revision of the Eighteenth Amendment would be appropriate.[64] It immediately became clear that Congress would not appropriate more money to extend the life of the Commission just to learn about the "crime problem" after it had learned nothing it wanted to know about the "liquor problem."[65] So that January, Clark, interested Commission members, and other advisors thrashed out a new, more limited goal in many letters and several conferences.[66] The new target for accumulating data was three years' worth of criminal cases and one of civil in each district. None of these data would be processed except the data on criminal cases in Connecticut, which would form the basis for a progress report to the Commission.[67] Meanwhile, Chairman Wickersham, working with materials furnished by Clark, would seek the foundation support necessary to finance completion of the study.[68]

While the search for funds went forward, fieldworkers poured the results of their labors into New Haven where Douglas and Samenow, aided by Thurman Arnold, newly added to the faculty, and others,[69] struggled to check, run, and analyze the Connecticut criminal cases. Their job was made doubly difficult by the need to first process materials on juveniles that they had agreed to collect for another commission consultant many months before.[70] But by May 1, although the New Haven staff, which had been "working nights for the last week or so," was "used up," the progress report was done.[71]

What the report showed was a bit of a surprise. It noted that, although the literature suggested the existence of numerous obstacles to effective law enforcement — "technicalities, delays and continuances, irrational juries, a cumbersome grand jury system, long trials, appeals on obsolete doctrinal points, and in general, the widely advertised results of what is generally called 'the sporting theory of justice' "[72] — in fact nothing of the sort appeared to be happening. Seventy percent of the defendants pled guilty when arraigned, most of those on the day the indictment or information was filed. Ultimately 90 percent of the defendants pled guilty and only 1 percent had a jury trial, generally lasting less than a day. Sixty percent of all cases were disposed of with a fine (80 percent of the Prohibition cases and 25 percent of the balance), with the amount "of the fine so nicely adjusted that in three years only five defendants were committed to jail for failure to pay." Eighty-five percent of the cases were disposed in two months.[73] Clark, Douglas, and Samenow had discovered modern federal criminal procedure.[74]

The three men were slightly bewildered by their discovery, which for them raised doubts about the administration of justice because the system "seems almost too efficient; because it presents the spectacle of a long line of orderly offenders, few of whom it is necessary to commit to jail either before or after trial, pleading guilty with systematic regularity . . . , raising no technical objections and so far as the records show, complaining about no invasions of their constitutional or other privileges."[75] But they proposed to stick with their figures, which to them suggested that the absence of delay was due to careful selection of the prosecutions brought, with an eye to eliminating or prosecuting under less serious charges possibly contested cases.[76]

At least one member of the Advisory Committee was enthusiastic about the limited results.[77] Unfortunately, the Commission was not. After nearly a month of sitting on the report, Wickersham, probably acting at Pound's request, asked for deletion of the conclusion that no delay in the disposition of cases had been found because "the statement is at variance with conclusions which were reached in other reports."[78] Although the other reports were virtually free of any data suggesting court congestion and delay, a slightly bitter Charles Clark agreed.[79]

Why Clark agreed is uncertain. Perhaps it was the realization that even with Wickersham's deletions, the report was a strong statement. It noted "the complete absence of procedural delays," a "negligible" incidence of contested cases and jury trials, a "negligible" amount of time required for the disposition of cases, and the prevalence of "minor offenses" for which "small sentences" were imposed.[80] These findings and the inference of selective prosecution negated the suggestion that the system was overrun with congestion and delay, at least for anyone who could read.

But, whatever Clark's reasons for agreeing to Wickersham's deletions, it was probably not any hope for future favors. Wickersham had generated a grant of $25,000 from the Rockefeller Foundation to the American Law Institute that might have financed completion of the study, but that grant was contingent on securing $25,000 more from other sources, and Wickersham had already run through his short list of alternative sources of funds with no success.[81] So in June 1931, as the fiscal year drew to a close, the fieldworkers madly finished their counting and everyone awaited the inevitable termination of the study.

When funding terminated on July 1, the staff of trained fieldworkers disappeared. Samenow, who according to Clark suffered from a personality that was not "pleasing" and was thus precluded from consideration for a permanent faculty appointment, left for practice.[82] Everyone expected that Douglas would complete the exodus by accepting Hutchins's seemingly magnificent offer to go to Chicago, but instead he stayed on as a visiting professor at a school he had never left.[83] Nevertheless, the excitement was over.

In October, Clark and Wickersham again approached the Rockefeller Foundation in an effort not to finish the original project, but just to process and tabulate data already collected.[84] Their effort succeeded and, as a result, Samenow was rehired to begin work on the accumulated data.[85] But with the small work force that could be afforded, the job went slowly. The cards were not all punched until summer 1932; Samenow's preliminary draft of the report on criminal cases was not finished until fall; and Douglas's redraft languished until just before Christmas.[86] While Douglas worked, Clark negotiated a complicated agreement with the American Law Institute to publish the two reports. The agreement required approval first by a committee of the ALI Council consisting of two members of the Commission and Judge Learned Hand, then by the Council, and finally by the membership — a process so full of potential traps that it plainly left Clark worried.[87] The report on civil cases was not ready until the end of summer 1933, at which time Samenow left for good.[88] Approval of both reports did not come until May 1934, and publication was delayed until the following fall.[89] Counting from the Hutchins and Clark meeting with Hoover, it had taken over five years to publish about one year's worth of research.

DESPITE THE SETBACKS and the enormous effort, Clark remained remarkably good-humored, as can be seen from an incident that took place at the very end of the study. Wickersham had been asked to write an introduction to the published volumes; his draft cut squarely into the representativeness of the study.[90] His reason for so doing was simple. Clark had already published an article in the *American Bar Association Journal* highlighting one of the study's most topical discoveries. He had noted that the diversity jurisdiction has been so swallowed up by the federal question jurisdiction and by cases brought by or against the United States that diversity cases represented less than 20 percent of filed cases. Moreover, of those diversity cases filed, 85 percent were simple contract or tort claims, and most of these were claims involving foreign corporations doing business in the forum states. Clark suggested that these findings supported a pending bill to treat a foreign corporation doing business in a state as a citizen of that state for purposes of the diversity jurisdiction.[91] Wickersham strongly opposed the bill[92] and so wrote his introduction to undercut Clark's conclusion. Yet, in the face of this rather direct attack on his scholarship, Clark, while seeking a change in the introduction, was able to remark that he thought he had adequately emphasized that the conclusions drawn in the study were his own. He continued: "Perhaps this thought is not important, but I have in mind to make it always clear that the figures are available to all commentators, whatever side of pending questions they take."[93] Such equanimity was a long way from the optimism of the days of the early reports on the Connecticut courts study. Yet the reasons for Clark's change of tone, if not obvious from the study of his enterprise, are relatively easily isolated: experience and a bit of bewilderment.

Clark's experience had been like virtually no other law teacher's. His Connecticut courts study was the first of its kind, although it admittedly had antecedents in the Cleveland Crime Survey. In it Clark had developed a variation on the staple methodology of the crime survey — the mortality table. Whereas the mortality table looked at how cases entering the system dropped out, in an effort to learn if criminals were being allowed to escape from justice, Clark's method in the Connecticut courts study focused on completed cases in an effort to learn what the system as a whole looked like over a given period of time. This methodological variant did exactly what it was designed to do; it generated what we now know to be a remarkably accurate picture of an urban court system. In supervising the development of this methodology, and then further refining it in the federal courts study, Clark had learned enough to have acquired the concerns of the newer social scientists about control of observation and their preference for the analysis of primary data. He worried about observer bias, prided himself on the fact that all his data were collected by investigators under his control, and even did some error estimation.[94] Clark had also absorbed some of the then current social science cant about the separation of data collection and data analysis.[95] And he was even a bit of a missionary, bringing social science to the most provincial law schools.[96] Yet, as he absorbed bits of the values of academic social science, somehow the early excitement derived from participation in a new and scientific inquiry was lost.

The published results of the Connecticut courts study hint at the reason for the loss of enthusiasm. After the first flurry of articles, virtual silence set in, just when there was little else to absorb Clark's time. Eight years later, further findings were published, largely because there was little else to do with the money left in the grant secured to support the research.[97] True, some new items of significance were disclosed — most obviously the development of a specialized personal injury bar and the tendency of more jury verdicts to be appealed and appealed successfully more often than nonjury verdicts. But the basic study was the same. Essentially uncontested matters — collections, divorces, and foreclosures — together with the largely settled matters, primarily tort cases, dominated the docket.[98] In so duplicating the results of the initial foray into the subject, the larger study exposed the routine nature of most scientific inquiry.

Routine inquiry need not be a problem. Indeed, fifty years later the fact that three times the effort was not likely to even double the results is not startling. When colleagues and friends were doing exciting things, like fighting with Pound and others about Realism and judicial decision making or attacking the Restatement project or looking at symbolic behavior in law, routine inquiry was a real problem. As the silence and resignation show, to Clark and his co-workers the fact that much more work had yielded precious little in terms of results was doubly depressing. It was depressing, first, because in contrast to the initial high expectations it seemed as if the field of investigation chosen by Clark had not been "one of the most fruitful" for scientific research, for the results did not "test the efficacy of our rules of procedure," nor did they suggest any "further detailed investigations of social problems" that might be undertaken, much less ways to trace "the potential law suits which never come to court."[99] It was depressing, second, because from the beginning — the Hutchins-Clark proposal for an institute of procedure — the courts studies were supposed to reveal the knowledge that would fuel the progress of reform, specifically the reform of the technical rules of procedure. Yet the increased effort by Clark and his co-workers had merely generated more evidence of the same conditions that seemed by and large irrelevant to the cause of reform as they knew it, since in a system where most cases are uncontested or settled, technical procedure played little part and thus to expend effort at its reform made little sense.

Taken together, the failure of the study to live up to the initial high expectations and the failure to provide fuel for the progress of reform suggested that the aims of the project, already reduced from solving the problems of the administration of justice[100] to "providing valuable information . . . to all those interested in the processes of law administration and in its improvement,"[101] ought to be further limited to gaining "experience statistics"[102] and to providing a stimulus for setting up "a permanent machinery to supply" "statistical data on judicial administration."[103] Such an aim was a long way from reform, and although Clark, who well knew exactly what his enterprise was worth as a piece of scientific research, accepted that reduction in aim, he surely did not revel in it.[104] And so in a real sense his experience was thus his undoing; it sapped the impetus for the doing.

By thus limiting his objectives, Clark may have succeeded in compensating for the debilitating effects of the limited results of his science. But limited objectives were no defense against the bewildering demands on one's science made by friendly insiders and by outsiders, friendly or not.

Of the insiders Samenow and Douglas were the workhorses of the operation. They apparently did their tasks without quarrel, maybe even with a bit of relish — indeed, both worked on more than one such research project at a time. The nearly two years of never quite knowing whether Douglas would leave for the University of Chicago were perhaps unsettling, but his prolonged indecision seemed to have no appreciable effect on his work. Thurman Arnold, however, was a quite different kind of co-worker. He had been brought to New Haven in part because of his ostensible interest in both the state and federal courts studies.[105] After his arrival Arnold was in fact of some help,[106] but as the project dragged on and he found new and more interesting things to do,[107] his participation became more problematical. Clark had difficulty in keeping him at his work, and Arnold began to question the legitimacy of collecting "mass statistics."[108]

Arnold's drift away from the enterprise could perhaps be rationalized by looking at the exciting new things he was doing. Outsiders, on the other hand, though less personally troublesome, were more intellectually so, as can be seen from their comments on the federal courts study's report on criminal litigation. Some were, of course, simply supportive, though whether reflexively or reflectively it is often hard to say.[109] In contrast, Learned Hand was thoroughly, but gently, skeptical about the enterprise; though he suggested that the results were "scarcely worth the extraordinary amount of intelligence and time they have cost," he knew his role and willingly bestowed his "unorthodox blessing" on the report.[110] The Harvard establishment presented a more disconcerting problem, however.

To some extent Clark had created his problems at Harvard. True to an ideal of objective social science and also a bit gun-shy because of the Commission's objections to the conclusions in the preliminary report, he sent out the draft of the criminal report virtually devoid of any conclusions or interpretive material. This action had the support of William Draper Lewis, executive director of the American Legal Institute, who was as worried as Clark about the problems of getting any conclusions approved by his diverse membership.[111] Many of the most thoughtful readers were not at all bothered by this mode of presentation. Mr. Justice Roberts, for example, was pleased with the "great discretion and fairness of appraisement," and Thomas E. Atkinson, a professor at Kansas, found the report "interesting" and "of great value."[112] But Clark's Harvard friends were not so charitable.

Monte Lemann, for example, found that the final report fell short of fulfilling the expectations created by the preliminary one.[113] Sam Bass Warner, who had done similar work himself, found the report a "jumble of figures without any special meaning or significance," suggested that Clark or Arnold or "some other genius . . . dream about it for the next six months and . . . completely rewrite it with a view to emphasizing the nuggets discovered," and then delivered the unkindest blow of all by suggesting it was "no better than a good Johns Hopkins report."[114] His colleague Edmund Morgan agreed.[115] Felix Frankfurter suggested that since the study presented neither "vivid illumination of the workings" of the lower federal courts nor "exploration of a new technique for securing such illumination," "scholarship would not be advanced" by publication of the report.[116] In support of his conclusion, he presented a memorandum written by an unnamed "professional friend," in reality Henry Hart, then in his first year of teaching, that was an outrageous hatchet job done with little understanding of the project.[117]

Clark was both unhappy with the criticism and slightly liberated by it. Exasperated, he complained to Warner, "A few years ago the cry was all for collecting many figures. Now it is to collect hardly any and interpret."[118] Yet he admitted that the cry for interpretation "clears the air and prepares the way for a report and set of conclusions which we have for some time felt we would like to make, but which, in view of the institutional nature of the study and its backing from diverse sources, we did not want to send out with the first draft."[119] Of course, when the conclusions arrived, some of the same parties complained—for example, Morgan. He argued that although the study disclosed no real obstacles to law enforcement, such as "technicalities, delay, . . . irrational juries [and] appeals on obsolete doctrinal points," neither did it "indicate their absence"; thus, it did not negate the possibility that the "long line of offenders pleading guilty with great regularity" was evidence that "the regular system of examining into the merits" was "so unsatisfactory that both the prosecution and defense sought compromise rather than trial."[120] Clark, by this time virtually shell-shocked, was ready to change his tune and not only to argue against appending conclusions to his study, but also to maintain that with the coming of the New Deal the prevailing practice had changed from the collection of facts to "action without even looking at the consequences," and that this change had done the study in.[121]

Clark's difficulties with his external audience were in one sense a bit bewildering, especially when one considers the content of the report. He had managed to examine 70,000 cases in thirteen well-selected district courts. Presentation was clear, if not expeditious. The pattern that emerged from the figures was again much like that of modern criminal procedure; most cases were disposed of on guilty pleas with relatively lenient sentences. As a result indictments were at times dispensed with, especially in liquor cases; few motions were filed; few trials were held; those trials held were of short duration; verdicts were appealed only when imprisonment was the sentence; and appeals were not often successful.[122] Interestingly, the report concluded that plea bargaining in the federal courts had begun about 1916 with the rise of federal criminal liability for what would otherwise be thought of as local law enforcement problems, such as auto theft, prostitution, and narcotics, and suggested that the practice be recognized and regularized.[123] All in all, the report was, and still is, quite informative and useful.

In another sense Clark's difficulties with his Harvard audience were all too explicable. Clark's findings differed significantly from those that had been written up in the Pound-Frankfurter survey, *Criminal Justice in Cleveland*. That survey painted the classical progressive reformers' view of criminal justice — organizational chaos, offenders escaping the law, unfettered prosecutorial discretion, procedural shenanigans at and after trial, even a "ring" of attorneys monopolizing misdemeanor cases in the Municipal Court of Cleveland and a set of "political attorneys" in the Court of Common Pleas who seemed to get better results for their clients than was the case for clients of less well connected attorneys.[124] Some of the difference in the two studies could be attributed to the difference in functions between the Cleveland Police Department and the various federal law enforcement officers whose cases fed into the federal courts. But, rhetoric aside, there were clear differences between the findings. In Cleveland only about half of the cases not sifted out by the prosecutor as in one way or another improvidently filed, were resolved with a guilty plea and anywhere from a quarter to a half of the cases tried resulted in acquittals. Such a difference might be seen either as consequential or as reflecting the differing roles of the state and federal courts in criminal matters and so ignored. However, it was difficult to ignore such differences when Frankfurter had concluded that, "[T]he most outstanding features of *Criminal Justice in Cleveland*, namely the practical breakdown of criminal machinery, has its parallel in other cities."[125] Clark's results suggested that any such conclusion was too strong.

Given the negative reaction to the careful work, based on rather extensive data in the criminal report, Clark must have sent out the draft of the civil report with trepidation. Here Clark had only 10,000 cases collected in haste during the last few months of the study.[126] And presentation of what data there were was complicated by the existence of separate law, admiralty, and equity dockets, each with its own procedural vocabulary, and by the overlay of federal civil actions for forfeitures and penalties. Even more important, but for the materials on the use of the diversity jurisdiction, precious little about the activities of the federal courts emerged beyond the prevalence of settlements, the limited incidence of jury trials, and the relative expedition with which cases, especially those permitting nonjury trials, were disposed of.[127] A very careful reader might have noticed the relative unwillingness of the federal government to settle cases,[128] but that was about all.

This time, however, except of course for a continuingly skeptical Learned Hand, the reviewers, especially those from Harvard, found the report thoroughly satisfactory.[129] Frankfurter commented, "Not only have you posed important problems — you have gone a long way towards shedding much light on them"; he even claimed to have gotten Clark started in the business of studying courts.[130] Lemann found the report both interesting and useful, and lamented that time and a lack of money had limited its scope; Warner found it both very good and understated.[131] Clark intuited a reason for the change in tune. In between circulating drafts of the first and second reports, he had published his piece on the diversity jurisdiction. As that piece supported the Frankfurterian-liberal reformist position on the legislation to limit corporate access to the diversity jurisdiction,[132] Frankfurter and his friends supported Clark's research; it was all as predictable as Wickersham's action had been. However, the existence of such a reason was hardly comforting and, taken together with the earlier objections, showed at best a perverse preference for the results of a poor job over those of a good one that conflicted with Clark's newly acquired scientific values.

However bewildering to Clark, the outsiders' reaction to the Study of the Business of the Federal Courts nevertheless illuminates the understanding of empirical legal research held by Clark and his contemporaries. Clark had spoken of the knowledge that was prerequisite to reform. In so doing, he spoke from within a tradition of progressive reform through the gathering of "the facts."[133] While Clark had altered that tradition, at least in its legal branch, by yoking it more firmly with the emerging quantitative social science of the time, he had at the same time affirmed its values in two important ways. First, he affirmed the activist aspect of the tradition that saw and focused scientific inquiry in terms of its usefulness in securing desired reforms. Second, he affirmed its model of the way the world to be inquired into was structured — congested courts, procedural shenanigans, and all — as well as its prescription of technical procedural reform as the way to eliminate the perceived defects in that structure. But, as noted earlier, somewhere in the course of his research Clark acquired some of the values of the new academic social sciences. In his work he affirmed aspects of those values as well, especially the young social scientists' concern for method that in part replaced the old model of the way the world to be inquired into was structured, and their recognition of a more attenuated relationship between scientific inquiry and desired reforms.

Clark was confused by the intersection of progressive reform and social science, as can be seen from his reaction to the later Connecticut courts' work.[134] There the results did not fit with the received understanding of how the legal world was structured and, moreover, suggested that the reforms that the research was done to support were largely irrelevant. Faced with this discontinuity between the expectations generated through his participation in progressive reform and the results of his research, Clark hesitated a while, but ultimately published the work anyway. In doing so he drew on his newer commitment to academic social science, although his analysis never fully broke free of the concerns of reform.[135]

In contrast, the troublesome outsiders who so bewildered Clark by their perverse preference for the bad over the good were not confused at all. They affirmed only the values implicit in the tradition of progressive reform, and their reaction to the federal courts study proved it. When, as in the criminal report, the study simply had knowledge to supply, when it was irrelevant, if not potentially undermining, to the cause of reform as the liberal reformers conceived of it, they were hostile; when, as in the civil report, it supported liberal reform proposals, they were pleased.[136] In so doing they reacted quite similarly to the way Clark had initially reacted to the enlarged Connecticut courts study, but they could not, and would not, react as Clark had ultimately done. They were completely oblivious to the values of the emerging social sciences; thus, the fact that Clark's fact gathering was a "scientific"

enterprise made no difference. Fact gathering that did not advance an immediate reform objective was scholarship not worth publishing, just as fact
gathering that did not fit their model of how the world was structured was an
"irrelevant jumble of figures." They would give or withhold their support for
the newer empirical research in law just as they had for the older, less structured research.

Thus, the origins of empirical legal research in the progressive practice of
searching for the facts that would provide the basis for reform partly impeded the research enterprise it had generated. Because the heirs of the old
progressive reformers wished the newer research to continue to fuel reform
as the old research had done, by providing the facts indicated by their model
of the way the world was structured, they refused to extend plainly expected
and needed support to the newer research, unless their wishes were met.
Deprived of support from these obvious allies, Clark and others who wished
to do empirical legal research might have turned to the emerging social scientific community for support; however, an attempt to gain support from that
community presented its own problems.

Business Failures and Auto Accidents: The Law Professors Meet the Social Scientists

The 1920s and early 1930s brought a significant influx of social scientists to
Yale. The impetus for this development was Yale's new President, James
Rowland Angell, an experimental psychologist by training. The vehicles for
mounting this innovation were several; ultimately the most important was
the Institute of Human Relations, thought up by Hutchins and the Dean of
the Medical School.[137] The Institute was a typical bureaucratic ploy, set up
independently of the various social science departments but designed to influence those departments by offering affiliation to their members and by
requiring its members similarly to have departmental affiliation.

Two of these social scientists—Dorothy Swaine Thomas and Emma Corstvet—were attached to the Law School.[138] Both were genuinely quite pleased
with their new associations,[139] and both were fascinated by statistics.[140] On
the basis of their training and the emerging statistical ethos in many areas of
social science, they both advocated and participated in the statistically quantifiable social science that was plainly the new wave of the time.[141] There,
however, the similarity ended.

Of the two, Dorothy Thomas was the more formally educated; she came
with a reputation as a methodologist of real sophistication;[142] Emma Corst-

vet, on the other hand, came with impeccable progressive credentials and a vital interest in social problems, accompanied by a then still fashionable antidegree bias and decent training in statistics.[143] Thomas was the first hired; in summer 1929 she came as a consultant to help decide what the Institute should be doing,[144] and stayed on as a part-time research associate and then as a full-time associate professor, starting in fall 1930.[145] Corstvet, lacking equivalent degrees, was first hired in late fall 1929 as a full-time research associate. Each was put to work on an existing project: Thomas on William O. Douglas's business failures project, Corstvet on Charles E. Clark's study of the compensation received by auto accident victims. The work on these two projects by these two women illustrates the problems faced by Clark and others when seeking support for the doing of empirical legal research by engaging in overtly collaborative efforts with members of the social science community.

DOUGLAS'S PROJECT was older and farther along when social science assistance in the form of Dorothy Thomas arrived.[146] Douglas, a 1925 graduate of the Columbia Law School, had taught bankruptcy starting in 1926 as a part-time instructor, then in 1927 as a full-time instructor at that school. He thought up the business failures project in summer 1928, right after he resigned from Columbia to protest Smith's appointment as dean and moved to Yale.[147] The original conception, announced in September 1928, was grand; its object was taken to be an inquiry into the "functioning of the whole credit system of the country." This inquiry was to take as its "point of departure administration of the bankruptcy laws." Douglas isolated two initial targets for the inquiry: the efficiency of the various methods of liquidating and salvaging a business and the extent of fraudulent practices in bankruptcy.[148] Although naming these two targets was the only specification Douglas could give of "the actualities of bankruptcy administration which in the past have been engulfed in so much misunderstanding and doubt as to bring the whole system at times under suspicion and disrespect,"[149] he did know what resources would be required in order to make his investigation: three years and $60,000 to pay for the expenses of two roving teams — one of economists "looking at the facts from the economic, business and social angle" and one of lawyers "looking at them from the legal, administrative angle."[150]

Where Douglas got the idea for the project is unclear, although it bears certain family resemblances to the original Hutchins-Clark Connecticut courts proposal first funded not six months earlier, and a hint of an idea first put forth in the Columbia curriculum study.[151] For some reason, funding was expected from the Social Science Research Council for work that was to have begun in the Southern District of New York.[152] That funding, however, did not appear. What did appear was the United States Department of Commerce, which expressed interest in Douglas's project, apparently because it fit into the Department's own "national retail merchants" study that was already in progress in two cities.[153] As a result of the Department's interest, the business failures project began, not in New York, but in Philadelphia, with a study of the causes of failure of retail grocers.

The size of the Philadelphia inquiry made in spring 1929 was small — thirty-five grocers.[154] Law students acting as dollar-a-year special agents of the Department of Commerce did the work of examining court records and interviewing bankrupts.[155] Given the size of the unscientifically chosen sample and the rather cavalier use of even such rudimentary notions as an "average," only in the loosest sense was the study scientific. Yet from an examination of this sample the investigators concluded that credit losses had contributed to the failure of only a few of these businesses, whereas "unscientific business practices" and "losses in real estate investment and speculation" had contributed to failure in many more of the cases. They also found, with some surprise, that despite adherence to a principle of creditor control of insolvency proceedings, most of the bankruptcies returned little to the creditors, that attorneys' fees ate up much of the limited assets available for payments to creditors, and that the entire process took a relatively long time.[156] It was a start.

While the Philadelphia study was underway, Douglas's project got the first of two unexpected boosts when, in spring 1929, a bankruptcy scandal broke out in the Southern District of New York.[157] Several lawyers and some district court personnel were indicted for bribery, subornation of perjury, and conspiracy to defraud creditors in a grand jury investigation that had disclosed widespread filing of collusive or solicited voluntary and involuntary bankruptcies.[158] The grand jury report accompanying the indictments suggested that a thorough investigation of bankruptcy administration in the district be made, and the United States Attorney, acting on that suggestion, petitioned the District Court for the Southern District of New York to institute such an investigation.[159] The District Court chose one of its members, Thomas D. Thatcher, to hold the investigation, and he invited the major local bar associations to participate. With the consent of the United States Attorney, the associations were ordered to conduct the investigation under the direction of "their counsel," Colonel William J. Donovan.[160] From the beginning, the investigation was directed not only at the corrupt practices discovered in the grand jury investigations, but also at reform of bankruptcy administration generally, and thus of the Bankruptcy Act. As part of this effort at bankruptcy law reform, Douglas was asked to prepare a comparative study of bankruptcy administration in the United States, England, Canada, France, and Germany, and an analysis of the various rules adopted by district courts for administering the Bankruptcy Act.[161] Douglas read most of the study as his "testimony" before Judge Thatcher. There were two principal findings of his study. First, English and Canadian practice often limited discharge when American practice did not, particularly in cases of the use of business funds for speculative or other nonbusiness purposes, and in cases of failure to keep adequate business records. Second, English and Canadian practice seemed on the whole more efficient, more businesslike, and less creditor-controlled than American practice.[162]

Although the purest of library research, Douglas's study for the Donovan investigation advanced the business failures project in two ways. First, its principal findings fit nicely with the findings in the Philadelphia grocers study. In Philadelphia, Douglas discovered the existence of objectionable practices by debtors that the English and Canadian statutes suggested might be corrected with legal controls. Similarly, the inefficiencies in bankruptcy administration that Douglas found seemed to be avoided in England and Canada. Second, Douglas's research gained him the appreciation of Colonel Donovan and a certain amount of public recognition among those persons interested in bankruptcy reform. Among those persons was William Clark, a United States District Judge for the District of New Jersey. He gave the business failures project its second boost when he convinced Douglas and the Department of Commerce to move their cooperative investigation to Newark and to expand it from grocers to all bankrupts, including wage earners.[163]

While Douglas's project was getting these twin boosts, he began another branch of his projected study of the efficiency of the various devices for liquidating or salvaging a business, with an investigation of the court records of equity receiverships brought in the United States District Court for the District of Connecticut.[164] This project and the New Jersey project, together with the results of the Philadelphia study, were sufficient to secure the agreement of the Institute of Human Relations to fund the business failures project generally, even though "as a matter of policy it was thought unwise to takeover a school or department project and put it on the Institute budget."[165] After a year's worth of work, Douglas had finally secured relatively stable financing.

With financing thus secured, Douglas took time to reexamine his conception of the project as a whole as he prepared his first written report on it. This time he abandoned the notion that his project was in any sense a study of the whole credit system of the country; it was a study of business failures pure and simple.[166] And with a year's experience he could specify a little better what he meant by a study of business failures. He contemplated three kinds of studies: one, of the causes of business failures, the Newark study; another, of "the efficiency of the administrative machinery employed in reorganizing or liquidating" a business, the equity receivership study plus parts of the Newark study; and a third, of "the incidences of the [business] failure as measured by the effect on the owners, the creditors, the employees and other groups in the community," a study not yet begun.[167]

Douglas accompanied this restatement of his project with a long report on a completed portion of the enterprise, the study of the forty-four equity receiverships instituted in the District of Connecticut in the previous ten years.[168] The report drew no real conclusions[169] but emphasized the high cost of fees paid to a seemingly inordinate number of officials — receivers, attorneys, appraisers, and the like — participating in the proceedings and the tendency of these officials, other than those attorneys acting as such, to be untrained for their duties.[170] He also noted that although the object of an equity receivership was to avoid the liquidation of the business that would occur in bankruptcy,[171] most of the receiverships undertaken had headed or seemed to be headed toward liquidation anyway.[172]

For some reason Douglas never followed up on the equity receiverships study directly; instead, he turned his energies toward the Newark study of the "causes" of business failures. The key to this study was to be a "clinic" at which by court order all bankrupts would have to appear and be examined by project investigators administering a loosely structured questionnaire, "evolved through conferences with judges, lawyers, economists, psychologists, sociologists and physicians," that was designed to isolate what commonsensically might be called the "causes" of business failures — what bankrupts' business practices had been and how they had used available funds before insolvency.[173]

At this point Dorothy Thomas began working at Yale. When she surveyed the project she concluded that methodologically it was "all mixed up" and set to work to "clean up" the project and "cut out" the ineffective parts.[174] Her initial efforts in this direction can be seen in an article that she wrote with Judge Clark and Douglas. The article outlined the procedures that were to be followed in the Newark study and then flatly stated that the effort could be seen only as "an immediate path-finding approach to an untouched field" designed to "indicate possible causative factors." Thereafter, effort would be needed to develop "more adequate techniques for controlling errors" and to produce data that would permit "inferences as to the causal connection of these various factors with bankruptcy." The study was merely preparatory for two reasons. First, it was only going to collect data from and about bankrupts, yet causation could be inferred only on the basis of comparable data about bankrupts and nonbankrupts. Second, although the method chosen for administering the questionnaire minimized several known problems with questionnaire studies generally, the survey would produce only a very limited amount of information of high reliability, and the method chosen to check the accuracy and completedness of much of the data obtained — cross-examination of the debtor by the investigator — would not likely yield data suitable for statistical treatment.[175]

Unfortunately, after only fifty-eight bankrupts were interviewed, "political problems" forced the closing of the bankruptcy clinic.[176] Rather than abandon the work in Newark, Douglas chose to collect his data by relying on some personal interviews with bankrupts and on questionnaires mailed to them with a cover letter either from the court or from the investigators.[177] He thus secured responses to his questionnaire from about half of a pool of nearly 1,300 bankrupts in the district. From a methodological point of view, however, the results he obtained were pure chaos. The only thing that could be salvaged was material helpful for "the development of a new [questionnaire] . . . in which most of the obvious sources of unreliability have been eliminated." Thus Douglas and Thomas produced an article, admittedly "somewhat pedantic," that examined two things in considerable detail. First, it described the refinement of the questionnaire in order to assure the "definiteness and completeness" of answers given and thereby ensure their representativeness. Second, it described the variations in the data secured by the various methods in order to "indicate the extent to which the [questionnaire] . . . itself was at fault in its failure to elicit definite replies."[178] After a second year of work Douglas had finally developed a reliable research procedure, although it was not one designed to find out what he wanted to know — the causes of bankruptcy.[179]

In fall 1930 the revised questionnaire was used in Boston "because of the interest and cooperation of the Hon. Thomas D. Thatcher," newly resigned from the district court bench and appointed Solicitor General and director of a special Department of Justice study of bankruptcy administration.[180] This time the questionnaire was administered by the bankruptcy referee in the regular examination of about 910 out of some 2,900 bankrupts filing petitions during the fiscal year ending June 30, 1931.[181] Preliminary results indicated that under the new procedures the revised questionnaire was working significantly better than the one used in Newark; it was producing "definite and complete answers to an extent that [would] . . . make frequency tables more truly representative of the groups studied."[182] Progress was being made.

Although the Boston study was as incapable of pinpointing the "causes" of bankruptcy as the Newark study, the results from the joint effort of Douglas and Thomas to refine the questionnaire were not conceived of as wholly methodological. The two expected that the data generated would supply material for additional articles: one based on the data from both Newark and Boston, "indicating the frequency of certain presumably causal factors in the production of bankruptcy," and another describing an attempt to develop "a method of investigating these factors in non-bankrupt cases."[183] Douglas worked on the first of these articles during the summer and fall of 1931. When he was finished he had two articles, not one.[184]

Curiously neither of Douglas's articles bore much relation to what might have been expected on the basis of the announced joint expectations. True, something like frequency tables appeared in both articles, and in neither did Douglas explicitly make the elementary mistake that Thomas had cautioned against — inferring causation from a study that did not include a control group — but the articles were only incidentally about the studies. They were about bankruptcy law reform, a topic that had heated up in the summer of 1930 with President Hoover's message on the subject announcing the beginning of Thatcher's study, which was in fact being run by Lloyd K. Garrison, one of Colonel Donovan's assistants in the earlier New York investigation in which Douglas had testified.[185]

In each article Douglas's argument was the same basic moral one: there are circumstances — such as inadequate accounting records, speculation, gambling, gross extravagance, or previous failures — that actually occur, as shown by the raw data from the Newark and Boston studies, in which discharge should not be allowed or in which the bankruptcy court should have the discretionary power, unfettered by notions of creditor control, to condition or suspend discharge, presumably in order to force the debtor to pay his debts out of after-acquired earnings.[186] Similarly, there are actual practices — such as lack of interest in the election of the trustee and inadequate examination of either bankrupts or applications for discharge — that are inconsistent with the assumed purpose of the Bankruptcy Act.[187] In each article the remedy for those evils was to look to the English bankruptcy act that Douglas had analyzed for the Donovan investigation a year or so earlier.[188] And so

Douglas proposed a series of technical amendments to the Bankruptcy Act, designed better to effectuate its assumed purposes and to deal directly with the occasions for granting of discharge when he thought circumstances made an absolute discharge undesirable.[189]

Even as phrased, Douglas's argument was at least implicitly causal. It implied that a change in the statute would cause a defined change in the behavior of businessmen and officials, unfortunately a causality that the very limited data Douglas chose to present on the operation of the English bankruptcy act seemed to belie.[190] But the argument was at least more sophisticated than the arguments made in the Philadelphia grocers study. That too was progress.

In two years' time Dorothy Thomas had made some small impact on the way empirical legal research was done at Yale. Similarly Douglas's arguments made some impact on the movement for bankruptcy law reform. When the attorney general submitted his bill for the reform of the bankruptcy laws, based in part on the study done by Solicitor General Thatcher, the accompanying report thanked Douglas for his help, and the bill included most of Douglas's suggested changes.[191] But despite this progress and despite published promises of more articles based on further studies,[192] and private assurances that a book was forthcoming,[193] no further studies were made by Douglas,[194] no book written. The business failures project was over.[195] Of its stated subjects of inquiry, the first, the causes of failure, had progressed only as far as learning the incidence of some of the purported causes of failure; the second, the efficiency of administration, had proceeded only far enough to make some simple observations based on the original forty-four equity receiverships, and on the indications of creditor interest disclosed in Newark and Boston; and the third, the effect of bankruptcy on others, had never even been started.[196]

LIKE THE BUSINESS failures project, the auto compensation study can be traced back to Robert Hutchins, who announced in February 1929 that he had been talking about doing a study of the extent and impact of injuries from auto accidents with members of the Committee to Study Compensation for Automobile Accidents.[197] This committee, chaired by Arthur Ballantine[198] and including several prominent New York and Philadelphia lawyers and judges, was organized in late fall 1928 by Ballantine and Shippen Lewis, who was to be director of the study.[199] The faculty promptly voted to undertake "the principal work of investigation" on the subject, provided that money for it could be found.[200]

In summer 1929, after Hutchins had left for Chicago, Clark picked up
the project. By then the funding problem had been solved with a grant of
$72,000 given to the Committee by the Rockefeller Foundation, through the
Columbia University Council for Research in the Social Sciences.[201] Clark
learned that Yale was to be not *the* but *a* principal investigator; he also
learned that he was to be a member of the Committee, as well as of its
executive committee.[202] In that role he soon found out that the dominant
members of the Committee were convinced that a system of statutory compensation, like that under the workmen's compensation laws, was the only
solution to the problems of personal hardship and court congestion caused
by lawsuits involving the by then increasingly common automobile.[203] The
Committee had already decided that its study was to have four parts: case
studies of the nature and impact of auto accidents on individuals; court
records studies of auto accident litigation; legal studies, largely directed at
the constitutionality of a compensation system; and insurance studies designed to flesh out the details of the compensation system. Most of the work
was split between Columbia and Yale.[204] Columbia professors executed or
supervised the third and fourth parts of the study. Clark supervised the court
records studies — not an onerous task, given his experience in such enterprises. Who was doing the "principal investigation" was thus hard to say,
especially since Shippen Lewis personally supervised the case studies of injured individuals.

The various studies were begun in late fall 1929. Work on the court records studies was not time-consuming, at least in New Haven. Clark used
previously compiled data from the Connecticut courts study; he did not
bother to update or augment that data to include additional information
collected for this study by workers in other jurisdictions.[205] It cannot have
been difficult at any of the other locations either, since the data sought —
number of cases, number of plaintiff victories at trial, dollar amount of
verdicts, and time from filing to trial — were quite limited and rudimentary.

Work on the case studies of injured persons initially presented no particular problems either. The general plan for this part of the research was to use
personal interviews in order to develop illustrative case studies as well as
statistical measures of the severity of injury, the amount of loss, and the
amount and timing of compensation. The first studies were done in Philadelphia; others followed in Connecticut, a state with a financial responsibility law, and Massachusetts, a state with a compulsory insurance law.[206]
No single form of questionnaire was ever agreed upon.[207] Rather, each re-

searcher was told the general objective and the specific data needed and was left to develop his or her own questionnaire and data collection technique.

Unlike Dorothy Thomas who found Douglas's study already going when she arrived, Emma Corstvet, hired just about the time work was to begin, was able to design her study from the start. In doing so she worked primarily with Shippen Lewis, not Clark. Given the object and the method of the study, she saw her problems much as had Dorothy Thomas: ensuring the accuracy and internal consistency of the data collected. Thus great effort was spent in developing a questionnaire "that really worked" and in careful cross-checking of answers with other available sources of information such as hospitals, employers, attorneys, and charities.[208] With the job of questionnaire development done, Corstvet and her three assistants began fieldwork in December 1929 and continued that work through September 1930.[209] The cases to study were obtained, without sampling, from the Department of Motor Vehicles' records.[210] When finished, Corstvet and workers in the other two jurisdictions had examined over 2,300 cases and made complete investigations of almost 1,200.[211]

The results did not surprise any of the participants. Only about 60 percent of the victims received any compensation, although about 30 percent of them received compensation in excess of total expenses, including lost wages.[212] Some slight tendency for the adequacy of compensation to be inversely related to the severity of the injury was also noted.[213] Careful research disclosed that deficiencies in the amount and delays in the timing of compensation were met largely by postponing or defaulting on payment of medical expenses or by using savings, and that in severe cases, when family income declined significantly, substantial debts were incurred for current living expenses.[214]

When the results of the various studies were compared, it appeared that the results from Boston, located in the only state with a compulsory insurance law, were significantly different from those elsewhere. A victim in Boston appeared to have a better chance of receiving compensation equal to or substantially in excess of losses than victims elsewhere, even victims of insured drivers. Clark was excited; while advising caution, because figures were "limited," and after careful checking to avoid "grievous error," he noted that the committee was "at the threshold of perhaps the most important conclusions to be drawn from [its] . . . case studies," for as a matter of "first impression . . . Massachusetts law causes the difference."[215] On the other hand, Corstvet, seconded by Dorothy Thomas, warned that researcher bias or discrepancies in researcher understanding of the object of research was likely to be a significant source of the differences.[216] Indeed, upon careful inquiry it turned out that the researcher in Boston had simply decided to include in her study only cases of "serious" injury.[217] So the Boston study had to be rerun in Worcester, where the results still turned out to be different from those elsewhere, although not as extreme as in the initial study.[218]

While the social scientists were gathering their data and debating the reasons for their differing results, the lawyers were planning their report and worrying about money. From the beginning, despite the known preferences of other committee members, Clark advocated making the Committee's product "a scientific investigation rather than a brief for a particular point of view."[219] Lewis, who was initially interested in using the case studies in a "fact brief of the Brandeis type," found that Clark's argument changed his mind; at least he agreed that the facts had to be "strong enough to speak for themselves."[220] However, Clark's opinion, even as strengthened by Lewis's, did not carry much weight with the Committee, which decided to put the statistical tables in an appendix and to present a Brandeis brief drawn from the case studies in a chapter in the text preceding the chapter interpreting the data in the appendix.[221]

At the same time that Clark was pushing for a real "scientific investigation," the Committee was running out of money. Within a year of receipt of the initial grant, Lewis was predicting that expenses would be $7,000 in excess of the $72,000 grant; five months later the estimated deficit had doubled.[222] Since the legal consultants had worked on a fixed-fee basis, a significant portion of this shortage was due to the case studies and much of that could be attributed to Yale. Corstvet had caught the error that had necessitated another study in Massachusetts,[223] and her study had cost anywhere from 50 to 600 percent more per case than any other.[224] Although the Rockefeller Foundation picked up the deficit,[225] Clark was both apologetic about Yale's part in creating the deficit and a bit bitter because of the nature of the report that the Committee finally chose to issue. In a letter to Lewis he defensively suggested that Yale had "tried to do this work thoroughly and carefully" and then observed that the cost had not been "excessive" when "compared with other research projects we have undertaken." He noted that there had been a bit of a conflict because at Yale "we have been most interested in the social and methodological implications of the study, while you have been most interested in the support which it gives to the Committee's thesis." And then he lamented that, as most sociological data would have to be left out of the report and would appear badly cut even in the appendix to which it was relegated, he and the Yale staff felt "as though we had worked hard in mining coal only to have most of it left at the mouth of the mine."[226] Lewis was hardly comforting when, in reply, he suggested that the effort had been worthwhile, for it showed that "a very careful study will reveal conditions similar to those revealed by less careful studies."[227]

The Committee's report was completed in December 1931 and published two months later.[228] After being "extensively discussed,"[229] it was forgotten to such an extent that a Yale Law School faculty member, hired only a year and a half after its publication and teaching in the field of torts, did not even know that Yale had had a major part in the research.[230] Meanwhile, the social scientists, who felt that the effort at Yale had "laid the foundation for . . . a detailed social study," began that study at the Institute of Human Relations.[231] Apparently it showed nothing that the earlier study had not also shown, for it was never published and thus could not even be forgotten.[232]

Why the Social Scientists Drifted Away

Years later when asked why she had stopped working with members of Yale's law faculty, Dorothy Thomas, who at first was extremely happy with her new association,[233] replied that it was because "nothing interesting" was going on.[234] That was, of course, not the only reason,[235] but within a year after the termination of the business failures project she severed all but her paper ties to the Law School by giving up the seminar in empirical legal research that she taught there. Her reasons for this decision are significant; she felt that she was getting too few students, each of whom had too little time for research, and that she was presenting ideas about the importance of careful, statistical research for an understanding of social and legal institutions that were "clearly against certain of the prevailing dominant attitudes in the law school."[236]

Emma Corstvet stayed active and interested in empirical legal research for several more years. During the year following the completion of the auto accident compensation study, she did an elegant study of the adequacy of accounting records kept by bankrupt and going concerns.[237] This was just the kind of study that Thomas thought should be the next part of the business failures project,[238] but which Douglas never got around to doing. The results were hardly conclusive, but given the difficulty of defining and measuring adequacy and the limitations of the available statistical tools, Corstvet nevertheless managed to show that more going businesses than bankrupt ones had adequate records.[239] After completing this study she became research assistant to Underhill Moore. She worked on Moore's studies for nearly three years until family responsibilities, acquired when she married Karl Llewellyn who was still teaching at Columbia, necessitated her moving to New York City.[240] Although for a while thereafter she commuted to New Haven for a few days a week, she too was through with empirical legal research.

Though she thereafter also worked briefly with Moore, Thomas ultimately turned her attention to population studies, an outgrowth of her interest in business cycles and her training in statistics; Corstvet turned hers to institutional economics, an outgrowth of her Wisconsin progressive education.[241] Of the two, Corstvet had had the better experience in working with the lawyers, largely because she did some research herself and because Moore, the lawyer she worked most closely with, was more interested in empirical research than the rest of the Yale Realists. But, neither social scientist really looked back, and the Realists' interest in empirical legal research was never to receive significant support from the social scientific community again.

As DOROTHY THOMAS and Emma Corstvet grew away from participation in empirical research at Yale, surely neither thought that she had been helped to leave her former activities by tensions generated from the interaction of the values of the emerging, social scientific community and those of the advocates of progressive law reform. Each simply found that other professional and personal interests and commitments were more satisfying and followed them. In personal terms that perception was correct, but here personal terms are misleading.

Both Thomas and Corstvet were a part of the emerging community of social scientists. In this community the relatively less rigorous Chicago School of sociology of Albion Small, Elsworth Faris, Robert E. Park, and Ernest Burgess was in decline, while the emphasis on quantification shared by Frank Giddings, William F. Ogburn, F. Stuart Chapin, and Luther L. Bernard was in an ascendancy that resonated with the similar efforts in the direction of quantification by James R. Angell and E. L. Thorndike in psychology, Harold D. Lasswell and Charles E. Merriam in political science, and Wesley Mitchell in economics.[242] Thus, both women had needs or objectives common to most of the young social scientists interested in empirical research at the time — accuracy of data collection, niceties of questionnaire design, and basic scientific predispositions. More important, though perhaps less obvious at the time, each also accepted the lengthening of the reform horizon that accompanied the growth of academic social science in America. In contrast, the lawyers in the supposedly joint research enterprise had an immediate interest in procedural and remedial reform. Ballantine's Committee acted out of a "felt need" to reform the mechanism for compensating the victims of auto accidents.[243] That Douglas acted from a similar motive can be seen in his continued attempts to refine his notions about what he was going to investigate: he felt the need, but that was about all. In particular, both the Committee and Douglas shared the same model of the world that their inquiry into the facts was directed at — court congestion, delay, procedural complexity, popular disrespect, and all that goes with the progressive notion of law reform.

Except for Clark, all of Ballantine's Committee were only interested in progressive law reform. That enterprise and empirical social science were historically offshoots of the same root,[244] but by the early 1930s, the two enterprises were simply discontinuous. The lawyers on Ballantine's Committee were not interested in, if they were even more than dimly aware of, the campaign to make social inquiry a science like the physical sciences. If the use of the best current methods — "careful selection of sample, careful rules of questionnaires, formal decisions on substitutions when parts of the sample were unavailable"[245] — brought good results, that was fine; but to be hobbled by method or the limits of available data, that was a different matter. Carefully collected data were less important than effective data. Facts were facts; for these lawyers, once enough of them were collected or the need for them had passed, study was over.[246] But for social scientists like Thomas and Corstvet, turning social inquiry into a science was a very important part of a developing professional identity that each participated in. Facts were not facts; some were meaningful and others doubtful. If the lawyers would let the exigencies of short-term campaigns for discrete reforms determine the nature and scope of social inquiry, if they would not attenuate their perception of the relationship between such inquiry and desired reforms, then there was no reason to continue the association. There were many other things to investigate, things that because of their susceptibility to methodological sophistication were truly more interesting.[247]

Douglas and Clark presented a less clear-cut problem for Thomas and Corstvet. Clark sat insecurely between social science and progressive law reform. Douglas's position was more ambiguous. His activities in the federal courts study suggest that he participated in, if not affirmed, some of the methodological aspects of professionalized social science. But the depth of his attachment to the values of that enterprise was another matter, as can be seen most vividly from his later activities in the campaign for bankruptcy reform.

Comprehensive bankruptcy reform was not to be had in the early 1930s, although eventually the provisions for wage earner amortization of debts that Douglas had urged were adopted.[248] Yet when such amortizations were approved, Douglas was opposed to them on the basis of "the facts" about bankruptcy, largely the same facts on which he had earlier supported amortization.[249] Of course, in the intervening years Douglas had learned something new; he had learned the opinion of his colleague Wesley Sturges,[250] as thoroughgoing a skeptic as the Realists ever produced,[251] that the basic problem for wage earners was "credit management" — an inability to limit intelligently the use of credit to a reasonable estimate of the amount of future income — so that amortization of consumer debts was simply a sentence to future abject poverty.[252] Douglas's "facts" could support that argument just as well as his earlier one in support of wage earner amortizations, for ultimately Douglas believed that his study had uncovered the causes of bankruptcy. Although he admitted that the determination of causation was "extremely hazardous," since cause and effect "curiously intermingle" and "appear differently to different observers," he was convinced that a "dominant characteristic" could be determined and, by implication, that from this "dominant characteristic" causal relationships could be inferred as a matter of something close to informed common sense. On the basis of these "dominant characteristics" and a comparison of the figures on the incomes of his bankrupts and some early attempts to define standard budgets for wage earners, Douglas concluded that amortization was impossible in most cases.[253]

Having interviewed Dorothy Thomas, I can easily imagine her tearing her hair out after learning of Douglas's argument. Whether his estimate of causality was right or wrong, as far as she was concerned Douglas went about his evaluation in the wrong way. Indeed, not only did he not follow the appropriate methodological rules, he reverted to the kind of armchair theorizing that methodological rules were designed to foreclose. Here the partial commitment of Douglas, a personal friend,[254] to empirical social science and its values was in some ways more disturbing to deal with than the noncommitment of lawyers like those on Ballantine's committee. For the flip-flop from one set of values to another only emphasized the ways in which careful, statistical research was not a part of the "prevailing dominant attitudes in the law school."

Finding the appropriate response to the less than total commitment of lawyers like Douglas to the norms of empirical social science was difficult for young social scientists like Thomas and Corstvet who were active missionaries for their young discipline. But, in general, their response was to gravitate toward the lawyers more committed to their science than most — Clark and Moore.[255] Yet, even here there were limits and so, in the end, other things seemed more interesting and, affirming the values of the social scientific community of which they were solely a part, Thomas and Corstvet drifted away to investigate those other things.

In a real sense the lawyers drifted away as well. In 1934 as the federal courts study was about to be published, Clark tried one more bit of empirical research, a still interesting study of the legal needs of the public and the activities of the bar in New Haven.[256] But when the data from this project finally appeared, Clark was too busy to write up the findings himself for he had started on a project that was to become the great intellectual passion of his life; he had become the Chief Reporter to the committee charged with drafting the new *Federal Rules of Civil Procedure*. Douglas, too, drifted away. As the business failures project wound down he turned his interest to the short-lived Yale-Harvard law and business joint degree program.[257] Thereafter came the chance to do a more traditional type of empirical research aimed at reform when he headed the Securities and Exchange Commission's study of the activities of bondholder protection committees in the reorganization of bankrupt corporations.[258] That work led to his being appointed a commissioner in 1936. And in 1939 both men were offered and accepted judgeships.

Whether this attempt at joint empirical legal research might have had any other conclusion is highly doubtful. Had the social scientists been regular full-time teaching faculty, perhaps their views would have carried more weight,[259] though later experience at Yale suggests to the contrary. Had the social science of the time been in a less prickly[260] phase methodologically, the task of meeting the social scientists' norms might have been easier. But even under the best of conditions the tension between progressive law reform and empirical social science was probably too great for the lawyer reformers and the social scientists to have engaged in much joint research without each first substantially compromising its own values, as an incident that Dorothy Thomas related aptly illustrates.[261] While at Yale she taught a seminar in empirical legal research. One semester, Thurman Arnold resolved to take it. He attended regularly until it came time for the students to present their research projects, at which point he objected to the student presentations on the ground that he had come to hear her, not them, and thereafter he stopped coming. Such insensitivity to the importance of student research for recruiting membership in the social scientific community may be understandable in someone as removed from that community as Arnold was, but, however understandable, such actions by the lawyers that casually undercut efforts to sustain and expand that community did not make it easier for individuals within it to continue to work with persons outside it.

Whether lawyers like Clark and Douglas, still interested in empirical legal research,[262] but caught between the values of progressive law reform and empirical social science might have been able to keep their enterprise going themselves may be less obviously "highly doubtful," but is, at least, quite problematic. To do so it would have been essential to secure funds, a task made difficult by the Depression.[263] The foundations had not seemed particularly eager to support empirical legal research, and at Yale general university funds were not to be had[264] and the Institute of Human Relations was not interested either.[265] One might have looked to the grantor of last resort, the federal government, as Clark in fact did.[266] However, as it turned out, that grantor was not particularly interested in social science research in law either.

BUT, MAYBE funding wasn't the real problem with sustaining empirical research in law. Maybe the problem was with relying on progressive law reform to fuel the research agenda. Maybe a lawyer who had broken free of that agenda could begin and sustain a commitment to empirical legal research and so serve as a model for others. One individual, Underhill Moore, did so break free and so I next return to Moore at Columbia. As a model, however, his research career suggests many cautions.

AFTER THE deanship fight at Columbia in spring 1928, Moore first turned down Cook's offer to come to Hopkins because he did not believe that either Cook or Oliphant could stick to his last and so the Trustees would close the Institute when results were not forthcoming. Then, having seen nothing more than dreams of empirical legal research in Robert Hutchins's eyes, he turned down an offer to come to Yale as well. Still, he was "quite lonely and out of it"[1] as a result of the "ructions" at Columbia and so when, in 1929, Hutchins's dream became a potential reality with the funding of the Yale Institute of Human Relations, Moore asked "the question: 'Where will my personal life probably be happier?' "[2] He answered it and left for Yale.

Studies in Banking Practice

Though Theodore Hope, the research assistant who had helped Moore develop his "institutional approach" designed to examine the extent to which judicial decisions reflect judicial acceptance and enforcement of community custom, preferred to go to Hopkins,[3] in their last years together at Columbia, the two men had isolated a subject for research and devised a questionnaire with which to pursue that research. So, in the fall of 1929 Moore confidently set his new research assistant, Gilbert Sussman, to work pretesting the questionnaire[4] and calmly left on a sea voyage to Europe on board the yacht of an insurance broker friend.[5] Moore's confidence was both short-lived and unwarranted, for when he returned, midway into his first semester at Yale,[6] problems with the questionnaire had already surfaced, problems intimately related to the research method, the subject for research, and, not incidentally, Moore's lack of experience in questionnaire design.

In Moore's "institutional approach" the otherwise despised law reports were peculiarly useful because they were full of countless "natural experiments," instances where the decisions on a given point of law "go both ways." In these instances one could attempt to discover the institutional, customary, ways of behaving and then match this behavior to the rule of law adopted in the jurisdiction.[7] Moore chose to research one of these instances: the liability of a bank for wrongful dishonor of a customer's check where the bank's defense was its decision to charge the customer's account, without notice to the customer, with the amount of that customer's overdue personal time note, which had been previously discounted for the customer by the bank and its proceeds credited to the account in question — in banking jargon of the time, the practice of debiting (without notice) direct discounts. On this quite abstruse and now largely unintelligible question of banking law[8] Moore isolated three decisions, a 1904 South Carolina case holding for the customer and 1920 New York and 1928 Pennsylvania cases holding for the bank, and set out to investigate banking practice in these three states during the relevant period of time.[9]

To begin this investigation Moore gave Sussman the task of pretesting Moore's questionnaire by administering it to all of the banks in the state of Connecticut.[10] Soon after Sussman began this task it became apparent that although Moore had done a very careful legal analysis of his fact situation, his questionnaire omitted any mention of the frequency of one of the suspected variables, the existence of security.[11] The omission was one of the problems that faced Moore when he returned from Europe. It was easily corrected and so Sussman returned to the field with a new questionnaire, one that both showed a growing awareness that behavior was a matter of more or less, and not yes or no,[12] and collected data on matters that were irrelevant to the study, but of general interest to Moore.[13] A more difficult problem that emerged was the recognition that, even as revised, the questionnaire would uncover not the behavior patterns in question, but only bankers' opinions about those behavior patterns. In one sense that problem, too, could be solved, at least in Connecticut, and Moore set about solving it. He sent Sussman to observe the activities of the bank employees who carried out the transactions Moore was interested in.[14] This study, which by its small sample showed a growing awareness of the limited purposes of pretesting methods,[15] generally supported the findings of the questionnaire study.[16] But sending Sussman into the field in Connecticut for the third time only accentuated another, much less tractable problem: money.

Moore had negotiated with Hutchins for the payment of salaries of two research assistants, one for doing empirical research and the other for more mundane tasks, including Moore's personal bookkeeping.[17] Some money for expenses other than the salary of these two assistants was included in what was plainly seen by Moore, at least, as a package deal,[18] but he had not really understood how expensive the planned fieldwork was going to be. The cost of fieldwork was brought directly home when, even before Sussman had finished with the third round of pretesting in Connecticut, Moore sent him off to Pennsylvania to study the practices of banks there before any more time could elapse between the 1928 Pennsylvania decision and the investigation.[19] In so doing Moore substantially depleted his available funds and thus jeopardized speedy completion of the research. So, while Sussman finished his work in Connecticut, Moore worked to get Hutchins's successor, Charles E. Clark, to supply more money in order to send Sussman to South Carolina. Moore's plea, made in the name of the "morale of everyone in the Bank Credit study,"[20] fell on deaf ears. To Clark, a budget was a budget, especially when he was "doubtful about the feasibility of tracing the life history of a case so far away as South Carolina and so long ago as 1900."[21] Moore turned to Yale's President James R. Angell, an acquaintance from back at the University of Chicago, for help in softening up Clark.[22] Although Angell agreed to help,[23] Clark did not seem to relent.

Part of the reason why the morale of everyone in the Bank Credit study needed lifting was that the results in Pennsylvania had hardly been a cause for great joy; they were, at the least, somewhat ambiguous. For this study Moore had sent Sussman to conduct interviews at a selection of the banks in the state, a selection made so as to overrepresent the banks in the Philadelphia area where the case had arisen.[24] From his experience in Connecticut Moore had substantially improved his questionnaire. It was narrower in scope and more naturalistic than the obviously legalistic Connecticut questionnaire.[25] But a better instrument had not brought better results. If anything, the reverse was true; the better instrument had brought more ambiguous results.[26]

Moore discovered that most discounted time notes were paid by the borrower's drawing a check, generally on his account at the bank holding his note, and tendering this check in payment of the note. This practice was all but universal outside of Philadelphia. A significantly smaller proportion of matured time notes were paid by the borrower explicitly instructing the bank that held the note to pay it by directly charging the borrower's account at that bank. No one could have been surprised by these results, which were essentially similar to the results in Connecticut.[27] But on the key question of whether a bank ever liquidated a matured time note without either a check of, or instructions from, the borrower, the results were inconsistent. They showed that in Philadelphia such action was at least as common as that of liquidating a note on the borrower's instructions, but that outside that city such unilateral action by a bank was virtually unheard of. Working with a decision from a court of statewide jurisdiction and getting this queer discontinuity in data, Moore concluded that only liquidation by check was a recurrent — in his jargon, institutional — transaction in Pennsylvania.[28]

Moore's conclusion seemingly suggested that in this circumstance at least, the law was not following custom, for the Pennsylvania decision had upheld the Philadelphia bank's defense. But Moore did not take time to puzzle over this implication; rather, despite the shortage of funds, he sent Sussman to South Carolina. For the investigation there, Moore chose a sample of ninety-three banks located throughout the state that had survived the twenty-five years since the decision[29] and secured appropriate letters of introduction, including some from the skeptical Clark.[30] At first Moore helped with the research. It soon became apparent that many of the banks chosen either lacked records back the twenty-five years or were unwilling to let Sussman look at the records they did have.[31] Thus, even working together the two men only managed to secure records at about half of their sample and even those records only generally spanned the first decade of the century. However, these limited records, bolstered by largely unstructured interviews with officers at the banks investigated and correspondence with other bankers in South Carolina, disclosed a uniform pattern. Matured time notes were never involuntarily liquidated by the bank holding the note. They were either paid in cash or by check and, on very rare occasions, on instructions. The reason was simple; most commercial credit was agricultural and intended to be liquidated out of the sale of harvested crops.[32] Harvest time was unpredictable and therefore maturities stated on notes were largely a matter of informed guessing.

These results were intriguing, but then the money ran out, the research stopped, and Moore and Sussman began the task of writing up the results of the year's effort. In so doing they had to deal with the criticisms of their enterprise offered by Dorothy Swaine Thomas.[33] She found the project "very obscure" in both writing and method, and urged Moore to give up the research because the method was too complicated and the data too problematical to yield good results.[34] He was quite obviously looking for help and eager to learn, but nevertheless kept on with the project, learning what he could from her, but also desiring to see what he could learn about what interested him.[35] Then, in the middle of writing, more money came in the form of $2,000 allocation from the budget of the Institute of Human Relations.[36]

Quickly, Moore sent Sussman and five assistants into the field in New York. This time Moore used two investigative techniques: first, a variant of the third Connecticut pretest study, in which the teller responsible for the transactions in question filled out work sheets and then the research assistant examined the results for "ambiguities and incompleteness," and, second, a questionnaire administered in small banks to the bank officer or teller in charge of the discounting of notes and, in larger banks, to the person in charge of loans or discounting. By using these two techniques Moore apparently hoped to avoid the problems of finding, getting access to, and using old records that had been encountered in South Carolina. He reasoned that a correspondence between the two measures of current practice would strengthen interview results about former practice. Other attempts were made to improve the reliability of his results. In both parts of the inquiry Moore tried to work with a scientifically chosen sample, although limited cooperation by interviewees made such attempts largely nugatory. And his questionnaire explicitly took into account the possibility that banking practice had changed in the ten years since the decision in question; it also showed a great deal of care in structuring the inquiry to get plain yes or no answers.[37]

The results of the New York study came in after publication of the initial parts of the whole study had already been begun.[38] In the more urban counties the dominant form for the liquidation of matured time notes was by means of a debit charge without instructions or a check from the borrower. In rural counties almost all notes were liquidated by check; some, on customer instructions; few, by bank debit in the absence of either. But, taken as a whole, the one most common transaction was that of the bank's debiting a customer's account on its own initiative. Thus, it might be argued that while there was some variation between studies, where bank debits were a known, if not always frequent, practice (Pennsylvania and New York), the court decision validated them; where such action was virtually unknown (South Carolina), the court decision failed to approve the practice.

With the completion of the New York work, Moore rushed to get his results in print, and in the process passed up a chance to get embroiled in the Realist Controversy, Llewellyn's feud with Pound over the existence and content of Realist jurisprudence.[39] In the resultant nearly 150 pages stretching over six successive issues of the *Yale Law Journal*, the convoluted, opaque prose dictated by the convoluted, opaque method developed two years earlier in "An Institutional Approach" thoroughly obscured the quite interesting results. Moore's cautious conclusion did little to remedy this obvious defect. He hazarded that his research had presented only "rough outlines" of the institutional patterns and his method for choosing a standard against which to compare those patterns and for measuring the degree of deviation of the pattern from that standard had fallen "far short of attainable precision." Yet he concluded that where the action of the bank deviated "slightly" from the institutional pattern of behavior, the court validated that behavior; where it deviated "grossly," the court refused to validate that behavior.[40] As that conclusion was precisely what he had set out to prove, a certain amount of joy was in order.

Moore had the six articles bound together and distributed the set to friends and acquaintances at Yale, Columbia, and elsewhere. Among the recipients were President Angell and Clark Hull, a psychologist associated with the Institute.[41] Moore surely knew the limits of the study[42] — most obviously the lack of any explanation of how the institutional patterns were brought to judicial attention, the lack of simultaneity of the events studied, and the singularity of the demonstration. What his audience thought about it, or whether their understanding was so thoroughly impeded by the structure and jargon of the research as to preclude thought, is quite impossible to say. Beyond pleasantries, no one commented on the research, at least by letter or in print, except perhaps for Llewellyn, who, begging off "mature critique" until a second reading, ignored the research and griped about how "unintelligible" the last third of the earlier "Institutional Approach" article has been.[43]

Encouragement, however, was not what Moore needed to keep his enterprise going. The results of this one study were a sufficient impetus for further work, if only money could be found to support that work. Thus, even before the debiting study was fully published, Moore knew exactly what further work he wished to do. He proposed to send "six men or women of Ph.D. or law journal caliber" into the field to investigate the institutional patterns underlining twenty-five "recent decisions in the field of Commercial Bank Credit in order to determine the causal relation, if any," between the pattern of banking behavior and the decision. The estimated cost of such an endeavor, excluding his and Sussman's salaries, would be a little over $11,000.[44]

The idea was a sensible one;[45] it was surely better to build on a small bit of successful research than to run off after something else. Whether it was equally sensible to continue to use Moore's framework for research was another matter. Dorothy Thomas thought not and told Moore so;[46] he thought otherwise, though of course he thought his method "perfectly clear."[47] However, money for further research was not to be had either directly from President Angell[48] or indirectly through the Institute.[49] Stymied, Moore decided to raise a small portion of the necessary funds by agreeing to do a new edition of his casebook[50] and to amuse himself with an informal study of the reasons for the failure of a local bank.[51] Then, with both of these tasks begun and in need of completion, the Institute decided in the fall of 1931 to support Moore's work with an allocation of $5,000, almost half of what he had said he needed.[52]

While Moore cleaned up the projects begun before Institute funds became available, he worked on two short articles. One, a study of the consequence of a bank's insolvency on its relationship with its commercial customers, a bit of pure doctrinal research, was an outgrowth of his work on the local bank failure.[53] The other, called "The Lawyer's Law," was an attempt to provide an intellectual framework, different than that provided in the Wigmore review, for the kind of study Moore had proposed before leaving Columbia and had carried out at Yale in the discounted notes study, as well as to intervene in the jurisprudential disputes that he had passed up earlier.[54] Of course, Moore had implicitly commented on these disputes earlier when in the "Institutional Approach" he had emphasized the role of institutional practices or custom in judicial decision making and selected for research a point of law in which the cases "go both ways." But this time, following the central thrust of the argument in the "Institutional Approach," Moore was more explicit. He began by emphasizing what he took to be the lawyer's central task: predicting judicial behavior. From this premise Moore argued that when a lawyer predicts judicial behavior, no matter what he says, he takes into account not just rules of law derived from judicial decisions, but also "every factor in the situation which he can differentiate from its context," and then makes an "intuitional judgment" on the basis of the whole.[55] Then, drawing, not always correctly,[56] on probability theory, Moore illustrated how the lawyer's predictions might be formally represented as the probability of the "future occurrence . . . [of a particular event] based upon the frequency of its past concurrence with other particular events." Finally he lamented that,

> [T]he lawyer's failure to see his problem as one of attempting to systematize and to make methodical the processes implicit in his intuitional judgments and his clinging to the traditional notion that his problem is

one of systematizing statutes and decisions have completely blinded those with scientific curiosity to take the direction which the inquiries into judicial behavior should take.[57]

Response to this justification of Moore's efforts was sparse. Herman Oliphant, then still at work at his studies for the Hopkins Institute, suggested that he and Moore were "pillars of conservatisms" with radicals like "Michael and Adler to the right and Frank to the left."[58] Robert C. Angell, a sociologist who had worked on family law at Columbia as part of the aftermath of the curriculum study, expressed more than a little skepticism at the willingness of lawyers to do the kind of work Moore advocated.[59] But with this piece out of the way,[60] Moore took to his research with some relish.

To begin, Moore sent a third-year student, C. E. Brandt, into the field to start the first of the projected twenty-five additional tests under the Moore and Hope method.[61] Moore chose to investigate a six-month-old Pennsylvania case holding that a bank was not liable to recredit a customer's account with the amount of a check certified, and thus paid, by a teller at the main office within a minute of receiving notice to stop payment based on an order placed moments earlier at the branch where the drawer normally transacted business.[62] The method of investigation was similar to that used in the New York debiting study.[63] All the Pennsylvania banks with branches were isolated and Brandt attempted to secure cooperation of each such bank to permit the officer in charge to complete a record of all the stop-payment transactions during an entire week. Better than three-quarters of the relevant banks cooperated in the study and over half participated for a second week as a kind of control group. The work sheet was designed to isolate the time it took to relay stop-payment orders between main and branch offices as well as to determine whether there was any difference in practice based on the depositor's mode of giving notice or the reason for the order. Although interviews were held with bank officers, the information gathered in the interviews was not used in the investigation except to clarify the data through an understanding of the internal organization of each bank.[64]

While Brandt worked in Pennsylvania, Moore set Emma Corstvet to work on a second inquiry.[65] Moore had isolated two recent cases on the narrow question of whether the depositor of a check, the proceeds of which were collected after the sequestration of the assets of, and appointment of a receiver for, the depository bank, was a general or preferred creditor of the bank.[66] This vexing, but quite topical, question turned on whether the check had been "deposited" or only "received for collection," a matter that under traditional doctrine was to be deduced from the terms, usually implicit, of the bargain between the bank and the customer. One of the important indicia of the terms of the bargain was the time at which checks drawn against the deposit would be honored. If the so-called "uncollected funds" were immediately available, then the check had been deposited and the customer was a general creditor; if available only at some later time, the check had been received for collection and the customer was a preferred creditor. Here then was a circumstance, as in the debiting study, tailor-made for testing Moore's institutional hypothesis, and this time without either the difficulties caused by using historical records to verify old practice or the theoretical problems raised by the lack of simultaneity of the events being investigated.

Unfortunately, in place of the theoretical and historical problems in the debiting study, Moore acquired two quite immense practical problems. One was the sheer volume and complexity of the records that would have to be examined in order to investigate whether and how often uncollected funds were drawn against. The other was the unwillingness of banks to let anyone examine the accounts of individual depositors, an examination necessary in order to make the investigation.[67] In order to avoid, at least temporarily, the second of these problems, Moore arranged for Corstvet to begin an "exploratory study" in the records of the failed bank in New Haven that he had previously studied.[68] Corstvet took a group of deposit slips for a nine-day period a few months before the failure and laboriously recreated the account of each of the nearly three hundred depositors, in the process checking potential variables such as age, occupation, age of account, average balance, and outstanding borrowings.[69]

The following year was spent tabulating and analyzing the data collected in the two studies.[70] The stop-payment study turned out to be the easier to complete. Although there were serious problems with the accuracy of some of the data collected by tellers filling out the work sheets, the accurate data showed that the modal, median, and mean time for a portion of the behavior investigated — the time from receipt of notice of the stop-payment order in the main bank to its communication to the tellers in that office — was at least as long as, and generally longer than, the time found in the case in question for completion of the entire process beginning with the giving of notice at the branch bank. Reasoning that the time for the entire process must necessarily be greater than that for any known part, Moore concluded, quite turgidly, that, as the teller at the bank in question certified the check only moments before learning of the stop-payment order, which was communicated, at the very least, as fast as and more likely faster than usual, the court, in upholding the bank's defense to the suit to recredit the customer's account, was acting in accordance with usual banking behavior.[71] Thus, the study again validated Moore's hypothesis.

Tabulation and analysis of Corstvet's exploratory study on the uncollected funds cases were in fact completed long before the stop-payment study was published.[72] Preparation for fieldwork in New York, the site of one of the decisions, was then started[73] and, with the help of President Angell, introductions to bankers in Ohio, the site of the other, were secured.[74] Then, suddenly, "theoretical difficulties" that Moore "could not dispose of" were discovered.[75] So, rather than spend "time and money when it was not clear precisely how the results could be interpreted," Moore stopped further research.[76] With this sudden jolt, after four years, the banking studies were over.

IT IS DIFFICULT to understand what theoretical problems, peculiar to the uncollected funds study, were so devastating as to have been grounds for terminating that research. Practical problems existed, even monumental ones, given the technology of the time. Two years later, just to publish the exploratory study, Moore and Corstvet had to make crucial, simplifying assumptions about both customers' bank balances and the time necessary for checks to go through the collection process and for funds to return;[77] replacing these assumptions with anything but more accurate opinions would have required months, if not years, of work. But these were not theoretical problems; they were the kind of practical problems Moore had met and overcome several times before. Thus, his own explanation for the termination of the uncollected funds study, and thereafter all of the commercial banking research, is at least a bit disingenuous.[78] If in the end Moore faced theoretical problems they were theoretical problems common to all the banking research and not peculiar to the uncollected funds study. What those theoretical problems were can be seen by looking again at the course of Moore's research in his early years at Yale.

In four years Moore learned a great deal about social science research. Indeed, the progress of his education can be seen in the progressive refinement of the technical detail of his banking studies. In Connecticut Moore started with a lawyerly questionnaire and a census methodology. Less than six months later in Pennsylvania his questionnaire had lost its lawyerliness and he was content to work with an informally defined sample. At the same time, as shown by the third Connecticut pretest, Moore had begun to doubt the reliability of questionnaire findings and thus began to study by direct observation. With the extension of work to South Carolina and New York, he began to worry about the problems created by nonsimultaneous events.[79] Then, in the written reports of those studies, concerns surfaced about the representativeness of sample, the consistency and accuracy of questionnaire answers and data interpretation generally.[80] With the stop-payment study, further problems with the accuracy of observation appeared as third-party recording of data turned out to be suspect. Moreover, interviews began to diminish in importance as an awareness of statistical technique began to surface.[81] Finally, in the uncollected funds study, first-party recording became very difficult and the results problematic to interpret.

The pattern to these progressive refinements in technique is really very simple — methodological objection, methodological improvement, methodological objection, methodological improvement, again and again. Moore was going through a short, informal course in contemporary social science method first at the hands of Dorothy Thomas and then under the direction of both Thomas and Emma Corstvet. The one was at the time working hard on studies of methods and accuracy of observation; the other had just finished work on the auto accident compensation study.[82] Both were quite obviously taken with the idea of teaching this particular old dog some new tricks.[83]

The process of learning about method by responding to the objections of Thomas and Corstvet was nevertheless a trifle exasperating as can be seen from a passage in "The Lawyer's Law." There, after Moore had completed setting out his framework, he noted the important role that other social science disciplines could play in improving on lawyers' intuitions, but was careful to insist that cooperative research must be focused not on an "amorphous and unorganized experience," but rather "of necessity" on "a problem set by one . . . [of the investigators] and the cooperation of the others must be aimed at the verification of his hypotheses."[84] Yet, exasperated or not, Moore continued to learn from his long drawn out lessons, acquired not just from the criticism of his own work, but also through his participation in Thomas's methodological seminar at the Law School[85] and his reading of books on method from the lists she recurrently prepared for him,[86] as well as through hours of discussion with Corstvet as she played out her role as Dostoyevski's washerwoman.[87]

As Moore learned the canons of social science method from Thomas and Corstvet, he also acquired something more intangible from them: the culture of contemporary social science. As noted earlier, both women were at the time a part of the leading edge of the movement to make social science "scientific" by making it numerical and quantifiable, or, in the accepted jargon of the day, behaviorist, not in the sense of Watsonian, but in the sense of proceeding from the structured observation of overt (separately identifiable and countable) behavior of individuals, rather than from the introspection of the investigator about the phenomenon in question based on its impressions, memories, or guesses.[88] As such they were taking part in what was simultaneously a methodological revolution and the establishment of a distinctive academic identity.

Moore was quickly drawn into and absorbed this culture. How quickly and how thoroughly can be seen from his study of the failure of the local bank. When it was completed in early 1932, Moore gave a copy to the Yale economist who had recently become director of social science activities at the Institute, with the observation that the work was not for the Institute since it was ad hoc and of no scientific value.[89] After reading it, the economist, less bothered by method than most of his social science colleagues, gently chided Moore that he was "far too modest in the characterization" of his work.[90] But for Moore the characterization was precisely correct and this fact suggests why he was ultimately faced with an insurmountable theoretical problem in the banking research.[91]

From the beginning Moore was interested in pursuing an essentially anthropological insight; law follows culture, not doctrine. He may have phrased his point as a hypothesis, but it was a conclusion. When push finally came to shove and it became time to show that one could do real scientific work in law, Moore produced a method to test his hypothesis that bore all the hallmarks of crank social theory[92] — formal overelaboration, arcane terminology, pseudomathematical precision — except one, imperviousness to criticism. Although the formal apparatus stayed the same, execution of the research changed with each criticism.

Moore started with something close to a crude anthropology: ask the natives what they do. And for a scientific demonstration, he relied on what would today be known as a natural experiment: the natives on one side of the river carry water on shoulder poles, those on the other side, on their heads; what accounts for this difference?[93] Through their criticisms Thomas and Corstvet reinforced the natural experiment form and tightened the observational method. Cases had to be decided simultaneously and investigation made as soon after the fact as possible. Direct observation was to be preferred and, if impossible, elaborate verification was essential. But ultimately even all of these methodological refinements were not enough, for still there could be troublesome problems of data interpretation, as, for example, was the case in the uncollected funds study. There, unlike the Connecticut pretests in the debiting study, no clear pattern emerged, so one could only wonder whether a finding that uncollected funds were drawn on in 6 to 25 percent of all transactions, depending on the time in the check collection process chosen as a yardstick, was high, low, or average.[94] With comparable data from other banks and other jurisdictions, even these practical problems could be solved, as Moore eventually all but admitted.[95] But, that work having been done, there would still remain the basic theoretical question underlying all the banking research: how similar were the two cultures? How similar was banking practice in New York and Ohio or New York, Pennsylvania, and South Carolina? Were the natives separated only by a river or by a gulf of one kind or another?

Given Moore's hypothesis and his subject matter, there was simply no way to answer that basic question by holding everything but banking practice constant, no way to be even vaguely assured that all of the other potential variables washed out. Even worse, Moore knew that the other variables did not wash out.[96] Therefore, lacking any but the crudest techniques for correlating multiple, simultaneously varying factors, Moore was quite squarely faced with the choice of either abandoning his four-year-long commitment to quantification — to science as he had just learned it — or abandoning his topic of research and instead finding one where it was easier to believe that most variables were controlled or controllable because there was only one culture being looked at.

Faced with this dilemma he chose to stick with social science, and with the kind of understanding of law he had been working to develop for over ten years, by affirming its methodological preconceptions and abandoning his chosen topic for research. In so doing, in choosing to do something that was, in theory at least, readily understandable to all academic social scientists who might care to know, he was not securing a complete answer to his theoretical problem. As he well knew, and as Emma Corstvet put it, paraphrasing him, "one cannot deny the possible existence of many intangibles, some of them important enough to threaten the overthrow of anything induced by a more strictly behaviorist approach; but . . . hope lies only in dealing with elements we can measure, running that risk [and struggling to measure]."[97] But he was cabining or limiting that problem. Thus, like Thomas, Corstvet, and dozens of other social scientists, Moore would struggle to measure, to adopt a "strictly behaviorist approach." He would therefore orient his research around that struggle. And so, he had in a real sense, become, if only in his head, a twentieth-century social scientist.[98] But in thus choosing to join with the social scientists, Moore ignored the question of what they would make of him. In time he would find out.

Studies in Traffic and Parking

When in 1933 Moore let "theoretical difficulties" call a halt in his banking research, he had already generally isolated a new topic to research. As part of a move to coordinate the Institute's program of research better by focusing its program on an in-depth study of the city of New Haven,[99] Moore volunteered to undertake a study of "the degree of correspondence between the behavior of the community . . . and the models of behavior set forth in statutes, ordinances, etc."[100] To carry this proposal forward he and Corstvet began several months of study of the recent statutes of Connecticut and the recent ordinances of the city.[101] Their plan, developed as they worked, was to do field observations both before and after implementation of a statute or ordinance. From the accumulation of "probably feasible investigations" Moore came to focus on changes in New Haven's traffic and parking ordinances because of the "relative simplicity" of the subject and because the Chief of Police, in his role as the New Haven Traffic Authority, was willing to cooperate.[102] And so in December 1933 Moore sent his fieldworkers, armed with Corstvet's meticulous directions,[103] out to watch drivers on the streets of New Haven.

The first study Moore set out to do was again a natural experiment. On two blocks in the heart of downtown an ordinance limited parking to a period of thirty minutes during the day, but not after seven o'clock. So for six days, just before Christmas, observers, placed on the street, timed the duration of parking for all people who parked in these two blocks during certain half-hour periods both before and after seven o'clock. In order to be sure that the two time periods were comparable, observers also monitored the flow of traffic and shadowed parkers to learn their ultimate destination. The second study, begun one month later, was a different kind of "natural" experiment, obviously planned with the connivance of the Chief of Police. This time Moore's fieldworkers spent five three-day, eight-hour periods of observation at a complex intersection about two blocks from the Institute.[104] Positioned on three of the five corners, the observers charted the paths taken by cars traveling through the intersection. The first time the intersection was unmarked; the second time a traffic circle was painted on the pavement, but in fact no ordinance establishing the circle had been enacted. Two months later the observers went out again. This third observation came after an appropriate ordinance had been adopted and while the circle was still painted on the street. For the fourth observation, stanchions were added to further emphasize the perimeter of the circle; for the fifth observation both the stanchions and the painted circle were removed, though the ordinance was not repealed.

On each of these studies Moore and Corstvet took their turns like everyone else and Mrs. Moore saw that no one froze by providing coffee and donuts.[105] Collecting the data was not the hardest part of either study by any means; interpreting it was much harder. The parking study showed that just over two-thirds of the parkers obeyed the time limit when applicable, while only half of the cars were parked for similarly short periods of time after the restriction was lifted. But even if one knew what significance to attribute to that fact, the number of observations was small and even after the effort to shadow parkers and count passing cars the best one could say was that there was "no clear indication" that the time periods "were not comparable." The traffic circle studies were even more problematical. In general, painting the traffic circle on the street, with or without an ordinance, caused people to deflect their normal path through the intersection so as to avoid the area where the circle was; removing the circle, even though the ordinance was still in effect, allowed traffic to return to its former pattern.[106] Adding stanchions to the painted circle accentuated its effect. But examining the data in detail indicated that three of the four traffic patterns studies did not entirely accomplish their goals[107] and the fourth had comparably few observations.

The effort to make sense out of these data brought two results. First, frustration set in, as evidenced by a plain hiatus in the studies and a decision to work into publishable shape the preliminary study done on the uncollected funds problem.[108] Second, in the process of preparing an annual report for submission to the Institute,[109] Moore acquired a slightly clearer understanding of exactly what he was interested in investigating when he talked about studying "social control."[110] Moore's report began by differentiating his work from traditional legal research. He emphasized the continuity of his new work with the banking studies. The earlier studies attempted to isolate "those factors in community life in significant causal relation or significantly associated with the behavior of the official government in laying down propositions of law and administering them."[111] The parking and traffic studies were directed at isolating precisely the reverse relationship: "that the established patterns of overt behavior which are unlike the model set forth in . . . [a] proposition of law . . . effect the degree of correspondence between subsequent behavior and the model in the proposition."[112] In other words, taken together, banking and parking would prove that law generally follows custom and, when not, custom modifies law. Moore also hoped to isolate "types of legal regulation" for which there would be a constant ratio between the frequency of behavior conforming to the legal rule before and after its adoption.[113]

Work on the uncollected funds articles occupied most of the following year,[114] but with the start of classes in the fall of 1935 parking studies were begun again in earnest. Initially, two more studies were completed. One took place on a block of mixed residential and commercial property located a short distance from the center of town. Parking was prohibited on one side only, with the prohibition changing sides each month. The second observation took place on a block considered comparable to the first, though it was closer to the center of town. Parking on the second block was permanently prohibited on one side and on the other side limited to thirty minutes.[115] In spring still another study was added, this time in the heart of downtown where, similar to the first study, parking was limited before seven o'clock in the evening to fifteen minutes and thereafter was unlimited.[116] Thus, by the time this fourth study was completed, Moore had collected two pairs of studies, each a variation on the natural experiment form, one pair with which one might contrast parking limited to fifteen minutes or thirty minutes against unlimited parking, the other with which one might contrast parking limited to thirty minutes or unlimited against parking totally prohibited. A pattern to his work was plainly emerging.

While Moore worked on gathering data, Emma Corstvet worked on analyzing the results.[117] Curiously she ignored the obvious pairing of the studies and instead treated each study separately. She began by attempting to determine parking duration by whether the subunits — side of street, block, day — could be combined. Once she had determined that such aggregation was appropriate, she turned her attention to determining whether the differences between the regulated and unregulated distributions were significant, using six different methods, some standard, some rather novel.[118] When she finished this task, Corstvet was convinced that the last study would have to be discarded as unusable because it had sampling problems.[119] The rest she found quite fine, if a bit small in scale. Having thus destroyed Moore's careful pairings, she proceeded to make several suggestions for further work. One was for reducing the existing data, which had been turned into graphic form, into mathematical form. Another was for doing further studies with larger samples so as to reduce the possibility of sampling error.[120] And then, her summary of the work to date complete, in fall 1936 Emma Corstvet quite reluctantly stopped working for Moore.[121]

The task of finding a replacement for Corstvet was difficult;[122] ultimately Moore had to accept Charles Callahan, a J.S.D. candidate with an interest in procedure,[123] instead of the professional social scientist he wanted.[124] But finding an assistant was the least difficult problem Moore faced while Corstvet worked at recapping the work to date. The others could conveniently be gathered under the heading "money" — Yale was notably short of it.

First, Moore fought and lost a battle with the Yale Corporation over whether they would give him a full-pay sabbatical semester, as had been the custom when he came to Yale, or one at half pay, as Yale had begun doing to save money.[125] Next he tangled, partly successfully, with the Yale Corporation and Clark over who would pay the salary of his research assistant at the Law School.[126] Finally he fought with the Institute's Executive Director who, in another reorganization of that organization's work, had decided to liquidate existing research projects whenever possible in order to create a "liquid research fund" to be used to support such projects as appeared to be most promising for the development of "a unified science of behavior and human relations,"[127] and so proposed to stop paying the salary of Moore's research assistant at the Institute and to stop funding Moore's research as well.[128] Ultimately the Institute agreed to pay part of the research assistant's salary[129] and contributed a pittance toward the research, but, as a result of these incidents, Moore, who concluded that "no one around here seems to be interested in . . . [empirical] research,"[130] was left deeply depressed.[131] He unsuccessfully sought funds for the research from numerous sources.[132] Yet, somehow he managed to begin in earnest the plan of further research that Corstvet had laid out for him. Moore would support his research with his own funds.

Taking Corstvet's advice Moore reran two of the studies: the one where parking restrictions were lifted each evening at seven o'clock, which she had suggested would have to be discarded, and another one where the no-parking zone changed sides each month, which she thought required a larger sample to be useful. Both reruns were a success,[133] but neither was in any sense a perfect experiment. It is by no means obvious that parkers during working hours are likely to be doing the same things, even if they are going to the same places, as parkers in the early evening,[134] nor that parking is such random behavior that, on a two-way street, the side on which parking is prohibited makes no difference. So in two more studies Moore tried to improve on his earlier research design.

In each of these new studies Moore took advantage of advance knowledge when parking restrictions were going to be first imposed.[135] In one of these areas, a warehouse district near the train station, his observers worked for three weeks before, and then again after, parking was limited to thirty minutes. In the other area, a spot on the edge of the campus away from town, observers similarly spent four weeks before and after the imposition of a sixty-minute limitation.[136] Unfortunately, what Moore gained in simplicity of design he lost to the possibility that parking behavior changed with the seasons as late fall went into midwinter.

Even with these studies Moore had by no means covered all of the possibilities. He had made no attempt to account for the effects of police enforcement of parking limitations. To remedy that omission, in the spring and summer 1937 he arranged to have a police officer assigned to his control who was set to work placing regular city parking tickets on cars at precisely determined times after the elapse of the period for permissible parking.[137] In this study, carried out at the site of the earlier study in the warehouse district, observers watched from inside buildings before regular tagging was instituted, while it was going on, and after it was discontinued.[138] By thus tagging cars in a place where law enforcement was apparently expected to be lax, Moore caused some problems with at least one local businessman who had to be threatened with jailing in order to convince him that the policeman and tags were real.[139] But the results were probably worth the effort and the businessman's aggravation, because they showed a small, though noticeable, shift in the direction of fewer parkings lasting thirty minutes or more.[140]

Taken together all the studies revealed several facts: where parking behavior did not already conform with a regulation, imposition of that regulation made some difference in the behavior of parkers; that this effect was consistent and more extreme the more extreme the limitation imposed; that the limitation did not seem to affect the ultimate destination of those individuals parking in the place, although it was obviously not clear whether the same individuals were parking for shorter durations or only parking elsewhere; and that systematic enforcement seemed to make the ordinances at least marginally more effective. A little further thought would have suggested that the most marginal effect found, the one in the study that Corstvet had decided was unusable and Moore had then rerun, might have been explained by the location of the study — across from the post office, a classic location for stops of less than the fifteen-minute limitation.[141] One might have called the effort a success and quickly written up the results. Moore, however, did no such thing.

By this time Moore had spent over $3,000 of his own money to finance his research and needed a loan to cover the expenditure.[142] So, having completed

Corstvet's plan of further research, for a year he turned his attention to analysis of the data collected. While in 1934 Moore thought only in terms of determining the "significant association" of various factors and ratios of difference in frequency distributions,[143] by 1936 he was determined to express his results as "simple mathematical functions" by which one might predict "behavior *after* the statute as a function of (i) . . . behavior *before* the statute, and (ii) the statute itself."[144] To this end he had shifted from two pairs of related studies to a collection of studies encompassing four different regulations: no parking, and fifteen-, thirty-, and sixty-minute parking. Even before he finished, he had isolated a mathematical relationship that he thought might hold for all the studies. It suggested that a parking regulation diminished the frequency of parking for durations longer than the limitation only for durations that exceeded the sum of (a) 37 percent of the difference between the longest duration observed when the area was unregulated and limitation and (b) the limitation.[145] Apparently, upon further analysis the relationship did not hold; at least it was never heard of again. But Moore and his assistants worked hard to develop other such relationships, deforming curves, aggregating data this way and that, and generally trying to learn exactly, quantitatively, what was the relationship between the phenomena they had observed and the parking regulations in question.[146]

An invitation to present a paper at the American Sociological Society meetings in the spring of 1938 gave Moore a chance to present his research findings,[147] but the paper was by no means satisfactory. At this point, Moore clearly wished to expand his research to other fields in an effort to increase the data base from which generalizations could be drawn, but, as still another reorganization at the Institute had completely eliminated the already limited support it was providing for his research — part of Callahan's salary — that was not possible. The Law School was able to pick up that salary but its assistance came with regular teaching responsibilities.[148] So, all that was left was the "painstaking, though undramatic, work" of reanalysis of Moore's data, a task that proceeded ever so slowly.[149]

While this reanalysis proceeded, Moore received an invitation to contribute a short piece to a projected volume on "American Legal Philosophies" being organized by Albert Kocourek, the junior editor on Wigmore's *Rational Basis of Legal Institutions*. Authors were asked to present their views on "the ultimate ideas of the origin, nature or ends of law"[150] from starting points as various as "ontology, epistemology, psychology, logic, value . . . [or] social fact."[151] Moore accepted "gladly, but with many misgivings."[152] Unlike most of the other participants in the project, Moore took Kocourek's suggestion seriously and used the occasion to "make a logical construct of the theory which underlies . . . [my] empirical work and indicates the relation of that kind of legal research to work in psychology and the so-called social sciences." The effort took all of the summer and fall of 1940 and on into winter 1941. Moore found the work "difficult far beyond expectation,"[153] but when he and Callahan had finished they had a piece that Moore was obviously proud of. Significantly, it was absolutely unlike anything else in the resulting "coffee-table" volume.

Moore began his essay with a flat, if a bit confused, espousal of the operationalist/logical positivist[154] requirement that all scientific, by which he meant causal, theories use operational or observable definitions. He therefore dismissed all "philosophies of law with which . . . [he was] acquainted" for not being "useful guides in attempting to formulate operational hypotheses as to the relations between law and other behavior." In place of the "sterility" of existing philosophies of law for generating such operational hypotheses, Moore proposed to set forth a theory of law "based on an analysis of the process of learning, through pain or reward, a response to a sign in a stimulus-response situation." His goal was to acquire "precise knowledge of the specific effects of law on behavior," in the belief that, "until such knowledge is available, any discussion of the relative desirability of alternative social ends which may be achieved by law is largely day-dreaming and any discussion of the 'engineering' methods by which law may be used to achieve those ends is largely futile."[155]

Having thus abused, if not disposed of, both traditional legal scholarship and the then newer forms of policy analysis, Moore presented his own theory. He first asserted that legal rules as well as legal behavior "may or may not be a sign to which a response has been learned." Then, importing legal phenomena wholly into the world of everyday events, Moore further asserted that it was improper to distinguish "between Law . . . and other behavior and artifacts" as was commonly done. Rather, Moore claimed, the more important distinction was between "behavior and artifacts which are signs" (i.e., those "to which human beings have been taught, through pain, humiliation, or reward, to respond") "and those which are not." He proceeded to distinguish learned responses from other responses, and review briefly the mechanism of learning through reinforcement. Then, reverting to concerns first expressed in the Wigmore review nearly twenty years earlier, he imported culture into the learning situation as learned responses or behavior patterns of those who teach, primarily parents, and attempted to account for changes in culture either as random behavior by reinforcing agents or as responses to new stimulus situations. Further, emphasizing cultural aspects of learning, Moore observed that as others were often responding to the same sign when an individual was learning his response to it, "the frequency with which . . . [the] behavior [of others] corresponds to the response being reinforced, may become a part of the sign" for the individual learning that response. He thereafter emphasized the wide variation in the range of stimuli to which "in life situations" responses may be learned and attempted to account for problems created by the verbal content of many stimuli. Moore further noted that not all things, be they legal rules, advertising messages, or other exhortations, purporting to be stimuli were necessarily such unless a response to them was learned, if only on the basis of recognizing the authority of the individual or organ issuing the stimulus.[156]

With the general description of his theory thus complete, Moore returned to a more narrowly legal context and observed, somewhat dogmatically, that "the common assumption that propositions of law are exhibited by the state to most people, that responses to them are conditioned in most cases by punishment inflicted by the state and that therefore law is a peculiar class of signs to which is given responses differing in degree from responses to other signs, is erroneous." "[M]ost propositions of law are not exhibited by anyone to the senses of most people"; "most responses which are thought of as responses to propositions of law . . . actually are responses to stimulus situations which do not include any proposition of law"; most responses given to propositions of law are not responses "learned through the punishment of the state" but rather have "been taught by parents"; and those instances "in which the state does carry out the process of conditioning a response," "cases of few deviational individuals" or cases where "the state is an innovator" that "attempts to obtain a response different from the responses being given by the great majority of people," "the process of conditioning a response to a law-sign" and other learning processes "are fundamentally the same."[157]

Having thus asserted his wholly naturalistic view of legal processes, Moore returned to the world of behavioral psychology in an attempt to produce a hypothesis for testing that was operational, in the sense he asserted at the outset. With some difficulty he derived as such a hypothesis the proposition that the change in behavior after the imposition of a legal regulation "varies directly . . . with the ratio, observed . . . before" the regulation was "introduced, between the frequency of behavior not corresponding to the" regulation "and the frequency of behavior corresponding to the" regulation.[158] In other words, behavior in conformity with a law is more likely where behavior has previously conformed without that law; or, stated negatively, the greater the disparity between the behavior designed to be altered by a law and the behavioral standard established by that law, the less likely behavior will conform to the law. And thereafter Moore summarily presented the results of the parking research, complete with three by-no-means elegant algebraic formulas, as partial support for the hypothesis.[159]

Although Kocourek's book was widely reviewed, Moore's contribution was generally either ignored,[160] found puzzling or perplexing,[161] or subjected to generally vituperative, though unperceptive, criticism.[162] Only four of the reviewers seem even to have understood the piece[163] and of the four only one offered even vaguely useful criticism—the quite contemporary suggestion that experimental method alone does not make a science.[164] Another at least understood the relationship between Moore's offering and his having come to intellectual maturity at a time when "science" was an important, new intellectual force.[165]

Moore's friends and associates did little better. Eugene Rostow, once a student, by then a colleague, understanding the piece to be a "preface" to a larger work, found it "an entirely articulate statement of the argument of . . . [Moore's] research," yet cautioned that the research might "confirm an infinite number of hypotheses" in addition to Moore's. Rostow, then, suggested that Moore "dramatize" his research "for law professors unfamiliar with other kinds of study" by distinguishing it from "other kinds of permissible scholarship in law"—studies of policy or doctrine.[166] The Director of the Institute found the piece "interesting" and "sound," but suggested that Moore make "a more careful study of the recent formulations of learning theory" by Clark Hull, a leading member of the Institute's staff, since Moore's results could be "predicted from the main postulates of Hull's system."[167] Hull in turn found Moore's contribution "important" and noted his "impression" that Moore's philosophy of law had "advanced very greatly within the last year or two, particularly in the psychological direction." He also offered a criticism of Moore's use of "operational," drawing on his own knowledge of the works of the Vienna Circle, and an extended discussion of "experimental extinction," the "one important lack" in a "remarkably realistic account of the psychology of behavior involving statutes."[168]

Moore quickly sought the aid of Hull,[169] and then he and Callahan set to work completing their analysis and presentation of the studies. In the course of the two and a half years they worked, World War II intervened and as a result Moore lost his office at the Institute[170] and his research assistant at the Law School.[171] Then, Callahan lost his teaching job at Yale.[172] Finally in December 1943, a full ten years to the month after the first observations were made, Moore's study, "Law and Learning Theory," finally appeared in 136 pages of the *Yale Law Journal*.

This time, after taking a brief, acid slap at "the failure of jurists and others to undertake . . . investigations of the quantity and degree of conformity [of behavior] to rules of law,"[173] Moore began a straightforward presentation of the work he had done. By subdividing two of his studies and saving the one Corstvet had earlier suggested should be scrapped, Moore managed to present ten studies of parking behavior spread over the four durational limitations — no parking, and fifteen-, thirty-, and sixty-minute parking. These studies plus the two tagging studies and the old traffic circle study were his data base. In presenting them Moore straightforwardly emphasized the variables controlled for and those left uncontrolled or tolerated as uncontrollable.[174] With these basics out of the way, he next turned to an analysis of the data he had acquired.

With respect to the parking studies Moore quickly passed over the marked shift of behavior in the direction of conformity with the regulation; instead, he highlighted two other findings. First, he noted that, although there was a marked shift of behavior for parking durations up until a "point" substantially in excess of the regulation imposed, the relative distribution of parkers among these shorter durational classifications was largely identical both before and after the regulation imposed. Only beyond this point was there any decline in the relative frequency of parking for a given duration. Second, he laboriously observed that, although on cursory inspection it appeared that there was no regularity to the difference between the number of cars parking in comparable periods before and after the imposition of a parking regulation, in fact, by carefully accounting for the actual use of the available time and space, one could observe a decrease in the percentage of available time used in regulated areas. Moore accounted for this decrease as the effect of the ordinance in making space available by simply eliminating parkings of long duration.[175]

Each of these observations was accompanied by precise mathematical formulas designed to quantify the relationships discovered, often through the use of somewhat peculiar variables, such as the cumulated percentage of unregulated parkings of a duration less than the "point." Thereafter, Moore explained the results of the tagging studies. Here he argued that the tagging had not made its impact on the behavior of all parkers, but rather that the difference in before and after behavior could be wholly accounted for by the effect of tagging on the behavior of individually tagged parkers who again parked in the same location. Finally, with respect to the traffic circle study, he argued that the decrease in behavior prohibited by the ordinance was great-est when compliance required the least deviation from the path normally taken through the intersection and least when compliance required the most deviation, in other words the degree of compliance was directly related to the ease of compliance.[176]

Having thus summarized his results, Moore turned to articulating an ex-planation of them in terms of their congruence with a more general theory of human behavior, which he labeled learning theory. This time his presentation was markedly different from the piece he had written for Kocourek. Where three years before Moore had explained learning theory in almost common-sense terms and had integrated into that explanation an appreciation for the cultural aspects of human behavior that dated back to the Wigmore review, Moore now spoke in the technical language of the academic psychol-ogist and reduced the cultural dimension of his presentation to a short almost afterthought that emphasized not the impact of culture on behavior, but of learned behavior as an explanation of cultural change.[177] He began by di-rectly presenting a slightly simplified version of stimulus-response psychol-ogy. Relying on presentations by Hull and two of his colleagues,[178] Moore emphasized the pattern: drive, cue, response, reward. "In order to learn one must be driven to make a response in the presence of a cue, and that response must be rewarded." He then noted that the bare outline of the theory would "suffice to explain only the most simple instances of human behavior"[179] and proceeded to complicate the presentation in three ways.

First he distinguished between "innate or primary drives" and "acquired or secondary drives," especially the acquired drive of "anxiety or fear." Sec-ond, Moore observed that responses may "extend over considerable time and space" such that one might refer to them as "chain responses." And third, Moore recognized that the multiplicity of drives may, taken together, simultaneously call for conflicting responses and that the verbal nature of some cues may create problems in isolating the learned response to the cue because the response might differ from the cue. Finally, Moore attempted to generalize from individual learning to group learning by the function of parental or group approval as a reward, the extinction of responses by the cessation of reward, and the part played by "technological and sociological invention or innovation" in learning "cue-response" relations.[180]

From this rapidly sketched theoretical framework, Moore proceeded to analyze each of his studies. In each case he began with the observation that the study was of the change in the frequency of a particular response brought about by the introduction of a cue calling for a conflicting response. In the parking studies Moore carefully identified the drives, cues, responses, and rewards of the individuals parking when the area was unregulated, "not a period during which a new response was being learned, but . . . a period during which each of the individuals . . . was giving a response which he had already learned." After eliminating problems based on the lack of knowledge of the quality and strength of the drives and rewards of individual parkers by assuming that they were distributed proportionately among studies and durational categories, Moore was left with one further problem. Learning theory would have postulated that the elapsed time of parking was a measure of the delay in securing the reward and thus an index of the strength of the reinforcement of the response of parking. However, elapsed time of parking nowhere entered into the equations that Moore had painstakingly derived to order his data. He explained this discrepancy between the theory and his data by suggesting that the strength of reinforcement was not determined by the absolute duration. Rather, it was determined by the relative duration between the cue and the response, "by the *conception which exists in the mind of the person giving the response*" as to the duration, a conception that "depends on his conception of his relative position in a distribution which includes not only his behavior but also the behavior of others who . . . are doing the 'same thing.' "[181]

With this problem out of the way, Moore asserted that the introduction of a new cue — the durational limitation — created a conflict in responses between parking in response to the errand to be done, and not parking in response to the anxiety aroused by the possibility of violating the durational limitation.[182] He then explained the changes in the frequencies of the various durations of parking after introduction of the limitation by suggesting that the point where the relative frequencies began to change corresponded to the time at which parkers began to feel anxiety arising from the subjective perception that they were about to violate the limitation. Because the response of not parking was in the circumstances more strongly reinforced than the response of parking, the apparent decrease in the duration of parkings beyond the point where anxiety appeared was thus the effect of the actions of parkers in passing up potential spaces. Finally, Moore suggested that, in the aggregate, the extent to which the response of not parking predominated was a function of the frequency with which individuals parked less than a given time even when the area was unregulated.[183]

Moore discussed the other two studies similarly, though in less detail. He explained the tagging study by observing that, since removal of the repeated parkings of tagged individuals totally eliminated the effect of the tagging program, that program presented no new cue to anyone but the individuals tagged.[184] To explain the traffic circle experiments, he postulated that the painted circle was a cue that in the presence of the secondary drive of anxiety called forth the response of keeping to the right to the degree that this response was more greatly rewarded by the reduction of anxiety than the response of driving directly through the intersection was rewarded by reduction of the drive related to crossing the intersection more quickly.[185]

Four friends read the manuscript before publication; none had much to say in response, although Rostow did observe that "the presentation was admirably clear, and the confrontation of difficulties direct and courageous. . . ."[186] Three reviews of the piece were planned;[187] in the following spring two materialized, one by Clark Hull and the other by Hessel Yntema, Moore's former colleague at Columbia and participant in the empirical research at the Johns Hopkins Institute of Law. Hull found the study "an original, fearless and convincing exemplification of the implementation of . . . [Moore's] philosophy" as stated three years earlier and a "courageous *tour de force*" given the "state of our ignorance concerning ultimate behavior laws."[188] He suggested a somewhat crude but effective simplification of Moore's data by which he quite directly related the point at which the limitation began to have an effect to a simple multiple of the duration specified by the limitation.[189] This relation, he observed, reflected "the habits of successful (and so, reinforced) disregard of law produced by our characteristically lax customs of law enforcement."[190] Yntema emphasized the importance of the study, both as a pioneering bit of research, and an exemplar of what might be done in quantitative studies of legal material of a normative nature. At the same time he questioned whether, in the face of limited resources for empirical research in law, it was wise to concentrate, as Moore had, on the regularities of behavior, rather than on admittedly abnormal "litigious behavior" that could be investigated through the use of "more expeditious, if less exact, techniques of objective inquiry," the kind of research Yntema had tried to do at Hopkins. In a similar vein Yntema wondered whether, contrary to Moore's assertions, it was not "legitimate to study legal propositions without reference to their conformity to or effect upon behavior,"[191] the kind of work that Cook had contemplated and that he and Cook had done since leaving Hopkins.

A thousand copies of the article were printed with a special introduction by the director of the Institute. Half of these were given away to individuals on the Institute's mailing list; the rest awaited buyers who never appeared. Beyond the two comments in the *Yale Law Journal*, the law reviews were similarly silent. Moore, who with the advent of the war, had canceled all of his subscriptions to social science journals[192] and turned his reading interests to military history and strategy,[193] was silent too.

Why

What then of Moore's singular case? Clark and Douglas tried to build support for empirical legal research from a traditional liberal concern for progressive reform based on gathering the "facts" about a problem and found that neither the reformers nor the newest fact gatherers, the empirical social scientists, were willing to support the research they wished to do beyond the limits of the perspective of each group. Beyond that, the lesson of their work was that no one was particularly interested in funding empirical legal research anyway. Moore's research obviously gave out, in the narrowest sense, for that same want of money and yet, on the basis of the experience of Clark and Douglas, Moore's research enterprise should have been the most fruitful. He did not seek support by threading his way between progressive reformers and social scientists, only and predictably to satisfy neither group; he threw his lot in with the social scientists exclusively. And he did not want tens of thousands of dollars — big pittances would have carried his enterprise along nicely, thank you.

Moore was thus singular both in his choice to trod the path alone and also in his wholehearted acceptance of the values of social science and its community of scholars. He was, or at least saw himself as, wholly within that community. His banking and parking research alone supports this assertion. The reform impulse at the base of either body of work is impossible, or at least extremely difficult, to perceive. But the degree of Moore's identification with the social scientific community is equally well demonstrated by his suggestion at the time of Angell's retirement as to the necessary qualifications for potential candidates for the university's presidency. The "first indispensable . . . requirement" was that the candidate be a "natural scientist," Moore asserted. He reasoned that neither undergraduate work nor graduate work "in the humanities and in disciplines such as economics" needed attention and that professional training would not "be changed very much for a long while"; therefore, if a natural scientist were chosen "there is at least a bare chance that he will have a vision of the possibility of the application of scientific thinking and scientific method to fields of experience to which they have never been applied" and "the will" to see that some of these possible applications will be carried out.[194] In other words, the university generally should follow the pattern of activity he had.

Given Moore's wholly naturalistic view of legal phenomena, his fierce determination to pursue research in that mode, and his commitment to the social scientific community, when it came to financial and intellectual support for his research the match should have been a natural one. But somehow from the beginning that match was never made.

Moore came to Yale because of the establishment of the Institute of Human Relations and with the support of Yale's President, James R. Angell, a social scientist himself, who also was an acquaintance from Moore's brief stay at the University of Chicago.[195] However, though Moore eagerly and immediately sought to participate in planning the research program of the Institute, instead of being in on the ground floor, he ended up an outsider knocking at the gate. That turn of events was clearly not his fault; rather it should be laid squarely at the doorstep of Robert Maynard Hutchins who oversold, and probably overestimated as well, the Law School's control over, and role in, the Institute's affairs.[196] Had Moore planned research that was methodologically mundane, the fact that he was an outsider when he finally appeared at Yale might not have made a difference. But his research was unusual and his method had all the hallmarks of having been put together by someone who had heard about social scientific research but had never seen or done any. In short, it immediately stamped Moore for what he was, a rank amateur.

For some people associated with the Institute, most notably Emma Corstvet,[197] but probably also President Angell,[198] Moore's status as an amateur social scientist made no difference. Rather, the important point for them was the fact that Moore was engaged in interesting research and was attempting to execute it as best he could. For most of the people at the Institute, however, the appearance of an amateur was a problem. The majority of these men and women were part of the second generation of academic social scientists in the American university. They had not created the discipline in which they worked, but had participated in it as graduate students in the new Ph.D. programs of the newly formed departments, as members of the academic societies that defined the discipline, as researchers within the bounds so defined, and as guides for their own graduate students who were headed down the same paths. In short, they were the first beneficiaries of the process by which the academic social sciences professionalized. An integral part of that process was the almost ritual gesture of excluding the amateurs from the profession through a combination of the adoption of technical methods and vocabulary, the imposition of "standards" for acceptable research, and, most effectively, the establishment of the Ph.D. as *the* requirement for academic employment.[199] As the Moore and Hope piece showed, Moore did not know the technical methods and vocabulary, had no inkling of what the standards were, and had never seen the inside of a modern social science Ph.D. program. His mere appearance at the Institute was thus a threat to the professional status of the social scientists; his work might well give their Institute a bad name.[200]

Reactions to this threat varied somewhat. Dorothy Thomas was plainly puzzled, even forty-five years later, how Moore, who had an obvious commitment to scientific research, could have looked for help with his research and yet finished the negotiable instruments studies without abandoning what was to her a patently unsatisfactory method.[201] In this respect, Douglas's attitude, which allowed Thomas to restructure his research technique, was preferable to Moore's single-mindedness.[202] But, matter of fact to the core, she taught Moore what she could, worked with him in their joint seminar, and, when she found more interesting things to do, moved on.

Others at the Institute, less charitable perhaps, or maybe only more insecure, simply chose to ignore him. Thus, nearly two years after his arrival, Moore's own work, though funded by the Institute and already visible in the published parts of the direct discounts study, was omitted from the director's virtually complete listing of research at the Institute issued at the dedication of its building.[203] A year later when the program to study the City of New Haven was first floated, Moore's potential contributions were again ignored.[204] Even individuals such as Clark Hull[205] who, from the beginning, were largely interested in and vaguely supportive of Moore's work,[206] assumed that seminars designed for the Institute as a whole would be of no interest to Moore[207] and ignored Moore's potential contribution to the joint research program he and others tried to design for the Institute.[208]

In time Moore's presence simply could not be ignored. It could, however, be begrudged. Thus, in the 1936 Institute reorganization plan, while Moore's research was noted, his interest in and potential contributions to other proposed research, though quite obvious, were still passed over.[209] Three years later, when the Institute's funds were reduced and its "commitment to certain lines of research" necessitated corresponding budgetary cutbacks, support for Moore's research was terminated.[210] The termination stood even though that research was squarely within the behavioral paradigm toward which the Institute's commitment had been made. Only begrudging acceptance, if acceptance is the right word for the activity of killing a line of research and then later supporting the preparation of the article tombstoning the corpse,[211] was offered and that only with an accompanying condescending attitude. The

Director, for example, suggested that Moore's presentation in the piece for Kocourek's symposium could be strengthened "somewhat by a more careful study" of Hull's work.[212] Hull was no less offensive when, in the response to the same title, he commented that Moore's account of "the psychology of behavior situations involving statutes" was "remarkably realistic" but, when discussing the "one important lack" in that account — a discussion of experimental extinction, a subject wholly tangential to Moore's article — presented his observations in such a way as to suggest that Moore might never have heard about experiments with white rats on electric grids.[213] Even when "Law and Learning Theory" was completed, the Director of the Institute could not resist emphasizing in his introduction to the separately bound version that Moore had not attempted to derive his empirical formulas by deduction from "any set of basic postulates," but had only made "a first crude beginning" with an attempt "to *describe* parking behavior . . . in terms of the concepts of behavior theory."[214]

Treated as an amateur by the social scientists, Moore might have been tempted to look elsewhere for support, but for him there was no elsewhere to look. The law school world generally was hardly hospitable. There his activities had made him the butt of some rather raw humor. His course on commercial bank credit was known colloquially as "the love life of a check";[215] his decision to begin empirical research, enshrined in the vision of Moore throwing out the contents of his filing cabinets and yelling, "It's my life's work . . . and it's all wrong";[216] his parking research, ridiculed with a story about him in shorts sitting on a camp stool in front of New Haven's Hotel Taft and when questioned as to what he was doing, responding, "Don't bother me. Can't you see I'm busy counting these cars?"[217] Indeed, the law school world had delivered to Moore such "misunderstanding and intellectual hardknocks"[218] that a merely kind letter from a former colleague[219] about a presentation Moore made at an AALS meeting[220] brought forth an expression of great pleasure.[221] In the more circumscribed world of the Yale Law School, the conflicting impulse toward research entertained by Clark and Douglas made it all but impossible for Moore to look to these men for support. And at Yale, at least, there was no other social scientific community to look to,[222] except that of the economists and political scientists — corners of the intellectual world where a little support was offered, but where, however peculiar it may seem given Moore's graduate work at Columbia and his work in banking, his interests never ran.[223] Disciples could, and to some extent did, provide some support. But good disciples were hard to recruit, as was emphasized by Moore's experience in finding a research assistant to replace Emma Corstvet and as his unsuccessful attempt to interest Friedrich Kessler in the soft social science of the always proposed, always in process, commercial bank credit book.[224] And even when potential disciples were recruited, they somehow never managed to gain a real enthusiasm for empirical research, but rather drifted away to other activities.[225]

Moore was thus left largely to his own devices. He pursued his own iconoclastic, idiosyncratic view of empirical research, drawing on ideas from Dewey, Robinson, and Veblen about what science was, and on what Dorothy Thomas and Emma Corstvet had taught him about research design. Thomas's emphasis on the niceties of observation and the subtler aspects of statistical method, left a particularly strong mark on the research, although in this she was aided by Moore's predisposition for detail, as shown in his earlier doctrinal research and continually emphasized in his teaching.[226] Her mark was also strengthened by Moore's surroundings at the Institute, for although treated as an amateur by the psychologists who came to dominate its affairs, Moore constantly turned to the members of this group for what little support they would provide. He needed their support and sought it, almost pathetically. They were the only game in town, the only peer group available. That they did not want or need him made little difference. Thus, he first shifted the form of his research to fit their idea of what research should look like, and then, when they announced a new game — community studies — not only volunteered to play, but also attempted to fit his research design more closely to their specifications, even to the extent of adopting a topic of research he was not particularly interested in.[227] Then, when the game changed again, he gave up the sociological/anthropological perspective on his research developed at Columbia at the end of World War I, a perspective that had twice led him to look directly at the relationship between law and custom, and adopted as his ideal the smooth stimulus-response curves of the experimental psychologists as well as their language and theoretical universe. He wanted to play in the worst of ways.

Of course, there is another way to see Moore's behavior. In one sense he was a captive of the social scientists at the Institute,[228] for as an amateur, strung along with occasional handouts of cash, he knew no better, and perhaps, just perhaps, they did. But if in bondage, it was a quite willing bondage. Moore wanted help with his work and wanted acceptance in the world where he thought real scientific research was being done. He searched elsewhere for that help and acceptance, in Malinowski's anthropology[229] and Timasheff's sociology,[230] for example. But always he came back to his quite lovely vision of what the scientific study of law meant, not the nineteenth-century science of Langdell, but the twentieth-century science of Eddington, whose book on relativity theory Moore had read the summer before coming to Yale.[231]

So, as long as experimental psychology was the scale against which success was measured in the world of social science at Yale, amateurs, at least, had to play by the apparent rules. Those rules forbade simple, contextual explanations of the kind tossed off by professionals like Hull. And so Moore, who thought he knew precisely why he was "busy counting these cars," produced a grand piece of research that Llewellyn, for example, thought proved Moore mad,[232] and that everyone else in the law school world either disliked, or ignored, or both.[233]

THERE WAS ANOTHER way to secure the intellectual support for empirical legal research. If an institute of social scientists would not provide support then law professors might build an institute of their own. And so, I next return to that other returned colonial officer, Walter Wheeler Cook, who tried to do just that when he convinced the Trustees of the Johns Hopkins University to establish the Institute of Law.

EMPIRICAL LEGAL RESEARCH AT JOHNS HOPKINS:

WALTER WHEELER COOK AND HIS FRIENDS

WHEN, IN MAY 1928, Columbia's President, Nicolas Murray Butler, chose Young B. Smith rather than Herman Oliphant to be Dean over the determined opposition of perhaps a minority, perhaps a majority, of the Columbia Law School's faculty, that faculty collapsed in disarray.[1] Of the losers William O. Douglas immediately resigned in protest; others, including Underhill Moore and Herman Oliphant, let it be known that they were, or were assumed by others to be, available to leave as well. The two main bidders in this market were Robert Maynard Hutchins, the Dean at Yale, and Walter Wheeler Cook, then at Johns Hopkins assisting that University with its plans to establish a nonteaching, research institute for law.[2] The bidding was fast and furious and some thought had reached unseemly numbers.[3] Quickly Douglas signed on with Hutchins[4] and Oliphant, with his old friend Cook.[5] Both buyers then focused on Moore.

Oliphant attempted to convince his colleague to come with him, arguing that the Hopkins project should be seen "in terms of our highest aspirations as to a Community of Scholars."[6] But, even after meeting with two members of the Hopkins Trustees, Moore was not moved, and so declined Cook's offer.[7] Hutchins, in contrast, offered a law school teaching post and a position at a yet to be organized social science research institute.[8] That did not move Moore either. Oliphant expressed "keen" disappointment at Moore's decision; he thought it "very clear" that Moore was "making a mistake in not heading up one of the practically independent research units of which the Institute is to consist."[9] Moore did not deny the importance of independent research units and felt that the lack of a teaching obligation and the absence of a professional school made the Hopkins plan "ideal."[10] He, however, explained his decision by reasoning that, given the financial instability of the

Hopkins enterprise, the lack of any firm idea on the part of the Hopkins Trustees as to the standard for measuring progress in research of the kind proposed, and the questionable ability of Oliphant and, even more so, Cook to stick to research during the first, lean years, the plan would never get carried out, with the result that the trustees, seeing the limited results, would withdraw their support and the participants would head off in other directions.[11] And so Moore waited until Hutchins secured the financing for the Institute of Human Relations at Yale and then took up Hutchins offer.[12]

Nearly two years later, when the Hopkins Institute was up and running, it filed an application with the Rockefeller Foundation for a grant of up to $5 million. In making the request Hopkins President Joseph S. Ames emphasized that law, as an instrument of social control, depended for its value on its "effectiveness," and that in studying the effectiveness of law "*all relevant facts* as to its origins, its relationship to social needs and conditions, its administration and its effects should be examined," not as a matter of "subjective opinion," but of "*objective facts.*" He then noted that the absence of "*sufficient data*" and lack of "*adequate techniques*" had made it seldom possible to make such an objective assessment and stated that the program of the Institute was designed to train "high-grade personnel" and to undertake "studies well suited to the present stage of scientific development in the field."[13] Finally, in an appendix he described in some detail the four principal studies underway at the Institute.

The first was a study of the judicial system in Ohio and in Maryland designed, first, to "get masses of comparative data concerning the grist currently being ground in the judicial systems of several rather diverse jurisdictions" in such a way that "there will result state-wide systems of judicial statistics" such as would be essential to "effective business organization and management of courts" and "improvement of the judicial machine," and second, to investigate "significant aspects of judicial administration," in particular, of court organization, procedure, personnel and of "new conditions" that "give rise to new problems" like auto accident or divorce litigation. A second was a survey of litigation in New York "to determine the amount of unnecessary slowness, cost and uncertainty" there was in litigation and "the causes of it." The third and fourth were studies of installment sales and of the concurrent jurisdiction of the federal and state courts, a fancy name for a study of litigation brought within, or otherwise potentially cognizable under the diversity jurisdiction of the federal courts.[14]

Each project represented an interest of one of the four principals at Hop-

kins. Leon Carroll Marshall, a friend of Oliphant's and an acquaintance of
Cook's,[15] and who had been at Columbia where he headed the Great Curriculum Study,[16] was in back of the Ohio and Maryland studies; Oliphant was
the man who had made contact with the group of lawyers pushing the New
York project; Cook had sponsored the installment buying project; and Hessel
Yntema, a junior colleague of Oliphant's at Columbia who had been invited
to join the group after Moore had declined,[17] had adopted the diversity
jurisdiction project. And each was quite a topical bit of research; indeed, the
installment buying project was a good deal ahead of its time. Moreover, if
Yale's proposal to the Rockefeller Foundation for the Institute of Human Relations may be taken as a standard,[18] the grant proposal might be seen as very
effective. Yet on reading it Max Mason, then Director of the Social Sciences
Division of the Foundation, scribbled, "this doesn't hang together."[19]

In the end the Rockefeller Foundation did not fund the Institute's proposal, though not because of its failure to hang together. And, though Moore's
estimate of the relative strengths and weaknesses of the Hopkins proposal
had a certain surface plausibility, it was no more prescient than his estimate
of the importance of the sounder financial basis at Yale. Yet, both events
suggest a weakness in the idea for the Hopkins Institute.

Since 1923, and probably before, Oliphant had been arguing that, in his
later words, "the time has come for at least one school to become a community of scholars, devoting itself to the non-professional study of law, in order
that the function of law be comprehended, its results evaluated, and its development kept more nearly in step with the complex developments of modern life."[20] Both Cook and Moore had heard and believed Oliphant's call,
although obviously they evaluated the Hopkins proposal differently. If this
idea, by no means necessarily implied by anything Cook or Moore had said
about science and law, was to succeed, it would be not because of its inherent,
moderate plausibility, but for two other reasons. First, *the* university, the
higher-education community, and *a* university, a particular institution of
higher learning, would have to accept and nurture the new school. Second,
the individual scholars who made up the school would have to take the idea
and make something of it, a matter of both developing *a* program of research
and executing it. None of these were trivial matters. Development and execution of *a* program were probably recognized for the problems they were from
the onset. To understand the problem presented by, if not *the* university, at
least *the* Johns Hopkins University, one needs to begin back a few years
before the Institute was founded with what was taken to be a problem at

Hopkins. Although envisioned as a part of the master plan for that university, Hopkins still had no law school.

Seeking a School of Jurisprudence

Or more properly a school of jurisprudence. That Hopkins needed such an entity is anything but clear. The best explanation for this need is that the fundraising campaign that the university undertook in 1910 specified expansion in four directions: engineering, education, public health, and law. The first three projects had gone forward in due course. The last floundered. This was particularly displeasing to one of the Hopkins Trustees, B. Howell Griswold, Jr., who had headed the 1910 campaign.[21] Griswold was a frustrated lawyer. Son of a reasonably wealthy railroad executive, after earning an undergraduate degree at Hopkins and a law degree at Maryland, he had practiced law for a while. But, after he married the daughter of a client, Alexander Brown, Jr., senior partner in Alexander Brown & Sons, America's oldest private banker, he abandoned law and became a banker in that firm, eventually becoming its senior partner.[22] At the time he became a banker, Griswold "made up . . . [his] mind that . . . [he] would not forget the law, which seemed to . . . [him] as a 'lovely lady' to whom . . . [he] had been quite 'attentive', one who had given . . . [him] rich rewards of happiness." Somehow this wish not to forget the law translated into an eagerness to provide for "a study of methods which . . . would prevent a sequence of error by repetition amongst the States of erroneous economic and social legislation and which might alter certain of the mechanics of Court procedure in a manner which would result in a much higher average of justice."[23] Griswold and the Hopkins Trustees tried to interest Victor Morawetz in such a project.[24] Morawetz was the son of a wealthy Baltimore physician who in twenty years of law practice had written the first great book on corporation law,[25] become a partner in a major New York law firm, advised J. P. Morgan in the organization of the United States Steel Corporation, and participated, often on behalf of Andrew Carnegie, in many of the great turn-of-the-century railroad reorganizations, including the Atcheson, Topeka and Santa Fe, of which he was Chairman of the Board of Directors for thirteen years. Then, at a relatively young age, he retired from practice and commerce and gave his life over to writing and working for improvements in the areas of law, finance, and education.[26] Morawetz was "very enthusiastic" about Griswold's idea,[27] but not enough to finance it. So there the matter stood for many years until, in spring 1923, Griswold had the occasion to advance the idea on the Chairman of the General Education Board, one of the Rockefeller philanthropies.

The Chairman, Wallace Buttrick, was also enthusiastic about Griswold's idea[28] and so sent Griswold to see the Board's president and chief operating officer, Wickliff Rose.[29] Griswold presented Rose with a plan for the school written by W. W. Willoughby,[30] the guiding light in Hopkins's tiny Department of Political Science. Rose seemed noncommittal, a matter that depressed Griswold,[31] but in fact was "interested" in the idea, which he saw as "quite new, quite out of line with other things" that the Board was interested in. So, while the Board thought the matter over, Griswold was sent to talk to the Laura Spelman Rockefeller Memorial, another of the Rockefeller philanthropies, which was planning a program in the social sciences.[32] This visit turned out to be ultimately futile,[33] and soon Griswold was back with the General Education Board where he was given to Abraham Flexner.[34] Flexner, who had pioneered reforms in medical education and who thought that, as *Fachschule*, schools of "medicine and law are . . . unfit for inclusion in a university,"[35] initially announced that he saw "nothing" in the proposal.[36] But, after reading Willoughby's plan, Flexner changed his mind and concluded that Griswold had "worked out definitely in his proposal a thing that had been vaguely floating in my [i.e., Flexner's] mind for years."[37] As a result Flexner suggested, without, of course, committing the Board by putting anything in writing, that if Hopkins would raise half the estimated $3 million endowment, he "felt" the General Education Board would contribute the rest.[38]

What was this plan that Griswold and Willoughby had dreamed up that so impressed even initially skeptical Rockefeller officials? Though the idea was articulated with occasionally different details,[39] the basic outline was always the same. Hopkins had made its name by combining research and graduate education in various fields and it would do the same thing in law by establishing a school of "advanced research and teaching, and not a professional institution for the preparation of students for the practice of the law." The school's purpose would be "to provide the information by means of which intelligent and effective action may be taken . . . to bring the great corpus of American law into closer consonance with the social, economic and political needs of the country." Its faculty would be "small in number, but composed of scholars of eminent distinction"; the student body would, "by reason of previous training, be qualified for advanced work and research," "including especially the preparation of a dissertation representing original and scholarly work," and be destined to be "teachers who will carry into other institutions, including professional law schools, the scientific and the broadened outlook which they will have obtained."[40]

The proposed subjects of study were thoroughly eclectic, including "The Law in Its Relation to the Facts of Social, Economic and Political Life," "Criminal Law and Criminology," "Judicial Organization and Procedure," "Legislation," comparative and analytical jurisprudence, both historical jurisprudence and legal history, "United States Constitutional Law," "Roman Law," and "Diplomacy and Diplomatic History."[41] The asserted need for such an enterprise — the growth in legislation and judicial decisions that together led to "existing confusion" — was admittedly the same one as had been used to justify the recently founded American Law Institute. Yet Griswold and Willoughby distinguished the object of the school from the "clarification and re-statement of existing law" that they saw as the object of the ALI. Hopkins would produce "men whose knowledge of the fundamental principles and history of law will be a direct force in securing wiser and sounder legislation" and who, by virtue of their "sound understanding of the economic and social needs of . . . [the] day, . . . will be beacons toward which those in authority and in search of light will turn for guidance."[42]

The plan was in its own way novel (a research and graduate training institution in law), familiar (progressive law reform), and enough like the formula that had brought success at the Hopkins Medical School, so that the interest of the Rockefeller philanthropies was understandable. The principals were, of course, excited and returned to Morawetz expecting that they might quickly garner his half of the implicit bargain with Flexner.[43] But it turned out that Morawetz was not as interested as he had at first seemed. At least in the interim he had acquired a more consuming interest — the ALI. As one of its founders and an active participant in discussions of the various restatements, Morawetz wanted Hopkins not to distinguish itself from the ALI, but rather to turn out reporters for the restatement project.[44]

Morawetz wished Hopkins to take on this role apparently because he was adamantly opposed to the draft Restatement of the Conflict of Laws that Joseph Beale of Harvard, the reporter on the project, had prepared. Morawetz objected to Beale's concept that the Restatement was offering an " 'international conception' rather than a statement of the law in force in the United States."[45] Why Morawetz cared about the question is a bit mysterious,[46] but whatever the reason, through the intermediation of Harlan Fisk Stone, Morawetz made an acquaintance who was equally opposed to Beale's draft and supported the same local law theory of the subject — Walter Wheeler Cook.[47]

Morawetz apparently found Cook's view that the "fundamental conceptions" underlying Beale's work were, "to say the least, unfortunate,"[48] sufficiently close to his own that he thought Cook possibly might be a "good
man" to be part of the Hopkins school.[49] So in fall 1925, Morawetz ascertained of Cook that Cook might be able to get a year's leave from Yale "to
engage in work" on the conflict of laws and then separately told Griswold
that he would contribute $10,000, Cook's salary, to "try out" Cook for the
year.[50]

For a while nothing much came of Morawetz's idea. Both men worked
on the Restatement project, which bothered others including Harlan Fiske
Stone, by this time a member of the Supreme Court,[51] and Cook's Yale
colleague, Ernest Lorenzen.[52] Then, in spring, Hopkins President Frank J.
Goodnow, who had been one of Cook's teachers at the Columbia political
science department, invited Cook to Hopkins to talk about the proposed
school of jurisprudence. Although Goodnow had "nothing definite to propose," he wished to invite "one or two" of the Hopkins Trustees.[53] Cook
jumped at the opportunity,[54] which got him a chance to meet Griswold.[55]
Cook found Griswold's ideas "quite chaotic,"[56] but after the meeting Cook
prepared a formal proposal for the new school that obviously delighted
Griswold.[57] This brought a further meeting with Griswold and Willoughby,[58]
a meeting with Morawetz, at which Morawetz told Cook of his suggestion
that Goodnow bring Cook to Hopkins for a year,[59] and a proposal from
Cook that he come for the year to work on two things: first, "the preparation
and publication of a discussion of the fundamentals" of the conflict of laws,
a project that Morawetz had "suggested"; and, second, "a book on Legal
Method — a discussion of modern views of logic and scientific method with
special reference to the work of the lawyer and judge." At the same time
Cook would help "work out carefully the details of the permanent plans for
the new school."[60] Though Morawetz was worried that Cook might have
other "engagements . . . which might absorb . . . [Cook's] time and distract . . .
[his] attention," so that Morawetz would fail to get the full value of his
contribution, with "reassurances" from Griswold[61] everyone was agreed.
Goodnow offered,[62] Cook accepted[63] and then asked for a leave of absence.[64]

Everyone was clearly excited by these events,[65] including Flexner who was
supposed to supply the money.[66] Why that was so is less obvious if one looks
carefully at the plan that Cook prepared in spring 1926 while negotiating for
the job. Although Cook said he had "tried to keep steadily in view the chief
aim or objective" of Griswold and Willoughby, only changing the "method
of reaching that objective in detail,"[67] the change "in detail" was quite signif-

icant. Griswold and Willoughby wanted a small graduate school; Cook, though asserting that "social as well as economic" changes in our modes of life "demand changed rules of law," the "vital readaption of our law," in fact proposed creating a small law school. He reasoned that graduates of existing schools "cannot be induced in sufficient number to undertake the work" of graduate research, and, even if they could, were "already so warped by the training for three years in the existing legalistic technique" that it would be at least difficult to reeducate them.[68]

Cook's was to be a four-year course for students who had had two years of college work,[69] designed "to fit men for the very highest type of legal research and at the same time meet the needs of students who intended to go to the bar for practice, but who wished a more scientific training than that now afforded by the existing schools." In other words, Cook wished to compress Hohfeld's separate schools for practitioners and for jurisprudes into one. However, Cook's school would eschew the traditional legal technique that Hohfeld had clearly wished to teach his lawyers and only belatedly and, almost as an afterthought, pick up any of Hohfeld's six great fields of jurisprudence — analytic, comparative, and historical. Instead, based on the notion that "Human laws are devices, tools, which society uses to regulate and promote human relations. The worth or value of a given rule of law can therefore be tested only by finding how it works . . . ," Cook proposed to focus the curriculum along "functional" lines by "first ascertaining just what the institution or relationship to which the law 'applies' is" and then studying the "effect of one rule or the other upon the human situation involved."[70] Thus, the difference between Griswold and Willoughby's plan and Cook's was not one of detail, though Cook clearly supplied a good deal of that, but of basic concept and thus of resources and results. There surely would be more students, more teaching, more faculty, and more endowment and likely would be less research, facts that Cook either chose to ignore or paper over.[71] Why no one seemed to notice this shift, even the astute Flexner, is by no means clear.[72] It may have been knowing self-deception, for Griswold, at least, worried that Morawetz, who, he said, wanted a "Kelvinator for freezing fluid legal ideas into clear solid concepts," would disapprove.[73] But, whatever the reason, some project was to move forward. With Yale's acquiescence in his leave, Cook came to Hopkins and set to work.

Freed from classes Cook managed to get a few things done. Results of the legal method project came out as "Scientific Method and the Law."[74] Sufficient work on the conflict of laws must have been done to keep Morawetz happy enough to agree to pay Cook's salary for the next year at the unheard rate of $15,000,[75] although none of this work reached print.[76] And a good deal of time and effort went into the proposed school of jurisprudence. Here there were really two projects, dealing with critics and garnering support. Of critics Cook had three, Griswold, Morawetz and Daniel Willard, the new Chairman of the Hopkins Board of Trustees.[77] Willard was worried that the plan would be "narrowed to restudy and classifying the law."[78] That problem was perhaps easy to avoid, though of course at the cost of troubling the hoped-for donor, Morawetz. And of course that is just what it did, for when Morawetz finally got to talking about this proposed school of jurisprudence, he became deeply worried that the proposed study of "the social and economic effects of existing law" was an indication that the school would be advocating changes in the existing social order.[79] Although cautioned by Griswold that he was only putting off an inevitable breach,[80] advice that, however true, ignored the fact that Morawetz was Cook's meal ticket, Cook tried to reassure Morawetz that "nothing was farther from our minds." Rather, the research would "accept the existing social and economic organization as a basic fact," determine whether existing rules of law "hinder" or "promote" this organization, and suggest better rules where existing rules were thus "defective."[81] Though comforting example from commercial law was provided,[82] whether Morawetz was truly comforted is not clear.

Comforting Griswold meant similarly trimming from obvious implications. Here Cook revised his plan to deemphasize the detailed curriculum that smelled like a law school, to hide as best he could the fact that it was "probable that a considerable proportion of the graduates of the School will go into practice,"[83] and to highlight research "by both faculty and students" into "law in action," though doing such research was said to require "the training of investigators competent not merely to indicate which is the 'better' of conflicting rules but also to show why it is better," a task that necessitated that "students . . . from the outset receive a different and broader training" than in existing professional schools. But if one was not lulled by the assertion that a detailed plan for the school could not be given, since the preferred procedure would be to have "the actual mode of reaching . . . [the] objective . . . be left to the small originating group," just as had been the case with the establishment of the Hopkins graduate and medical schools,[84] one could see that the curriculum was not one whit changed. Nevertheless, Griswold seemed to have been satisfied.

In organizing support for the proposed school, Cook tried to pressure Goodnow and Griswold quite directly[85] and to bolster his case with the imprimatur of important public figures, both from the bench and bar. For this purpose he prepared a special statement of "objectives" that he then sent to judges, university presidents, and prominent practitioners for suggestion and criticism.[86] Most were generally supportive.[87] Some saw problems. For example, it took two letters to convince Cardozo of the merits of the scheme;[88] the Vice-President at Chicago, a Law School faculty member, was not quite sure that the research in question belonged in a law school;[89] and President Angell of Yale, though "extremely sympathetic," cautioned that while it was desirable to introduce social science conceptions into the law, "it will . . . be many a long day before any large adoption of their technique can be hoped for with the expectation of greatly improving on present procedure."[90] Elihu Root, however, was more deeply skeptical. Noting that students who had a fourth year of law school were "frequently . . . less fit for the fighting part of life" than before that year, he suggested that although "research into the rational bases of the law as it ought to be" was something he supported, it was desirable to recognize the "natural line of cleavage" between those who do such research and those who "teach young men how to apply and maintain the law as it is," though, of course, the interactions of the two groups "may be of the highest value."[91]

Cook also sent copies of his new plan for the school and the separate justification for it to the General Education Board.[92] There he met not with Flexner but with Wickliff Rose, who three years earlier was supposed to be interested in the proposal. Rose succeeded in whipsawing Cook still further by taking the research emphasis in the proposal seriously, but suggesting that a purely research institution "might tend toward sterility," a comment that forced Cook to track back toward his original proposal. Rose further suggested that the social science departments at Hopkins might not be adequate to Cook's needs, a matter that Cook admitted he had not considered "in detail."[93] Yet when Cook tried to respond to these criticisms,[94] Rose politely shut the door with the curt response that until the Rockefeller philanthropies decided "what organization should handle the matter of legal education, the General Education Board was not disposed to take up further proposals" in the field.[95] It was a disheartening conclusion to a long year of work.

After Cook's usual return to his Adirondack summer hideaway and a late summer stop at the 1927 Social Science Research Council conference on research, which gave Cook an opportunity to tangle with Morris Cohen over the utility of Aristotelian logic,[96] Cook returned to Hopkins. There he continued work on the conflict of laws[97] and produced still another draft of the plan for a school of jurisprudence.[98] Neither forestalled the inevitable break with Morawetz.[99] So, with both potential donors out of the picture, Cook found himself in a "somewhat difficult position" with respect to Yale. He therefore proposed that he would accept a "Research Professorship of Law," provided that Hopkins would establish one or two more such professorships and secure "the right kind" of individuals to fill them. Cook was thus "willing to risk the matter of raising the remaining funds for the School," if Hopkins was willing "to commit itself permanently" to the amount necessary to fund these professorships, estimated at $50,000 per year.[100]

No one bit at Cook's suggestion[101] and Cook seems not to have pursued it or anything very vigorously at this time for he was obviously distracted from work by the fact that his wife was dying. Then, in early May, President Butler passed over Oliphant for the deanship at Columbia and the mad scramble for money and bodies began. Griswold tried to tap at least one more foundation[102] and, with the help of Willard, played "pigs in clover" with the various disaffected Columbia faculty,[103] while Hopkins's then Acting, soon to be permanent, President, Joseph S. Ames, worried about the security of financing[104] and Moore worried about the effect on his life of that insecurity.[105] Willard, making his first deal in his new role, and Griswold finally decided on Cook, Oliphant, Marshall, and Hessel Yntema, who as a junior replacement for Moore was to be paid only $10,000 and to work up to the $15,000 that all the others were to be paid.[106] Griswold, Willard, and a group of the Trustees and local citizens[107] agreed to underwrite the expenses of the Institute in the amount of $75,000 and assured the faculty that $3 million in endowment, an amount at then current capitalization rates sufficient to double that income, would be available within a year.[108]

Exactly what the balance of the agreement was is hard to say. For example, whether Hopkins had added four tenured faculty to its ranks is unclear. Cook once said his appointment was for a "limited period of time," the point of the regular appointment being that it protected his Carnegie pension.[109] Though Cook's actual appointment was not for a term,[110] Marshall's appointment was for five years "at first,"[111] and Griswold said Hopkins's commitment was for three years.[112] Likewise, while all agreed that the entity they were forming was to have a governing board consisting of Hopkins's President and the four scholars,[113] that governing board never seems to have met. And though the Trustees, and not the four scholars, committed themselves to take active steps to raise an endowment of $3 million,[114] what the four members of the "originating group," an intentional invocation of the four founders of the Hopkins Medical School, committed themselves to do beyond "research" was not apparent. The *Baltimore Sun*, parroting the University's press release, indicated only that at the outset there would be no students and that the faculty would study "criminal laws in the light of modern social science thought," "the law in relation to business," and "the activities of legislative bodies."[115] The *American Bar Association Journal*, parroting that same release, suggested that "the faculty . . . [would] concentrate on their own research problems and upon the formulation of their course for future action."[116] In a real sense both were right.

IS THERE ANYTHING remarkable in the founding of the Institute of Law such that I may be pardoned for this shaggy dog story or fish on a plank recipe? In one sense it is but another version of the stories of drift and default and accident that Willard Hurst keeps drumming into our heads.[117] But, in another sense, the story is a significant one for evaluating the importance of university or at least Hopkins's support for Oliphant's idea about the desirability of creating a community of scholars engaged in the nonprofessional study of law.

Start with this basic proposition: no one got what he wanted when the Institute was established. Griswold and Willoughby wanted a graduate department devoted to progressive law reform. Theirs was to be a school of advanced teaching and research that would provide the information necessary to modernize American law. Cook wanted a Hohfeldian school of jurisprudence that would first consider what it was to be scientific and then follow out a new functional curriculum geared to that scientific examination of the law. His was to be a school for training practicing lawyers, skimming off the best of the crop to pursue the highest type of legal research and obviously to spread the word to other law schools. Morawetz wanted a training school for restaters. His was to be a school where rules were clearly stated and social and economic policy eschewed. And Hopkins wanted the law school it had hoped for since 1910. Instead, Ames and Willard, the new team at the helm, got an indescribable thing unlike any other piece of that basically tiny university[118] (and a fundraising obligation to boot), and everyone at the Institute got a chance to try out the ideas about "scientific research" in law that Cook had been trumpeting for six years.

Unfortunately Cook's ideas were a part of the problem. While they had the advantage of preserving the law professor's professional identity, they also had the disadvantage of making conservative lawyers like Morawetz and Root just a little uneasy. And they offered absolutely no innate direction for research beyond that provided by a method so general it ruled out only pure philosophical speculation and *maybe* traditional boundary maintenance based on case parsing of the kind Cook did at the beginning of his career. All good men and true could agree with Stone that this traditional activity, "the Ames contribution," was "a valuable one in its day, but we have been ready for the next step a long time."[119] However, it was left to Cook, Oliphant, Marshall, and Yntema to decide what that next step was to be, to develop *a* program and execute it. Given the nondirectionality of Cook's ideas about scientific method, all these men had to bring to the question was their own dissatisfaction with legal education, a dissatisfaction even Morawetz shared.[120]

Still, beyond their common dissatisfaction with legal education the four men did share one thing. They agreed that each faculty member was to head up a "practically independent" research unit. How that fact would help them with the job of developing a plan is hard to see, except in one perverse respect. The education of three of the four participants, as Cook said over and over, fitted its students only to parse cases and concepts,[121] an activity that Cook also admitted "a very large part of . . . [his] own energy would go into."[122] Sharing that education would bring to the enterprise some commonality. However, all the plans to date had provided for studying, for example, "the law in relation to business" and "criminal laws in the light of modern social science thought." If three of them were to follow where their training led them, who would look into the affairs of the businessmen and criminals? The matter, of course, might be simple. If one looked at the one example of a functional study of the law in relation to business that was always used in Cook's materials[123] — Oliphant's study, "The Theory of Money in the Law of Commercial Instruments" — one would notice some nice theory and some interesting assertions about commercial practice but absolutely no facts about such practice and no sources cited beyond cases, statutes, and traditional legal commentary. If this was scientific research, then maybe all could engage in it, but if so, this surely was not a matter of "taking to the field" as Clark had sent Samenow to do.

That it was not clear what kind of a program would emerge from the work of the originating faculty only made more crucial the question of whether Hopkins would accept and nurture any program that ultimately came from one of its trustees and not from its faculty. On this question there was little evidence beyond what the budget documents suggest that Hopkins expected to get for its trouble. Beginning with Willoughby's first draft, the chief items for which endowment support was sought were "men and library."[124] This vision was not very different from that behind Herbert Baxter Adams's Department of History forty years earlier, with its seminary room and the "studies in" series.[125] Just how $3 million, a figure that suggests that Hopkins still wanted a school like one of those proposed,[126] was going to pay for any empirical work *and* for a faculty of somewhere between eight and sixteen[127] is more than a little difficult to understand. So what Hopkins expected was no clearer than was what the originating faculty would do. Whether those circumstances made a difference only time would tell.

Making Sense of an Institute: 1928–1929

When the four faculty members of the newly formed Institute of Law assembled in Baltimore in the fall of 1928, they had before them three tasks. The first, the task of deciding what they as the Institute were going to do, they knew and accepted. The second, the task of raising an endowment for the Institute, they knew but denied was their obligation. The third, the task of trying to figure out whether there was a theory that could make sense of whatever program they adopted, they probably did not realize. And so they focused on the first task. This task was not, however, just a matter of figuring out how to put the left foot in front of the right. A formal program had to be worked out, if only because of that pesky second task. If an endowment were to be raised, it would be raised with the aid of a program document and, whether or not the four had the "obligation" to raise funds, they alone could specify, which for practical purposes meant write, that program. Doing so was, in part, a matter of pure organization and to that task Marshall turned.[128] The group would, he proposed, work as a committee of the whole, as had the faculty at Columbia during the curriculum study, on the basis of detailed typed reports held for later discussion,[129] and he began churning out such reports with the clear purpose of making concrete the Institute's program.

As Marshall saw it, given that the group's "assumption" was importance of "law-in-action — the human effects of law," the group needed to "keep close to life and to reality."[130] Thus, the Institute should emphasize "experimental, objective inquiry" for which one would need "several types of experts: field workers, statistical workers, clerical workers; masses of raw materials; [and] conferences, cooperation with various individuals and institutions," an expensive program, but one having "*practical* bearing and effect upon the field of social control."[131] Marshall knew how this emphasis limited the selection of problems and how costly was "the inductive gathering of social data."[132] To drive home questions of cost, he produced lists of needed faculty[133] and a draft budget for not a $3 million but a $7 million endowment to support a faculty of six to ten, a group of associates and assistants of ten to thirteen, and support staff of sixteen.[134] Curiously, at the same time that he created his grand project, Marshall questioned the assumption of "team work" and "organized" research, pressed the importance of the "lone wolf" investigator,[135] and recognized that Yntema[136] wanted to translate the Year Books and he [Marshall] wished to create teaching materials.[137] So again there was that question, Who was going to do the work of the grand projects on "social control"? That was not clear, but what was clear, was that so long as Oliphant was around there would be no shortage of such projects.

Oliphant put his research assistant on the subject of "justice and the poor," and she turned up nine projects including *in forma pauperis* statutes and a survey of the kind of claims low-income people had.[138] Simultaneously Oliphant produced a list of thirty-five projects ranging from a "job analysis and technique for preparing briefs containing non-legal social science material,"[139] through "do we have a crime wave," differences in divorce outcomes when children are present, the Japanese adoption of the jury system, "educational campaigns to prevent legal mishaps," courthouse structure and curing long transcripts on appeal, to the effect of the income and estate taxes on the form of the business unit, and the effect of utility rate structure on "social energy" and the location of industry.[140] Marshall threw in law and accounting,[141] Cook offered courts of specialized jurisdiction, modern legislation and "the small loan problem,"[142] and staff members contributed too.[143] Outside academics were likewise surveyed for their suggestions,[144] though none really had any significant ideas.[145] And to fill out the pattern, a systematic survey of the research actually being undertaken in the United States was begun.[146]

By December an enormous fundraising document, written primarily by Marshall, but contributed to by all, was complete in draft.[147] Oliphant, who could not have written it had he wanted to, since he had spent all fall writing up a summary of the results of the Columbia curriculum study,[148] nonetheless critiqued it carefully. He noted that the work of preparing the document had brought the group "face to face" with its "central problem" which he formulated variously as an inability to specify "how we are to go about making any improvement in the now prevailing conditions in the formulation and administration of law" or, more trenchantly, "we do not state what we are going to do" except for the preparation of teaching materials or improving "the methods and facilities for research." More devastatingly, he opined that others could easily read the document and conclude that "Oliphant and Cook are riding their method hobbies while Oliphant and Marshall are up to their old job of laying plans for somebody else to do some work." "Our phrase, law-in-action, and all of our synonyms for it add noth-ing to Pound's 'Sociological Jurisprudence' nor do we advance the matter by talking about 'vital problems' or 'social significance . . .' so long as we do not attempt to state of what the vitality or significance consists."[149]

Unfortunately, Oliphant's own statement of what "law-in-action" was did little more than emphasize the truth about his method hobby.[150] So his cri-tique had little impact on the ultimate document that was sent out to dozens of hopefully interested lawyers, judges, and academics in February 1929.[151]

That document consisted of a foreword jointly signed by Goodnow and Griswold and a statement with ten appendixes by the faculty. The fore-word tracked earlier fundraising documents in emphasizing that the Institute would study "law as it is and as it ought to be" in such a way as to be "objective and experimental in method, practical in approach, and coopera-tive with the other social sciences in plan and execution." After noting the "increasing bulk, conflict and confusion of law" and the "changed [social] conditions" of the day, it carefully set aside claims that practicing lawyers, "the professional law school," the American Law Institute, legislative bodies, judicial councils, or "university departments in the social sciences" might already be doing the Institute's work and emphasized the appropriateness of Hopkins as a site for the Institute, including the lack of "pressure . . . to secure quick results." It then concluded by affirming that any "approach to the great and almost uncharted area of legal research must be made with care and foresight," and that members of the faculty, "fully conscious of this," had "limited the scope of their initial program to proposals which have the three essential requirements of promising intrinsically valuable results; of being capable of accomplishment at the present time; and of being of such a character as will facilitate the future expansion which is desirable and necessary."[152]

Unfortunately, the faculty's "Immediate Program" showed little conscious-ness of this care and foresight. After noting that "the *permanent* program of the Institute should be matured slowly and after careful experimentation," it emphasized that there were "so many opportunities for constructive work in social engineering and for fundamental research in social organization that there is embarrassing abundance of opportunity for a vigorous *immediate* program of action."[153] This program was to consist of "continuing scientific analysis both of the basic functions of law and of its deficiencies in perform-ing those functions"[154] and two other "major activities" "reasonably limited in scope": "(1) the training of high grade personnel and (2) scientific research looking definitely toward analysis of areas of major maladjustment, toward stimulation of the flow of scientific data, toward greater integration of law with the other social sciences, and toward the improvement and utilization of scientific method."[155] The first activity was quickly disposed of with all detail relegated to an appendix. It was the final tombstone of Cook's law school.[156] The second was more difficult and hardly reasonably limited in scope.

Since, in fact, no one had settled on what he would do and almost everything of substance going on was admittedly underway before the Institute was formed, the best the group could offer was to lay out "principles" for the choice of future projects and to give examples of possible projects. The principles identified were three: "the availability of personnel," said to be a "major" problem; the "social significance of the subject matter," said to be important because the Institute was "vitally interested in the study of the human effect of law," and "the scientific significance of methods and techniques," said to be important because "the judgments on social and legal questions should rest, as far as reasonably may be, upon objective data rather than upon unanalyzed subjective attitudes." Somehow these three principles generated five types of research projects each complete with examples. First, for "projects lending themselves readily to realistic treatment and to keeping close to practical affairs," "projects which promise to yield results of practical value in social control," the faculty listed accident litigation, specialized tribunals such as small-claims courts, commercial arbitration, bankruptcy, and modern legislation. Next, for "projects looking toward making available greater qualities of dependable comparative data," there was the collection of "detailed histories of typical pieces of litigation," the survey of "the judicial machine in . . . some . . . state" and the business of legal aid societies. For "projects involving the use of the experimental method," there were listed only a comparative study of "the legal and practical position of boards of directors" and the hope to try "experimentation under controlled conditions." Thereafter came "projects looking toward the improvement of existing techniques," which included the study of common-law remedies, the gaining of "an understanding of what is involved in scientific thinking," "the preparation of materials of instruction which fuse law and accounting," and the study of "available procedures for getting non-legal social science materials before the courts." And lastly, for "projects looking toward a greater integration of law with the social sciences," there were identified a study of employment agency charges, the study of new industries such as radio broadcasting or aviation, and the legal and economic position of management in business and the whole field of trade regulation, both of which were also targets for the preparation of materials of instruction.[157]

Although each of these five kinds of projects was the subject of a separate appendix, little in the way of plan or information could be derived from these attempts at amplification.[158] And a careful reader would have noticed something curious. Despite assertions about the importance of "keeping close to practical affairs" for an institute "vitally concerned with the human effects of law" and largely interested in experimental, objective, realistic inquiry, four of the five projects actually listed as being underway were the purest of library research: Yntema's study of common-law remedies and Cook's, of scientific method, and Marshall's preparation of materials on law and accounting and Oliphant's, on trade regulation.[159] Even more curious was the fact that, while all of the proposed projects that were not obviously methodological or pedagogical in nature could be identified with one or another of the faculty, only two fit at all with known previous interests of anyone. For example, although he had suggested the topic, Cook had never taken any interest in specialized tribunals; similarly Marshall had no preexisting interest in surveying the judicial machine or Oliphant in commercial arbitration or bankruptcy or legal aid. Even the two exceptions are themselves illustrative. It is difficult to see exactly how Oliphant would head into the field, as Clark's research assistants had done, to study modern legislation regulating business, just as it is difficult to see in what field Marshall would find data on the legal and practical positions of boards of directors.[160] Both were classic library projects that easily might be supplemented with a few interviews. Of course, both might be turned into quite mammoth interview projects,[161] but there was nothing in the description of either project to suggest that such would be the case. Thus, exactly where the impetus to study the human effects of law would come from was not obvious on the face of the document.

Be that as it may, the document was done, ready for the professional fundraiser, the John Price Jones Corporation, hired by Hopkins to raise money for the University in general and the Institute in particular,[162] to do its magic with. Copies were sent to foundations,[163] lawyers, judges, and academics.[164] The responses of the lawyers and judges were used to select members of a national advisory committee, and these responses, suitably laudatory after being suitably edited, were subsequently published as another fundraising document.[165]

All of these preliminaries out of the way, it was time to set to work. Doing so was, of course, more complicated than might at first seem to be the case. Not only was the question of what to do an open one but so too remained the not unrelated question of what resources there would be to work with. The likelihood that there would be an endowment within a year as had been hoped the previous spring was rapidly decreasing even as the Hopkins administration was looking for a budget from the Institute for the following year. The task of assembling the budget and thus possibly firming up faculty activities fell to Cook, who had been appointed Director for a year[166] under a system, an outgrowth of the troubles at Columbia,[167] where each faculty member would take the job for a year in rotation.[168] Cook had each member draft and circulate a personal budget. The returns disclosed some truly grandiose plans. Marshall wished to try "to visualize a 'functional' society" and study "business organization and management and/or control in relation to" such a society, a project that he conceded might be "fairly 'general.' "[169] Not to be outdone, Oliphant wanted "to blast out some general maps of the whole field" of "the 'administration of justice' — whatever that means."[170] Each document had more ideas in it than time available, yet each author managed to pare his wish list down, subject to the availability of funds and personnel. Marshall planned to study the rayon industry;[171] Yntema, common-law remedies, Roman law, and the comparative conflict of laws;[172] Oliphant, materials on trade regulation;[173] and Cook, legal method.[174] And yet even these choices were hardly definite for, as Oliphant candidly admitted, he could "state fifty other projects equally useful and inviting so no skies will fall" if his chosen activity was not done.[175]

While budgets were being prepared, Oliphant[176] met with a group of New York lawyers led by Edward S. Greenbaum who were interested in collecting the "life histories" of cases in order to learn the reasons for the cost, delay, and uncertainty of litigation.[177] In his budget, written after that meeting, Oliphant noted that he planned to "lend a hand" in that project which, he explained, would primarily be carried by "Greenbaum and his crowd."[178] Just how Oliphant and Greenbaum managed to get together is unclear, but another curious, though more easily explicable, thing happened about this time. Carrington T. Marshall, Chief Judge of the Ohio Supreme Court, Chairman of its Judicial Council, and Leon Marshall's older brother, asked the Institute to help "a state judicial council which is engaged in making a survey of its judicial machine."[179] Yet this project was hardly central to Marshall's activities for he did not even list it in his plans for the next year.

Too much should not be made of these straws in the wind. Such ideas were to be found everywhere at the time, as Clark's activities indicate. Indeed, about this time Cook was fiddling with a similar idea, a comparative study of English and Maryland practice with respect to settling issues before trial, a project that Maryland's Chief Judge, Carroll T. Bond, was interested in.[180] And Yntema's research assistant, George H. Jaffin, a recent Columbia graduate, who came with the group to Hopkins, rather than pursue more traditional graduate study at Columbia,[181] proposed a study of the diversity jurisdiction of the federal courts, which contemplated "a statistical study of . . . [diversity] litigation at the source — the trial court."[182] Simultaneously everyone was moving in several directions at once. Oliphant planned a study of employment agency practices, following a Supreme Court decision holding an attempt to regulate their fees unconstitutional.[183] And Cook tried to formulate a proposal to study the defense received by poor persons accused of crimes, a study he planned to leave to "a man of first rate ability, with experience both in practice and teaching," hired specially for the event, though at one-third of his salary.[184]

Such rather abstract scheming continued until Goodnow, Willard, and Griswold met with officials of the Rockefeller Foundation in late spring. The trio came to collect on Flexner's assurance, given four years earlier before his "retirement,"[185] that the Rockefeller philanthropies were very interested and willing to discuss large grants.[186] They spoke on the basis of an artfully contrived position paper that emphasized research, tried both to sidestep the question of who would be added to the faculty and to provide assurance that good people were available, and attempted to avoid critical discussion of professional legal education or of research plans at Harvard and Yale and, at the same time, to sell its own project.[187] Unfortunately, they walked into a discussion about Hopkins's use of past funding from Rockefeller and the relationship of such funding to "the program of the University" as evidenced by current requests.[188] The men did their best to make sense out of the various proposals,[189] and thereafter to turn discussion to their request that the Foundation contribute about $4.5 million to Hopkins, including capitalization of the $75,000 per year guarantee offered by Griswold and others out of a total budget of $7.5 million for the Institute. However, this topic only further upset Foundation officials who noted that, if subsequent fundraising failed, the University would simply be transferring its obligation under the guarantee to the Foundation, having raised nothing more than a pledge of the cost of a building. These officials were not calmed by Goodnow's assurance that local endowment would be forthcoming once the "nucleus of the Institute were stabilized and the prestige of Foundation approval secured." Rather they suggested that "stabilizing the initial stage of development" was the University's job since it "had committed itself by the initial guarantee."[190]

A formal, cold letter from the president of the Foundation, emphasizing, at the cost of some honesty to the record, that no promises had been made, followed.[191]

This disastrous meeting led to a new round of minimum or "bare bones" budget making.[192] The overall total was reduced by about 10 percent to $107,000,[193] an amount still well over the amount of the Trustees' guarantee. Nevertheless it was promptly approved by the University.[194] The individual budgets showed that the Foundation's cold water had brought a limited amount of closure with respect to projects to be done. Cook, of course kept alive the conflicts and legal method books, but now he added work on, and isolated assistants for, "the function of pleadings in bringing out the issues for trial," a study to be conducted with Chief Judge Bond, and a study of small-claims courts.[195] Oliphant scrapped work on the materials on trade regulation and settled on helping with the New York survey and a similar survey of "the items of business" coming into typical law offices.[196] Yntema kept his work in Roman and comparative law, conflicts of law and legal history, but adopted Jaffin's project on the diversity jurisdiction.[197] Only Marshall's work seemed no more definite; he proposed to look quite generally at the legal and economic situation of modern management in large-scale enterprise and added on a patent study that was dependent on the talents of a specific research assistant.[198]

Oliphant, always alive with suggestions, saw the problem with the Foundation as encompassing skepticism over whether the faculty would "produce" and thus whether it might thus be better to support "established schools." He proposed to answer these questions, "within the limitations of our present funds and the time at our disposal," by concentrating the efforts of himself and his colleagues on collecting "a few . . . distinctive bodies of basic field data" that could be obtained by using "a large group of persons" who "without cost" could be "put to work gathering . . . [that] data . . . by means of questionnaires." The idea would be "to help each other do the initial planning of the questionnaires" and then each be given full authority and responsibility to "get one of . . . [the] questionnaires into rough working order and (if possible) to get *some* returns trickling in by November" when the Rockefeller Foundation Trustees would meet to discuss the Hopkins application. As possible subjects for this enterprise he presented his usual astonishing array of projects, including "What is the American Lawyer and what is his place in American life?," taxation of interstate corporations, defense of the poor, forfeiture of real and personal property in installment sales, management contracts, and courthouse architecture.[199] But his colleagues were not moved to act on his suggestions[200] and the year moved to a close.

WHICH IS NOT to say that nothing but planning and administration got done during the year. Much of each continued to occupy everyone's time after the Rockefeller Foundation meeting.[201] But some scholarship got started or completed as well. Much of this scholarship obviously antedated the founding of the Institute.[202] And some was an example of pure puffery.[203] But two completed projects were of significance. The first was the mailed questionnaire survey of legal research in the United States that Oliphant had set his research assistant to doing in early fall.[204] Although the results were hardly surprising, the overall picture of limited work and that work largely in doctrinal areas possessed a certain real verisimilitude.[205] The other was the publication of a translation of a book by a French political economist Jacques Rueff, *From the Physical to the Social Sciences*, the methodological "bible" among all the juniors at the Institute.[206]

Rueff's little book asserted three things: truth is discovered as a matter of the coherency of related propositions tested by principles of identity and causality; scientific truth is relative to what is known at a time and place; and causes are explanations or rationalizations or hypotheses good only so long as they satisfactorily explain the phenomena in question. From these three assertions he concluded that the physical sciences and the social sciences alike share one common method and so are equally sciences. This established, he then shifted to the point of the book, the proposition that both mathematical economics and ethics were sciences.[207]

Oliphant and one of his research assistants attempted to take these ideas and apply them to law. His argument was simple. He began by asserting his conclusion that "there is now no such thing as a science of law unless one is willing grossly to abuse the word 'science.'" He chose not to defend this conclusion directly but instead he immediately began to identify three methods of judicial decision making in novel cases—the transcendental, or decision based on a major premise founded on "principle"; the inductive, or decision based on a major premise derived from an examination of decided cases; and the practical, or decision based on a major premise founded on "policy" or commonsense experience. Oliphant proceeded to attack the first method on the ground that "for any case wherein there is a clash of two groups having conflicting interests, two conflicting major premises can always be formulated, one embodying one set of premises, the other embodying the other." This ability is founded on the fact that "[t]hose of us who have different and conflicting interests know social 'reality' differently," so that this method of decision shows "fundamental futility." He then attacked the second or inductive method as Cook had, on the grounds that, unless the decided case was included in the phenomena on which the induction was based (in which circumstance the case was not novel), the premise induced could not cover the case to be decided. Then, rather than turn immediately to the third method, Oliphant summarized. "Both of these two logical approaches . . . beg the question they are set to solve. . . . In each case, the decision reached will depend on the major premise adopted. This in turn will depend upon which of two conflicting interests will be served." Deciding by choosing premises "is not objectionable as method; the abuse lies in applying logic in the proper sphere of the empirical. When logic is so applied, there is nothing to insure that the major premise chosen bears any relation to prevalent social values — the essence of justice."[208]

Exactly what Oliphant meant by this argument was anything but clear as the presence of two conflicting interests tends to undermine the notion that there is *a* "prevalent social value" and the subject to be investigated in "the proper sphere of the empirical" was completely unspecified. Oliphant may have recognized at least the latter part of this deficiency for thereafter he asserted, as Cook had before and Dewey before that, that the "proper function" of syllogistic argument was "not to prove the conclusion desired, but to make explicit what is already implicit in one's position on a question." Thus, since the syllogistic process was "perfectly automatic, new knowledge must depend primarily on the phenomena selected for correlation and explanation." As a result, it was "imperative to agree upon what the phenomena are" and, in particular in the social sciences, "to concentrate upon an order or range of phenomena enabling us to deal impersonally, and, so far as possible, objectively with factors hitherto regarded as necessarily subjective and imponderable." Oliphant conceded that "[i]t may well be that substantial agreement upon social phenomena can never be reached" and thus that the social sciences will forever differ from the natural sciences where "the extent of . . . agreement . . . [upon what the phenomena are] accounts for the degree of solidarity of thought." Still, since, as Rueff had argued, "causal explanation is the only one the human mind understands" and "the process of explanation [in the physical sciences] proceeds from the observation of phenomena to the 'creation' of causes," progress in the social sciences, including law, necessitated concentrating on studying a range of questions on which agreement could be had as to what the phenomena are.[209]

If this argument cleared up one of the previous problems — "the proper sphere of the empirical" — still there remained the questions of how agreement, even limited agreement, on what phenomena were was to help in the "creation" of causes and of how the causes so created related to deciding cases. Oliphant ignored these questions and instead picked up where he had left off with his third method of legal decision, the practical. This method was not attacked directly, rather it was characterized as relying "on 'common sense' — a sort of intuition . . . which assumes to know how to decide the practical questions of life merely as a result of having lived in life." Oliphant then asserted that, when decisions under the first two methods were not the product of "the operation of sheer chance," they were the product of "the operation of practical factors . . . conscious or unconscious." Thus, all three methods of decision were in reality the same, though only in the third were "practical considerations" "consciously" undertaken and in none were such considerations looked at "methodically." As a result "so far as law has an empirical branch, its precarious existence is largely either unsuspected or is the haphazard product of a 'common sense' empiricism which professes no order and no methods" and therefore, "[u]nless . . . one is prepared to call a body of learning which has substantially no empirical branch or techniques a science, there is no science of law."[210]

In Oliphant's work one could see bits and pieces of Cardozo on *The Nature of Judicial Process*, Cook on logic, scientific method, and law and maybe a bit of Oliphant's own previous work on legal education. Hints of what would be Llewellyn and Frank on judicial decision making could be found as well. Still, these were not the important parts. What was important was the fact that one could draw out of this welter of ideas an argument that relied on an identification of the empirical with the scientific that Cook had not made.[211] Beyond that the details were only confusing, though often suggestive. Half a century later the reader cries out for the distinction between relations of identity or class membership like those that are central to syllogistic reasoning and relations of causality, but of course to make such a distinction, even if available to Oliphant, would have undermined his clear desire to shift legal discussion from exercises in classification to questions of cause and thus consequence. Yet, without such a distinction, just exactly what was to be investigated and why that investigation was to be empirical was radically unclear.

The admission that law was not a science but a species of handicraft, as Langdell derisively put it,[212] or an art like fencing or dancing, as Veblen observed,[213] would not have made a great deal of difference for practical affairs, unless one followed the implicit advice of both men and evicted its study from the University. That, of course, would have been a serious problem for legal academics like Oliphant and the Hopkins faculty. Yet to investigate the practical consequences of adopting a rule of law, the implicit, though unstated, subject for empirical inquiry and an admittedly causal question, would say nothing about how to decide a novel case unless one assumed an "all-men-of-good-will" ethics, an assumption that the assertion of the existence of conflicting premises based on conflicting values made dubious. And, the notion of concentrating empirical efforts in areas where agreement could be had, offered little more promise, since those areas were unlikely to spawn novel cases unless one took seriously Oliphant's often stated, but never elaborated or defended, notion that much legal principle was "medieval"[214] and thus that exposure of "modern" circumstances would bring individual decision makers to choose different premises.[215] Still with all these defects the piece had a ring and a pace to it. And, more important, it pointed in a definite direction. It suggested that, as Cook put it elsewhere, "only a small part of the work of the staff of the Institute will be with books in libraries; by far the larger part will be concerned with the difficult, time-consuming, and expensive task of gathering and interpreting the facts concerning the operation of our legal system."[216] That suggestion, together with the choice of projects by some members of the staff, was a hopeful sign. The year's worth of effort had accomplished something.

Starting a Research Program: 1929–1931

During the summer of 1929 when everyone had left Baltimore, Frank Goodnow retired as Hopkins's President. He was replaced by Joseph S. Ames, a physicist who had spent all of his academic life at Hopkins in its college of arts and sciences, peculiarly called the Philosophical Faculty, first as a student, then as a faculty member, finally as the Dean.[217] Only on becoming Provost in 1926 had he assumed any wider affiliation. He was deeply devoted to the University and its vision of being "an institution for advanced work," "not comparable with . . . any other American University." It was, he said, "a place where new ideas are welcome, and where results will be obtained."[218] It was to Ames that the Institute would now report; it brought new ideas and at least Oliphant understood that it needed to show results.

NO MATTER WHAT their budgets said they might do, when members of the faculty drifted back to Baltimore in the fall of 1929, they in fact began to spend increasing amounts of time on the research studies that had been brought to them by Marshall's brother, the Study of the Judicial System of Ohio; by Greenbaum's group, the Survey of Litigation in New York; and (to a lesser extent) by one of their own research assistants, Jaffin's study of the diversity jurisdiction. In so doing they acted as if they were acting on Oliphant's identification of science with empirical inquiry and his emphasis on the need to show quick results.

Of these projects, Jaffin's was the farthest along for he had spent the summer preparing one questionnaire designed to gain the opinions of lawyers who practiced in the federal courts on the merits or demerits of various proposals to modify the diversity jurisdiction,[219] and another designed to learn the reasons why lawyers who brought cases in the federal courts during a two-year period chose federal rather than state court.[220] The former was a wholly innocuous document that might well have helped to determine whether the debate on the diversity jurisdiction was really a fight among a few partisans, with the mass of the profession relatively unconcerned. The other was a rather good attempt to catalog exhaustively the various factors, including time and cost, procedural variations, applicable law, local prejudice, and variation in judicial ability, that might weigh in a decision to bring suit in federal court and then learn which factors counsel thought had influenced the choice actually made. This latter survey instrument posed serious problems of interpretation for it would gather only post hoc rationalization of actions already taken and it missed one significant possibility — status to the lawyer of simply practicing in federal court — but on the whole it would have produced far more light then heat. Yntema sent Jaffin's two documents out for comment just as Clark had done.[221] Little is known about the replies received, although Yntema found that "this step was one well warranted."[222]

Although Oliphant had begun drafting a questionnaire for Greenbaum's group the previous spring,[223] and although that questionnaire had been pretested over the summer and revised several times,[224] it was not ready similarly to circulate for comment until late in fall.[225] Oliphant envisioned a broader project than that Greenbaum had brought to him. It would look at both the importance of "litigation in the whole process of law administration or scheme of regulating life by law," including its importance to the income of practicing lawyers and the factors influencing its incidence and trends in its volume, and the extent and causes of delay, expense, and uncertainty in it. The questionnaire was designed to be filled out by lawyers or their "subordinate or clerical personnel" and was to be limited to "commercial contract and negligence litigation."[226] It was tolerably clear, not unreasonably detailed, though without adequate space for the answers to be supplied, and notable for inquiring as to whether one of the costs of litigation was the destruction of "valuable business relationships of the parties."[227] The project's emphasis was to be "in amassing specific data on a large number of cases rather than gathering all the facts as to a few" in the hope that such a procedure would "afford a sufficiently broad base for reliable statistical inferences."[228] The difficulty of doing any such thing without a sensible sampling technique or an actual census was not noticed by Oliphant and there was no Dorothy Thomas available to point that problem out to him. Still, one could discern that Oliphant had clear hypotheses to test when looking at "the grist as it is ground."[229]

At the same time Yntema and Marshall pushed along the Ohio study.[230] Over the summer support of the Ohio Bar Association had been sought and secured[231] and Jaffin had gone to work preparing a questionnaire.[232] This instrument focused on parties, the type of case, the mode of disposition and amounts recovered and collected some rudimentary information on dates on which various key events occurred.[233] In its narrowness the questionnaire accurately mirrored the twofold thrust of the study: to gain a "comprehensive" view of the administration of justice in the state and "to prepare the way for the installation of a permanent system of judicial statistics," an objective that led to a remarkably detailed listing of types of cases.[234] Two specific studies were to begin the process of acquiring this comprehensive view. The first was the collection and analysis of all of the civil cases (excluding divorce) for which judgment was rendered in the Court of Common Pleas (statewide court of general civil jurisdiction) in Ohio during 1930.[235] The second was the collection and analysis of two past years of cases in the Ohio Supreme Court as well as all cases in the Circuit Courts of Appeals (intermediate appellate court) for that same year 1930. In addition, from the outset hope was expressed that a start could be made on a study of the municipal courts in the larger cities since "from the point of view of the impact of the system of justice upon human welfare, the work of the municipal courts is strategic. Presumably, economic and racial situations are involved which are only sporadically and indirectly reflected in the work of the higher courts."[236]

Since the initial focus of the study was not on the details of litigation procedure, as had been the case in Clark's study, but on types, volumes, and results, the rudimentary nature of the data sought meant that outside critical comment was hardly essential, as it had been for Jaffin and Oliphant, and so the study was announced with some fanfare in December 1929.[237] A week later Yntema suggested that it was time to begin a similar study in Maryland.[238] Cook would head the study and put together a comprehensive plan for the next three to five years, while Marshall and Yntema duplicated in Maryland the work planned for Ohio.[239] With some prodding by Yntema[240] Cook began to work.[241] Two months later, after much finagling, the Governor of Maryland formally asked Hopkins to undertake the study and Chief Judge Carroll T. Bond of the Maryland Court of Appeals, on behalf of the state's Judicial Council, endorsed the idea. And so, just over three months after the Ohio study was announced, its Maryland twin received its fanfare too.[242]

During the three months that it had taken to get the Maryland study organized, real plans had been made. Jaffin again created questionnaires that paralleled the Ohio questionnaires covering law and equity cases (excluding divorce) in the Circuit Courts of Maryland.[243] These forms were to be used for "a year; possibly longer" starting July 1, 1930. Additional studies were projected including studies of divorce, criminal litigation and appeals,[244] as well as a study of small-claims courts.[245]

The same week that the Maryland study was announced Oliphant and Greenbaum finally announced their New York study when they sent out 21,000 questionnaires to New York City lawyers.[246] Unable to collect the endorsements of the study from the local bar associations, they nevertheless assembled personal endorsements from Governor Franklin D. Roosevelt, from leaders of the New York bar,[247] from Judge Cardozo and the presiding judges of the local Appellate Divisions, and from the United States Attorney.[248] Completed questionnaires soon began to come in and in due course the group made plans to use "unlocated" (i.e., unemployed) law school graduates to collect cases from insurance companies, public utilities, and large law offices.[249]

Two months after the announcement of the Maryland and New York studies, the Institute convened a "Conference on Studies in the Administration of Justice" in conjunction with the annual meeting of the American Law Institute.[250] The conference was designed to showcase the Ohio and Maryland studies, though Greenbaum was given the opportunity to read a brief paper on the New York project at the following luncheon,[251] as well as an attempt to interest other state judicial councils to undertake similar studies under the Institute's auspices. But more than anything else it was a defense of the Institute's entire research enterprise.

It may seem strange that an enterprise less than a year old and from which nothing had been published required any defense, but one needs to remember how small the world of elite law schools was at the time and thus how fast "the word" could pass. And Hopkins's work had already been given some prominent knocks. Most notable were those from Felix Frankfurter. Though Frankfurter asserted that he was "deeply sympathetic with what is afoot in . . . [the] Institute," he never seemed to offer the enterprise much support. He refused to participate in Oliphant's survey of research, finding it "a perfectly fruitless endeavor, if not mischievous."[252] Asked to comment on Jaffin's study and questionnaire, Frankfurter pronounced the method of approach "invalid and fruitless," not to mention "in its details mischievous from the point of view of one who desires that these problems be subjected to rigorously scientific critique"[253] and "an index of the direction and the tendencies of . . . [the] Institute" which "seem . . . to violate the scientific ideal to which . . . [it is] committed."[254] And asked to comment on Oliphant and Greenbaum's study and questionnaire he asserted, apparently off the cuff,[255] that the questionnaire was open to the same objections as were offered with respect to Jaffin's diversity jurisdiction questionnaire.[256] All this from a man who asserted he was "not obstructive or negative by temperament," but rather cared "so much about searching explorations into the inadequacies and ineptness of so much of our legal administration" that he disliked "to see effort go in directions that . . . [are] sterile either in their objectives or in their procedure."[257] Others, such as Charles E. Clark, were less given to posturing but only moderately more sympathetic.[258] Exactly what was bothering Frankfurter about the Institute is unclear, but his willingness to share his and others' comments with influential friends outside of Harvard made matters even worse.[259] Perhaps it was simply the fact that the Ohio study was going over ground that the Frankfurter-Pound Cleveland Crime Survey had covered several years earlier and so casting doubt on the "scientific" nature of that study which Frankfurter proudly trumpeted in his introduction.[260]

When Marshall and Yntema began to defend the Institute's research, they emphasized the choice to focus its efforts on "the formulation and installation of adequate systems of judicial statistics" so as to "make available the needed data upon which to base the more specific studies."[261] Yet, quickly, this sensible priority got reversed so that the primary objective was to "get masses of comparative data concerning the grist currently being ground in the judicial systems of several rather diverse jurisdictions," including data on "the individual and social situations out of which cases arise," and the by-product of that effort was the development of "a state-wide system of judicial statistics." And still later a set of specific studies overwhelmed the whole, at least in terms of their number and scope.[262] It was not an auspicious start to any defense.

Marshall's exploration of judicial statistics demonstrated that there was no such thing, at least for civil matters, and so he asserted that the judicial council movement was a hopeful development as it stood as a "sponsor" for judicial statistics. He then argued that statistics should include data on "the human element in each case" and on "the social situations which are relevant" because judicial statistics ought to be collected, not just for court administrators, but for "scholars, judges, legislators and others interested in the improvement of the judicial machine — in ascertaining those points at which some type of readjustment is expedient either because this readjustment will more efficiently serve old social forms and needs or because the readjustment is necessitated by the development of some new social situation."[263] That assertion was fine except that thereafter Yntema all but qualified it out of existence.

Yntema began by defending the use of court clerks as his fieldworkers,[264] then turned to the question of "what information we should secure." Here, he emphasized that the information compiled should relate to both "the actual operation of the machinery of justice" and "the practical effects of the administration of justice upon the individuals affected thereby."[265] Although Yntema asserted that this second aspect of the inquiry was the primary one and that thus "the analysis must basically be worked out in units representing human life," he followed this assertion with a long, seemingly contrary, argument to the effect that analysis "must correspond with the units in which we normally analyze the technical processes of litigation."[266] This shift in focus was acceptable because "certain aspects of the technical legal data . . . reflect more or less the human situation. Especially is this true of the cause of action, which is the form in which the law has traditionally cast life."[267] And so, apparently Oliphant's long plea for a functional curriculum was not all that important; life really did follow law.

The entire mess could have been avoided had both men stuck to their initial position that the terrible state of existing statistics made it essential to develop a baseline of knowledge about an entire "system of the administration of justice." That was, however, not a sexy objective; it was far from examining "practical effects of the administration of justice upon the individuals affected thereby." Perhaps in time the contradictions in the enterprise between the mundane nature of the data and the grand aspirations for knowledge would get resolved.

Meanwhile, Jaffin had been very busy preparing the data sheets for use in the intermediate appellate courts as well as ones for the divorce study and the criminal courts study that were about to begin. Along with this task was that of revising the data sheets in Ohio because the clerks "especially in the larger cities" could not get information on the occupations of the parties,[268] preparing data sheets for a study of the Municipal Court of Cleveland,[269] and designing a questionnaire as part of an attempt to obtain information on the social and economic backgrounds of litigants in divorce actions.[270] At the same time that all these studies were being begun, existing studies were being scaled back, for example, the period for collection of Common Pleas cases in Ohio had to be cut from twelve to six months so that the work of the clerks was not "over-crowded" when work started on the collection of divorce and criminal statistics.[271] Others were recruited to help with the grand project. A study of the cost of litigation, seen in terms of the expenditure of public money in support thereof, had been begun by one of Marshall's research assistants and academics in law in various schools in Ohio agreed to begin some of the special studies that were contemplated.[272] In between drafting new data sheets, Jaffin did a little work on the diversity jurisdiction.[273] And Oliphant and Greenbaum started sifting their first results which brought to light the problems of classification of data that had been put off by adopting the questionnaire format.[274]

Over the summer of 1930 the now completed data sheets began to be used to collect a true mountain of data in both Ohio and Maryland.[275] Projected special studies continued to multiply uncontrollably as Marshall was able to induce several graduate students to make Institute studies the basis of their Ph.D. theses[276] and to convince faculty at several schools, not just the law schools tapped earlier, to undertake studies.[277] The New York study also worked at amassing data, expanding its efforts in the direction of examining case files to collect data on satisfaction of judgments, settlement of tort claims, default and summary judgments, and trial calendar management.[278]

Checking, coding, and running all these data occupied much staff time for the entire year so, when it came to report on what had been done, there was the problem of what might be said. Ames cautioned that annual reports should be limited "to facts and omit all promises."[279] The report prepared by Marshall, who was Director for the year, eschewed promises, and almost everything else. Of course, he could do little more, for, in all but two of the Ohio and Maryland studies, a decision had been made to look at cases begun during a given period.[280] The choice was, in effect, dictated by the desire to use court clerks and develop systems of judicial statistics. But that choice also meant waiting through all the time that it took to complete the relevant cases. So Marshall patiently set forth his objectives for the nth time, listed the case reports he expected to have in the fall,[281] listed all the special studies contemplated, offered a brief financial statement, and included copies of the twenty-six data collection sheets Jaffin had created.[282]

In contrast to Marshall's spare presentation, Oliphant produced an elaborate document full of charts and graphs. The reason for this difference was not in the data each had analyzed. Oliphant had collected only 5,500 of the 20,000 life histories of cases he wanted and his research assistants had collected or were still in the process of collecting (it was not clear which) limited procedural data on 100,000 civil cases. Other than the rudimentary analysis done especially for the report, little analysis had been undertaken on anything but a special study of trial calendar practice undertaken with the New York Chamber of Commerce and a committee of the Association of the Bar of the City of New York.[283] Thus, it was clear that the New York study was no farther along than Ohio or Maryland. But there was a reason for the elaborate presentation. This was the first time the Survey of Litigation had made it into print.

Oliphant began this debut by asserting that the point of the study was to examine the common complaint that litigation was "excessively slow, costly, and uncertain as to its outcome." As to the cost of litigation, he supplied figures from "an early stage of a study of the cost of civil litigation in New York City" giving $17 million as the total governmental outlay; figures from municipal court cases, "which are probably not far from representative," showing that for claims of $100 to $600 the cost of litigation for both plaintiff and defendant was about one-third of the amount at issue; and a table, based on a year's worth of city court judgments and 44.41 percent of a year's worth of supreme court judgments, showing that only 8.9 and 17 percent respectively of those judgments were satisfied in whole or part.[284] For delay he offered figures, "[t]he results of one early probing" of lawyers reports of cases, showing the percent of cases in various courts by elapsed time between filing and final disposition.[285] For uncertainty the best Oliphant could do was a quote from the report recommending the founding of the American Law Institute, though he did suggest that there was a "large number of factors which observation and experience point to as to contributing to the fortuity of civil litigation." The balance of the report was similar; a collection of probes, assertedly representation figures, expert opinion, and the like, fitted (they were not thrown) together to support a "study, whose product might guide changes, upon the way in which *particular* procedural

rules and structures actually work," so as "to locate with increasing exactitude those points in the total sequence of a piece of litigation . . . at which
(1) delays pile up, (2) costs accumulate and (3) factors causing uncertainty of
outcome enter."[286]

Oliphant then described his program for reform. He reasoned that, since
half of litigation was debt collection and a third tort claims, if these two kinds
of cases could be "treated as to be eliminated or promptly disposed of, court
congestion and delay would largely disappear, with costs and uncertainty
reduced."[287] And, as "hypotheses for study," he suggested that "the number
of groundless accident *cases brought* and the number of groundless *defenses
asserted* in collection cases should be reduced"; that since collection litigation "lends itself to ministerial treatment," such treatment should be made
"more general and expeditious"; that much of the accident litigation that can
be disposed of without trial can be disposed of earlier;[288] and that "a most
substantial and readily alterable factor adversely conditioning the functioning of courts is lack of proper housing, modern organization and facilities."[289] How these were or could be treated as hypotheses was not apparent,
but Oliphant plowed on listing and examining in turn three "foundation"
studies that were to be continued, those of cost, delay, and uncertainty; four
"strategic" inquiries (presumably to be initiated), to identify suits and defenses without merit, to find ways to reduce these, to look at "settlements as a
business policy," and to examine contributory negligence; five "crucial" studies (also presumably to be initiated), to identify cases requiring ministerial
treatment, to provide earlier and fuller definition of issues and evidence,
and to examine calendar practice, preliminary hearings, and summary judgments; as well as three "final" studies, to examine collection of judgments,
jury trials, and facilities for judicial business.[290]

If one allows for a deep procreditor bias, most, if not all, of these studies
were quite sensibly described, or perhaps the better word is argued. For,
although there were interesting facts presented along the way and occasionally quite penetrating insights into modern litigation,[291] it was usually the
case that it was unclear what the study might *prove* and occasionally difficult
to see exactly how one might collect data on the issue. One example should
illustrate.

After noting that, in order to understand "the flood of litigation," one
needs first to make a "detailed analysis of the kinds of cases and defenses
making up the stream of litigation . . . and to ascertain the rate of increase or
decrease" of each, Oliphant then opined that "[h]ow changes in social conditions and practices, *e.g.*, the rise of installment buying, affect the work of

courts needs to be understood." He then turned to the need to look at each class of case and defense to identify "the portions of them which should never reach the courts determined by applying as tentative guides such tests as: whether one party habitually wins; whether they typically are disposed of in a way indicating lack of substantial merit and what the tabulated opinions in our reports of cases as to the merits of particular types of actions show." He thus began with a massive but possible statistical project, though not one on which the life histories that he and Greenbaum had collected would provide much help, then he identified an interesting but completely methodologically indistinct project, and finally he proposed a third, possible, if more difficult to operationalize, and more controversial, project, all of which were clearly seen as preliminary to the important question — "Ways to Reduce the Number of Such Suits and Defenses."[292]

And what were the ways to reduce "Such Suits"? Here Oliphant wished to talk about the imposition of costs on losing parties. "How effective in preventing groundless suits is this rule in actual operation? Are unsuccessful plaintiffs having to pay costs?" On this question he offered the results of an examination of judgments for costs entered against plaintiffs in two courts, apparently done by Survey personnel, showing only a quarter or less of such judgments were satisfied and then undercut his own data by noting that "a canvass of the judgment of a number of law firms representing insurance companies in accident litigations yields a composite judgment that only from one to five percent of judgments against plaintiffs for costs in accident litigation are collected." Thereafter he opined that if further study of the rule respecting costs of suit

> confirms this initial indication (and the common opinion) that it is scarcely operating, it is of prime importance to ascertain the reasons for its failure to operate and the modifications required to make it do so. Sample angles of this study which require development: how costs operate in other jurisdictions . . . ; to what extent they now do, or should be made to vary with the actual expenses of the party, the nature of the controversy and the amount involved, therein; how groundless cases may be picked out at an early stage and whether, if such cases are to proceed, the attorneys should be made personally liable for . . . costs unless security for their payment is posted.[293]

So again Oliphant had identified three more projects: the first was probably library research; the second, an exercise, at least as to what "they now do," that could probably be done from the life histories; and the third, if we assume the success of the effort previously noted of identifying groundless cases, absolutely impossible to operationalize except as an experiment, and an highly unlikely one at that. Even more important, of course, by looking only at cases actually brought no one would ever know the effect of the rule in reducing the number of groundless suits since by hypothesis it has failed in that function in every case examined.[294] And so, as the first publication of the Survey came an interesting, massive, but wholly un-thought-out agglomeration of data, hypotheses, projects, and opinions, all with the deep odor of bar association reform projects, whatever be Oliphant's disclaimer that the point of the Survey was "seeking the truth," not "seeking the changes to which it might point."[295] And this, not quickly to show that the faculty could "produce," as Oliphant had indicated was desirable, but after two years effort.

AS SHOULD BE OBVIOUS, since all of the data collection on the court studies was done by others, much of the time of the faculty members of the Institute for these two years was spent in other activities. What were they doing?

There was a certain amount of administration.[296] Cook clearly did not like doing,[297] nor was he very good at, it.[298] Marshall, in contrast, seems to have thrived on it and done fairly well,[299] so that administration flowed smoother after January 1930 when Marshall succeeded Cook as Secretary.[300]

Further attempts were made to rationalize the goings on, principally by Oliphant. He first proposed that the Institute frankly focus its activities on law administration rather than substantive law because changes in law administration were far more effective in changing "the law-in-action" than changes in substantive law, a position that Marshall at least doubted.[301] Later Oliphant proposed that the four divide up their energies so that Yntema would focus on "unspecialized courts," courts of general jurisdiction; Cook, on specialized courts or agencies; Marshall, on business and economics; and himself, on legislation, all in the name of no longer avoiding "basic and apparently delicate questions as to just how the Institute . . . [would] be run" as the group came "to work shoulder to shoulder on administration of social control in a single state."[302] But such grand attempts at creating order slowly died out as order set in by default, as it were. In its place came writing, real scholarship, in some sense the point of having an institute whose faculty was freed from teaching obligations.

What did each choose to pursue? Cook continued to work on scientific method, offering a series of lectures at the University of Illinois Law School and one each at the New School for Social Research and the Brookings

Institute that were said to "form the basis" of the long planned book on scientific method and law.[303] And he managed to get out the first piece of work on the great conflict of laws project in seven years.[304] It was an attack on Story's territorial theory of the conflict of laws that utilized Hohfeld's categories, in modified form, to show that the assertion of jurisdiction by one state over a "thing" always effects the "rights" of persons in another state who have "rights" in the thing and thus that the acts of a state can have effect without the state's boundaries contrary to Story's assertions. He also ac-quired a research assistant who initiated a study of installment sales.[305]

Marshall had done little during the first year other than clean up his old commitments from the University of Chicago's business school.[306] Those commitments out of the way, he kept scouting around for some management or industry to study,[307] and spent much time working to raise money to finance the Ohio study.[308] These two together seemed to keep him busy enough that he turned down Pound's invitation to run a study of the "Eco-nomic and Social Consequences of Prohibition" for the Wickersham Com-mission,[309] though for a prolific writer he in fact published very little.[310] Oliphant continued his eclectic course. He published a piece on labor law[311] and he tried out some ideas on legal education in a brief piece notable only for his recognition that the call for a functional classification of legal mate-rials assumed that "correlating the study of law with the other social sciences will aid in making the law more plastic to changing social conditions and . . . that such increased plasticity is a major contemporary need."[312] At one point he presented a long, thoughtful proposal for studies in legislation that cov-ered a broad range of questions from legislative staffing, through its changing content to its enforcement and effect.[313] And he tried to supervise the Survey of Research and a study of worker's compensation in New York, to get another translation project going and to work on the activities of trade asso-ciations in policing their members' credit payments. He even proposed a study of what we now know as the free press–fair trial issue.[314]

The more prosaic Yntema at first contented himself with pushing along the legal remedies material[315] and plans for the development of comparative law at the Institute.[316] Much of his work was, however, more closely related to the studies. He published a piece on research method,[317] and with Jaffin the first part of the diversity jurisdiction study.[318]

The former, a paper given at the AALS Round Table on Remedies (of all things), was a pep talk for empirical research generally, and court studies in particular, as designed to provide "the description of the actual operation of law, both substantive and procedural, on an observational basis widely representative of varied times and places." But it had a hidden point. It was again a public defense of the Institute's program, this time against Frankfurter's private charge that by focusing on the need to "adapt the law to modern conditions," science, "timeless, universal, uniform for all times and places" was being sacrificed for relevance. Here Yntema sensibly denied the truth of implied dichotomy and emphasized that whatever the subject matter of research, the "university ideal" of free inquiry was the relevant standard, especially since so little was known at the time that "methodological criteria" needed to be "generous and experimental."[319] Unfortunately the latter, designed to be an explanation of the study that the two planned, was overwhelmed by a similar attempt to meet Frankfurter's positions and criticisms.

Frankfurter had argued for the abolition of the diversity jurisdiction on the grounds that, as a practical matter, diversity cases were flooding the federal courts, requiring the appointment of many judges, thus debasing the prestige of the office.[320] He held that the diversity jurisdiction was no longer justifiable on the grounds of local prejudice since the chance of such prejudice was eliminated by the now national economic structure and substantively harmful in that, through the rule in *Swift v. Tyson*, it gave nonresidents an advantage denied to residents. This argument the two found to be oversimplified, in that it ignored the possibility of regional or subject matter variation in prejudice; unfounded, in that it assumed crucial facts such as the actual distribution of litigation; and designed for persuasion, rather than for "scientific purposes." The study of the diversity jurisdiction that Yntema and Jaffin had designed would, it was asserted, supply the missing factual basis of the argument by looking at all the cases, state and federal, in a jurisdiction, both those that could be brought in both court systems and those that could not, in an attempt to find out what, if any, of a range of factors — quality and powers of the judge, character of the jury, substantive law, procedural law, state of the docket, cost, convenience, or lawyer specialization — might account for the choice of one court system over another where choice was possible.[321]

It was a neat research design, if a somewhat too grand undertaking.[322] Unfortunately the design was all but lost in a defense of the choice not to concentrate efforts in the federal courts alone but to deal with lawyers' reasons for choosing one forum over another,[323] as well as an all too ponderous and altogether abstract explanation of the scope of the study, choice of sample, and choice to attempt correlation of variables rather than pure description. There was, however, a punch line to the story and with a punch that could only have been Jaffin's. Frankfurter, relying on a look at the Federal Reporters had estimated that diversity litigation was 27 percent of all litigation. A recheck of this figure yielded a far different proportion of district court opinions and, more important, a check of the Attorney General's Reports turned up still different numbers. In twenty-five years private civil cases had declined in their proportion of the total case load of the federal courts from one-quarter to one-tenth; approximately half of these cases were diversity cases, which thus made up only about 5 percent of total litigation.[324] There was an obvious retort of course.[325] But the starkness of the mistake allowed for the observation that even if, as Pound had suggested, it was foolish to have "faith in masses of figures as having significance in and of themselves,"[326] it was still important to see "that the sample should be appropriate to the purpose and that the sums should be faithfully done. These . . . are not merely statistical precepts; they apply with as much force to the manipulation of the symbols which are words."[327]

It was a sensible lesson, not that there is any reason to believe that anyone had been taught. Had Yntema stuck to his figures, it might have been an even better lesson. But it was the symbols which are words that, however, occupied a good deal of the time of Yntema and also Cook, for both took the hiatus that data gathering provided to get embroiled in what was later to be called the Realist Controversy.[328]

Despite common assumptions that this was a dispute that, *in print* at least, was between Llewellyn and Pound, it began *in print*, somewhat earlier with Mortimer Adler's review of Jerome Frank's *Law and the Modern Mind*.[329] Adler, who was to be paired with Llewellyn in the review,[330] chose to attack Frank's work as an example of "legal realism" and thus to attack, though not in detail, Cook, Oliphant, and Yntema. The review, like Llewellyn's, was all over the place, but made a point of asserting three propositions: first, that Frank's exposition of science as an "empirical procedure, free from the heavy weight of formal logic and untainted by Platonism," ignored an opposed conception of science as a rational activity; second, that his genetic explanation of the myth of legal certainty as "the basic craving for a father-substitute" was, whether true or false, irrelevant to the question of whether legal certainty was a "myth"; and, third, that Frank's denial of the possibility that legal certainty could be found in syllogistic logic, ignored both that formal logic was not an account of "the psychological phenomenon of human thinking" and that there were two sciences of law, one the "law in discourse," the logical development of certainties, formally true arguments for various alternative rules of law, and the other, "law as official action," the empirical development of probabilities, estimates of the likelihood of actual judicial decisions.[331]

Frank liked the review for its "berserker quality."[332] Cook obviously did not and, when Oliphant was unwilling to reply,[333] Cook came to the aid of his former student.[334] Cook ignored Frank's psychoanalysis[335] and focused on science. He expressed doubts that Adler's law in discourse could contain a plurality of doctrines *about law* since purely formal sciences were about nothing concrete, and then asserted that, even if the defined classes that constituted the propositions of the law in discourse were "a useful tool in the development of a real science of law," these classes could be applied only by taking into account their character as empirical generalizations, so that even after agreement was reached on the applicable rule of law, legal certainty would depend on the choice of the category in which to put the facts of a particular case.[336]

Frank, who admitted that his and Cook's aims were "substantially identical" with respect to trying to get lawyers to think like scientists, although he doubted that one could, "by purely intellectual processes, change people into pragmatists,"[337] expressed "biased admiration" for the review.[338] Holmes liked it too,[339] as did Dewey,[340] whose praise "pleased" Cook.[341] Morris Cohen, though in "thorough sympathy" with Cook's position on the need for an emphasis on the factual side of law, tried to get Cook to admit that the rule of law adopted as the major premise of the syllogism in a case determined the actual decision, as a necessary though insufficient condition.[342] But Cook was unwilling to concede even this much, arguing that in any case of doubt, "the judge has read new meaning into the middle term" and thus "has 'made' his major premise as well as his minor."[343]

This question of the determinative force of the choice of the major premise in a case[344] was in large measure the central issue in this debate, for the next attack on Realism came from Cohen, first in an article on Holmes[345] and then in his book, *Reason and Nature*. Cook tackled the book in a brief review.[346] Curiously, Cook was more restrained than in his reply to Adler, making but three important points. First, Cook admitted that, as Cohen had argued, empiricism and rationalism were necessary complements. He nevertheless offered the sensible observation that Cohen "leans very largely to the 'rationalist' side." Second, he noted that, contrary to Cohen's assertion, not all scientists make the assumption that the logically necessary relationships between mathematical expressions of physical phenomena hold true of the phenomena themselves, at least until verified by "observation or experiment." And, third, he reiterated his criticism, stated in the earlier letter, of Cohen's notion that legal rules adopted as premises determine conclusions.[347] Considering the vigor with which Cohen had expressed his views and with which

Cook had earlier entered into academic debate, the reason for the kid gloves was not obvious.

Yntema, who had previously written a quite laudatory piece on Holmes,[348] could not be so brief, so gentle and detached, or ignore Cohen's attack on Holmes, much less avoid taking a few shots at Adler. Unfortunately his rambling, often highly allusive style obscured much of what he said, but a patient reader might have discerned three sensible points. First, he asserted that Adler's law in discourse traded on "the indelible, cultural associations of the concept" of law and appeared "to represent a familiar, postulational mode of contemplating legal problems . . ."; second, he observed that Cohen's critique of empirical legal science, which challenged it "in the name of reason and justice," had failed to see that beneath "its empirical devices" is "the quest of science to ascertain justice"; third, he offered that Cohen's "normative legal science" is, "in effect," "the literary and speculative tradition of jurisprudence" "rationalized." Thereafter, he isolated his argument with Adler and Cohen down to the question of "whether legal science will not profit by objective, detailed, descriptive study," given that a "distinction is to be made between the objective description and its professional use; that judges decide and science asks why; that the verification of theory by fact will not destroy but rather fortify the applicability of norms of Ought in the realm of reform, propaganda, and practical government."[349] One is reminded again of Frank's comment to Cook about changing people into pragmatists.

The balance of the fight was left to Llewellyn, who answered Pound's generalized charges empirically, as it were.[350] The faculty at Hopkins was satisfied at that division of labor. Cook, of course, was in his own way beholden to Pound for his support in the early years and Yntema was a recent Pound student, having completed his S.J.D. under Pound ten years earlier.[351] Oliphant seemed not to care about the entire controversy and, of course, Marshall was uninvolved. This satisfied everyone except George Jaffin, who thought the crew bewilderingly cowardly[352] and took a swipe at Pound in an article he had been working on for several years. The topic was the labor conspiracy cases. In a peroration Jaffin suggested that the doctrine that intentional infliction of injury is actionable unless justified "needs more than formulation; it needs content and until content is injected it remains bare — an empty formula, like Pound's 'balance of interests,' full of 'sound and fury.' What constitutes justification? How do you 'balance' the imponderable interests?"[353]

DURING THESE two years of designing studies and explaining them to others and also of engaging in exciting intellectual controversy while data collection proceeded, the question of financing the Institute and its projects was in some ways nigh onto an obsessive one, though in a real sense the faculty was largely uninvolved. Money was the Trustees' problem. At the same time although there was much activity by the Trustees and the University's President directed at the question of finance, little was accomplished.

In summer 1929 Hopkins was informed that the officers of the Rockefeller Foundation were "disinclined to recommend any grant to the Institute at the present time." The reason apparently given was the one hinted to at the meeting that spring: that the Foundation thought it was Hopkins's obligation to raise the initial endowment given that the Institute was launched on a permanent basis with guarantees rather than permanent funds.[354] The University responded by setting up a fundraising committee of the Board of Trustees headed by Edwin Baetjer, one of the original guarantors of the Institute's finances, and a bachelor, corporate lawyer in Baltimore.[355] The choice was obviously made with the object of liberating the chairman of some of his assets, but it was not clearly otherwise inspired. Baetjer was said to be hostile to "the inductive approach to law" and thus pushed the social sciences out of the funding literature and instead emphasized the Institute as a fact-finding operation. He also was less than satisfied with the composition of the Institute's staff, worrying that no distinguished lawyer or judge was at the Institute,[356] a worry that led to approaches first to Brandeis[357] and then to Cardozo[358] with the surprising suggestion that each leave the Supreme Court and join the Institute.

Baetjer favored discrete approaches to men of established wealth, for example, the du Ponts,[359] and so he ignored a recurrent faculty suggestion that the Institute recruit a group of associates who would pledge $1,000 per year.[360] Such a posture had its costs. For example, his initial approach had been to seek general endowment. But, when one of the du Ponts objected to that approach on the ground that it will be "better" for the Institute "to show its worth under penalty of demise,"[361] the University trimmed its sails[362] with the result that the entire fundraising campaign lost what little coherence it had.[363]

Unfortunately, in addition to the difficulties following from Baetjer's intellectual and philanthropic preferences, he was a less than tireless worker[364] who expected much of others. So, great amounts of faculty time was absorbed creating sample budgets for various potential studies that Baetjer wished to include in the fundraising literature.[365] Still, with the help of Donald Hammond, the staff member of the John Price Jones Corporation assigned to the University for the project, Baetjer got out fundraising literature,[366] managed to obtain a good deal of national publicity,[367] and put together a campaign dinner that featured a speech by Roscoe Pound and remarks by Maryland's Governor and, more than a trifle ironically, Mr. Justice Pierce Butler.[368]

By early spring 1930 the results of fundraising efforts left the University confident enough to approach the Rockefeller Foundation once again. It had, it said, over $1 million in cash and pledges, including $450,000 for a building to house the Institute and $50,000 for a basic library.[369] Unfortunately, when Ames, Griswold, and Willard went to see the Foundation, they learned that the request had been submitted too late for Trustees' consideration that spring.[370] So the faculty, set to putting together another bare-bones budget, this time for 1930–31.[371] The result was a peculiar understanding of economy. Oliphant agreed to cut his request for the Survey from what was needed for expansion to what was needed to keep it in a "reasonably healthy" state,[372] and the group as a whole magnanimously agreed to cut the outlay for research assistants and typists by 10 percent.[373] But against this economy was set the fact that wholly new disbursements, all for the court studies, amounting to $75,000, were planned.[374] Somewhat surprisingly the University approved the entire sum.

The choice to make a grand budget request had been intentional. Marshall had earlier recognized that "conservative (or even sound) financing" would dictate a budget of no more than that for 1929–30, but argued that at that time in the Institute's history "a situation which does not expand runs the danger of a charge of decadence."[375] Marshall's diagnosis was that the group faced "dangers arising from inertia in attacking financial problems" and so he proposed that the group do some fundraising of its own[376] and urged that "active work . . . [go] on through the summer" so as to drive *present activities to completion.*"[377] The group clearly agreed on the need to expand in order to avoid decadence, but it seems not to have thought much of Marshall's diagnosis and prescription, for little was done about fundraising and the faculty dispersed as usual for the summer, Yntema only attending the Social Science Research Council's Conference on Legal Research.[378]

These decisions were troubling to President Ames, especially the budget request well in excess of the guarantee fund. Hopkins's finances already had been badly battered by the Depression and it was not alone.[379] The donor of the building that was to house the Institute was also in serious financial shape and wished to be released from his pledge.[380] And there were other problems. For example, although Ames recognized that Baetjer was a disaster as a fundraiser,[381] Willard would not remove him as chief of the fundraising operation[382] and the Rockefeller Foundation continued to drag its heels pleading the press of other matters.[383] When in fall 1930 it finally acted, it curtly said no for the second time, again emphasizing the need for the Institute to secure permanent support.[384] A somewhat warmer response, tempered by a mysterious reference to "complications which appear to be involved in the present situation," was offered to Marshall, but exactly what good the "general sympathy" of the Foundation for "the Institute's fundamental objectives" was,[385] unaccompanied by some cash, is hard to see.

Somewhat understandably things were allowed to limp along. Thus, even though the success of the fundraising in Ohio was due to the personal efforts of Marshall and others in contacting numerous individuals for small donations,[386] Baetjer still opposed such a method of fundraising[387] and so dignified approaches continued to be made to men of great wealth. Unfortunately, these were netting little cash.[388] For example, Irénée du Pont, though contacted elaborately,[389] quickly concluded that $25,000 was his limit, expressing the helpful conclusion "that if other people of means gave in like proportion, the Institute could be readily financed."[390] A year's worth of work on Secretary of the Treasury Andrew Mellon[391] seemingly netted nothing either. And there was even trouble collecting on a small appropriation from the Maryland legislature given to support the Maryland study.[392] Finally however, Oliphant who had become Secretary/Director of the Institute in January 1931 began to take hold a bit. He turned to fundraising for his Survey of Litigation and, beginning with William Nelson Cromwell,[393] managed to collect pledges sufficient to lay "an effective basis for financing" the Survey.[394] The New York study like Ohio would run on its current, separate receipts for the coming academic year. What the rest of the Institute would run on was by no means clear.

Winding Down the Institute: 1931–1933

In midsummer 1931, after the faculty had scattered as usual, President Ames quite accurately identified the Institute's problem.[395] As he saw it, given all the data that would soon be available for analysis, "our main trouble is going to be to stay alive long enough to reap the fruits which are due us."[396]

During the previous year the Institute faculty had spent almost every penny of the enormous budget that the University had approved. At the same time the bottom had dropped out of the University's endowment when its major asset, an interest in the Baltimore street railway, became valueless with the bankruptcy of that entity.[397] The chaos at Hopkins was palpable and so the academic year had closed without settling on a new budget for the Institute at all.

Given this financial stringency, the point of getting the Ohio and New York studies separately financed was not just that they stood a better chance of getting completed, but also that at least as pro forma matter, it removed at least $25,000 from the Institute's budget.[398] And even a pro forma improvement in the Institute's financial situation was in order when, though within its 1930–31 budget, nevertheless it had run a deficit of nearly $100,000 and its accumulated deficit for three years was possibly $200,000.[399]

The matter of a budget still hung fire in September when, for a change, some good financial news was had. After all the work by Ames and Willard, Andrew Mellon donated $75,000 to the Institute. In response, Ames established a budget ceiling of that amount, on the rationale that the accumulated deficit approximately equaled the pledges in hand, and left the details to the faculty.[400] Making a budget on that basis was not going to be easy as faculty salaries alone totaled three-fourths of that amount, but it was aided by the departure of several research assistants, including the hardworking Jaffin, who acted on their own sense of impending financial disaster or faculty counsel in that direction.[401] Even this cutback in personnel was not enough. Oliphant's optimistic estimate of his ability to raise money for the Survey of Litigation proved to be just that. And so he, with Ames's help, connived to pull off a classic funding scam. He managed to secure a $10,000 "emergency" grant from the Rockefeller Foundation without telling it that funds were being sought from the Carnegie Foundation.[402] Then, with the aid of a letter from Paul D. Cravath,[403] he got $5,000 from the Carnegie Foundation without telling it that funds had been secured from the Rockefeller Foundation.[404]

Almost immediately Ames moved to settle the Institute's finances for 1932–33 and a subcommittee of the Executive Committee was instructed to confer with Marshall on both budget and the question of "what tangible results can be expected within" academic 1932–33.[405] The committee collected some information[406] and was told of the status of the various studies.[407] Although the Trustees had earlier discussed closing the Institute as one way of helping to meet Hopkins's overall financial crisis, the subcommittee recommended continuation at the present budgetary level.[408] Ames struggled with his personal recommendation to the Trustees.[409] He finally settled on a proposal to make Marshall the Director, limit his budget to be no more than $35,000, and "regretfully" advise Cook and Oliphant that it was "not feasible to retain their services beyond October 1, 1932." In the interim salaries were to be reduced to $12,000 per year and staff was to engage in no "re-munerative outside activities." Ames's rationale for at least some of these actions was stated in the penultimate draft. "Present economic conditions . . . have forced upon the University the most rigid economy in administration and policy. . . . Every effort is being made to preserve and maintain, if possi-ble, the efficiency of previously proved and established divisions essential to the whole University."[410] The Institute was not "previously proved," much less "essential to the whole University."

The faculty was informed of at least some of Ames's thinking.[411] Cook and Oliphant sent a letter to Willard recounting in great detail their understand-ing, based on meetings with him, particularly the meetings including Under-hill Moore, of the terms upon which they had been hired, namely as fully ten-ured faculty members.[412] And lines at Hopkins were quickly drawn. Ames recruited the titular leaders of the Faculty of Philosophy, Jacob Harry Hol-lander of political economy and Arthur O. Lovejoy of history, as well as the dean of the Medical School to speak to the Trustees,[413] and lobbied individ-ual Trustees himself.[414] The Faculty Academic Council weighed in,[415] as did individual departments including political economy, engineering, and public health.[416] Support from these quarters was not hard to secure since the rest of the University's faculty had agreed to a 10 percent cut in salaries,[417] which, in the Philosophical Faculty, at least, were not obviously adequate before that cut.[418] Only the tiny Department of Political Science, consisting of Willough-by and one other soul, supported the Institute.[419]

Cook stated his case for the Institute in terms of "that freedom of research which is essential to all sound and fruitful scientific work" and of the Univer-sity's prior commitment to carry on the "experiment," "to study the law in action as distinguished from the law in the books . . . in a truly scientific spirit, untroubled by demands for quick results and quantity output."[420] Ames responded in terms of his opposition to the "policy of running into debt at the expense of the *real* University" and hinted darkly that he had "strong convictions in regard to the whole Institute itself, the character of its work, the quality of its men and so on," that he would rather not put in writing.[421] Then Griswold belatedly weighed in on the side of the Institute.[422]

While the matter hung fire, the faculty put together still another report of its activities over the past three and a half years, a report that it sent to its national advisory committee in an obvious attempt to garner support.[423] The document proudly announced that, although it was "too early to estimate how far The Institute of Law has realized its purposes, . . . its most important contribution thus far has been to indicate the validity of the scientific ideas which led to its establishment."[424] After listing specific achievements,[425] it concluded only that, given its "trained staff and its general position in American legal education, . . . it will be possible within the near future . . . to estimate more adequately the large potentialities of . . . [its] research for the improvement of existing conditions and the advancement of legal science."[426]

Appended to this surprisingly tepid statement was a list of publications, excerpts from recent supportive correspondence, and a financial statement. While the last two items were unremarkable, except insofar as one disclosed to the knowledgeable reader that Marshall had raised approximately $150,000 for the Ohio study,[427] the first was a seventeen-page list of publications by the faculty and research assistants in the past three and a half years and those expected in the next six months. It was an impressive list, at least if one ignored the fact that it ranged through scientific method, the conflict of laws, undergraduate education in business, economics, and the secondary school social studies curriculum, in addition to the Ohio, Maryland, and New York projects. What indeed did hold the Institute's program together?

In the end, of course, the matter was compromised. The Board voted to reduce the amount available for the operation of the Institute for 1932–33, to $64,000, to terminate the Institute thereafter unless funds for its continuance were secured by the start of that academic year, and, if such funds were not endowment funds, "to determine whether the Institute shall be closed or be operated on some reorganized basis."[428] Marshall was made the Acting Director for the duration, replacing Yntema who had succeeded Oliphant in the alphabetical rotation.[429] All the faculty took a salary cut to $10,000.[430]

Marshall took over at once, first doing damage control[431] and then turning his attention to fundraising. From the beginning there was dark news. The Rockefeller Foundation, which had previously been informally approached by Ames for an emergency grant for one year,[432] turned down a real application for three years at $50,000, even though the Foundation privately concluded that "[i]t would appear to be altogether unfortunate for this important undertaking to collapse" and that "the undertaking will probably fail at once" without its aid.[433] Marshall and Ames went to the Executive Committee of the Hopkins Trustees with an analysis of this predicament. Marshall opined that there was sufficient money in the budget of the Maryland study except for publication, that New York was likely to be turned over to a group of lawyers Oliphant was organizing, and that Ohio was in fine financial shape. He concluded that no foundation or combination of foundations would endow the Institute or carry it for three to five years or even make grants for specific projects. The same was true for individual donors who would wish to see the central activities covered first.[434] This settled, he identified four options: abandon the Institute, maintain a shell, reorganize on the basis of a small staff and small budget, or continue the status quo but with a limited budget.[435] The Executive Committee, of course, put off any decision and appointed a committee of three, chaired by Willard to work on fund-raising.[436]

Marshall made the rounds of the foundations again and with the same conclusion.[437] He met with the Committee.[438] New plans were developed[439] and new fundraising materials prepared.[440] The futility of it all should have been obvious, but somehow Marshall never seemed to lose his drive or optimism. His colleagues, on the other hand, wrote to the Trustees that they had "come to the conclusion that it will be inexpedient for us to continue on the staff of the Institute of Law after June 30, 1933."[441] If the Institute was to survive, it seemed as if it would be Marshall's Institute.

While teaching at the Northwestern summer school, Cook began the search for a job with a letter to Pound.[442] Yntema had gingerly started that enterprise several months earlier and in the same quarter.[443] How much job hunting the others did is unclear. But the sense of winding down was apparent first in Oliphant's efforts to get his New York lawyers to take over the Survey of Litigation on a permanent basis, an effort that led to the founding of the New York Law Society,[444] then in Yntema's choice to take a leave of absence for the second semester to work on Roman law in Europe.[445] Only Marshall seemed to work on as if something good might yet happen.

And work he did. On the intellectual side he spent much time and energy selling the Institute's classification of offenses so as to make the collection of criminal statistics uniform.[446] And at the same time he worked to keep the Ohio study pushing forward. Much of that work was editorial, for manuscripts were coming in. But some was pure administration too; pushing the mountain of civil case records through processing[447] was a matter of time and money and keeping authors motivated.

There was also the matter of what to do with the Institute. Although the endowment specified in the Trustees' resolution had not materialized,[448] Ames told Marshall that he wished to continue the Institute on some basis.[449] Marshall produced a plan that included bringing in "new faculty."[450] Ames liked the plan in general, if not in detail, and recommended it to Willard,[451] who also approved. But Willard felt that he needed the approval of the faculty as a whole in order to alter the Trustees' previous resolution. Faced with unanimous opposition of a group of senior faculty assembled for the purpose of discussing the matter, Willard was "disinclined to push . . . [it] any further."[452] And so in February the Trustees implemented their earlier resolution.[453] The Institute was dead.

Immediately the gloating[454] and the recriminations started. The recriminations centered around Cook. On the same day that Ames informed the faculty that the Institute was dead, he asked whether the Maryland study could be completed.[455] Cook exploded. Given "the limitations as to funds during the current year and to some extent last year, as well as the character of the work undertaken," nothing of the sort could be done. The Maryland study was to be "not 'just another survey' of a relatively superficial character, but something much more fundamental." There would not even be funds sufficient to process the civil cases, a study that Cook regarded as "the most important of the studies undertaken."[456]

Cook mailed copies of this letter to Willard and Griswold and took the occasion to remind them that he refused to make any complaint or apology "for the form which the plans for the Maryland Study took, based, as those plans were, upon the assumption of adequate time and reasonably adequate funds to do a worthwhile piece of work" and that, when the Institute was founded, they had given promises that there would be no pressure to produce results and that they would provide support when the cry went up that there had been no results.[457] Griswold, who was deeply unhappy at the closing of the Institute,[458] did not reply. Willard tried his best to minimize the question of results but instead chose to rest his case on "the condition of the University, or more particularly . . . the Philosophical Faculty."[459]

Recriminations extended elsewhere. Given the timing of the closure of the Institute there was a question of whether it violated the rules of the American Association of University Professors.[460] As Cook was at the time the group's president, he refused to start an investigation of the matter "because given his office" it would be "impossible" for the other officers to handle it "without involving everyone in embarrassment."[461] That, however, did not stop him from engaging in a running feud with Arthur O. Lovejoy, an AAUP founder and former president, that proceeded in letters delivered indirectly through the Association. Here Lovejoy argued that the Institute's faculty had received quite adequate notice the previous spring and that in any case they never had tenured but only term appointments,[462] and Cook argued that, as Lovejoy had no firsthand knowledge of the relevant meetings with the Trustees, he could not know whether Cook's appointment was tenured or not and that the question was not what his "rights" were but what, given "the unprecedented and totally unforeseen situation," was "fair" for Hopkins to have done in view of the fact that he and the rest of the faculty had given up tenured appointments elsewhere to come to Hopkins and were now "sent out with no prospect of making other academic connections."[463]

Behind Cook's argument there was a real problem. Of the four, Oliphant landed on his feet first. Through a mutual friend he was introduced to Henry Morgenthau, who was to be chairman of the Farm Credit Administration in the new Roosevelt administration, and the day of the President's inauguration he resigned his Hopkins post to become General Counsel to that agency.[464] No one seemed to worry much about Yntema, and Marshall could clearly take care of himself. But Cook's future was a real problem. He was already sixty years old. Although his children from his first marriage were of college age, two years earlier he had married the Institute's librarian–research assistant[465] and his Carnegie Foundation pension would lapse if he did not find a position in an accredited institution.[466]

Though Cook's friends were loyal, they were not necessarily numerous for he had burned a lot bridges in his life. Pound tried once again to find Cook a place at Harvard as well as at Chicago,[467] and both Frank and Pound tried to open up a place at Michigan.[468] Oliphant and Yntema worried,[469] even if, as was probably true, they could do little at the time. But more typical surely was the action of Ames, who though he said he was "doing all in his power" to help Cook,[470] left no evidence of that effort, much less of one of the kind he and Willard made on behalf of Marshall.[471] Indeed, Ames plainly vetoed attempts to keep Cook on in any capacity either as a replacement for Willoughby who was retiring,[472] or even temporarily to complete the Maryland study under the auspices of the Judicial Council.[473] What would happen to Cook was thus a real problem.

CURIOUSLY, during all this turmoil and uncertainty a surprising amount of research got completed. On the Maryland study there were four publications,[474] the New York study produced three pieces of work,[475] and the Ohio study generated a volume of material that was astounding—six studies in each of the two years.[476] In addition reams of data that were not published got processed, coded, and run in all three states.[477]

Individually the four faculty members were productive as well. While pushing along all of the Ohio publications Marshall managed to get out four pieces of his own,[478] including a plan "to get the teachers of law at work finding out what law-in-action in the trial courts really does,"[479] by putting their students to work over vacation collecting case reports in their home counties and then processing the material locally where possible or centrally where not.[480] And though Marshall confessed that he "had rather expected that the professional law school teachers would not see very much in the idea,"[481] he convinced teachers in Iowa, North Carolina, Ohio, and West Virginia to try it out.[482]

The others also pushed along their own projects. Cook published an important piece of the ever receding conflict of laws project,[483] did two more lectures on scientific method,[484] and took time to argue about the nature of formal proof with Jerome Michael.[485] Yntema, who probably did more work on the Ohio study than Marshall gave him credit for, tried to intervene in the diversity jurisdiction controversy with an extraordinarily calm piece analyzing the arguments put forth by all and sensibly concluding that most were irrelevant and the balance unproved,[486] and again tried to intervene, far less successfully, in the scientific method controversy.[487] And Oliphant tried out the parallels between legal and medical education,[488] a bit of debunking on criticisms of law and justice, which was in its own way quite sage,[489] and tried once again to publish a more theoretical defense of the Institute's enterprise.

In this last work Oliphant attempted to meet two arguments against "applying scientific methods . . . to the study of law."[490] The first was "that most of the data indispensable for scientific work on social questions are not facts quantitative in character and, in consequence, lending themselves to precise quantitative manipulation and expression." Here, he argued contrary to Rueff and (implicitly) Cook, that there was not a single scientific method from which there were various deviations but various sciences with various methods some of which, like astronomy and geology, were not experimental but observational. Each science varied in method "because the contemporary problems upon which . . . [each is] engaged happen to require different degrees of exactitude in measurement and observation," depending on "the academic or practical use to which it is put." "[T]he upper limit of exactitude" which each science needs "to be capable of producing" is a function of "the discriminating capacity of the social agency available for effectuating changes indicated by their studies (e.g., the legislature)."[491]

Of course, none of this said anything about what made any method "scientific." Here Oliphant emphasized that a scientific method "impersonalizes the observation it seeks," which is to say seeks to make observations that do not vary significantly from what would be observed by "the mass of men," and that the supposed distinction between "facts which can yield objective results, and opinions or judgments which can yield only subjective ones" was in fact no distinction at all but a series of "gradations" based on "the number of items of sense experience constituting the basis of inference in each case and of the frequency with which the person involved is called upon to draw the inference." Generally, the more the stimuli and the less frequently the inference is made the more factual an inference will be, but, as it is a matter of gradation, "from the stand point of scientific method, how far . . . toward the factual end of the gradation" we can go in selecting data upon which to build statistical or other general inferences depends entirely upon the purposes we have in mind."[492]

Oliphant then turned to the other objection to scientific method in law: "that no genuine social science can be built up . . . because, unlike the situation in the physical sciences, social ends, purposes, desires and ideals are inextricably involved in all social sciences, i.e. that there can be no such thing as a social science because there is no way of fixing ultimate social values as standards." He began to meet this argument by distinguishing as Yntema had between "the rational and empirical side of science." He speculated for a while about the possibility and limits of grounding the rational side of science but ultimately found the question did not require an answer, because, on the empirical side of social science, there are "some objective techniques, processes and procedures" and therefore there is "as much science in this department of human thought and experience as in any other." And he opined, "We in law have objective methods of inquiry and plenty of problems and an abundance of materials to study. As we work on these problems with these methods, we may lose much of our speculative despair as to ultimate social values."[493]

There was, of course, a deeper problem — the charge that underlay the objection based on the need to take values into consideration, namely that "a student of law is deficient in moral sense if he merely observes and records the uniformities of social behavior with which the law is concerned." Here Oliphant entered a simple denial and invoked the division of labor. First, "law as a science whose object is detached scrutiny and description of actual conduct is different from law as a part of the art of government," so that "one may take uniformity of conduct (good and bad) of men generally and of those in the governing group to be the subject-matter of the science of law as a venture in scientific description without denying that how men *should* act and judges *should* decide is a legitimate but different branch of scholarly interest and activity." Thus, the choice to do empirical research

> may . . . be substantial evidence . . . [of the researcher's] desire to get on with what is his proper job at least, *viz.*, to identify rather than to

evaluate the social consequences of particular legal measures and devices. . . . Such identification is now one of the threshold tasks in reducing the excessive amount of muddling and guessing which there is in law
and its administration. When that task is well underway, there will be
other seasons and other specialists more appropriate for doing the difficult task of evaluation.[494]

It was a new note to the Hopkins song, beyond Cook's version of Dewey
and science as a method of inquiry, beyond Yntema's work building out from
Cook by distinguishing a rational and an empirical science of law. Oliphant
calmly pushed the rational science of law to one side. Science was not a
generalized method but an objective observational or experimental inquiry;
it was the world that Dorothy Thomas lived in defined inside law in ways
that Charles Clark couldn't have (and needn't have) done. Empirical social
science had finally penetrated legal theory. Thus, whether this was an adequate defense of Oliphant's actual enterprise or even an adequate response
to the criticisms of the entire Hopkins enterprise leveled by Cohen, Adler,
Frankfurter, Pound, and others is irrelevant for present purposes. The song
was changed and it was sung optimistically, however strange that optimism
might seem to be in view of the real circumstances of the Institute.

AND SO THE Institute wound down. At the end real work seemed to diminish markedly for most of the faculty. Oliphant worked to park the New York
study with his group of lawyers, though at the time he left they were still not
ready "to continue the work,"[495] but beyond that he seems not to have
pushed the project along. Yntema accomplished very little if anything in the
month or so before he departed for Europe. Although Cook tried to reassure
Judge Bond that, even though the Institute was closing, work would continue
in the Maryland study and thus, of course, keep the flow of funds from the
State of Maryland[496] and told the same thing to Pound,[497] there is no evidence that he personally did much at all in that direction. Only Marshall,
who made the usual job inquiries,[498] spent his last months on the Institute's
activities, then presented Ames with a budget for the Ohio studies, since there
was still money available for this work,[499] and headed to his summer home.
An obviously harassed Ames thanked him "with the utmost sincerity, for . . .
[his] cooperation in every respect during the past five years."[500] Other leave
takings were obviously less cordial. Ames arranged for Cook and Yntema to
receive small stipends during 1933–34 and to put Cook on leave of absence
so as to protect his Carnegie pension,[501] but that was all. He firmly refused

entreaties from a delegation of Maryland lawyers, headed by Judge Bond and the Chief Judge of the local trial court, who offered to raise money in order to keep Cook on at Hopkins so that he might finish the Maryland study[502] and testily told Yntema to go find himself a law school teaching job.[503]

Marshall landed at the Brookings Institution as a visiting scholar, where he tried to carry to completion the Ohio study.[504] Two more volumes ultimately appeared.[505] From there he moved first to the National Recovery Administration, then back to Hopkins as a visiting professor in the Department of Education and then finally landed at American University.[506] Yntema took Ames advice and soon found a position at the Michigan Law School, "taking up again the thread of historical and comparative work in which . . . [his] interests" in law lie.[507] Cook, as everyone was afraid of, had more trouble. Harvard turned up nothing[508] and no other "suitable" position appeared. So he became the part-time but paid General Secretary of the American Association of University Professors and worked in his Hopkins office the rest of each day.[509] After Oliphant moved with Morgenthau to the Treasury Department, Oliphant secured another post for Cook as chairman of the Committee on Enrollment and Disbarment of the United States Treasury Department where he apparently managed to clean up a real mess. Finally, after two years Cook went to Northwestern where he taught until retirement.[510]

Four years later Griswold was still angry, convinced that his original idea had been a good one.[511] Hopkins, which upon the demise of the Institute had quickly released its donors from their unpaid pledges,[512] some six years later quietly deposited in its general account the $17,000 balance still remaining of the funds for the Ohio study.[513] And, as for the rest of the world, its comment was curiously uttered by the Carnegie Foundation when it turned down Marshall's application for $3,000 to $5,000 to finance his law school data collection project. It noted that "the Trustees feel that the grant just made to complete the program of the American Law Institute will have to represent the contribution of the Corporation in the legal field for this year."[514]

Evaluating the Demise

What caused the demise of the Institute of Law at Hopkins? The answer to this question seems so obvious as to make pointless the exercise of formally asking it. The lack of money caused the Institute's demise. That answer is, it seems to me, so radically wrong that it should be dealt with expeditiously at the outset. Griswold asserted that at the time the Institute folded there was "$100,000 to $200,000 still due as contributions" that were "good as gold."[515] Even if this assertion is treated as a bit of an exaggeration, both Griswold and Baetjer had made commitments, clearly good, totaling about $30,000 for each of the next two years, whatever might have been the status of the pledges of the other guarantors. Those funds would have covered Marshall's slimmed down Institute; the Ohio study still had funds left; and the Maryland bar, a source never previously tapped, was willing to pay Cook's salary to finish the Maryland survey. And the accumulated deficit could not have bulked large in the minds of Ames and the Trustees when the funds that might have paid that deficit, and that were counted as covering that deficit when budgets were made, were written off without even asking already committed donors to help. Nor can the lack of funds explain limiting the Institute's budget to $75,000, Secretary Mellon's donation, in a year when Griswold and Baetjer together added their $30,000 to the Institute's finances. Admittedly, with limited sums only limited things could have been accomplished, but at least Marshall and Cook were willing to go on with something limited. Maybe, two years down the road the result would have been the same. But in 1932–33 the lack of money was not what killed the Institute, at least not in the way that Moore's efforts were slowly starved.

A SECOND EXPLANATION for the demise of the Institute also needs to be disposed of at the outset, though at greater length. That explanation asserts that the Institute's work product was intellectually inferior. As Llewellyn put it twenty years later, "I doubt whether in all of the quest for social science there has ever been such hastily considered, ill-planned, and mal-prepared large-scale so-called research. . . . Certainly, among the major sins were inquiry running wastefully beyond clear hypothesis, unnecessary large scale work where clear and shrewd sampling would have sufficed [and] heavy quantifying where it did not pay. . . . [They] counted and counted among the court records of Baltimore and Ohio. I read the results, but I never dug out what most of the counting was good for."[516] An examination of the published product of the Institute's court studies, a pile of books over two feet high, suggests that that criticism is wide of the mark.

What exactly did the Institute learn? In the spring of 1931 Yntema summarized its knowledge this way. "Civil justice today seems typically an administrative machine for the collection of claims or the encouragement of private settlement and a-typically to culminate in the declaration of rights in disputes brought into court by those who seek justice; criminal justice is a still more intricate machinery of police, in which the court is a subordinate unit."[517] This can be translated into the vernacular of a more recent time as "In the halls of justice, the only justice is in the halls."[518] Three things need to be noted about this statement. First, in the strictest of senses, in 1931 it was not news. Clark's preliminary findings in Connecticut made precisely the same findings for civil cases and his federal courts study did likewise for criminal cases. If one knew that Connecticut was typical of state jurisdictions and that federal criminal practice differed not one whit in its essentials from state criminal practice, then the entire Institute enterprise was futile. But, of course, no one knew that in 1929, when the relevant work was begun, nor, as the reaction at Harvard to the federal courts study indicates, were these conclusions obvious in 1931. Indeed, they are still good for a class or two with students today.

Second, in the strictest sense, in 1931 it was hard to say that the Hopkins effort had shown anything. All that was available at that time was Oliphant's preliminary report of his New York work[519] and Marshall's similarly preliminary report on Maryland criminal cases.[520] As no final work ever appeared for New York, in either Maryland or Ohio for civil cases, or in Maryland for criminal cases, one has to take on faith that Yntema's conclusions were born out by the unpublished data. But, of course, those conclusions are exactly what we know now to be the case; they were equally likely to have been the case then. Indeed, the chance that the data showed anything else is minuscule.

Third, again in the strictest sense, the Hopkins studies gathered no information about "the intricate machinery of police," though Marshall and two collaborators eventually published some little bit about the incidence of crime in Ohio based on existing police records.[521] Here there is no "but of course." At that time no one in the law school world, at least, knew the importance of *the* police in criminal justice without which the role of the prosecutor is but incompletely understood and that of the court completely misunderstood; thus no one could have truly understood the degree to which criminal justice was a matter *of* police, so that Yntema's statement is but a shrewd guess to the extent it goes beyond noting the subordinate role of the court.

A fourth preliminary matter should be noted that Yntema could not have known in 1931. The actual completed work published by the Institute bulks largest in two areas that Yntema never mentions, divorce and the so-called minor or specialized tribunals or jurisdictions — justice courts, equity receiverships, the public service commission. And here the work was on the whole both better and more original than was the published product relevant to the grand investigation of courts of general civil and criminal jurisdiction. Yet, taken as a whole, the entire product is a grand testimony to the deadening routine that is the administration of justice and at the same time to the local variations that can be found beneath the overwhelming routine that are traceable in large measure to local personalities and conditions.

First, the routine. The best example here, indeed the best product of the Institute, is the two volumes on divorce litigation published by Marshall and Geoffrey May, a research associate brought from Russell Sage for the project.[522] These were, it must be remembered, the early years of "the divorce problem" when a great deal of social science effort was going into the causes of divorce or "family disorganization," as it was called. While lawyers and judges acquainted with the practice of what is euphemistically called "family" law (or, in New York, more bizarrely "matrimonial" law) surely were not surprised with the basic picture painted by the findings,[523] these findings were striking in the way that they showed the steady progression of essentially mutually agreed divorces through the courts. In Maryland, for example, of the two-thirds of filed actions pursued to judgment, in only 5 percent or less of the cases was any contested hearing held and these were relatively concentrated in cases where a legal separation alone, with or without alimony, and not complete divorce with the possibility of remarriage, was being sought.[524] In the over 40 percent of the cases in which answers were filed and thus formal contests evidenced, most were disputes over the terms of the property or custody arrangements, as evidenced by the filing of the overwhelming percentage of the known property or custody agreements in such cases. And an examination of these agreements even disclosed the shamefully low level of support and alimony agreed to or decreed. The existence of a peculiarity in Maryland procedure requiring that transcripts of effectively uncontested cases be made and filed allowed a view of the summary nature of the evidence offered in the hearings, as well as of the violence, alcohol abuse, and adultery that both caused and accompanied divorce.[525]

The criminal cases in Ohio published by Charles E. Gehlke of Western Reserve, again a collaborator secured for the project, showed a similarly well functioning administrative machine, though one that differed in detail from that disclosed in Clark's federal courts study, less from the Pound-Frankfurter Cleveland Crime Survey. Statewide only slightly over half of the defendants pled guilty. Surprisingly, in nearly 20 percent of the cases the grand jury refused to indict, in 5 percent the defendant was never available for trial, and in slightly over 10 percent the case was dismissed by the prosecutor. That left 10 percent of all cases tried with about 30 percent of those cases ending in acquittal. Only those cases ultimately dismissed tended to drag on and on. For those who pled guilty or were tried, cases were generally disposed of in a month to a month and half. Here, where more cases were felonies, a not surprising one-half of those pleading or found guilty were imprisoned, and only 20 percent received a fine and the same proportion probation. Less than 15 percent of the pleas involved a classic plea bargain, a plea to a lesser offense. Not surprisingly those charged with property crimes were more frequently convicted, either on plea or after trial, than those charged with crimes against the person.[526] But overall the picture fit with earlier work and with the sense of an administrative procedure in which the judicial determination of guilt or innocence was a distinct sideline activity.[527]

Other studies also emphasized the administrative side of adjudication. A nice Ph.D. thesis on the Maryland Public Service Commission demonstrated that the immense majority of matters dealt with were minor, routine, and expeditiously disposed of, while only a few large cases dominated the Commission's attention for long periods of time.[528] And a wonderful, emphatic study of justice of the peace courts in the county surrounding Cincinnati, also graduate student work, showed the use of these minor courts for routine debt collection and equally routine — "fined $5.00 and costs" — minor criminal law enforcement.[529] Yet nearly all of these studies[530] pointed up the other half of the findings of the Institute's work: the minute variations in local practice and person that make justice, civil or criminal, an individualized thing.

The "problem," if that is what it was, of the variability of justice within a state was going to surface once one got beyond urban areas where Clark began, or the federal criminal courts, made relatively homogeneous by the peculiar list of federal offenses and the north and central bias to that study. With hindsight it was an obvious finding. Nonetheless, it was a troubling finding, first, because it made presentation of results very complicated, often benumbingly so and, second, because the purpose of the studies was to show *the* law in action. That fact meant that there had to be not just a central tendency, but a relative uniformity or at least an explanation for such lack of uniformity as appeared. Unfortunately, the higher the power of the microscope the more random the activity appeared.

For example, the Maryland divorce study turned up a surprising variation, the relative predominance of nonresident defendants in two counties. That could be explained by their proximity to Washington, which apparently had a harsh divorce law, but it was more difficult to explain, except in very personal terms, why divorces were denied six times more often in Cincinnati than in other urban counties or why they took twice as long to process in

Youngstown, Ohio.[531] Such variation, though highlighted "not in a spirit of criticism," since "[d]iversity is not necessarily objectionable, [i]f it is a manifestation of intelligent, high minded experimentation,"[532] was obviously no such thing. But what was to be made of other variations was by no means clear — for example, in the justice of the peace study, which turned up individual justices engaged in stamping out petting parties, fleecing passing motorists, acting as a collection agency, or simply doing nothing at all.[533] It was not easy to chalk up all the variation to democracy in action at the local level when law was supposed to bring the uniform treatment of all citizens.[534]

Of course, the "problem" was both an artifact of the methodology used and discovered because of that method. Here, the Ohio criminal courts study makes that clear. Data were separately collected and processed for each county and only then aggregated into five groups — the eight predominantly urban counties and four groups roughly comparable in population but differing systematically in density of population from more to less rural.[535] Aggregated, the data were reasonably smooth along the classic American urban-rural axis. But within groups chaos often reigned, more chaos than the statistical unreliability of small numbers[536] might likely account for. All this "noise" would have been eliminated if the data had not been run county by county — and all of the value. Yet, all that detail created simple problems of presentation that at times seem to overwhelm the book and, given that the study was of court records and not of courts, made it impossible to do more than suggest repeatedly that the variation indicated areas that were ripe for further investigation.

The sense of simple technique overrunning understanding, of losing the forest in the trees, that Llewellyn decried is surely there, but ought not to be allowed to overwhelm the positive achievement of these studies. The work in Ohio was for the most part solid;[537] little beyond the divorce study was published in Maryland and thus could not be weak. The entire judicial statistics enterprise that so occupied Marshall's time is harder to evaluate. Hindsight, of course, suggests that systems of statistics, other than perhaps those on individual judicial work load where a strong central executive can wield some authority, have done little to aid court management, much less disclose social problems as they occur, as was hoped. But, of course, hindsight is not what is important here. As a matter of foresight Marshall's idea was surely plausible.

What one should say about the balance of the Institute's work product is less clear. Three articles stand out. Cook's two on the conflict of laws are basic to our understanding of the subject today, and one of them, that on substance and procedure, still repays rereading. Similarly, Oliphant's "Facts, Opinions, and Value-Judgments," though, as is the case with most of his work, more suggestive than finished, is really only one of two serious attempts (the other is Moore's) by the Realists to articulate an understanding of the twentieth-century notion of science as a purely empirical activity as it might apply to law. It too still repays rereading. In contrast, Cook's more finished work on the subject not only breaks no new ground, but ultimately reaches a dead end in his unpublished Storrs lectures delivered the year after the Institute was closed, an undigested mix of Dewey's pragmatism, operationalism, and logical positivism, all assembled to prove the same proposition as before: that in any new case for decision both the lawyer and the judge infuse the middle term of the syllogism with new meaning that, for the judge at least, ought to be done only after paying attention to the social consequences of the choice.[538] Yntema's work on the concurrent jurisdiction, preliminary to the never done empirical work, is good, topical analysis, but nothing more, which is of course better than his jurisprudential work, aptly described as confused. Thus, with exceptions, the lot is undistinguished, a sad statement for individuals freed from teaching responsibilities for five years. But still, the common judgment of the Institute's work rests not on any of this work but on the published product of the state surveys and those, to the extent published, were good.

IF NEITHER money nor work product can account for the demise of the Institute, then what can? While there are other relevant factors,[539] I think it is important here to emphasize the overriding importance of the University that Cook and his friends found themselves in.

Looked at carefully the Institute's program was nothing more than a mishmash of what each individual, each "practically independent research unit," to use Oliphant's words when trying to sell the idea to Moore, wanted to do. To the end there was no theoretical or even less grandiose idea that might have grounded the Institute's research and, as is shown by Cook's continual attempt to sell his understanding of Dewey on science both before and after first Yntema, and then Oliphant, attempted to see the connection between scientific method and empiricism, no agreement even on what a scientific approach to law meant. Instead, as Oliphant once recognized, the group made do with a bunch of slogans—social control, law as a human device or tool, the need for the readaptation of law to life, law-in-action, the human effects of law, vital problems, social significance, research keeping close to practical affairs, the judicial machine, functional organization, cooperation or integration with the social sciences, a community of scholars — and a grab bag of problems, most of which could be identified with one or the other stream of progressive reform, for example, the lawyer's narrow stream, as in the New York study's obsession with cost, delay, and uncertainty or in Jaffin's study of concurrent jurisdiction, or the broader stream, as in the never completed study of installment contracts or Marshall's wish to study boards of directors. It is not clear where in particular these slogans or problems come from or what they meant to the crew, any more than it is clear where Clark and Hutchins got the idea that the facts were a prerequisite to reform, and in a real sense it does not matter. What matters is that with no explicit theoretical idea of what they were looking for, or even an implicit one as Moore had had, and no principle of self-limitation — the study — as Clark had had, there was no way to create *a* program. As a result, execution — the jumble that Llewellyn perceived — came to dominate the program and not the other way around.[540] To one with a marked catholic taste, that was not a bad thing because many of the projects were not dumb ideas and might have amounted to something. But at Hopkins this lack of focus created problems. One had to do with funding, another with the University itself.

The assertions George E. Vincent, the Rockefeller Foundation's President, to the contrary not withstanding, no matter what its files showed, Flexner's discussions with Griswold had created a reasonable understanding that the Rockefeller Foundation would supply a considerable amount of the endowment for the Institute. And the Foundation knew this; its constant assertion of its interest in the project is quiet testimony and not just a reflection of private valuations of merit. And yet, time after time, Ames went to the well and came back with an empty bucket. That Ames and others at Hopkins were bewildered by the juxtaposition of these two facts can be seen, in part, by Ames's return to the well even though the obvious, stated condition for Foundation support had not been met. Something didn't add up. What that something was Ames never learned, but it was both a specific and a more general something. The specific thing is this. The Foundation was offended at the bidding between Hopkins and Yale over the services of Cook, Marshall, and Oliphant, bidding that was especially hard to swallow since it came after a request to the Foundation for endowment funds to improve salaries in the Philosophical Faculty, salaries that were not even within spitting distance of those being offered to the Institute's faculty.[541] Thus, the Foundation was unwilling to use its funds in effect to bail the "winner" out of a bad bargain lest the Foundation seem to be condoning sharp practice.

The more general thing was a significant shift in the Rockefeller philanthropies at this time. It is not insignificant that the assurance of Foundation support came from Abraham Flexner. Flexner, who had made the Hopkins Medical School into an important center for medical education and research, believed in science as a solution to contemporary problems and in funding flagship institutions to take the lead in showing other schools how teaching and research ought to be done. His was a kind of personal, hands-on philanthropy, pursued, of course, with other people's money. Flexner retired just as the Institute was being founded, or so it was said in the public press. In fact he was fired as part of an administrative reorganization at the Foundation[542] that saw its program shift from one modeled on Flexner's approach to one designed to fund "the advance of human knowledge" in order to "advance social integration."[543] In order to avoid unseemly, in-depth institutional entanglements of the kind that Flexner was constantly embroiled in, Foundation officials grouped subject matter into divisions that would monitor the growth of knowledge in an area and make grants accordingly.

No one at Hopkins understood this shift, indeed the University's recurrent approach to the Foundation — we are a good university that has good faculty wanting to set up a good, new institution to help in the resolution of social problems — indicates the extent to which the pitch was being made with Flexner's understanding of the philanthropic enterprise in mind. Under such changed circumstances, the inability of Goodnow, Willard, and Griswold to articulate a program for the University as a whole at the time of their first meeting at the Foundation in response to a question that can be translated colloquially as, "Do you guys know what you're doing?" and the inability of Cook and company to articulate a program for the Institute that "hung together" took on new and important meaning. Knowing what one was doing and having the ideas hang together were now independently important and their absence only reinforced the sense that the behavior of all parties had not been thought out but rather was opportunistic, if not also grasping. A proper foundation let misbehaving supplicants dig themselves out of such a mess.

The lack of Rockefeller support for the Institute might not have meant much at some universities, but at Hopkins it was unfortunately important in the negative way that it put the Institute at the mercy of the Philosophical Faculty. Mincing words here is not possible. The Institute died because the Philosophical Faculty, the group that the Rockefeller Foundation felt was too weak to support the Institute's program intellectually,[544] wanted the Institute killed.

Whence commeth the Philosophical Faculty's enmity? As Hopkins's president, Goodnow had not been particularly supportive of the Philosophical Faculty in the sense of putting resources there, and the group as a whole was not obviously enthralled with him.[545] The Institute was clearly Goodnow's project as far as the University was concerned; only Willoughby of the faculty pushed it. And the faculty as a whole could never have liked the Institute. In the rarified atmosphere at The Hopkins, law, a mere professional school, was déclassé, an entrée into the pursuit of filthy lucre, the teachers of which were paid salaries grossly disproportionate to the value of the subject taught when measured by philosophical standards.[546] Moreover, the mere existence of the Institute was a signal that key members of the faculty cannot have liked. Hollander was an economic historian[547] and political economy was neither economics nor commerce; indeed, both were fighting words to the small band that tried to keep the field of political economy going after political science and economics had split apart as disciplines. Lovejoy was a historian of ideas and hardly a Deweyite.[548] Indeed, Dewey's idea of science suggested that Lovejoy's almost Hegelian understanding of the unfolding of ideas over time was so much hot air, that people didn't think that way and thus that their ideas did not unfold, but rather grew in pragmatic response to changed conditions. When one adds the source of the idea, the intellectual challenge, and the pure affront of paying grand salaries to newcomers while the old, faithful faculty starved, at least in relative terms, there are the makings of real anger.

In a faculty with a serious tradition of self-governance, such anger was dangerous, for the only real counterweight was the president. However, Ames was anything but a counterweight; he was really a member of the Philosophical Faculty party.[549] Indeed, his only real innovation in the seven years he was President was a plan to strengthen the Philosophical Faculty by adding to it postdoctoral and graduate fellows.[550] Thus, although Ames clearly liked Marshall and was willing to live with the compromise the Board of Trustees struck, at least to the extent of keeping Marshall,[551] his feelings were more accurately put when, in response to praise for letting the Institute die, he told Hollander, the man who gave the address at the dinner honoring Ames's sixty years at the University,[552] "The faculties of the University are really *the* University."[553]

Without Ames's support for the Institute, the Philosophical Faculty could easily make money an issue, if a peculiarly phony one. In mounting a response to that issue, the Institute's faculty had nowhere to look for effective support. The Institute was not Willard's idea, it was Griswold's. But at the time of the original funding crisis Griswold admitted that he hadn't talked to the Institute's faculty in two years.[554] That was understandable for he had put all of his energy into saving his banking business from the ravages of the Depression,[555] but that was of no assistance to the Institute he had helped dream up. And, although the faculty spoke of the Institute's prominent "position in the world of American Legal Education,"[556] that position was anything but secure. Rockefeller Foundation officials recognized that "[v]iolent differences of opinion" about the Institute existed "among people competent to have judgment, ranging all the way from enthusiasm to complete doubt of place and people engaged."[557] One has the sense that the balance of "respectable" opinion was negative. Frankfurter had been sniping; Clark too. Indeed, from the outset there was sufficient static that both Oliphant and Cook wrote to Angell and Hutchins respectively to say "Did I do anything wrong?"[558] And sniping apparently emanated from both Michigan and Harvard generally.[559] Moreover, the bigwigs in the profession were anything but uniformly supportive. Wickersham,[560] Newton D. Baker, a trustee,[561] and William W. Cook, Michigan's great benefactor,[562] all weighed in negatively, and then there were two more Trustees, Howland and Burlingham, who had been in contact with Frankfurter and seemed to share his views.

With nowhere to turn for support, the Institute was essentially defenseless against the University that Cook looked to as a sponsor for scientific research in law. Here Cook, the AAUP activist, the patriot of the community of scholars, made a mistake that Veblen had not and that Dewey's philosophy should have guarded him against. The University was not interested in scientific research any more than it was interested in any number of other things, like docile students, quiet alumni, a positive balance sheet, and not rocking the intellectual or internal social boat. For *the* University didn't exist and thus what Cook thought of as *the* University could only be understood by looking at what its pieces and people did. At Hopkins the most relevant piece of *the* University was the Philosophical Faculty. That group was envious of the Institute's fancy salaries, scared that its University was falling apart, and angry that a group of newcomers was receiving such special treatment. And so it struck out at the seemingly strong — but, in fact, defenseless — offending entity as soon as it could.

THE DEMISE OF the Institute of Law in the summer of 1933 was not literally the demise of the Realists' involvement in empirical research. Publication of the federal courts study was still a year off; of the Connecticut courts study, four years off. Clark would start one more study before becoming totally absorbed in the federal rules project, and Moore, of course, would work on for ten years. Nor was it the demise of the law professor's interest in legal research. But three successive examples of beginnings full of high hopes, middles full of unexpectedly hard work and a certain amount of disillusion, and ends full of what might best be described as painful decline, followed by the call "strike your tents men; time to move on," ought to suggest that maybe, just maybe the problem with empirical research in law is not accidental but systematic. I next turn to look at some factors that might be seen as systematic, before looking at the revival of empirical legal research in the years following World War II.

EMPIRICAL LEGAL RESEARCH SINCE WORLD WAR II:

THE REINVENTION OF THE SQUARE WHEEL

THE SAMENESS of these three stories of empirical legal research ought to cause one to wonder what there was about the Realists' efforts that would bring a recurrence of cases of modest success followed by . . . well . . . nothing. It was as if someone had invented the square wheel; some movement of the horse cart was possible, but not much. After World War II when the topic of empirical legal research came up, the commentary recognized that what had come before was not a success story, that something had gone wrong.[1] Not all verdicts were as harsh as those of Llewellyn on Hopkins and Moore,[2] but there were few voices raised in praise of the Realists' work.[3] Overall the dominant note to this postwar commentary was that of what might best be called sober disappointment[4] coupled with some optimism that "we" had learned a few things and so could do "better." Before looking at that doing "better," one should attempt at least a preliminary evaluation of the strengths and weaknesses of the Realists' empirical work, if only to understand the pattern that provided the baseline for that doing.

Why the First Square Wheel Did Not Go Far

The reasons for the decline of the Realists' efforts at empirical legal research are numerous and, in one sense, accidental. They are accidental because the background against which the story must be seen was surely as favorable to an attempt to do, and institutionalize the doing of, such research as anyone had a right to expect. Socially and politically it was a time when scientific research was a good thing. Herbert Hoover, the great engineer, was President. He, who would bring his practical, objective science to bear on American government, who in the Department of Commerce had fostered the collection of incredible quantities of "facts,"[5] and who continued to foster detached inquiry into social problems,[6] at least gave social scientific enterprises a setting in which they could try to flourish. And other elements of the social scene helped too. Taylorite scientific management was a significant force in business;[7] the progressive tradition of commissions of detached inquiry was still prevalent; and even the general public was, it appears, fascinated by statistics.[8]

Academically the background was equally favorable. The social science disciplines had just finished their fragmentation along methodological lines from a unified science of political economy into their now invariable universe,[9] but the concomitant fragmentation of academic departments was still underway.[10] This was the time of the early reception of quantification into social science, when counting seemed enough and statistics as it is known today was in its infancy. Thus, method in the social sciences was only beginning to adopt the now familiar norms,[11] and indeed major methodological works were still being written canonizing all then generally accepted methods within given disciplines.[12] Graduate education was expanding rapidly, in part to supply the needed Ph.D.'s to staff the new social science departments in every educational nook and cranny in the country. Professional education, especially in medicine, but also in law, was still in the process of reform.[13] Foundation interest in support for education, especially professional education, was at a high point.[14] On a more narrowly institutional level, Columbia, it appears, was still suffering from growing pains; Yale, just becoming a university; and Johns Hopkins, still trying to duplicate its medical successes.[15] Thus, there was great potential for new educational openings in general and openings toward an active, diversified social science community as well.

Professionally, the background was admittedly nowhere near as favorable. The enormous American Law Institute scholarship engine had already been set in motion, its wheels well greased with money that might have been captured for empirical research in law, but that instead lined the pockets of more traditional legal scholars.[16] That organization provided now tax deductible opportunities for slightly left of center, upper-caste lawyers to socialize in an atmosphere that reinforced the notion that theirs was a learned profession and thus further separated them from the stench of the *Untermenschen* of the profession. Even more debilitating was the notion fueled by the ALI's mere existence that library, not field, research was *the* method of legal research among the group in the profession that was the most likely to support empirical research in law. And the profession as a whole, or at least that upper portion about which something is known, was surely not interested in social science intrusions into the "practical" training for the practice of law, although at least parts of the profession were not adverse to using "scientific" methods when such methods seemed to advance the profession's interests.[17] But the professional background could hardly be expected to be favorable at any time; union spokesmen can be expected to oppose innovations in the craft that smell of automation or, in that marvelous English word, of redundancy, and this is as true of unions of persons whose craft skills are mental as of those whose skills are manual.

If the social, political, and academic, if not professional, background was largely supportive, what then were the reasons for the decline of empirical research in law and thus of the scientific side of Realism? These were the usual accidents of time and of person (though there is a nonaccidental aspect to the matter of person) and the nonaccident that was the nature of the research enterprise itself. First, time.

IN SOME SENSE the Depression did the dirty work. If business had continued its short-lived, post–World War I boom, there might well have been enough foundation money for starting much empirical research in law. But the Depression came, and instead of watching the foundation largess almost fall out of the trees, Charles Clark saw the money tree wither. Virtually untrained in the then developing art of grantsmanship, both he and Underhill Moore looked for money to support their predetermined research objectives rather than attempting to orient their research toward grantors' interests. Thus, Clark was reduced to twice asking George Wickersham if he could find money.[18] Moore was left to get what little support he could from the increasingly frugal Institute of Human Relations and then, when that money was gone, to finance research out of his own funds.[19] The Hopkins Institute had to scrounge as well, though clearly there was money to continue its activities at some level. But, if there had been no Depression, then the Philosophical Faculty would have had far less potent arguments with which to attack the Institute as Hopkins cut back its educational programs in an effort to stem the flood of red ink.[20] Thus, the Depression brought home the financial realities of modern social science research and belied the Realists' initial feeling that the diversity of social science presented numerous opportunities.

DESPITE THE OBVIOUS importance and impact of the "accident" of the onset of the Depression, the "accident" of person, was probably more important. Each brought strengths and limitations that shaped the Realists' empirical research in important ways. Consider first, if only briefly, a man offstage for most of this story — Robert Maynard Hutchins. Empirical research began at Yale because Robert Hutchins was there. He helped Clark with the idea for the Connecticut courts study and as dean saw to it that that idea was funded. He and Clark then made the trip to Washington to see Herbert Hoover about studying the federal courts, a call that seems to have led to Clark's later working for the Wickersham Commission. Hutchins hired first Douglas and then Moore. He made the connection that got Clark a piece of the auto accidents study and, let us not forget, he teamed up with the dean of Yale's Medical School to found the Institute of Human Relations where Douglas and Moore got some funding and Moore, at least, got ignored. All of this in a little over three years' time. He was a whirlwind and, though there was a pattern to his flight, it was the pattern appropriate to a whirlwind. Hutchins would do anything he could to shake up legal education in general and the Yale Law School in particular. Start something and then, if necessary, see what it might be turned into.[21] Except that, before it came time to see what all of these starts could be made into, Hutchins left for Chicago and it was Charles E. Clark who inherited it all.

What Clark inherited can be charitably described as a mess of opportunities; but what did he do with them? While he passionately believed in "fact research," as he called it, and loudly lamented its decline, Clark was able to do little to keep any going. Not only was next to nothing new started, that next to nothing was started while there were plenty of ideas for research projects just lying around.[22] True, both the two procedure studies and the auto compensation study were eventually completed. But, Clark started only one study himself and it went nowhere.[23] Yet, to look only at Clark's research and not more broadly at his deanship is to miss his substantial achievements. He held the Yale Law School together through years of declining resources while federal agencies made extraordinary demands on everyone's time.[24] At the same time he managed to recruit a faculty of unusual talent and, ultimately, achievement. And, though he was unable to generate any real educational innovation during his deanship,[25] he saw to the development of an effective committee system, necessary to run the Law School, which had doubled its faculty in the ten years following Hutchins's selection as Acting Dean.[26]

Clark's achievements and failures trace as telltale a pattern of activity as did Hutchins's. The procedure studies were completed in large part because Clark saw to it that they were completed;[27] the thought that something once begun might not be completed was inadmissible to him. And the auto compensation study was so finely wrought that it is a monumental example of a concern for careful work overwhelming the rather mundane purpose for which it was done. Such changes in the educational program of the Law School as were undertaken were all considered, reported, and justified almost to death by a committee structure Clark had created. And although his faculty was unusually talented, with one or two exceptions it was not audacious, any more than Clark was an audacious dean. Taken together, these events reveal a man who in his approach to problems and in his style, if style is the right word, was always careful, measured, though not plodding, and above all thorough. That was Clark's way — lawyerly, in a word.[28] It was a style appropriate to times of consolidation or decline, when order and the husbanding of resources are appropriate. Thus, it is not surprising that Clark's achievements as he guided the Law School through the Depression were largely administrative. But with respect to new activities and partial programs it was a style with limitations.

The limitations of Clark's style were two. The first can be seen in several incidents. Despite Clark's worries that Douglas would leave for Chicago, when Douglas's bankruptcy studies were finished his interest was allowed to drift, drift probably induced in part because of his rather stern introduction to real social science method administered at the hands of Dorothy Thomas. Moore too was left to move along his own track, although the cantankerousness of these two neighbors probably made it impossible for Clark to have moved Moore in any particular direction, even if he had wanted to do so.[29] Here and elsewhere it can be seen that realizing on potential assets was not Clark's forte. Given a sensible project, he could execute it; create one out of scraps and pieces, he could not. All the care and thoroughness he could muster were of no help in such a task. Ultimately, it was just not his style.

The second limitation was related to the first. Just as Clark could not create out of scraps, he could not lead out of diversity, either. His idea of leadership was leadership by demonstration.[30] He could, and did, show what kind of activities he thought were appropriate for legal scholars — a rather promising combination of empirical study and policy analysis[31] that might have led away from the kind of data-free social science that is the dominant mode of law school legal analysis today. He made his silent point over and over again, especially in the procedure studies, but if no one wanted to learn from the demonstration, Clark was not the dean to think up new and exciting things to do that might tempt others to follow his lead despite themselves. He was too thorough for that kind of serendipity. His work was self-describedly "practical."[32] It was sophisticated in a technical way, but as such it was hardly the sort of thing to galvanize others into action.

The consequence of Clark's brand of educational leadership was striking. The faculty Clark inherited was alive with energy and activity;[33] it plainly knew that it was special. It did not lack for ideas; if anything, it had too many. What it lacked was direction.[34] Scraps and pieces pointed in the direction of empirical legal research. Clark tried to show the way in his own research, but he could not work with scraps and pieces, and regrettably his faculty was not patient (one almost wishes to say humble) enough to learn from his careful, but not flashy, examples. And so the momentum of the faculty was allowed to spend its force, as well as to grow, in pursuits other than empirical research, as the Depression and the nature of the research enterprise made that kind of research less attractive.

Moore's temperament equally influenced the course of his research, though in a more complicated way than Clark's temperament influenced both the course of his own research and of research generally at Yale. All the published accounts of Moore emphasize his gruffness as well as a teaching style that combined a withering, remorseless logic with a totally domineering manner.[35] Published accounts, however, largely fail to capture other quite different aspects of Moore's personality. For example, it is perfectly clear that when he chose to do so the gruffness could completely disappear and Moore could become unbelievably gracious and charming.[36] Instead of viciously attacking, he could at times spend long hours building up individuals; instead of intimidating he could rationally persuade.[37] And students like Douglas[38] and Wesley Sturges, who could, or were permitted to, cut through the gruffness, could also find something special, and expressed in quite personal terms a lasting debt to Moore for, in Sturges's words, "initiating" them in "a pattern of thinking" that kept them free from the ways of "an earlier tradition."[39] Even students with humbler legal minds who stuck it out in courses whose content was overly detailed and technical[40] somehow came to sense that something was present in addition to the shouting.[41] However disparate these aspects of Moore's temperament may seem, it would be a serious mistake to simply write him off as a paradox and leave it at that. For something did hold his personality together. Despite the gruffness and the aura of the aging, self-assured, late-Edwardian gentleman that his portrait shows, Moore was basically quite shy and a bit sensitive.[42]

Once Moore's basic shyness is recognized, the course of his research, not just parking but banking too, becomes easier to understand. As Moore once observed, he had come to Yale in answer to "the question: 'Where will my personal life probably be happier?'" He had found that "the ructions at Columbia had been such that . . . [he] could no longer be happy there" and so he left.[43] Despite his shyness, Moore needed, and looked for, the sustained intellectual contact as a stimulant for his ideas that he had once found at Columbia in the immediate postwar years.[44] Yet, because he was basically shy, his approach was seldom direct. He all but "hung around" the Institute of Human Relations, always wanting to be counted in, but always overlooked because he never did much to call attention to his presence. While he learned much from Dorothy Thomas, he put it in practice so slowly that she lost interest. Likewise, though he had been acquainted with Hull for nearly ten years, at the time of his piece for Kocourek's volume in which he drew heavily on Hull's learning theory, Moore quite obviously wrote without ever having talked at length with Hull about that theory and its contemporaneous refinements. Over and over he looked for help, for intellectual stimulation, but from a distance.

While shyness might not have been a handicap in many academic endeavors, the nature of Moore's enterprise made shyness a positive disability. Had he been working in a well-plowed field, he might have received the necessary stimulation and guidance simply by being around other scholars and keeping up with the journals. But he was not working such a field; he was cutting "first growth timber."[45] So for his needs Moore had to rely on the Law School, or the Institute, or go it alone.

Relying on the Law School for intellectual stimulation and guidance was impossible for several reasons. First, in simple personal terms, there was no one there to look to. Charles Clark, the most obvious candidate, and Moore simply could not get along.[46] Douglas, the next most obvious choice, while a friend of sorts to the end, was quite obviously not sufficiently committed to empirical research over any long haul to fit the bill. And Thurman Arnold, although plainly a good buddy,[47] was simply not serious enough about anything for Moore's taste.[48] Beyond Arnold there was simply no one,[49] except for Arthur Corbin. Now while there was a special bond between Corbin and Moore that derived from their having both begun teaching in the first decade of the twentieth century during the years when law teaching was undergoing the process of professionalization and from a shared commitment to sustained and not faddish scholarship,[50] that special bond provided no more than the basis for a tolerant friendship.[51] That was hardly the kind of support that Moore needed and sought.

What Moore needed was the support of a common intellectual community such as might have been built around sustained commitment to the kind of research that Clark and Douglas, Corstvet and Thomas, and yes, even Thurman Arnold for a while,[52] engaged in. But the one thing the really grand crew at Yale was not noted for was sustained commitment to anything. Clark's dogged pursuit of procedural reform came the closest to Moore's ideal of committed scholarship, but Clark broke the traces and ran back to property or over into constitutional law with some regularity and even in procedure Clark's scholarship soon gave way to cheerleading for the new Federal Rules. Douglas went from business associations to bankruptcy to securities in seven years. Arnold changed horses at every stream. Hamilton could never decide whether he was studying economic organization or constitutional law. Surges covered a permanent shift from creditor's rights to arbitration by publishing virtually nothing for nearly ten years. Rodell's idea of consistent effort was to write regularly for the same magazine. Moore, in contrast, when at the end of a session with his research assistant spent fleshing out sections of the Negotiable Instruments Law in a way easily "ten times . . . better than the regular literature on the topic," quickly turned aside the suggestion that they should write up and publish the analysis with the observation " 'You know, we're not trying to show everybody how smart we are.' "[53]

Lacking intellectual support in the Law School, Moore was driven in the direction of the Institute of Human Relations. There, as an amateur he was not particularly welcome; yet, being shy, he was uncomfortable about elbowing his way in. When an even tangentially common interest made discussion easy, as when an engineer offered some research on automobile speeds, Moore opened up quite directly.[54] But short of that kind of invitation he had a hard time starting any discussion. Thus, Moore's temperament only served to make it easier for individuals at the Institute to ignore or begrudge his presence. As a result, he was largely left on his own, led to rely on himself and his research assistants for much of his intellectual support.

Unfortunately, although Moore was a formidable personality and a fine, widely read intellect, left to his own devices he was hardly a juggernaut capable of both completing his research and understanding and remedying the defects in the original design of that research.[55] Indeed, his ideas about reasonable methods of research were anything but naturally sound. Twice he simply made wrong choices when problems developed with the research. First, in the banking studies, where he began with a wonderful topic for research and a bizarrely overdetailed method, he failed to see that the desirable improvement was not to tighten observational techniques, which were already as rigorous as the subject matter warranted, but to loosen the overt reliance on quantification and simplify the elaborate structure of method. Then, in the parking studies, where he again chose a sensible topic for research, he began with a clear, clean, though not perfect, explanation of his results and, in the name of better understanding, produced for Kocourek a less clear, less clean, and less than perfect explanation of those results and, yet again in the name of better understanding, in the end produced a truly opaque and convoluted explanation that was still not perfect. And Moore did this because he failed to recognize that the behavior that to him seemed so simple was in fact too complicated for Hull's psychological model. As a result, he never saw that what his study needed was not complicated mathematics, but the simplification of data in the direction of the ethnographic studies that he had been quite obviously interested in at least as far back as the time of the review of Wigmore's book.

Why Moore made these critically wrong choices is easy to see. Too shy to seek real help, he followed the natural bent of his mind, which was toward the methodical and technical. He thus quickly learned and understood statistical technique and the rudiments of experimental design,[56] but never the theory behind it, for he was not a theoretician, even at a low level. For example, although, in his own awkward way, he often tried to contribute to the jurisprudential debates of the time, his record in this territory, which he knew comparatively well, was hardly impressive.[57] So to say that he could have intuited that the problems with his research lay in the dominant statistical ethos of the social science that he knew (and that perversely came to offer help when he really needed it), then could have dug his way out of that ethos in order to recover the ground of this thought from some twenty years earlier, and finally could have built anew on that thought (all much harder tasks in less familiar intellectual terrain than moving along the jurisprudential peanut of the day) is to suggest the impossible.[58] He was by temperament and training committed to scientific research in law, committed enough that he could not fall away from it as Clark and Douglas had done, but he was not therefore the man to see beyond the particular science he had found his way into.

Unbelievably, the faculty at the Hopkins Institute was even less suited to the task it faced than was Moore to his task or Clark to his. Indeed, it would be hard to have collected a more ill-suited crew to man the Institute if one had tried. Ames put it this way, "I am very doubtful whether, . . . [if] the Institute is re-established any of the previous members of the faculty would be considered as the best men to undertake the venture."[59] While Ames was himself part of the problem,[60] in this assessment he was surely correct.

Consider first Cook. He was phenomenally difficult to deal with, perhaps more difficult than Moore or Clark. Frank offered faint praise when, in recommending Cook for a teaching post, he offered assurance that there was "no fear that Cook would try to push himself forward at the expense of anyone else; the years when he might have done that are gone by."[61] Others, even willing prospective employers, felt that he would be "a hard man to get along with."[62] Deeply insecure and self-centered,[63] except in his own home where he was a warm and affectionate husband and father,[64] he was incapable of ever forgetting a slight[65] or of giving credit where it was due, either to his intellectual forebears in law[66] or to his co-workers.[67] A relatively tall man, he seems to have kept the world at bay by the expedient, easy for tall people, of constantly teaching,[68] in effect talking down at, not with his audience.[69] The insecurity that kept him on "Cook's tours of the law schools"[70] in search of, if not a higher salary, at least a "better" place,[71] made him look at only "suitable" law school teaching positions in 1933,[72] and made him deeply concerned about his pension long before he had a new, young wife.[73] And it was his self-centeredness that made Marshall observe, first, that in order to "carry anything through," Cook needed "a definite reward, particularly . . . monetary," and, second, that "although he had done "little" on the Maryland study, Cook would "kick up an awful dust unless . . . his name appear[s] on the finished product."[74] Thus, while recognizing correctly that the question of terminating his tenure was not a matter of his or anyone's "rights" but of what was fair in the circumstances, only he could have thought, even for an instant, that a proper solution was for the rest of the Hopkins faculty to take a little extra pay cut to preserve his job![75] This, to a faculty that had already been administered a 10 percent pay cut from salaries that even the Rockefeller Foundation knew were inadequate and which were one-half to one-third of his original salary and thus still only three-quarters to one-half of his reduced but still handsome salary.[76] Add to insecurity and self-centeredness the fact that he disliked and was terrible at administration,[77] disliked fundraising and clearly believed that it was the University's job,[78] and admitted that, though he thought empirical research was important, he was uninterested in doing any[79] and one clearly has the perfect founder for a small experimental research institute dedicated to the scientific study of law.

Marshall had his own weaknesses too, at least in the context of working in the same organization as Cook, though some of those defects would have been strengths in any other context. He was friendly and open and chubby, an energetic workhorse who was careful of details in the execution of projects.[80] He was thus a good administrator who took to fundraising as a natural task and who attended easily and effectively to the political jobs of making contacts, coordinating with others, and recruiting assistance.[81] Ames clearly appreciated these qualities;[82] Cook surely did not, any more than he appreciated Marshall's intellectual equipment, for in contrast to Cook's patient analytic work, Marshall was prone to breezy overstatement and glossy optimism. It was he who kept emphasizing that the group was collecting "masses" of data,[83] and he who kept trumpeting the importance of judicial statistics,[84] the latter a reflection of his economics-business background where collection of mass statistics by such entities as the Bureau of Economic Research and Hoover's Commerce Department was the norm for understanding the world. And he was full of ideas, most half-baked and ultimately untouched. While not incapable of slighting a collaborator,[85] he surely would not have put his name on anything that he did not have a substantial part in. And his personal security, a security that seemed to verge on casualness in the search for a new job,[86] even though he too had a substantial family, bespoke an attitude of "what advantage can we get out of this difficulty."[87] Cook and Marshall were thus about as different as two men could be. Marshall was guaranteed to antagonize Cook, antagonism that clearly became more acute after Marshall took the job of Director in a way that violated Cook's sense of faculty democracy and brought back to him and the others memories of Butler's imposing Smith on the faculty at Columbia.

Then there was Oliphant, a wild man who once drove a yellow Stutz Bearcat.[88] He was as much of a prima donna as Cook and seems to have had a deep and abiding need both to do his own thing and to do that thing in some area that allowed him to be free from anyone's looking over his shoulder.[89] He thus twice tried to divide up the faculty's activities so that no one would be interested in his work.[90] His way of coping with being a member of so small a group was to stay by himself as much as possible. Thus, much of his work was a mystery to the staff in Baltimore[91] and I suspect to his faculty colleagues as well. The world of New York legal practice and the political power it breathed attracted him in the way that only an Indiana farm boy could be attracted. He had a million ideas, which he, at least, was self-conscious enough to understand were usually for someone else to do. But that self-knowledge did not mitigate the fact that they were for someone else to do and that, when it came to doing, he tended toward the suggestive and slapdash, rather than the careful and followed through. Indeed, Oliphant seemed to be incapable of following any project through to completion, if completion took any significant amount of time.[92] And, while he seems not to have been the kind of person who would antagonize either Marshall or

Cook, rather than balancing their weaknesses, he all but duplicated Cook's self-centeredness with his own inability to work with others and shared with Marshall both breeziness and the tendency to think of things for others to do.

Finally there was Yntema, an admitted perfectionist where scholarship was concerned,[93] a bit of a perpetual student and so withdrawn that he taught facing away from the class with his hand over his mouth.[94] Even if he were not the junior partner and treated as such, he could not have made up for anyone's weaknesses and exhibited few strengths.

Now these strengths and weaknesses, personal animosities and jealousies need not have been liabilities. Other groups have functioned well in similar situations; for example, I am reminded of Fred Konefsky's story that, after a performance, the Budapest String Quartet often went to a restaurant and requested four tables for one. But at the Institute these personal traits were a liability. The analogy to the Budapest Quartet is here instructive. They had a focus, an idea that held them together; at the very least each had the same Beethoven quartet on the music stand. At the Institute, from the beginning everyone had different music.

When the Institute was formed no one had any idea what the faculty of four was going to do *as an Institute* and so for over a year they kicked the question around at their regular faculty meetings and at the afternoon teas hosted by Marshall's secretary,[95] who came with him from Chicago via Columbia. It is charitable to say that little came out of these efforts. Although one can detect in Marshall's suggestions a bias in the direction of investigating the managerial problems inherent in large business organizations of national scope, it was clear to him and everyone else that this was not a program for the Institute as such. Oliphant's ideas were all over the place, though in some vague sense they focused on the way that organizational devices make substantive law reform effective. That focus might have provided a program for the Institute, except that Marshall did not believe in the truth of the empirical observation that underlay Oliphant's focus,[96] Yntema did not really want to do anything other than historical and comparative law, and Cook, nothing but scientific method and the conflict of laws. So, for a year everyone talked and everyone worked on whatever each had brought to Baltimore. A crucial year was thus lost and an effective precedent set: every faculty member would do what he damn well pleased.

Now that decision fit the personalities of Cook and Oliphant, and maybe Yntema as well, but it suited the Institute not at all, for it meant that the Institute's program essentially would be the product of chance. Oliphant fell in with Greenbaum and his New York lawyers; Marshall talked to his brother who had a new Judicial Council to run and nothing for it to do. And so the Institute started off in a direction, court studies, that only Cook was possibly trained for — he, at least, had taught pleading and practice — and no one was interested in a priori. Given that Marshall was the best administrator and only natural fundraiser, his study, into which he somehow dragooned Yntema's body but not his interest,[97] came to dominate the Institute's affairs and to take a direction, the development of a systematic statistical base, that his economics background suggested to him was important, but that was guaranteed to strike the interest of few, if any, lawyers and none of his colleagues. It thus made no difference whether court studies were a good or a bad idea or whether the work product of the Institute was good or bad; it was the wrong idea and the wrong product. It was not going to sell. And even worse it was going to put Marshall in the center ring that Cook needed to occupy and that Oliphant needed to have empty.

The result was that the best anyone could do to create the semblance of a program was to get a court study for Cook to direct, but not really take part in. But, not being essentially duplicitous individuals, no matter how many times they tried, no matter how many times they talked of the importance of training researchers and of basic studies of scientific method as an integral part of the research program, no matter how much paper they used, they still could not paper over the problem that Max Mason identified: the Institute's program did not "hang together." Indeed, one could not even make the court studies hang together, or at least no one tried. Oliphant was interested in cost, delay, and uncertainty, classic topics for progressive law reform. Marshall was interested in knowing how the judicial machine really operated. He did not care about uncertainty or cost and only a little about delay, for he did not have the foggiest idea what was really going on in the courts, any more than Oliphant cared about how the judicial machine as a machine operated, for he knew: it operated with cost, delay, and uncertainty.

That the research program of a department does not hang together is probably fine; at least it is expected. But it was an institute, a research entity, at Hopkins, a place known for its research, that was being sold. Without a program that made sense *as a program* no one could sell the Institute. But, given the four faculty members, there never could be a program or more accurately it was guaranteed that any program that emerged would only increase the centrifugal forces inherent in their personalities. And so no endowment came because no one could explain what it was going for, the Philosophical Faculty naysayers gathered in a Greek chorus, and Cook, Oliphant, and Yntema resigned when Marshall was made Director. It was the closest they had come to doing something together — they united in opposition to something that had nothing to do with the program, except to say symbolically that it had not emerged.

WHILE ALL OF THESE MATTERS of personality are sensibly seen as accidental — they might have been otherwise — it is important to note here briefly, for it will be more important later, that in one sense none of this was accidental. Looking only at the law professors, three — Cook, Moore, and Oliphant — were classic malcontents. All three were unhappy with the law schools they found themselves in and unhappy with what they taught, difficult to deal with, and sure that they knew exactly what needed to be done. Clark, though not a malcontent, was anything but happy with legal education.[98] I do not think it accidental that the major participants in the Realists' empirical research activities were this unhappy with the world of the common law professor.[99] While malcontents often drift away from the activity that makes them unhappy, they can also attempt to improve their situation by remaking that activity. Each was thus available to other pursuits. On this view one might argue that what was accidental to this story was empirical social science. If what was "hot" in the academy in the twenties and thirties was humanities scholarship, this book would be titled "American Legal Realism and the Humanist Tradition." Although there is some real truth to the notion that as a group the Realists were classic malcontents who would have been unhappy in any army and not just Christopher Columbus Langdell's army, the notion that any fad would have grabbed their interest is implausible, at least to the following extent. Empirical social science was attractive because its wisdom opposed the law's traditional wisdom; it pressed in the direction of inquiry into a world of social actors and social actions and so away from the inquiry into the world of legal concepts that each found somehow unsatisfactory. As such it fed the malcontentedness. Humanities scholarship which emphasizes great works of the human mind would not have fed the malcontentedness.[100]

WHILE MATTERS OF TIME and to an extent of person may be seen as accidental, the nature of the Realists' research enterprise can not be. Here proceeding as before is unhelpful. Instead, we must turn our story back toward its beginning and return to Walter Wheeler Cook, first at Columbia and then at Hopkins, for it is he alone among the Realists who had a well worked out understanding of what it was to apply scientific method to law. However, in examining Cook's ideas, it is important to remember that he was not an original thinker. Reviewing his work on scientific method in law for the twenty years following Dewey's lectures, one is struck by how little the argument changes and by how much the trappings, the examples and authorities, that accompany that argument reflect the science-for-intellectuals literature of those years. Thus, the great book on scientific method never appeared because Cook had nothing unusual to say on that subject. All of which is not to say that his work in the field, both articles and a wonderful set of materials for law students,[101] was not useful. Precisely the contrary is the case. Cook literally dragged the modern idea of science into law. This was a significant achievement as was his conflicts work, where it can be honestly said that he remade the field in his own image.[102] Cook saw to it that law could not ignore science, but at the same time he was only embroidering ideas that Dewey had articulated first.

The three ideas of Dewey that Cook pushed were that science was a method of pulling together experience with problem-solving objectives; that the syllogism was not a reflection of the thought processes of humans, though it was a method of ordering thought; and that when thinking about anything "new," solving a new problem or coming to understand a new fact, one necessarily created new premises or categories, gave new meaning to the terms that would ultimately be dressed up in a syllogism. In Dewey all three were really different sides of the same irregularly shaped rock; the pragmatic understanding of truth as what works, what is validated by experience. But in Cook the matter was different. Because case analysis had long been thought to be part of a syllogistic judicial logic, the last two points got split off into the great juristic debate for which Realism is so well known, a debate about the nature of judicial decision making that hid a debate about the substance of judicial decisions.[103] This debate is the one on which Cook focused his efforts. In truth he was less interested in the methodology of science than in demonstrating that the assumed deductive methodology of judges was nothing of the kind, but necessarily hid a choice as to what rule to apply in any given case. And so Dewey's first point was left to hang alone, generously translated by Llewellyn into his aphorism, "see it fresh, see it clear,"[104] but more generally seen as opening the possibility of doing empirical research.

Now there is nothing wrong with splitting up Dewey's ideas in this way. I doubt that if the matter had been brought to his attention Dewey would have strongly objected.[105] Nor do I think that much should be read into Cook's choice to see Dewey as he did. That choice was less a response to any theoretical or methodological problem than a response that fit with, and so made sense of, Cook's life and interests. At the same time, however, that choice implicated answers to two of the questions that any academic discipline needs to face, if only implicitly: "What is appropriate scholarship/research in this field?" and "How does one make sense of, give meaning to, or come to understand the results of that scholarship/research?"

Nineteenth-century legal science answered these two questions simply: it treated them as if they were one question. Legal scientists examined case reports and from the cases derived (in an unspecified way) doctrines that were fit into a system of principles that governed the actions of judges because they formed the law. This is the world that Cook worked in at the start of his career. Cook's view of Dewey suggested that new answers need be given to the same two questions, for now there were at least two kinds of research: case law research and empirical studies. On the one side, Cook's own work suggested a modest, but significant change in the nineteenth-century understanding of case law scholarship/research. Case law research would yield not doctrines but rules (a class of objects with a smaller compass), and those rules would be organized not with reference to principles but rather with respect to considerations of policy, of social advantage. But on the other, the empirical side, Cook offered little help in answering questions about how to understand the results of research or even about when it was appropriate to do empirical work, a question that nineteenth-century legal science did not have to answer because it offered no choices about what kind of research to do. As Cook was not much interested in empirical work, he left the job of figuring out answers to those who were. Thus, these were the questions that Oliphant and Yntema would try to answer at Hopkins and that Clark and Douglas would meet at Yale; consequently the story of their attempts to do so bulks large in this book.

Cook's choice to see Dewey in this way, to reorient modestly case law research and, at the same time, to leave the place of empirical research in law undefined, had, as they say, its benefits and its costs. Some of the benefits become clear if one remembers that the great juristic debate, the debate over judicial decision making, was in part a debate over how to look at law — from the inside or from the out. Nineteenth-century legal science took the position of the insider. Progressive reformers like Pound and Wickersham did so as well; they would reform the rules because from the insider's perspective it was important to have better rules. Moreover, complaints about Llewellyn's temporary divorce of the "is" and the "ought" from the likes of Dickinson or Fuller or about the failure to pay attention to the rational science of law from Adler or Cohen can easily be understood as complaints about proper behavior. As far as these critics were concerned, Llewellyn and empiricists like Moore were not acting like proper legal academics. Proper legal academics made their observations and offered their criticisms from the internal perspective from which law was about norms.[106]

Holmes's prediction theory undercut all of this, for that theory suggested that it was plausible for a party inside the system to act as if he were observing the system.[107] Moore's and later Oliphant's identification of empirical social science with the position of the outside observer only made things worse, for, since science was "objective," this identification suggested that the legal science of the insiders produced not the objective truth that it had always purported to produce but something else. That suggestion was more than a might disturbing, even to the crew at Hopkins. Cook, for unclear reasons, hated Beale's vision of the conflict of laws and Oliphant seemingly believed in the progressive reformer's concern about congested courts and went to Washington to engineer social change with such measures as the excess profits tax. Thus, each had to decide what it was that the insider's perspective produced, because for each that perspective was important. If these activities — doing the conflict of laws or seeking to relieve court congestion — were meaningless, then a great deal of academic legal work was pointless. Known pointless activity is always to be avoided and so both men had reason to work out a way to avoid this obvious conclusion. Still, Oliphant never did figure out what to do with the inside reformer's perspective. He just brushed it aside. And later Cook could deal with the problem only by insisting with Dewey that ethics, the policy that made sense of legal scholarship, might have an empirical dimension. Yet, the feebleness of these attempts to avoid the obvious ought not to be dismissed as evidence of feeble brain power; rather, like Cook's equally feeble attempts to criticize Freund's book twenty-five years earlier, they should be recognized as an indication of the significance of the question at issue. An answer needed to be offered, even an inadequate one.

While Cook's view of Dewey did not provide the necessary answer to the question of what was produced by the insider's case law scholarship, it had one distinct advantage. At least, it could keep that question at bay. One did not have to consider what case law scholarship might mean, for in Cook's view science was simply a method: it was just pragmatic thought in another guise. Anything could be done scientifically: one simply adapted the available tools to the materials and objectives at hand and set to work at whatever project one wanted.[108] Thus, case law work and even law reform could go on pretty much as before, because, if properly done, it too was scientific. And so, though Dickinson and Fuller, Adler and Cohen did not see it, Cook could preserve the world that they were comfortable in; indeed, he defended their world when it seemed to them that he had attacked it. Theirs might not be the only activity for legal scholars, but it could be insulated from those who adopted the outsider's perspective. Using the results of empirical work much as they had used the results of Hohfeld's work, the insiders could continue to pay pretty close attention to the norms they had always paid attention to.

But, it was not just the scholars who defended the insider's perspective who would benefit from keeping troublesome questions at bay. Realists like Cook and Oliphant or Douglas and, maybe even, Clark might similarly benefit. As Cook demonstrated, he could talk, indeed all but hector, science; do the conflict of laws; and keep his head on straight because he was doing the conflict of laws scientifically. He was checking the doctrinal formulations against what they were supposed to represent: the activities of the appellate courts that we call law. Similarly, Oliphant could find that settled automobile accident claims were a major part of the civil docket in New York and yet advocate the more stern administration of the rule assessing costs against losing parties in the name of relieving congestion by keeping frivolous suits out of court; Douglas could fail to discover whether gambling and property speculation were important causes of bankruptcy and yet work to bar discharge for such activity; and Clark could find that procedure seemed to play little role in civil litigation and yet work to reform federal procedure by drafting and urging the adoption of the Federal Rules. Each proceeded scientifically with respect to both his empirical research and his policy prescriptions; with Cook's view of Dewey as a guide, the latter enterprise need never find its concerns questioned in the name of the former.

To provide this major benefit, to open up the possibility of a broad future for diverse kinds of scholarship while cutting off only a limited aspect of the past — the implicit claim of case law scholarship to be the only form of scholarship — as did Cook's view of Dewey, was not a priori a bad thing. Indeed, with some hindsight and a heavy dose of imagination one could say that in this way Cook enabled law to avoid the awful morass of statistical method in which social science still finds itself. But there were costs to Cook's action and those costs were all on the empirical side of law. If science was just a method, then one needed, or at least would likely find it more comfortable if one had, a separate point to or explanation for the choice of one's research topic. The problem posed was simple. If traditional method and materials of the law, case law analysis, was, when properly pursued, adequately scientific, then what reason was there for a properly professionalized law teacher, moderately content in the accustomed groove of scholarship, to do anything else?

And so, empirical legal research was faced with the need to justify its choice to put down the pipe and get out of the armchair.

This matter of justification was both a question of occasion and that of meaning or understanding of the results of research. Here then was the role for, and of, progressive law reform as Clark, Douglas, Hutchins, and others knew it. It offered both occasion and meaning. Based as it was on an all-men-of-good-will ethics, progressive law reform functioned on the conceit that the true conditions were unknown, but if known would galvanize society into making the necessary changes to set matters right. In Pound's terminology, if men knew what the law in action was, then men would adjust the law on the books to conform to the jural postulates, the commonly accepted understandings of what good law ought to be.[109] The need to know what was "going on," to see the law in action so as to reform the law in the books, thus provided the reason for engaging in empirical legal research. It was a way of finding the facts that would bring reform. And yet, as an occasion for doing or a matter of giving meaning to or understanding the results of empirical research, this idea was less than ideal.

Progressive law reform was not a capacious enterprise. Control of the agenda of law reform was largely within the profession, in the hands of the leaders of the bar like Wickersham and Ballantine, Burlingham and Greenbaum, and of the few academics, like Frankfurter, who, being from the "best" schools, were allowed entry into such circles. These individuals defined what research was sensible to pursue and what results were intelligible, and they could help to make their opinions about sense a reality through informal relationships with funding sources, as Cravath had done for Oliphant at Carnegie, because in most quarters theirs was *the* view of law reform. In professional hands law reform was quite obviously directed toward "safe" channels, whether from a limited social vision, from solid political preference, or from a Kolkoesque desire to avoid worse alternatives.[110] Thus, reform remained a surface notion in which all, or most, of the defects in the law were procedural or remedial; the courts, congested, and the rules, uncertain; and in which higher standards for admission to the bar were the cure to both overcrowding and unethical practices by lawyers.[111] Quite obviously, this view aided the social and economic position of both these lawyers and their clients. But, more important, this view placed direct limits on what research might be done, what its results might mean, and how it was to be pursued.

Clark and Douglas felt the limits that the profession's definition of reform placed on research quite directly when trying to explain the absence of court congestion, when trying to outline the contemporary significance of the diversity jurisdiction, and when justifying all the work done on the auto compensation study. Douglas reflected these limits when giving up the business failures project. But the indirect limits that derived from the limited purpose for which reform needed facts were just as serious. The facts had not just to fit with the campaign for reform, they had to fit the pace of reform, its budget both in time and money. However, empirical legal research in the model of academic social science was an unruly horse with its own pace and content.

As Douglas remarked a year or so after he gave up the business failures project, "All the facts which we worked so hard to get don't seem to help a hell of a lot."[112] If what was wanted was the facts on which to base the argument for reform, quantitative empirical research either produced too many, as in the courts studies, or worse, a very few at an enormous cost, as in the business failures or auto accidents projects. And then there was the matter of time. Of the completed studies that Clark and Douglas engaged in, the shortest, auto compensation, took three years, and the median time was nearly five years. At least after the technical revolution in social science methodology that Thomas and Corstvet represented, empirical research was time-consuming and costly. Neither fit well with the need for facts to fuel reform. Reform had to have its facts when the political time was ripe and at as low a cost as possible. It thus presented real limits as a reason for doing and as a means for understanding empirical research in law.

These limits can be seen at Hopkins as well. Here Cook's ideas played out more directly than at Yale. Since anything could be done scientifically, each "practically independent" research unit would have to decide just what it would do. Into this intellectual vacuum all the research assistants inserted Rueff's *From the Physical to the Social Sciences*.[113] But on its own that book really led nowhere either; it simply said that empirical social research on the model of the physical sciences was possible. Everyone basically knew that; the question was precisely what empirical legal research to do. So everyone who wished to do such research, as Cook plainly wished everyone but he would do, was remitted to happenstance to answer the question.

Oliphant fell in with the New York City law reform crowd, or at least a piece of it, and the Survey of Litigation reflects that fact. It was focused on cost, delay, and uncertainty in litigation, the staples of law reform for years. And what got completed and published reflected that fact. Calendar practice reform worked, and so at least part of that study made it into print.[114] But then, when the focus of reform shifted to Governor Franklin D. Roosevelt's new statewide committee, the Commission on the Administration of Justice in New York State, really a miniversion of the Wickersham Commission,[115] nothing else got pushed to completion. This was not just because Oliphant left, but because his study, whatever its results, was no longer needed. Reform could proceed without it.

Curiously, Marshall managed to stumble onto a different occasion for doing empirical legal research. Through contact with his brother, Marshall found judicial administration. It was then a new enterprise consisting mostly of Herbert Hartley and his American Judicature Society[116] and the nascent Judicial Council movement.[117] Judicial administration was really a branch of Taylorite management. Its watchword was efficiency. It did not want reform; it wanted control. Its problems were not cost, delay, and uncertainty; its problems were lack of uniformity of treatment, the lack of production standards, and jurisdictional chaos. It was a group largely with its own agenda that drew its membership from judicial and other official administrative bodies, as can be seen from the meeting that Marshall had with the Bureau of the Census and the FBI and from the conference that he arranged for representatives of the state judicial councils.

Examples of that agenda can be seen in the work of the Ohio study. Although at this time not a single study of the municipal courts in Ohio cities had been published, much less any that might suggest that lack of uniformity was a problem, Yntema created a draft uniform municipal court act.[118] And although the appellate court study was not yet done, much less when published did it indicate the need for a simplified procedure, Silas Harris generated an appellate procedure reform act that mainly made it easier for the judiciary to process the paper that is appellate litigation.[119] And once the business of classifying criminal cases got completed, the momentum for finishing the court studies was somehow lost, despite the fact that there was money left to have subsidized the enterprise. As a matter of court administration, a case is a case; a defense, a defense. The details did not matter any more than did the role of the prosecutor or the age of children of divorcing spouses, unless the details somehow contributed to inefficiency.[120]

If neither law reform nor judicial administration could successfully provide a stable foundation for engaging in empirical legal research because each limited the occasion for and constrained the meaning of such research, it was at least possible to retrace one's steps back to Dewey's lectures at the Columbia Law School, reject Cook's action in splitting up Dewey's three ideas on science, and, instead, reunite the three. Seen in this way Dewey on science turned science into a critique of nonempirical forms of knowing and so pointed in the direction of a particular application of the method of science, namely (quantitative) empirical studies. Moore, in effect, reunited Dewey in this way, though not being a theoretician he left few clues to the precise dimensions of this other view of Dewey beyond his research and scraps in his correspondence.[121] He probably envisioned an empirical science of law, not directed at reform of existing law, nor at making its administration more efficient, but rather somehow united with the training of lawyers based on the knowledge acquired through the empirical studies.[122] If this was his vision, it was in some ways a quite attractive vision that Clark shared as well.[123] But its underpinning, Moore's nascent empirical science of law, like Cook's alternative, had benefits as well as costs.

The primary benefit was seemingly extraordinary. By its own terms the view of science as a critique of nonempirical ways of knowing that Moore followed opened untold doors for the understanding of law and so directly answered the question, "What is appropriate scholarship/research in this field?" in ways that Cook's view of Dewey could not do. It said, "Tell me what of the old wisdom you think is untrue and I will help you learn the truth." That was a heady offer. The world did not have to think that the problem was very interesting. Indeed, many then and since have surely found that neither Moore's banking nor traffic studies were intrinsically interesting, though at least the banking studies were such for Moore and for any serious student of the changes that had taken place in American banking in the years when a real national currency began to displace the draft and the note from their nineteenth-century role as a medium of exchange that supplemented gold. All that was necessary was that the researcher find the problem interesting. Models were not particularly constraining, though that was not an unmixed blessing; acceptable techniques were still moderately fluid; and in few circumstances could one be told, "Don't bother; it's been done before." All that was asked in return was that, in Corstvet's words, one struggle to measure.

To this benefit must be added two others. First, to see and follow this view of science was "to catch a wave," as the vernacular puts it. Empirical methodology in the social sciences was growing. The swell was noticeable enough that reaction was already beginning to be heard,[124] and soon there would be a great crest. The ride in front of that crest promised to be spectacular. Second, there was the pesky problem of the insider and the outsider view of law. Here, as in the case with Cook's view of Dewey, the basic problem was identifying what it was that case law analysis, legal science, might produce. Moore managed to avoid this problem by identifying his work with that of the practicing lawyer, Holmes's predictor, and then abandoning the internal perspective altogether. Whatever case law analysis produced it was not scientific knowledge. Avoidance was perhaps a sensible strategy, for science as a critique of nonempirical ways of knowing was a most corrosive idea. It suggested that case law analysis, built not even on what courts did but only what they said and so purported to do, was meaningless, unless checked for its correspondence with some action in the world. Better to push the activity outside science and leave it there. To do so was a benefit, even if (and maybe better because) it infuriated the practitioners of legal science.

If these three things—a grand opening toward knowledge, an exciting wave of empiricism and avoidance of a problem of the meaning of the insider's work—were the benefits of seeing Dewey on science as Moore seemed to do, then what were the costs? Here I believe two need to be identified: the matter of understanding and the matter of a place to work.

First, understanding. On Cook's view of Dewey, progressive reform or judicial administration would provide both the occasion for and the meaning of the results of empirical work. On Moore's view, occasion was not a problem; there was no other choice if one was going to be scientific—a pipe and a chair were not an alternative to work in the field. But meaning was still a problem.

While Moore's view of science allowed one to study anything, it was remarkably thin in the help that it offered with the task of coming to understand the meaning of what one learned. Consider the court studies. This work at both Yale and Hopkins pointed to the routine administrative character of much of what passes through the modern court system. Today, we accept that finding as if it were obvious, although we do not truly understand it, in the sense of having a theory that explains why we should expect such a finding, and we clearly fight it, as seen by our continuous attempts to create judicialized due process to control mass processing of cases and to teach about civil procedure as if a trial were its point. But in 1930 there was not even a basis for acceptance.

Why this is so is simple: Moore's view of science brought with it few ideas with real explanatory power. On the sociology side there were ideas about law as social control, the dislocations that followed from the growing complexity of modern life and of cultural lag and on the law side, of the "gap" between the law on the books and the law in action from Pound's sociological jurisprudence, and of the congested courts from progressive law reform. None of these ideas was really capable of shedding light on the findings in the court studies. The complexity of modern life suggested that the courts ought to be congested, but since complexity was supposed to bring disorder in both sociological and progressive legal theory, finding basically efficient admin-istration in the court system was hard to explain. Nor did these findings fit with any notion of law as a part of culture that lagged behind the develop-ment of material life. If anything, efficient, mass processing of cases showed that law was not lagging, but keeping up with life. And then there was social control. Efficient operation aided social control, I suppose, but routine pro-cessing of vast quantities of cases suggests that such aid was overall not much.

As for the gap between law in the books and law in action, clearly there was a good deal of that to be found, and not only in the court studies, but also in Moore's research. Still, it was never clear exactly what one was supposed to do when one found a gap other than to close it up, either by recognizing the limits of effective legal action and so limiting what one asked from law or by adopting social engineering methods that would develop better law that would come to grips with life and so reduce the gap that way. Pound's phrase was a call to action, not an aid to understanding. Thus, it was hard to tell what action to take when one found that the courts were efficiently con-gested. Pound had no answer for that one: it must be, as Morgan argued, that the law was so far out of touch that it had left litigants with no other choice than to avoid law as best they could.

Even less did Pound's idea offer an explanation for Moore's research that suggested that the gap was to be expected, unless law was simply affirming customary behavior, since, where law did not follow custom, custom modi-fied law.[125] Nor were the dislocations that followed from the complexity of modern life or cultural lag of much help in understanding bankers and park-ers. And then there was social control. Here Moore's work suggested an important qualification — that law as an instrument of social control was likely to always be at least modestly ineffective — to what was at best an un-thought-out idea in sociology and here, where help could have been had, there was no one to talk with at Yale.

Thus, since Moore's social science had brought with it no conceptual schema that could explain the results of the Realist's research, that research could not form the basis for stimulating more work. While true, the results were just a jumble of facts, as Llewellyn asserted. Even worse, the lack of a way to explain the facts meant that some of the most interesting ones, such as those about the difficulty of proving embezzlement or the low level of sup-port in divorce actions, got lost. There was no way to distinguish these facts from any other facts and, since reform didn't dictate what facts were impor-tant or unimportant, all facts were treated as equal and equally forgettable.

There were, of course, alternative conceptual frameworks for understanding the court studies or Moore's banking and parking research. Most notably there was a nineteenth-century enterprise that could be seen as a kind of empirical legal research. That was the largely historical scholarship of such individuals as Sir Henry Maine, Sir Paul Vinogradoff, Otto von Gierke, Theodor Momsen, and Fustel de Coulanges, the historical sociology of Max Weber and the less historical sociology of Eugen Ehrlich. This rich and suggestive literature, some of it even available in English translation, was ignored by all of the Realists in their empirical work.[126] In one sense that is a real loss because this work led in a direction away from narrowly quantitative studies, but at the same time was richly and rigidly objective in its treatment of sources and, in history, in its insistence on the use of original sources. It was thus methodologically looser than American sociology was becoming and methodologically tighter than the more speculative work of first Frank and then Arnold and Robinson.

Unfortunately, this work was closed off to the Realists interested in empirical research for reasons of language, discipline, approach, and source. First, language. Much of the material was available only in German or French; American law professors did not work in those languages and the fact that the only American legal scholar well versed in European sources was Pound made the Realists doubly unlikely to look at them. Next, discipline. The largest amount of this scholarship, even the scholarship available in English, was in history, generally ancient or medieval history at that. It is important to recognize that only one of the Realists, Walter Nelles, was a historian. Unfortunately, but understandably, the Realists conflated history with one of its types, doctrinal history, and so eschewed history altogether because for them it had the wrong resonance. It brought to mind the research of Langdell, Thayer, and Ames, and they were the enemy, the revered elders whose work Cook and Hohfeld had attacked for not getting it right. History was part of their legal science and it was thought that that legal science had proved inadequate to contemporary circumstances by fixing law on a deductive method that paid little attention to the changes in American society and the necessity of law to adapt to those changes. That the relevant European historical scholarship offered anything but this lesson is beside the point. The Realists paid little attention to the good American historical scholarship of Henry Adams, Charles Beard, and James Harvey Robinson. There was thus still less chance that they would pay enough attention to the best European historical scholarship and so come to understand that these authors suggested other ways to look at law in a society. To do this the Realists would have had to open these less easily accessible books and, since they had not opened the more accessible American literature, that was not going to happen.

Third there was approach. The sociology of Weber and Ehrlich was the wrong sociology, even if it had been known. Theirs was seen as a product of the same loose sociological method that was shared with Sumner, the American understanding of Herbert Spencer, and numerous pundits of the political economy whom each of the Realists had encountered in college. Reaction to the relentless, almost apologetic conservatism of this group, its sense that the American economic and social system was adequate, even essential to progress, provided most of the push for doing quantitative empiricism in American sociology. This reaction to what was seen as social speculation, not social science, made the loose work of these European scholars less available than it might otherwise have been.

Last there was source. One must remember, the Realists were American law professors. Here, in particular, the view of intellectual history as accounting for all possible dialogues with all available ideas must be resisted. If one was an American lawyer, one did not look to European sources, beyond an occasional glance at English ones. After all, at this time American exceptionalism was still not dead; indeed, Americans had just attempted to avoid a European war because it was none of our business what those decadent European states with their antique political systems did to each other and, only shortly before that, endured a bit of a national crisis of conscience when we acquired an empire just as had those same decadent European states. So, whatever the merits of the models for the empirical study of law that could be found in the best of the European scholarship at that time, such ideas were not available to the Realists. Theirs would be a red-blooded American's quantitative empiricism even if the collection of totals and analysis of percentages benumbed the brain.

However, the cost involved in the lack of a conceptual schema for understanding research was not the only cost to adopting Moore's view of Dewey on science. There was also the question of place, of where to work and thus of how that work would be received, a question easily subdivided into looking first at the university, next at its departments, and last at the law school. To begin with, the university then (and even more so now) had no particular interest in an empirical science of law any more than Hopkins had a particular interest in Cook's Institute. And, indeed, it probably had less interest in this activity that was exemplified by Moore's science. At least the empiricists in Cook's Institute were fitting their research into the interests of powerful outsiders active in law reform and judicial administration. In some vague sense that fact was helpful to the university, for at the time scholars like

Charles E. Merriam[127] or William F. Ogburn[128] were busy forming the now much derided "multiversity" out of the earlier "Wisconsin ideal." Their creation, structured as it was toward public issues and public service, had no use for an empirical science of law because that science had no apparent use, except one too far down the trail to be worth much in the way of support. The university, of course, would not actively oppose such a science, but it surely would not go out of the way to support it either.

Nor was the empirical science of law attractive in any particular corner of the university. By the late thirties and early forties university departments in the social sciences were no longer still forming, but had thoroughly balkanized and solidified. Individuals in these departments, it should be remembered, found Moore's research for the most part unintelligible, for it was not their science. It was *drawn to a nonexistent paradigm within a nonexistent culture.* These individuals might help research like Moore's become more like something they knew and could understand, but taking it on its own terms was really quite impossible. That the research was scientific, empirical and all that, may have been enough in the early twenties,[129] but it was not enough fifteen or twenty years later. By then, research had to be a part of a definable academic discipline and by its nature this was the one thing that the Realists' research could not be.

And then there was the law school. Here Moore's work is again a good example. All the inhabitants of the law school world found Moore's empirical science of law, neither doctrinal nor directed at reform and sustained really beyond imagination, weird, thus perhaps dangerous. For those who were satisfied in their jobs because it was all they could handle, men like Vance and maybe Lorenzen, Moore's empirical science of law was frightening. Thus, they disliked it, even if they did not oppose it.[130] For those like Corbin and Llewellyn, satisfied because the law school world gave ample room for using their quite extraordinary talents to uncover substantial insights about doctrine and its use, Moore's work was simply unnecessary. A suggestion to go to Cincinnati to "observe the operations of bank tellers at close range"[131] was pointless when a call to a friendly banker coupled with a bit of imagination would provide the same information. Thus, these men, like Friedrich Kessler to whom the suggestion was made, mostly ignored Moore's work.[132] For men like Hutchins and Douglas, who found the world of law teaching both a bit empty and largely devoid of sustained commitment to absolutely anything except the law school, Moore's work was largely puzzling. They were surprised when they woke up in a university.[133] But the university they woke up in and thus responded to was a university in which scholarship like that Moore espoused was becoming a lost ideal. Despite the quite obvious similarities, somehow his work was not the kind of work these younger men saw around them and so they tolerated it, but at a distance. Thus, the empirical science of law built on Moore's view of Dewey left all concerned very ambivalent.[134] Not surprisingly many, if not all, felt the need not to confront it but to distance it, as they distanced Moore's work with a slightly derisive humor — "the love life of a check,"[135] or "can't you see, I'm busy counting these cars."[136] None felt the need to imitate it.

Surely, in the thirties at least, the costs of adopting Moore's view of Dewey on science exceeded the benefits. It was too early for the American, bastardized version of Weber's value-free social science or the structural functionalist ideas of Merton and Parsons to be of aid to Moore's science, built as it was on Thomas's and Corstvet's desires for objectivity and the notion of custom, not function or structure. And so, of two possible formulations of Dewey on science, Cook's survived by default. Empirical research in law would by nature, really necessity, be attached to reform or judicial administration or some other, later impulse coming from the insiders' view of law as norm. Were there no such impetus, there would be no empirical research.

Three Attempts to Build a Round Wheel

The impetus to do empirical legal research never really died out in at least the elite law schools. Indeed, the same year that Moore's parking research was finally published McDougal and Lasswell published their great piece on legal education for public policy in which social science played a large part, albeit the role envisioned was that of the lawyer as a consumer rather than a producer of empirical legal research[137] and a year earlier a committee of the Social Science Research Council that included among its members both Clark and Marshall published a "call for sustained research in institutions around the country" into topics in "judicial administration," a category that encompassed both the Yale and Hopkins work.[138] So when, after the war was over and the returning GIs were educated, the idea of doing some empirical research jointly with the social scientists but in a law school setting was raised, no one was surprised. Of course, because we were all Realists now and so had learned from past mistakes, we would do "better."

Chicago's Law and Behavioral Science Program

The first bit of that better research began in spring of 1951 soon after Robert Hutchins resigned his post as Chancellor of the University of Chicago to become an associate director of the newly wealthy Ford Foundation.[139] One of the members of his former faculty, Edward H. Levi, filed a grant application with the Foundation to create a "graduate research and clinical center" at the Law School. This application, part of an attempt by a new dean from a new generation to energize his law school, proposed to "bring the knowledge of the social sciences to bear upon the facts of the law, and to reformulate such knowledge into acceptable statutory law," and so it provided for a research staff of graduate fellows to work in "criminology; law and economics; philosophy of law, international law and comparative law," a clinic "to bring the law school sample cases illustrating the way the legal system is operating, and the facts with which the legal system must deal," and a law revision group designed so that "the law school research and clinical center will have an immediate effect upon the development of the law."[140] The document was a good lawyerly job that attempted to cover the fact that, as was the case with the Hopkins Institute's ideas twenty years earlier, the three pieces were not terribly closely related. Given that precedent, it is not surprising that the Ford Foundation staff, though recognizing that "legal research is currently and traditionally starved," likewise was "not impressed" but found the proposal, "a hodge-podge so far as Foundation interests are concerned."[141] Nevertheless, Hutchins kept it alive.[142]

During the next year the Foundation attempted to decide what kind of a program it wanted and Levi and the Foundation tried to put together something mutually satisfactory.[143] While doing so, however, Levi's conception of the proposal shifted in the direction of a focus "on the effect of law upon behavior and of behavior on law," and a design "to secure a body of facts and a set of generalizations about human behavior in situations in which law is involved in one way or another,"[144] a phrasing that betrays the appearance of Karl Llewellyn at the Law School.[145] Possible areas for research similarly shifted to law observance and infringement, social institutions, individual rights, and the administration of justice, each with a long list of possible topics.[146] Dubious of Chicago's claim to the Foundation's largess, Foundation officers visited three other law schools — Columbia, Harvard, and Yale — only to conclude that Chicago *was* the place to put Foundation money[147] and so worked with Levi to generate an acceptable proposal.

The resulting grant application[148] began with a quite bold statement: "The subject matter of law is human behavior."[149] In pursuit of this observation Levi proposed to choose three research topics from a list of five: the youthful offender, obscenity, the association between beliefs about tax burdens and attitudes toward government spending, the jury system, and arbitration, and to spend $400,000 over two and a half years.[150] The choice of which of the five to pursue seemed not to be very important for it was expected that the studies chosen that "deal with . . . behavior either in problem situations or where . . . customary behavior without the added sanction of formal rules is deemed insufficient" would "tend to subdivide and to give rise to additional but related studies."[151] The application was careful to note problems that might have been seen in the Realists' efforts at empirical research and to indicate solutions.

> The program which is suggested requires inter-disciplinary research. Inter-disciplinary research while often most fruitful is also most difficult organizationally as well as conceptually. The suggestion is that by concentration on actual situations which raise simultaneously legal and behavioral science problems, some of these difficulties will be obviated. But those who have had experience with this kind of work surely will attest to the fact that it is of great importance to have a group so situated that its members learn from one another, and with projects so arranged that techniques and data relevant to one may be also relevant to another. It is of the utmost importance that the doing of the research be a common experience for the group as a whole, and that there be a carry-over of insights and knowledge from one project to another. In the course of time much will depend upon the formation of an atmosphere and a growing sense of what is involved in doing this kind of cooperative intellectual work in a field in which precedents are almost nonexistent.[152]

The Foundation's directors duly approved the application[153] and equally duly three projects were chosen to work on: the jury, arbitration, and attitudes concerning the income tax.[154] The last two were directed by Soia Mentschikoff and by Walter Blum and Harry Kalven, respectively; the jury study, commonly identified with Harry Kalven, by first, Bernard Meltzer and then, Philip Kurland,[155] though Levi had "direct responsibility" for guiding it,[156] and only finally by Kalven.

Program funds were used to add two sociologists, Hans Zeisel and Fred L. Strodtbeck, and one psychologist, Alan Barton, to the faculty as well as to secure the cooperation of several university faculty members, including Edward Shils.[157] From the beginning the jury study seems to have dominated the enterprise, whether because of the potential breadth of the topic or Levi's direct interests, it is not clear. Emphasis was placed on "(1) problems of jury selection; (2) the effect upon the juror of the manner of his reception into the trial system; (3) the impact of the trial and of the instructions of the judge upon the jurors; (4) the nature of the jury's deliberation; and (5) comparison of jury trials with alternative adjudication procedures."[158] A great number of research techniques were used including intensive interviews with actual jurors after real cases; similar interviews and analysis of recorded deliberations of jurors drawn from regular jury lists who had listened to recorded trials;[159] and questionnaires administered to judges asking whether they agreed or disagreed with jury verdicts in cases they heard, to jurors attempting to isolate relationships between juror characteristics and votes for conviction or acquittal and checking attitudes to jury service, and to lawyers looking at reasons for waiver of jury trial and to expectations as to damages.[160]

The arbitration project on the other hand was smaller. It centered on "(1) factors responsible for the growth of machinery of arbitration in trade and exchange groups; (2) the judicial machinery found in such groups and the values inherent in the forms utilized; (3) the decision-making process of arbitration; (4) the extent and history of commercial arbitration." Methods were suitably eclectic, though obviously a bit more oriented toward library and archival research. Still interviews and questionnaires were sent out to trade associations to learn the extent of commercial arbitration; in addition "[i]n analyzing the process of decision by arbitrators . . . techniques of interview, observation, recording and experimentation, including psychological testing for personality structures and values" were used. The intensive phase of the study focused on "the American Arbitration Association as an example of a group providing general machinery for use by the public, and . . . the New York Stock Exchange as an example of [arbitration in] a tightly knit institution."[161]

Work on both of these projects seems to have moved along quickly. At least, after two years Levi thought that enough progress had been made, thus "fulfilling the hopes and expectations" with which the program was undertaken, to apply for a renewal of the grant for five years. An amount of $1,250,000 was sought for the research program; $375,000, for a program of fellowships for "law teachers and graduate lawyers, social scientists and foreign scholars"; $650,000, for foreign and international studies; and $1,500,000, as a contribution to the cost of a new building, this last tagged on with the argument that space needs of the research had interfered with the existing Law School program and made acute the existing need for such a building. The application stressed that the program was "a central part of the program of the law school itself," and that the three studies involved "basic research, the development of new techniques, the acquisition of data and the development of new substantive ideas," and "formed a program of law and behavioral science research rather than a set of isolated inquiries."[162] The Foundation took the application very seriously, appointing a committee of three outside evaluators[163] in addition to seeking comments from members of the project's existing advisory committee. The outsiders were uniform in their praise of the jury project.[164] Views of the arbitration project were more mixed[165] and those of the tax project more negative.[166] Importantly, all the evaluators of the Law School's work commented on what one referred to as the "complete co-operation among all the people engaged in the various projects regardless of whether they come from law or other disciplines" who have "learned to talk and work together."[167] The Foundation was suitably impressed and though it refused to contribute to the Law School's building fund, it did make a four-year grant of $1,000,000 for research (including $120,000 for faculty salaries and $200,000 for fellowships and comparative legal study).[168]

With the renewal of the grant the Chicagoans pushed research forward as best they could. In due course the tax project got closed as it became clear that tax issues, at the level of sophistication that Blum wanted to discuss them, were too complicated and subtle to get useful answers from such a crude method as public opinion polling, whether by interview or questionnaire.[169] But the jury study, the largest of the research projects, grew and grew. Data collection continued for four years and ultimately the study cost over $400,000, almost half of the second grant. A study of "court congestion and delay" in the New York courts, part of the work of the Temporary Commission on the Courts in New York, was accreted.[170] Dozens of lectures were given explaining the project and reporting its findings. Articles reporting small pieces of the work dribbled out, despite the "general policy of holding major publications until the end of the project."[171] Those major publications were to be eight books.[172] Eventually two of these books were published, Rita James Simon's *The Jury and the Defense of Insanity* and Kalven and Zeisel's *The American Jury*, a study of the jury in criminal cases.[173]

The other major project, commercial arbitration, had finished its data collection by 1958[174] and planned four volumes.[175] None appeared, although the articles on the history of arbitration[176] made it into print, as did a summary of the project and a more technical piece.[177]

IF ONE IS to evaluate the effect of all of this Ford Foundation largess being concentrated in one place and on law and the behavioral sciences, then one needs to recognize at the outset that whatever the grant applications said about these efforts as forming a single program, whatever the evaluators said about the group of researchers working together, and whatever may have been the case in the earliest years, by the middle at least, there was no program. There were several different activities funded out of the same grant. Indeed, in the end reports to the Foundation even gave up the pretense of there being a program, choosing instead simply to quote from the report of the director of each of the individual projects.[178] Another thing needs to be made clear as well. Although the renewal grant application provided a separate special memo on the impact of the program on the Law School as a whole, and reports always emphasized the number of faculty members that took part in the program's activities, in fact the program had almost no long-term impact on the Law School.[179] The preexisting faculty interest in law and economics that the initial application trumpeted as indicative of the Law School's already existing commitment to the social sciences[180] simply reasserted itself after the waters calmed. Indeed, the only surviving bit of law and social science at the school, the Center for Studies in Criminal Justice, was created by Norval Morris after the Law and Behavioral Science Program was largely over and works in an area where the program hardly ventured.[181] Even more telling was the fact that not until that later time did Hans Zeisel even offer a course on social science method to regular law students and that *at their request and urging.*[182]

All this aside there were real achievements. First and most obvious is the jury study, which produced one of the real monuments of the law and social science literature. While *The American Jury* may not have been worth all that money, it was worth much. And no one should forget its shadow. Rita Simon's book explicated a new and interesting research method, even if it did not set the law on fire. The commercial arbitration study was obviously less successful, though the two articles on the history of arbitration are helpful, as is Mentschikoff's summary. And even an interesting article came out of the failed attempt to look at attitudes toward the income tax.[183] And then there is the inestimable benefit of having attracted Hans Zeisel's patient, engaging attention to the law.

The fellowship program that accompanied all the research is more troublesome.[184] Although reports to Ford indicated that for a "few" the experience had "not been effective," they asserted that for "the greater number" it was a "useful (sometimes perhaps invaluable) and deepening experience."[185] There is reason to question that evaluation, at least as far as reversing the quantities. The twenty-two fellows include some individuals who later became very well known for their work in the area;[186] still many more, and not just the law professors, seem to have done little in the area since. Possibly this is because, as was admitted, most of the research projects were already past planning and into data collection and writing with the result that it was "somewhat difficult to make available the project experiences" to the fellows.[187] But perhaps not.

And why might that be? The record of publication of the Law and Behavioral Science Program is interesting, even revealing. The one piece that was finished expeditiously was the study of court congestion. Authorized in August 1957, it was published exactly two years later. The resulting book, Zeisel, Kalven, and Bucholz, *Delay in the Court*, is a fine piece of work,[188] but it is interesting that this work was the only bit of the program narrowly tied to the efforts at law reform that seemed to animate Levi's original proposal to the Ford Foundation. And then there is the note in a list of program publications that one of the last two publications of the commercial arbitration project was an American Bar Foundation publication on the unification of international private law![189] What seems to have moved projects quickly to completion is their relationship to rather traditional law professorial agendas. Perhaps that message came across to the fellows.

The Walter E. Meyer Research Institute of Law

Soon after the jury project got started, the Walter E. Meyer Research Institute of Law came into being. Created as the result of a bequest of a wealthy, bachelor lawyer, Meyer existed because David Cavers, then Associate Dean at the Harvard Law School, was curious about, and took the time to cultivate, an alumnus who regularly made contributions for "research" at that school.[190] By its terms the bequest was to establish a foundation for "investigation, research and study to throw light on matters which will be of aid in securing to humanity a greater degree of justice."[191] Named as among the trustees were Cavers, as a representative of Harvard, and unnamed faculty members at the Columbia, New York University, and Yale law schools.[192] Eugene Rostow, then Dean at Yale, argued against forming any foundation and instead proposed dividing the assets of the trust among the three schools (Harvard, Yale, and Hebrew University) that were named as beneficiaries in default of the foundation's formation[193] and Cavers suggested that the funds be used to establish research chairs at each of the four schools.[194] Both plans were opposed by the executors, two nephews of the decedent, who were agreed to as additional trustees, and who favored some kind of project-related research, and so both were dropped.[195]

Outside advice was then sought in order to determine just what the foundation, when established, ought to do with its money. Willard Hurst suggested putting all the funds into providing young scholars with grants in an amount necessary to free them from at least half their teaching responsibilities for a period of years, as well as to provide them with full-year sabbaticals every four or five years, all as a way of "trying to modify the institutional traditions of law schools" in the direction of supporting more research. Hessel Yntema, not wholly surprisingly, suggested that the Meyer money be used to set up an operating institution not unlike the Hopkins Institute. Neither idea was appealing to the trustees who worried more basically about whether, as Hurst and another advisor, Myres McDougal, put it, given the "climate and set of attitudes concerning research in the legal field," law teachers could be interested in projects within the terms of the will and whether collaboration with social scientists was really possible.[196] Arguments over the distribution of research funds continued to focus on whether or not to include other law schools.[197] This position finally carried the day with the adoption of a grants policy promising support for research by "[m]embers of American law faculties and others engaged in scholarship about law" directed at "the functioning of law as an instrument of justice" with the hope of "drawing legal scholars and other students of social behavior together and further[ing] the understanding and advancement of justice through law."[198]

Worried about a great influx of applications, the Trustees circulated the policy statement only to law school deans and a few social scientists.[199] Such worries were, however, unfounded. Indeed, the fact that grant applications were hardly numerous[200] led Cavers, the Meyer Institute's President, to express "some disappointment"[201] that extended to the scattered value of the work supported as well. And soon the call was again heard, this time from Acting Dean Miguel DeCapriles of New York University, to divide a major portion of the Meyer funds between the four law schools and be done with it. Predictably Rostow favored the proposal, but instead the Trustees agreed to attempt to focus their program, now expressly designated as attempting to "press beyond conventional scholarly analysis of appellate decisions," in two infelicitously described areas — "Law and the Common Man" and "Justice in the Big City," really a focus on auto accidents, criminal justice, and family and consumer problems and on urban law respectively. This reformulation of policy seems to have at least coincided with, if not increased, interest in the program; grant applications nearly doubled in the following two years with a relatively similar increase in disbursements.[202]

The combination of some successful litigation concerning the value of what was originally the trust's only asset,[203] some good investment management, and a booming stock market meant that, after a little over five years operation of a trust specified to have a maximum duration of twenty years, and the appropriation of funds in the amount of over $1.5 million, the trust, originally valued at $1.2 million, still had uncommitted assets of $2.9 million. With the addition to this corpus of a grant of $500,000 from the Ford Foundation to fund investigation into urban problems, research had a bright future.[204]

Then, in the fall of 1964, Rostow requested that the Trustees make a capital grant to Yale of $500,000 to be used for either a chair for a behavioral scientist or in urban law, or as matching funds for a grant for a program in urban law then being sought from the Ford Foundation as part of a $5 million fundraising drive. Though Cavers noted that the chairs for which funding was sought were not conceived as research chairs and that the other three law schools would line up for their share further depleting the Institute's funds, the Trustees voted a $400,000 grant. The other three schools postponed their claims for two years, so as to allow the Institute to earn income and thus make additional grants; still, in one fell swoop, the Meyer's stock of effective disposable assets was down to $800,000 plus the Ford grant and the future was none too bright.[205]

As it turned out, however, though applications remained at previous levels, continued astute financial management together with an unexplained, and not intentional, shift to making smaller grants meant that four years later the Institute was left with effective disposable assets of about $1 million.[206] Yet clearly the Institute's trustees understood that the program was going to end relatively soon and so in spring of 1967 they organized a series of three "consultations" directed generally at the role of research in law, including needs, methods and instrumentalities, in the near to medium future.[207] While a lively discussion, the effort led in no particular direction. Later discussions among the Trustees developed the idea that remaining funds should be devoted to creating "an entity with broad responsibilities for promoting and guiding efforts to organize and pursue law-related research," defined as research such that "among the principal questions it posed, were those which persons with law training would be the most competent to handle."[208] Thus was born the Council in Law-Related Studies (CLRS).

The new entity was to be patterned after the Social Science Research Council. It would arrange ad hoc committees of scholars organized around problems that its board had decided were ripe for research. Cavers, who was about to retire from teaching, agreed to be the Council's president and in the summer of 1969 the Meyer Institute was inactivated as a grant-giving entity and approximately half of its funds were given to CLRS for its program, the balance being reserved for future grants if that program proved successful.[209] The Council chose to attempt to focus research efforts in three areas: pollution control, jail conditions, and drunken driving. The first proved to yield the most satisfactory results and the last the least interest, but overall the response of law professors was thoroughly disappointing. Only when the Council added a program related to the study of the effectiveness of no-fault insurance did significant interest appear.[210]

After two years, the Meyer Institute advanced funds to CLRS for two more years of work, but clearly the days of both organizations were numbered as other foundations could not be interested in supporting CLRS's work and Meyer was down to its last $200,000. A decision was then made to attempt to increase law professors' interest in the projects of CLRS and in law-related research generally by, in effect, merging the Council into the Association of American Law Schools. Although approved by all the necessary boards of directors and supported by the Ford Foundation with a grant of $150,000, this idea foundered and then died when no qualified law professor could be found who was willing to take the job of heading the program. And so a decision was made to fold the Meyer Institute into the Council and to wind up the Council's affairs by dispersing $100,000 to the Social Science Research Council for the support of its Social Science and Law Committee and the balance of $170,000 to the American Bar Foundation for small research grants to younger law professors.[211]

AT THE TIME CLRS was created one of the Meyer Trustees noted that the Meyer Institute had been created "with the intention of generating an interest in legal research that did not then exist" and ventured an opinion that the Institute had "succeeded in that endeavor."[212] While the history of CLRS suggests that "succeeded" may not quite be the right word, it would be a mistake to treat the Meyer's work as a failure. Excluding the grants to the four law schools, but including the grants and research funded by CLRS, Walter E. Meyer's $1 million gift together with the Ford Foundation's contribution funded research in the amount of $2.8 million.[213] Those research grants supported, in whole or in part, some of the most interesting law and social science done during the sixties. Indeed, the list of Meyer supported projects is quite astonishing: Bruce Ackerman's Delaware River study,[214] Guido Calabresi's *The Costs of Accidents*, Alfred Conard's work on compensation of auto accident victims,[215] Kenneth Culp Davis's *Discretionary Justice*, Walter Gellhorn's *Ombudsmen and Others*, Joel Handler on lawyers,[216] Keeton and O'Connell on no-fault insurance,[217] Richard Kuh on pornography,[218] Stewart Macaulay on auto dealers and their manufacturers,[219] Maurice Rosenberg on the pretrial conference[220] and on delay in personal injury litigation,[221] H. Lawrence Ross's *Settled Out of Court*, Jerome Skolnik's *Justice without Trial* and student law review comments on police interrogations[222] and the imposition of the death penalty.[223] What the endowment grants to the four law schools produced, especially at Yale where no program in urban law survived and no research professorship was established,[224] is more problematic. Yet the real failure of CLRS is, I think, the more important fact. It could not institutionalize its program, even with so broad and nebulous a concept as "law-related" research. The law professors would take the Meyer money but their actions were in large measure adventitious. They implied no commitment to empirical legal research as a way of understanding law.

The Russell Sage Program

At the same time that the Meyer Institute was active, a succession of presidents at the Russell Sage Foundation, an old philanthropy interested in social work until about the time of the Korean War, turned its program in the direction of the social sciences, specifically seeking the insight the social sciences could bring to the professions. Medicine was the initial focus of this program, but in the late fifties and early sixties, as the National Institutes of Health began to provide money for research into the application of the behavioral sciences to health problems, the Foundation's interest shifted in the direction of law. The law program was fashioned by Leonard S. Cottrell of the Foundation's staff. As the program emerged it seemed both to target individual schools as places that could develop law and social science programs and, through residencies, fellowships, and research grants, to work to create a constituency of scholars in law and social science in the law schools. In one respect that program was successful.[225]

The Sage program effectively began in 1961 with a grant to the University of California at Berkeley to help set up the Center for the Study of Law and Society. It was to be a center for "research and training for work in the field of law and the social sciences."[226] Simultaneously, a smaller grant went to the University of Wisconsin to employ two sociologists to work with the law faculty in the development of a program of teaching and research in sociology and law.[227] This program, ultimately supported for eight years in an amount totaling $600,000, soon shifted its focus in a way that bore all the indicia of Willard Hurst's suggestions to the Meyer Institute Trustees. Wisconsin used its money to train young social scientists in legal method and young law professors in social science method and to move each along the road to a publishable research product in the area.[228]

In 1964 a major Sage grant was made to Northwestern in the amount of $465,000 over six years.[229] This program provided fellowships for students in both law and the various social sciences who were interested in doing law and social science research. Other grants totaling $765,000 were for student fellowships at Columbia,[230] for a program of interdisciplinary research and teaching focused on judicial administration at Denver,[231] to support the appointment and teaching of a sociologist, Lloyd E. Ohlin, on the Harvard Law School faculty,[232] for a Center for Studies in Criminology and Criminal Law at Pennsylvania,[233] and for a law and psychology program at Stanford.[234]

Starting in 1963, the Russell Sage foundation opened a second front in its program. It began to fund residencies designed to provide additional education in another discipline and facilities to carry out research projects for young academics in both law and the social sciences.[235] The residency program was administered in two ways. One million dollars over thirteen years was invested in a program that allowed recipients to seek training and research opportunities wherever appropriate.[236] Over half a million over seven years starting in 1967 was put into the attempt to assemble a "critical mass" of such scholars around Stanton Wheeler at Yale.[237] Finally, a third aspect of the Foundation's program should be noted. Over fifteen years about $1.3 million was put directly into research grants, a surprising amount of it jointly with the Meyer Institute.[238]

How would one evaluate the Russell Sage program? Looked at as a collection of parts, the results were, as might be expected, mixed. Consider first the institutional grants. The Berkeley program into which Russell Sage pumped about $450,000 over twelve years was a resounding success in its output of research and its training of graduate students. Yet, it was only after the demise of the School of Criminology at Berkeley and the establishment of the teaching program in Law, Society, and Criminal Justice that it began to have more than incidental contact with the Law School.[239] And, as evidenced by the still tenuous relationship of that teaching program, now known as the Jurisprudence and Social Policy Program, to the Law School and the relatively low level of activity by that University's law faculty in terms of the production of empirical research, propinquity to even a strong program guarantees nothing.[240]

By any account the Wisconsin program has been a success as well, whether one measures by looking at the list of alumni of the program,[241] the amount of research produced,[242] or the continuance of work both in the Department of Sociology and in the Law School that is identifiably law and social science. Given that all of the original sponsors of the Northwestern program left, though one returned, and that the program not only continued, but turned itself into a formal J.D.-Ph.D. program, and given the quite astonishing list of alumni of the program, many at the forefront of the younger generation of law and social science scholars,[243] this program too must be judged a success. What its impact on that Law School was, other than as a matter of curriculum, is much less clear, at least if measured by the research of the Northwestern faculty other than Rosenblum and John Heinz. Other grant programs, however seem to have been less successful, at least if success is measured by impact on law faculty or significant law and social science research output, though, of course, where student teaching was a major concern, as at Denver and to a lesser extent Harvard, such measures are less relevant.

The fellowship program is a similar matter. The roster of individuals who were given fellowships in this program is truly astonishing; a surprising number of the scholars of middle age now active in the field must be included and many note that the program effected a marked shift in their interests in the direction of greater commitment to work in law and social science.[244] Still it must be observed that the program at Yale seems to have had little impact on that Law School, at least if measured by the failure of the school to continue it after the Russell Sage funds were exhausted or by the general research output of the faculty.

Lastly there are the individual grants. An external review committee found this aspect of the program "least successful," noting that of the thirty or more projects examined "only about one-third made" some contribution to the state of the art or the specific topic and "only a handful" made significant contributions.[245] On the whole that evaluation seems correct, though it should be noted that Russell Sage supported Jerome Carlin's work on lawyers' ethics,[246] Jack Getman's study of NLRB elections,[247] the Heinz and Lauman Chicago Bar Survey,[248] Ianni's study of a Mafia family,[249] Earl Johnson's *Justice and Reform*,[250] and Douglas Rosenthal's *Lawyer and Client: Who's in Charge?*, a not insignificant list.

Looked at not as a discrete collection of parts, but rather as a whole, the Russell Sage program assumes a different aspect. In 1976, as Russell Sage was about to terminate its program in Law and Social Science and concentrate its energy in policy study, the Chairman of its Board of Trustees emphasized the rhythm of change in an institution, which he ascribed to changes in executive leadership.[251] It is not clear how much of the changes in the Russell Sage program are due to changes in executive leadership,[252] but it is clear that there was a certain rhythm to the Law and Social Science program.

Russell Sage's activities show a pattern of intentionally fostering growth in an academic area and then moving on. This is what the Foundation did in law. First, centers of study were established.[253] Then, once a cadre of individuals who identified themselves professionally with law and social science had emerged, they, with Russell Sage's help, were enabled to find the visible focus of their efforts, the Law and Society Association, and its publication, the *Law and Society Review*.[254] Next this core of scholars was helped to expand through the support of a large number of very junior scholars, who were expected to spread throughout the country. Finally, a little research support was added to the modest funds that then existed.[255] With such a script Russell Sage was phenomenally successful, aided, of course, by the appearance of the National Science Foundation. The NSF began its concentration in the law and social sciences in 1967–68, about the time the residency program was hitting full stride, and followed that concentration with its formal program in 1971–72, about the time that the Sage program was beginning to wind down.[256] These events moreover cannot be seen as unrelated. If Sage had not aided in the creation of the nucleus of scholars to do the work, there would never have been an NSF program.

At the same time there is something anomalous and significant to be noted to the development that the Russell Sage program initiated. In all but one place the law professors were ultimately unaffected. Only at Wisconsin did the program make significant inroads into the Law School over the long haul and then only into half of that Law School, thereupon proving correct Willard Hurst's advice to the Walter Meyer Trustees, get them young, and Harry Kalven's later observation on the jury study, do not expect propinquity to make a difference. Everywhere else that Sage put its money, though bits of law and social science remain and even got renewed, overall, the law schools continued on much as before.

Why the Wheel Remains Square

There is a sameness to these stories of attempts to do or foster empirical legal research in law schools or by law professors. If it is not inappropriate to invoke the memory of Harry Kalven, one might capture the team's overall performance as "one hit, no runs, innumerable errors." The National Science Foundation's Law and Social Science program keeps the Law and Society

Association functioning, and, on the whole, the results are positive for the accumulation of knowledge.[257] But the law professors are clearly marginal in the program's list of applicants and in the Association's membership (except as its president) and those law professors active in the Association are marginal in the law teaching profession, despite the notoriety of a few individuals. Why is this the case? Why has empirical legal research not caught on, not taken hold in the law schools?

IT SHOULD BE remembered that this failure cannot be ascribed to that old bugaboo — theory — for the law professors have available to them the most capacious of theories: Cook's model of a science of law.[258] Although no one has yet dared to set up another freestanding institute,[259] the list of research projects that would have fit within its bounds is quite astonishing. There is first the entire list of projects funded under the Walter Meyer Foundation and then, more specifically, both the jury study, a classic bit of conservative law reform designed to shore up an ancient institution, and the Law and Modernization project,[260] the comparative law that Yntema had envisioned as part of the enterprise. And, of course, the Russell Sage money and the SSMILE program[261] were designed, if not to create freestanding institutes, at least to create centers within individual law schools that would foster empirical research without necessarily attacking everything else going on in the building. And yet, the history of these projects suggests that, though Cook's model of a science of law is attractive, it still does not work. Somehow law and social science is a square wheel; somehow since 1922 we have been reinventing that square wheel. To understand why that is so, one has to go back to where this journey started, to the turn of the century with Cook and Moore on the prairie.

Out there in the West, as they called it, where the wolves howled at night and the trains came only once a day, a profession was formed.[262] The "leaders" of the "profession" talked up a storm in Cambridge, Chicago, New York, and wherever the American Association of Law Schools met and forged transatlantic alliances in pursuit of the project of developing legal science.[263] But without indians, chiefs make relatively ineffective war. It was in places like Grand Forks, Lincoln, Columbia, Lawrence, Iowa City, and Madison where the important battles were fought and the profession was made. It was first the missionaries and then the colonial officers like Cook and Moore who made the revolution that is always ascribed to the bearded genius of Austin Hall.

This is not the time or place to again run over the arguments and evidence in support of the proposition that the law teaching profession was created at this time.[264] Rather, I wish only to note that, as part of that process of professionalization, the law teachers came to agree on a subject matter for their science. It was to be largely private, common law embraced as a scientific — that is, a rationally ordered and justified — system. Put slightly differently, although there may have been a great deal of talk about teaching people to think like a lawyer, whatever that might be, the real subject matter was going to be law as rule, the rules of law. Law professors were not going to teach the other sciences; they were not going to teach about law; they were going to teach law.[265] This is the understanding upon which all the pre–World War I casebooks, some great — Gray's *Property*[266] and Thayer's *Constitutional Law*[267] — some not so great, were built; this was the understanding that Cook and Moore took with them to the prairie. If one was going to take a broader, or even a different view of law as both men had been taught, then one was going to teach political science or history or economics or what have you, not law.

The reasons for this choice — the lack of other intellectual claimants to the subject matter, the fit with understandings of law deep within American culture, the sense of fit with the practicing lawyer's definition of his profession, and the mesh with the ideology of the rule of law — need not be rehearsed here either.[268] They are important in their own right but unimportant here. What is important is the fact of that professional self-definition and the equally obvious fact that by World War I, the intellectual task that that definition implied — the collecting, ordering, and logically justifying the rules — was done. It had been done in treatises, casebooks, and articles; all that was left was for a grand restatement of the law and the patient noting of minor changes in the rules.

I do not wish to suggest that this was a bleak prospect for the professional law teacher; I doubt whether most even looked at that prospect. There were new cases to learn, new courses to teach, and a long, hot dry summer in which to try to write an article about whatever interested or puzzled one in the classroom. But the task was not that of the pioneers, the missionaries, for the frontier was closed; rather the task of the colonial officers was more like that of occupying a fort, long secured — the doing of regular maintenance tasks reasonably well.

For most people that task was fine. For some, for the more restless, adventurous, or maybe just cantankerous, it was not. Cook and Moore had each done a casebook and a few articles and then fell strangely silent. Thereafter, each chased after will-o'-the-wisps; Cook, first Hohfeld, then Dewey;

Moore, a more generalized science. And each caught one such phantasm and it changed his life. This is graphically true of Moore, but is equally true of Cook. He talked science and talked science and talked science until law and scientific method was Cook and his great work in the conflict of laws was essentially lost. But a professional identity, a sense of personhood, of what one is, once forged is a tough thing. It would be foolish, as well as erroneous, to suggest that Cook and Moore simply took on a new professional identity, the way one changes clothes after work. Both still bore marks of their colonial service long after the prairie dust was cleaned out of cuffs and lost in memory.

In Cook, of course, this is more obvious. Not only did he never give up case law, but, by splitting up Dewey's thoughts on science in the way he did, he managed to preserve as much of the earlier professional identity as possible. One could still be a law professor and do doctrine, so long as one did it scientifically. If one wished, rules could still be the centerpiece of the science of law, just as they were of legal science, and, if one did not so wish, one could find support for one's activities in the law reform agenda of the day or the judicial administration movement or somewhere. Such was the tyranny, the second-class citizenship that was implied by "law and," a phrase Cook never used and yet still invented.

The case for Moore is seemingly different. He, of course, sprung completely free of his professional identity to become a social scientist pure and simple. However, there is a problem with this interpretation of Moore's career. Only saints and hermits develop professional identities that are self-contained and Moore was neither. For all others, professional identity is a phenomenon of group behavior. Moore had no group. The law professors could not understand his work because it had lost touch with their identity, an identity that, of course, implied appropriate work. Counting cars was not appropriate work. And the social scientists could not understand his work on its own terms either; it was outside their ideas of appropriate work, their paradigms, as well. Thus, the quiet depression that seems to have overcome Moore in the few years after publication of "Law and Learning Theory"[269] seems to me to be less that of self-recognized failure than that of the internal exile. He could still do old fashioned legal analysis, but publishing it was a pointless exercise in showing "everybody how smart we are." Strangely, in the absence of a new professional identity, somehow the old one still tugged just a bit.[270] It could not be wholly escaped for it surrounded one day after day. The dust of the prairie was somehow still in his cuffs and its memory not eradicated.

But for one example, an example that makes the point as well, the entire subsequent course of empirical legal research in the law schools follows Cook's model. For law, empirical social science is a method, a way of finding out what one needs to know in order to go back to the main business of doing law, of doing rules. Thus, when the money runs out, the waters of the pond become still again. After the jury study nothing happened at Chicago or other law schools and not because juries are uninteresting subjects for research or because Kalven and Zeisel told us all we need to know about them (they did not even publish all they knew!), or because we all know that delay has a positive function in personal injury cases or because the insanity defense is a done topic. Indeed, jury studies go on elsewhere in the academy, delay is constantly derided in personal injury litigation, and insanity remains a fascinating topic. Luckily, after the Walter Meyer money gave out there was a National Science Foundation program to pick up the funding slack and yet the list of law professors funded by Meyer to do empirical research who ever did any later, much less who are known for their empirical research, is short indeed.[271] And with one exception Russell Sage concluded that the money it had given to law schools, while not wasted, had proved to be of no lasting impact. That exception was Wisconsin, where arguably a group of scholars — though by no means an entire law school — forged a new professional identity as social empiricists in law, or some such god-awful phrase. Pouring money into people and their education as Sage did may pay off. Pouring money into research did not.

Thus, it would seem that, though the Hopkins Institute was a washout, Cook won in the end. Its program may not have made sense, it may not have hung together, but it sold. The twentieth-century notion of science as an empirical activity could be brought into law and nothing really upset if it was kept at its proper Japanese-wife distance: law and . . . Any closer and the problems created by seeing science as a criticism of other ways of knowing simply overwhelmed the daily business of being a law professor as Moore proved. Science was too threatening. It suggested that the words of law might not be too important, that the special preserve of the law professor might not be too special and that, since law was not just rules, the rule of law might not be just a matter of following rules either. That threat was simply too much for the professional identity of the law professor; it could only be attacked mercilessly or distanced with derisive laughter. Llewellyn did them both.[272]

But to mention Llewellyn, and not say Vance or Lorenzen of Moore's colleagues, is to recognize that professional identities do change over time. The professional identity that Moore and Cook learned on the prairie is not the same one law professors have today. Scholarship in the high-Germanic mode of Wigmore and Williston, scholarship whose purpose is the patient organization and classification of the rules, is dead. We do still restate the law and write treatises, but somehow those activities are different than they were eighty years ago. The American Law Institute is a club with its own rules and sells its own sense of having arrived; treatises are a by-product of something else—the need for cash to put children in private schools, the existence of the material sitting there anyway, the demand of the profession for easy, reasonably accurate access to the rules in specialized fields. The norm of scholarship has shifted and the identity of the law professor as well.

As Cook and others using Hohfeld's tools showed, justification by logical entailment helped not at all in those cases where help was most needed—the so-called new case. And so was born policy analysis. It is not unimportant that the bastard form of Pound's interest analysis that is policy analysis fits well with Cook's rendition of science. Empirical knowledge is always relevant but never determinative; policies can always trump facts or make them irrelevant. And so it is the rule that remains the centerpiece of discussion. Thus, it is appropriate to raise Llewellyn's name, for policy analysis is the legitimate child of case law Realism practiced by Cook and mastered by Llewellyn, Corbin, Gilmore, and all the heirs of Realism. It is a capacious home for law reform and for participation in the "important" legal activities of the day. It is the home that Realism made for its heirs when the Realists marched to Washington to participate in public life, their only real alternative to Moore's empirical science of law.

I SUPPOSE THAT in a study brought to a conclusion through the generous assistance of the National Science Foundation's program in Law and the Social Sciences I am duty bound to suggest a way to put empirical social science in the center of the law school world. I hope that this study has convinced its readers that that is exactly what I cannot do. Professional identities are strong things. Though the tall-grass prairie is almost all gone, we still forge the law professors alone in a room with 80 to 100 recalcitrant twenty-two-year-olds who bring with them the cultural understanding that law is about rules and who get a pile of appellate cases to chew on. The centrality to that experience of the notion of law as rule is as overwhelming as the smell of limburger cheese. Until some genius comes up with some reason for seeing law as something else, matches it with an appropriate professional identity, and sells it in a culture where currently the only alternative understanding of law available is that of the rule of law's evil twin brother — law as who you know (hardly an inspiring conception) — we shall live with Walter Wheeler Cook's version of John Dewey on science because, even if it does not hang together, at least it fits. Until one takes the "and" out of "law and . . ." there is no point in talking.

In the meantime, while waiting for the arrival of that genius, it may be sensible to remember Charles E. Clark. His actions in leading by example may not have been effective at Yale, but he expressed care, concern, and patience in carrying his work to a conclusion, an object lesson to a profession full of mayflies. Remember too Walter Wheeler Cook. He may not have been the most secure, other-directed law professor in the world, but he had an idea he passionately believed in, an object lesson to a profession where ideas passionately believed in are few and far between and most often silly. And remember especially Underhill Moore. He may not have been the premier intellect of the crew or charitable to his dean, but the essence of the man was his extraordinary flinty integrity and seriousness of purpose, an object lesson anytime, any place, in any profession.

ON THE HISTORY OF INTELLECTUALS,

INCLUDING LAWYERS

WHEN PREPARING this manuscript for publication my good series editor suggested that I insert in the introduction the obligatory sentences that state the contributions made by the book to the relevant literatures. For a change I did what I was told. I did not, however, identify the literature to which I most hope that this book will be a contribution. Though it should be no surprise to anyone who has read that introduction, I will state it directly now. This book is intended to be a contribution to intellectual history generally because it attempts to show what it is to be an intellectual in America in the twentieth century.

Why make such a broad claim? Simply this. It is an important thing for any culture to know where the ideas in its past and present came from. It is an important thing for any culture to understand what those ideas meant in their time and place and how that meaning has changed, if it has, over time. It is important for any culture to have intellectual heroes (and goats), individuals who exemplify what it is to be a serious (or frivolous) intellectual. However, it is a serious mistake to imagine that the way that we have come to save this part of our past, the discipline that we call intellectual history, bears much relationship to how that past was lived, and we will seriously distort our measure of the worth of contributions made by present intellectuals if we hold them to the standards that we in the discipline have manufactured in an attempt to learn about the ideas in our past.

It is my hope that this book exemplifies my wish to set us on a different, better path for thinking and learning about the ideas in our past. I have suggested three heroes — Cook, Clark, and especially Moore. I have attempted to identify, when possible, where their ideas came from. I have tried to show how those ideas changed over time. I have even attempted, at some length, to explain why those ideas took the shape that they did and how they worked out in the practices that these thinkers believed that their ideas implied. I have done that work and present it as an example of what intellectual history ought to be.

It will, I suspect, be easy to dismiss my work for just what it is, an example, and not a particularly representative one at that. "After all, these people were only law professors and we all know that law is not really a discipline," it will be said. There is no way for me to meet this criticism. They were only law professors and not particularly intellectually self-conscious ones at that. But law is a discipline, if a particularly silly one. There is little difference between seeing that, "If Sunstein says this and Michelman that, then it must be the case that . . ." and Shazaam!, a newly minted assistant professor has an article, and seeing that, "If Jevons says this and Seligman says that, then it must be the case that . . ." and Shazaam!, a newly minted assistant professor has an article. There is a dialogue in law, though a particularly inane one, just as there is a dialogue in economics, or sociology, or anthropology. Which is to say that there are many monologues that intersect at the edges, a working within a framework intelligible to others and an attempt to distinguish one's self and one's scholarship from the selves and scholarship of everyone else working in that framework.

So, what I offer as an example is, I wish to suggest, more than just even a representative example of what it is to be an intellectual in the twentieth century. It is an attempt, an invitation to open a discussion about what intellectual history, even the "new intellectual history," is and has become as this century closes. Because I too doubt, to paraphrase Jerome Frank, that one can, by purely intellectual processes, change scholars so that they see the ways that intellectual history must, if it is to be history, accept, indeed embrace, both biography and social history, I have offered an example to engage thought. Because I am nevertheless an optimist, I issue this invitation for discussion. It is time that we consider giving up the history of ideas, giving up intellectual history as a history of the ideas of humans set apart from the rest of their lived experience, and to begin to write the history of intellectuals.

Indeed, let me make my statement even stronger. It is just as reductionist to turn the activities of intellectuals into either topics — republican theory, welfare economics, or social thought — or disciplines — economics, sociology, or law — with problems and coherent schools of thought, as it is (or was) to reduce the actions of individuals to their place in the drama of the ownership of the means of production. Such a view of intellectual life is both overdetermined — there are dozens of influences and sources of ideas for any thinker, mostly overlapping — and underdetermined — there are all sorts of problems that could be implied from what Jevons and Seligman said. People cannot be reduced to their ideas any more than societies, to their economies.

Choice is exercised in seeing what is implied as a problem in a topic or discipline and behind that choice is an enormous amount of chance and misunderstanding, an article read carefully because the reader was trying not to think of something painful in that reader's homelife, a dislike for another's work because that other seems "not on the up and up," the mistranslation of a key concept from one framework of inquiry to another. Intellectual history must both show that choice and account for that chance, with the enormous amount of discontinuity that both choice and chance imply. Look only at this book. It comes from an unexpected encounter with some materials that were not what I was looking for at the time. Those materials played into an interest in Realism I had first developed, then lost six years earlier, as well as a dislike for contemporary legal and social science scholarship and an appreciation for the rigors of quantification. All of this was focused by a chance observation of a colleague and a feeling of boredom in the middle of a different research project that, at the outset, I knew I was simply the "perfect" person to do. I have a hard time believing that the selection of Ph.D. topics, often the basis for a life's work, is any less serendipitous, given discussions I have had with the occasionally proud owners of such a degree.

I know that what I seek from my readers is deeply postmodern and that I have denied having a postmodern bone in my body, but let me offer this simple plea. Let us simply stop the pretense that it is the dance of reason that we chronicle in intellectual history, if only in the name of more accurately representing the thinkers of the past as that humanistic ideal — people trying their best to get from Monday to Tuesday in as honorable a job as they have managed to find. Let us stop looking for the dance of reason and record the whole dance of life.

MORTIMER ADLER b. 1902. Ph.D. 1928, Columbia. Inst. (philosophy) 1923, Columbia; assoc. prof. 1930, prof. 1942–53, Chicago. Dir. 1952–, Institute for Philosophical Research. Dir., editorial planning, 1966–, chair, board of editors 1974–, *Encyclopaedia Britannica*, 15th ed.

JOSEPH S. AMES b. 1864. A.B. 1886, Ph.D. 1890, Johns Hopkins. Assoc. (physics) 1891, assoc. prof. 1893, prof. 1899, provost 1926, pres. 1929–35, Johns Hopkins. d. 1943.

JAMES ROWLAND ANGELL b. 1869. A.B. 1890, A.M. 1891, Michigan; A.M. 1892, Harvard. Inst. (psychology) 1893, asst. prof. 1894, assoc. prof. 1901, Minnesota; prof. 1905, sr. dean 1908, dean of faculty 1911, Chicago; pres. 1920, Carnegie Corporation; pres. 1921–37, Yale. d. 1949.

THURMAN ARNOLD b. 1891. A.B. 1911, Princeton; LL.B. 1914, Harvard. Private practice 1914–27. Lect. 1921, Wyoming; dean 1927, West Virginia; prof. 1930–38, Yale. U.S. Assistant Attorney General, antitrust, 1938–43. Judge 1943–45, United States Court of Appeals, District of Columbia Circuit. Private practice 1945–69 (Arnold, Fortas & Porter). d. 1969. *The Symbols of Government* (1935); *The Folklore of Capitalism* (1937).

EDWIN BAETJER b. 1868. LL.B. 1890, Maryland. Private practice 1890–1945 (Venable, Baetjer & Howard). Chair, board of directors, 1932–45, Dun & Bradstreet. Trustee 1912–45, Johns Hopkins. d. 1945.

ARTHUR A. BALLANTINE b. 1883. A.B. 1903, LL.B. 1906, Harvard. Private practice 1906–60 (Root, Clark, Buckner & Ballantine). Inst. 1907–9, Harvard; inst. 1907–14, Northeastern. Asst. secy. 1931–32, undersecy. 1932–33, Department of the Treasury. d. 1960.

JOSEPH H. BEALE b. 1861. A.B. 1882, A.M. 1887, LL.B. 1887, Harvard. Private practice 1887–92. Asst. prof. 1892, prof. 1897–1937, Harvard; prof. and dean 1902–4, Chicago. d. 1943. *A Treatise on the Conflict of Laws* (1907, 2d ed. 1935).

WALTER BLUM b. 1918. A.B. 1939, J.D. 1941, Chicago. Government practice 1941–43. Asst. prof. 1946, prof. 1953–, Chicago.

NICHOLAS MURRAY BUTLER b. 1862. A.B. 1882, A.M. 1883, Ph.D. 1884, Columbia. Asst. (philosophy) 1885, tutor 1886, adj. prof. 1889, prof. and dean 1890, pres. 1901–45, Columbia. d. 1947.

WALLACE BUTTRICK b. 1853. Diploma 1883, Rochester Theological Seminary; D.D. 1898, U. Rochester. Baptist ministry 1883–1902. Secy. 1902, pres. 1917, chair

1923–26, General Education Board; trustee 1917–26, Rockefeller Foundation. d. 1926.

CHARLES E. CALLAHAN b. 1910. B.S. 1932, J.D. 1934, Ohio State; J.S.D. 1937, Yale. Private practice 1934–35. Lect. 1938, asst. prof. 1939, Yale; assoc. prof. 1943, prof. 1948–74, Ohio State. d. 1974.

DAVID F. CAVERS b. 1902. B.S. 1923, Pennsylvania; LL.B. 1926, Harvard. Private practice 1926–29. Inst. 1929, Harvard; asst. prof. 1930, West Virginia; asst. prof. 1931, prof. 1932, Duke; prof. 1945–69, Harvard. Pres. 1958–69, Walter E. Meyer Research Institute of Law; pres. 1969–76, Council on Law Related Studies. d. 1988.

CHARLES E. CLARK b. 1889. B.A. 1911, LL.B. 1913, Yale. Private practice 1913–19. Asst. prof. 1919, assoc. prof. 1922, prof. 1923, dean 1929–39, Yale. Reporter 1935–38, 1942–56, Advisory Committee on Civil Procedure of the Supreme Court of the United States. Judge 1939–63, United States Court of Appeals, Second Circuit. d. 1963.

MORRIS R. COHEN b. 1880. B.S. 1900, CCNY; Ph.D. 1906, Harvard. Inst. (philosophy) 1906, prof. 1910, CCNY; prof. 1938–47, Chicago. d. 1947.

WALTER WHEELER COOK b. 1873. A.B. 1894, A.M. 1899, LL.M. 1901, Columbia. Inst. (American history and jurisprudence) 1901, asst. prof. 1902, prof. (law) 1903, Nebraska; prof. 1904, Missouri; prof. 1906, Wisconsin; prof. 1910, Chicago; prof. 1916, Yale; prof. 1919, Columbia; prof. 1922, Yale; prof. 1926–33, Johns Hopkins; prof. 1935–43, Northwestern. d. 1943. *The Logical and Legal Bases of the Conflict of Laws* (1942).

ARTHUR CORBIN b. 1874. B.A. 1894, Kansas; LL.B. 1899, Yale. Private practice 1899–1903. Inst. 1903, asst. prof. 1904, prof. 1909–43, Yale. d. 1967. *Contracts* (1950).

EMMA CORSTVET (LLEWELLYN) b. 1898. B.A. 1918, Wisconsin; student 1918–19, Bryn Mawr; student 1923–24, London School of Economics. Res. assoc. 1924–27, Laura Spellman Rockefeller Memorial; res. assoc. 1929–36, Yale; faculty member (economics) 1938–65, Sarah Lawrence. d. 1984. [Sarah Lawrence has the sensible practice of refusing to assign rank to its faculty.]

JOHN DEWEY b. 1859. A.B. 1879, Vermont; Ph.D. 1884, Johns Hopkins. Asst. prof. (philosophy) 1884, Michigan; prof. 1888, Minnesota; prof. 1889, Michigan; prof. 1894, Chicago; prof. 1904–52, Columbia. d. 1952.

WILLIAM O. DOUGLAS b. 1892. A.B. 1920, Whitman C.; LL.B. 1925, Columbia. Private practice 1925–27. Lect. 1925, prof. 1927, Columbia; prof. 1928–36, Yale. Dir. 1934–36, Securities and Exchange Commission Study of Bondholder Protective Committees. Member 1936–37, chair 1937–39, Securities and Exchange Commission. Justice 1939–75, U.S. Supreme Court. d. 1980.

ABRAHAM FLEXNER b. 1866. A.B. 1886, Johns Hopkins; A.M. 1906, Harvard. Staff 1908–13, Carnegie Foundation for the Advancement of Teaching; asst. secy. 1913, secy. 1917, division dir. 1925–28, General Education Board. Dir. 1930–40, Institute for Advanced Study. d. 1959.

JEROME N. FRANK b. 1889. Ph.B. 1909, J.D. 1912, Chicago. Private practice 1912–33. General counsel 1933–35, Agricultural Assistance Administration. Private practice 1936–37. Member 1937–39, chair 1939–41, Securities and Exchange Commission. Judge 1941–57, U.S. Court of Appeals, Second Circuit. d. 1957. *Law and the Modern Mind* (1930); *Courts on Trial* (1949).

FELIX FRANKFURTER b. 1882. A.B. 1902, CCNY; LL.B. 1906, Harvard. Atty. 1906, Office of the U.S. Attorney, S.D.N.Y.; atty. 1910–14, War Department. Prof. 1914–39, Harvard. Justice 1939–62, United States Supreme Court. d. 1965.

ERNST FREUND b. 1864. J.U.D. 1884, Heidelberg; Ph.D. 1897, Columbia. Private practice 1886–94. Inst. (political science) 1892, Columbia; asst. prof. 1894, assoc. prof. 1898, prof. 1902–32 (law), Chicago. d. 1932.

FRANK J. GOODNOW b. 1859. A.B. 1879, Amherst; Ph.D. 1882, Columbia. Inst. (political science) 1883, adj. prof. 1887, prof. 1891, Columbia; pres. 1914–29, Johns Hopkins. d. 1939.

LEON GREEN b. 1888. A.B. 1908, Ouachita C.; LL.B. 1915, Texas. Private practice 1912–20. Prof. 1921, Texas; dean 1926, North Carolina; prof. 1927, Yale; dean 1929, Northwestern; prof. 1947, Texas; prof. 1958, U. California, Hastings; prof. 1959–79, Texas. d. 1979. *The Rationale of Proximate Cause* (1927); *Judge and Jury* (1930).

EDWARD S. GREENBAUM b. 1890. A.B. 1910, Williams; LL.B. 1913, Columbia. Private practice 1913–70 (Greenbaum, Wolff & Ernst). d. 1970.

B. HOWELL GRISWOLD, JR. b. 1874. A.B. 1894, Johns Hopkins; LL.B. 1897, Maryland. Private practice 1897–1904. Member 1904, sr. member 1924–46, Alex. Brown & Sons. Trustee 1911–46, Johns Hopkins University. d. 1946.

ROBERT L. HALE b. 1884. A.B. 1906, A.M. 1907, LL.B. 1909, Harvard; Ph.D. 1918, Columbia. Private practice 1909–12. Lect. (economics) 1915–22, lect. (law) 1919, asst. prof. 1928, assoc. prof. 1931, prof. 1935–49, Columbia. d. 1969.

WALTON HALE HAMILTON b. 1881. A.B. 1907, Texas; Ph.D. 1913, Michigan. Inst. (economics) 1910, asst. prof. 1913, Michigan; asst. prof. 1914, Chicago; prof. 1915, Amherst; prof. 1923, Robert Brookings Graduate School; prof. (law) 1928–48, Yale. Private practice 1948–58 (Arnold, Fortas & Porter). d. 1958. [Hamilton was admitted to practice in Georgia by special act of that state's legislature.]

WESLEY N. HOHFELD b. 1879. A.B. 1901, U. California, Berkeley; LL.B. 1904, Harvard. Private practice 1904–5. Inst. 1905, asst. prof. 1907, assoc. prof. 1908, prof. 1909, Stanford; prof. 1914–18, Yale. d. 1918.

JACOB HARRY HOLLANDER b. 1871. A.B. 1891, Ph.D. 1894, Johns Hopkins. Assoc. prof. (political economy) 1894, prof. 1904–40, Johns Hopkins. d. 1940.

THEODORE S. HOPE b. 1903. A.B. 1925, Harvard; LL.B. 1928, Columbia. Res. assoc. 1928–31, Johns Hopkins. Private practice 1931–(Donovan, Newton, Leisure & Irvine).

CLARK HULL b. 1884. A.B. 1913, Michigan; Ph.D. 1918, Wisconsin. Inst. (psychology) 1916, asst. prof. 1920, assoc. prof. 1922, prof. 1925, Wisconsin; prof. 1929–52, Yale. d. 1952.

ROBERT M. HUTCHINS b. 1899. A.B. 1921, LL.B. 1925, Yale. Secy. 1923–27, Yale Corporation. Lect. 1925, prof. and dean, 1927, Yale; pres. 1929–54, Chicago. Assoc.

dir. 1954–57, Ford Foundation; pres. 1957–77, Center for the Study of Democratic Institutions. d. 1977. *The Higher Learning in America* (1936).

GEORGE H. JAFFIN b. 1906. A.B. 1925, CCNY; LL.B. 1928, Columbia. Res. assoc. 1928–31, Johns Hopkins. Private practice 1931–37. Atty. 1937–76, Securities and Exchange Commission and Department of Justice.

HUGER W. JERVEY b. 1878. A.B. 1900, A.M. 1901, U. of the South; LL.B. 1913, Columbia. Prof. (Greek) 1903–9, University of the South. Private practice 1913–28 (Satterlee, Canfield & Stone). Assoc. prof. 1923, prof. 1924–46, dean 1924–28, Columbia. d. 1949.

HARRY KALVEN b. 1914. A.B. 1935, J.D. 1938, Chicago. Private practice 1939–42. Inst. 1945, asst. prof. 1946, assoc. prof. 1949, prof. 1953–74, Chicago. d. 1974.

ALBERT KOCOUREK. b. 1875. LL.B. 1897, Michigan. Private practice 1897–1952. Lect. 1907, prof. 1914–52, Northwestern. d. 1952.

MONTE LEMANN b. 1884. A.B. 1902, Tulane; A.B. 1903, LL.B. 1906, Harvard. Private practice 1907–59. d. 1959.

EDWARD H. LEVI b. 1911. Ph.B. 1932, J.D. 1935, Chicago; J.S.D. 1938, Yale. Asst. prof. 1936–40; prof. 1945–75, 1977–85, dean 1950–62, provost 1962–68, pres. 1968–75, Chicago. U.S. Attorney General 1975–77.

SHIPPEN LEWIS b. 1887. A.B. 1907, LL.B. 1910, Pennsylvania. Private practice 1910–52. d. 1952. [Brother of William Draper Lewis.]

WILLIAM DRAPER LEWIS b. 1867. B.S. Haverford, 1888; LL.B. 1891, Ph.D. 1891, Pennsylvania. Lect. (economics) 1891, Haverford; prof. (law) 1896–1924, dean 1896–1914, Pennsylvania. Executive dir. 1923–47, American Law Institute. d. 1949.

KARL N. LLEWELLYN b. 1893. A.B. 1915, LL.B. 1918, J.D. 1919, Yale. Private practice 1919–22. Asst. prof. 1922, assoc. prof. 1923, Yale; assoc. prof. 1925, prof. 1927, Columbia; prof. 1951–62, Chicago. d. 1962. *The Bramble Bush* (1930); *The Common Law Tradition* (1960).

ARTHUR O. LOVEJOY b. 1873. A.B. 1895; A.M. 1897, Harvard. Asst. prof. (philosophy) 1899, assoc. prof. 1900, Stanford; prof. 1891, Washington U.; prof. 1908, Missouri; prof. 1910–38, Johns Hopkins. d. 1962.

LEON C. MARSHALL b. 1879. A.B. 1900, Ohio Wesleyan; A.B. 1901, A.M. 1902, Harvard. Prof. (economics) 1903, Ohio Wesleyan; asst. prof. 1907, assoc. prof. 1908, prof. 1911, dean. 1911–24 (College of Commerce), dean 1918–24 (School of Social Work), Chicago; vis. prof. (law) 1926–27, Columbia; prof. 1928–33, Johns Hopkins; prof. (economics) 1936–66, American University. Director, Division of Review, National Industrial Recovery Administration 1935–36. d. 1966.

MAX MASON b. 1877. B.Litt. 1898, Wisconsin; Ph.D. 1898, U. Göttingen. Inst. (math) 1903, MIT; asst. prof. 1904, Yale; prof. 1908, pres. 1925–28, Chicago. Division dir. 1928, pres. 1929–36, Rockefeller Foundation. d. 1961.

SOIA MENTSCHIKOFF b. 1915. B.A. 1934, Hunter; LL.B. 1937, Columbia. Private practice 1937–49. Vis. prof. 1947–49, Harvard; prof. 1951, Chicago; dean 1974–82, Miami. d. 1984.

W. UNDERHILL MOORE b. 1879. A.B. 1900, A.M. 1901, LL.B. 1902, Columbia. Private practice 1902–7. Prof. 1906, Kansas; asst. prof. 1908, assoc. prof. 1909, prof. 1910, Wisconsin; prof. 1914, Chicago; prof. 1916, Columbia; prof. 1929–47, Yale. d. 1949.

VICTOR MORAWETZ b. 1859. LL.B. 1879, Harvard. Private practice 1880–1908 (Seward, DaCosta, Guthrie & Morawetz). With Francis Lynde Stetson, represented Andrew Carnegie in the formation of the United States Steel Corporation. Chair, board of directors, 1893–1909, Santa Fe Railroad. d. 1938.

EDMUND M. MORGAN, JR. b. 1878. A.B. 1902, A.M. 1903, LL.B. 1905, Harvard. Private practice 1905–12. Prof. 1912, Minnesota; prof. 1917, Yale; prof. 1925, Harvard; prof. 1950–66, Vanderbilt. d. 1966.

HERMAN OLIPHANT b. 1884. A.B. 1907, Marion Normal; A.B. 1909, Indiana; J.D. 1914, Chicago. Inst. (English) 1907–11, Marion Normal; inst. (business law) 1914, asst. prof. 1915, lect. (law) 1914, asst. prof. 1916, assoc. prof. 1917, prof. 1919, Chicago; prof. 1921, Columbia; prof. 1928–33, Johns Hopkins. General counsel 1934–39, Department of Treasury. d. 1939.

ROSCOE POUND b. 1870. A.B. 1888, A.M. 1889, Ph.D. 1897, Nebraska; student 1889–90, Harvard Law School. Private Practice 1890–1901. Commissioner of appeals 1901–3, Nebraska Supreme Court. Private practice 1903–7. Asst. prof. (American history and jurisprudence) 1899, dean (law) 1903, Nebraska; prof. 1907, Northwestern; prof. 1909, Chicago; prof. 1910–47, dean 1916–36, Harvard. d. 1964.

THOMAS REED POWELL b. 1880. A.B. 1900, Vermont; LL.B. 1904, Harvard; Ph.D. 1913, Columbia. Private practice 1904–6. Lect. (political science) 1907, Columbia; assoc. 1908, Illinois; lect. 1911, assoc. (law) 1912, assoc. prof. 1913, prof. 1920, Columbia; prof. 1925–49, Harvard. d. 1955.

EDWARD S. ROBINSON b. 1893. A.B. 1916, Cincinnati; A.M. 1917, Carnegie Tech; Ph.D. 1920, Chicago. Inst. (psychology) 1919, Yale; asst. prof. 1920, assoc. prof. 1923, Chicago; prof. 1927–37, Yale. d. 1937. *Law and the Lawyers* (1935).

FRED RODELL b. 1907. A.B. 1928, Haverford; LL.B. 1931, Yale. Legal advisor 1931–33, Gov. Gifford Pinchot, Pennsylvania. Asst. prof. 1933, assoc. prof. 1936, prof. 1939–80, Yale. d. 1980. *Woe Unto You, Lawyers* (1939).

ELIHU ROOT b. 1845. A.B. 1864, A.M. 1867, Hamilton; LL.B. 1867, NYU. Private practice 1867–1937. U.S. Attorney, S.D.N.Y. 1883–85. Secretary of War 1899–1904. Secretary of State 1905–9. U.S. Senator 1909–15. d. 1937.

WICKLIFF ROSE b. 1862. A.B. 1889, A.M. 1890, U. of Nashville. Inst. (history) 1891, prof. (philosophy) 1892, Peabody College and U. of Nashville; prof. (history and philosophy of education) 1902–4, Tennessee; dean 1904–7, Peabody College and U. of Nashville. Gen. agent 1907–10, Peabody Education Fund; admin. secy. and member 1910–14, Rockefeller Sanitary Commission; trustee 1910, pres. 1923–28, General Education Board; trustee 1913–28, Rockefeller Foundation. d. 1931.

EUGENE ROSTOW b. 1913. A.B. 1933, LL.B. 1937, Yale. Private practice 1937–38. Asst. prof. 1938, assoc. prof. 1941, prof. 1944–84, dean 1955–65, Yale. Undersecy. for political affairs 1966–69, Department of State. Dir. 1981–83, Arms Control and Disarmament Agency.

CHARLES U. SAMENOW b. 1908. A.B. 1927, J.D. 1929, Yale. Res. assoc. 1929–33, Yale. Special asst. to the administrator 1936–68, Rural Electrification Administration. d. 1974.

HENRY W. SCHOFIELD b. 1866. A.B. 1887, A.M. 1890, LL.D. 1890, Harvard. Atty. 1891–92, Office of the Solicitor General. Private practice 1892–1900. Asst. corp. counsel 1900–1901, City of Chicago. Prof. 1902–18, Northwestern. d. 1918.

RITA JAMES SIMON b. 1931. A.B. 1952, Wisconsin; Ph.D. 1957, Chicago. Res. fellow (law and sociology) 1957, Chicago; inst. (sociology) 1961, Columbia; inst. 1961, Yale; asst. prof. 1963, assoc. prof. 1966, prof. 1968, prof. (law) 1971–74, dir. of law and society program 1975–80, Illinois; prof. (law) 1983–, dean, School of Justice 1983–89, American U.

YOUNG B. SMITH b. 1889. B.S. 1909, Georgia; LL.B. 1912, Columbia. Private practice 1912–16. Asst. prof. 1916, assoc. prof. 1918, prof. 1919, dean 1927–52, Columbia. d. 1960.

HARLAN F. STONE b. 1872. B.S. 1894, Amherst; M.A. 1897, LL.B. 1898, Columbia. Private practice 1898–1924 (Slaterlee, Canfield & Stone). Lect. 1899, prof. 1902, dean 1910–23, Columbia. U.S. Attorney General 1924–25. Justice 1925, chief justice 1941–46, United States Supreme Court. d. 1946.

WESLEY STURGES b. 1893. Ph.B. 1915, Vermont; LL.B. 1919, Columbia; J.D. 1923, Yale. Asst. prof. 1920–22, South Dakota; asst. prof. 1923, Minnesota; asst. prof. 1924, assoc. prof. 1926, prof. 1928, dean 1945–54, Yale; dean 1961–62, Miami. d. 1962.

GILBERT SUSSMAN b. 1905. A.B. 1926, Oregon; LL.B. 1929, Columbia. Res. assoc. 1929–34, Yale. Atty. 1934–45, Department of Agriculture and Bonneville Power Administration. Private practice 1945–85. d. 1985.

THOMAS W. SWAN b. 1877. A.B. 1900, Yale; LL.B. 1903, Harvard. Private practice 1903–16. Dean 1916–26, Yale. Judge 1926–75, U.S. Court of Appeals, Second Circuit. d. 1975.

DOROTHY SWAINE THOMAS b. 1899. A.B. 1922, Columbia; Ph.D. 1924, U. London. Res. fellow (statistics) 1924, Federal Reserve Board; res. fellow 1925, Social Science Research Council; res. fellow 1926, Laura Spellman Rockefeller Foundation; asst. prof. 1927, Columbia Teachers College; assoc. prof. 1931, Yale; prof. 1940, U. California, Berkeley; prof. 1948–70, Pennsylvania; prof. 1972–77, Georgetown. d. 1977.

GEORGE E. VINCENT b. 1864. A.B. 1885, Yale; Ph.D. 1896, Chicago. Asst. (sociology) 1895, asst. prof. 1896, assoc. prof. 1900, prof. 1904, dean of faculty 1907, Chicago; pres. 1911–17, Minnesota. Pres. 1917–29, Rockefeller Foundation; trustee 1914–29, General Education Board. d. 1941.

SAM BASS WARNER b. 1889. A.B. 1912, LL.B. 1915, Harvard. Private practice 1915–17. Prof. 1919, Oregon; prof. 1928, Syracuse; asst. prof. 1929, prof. 1932–45, Harvard. Register of Copyrights 1945–50. Newspaper publisher 1952–79. d. 1979.

GEORGE WICKERSHAM b. 1858. LL.B. 1880, Pennsylvania. Private practice 1880–1909 (Strong & Cadwalader). U.S. Attorney General 1909–13. Private practice 1914–36 (Cadwalader, Wickersham & Taft). d. 1936.

JOHN HENRY WIGMORE b. 1863. A.B. 1883, LL.B. 1887, Harvard. Private practice 1887–89. Prof. 1889, U. of Keio, Tokyo, Japan; prof. 1893, dean 1901–29, Northwestern. d. 1943. *A Treatise on the Law of Evidence* (1904, 2d ed. 1923, 3d ed. 1940).

DANIEL WILLARD b. 1861. Student, Massachusetts Agricultural C. 1878–79. Railroad employment 1879–1910, various railroads; pres. 1910, chair, board of directors 1941–44, Baltimore and Ohio Railroad. Trustee, 1914–44, chair 1926–41, Johns Hopkins. d. 1944.

SAMUEL WILLISTON b. 1861. A.B. 1882, LL.B. 1888, Harvard. Private practice 1889–90. Asst. prof. 1890, prof. 1895–1938, Harvard. d. 1963. *The Law of Contracts* (1920, 2d ed. 1936).

W. W. WILLOUGHBY b. 1867. A.B. 1888, Ph.D. 1891, Johns Hopkins. Private practice 1891–97. Asst. prof. (political science) 1894–95, Stanford; prof. 1897–1933, Johns Hopkins. d. 1945.

HESSEL YNTEMA b. 1891. A.B. 1912, A.M. 1915, Hope C.; A.M. 1913, Ph.D. 1919, Michigan; B.A. 1917, Oxford; S.J.D. 1921, Harvard. Inst. (political science) 1917–20, Michigan; lect. 1921, asst. prof. (law) 1923, assoc. prof. 1925, prof. 1928, Columbia; prof. 1928, Johns Hopkins; prof. 1933–66, Michigan. d. 1966.

HANS ZEISEL b. 1905. Dr. Jur. 1927, Dr. Rer. Pol. 1928, U. Vienna. Research in sociology, advertising 1928–52. Prof. (law and sociology) 1952–74, Chicago. d. 1992.

A Note on Sources

Much of my material comes from archival sources. To simplify citation I have adopted the following abbreviations. I also note something about the character of the major archival sources.

BHG   B. Howell Griswold Papers, Ferdinand Hamburger, Jr., Archives, Milton S. Eisenhower Library, Johns Hopkins University, Baltimore, Maryland, Record Group Number 08.020, Institute of Law, subgroup 3, B. Howell Griswold.

CAR   Carnegie Corporation Archives, Carnegie Corporation of New York, New York, New York.

CCB   Charles E. Clark Papers, Beinecke Rare Book Library, Yale University, New Haven, Connecticut (contains materials on Clark's empirical research and on the Connecticut Judicial Counsel and a plan to revise the membership rules of the American Bar Association).

CCL   Charles E. Clark Papers, Department of Manuscripts and Archives, Sterling Memorial Library, Yale University, New Haven, Connecticut (contains limited materials for the period 1925–29 and after 1939; no materials on his deanship).

CUA   Student Transcripts, Office of the Registrar, Columbia University, New York, New York.

DCP   David Farquhar Cavers Papers, Special Collections, Harvard Law School Library, Langdell Hall, Cambridge, Massachusetts (contains complete records of the Walter E. Meyer Research Institute of Law and its successor, Council on Law Related Studies, as well as Cavers's manuscript history of the Institute).

FFP   Felix Frankfurter Papers, Special Collections, Harvard Law School Library, Langdell Hall, Cambridge, Massachusetts.

FRD   Archives, Ford Foundation, New York, New York (terrible quarters, for a wonderfully helpful staff in a very well organized collection). All materials are from grant 52-152, except where otherwise noted.

HFS   Harlan Fiske Stone Papers, Rare Book and Manuscript Library, Butler Hall, Columbia University Libraries, Columbia University, New York, New York (covers the period of Stone's deanship).

HOP   Presidential Papers Series, Ferdinand Hamburger, Jr., Archives, Milton S. Eisenhower Library, Johns Hopkins University, Baltimore, Maryland, Record Group Number 02.001, Office of the President, series 1, file number 142.1, Institute of Law.

IHR   Records of the Institute of Human Relations, Department of Manuscripts and Archives, Sterling Memorial Library, Yale University, New Haven, Connecticut (the Institute's central office files).

IOL   Institute of Law Papers, Ferdinand Hamburger, Jr., Archives, Milton S. Eisenhower Library, Johns Hopkins University, Baltimore, Maryland, Record Group Number 08.020, Institute of Law, subgroup 1, Institute Records (largely the files of the Institute's fundraiser).

JHH   Jacob Harry Hollander Papers, Ferdinand Hamburger, Jr., Archives, Milton S. Eisenhower Library, Johns Hopkins University, Baltimore, Maryland, Record Group Number 08.020, Office of the President, series 1, file number 142.1, Institute of Law.

JRA   James Rowland Angell Papers, Department of Manuscripts and Archives, Sterling Memorial Library, Yale University, New Haven, Connecticut (voluminous and interesting).

KAN   University Archives, Kenneth Spencer Research Library, University of Kansas, Lawrence, Kansas.

LCM   Leon C. Marshall Papers, American Heritage Center, University of Wyoming, Laramie, Wyoming (vast).

MOH   Manley O. Hudson Papers, Special Collections, Harvard Law School Library, Langdell Hall, Cambridge, Massachusetts.

MSU   University Archives, Lewis Hall, University of Missouri-Columbia, Columbia, Missouri.

NEB   University Archives, University Libraries, University of Nebraska-Lincoln, Lincoln, Nebraska.

RMH   Robert Maynard Hutchins Papers, Department of Special Collections, Joseph Regenstein Library, University of Chicago, Chicago, Illinois.

ROC   Rockefeller Foundation Archives, Rockefeller Archive Center, Hillcrest, Pocantico Hills, North Tarrytown, New York (contains records of the many Rockefeller philanthropies).

RPP   Roscoe Pound Papers, Special Collections, Harvard Law School Library, Langdell Hall, Cambridge, Massachusetts (voluminous, well organized, though lacking outgoing correspondence for the early years).

SHF   Samuel H. Fisher Papers, Department of Manuscripts and Archives, Sterling Memorial Library, Yale University, New Haven, Connecticut (Fisher was a member of the Yale Corporation).

SSRC   Archives, Social Science Research Council, New York, New York.

TRP   Thomas Reed Powell Papers, Special Collections, Harvard Law School Library, Langdell Hall, Cambridge, Massachusetts.

UMC   W. Underhill Moore Papers, Rare Book and Manuscript Library, Butler Hall, Columbia University Libraries, Columbia University, New York, New York (covers Moore's life from about 1900 to 1919).

UMY   W. Underhill Moore Papers, Department of Manuscripts and Archives, Sterling Memorial Library, Yale University, New Haven, Connecticut (serial letter files 1919–43).

WIS   University of Wisconsin Law School, General Correspondence, Division of Archives, Memorial Library, University of Wisconsin, Madison, Wisconsin.

WWC   Walter Wheeler Cook Papers, in possession of W. Willard Wirtz, Washington, D.C. To be donated to the Northwestern University Law Library.

Two of my own previously published works on this subject are cited frequently enough that I have created special citations for them.

"Underhill Moore" "American Legal Realism and Empirical Social Science: The Singular Case of Underhill Moore," *Buffalo Law Review* 29 (Spring 1980): 195–323.

"Yale Experience" "American Legal Realism and Empirical Social Science: From Yale Experience," *Buffalo Law Review* 28 (Summer 1979): 459–586.

Preface

1. Twining, *Karl Llewellyn and the Realist Movement*, p. 66.
2. Ibid.
3. Stevens, "Two Cheers for 1870: The American Law School," republished in expanded form as Stevens, *Law School*.
4. Kalman, *Legal Realism at Yale*.
5. Schlegel, "The Ten Thousand Dollar Question."
6. Verdun-Jones, "The Voice Crying in the Wilderness"; Verdun-Jones, "Cook, Oliphant and Yntema." See also Verdun-Jones, "Jurisprudence Washed with Cynical Acid"; Verdun-Jones, "The Jurisprudence of Jerome N. Frank"; Verdun-Jones, "The Jurisprudence of Karl Llewellyn."
7. Purcell, *The Crisis of Democratic Theory*.
8. Duxbury, "Some Radicalism about Realism"; Duxbury, "Jerome Frank and the Legacy of Realism"; Duxbury, "Robert Hale and the Economy of Force"; Duxbury, "In the Twilight of Legal Realism."

Introduction

1. See generally Furner, *Advocacy and Objectivity*; Haskell, *The Emergence of Professional Social Science*; Oberschall, "The Institutionalization of American Sociology"; Ross, *The Origins of American Social Science*.
2. See Bingham, "What Is the Law?"
3. Duncan Kennedy supplied me with the felicitous phrase. Although he has since disowned it (and "the fundamental contradiction"), I still like it (and "the fundamental contradiction").
4. Purcell, *The Crisis of Democratic Theory*, tells part of the story.
5. I see no reason to document these attitudes toward Realism in great detail for they are ubiquitous. Hart, *The Concept of Law*, pp. 132–44, expresses the first with some reserve; Gilmore, "Legal Realism: Its Cause and Cure," expresses both of them; Reuschlein, *Jurisprudence: Its American Prophets*, also expresses both, unusually vituperatively.
6. The tense here is also a matter of consequence. If Realism "is" a jurisprudence, then it participates in the timeless chatter of the idea computers. If Realism "was" a jurisprudence, it is a historical curiosity fixed in and understood as a part of its time and place. It is amusing to note that the choice to see something as a timeless idea is more comfortable and less threatening than to see that thing as a historical phenomenon that might have reasons for its appearance and, through its disappearance, shed light on our world.

7. Llewellyn, *The Common Law Tradition*, pp. 509–10.

8. Pound, "The Call for a Realist Jurisprudence."

9. Llewellyn, "Some Realism about Realism: Responding to Dean Pound."

10. Dickinson, "Legal Rules: Their Function in the Process of Decision." See also Dickinson, "Legal Rules: Their Application and Elaboration."

11. Fuller, "American Legal Realism," p. 461.

12. Mechem, "The Jurisprudence of Despair," p. 692.

13. Kennedy, "Realism, What Next? I," p. 213. See also Kennedy, "Realism, What Next? II."

14. Lucey, "Natural Law and American Legal Realism," pp. 532, 533.

15. McDougal, "Fuller v. The American Legal Realists."

16. Garlan, *Legal Realism and Justice.*

17. Patterson, *Jurisprudence: Men and Ideas of the Law*, p. 539.

18. Bodenheimer, *Jurisprudence: The Philosophy and Method of the Law*, p. 1161.

19. Reuschlein, *Jurisprudence: Its American Prophets*, pp. 185, 188.

20. See Friedmann, *Legal Theory.* "[T]he realist movement is not a philosophy of law, it is a method of approach which wants to find out what law is, not what it ought to be. In exploring law it is positivist, and puts its faith in science." Ibid., p. 296. "Realist jurisprudence thus appears in its true perspective namely as an attempt to rationalize and modernize the law — both the administration of law and the material for legislative change — by utilizing scientific methods and the results reached in those fields of social life with which the social law is inevitably linked." Ibid., p. 303.

21. Schlegel, "The Ten Thousand Dollar Question."

22. . . . and for most other texts as well, I believe.

23. Rumble, *American Legal Realism.*

24. Purcell, *The Crisis of Democratic Theory.*

25. Twining, *Karl Llewellyn and the Realist Movement.* For Twining's later views, see Twining, "Talk about Realism."

26. Twining, *Karl Llewellyn and the Realist Movement*, p. 67.

27. Stevens, *Law School.* For a more complete version of my views on this book, see Schlegel, "Langdell's Legacy."

28. Kalman, *Legal Realism at Yale.* For a more complete version of my views on this book, see Schlegel, "The Ten Thousand Dollar Question."

29. Horwitz, *The Transformation of American Law 1870–1960.* For a more complete version of my views on this book, see Schlegel, "A Tasty Tidbit."

30. It should be apparent from the correspondence and personal interaction of the individuals who play major roles in my story that it is sensible to see them all as Realists. To date I have made no exhaustive attempt patiently to trace out the personal relationships of this group of individuals in order to give a definitive answer to the question, Who were the Realists? Nor shall I do so, for I think that such an activity would be wasteful of my time. All I wish to do is to identify a central social core or overlapping cores of individuals and work from there. Arguing for the inclusion or exclusion, the centrality or marginality of this or that individual is the kind of silly scholastic debate that gives academic history a bad name with sensible readers. This observation should also make clear that I do not object to the specific inclusions or exclusions made by the writers discussed earlier. I object to their failure to identify a sensible social core or cores of individuals by considering all of what the group has done and to maintain attention on that group. And I object to their failure to see that Realism is not just, and maybe not even most importantly, a jurisprudence, but is

other things as well. There is nothing wrong with presenting partial pictures seen as such. What is wrong is presenting partial, largely contextless pictures as the whole picture.

Prologue

1. I see no point to identifying individual sources for what follows. In assembling this narrative I have used Currie, "The Materials of Law Study"; Kalman, *Legal Realism at Yale*; Horwitz, *The Transformation of American Law*; "Yale Experience"; "Underhill Moore"; Stevens, *Law School*; Twining, *Karl Llewellyn and the Realist Movement*. None of these sources, not even my own, tells this story in precisely this way.

2. The most complete rendition of this other story is Horwitz, *The Transformation of American Law*. Other prominent ones are Singer, "Legal Realism Now," and Mensch, "A History of Mainstream Legal Thought." A good but relatively obscure one is Fisher, "The Development of Modern Legal Theory."

Chapter 1

1. Powell, The Harvard Law School, n.d. [ca. 1935], TRP.
2. I have collected brief biographies of my cast of characters in an appendix. The story of Stone's resignation as dean, though not of the fight over his replacement, is recounted in Foundation for Research in Legal History, *A History of the School of Law, Columbia University*, pp. 272–75. That book, often attributed to Julius Goebel, was written almost entirely by Samuel F. Howard, Jr., one of Columbia's assistants in law hanging around for a year after completing his LL.B.

> Professor Goebel was asked to write the Law School history; he was not interested in the matter, and suggested that the task be assigned to me. I was interviewed by the Columbia College professor who at the time was in charge of the overall project, and got the job. At the end of the semester, accordingly, my associateship was terminated and I became a member of the staff of the Foundation for Research in Legal History, to devote my full time to the projected history for a year.
> ... Professor Goebel, who had other fish to fry, gave me a free hand to do what I pleased. He let me work in his office at Kent Hall (to which he came only to pick up his mail); he arranged for the Law School secretarial staff to type my manuscript as I wrote it; and he read over the typescript and pointed out some typographical errors I had overlooked; but that was the extent of his supervision. He had the "final cut," as they say in the moving picture business, but he did not try to exercise it, and he did not try to tell me what to write or how. (Howard to Schlegel, 3/23/80)

3. Columbia University, Courses in Law and Special Conferences in Jurisprudence, n.d. [1922], RPP.
4. The series was the brainchild of Wigmore, Roscoe Pound, Ernst Freund, and C. H. Huberich, who convinced the Association of American Law Schools (AALS) to provide editorial direction to a project already begun by Wigmore's publisher. They justified the project on the basis of the profession's being "almost wholly [sic] untrained in the technique of legal analysis and legal science in general" such as would be

needed in the coming "period of constructive readjustment and restatement of our law." AALS, *Handbook and Proceedings, 1910*, p. 49. Four years later the publisher was complaining that only one-third of the Association's member schools were subscribers. AALS, *Handbook and Proceedings, 1914*, p. 8. Ten years later when the last book in the series was published, the same lament could still be heard. AALS, *Handbook and Proceedings, 1925*, p. 90.

5. See Walter Wheeler Cook to Harlan F. Stone, 9/15/22, HFS. Pound's basic text on the subject was his "The Scope and Purpose of Sociological Jurisprudence."

6. Columbia University, Courses in Law and Special Conferences in Jurisprudence, n.d. [1922], RPP.

7. Cook to Stone, 9/15/22, HFS.

8. Ibid.

9. Underhill Moore to Cassius J. Keyser (Columbia, Department of Mathematics), 2/6/24, UMC.

10. See "Underhill Moore," pp. 201-18.

11. It has become fashionable to attack Grant Gilmore's assertion that Langdell was "an essentially stupid man." *Ages of American Law*, p. 42. The major job of rehabilitation is Grey, "Langdell's Orthodoxy," but Speciale, "The Beginning of Anti-Formalism in American Legal Theory," moved the ball earlier as did Chase, "The Birth of the Modern Law School." By now the point is made everywhere. See, for example, Reimann, "Holmes' *Common Law* and German Legal Science," pp. 106-10. I remain unconvinced. Langdell was shrewd; one would have to be to make a fortune speculating in western farm mortgages. See Eliot, "Langdell and the Law School." But the man's total output of legal theory is about a page of print. Langdell, "Preface," and Langdell, "Harvard Celebration Speech." A careful reading of all his annual reports shows that he was a quite batty numerologist. Conceivably, all that need be said about legal theory could be said in a page or two. But more likely all that Langdell could say about legal theory was a page or two. Formalism may not have been as stupid an idea as the Realists made it out to be, but in coming to understand why it was not silly, in turning formalism into classical legal thought, one ought to be careful with respect to which formalists one simultaneously rehabilitates. Some formalists, like some Realists, may just have been dumb. At least, if it takes one hundred pages to turn Underhill Moore from a campstool, car-counting loony into something else, then more ought to be required than showing that a page or so of print was an example of "orthodoxy" in order to suggest that a man who spoke little did so for reasons other than that he had little to say.

12. Being at Harvard aided Langdell in two ways. First, during the first fifteen to twenty years Langdell could exploit Harvard's traditional position, and thus an essentially captive market, as the finishing school for relatively wealthy young men from upper New England generally, and Boston in particular, who wanted to be lawyers. See, for example, Warren, *History of the Harvard Law School*, 2:358. As a result Langdell had the time to let the innovation mature and then to produce a half generation of student converts who might spread the word. Second, because of Harvard's central position in the movement to create the American university and its success in doing so (see Veysey, *The Emergence of the American University*), it provided Langdell with a new and ready market for his innovation: all the presidents of all the lesser universities for whom success was creating a little Harvard on the prairie.

13. Stevens, *Law School*, p. 440, acknowledges the important role of Ames, Langdell's first convert, in the success of Langdell's revolution, although he does not pin-

point exactly what Ames contributed. Apparently Ames was a more dynamic teacher. He made the shift from Langdell's casebook, which was organized on historical principles, to a casebook organized in a more analytical format as the treatises had been and shifted the justification for case law teaching from the teaching of doctrine to training for thinking like a lawyer. Even more important, Ames, unlike Langdell, was a missionary for the new system.

14. Pomeroy, "John Norton Pomeroy," pp. 99–101, 106.

15. See Foundation for Research in Legal History, *A History of the School of Law, Columbia University*, pp. 135–58, for the story of Keener's takeover of the Columbia faculty.

16. See, for example, Phelps, "The Methods of Legal Education"; Keener, "The Methods of Legal Education."

17. Wigmore and Abbott introduced the case method at Northwestern in 1893. See Roalfe, *John Henry Wigmore*, p. 35. Then in 1895 Abbott moved and introduced the method at Stanford, where he was dean for ten years. Francis M. Burdick was another conqueror. He introduced a system of text and cases at Cornell in 1887. See Foundation for Research in Legal History, *A History of the School of Law, Columbia University*, pp. 203, 162.

18. See Johnson, *Schooled Lawyers*, pp. 115, 121–33, 138–44. Richards brought case study to both Iowa and Wisconsin.

19. The excitement even comes through the dreary pages of Roalfe, *John Henry Wigmore*, pp. 34–44. It is strangely missing from Johnson, *Schooled Lawyers*, largely because he views the coming of "schooled lawyers" on the Harvard model at best ambivalently. Foundation for Research in Legal History, *A History of the School of Law, Columbia University*, 145–55, succeeds in capturing the excitement at Columbia in spite of itself.

20. The demonstration of this proposition in a small compass is quite obviously difficult. Some evidence can be garnered by looking at the first "stud book." AALS, *Directory of Teachers in Member Schools, 1922*. If we look only at the first half of the listings, the following individuals, grouped by the school from which they received their final law degree, with their post fifteen years later indicated in parenthesis — some quite obvious successes, others "dropouts" of one kind or another — seem to fit the pattern.

Harvard
   Henry W. Ballentine (Cal., Berkeley)
   Morton C. Campbell (Harv.)
   Elliott Cheatham (Colum.)
   E. Merrick Dodd, Jr. (Harv.)
   Henry H. Foster (Neb.)
   Everett Frazer (Minn.)
   Ralph W. Gifford (Colum.)
   Eugene Gilmore (Wis.)
   Herbert F. Goodrich (Penn.)
   William G. Hale (So. Cal.)
   Henry Craig Jones (Iowa)
   Steven I. Langmaid (Cal., Berkeley)
   Edwin R. Leedy (Penn.)
   Charles W. Leaphart (Mont.)

Columbia
  Percy Bordwell (Iowa)
  Charles K. Burdick (Cornell)
  Homer F. Carey (Northwestern)
  Walter Wheeler Cook (Northwestern)
  Noel T. Dowling (Colum.)
  Edward W. Hinton (Chgo.)

A clear class difference can be seen in the ultimate employment of individuals from the "also-ran" law schools.

Chicago
  Leslie Ayer (Wash.)
Michigan
  Edmund C. Dickinson (W. Va.)
  Alvin E. Evans (Ky.)
Northwestern
  Earl C. Arnold (Vand.)
Yale
  Millard Breckenridge (N. Car.)
  George W. Goble (Ill.)
  John E. Hallen (Ohio St.)
  Albert J. Harno (Ill.)

21. Of the major appointments at Columbia between 1900 and 1925, only Moore, Cook, and Nathan Abbot had done any significant teaching elsewhere; at Harvard, only Pound, Edmund Morgan, and Edward Thurston. See generally Sutherland, *The Law at Harvard*, and Foundation for Research in Legal History, *A History of the School of Law, Columbia University*.

22. See "Underhill Moore," pp. 192–95, for examples.

23. Ibid.

24. A short history of the AALS can be found in Seavey, "The Association of American Law Schools in Retrospect." Aspects of its history are treated throughout Stevens, *Law School*.

25. Thayer, "The Teaching of English Law at Universities" (emphasizing the scholarly role of the professional law teacher). This lecture was quite obviously inspired in part by Dicey, *Can English Law Be Taught in the Universities?*, and Bryce, *The American Commonwealth*, 1:623.

26. See Hurst, *The Growth of American Law*, p. 263 (Langdell on the law professor as "juris consult").

27. Ames, "The Vocation of the Law Professor," pp. 368, 369, 366. (The address was given in 1901 and privately printed thereafter.)

28. Hohfeld, "A Vital School of Jurisprudence and Law," in its baroque detail, is perhaps the apogee of this notion of professional vocation as well as an important early statement of the case for a still more analytic, less genetic scholarship than that pioneered by Ames. Lewis, "The Law Teaching Branch of the Profession," is about the last statement of the notion in any form that Ames would have recognized.

For the impact of the Germanic model of legal scholarship on these law teachers, see Ames, "The Vocation of the Law Professor," pp. 368–69. See generally Herbst, *The German Historical School in American Scholarship*.

29. On the limited libraries of provincial law schools, see Wigdor, *Roscoe Pound*, p. 121; Pattee, "The College of Law," p. 142.

30. See, for example, "Underhill Moore," pp. 172–75, 211–19.

31. One can discount the purely verbal expressions of the notions of colonial service and scholarly vocation as simply that — much talk, the unimportance of which is shown by the little action that accompanied it. And as is often the case with such an objection, it has more than a bit of merit. The histories of major law schools such as Harvard and Columbia are replete with faculty whose commitment to anything more than a very episodic scholarship is highly dubious. Any attempt to account generally for the process of professionalization of law teachers before World War I would have to account for these negative cases too. But, for present purposes, all that is important is that, whether these two notions are dominant or only subsidiary themes over the profession as a whole, they adequately explain Cook's and Moore's early professional activities. And that they do.

32. Fuchs, "Walter Wheeler Cook," p. 185.

33. Cohen, "Prof. Underhill Moore and His Influence on the Growth of the Law School."

34. See Foundation for Research in Legal History, *A History of the School of Law, Columbia University*, p. 161.

35. The department included John W. Burgess, Frank J. Goodnow, John Bassett Moore, and Munroe Smith. See generally Hoxie, *A History of the Faculty of Political Science, Columbia University*.

36. Horace E. Deming to Edmund J. James (President, University of Illinois), 1/17/10, UMC. On Moore's employer, Horace E. Deming, and his practice, see "Underhill Moore," p. 241.

37. Transcript, "Walter Wheeler Cook, Flushing, N.Y.," 10/10/91, CUA.

38. "New History Professor" (announcement of Cook's appointment at Nebraska).

39. See "Walter Wheeler Cook" (continuing teaching in mathematics); Transcript, "Walter Wheeler Cook, Columbus, O.," 11/12/97 (Political Science); Transcript, "Walter Wheeler Cook, Columbus, O., June 4, 1873," 11/3/97 (Law School), CUA.

40. See Transcript, "Walter Wheeler Cook, Columbus, O.," 11/12/97, CUA.

41. Foundation For Research in Legal History, *A History of the School of Law, Columbia University*, p. 158, sets forth the requirements for the degree.

42. "New History Professor"; University of Nebraska, *Catalog for the Year 1900–01 and Announcements for the Year 1901–02*, pp. 183–85.

43. See Wigdor, *Roscoe Pound*, pp. 3–5.

44. University of Nebraska, *1869–1919*, p. 132, puts the faculty at 56 in 1900 and the student body at 2,250 in the same year.

45. Ibid., pp. 130–31. Andrew's work at Nebraska is sensibly depicted in Wigdor, *Roscoe Pound*, pp. 104–5.

46. See University of Nebraska, *1869–1919*, pp. 42–47, 105–12.

47. Griffin, *University of Kansas*, pp. 242, 224–26.

48. Stephens, *A History of University of Missouri*, pp. 361, 328, 361, 366 and 368–69, 383–84, 368.

49. Griffin, *The University of Kansas*, pp. 197, 284–86, 654.

50. Moore to Harry Richards (Dean, University of Wisconsin Law School), 2/28/07, WIS.

51. Moore to Richards, 2/28/07 (assigned text and cases but used cases in class), WIS; Kansas Law Class of 1908, Twenty-fifth Annual Reunion Booklet, 1933, UMY.

52. Fratcher, *The Law Barn*, pp. 92 n. 36, 9, 34, 11, 62.

53. Ibid., pp. 52–53.

54. Griffin, *The University of Kansas*, p. 287.

55. See "Notes and Personals" (1908), p. 246 (courses on agency, bills and notes, bailments and carriers, damages, partnership, and insurance).

56. University of Missouri, *Announcements of the Department of Law, 1905–06*, pp. 10–13 (courses on criminal law, domestic relations, torts, agency, equity, bills and notes, constitutional law, wills).

57. Moore, "Significance of the Term 'Contract' in Article I, Section 10 of the Constitution."

58. Ewart, *The Principles of Estoppel by Misrepresentation*. Ewart's career is critically discussed in Risk, "John Skirving Ewart: The Legal Thought."

59. Cook, "Agency by Estoppel," p. 38.

60. 1 B. & Ald. 323, 106 Eng. Rep. 250 (1818).

61. Cook, "Agency by Estoppel," pp. 43, 38, 44–46.

62. See Kennedy, "Toward an Historical Understanding of Legal Consciousness"; Horwitz, *The Transformation of American Law, 1870–1960*.

63. See Cook, "How May the United States Govern the Philippine Islands?"

64. See Baldwin, "The Constitutional Questions Incident to the Acquisition and Government by the United States of Island Territory"; Langdell, "The Status of Our New Territories"; Thayer, "Our New Possessions."

65. See Whitney, "Another Philippine Constitutional Question." Edward B. Whitney was a lawyer active in reform circles. See "Edward S. Whitney."

66. Cook, "How May the United States Govern the Philippine Islands?," pp. 69, 70.

67. Ibid., pp. 71–72, 73.

68. See Freund, *The Police Power*.

69. Cook, "What Is the Police Power?," p. 330.

70. Ibid., pp. 327, 328, 329, 330, 331.

71. Ibid., pp. 331, 332–33.

72. Ibid., p. 334.

73. An easy entry into this topic is Warren, *The Supreme Court in United States History*, 2:713–18.

74. Cook, "What Is the Police Power?," p. 336.

75. Curiously Pound's biographer never mentions this aspect of Pound's life. Before taking the deanship at Nebraska Pound *was* the program in jurisprudence in the department, teaching elements of jurisprudence, ancient law, Roman law (3 courses), common law, history of English law, canon law, and criminal law, a list that facially obligated him to teach eighteen hours per week. See University of Nebraska, *Catalog for the Year 1901–02 and Announcements for the Year 1902–03*, pp. 93–94, 191–93.

76. Ibid., pp. 93–94, 192–93 (American history); 230–32 (law).

77. M. B. Reese to Chancellor and Board of Regents, n.d. [ca. 6/3], NEB.

78. University of Nebraska, *Catalog for the Year 1903–04 and Announcements for the Year 1904–05*, pp. 96–98 (American history); 255–56 (law).

It is difficult to make much out about the details of Cook's relationship with Pound when both were at the Nebraska Law School. For all the story about Pound's reviving the Law School (Wigdor, *Roscoe Pound*, pp. 104–9), Cook began teaching there before Pound did and Pound stayed firmly anchored in the Department of American

History and Jurisprudence, arranging that his and Cook's courses there be offered jointly at the Law School. See University of Nebraska, *Calendar, July 1, 1903–July 1, 1904 and Announcements 1904–05*, pp. 278–79. Years later Pound talked of Cook as "my right hand man" in the job of reorganizing the Law School (Pound, "Some Comments on Law Teachers and Law Teaching," p. 527), though in fact Cook was there for only the first of Pound's three years as dean. My guess is that the social distance between the greenhorn and the local boy well enough connected to have been appointed Commissioner (i.e., temporary judge) of the Nebraska Supreme Court and founding Secretary of the Nebraska Bar Association was too large to cross.

79. Cook to The Regents of the University, 6/4/04, NEB. Cook's salary was to be $2,000. See Cook to R. H. Jesse (President, University of Missouri), 6/4/04, MSU.

80. University of Missouri, *Law Department, Announcements, 1904–05*, pp. 10–14.

81. See "Underhill Moore," p. 227.

82. Ibid., pp. 227, 232, 228.

83. Moore, "Book Review" (review of Meecham and Gilbert, *Cases on Damages*).

84. See Moore to Harlan F. Stone, 2/22/16, UMC.

85. See Schlegel, "Langdell's Legacy"; Schlegel, "Between the Harvard of the Founders and the American Legal Realists."

86. Cook, "What Is the Police Power?," p. 330.

87. See Schlegel, "Between the Harvard of the Founders and the American Legal Realists."

88. Moore was informed that his dean felt that he was "not well adapted for work in . . . [the] Law School." Frank Strong (Chancellor) to Moore, 1/15/07. A student petition urged Moore's retention. University of Kansas, School of Law, Petition of Law Students, n.d. [spring 1907]. And Moore was rehired with that Dean's approval apparently. Strong to Moore, 6/18/07, KAN. Moore apparently earned the Dean's enmity by flunking 15 to 20 percent of his class, at a school that was "a dumping ground for athletes." Moore to Harry Richards, 2/28/07, WIS. This probably did not sit well with a man described as the "patron saint of KU football."

89. See generally Curti and Christensen, *The University of Wisconsin, 1848–1925*, 2:122, 11, 23–24, 71–72, 306, 497, 500–502, 509, 533, 538, 540–45, 9–11.

90. See Karl, *Charles E. Merriam and the Study of Politics.*

91. See Johnson, *Schooled Lawyers*, pp. 131, 114–15, 127, 131.

92. "Notes and Personals" (1908), p. 246 (courses on bankruptcy, bills and notes, criminal law, conflict of laws, suretyship).

93. Eugene Gilmore and Howard L. Smith.

94. See Ellsworth, *Law on the Midway.*

95. Goodspeed, *A History of the University of Chicago*, pp. 334–35.

96. Moore's starting salary at Chicago was $5,500, a substantial jump from the $4,000 he would have made had he stayed at Wisconsin. With the advancement came a further decrease in teaching load. "Notes and Personals" (1914), p. 587 (courses on bills and notes, municipal corporations, suretyship, and mortgage and half of the course on contracts).

97. Floyd Meecham and Harry Bigelow.

98. See Roalfe, *John Henry Wigmore.* Henry Schofield and Blewett Lee were the most notable of the practitioner-teachers.

99. Chicago is hardly known as a summer colony; still, during these years its summer session drew Henry M. Bates (Michigan), Frederick C. Woodward (Stan-

ford), Edwin R. Keedy (Indiana), Harry S. Richards (Wisconsin), Clark B. Whittier (Stanford), William P. Rogers (Cincinnati), Percy Bordwell (Iowa), Chester Vernier (Illinois), Dudley O. McGorney (Tulane), and Austin Wakeman Scott (Harvard). While none of these was Patti or Caruso, for its class it was a real watering hole.

100. See, for example, Cook to Pound, 7/20/09, RPP; Wesley N. Hohfeld to Pound, 9/24/12, RPP.

101. Smith and Moore, *Cases and Materials on the Law of Bills and Notes* (1910).

102. Norton, *Handbook of the Law of Bills and Notes*. At the same time he published Moore, *Illustrative Cases of the Law of Bills and Notes*. He also tried to get the job of editing Ames's casebook on the subject. Moore to Richard Ames, 5/31/12, UMC.

103. Moore, "Negotiable Instruments." (This article was in the American Law and Procedure series, edited by James Parker Hall, Dean at the University of Chicago. The series contained articles by Walter Wheeler Cook, Albert Kales, and Roscoe Pound, among others. To the consternation of these individuals, this work, originally designed for nonlawyers, was in fact utilized by the La Salle Extension University as a part of its correspondence course in law. See Hall, "Communications.")

104. Hohfeld to Pound, 3/15/12, RPP.

105. Hohfeld's obituary establishes that Hohfeld taught at Chicago in 1910. See the *Yale Alumni Weekly* 28 (1918): 162. Hohfeld to Pound, 12/26/10, RPP, confirms Pound's teaching that summer before moving to Harvard.

106. Hohfeld to Pound, 3/15/12, RPP.

107. Hohfeld, "Nature of Stockholders' Individual Liability for Corporation Debts"; Hohfeld, "The Individual Liability of Stockholders and the Conflict of Laws."

108. Hohfeld to Pound, 3/15/12, RPP.

109. Cook, "The Place of Equity in Our Legal System," pp. 174, 174–76, 175, 177, 178.

110. Schofield is basically unknown today. His real specialty was utility franchises. For a brief biography and a sense of the man, see Wigmore's foreword in Schofield, *Constitutional Law*.

111. Schofield, "Discussion," pp. 178, 179, 180.

112. See Cook, "The Place of Equity in Our Legal System," p. 178, citing Pound, "The Decadence of Equity."

113. Schofield, "Discussion," p. 181.

114. Hohfeld to Pound, 5/20/13, RPP.

115. Hohfeld, "The Relations between Equity and Law," pp. 539, 544, 539 n. 3, 540.

116. Hohfeld, "A Vital School of Jurisprudence and Law," pp. 96, 97.

117. Ibid., pp. 83, 86, 99–100, 103, 104, 107, 99.

118. See Singer, "The Legal Rights Debate in Analytical Jurisprudence from Bentham to Hohfeld," pp. 975, 989 n. 22.

119. See Twining, *Karl Llewellyn and the Realist Movement*, p. 387 n. 330.

120. Bates, "Address of the President," p. 29.

121. Beale, "The Necessity for a Study of Legal System," pp. 47, 48.

122. Hohfeld, "A Vital School of Jurisprudence and Law," p. 98.

123. Ibid., pp. 114, 128, 129, 80, 110, 112–13. Robert Gordon brings to my attention the similarity between Hohfeld's school of jurisprudence and both the program of the School of Political Science at Columbia and the public law curriculum at Oxford.

124. See Larson, *The Rise of Professionalism*; Schlegel "Between the Harvard of the Founders and the American Legal Realists."

125. See Ames, "The Vocation of the Law Professor," pp. 368–69.

126. See Kirkwood and Owens, *A Brief History of the Stanford Law School, 1894–1946*, pp. 19, 22–23, 28–29.

127. See Cook, "The Powers of Courts of Equity."

128. Cook began by distinguishing rights *in personam* and *in rem*, from actions *in personam* and *in rem*, judgments or decrees *in personam* and *in rem*, and procedures *in rem* or *in personam*, for the enforcement of judgment or decrees. Ibid., pp. 40–54. In his basic definitional work Cook followed Hohfeld's earlier work quite closely, emphasizing sense of "right," limited to circumstances where another person has a correlative "duty," though. Cook differed from Hohfeld in discussing remedial rights. See ibid., pp. 44–45, and Hohfeld to Cook, 2/13/15, WWC. Cook followed Austin and others by finding that rights *in rem* were those against other people generally and that rights *in personam* were those against a limited determinate number of persons. Actions and the resulting judgments or decrees were, however, to be distinguished so that those *in rem* were those where the object was to exercise power over a specific thing or *res*, whereas those *in personam* were where the object was to enforce a personal liability. Procedures for the enforcement of judgments or decrees were treated similarly so that the procedure of seizing property for sale was procedure *in rem*, while procedure like that of imprisoning for contempt was *in personam*. Cook, "The Powers of the Courts of Equity," pp. 41–42, 44–50, 51–54.

129. Cook, "The Powers of the Courts of Equity," p. 53.

130. Thus rights *in rem* could be adjudicated by actions *in rem* or *in personam* and likewise with rights *in personam*. Ibid. However while judgments *in personam* could be enforced by procedure *in rem* or *in personam*, judgments *in rem* were curiously left hanging. Ibid., pp. 53, 54.

131. Ibid., pp. 108, 115. Similar conclusions were reached from comparisons of the common-law writ of partition with the bill in equity for partition and of bills in equity for the specific performance of contracts for the conveyance of land with the common law actions of ejectment, replevin, and detinue. Ibid., pp. 119–33.

132. This is a 1908 reprint of a series of articles written between 1888 and 1897 under that title.

133. Cook, "The Powers of the Courts of Equity," pp. 122, 120 n. 39, 123, 125.

134. Ibid., pp. 128, 129. See, for example, ibid., p. 138, where in the case of the right of the holder of an instrument to recover on that instrument even though it was obtained by fraud, an action bought to cancel the instrument is an action *in rem* and not an action *in personam* to enforce a personal liability for deceit.

135. Ibid., pp. 121, 131, 119, 233, 117 n. 32.

136. See Hohfeld to Cook, 2/13/15 ("Gradually . . . the fact that the Harvard men didn't say the last word . . . will become apparent to all"), WWC.

137. Cook, "The Alienability of Choses in Action," pp. 819, 821–34, 834–36, 834.

138. Williston, "Is the Right of an Assignee of a Chose in Action Legal or Equitable?," pp. 97, 100, 90, 108. The three classic cases were the debtor's right of setoff against the assignor, the rights of holders of latent equities in the chose, and the rights of partial assignees.

139. Cook, "The Alienability of Choses in Action: A Reply to Professor Williston," pp. 451, 452.

140. Curiously, the first failure turned out to be nothing more important than

Williston's using "rights" where Cook had used Hohfeld's complete system. But the point allowed Cook to give a rather preachy minisummary of Hohfeld's system and an encomium for "exact, scientific analysis of fundamental legal conceptions and an equally exact and scientific terminology." Williston's second failure was that of using "legal rights" and "equitable rights" rather than recognizing that the assignee's "rights, privileges, powers and immunities" were "legal as well as equitable." Ibid., pp. 455–59, 453, 455.

141. Ibid., p. 460. Much of this argument was a replay of his *Columbia Law Review* piece, and here again Cook utilized Hohfeld's argument that as between equity and law there are only two kinds of relations, exclusively equitable and concurrently equitable and legal, for when exclusively legal relations are "in conflict with some paramount exclusively equitable . . . relation . . . [that relation] has the effect of annulling the legal . . . relations in question." Thus "because Professor Williston does not recognize that a right . . . may be at the same time both legal and equitable, . . . he fails to see that to say that right is legal is not necessarily to say that it is exclusively legal and so not equitable." Ibid., pp. 461, 463.

142. Ibid., pp. 467, 475. See also ibid., pp. 477 (need to look at the "real reasons back of the rule"), 479 (real problem involved is one of purely business policy), 488 (decision needs to be put on grounds of "policy").

143. Ibid., p. 485.

144. See Williston, "The Word 'Equitable' and 'Its Application to Assignment of Choses in Action,'" pp. 823, 827, 829, 833.

145. See "Underhill Moore," p. 230.

146. Foundation for Research in Legal History, *A History of the School of Law, Columbia University*, pp. 10, 231, 241–55.

147. See "Underhill Moore," p. 204.

148. Veblen was not at Columbia but at the New School for Social Research, an establishment of dissident Columbia faculty members. He was, however, a part of the intellectual community that had its center first at Columbia and then at Columbia and the New School.

149. See Moore to Harlan F. Stone, 2/22/16 (E. W. Hinton); Moore to Stone, 4/16/16 (Cook), UMC.

150. See Ross, *The Origins of American Social Science.*

151. Pierson, *Yale: The University College,* p. 259.

152. Hohfeld to Pound, 10/23/13, RPP.

153. See Twining, *Karl Llewellyn and the Realist Movement,* p. 34. Hohfeld was clearly looking for a job (see Hohfeld to Pound, 5/22/13, 7/15/13), and said he saw Abbott and Pound as more directly responsible for his getting this one than Corbin (Hohfeld to Pound, 10/17/15, RPP).

154. See Kalman, *Legal Realism at Yale,* pp. 99–100.

155. Hohfeld to Roscoe Pound, 9/24/12 ("easily the best of the best of the men now at the University of Chicago Law School"); Hohfeld to Pound, 7/17/16 ("high admiration and regard" for Cook; "on my list of calls"), RPP.

156. *Yale Daily* 39, no. 177 (5/16/16): 1, 5.

157. Pound to Cook, 5/27/16, RPP.

158. Moore to Hinton, n.d. [fall 1916?], UMC.

159. See, for example, Hohfeld to Pound, 3/15/12, 9/24/12, RPP. Hohfeld to Cook, 2/13/15, WWC.

160. Cook to Stone, 2/18/19, HFS; see also Cook to Moore, 3/24/19 ("My chief

concern is to find out at which place [i.e., Yale or Columbia] the greatest progress is to be hoped for in really doing constructive things during the next twenty years"), UMC.

161. Hohfeld to Pound, 5/20/17, RPP.

162. Kalman, *Legal Realism at Yale*, p. 100 (quoting Fleming James).

163. *Yale Alumni Weekly*, 3/23/17 (supp.).

164. Ibid., pp. iv, ii, i.

165. See, for example, Hohfeld to Pound, 5/20/17, RPP.

166. Hohfeld to Cook, 2/13/15, WWC.

167. Hohfeld to Pound, 5/20/17, RPP.

168. Hohfeld to Pound, 1/21/18, RPP.

169. Cook to Moore, 2/4/17; Moore to Cook, 2/5/17, UMC.

170. Cook to Moore, 2/18/17, UMC.

171. Hohfeld to Pound, 4/10/18, RPP.

172. Hohfeld to Pound, 6/9/18, RPP.

173. Pound to Hohfeld, 9/3/18, RPP.

174. See *Yale Alumni Weekly* 28 (1918): 162.

175. Cook to Manley O. Hudson (colleague while at Missouri), 10/25/18, MOH.

176. Cook to Moore, 11/6/18, UMC.

177. Jerome Frank to Cook, 12/23/18 ("a great shock to anyone interested in the future of Anglo-American law"; "he has permanently clarified our legal system, both from the point of view of practice and pedagogy"); Herman Oliphant to Cook, 12/27/18 ("depressed" though "I did not know the man." "[L]egal scholarship has lost not merely a devoted disciple. It has lost a leader of the first order. He was making the most important and probably the only distinctively new contribution to the law since the earliest days of Harvard"), WWC.

178. Pound to Cook, 10/29/18, RPP.

179. Cook to Pound, 11/6/18, RPP. Pound was right on length of acquaintance, whatever might be the matter of "intimacy." Llewellyn too took a possessive view of Hohfeld's memory. See Twining, *Karl Llewellyn and the Realist Movement*, p. 97.

180. Cook, "Hohfeld's Contributions to the Science of Law." This essay was later reprinted as the introduction to a bound complete version of Hohfeld's works. Hohfeld, *Fundamental Legal Conceptions as Applied to Judicial Reasoning.*

181. Llewellyn, "Wesley Newcomb Hohfeld — Teacher."

182. Cook, "Hohfeld's Contributions to the Science of Law," p. 722.

183. Cook to Moore, 3/24/19, UMC.

184. Moore to Hinton, 5/7/19, UMC. Which is not to say that Moore had not considered going to Yale. See Edwin M. Borchard to Moore, 4/17/19; Ernest Lorenzen to Moore, 4/16/19, UMC.

185. *Columbia Alumni News* 10 (5/23/19): 931.

186. Foundation for Research in Legal History, *A History of the School of Law, Columbia University*, p. 263, identifies Cook's Columbia salary. I infer Cook's Yale salary from Hohfeld to Pound, 5/20/17, RPP.

187. See, for example, Cook, "Recognition of 'Massachusetts Rights' by New York Courts"; Cook, "What Constitutes an 'Injury' to 'Real Property'?"; Cook, "The Associated Press Case"; Cook, "The Conclusiveness of State Judgments under the Full Faith and Credit Clause."

188. See, for example, Cook, "Recognition of 'Massachusetts Rights' by New York Courts"; Cook, "Full Faith and Credit to Judgments of Other States"; Cook, "The Powers of Congress under the Full Faith and Credit Clause"; Cook, "The Conclusive-

ness of State Judgments under the Full Faith and Credit Clause"; Cook, "Specific Intent with Acquisition of Domicile."

189. Hohfeld to Pound, 7/12/14, RPP.

190. Cook to Stone, 2/18/19, WWC.

191. Cook, "Estoppel by Misrepresentation and the Recording Acts," p. 690. See also Cook, "Conversion by Innocent Agents"; Cook, "The Associated Press Case."

192. 245 U.S. 229 (1917).

193. See, for example, Cook, "The Associated Press Case."

194. Cook, "The Privileges of Labor Unions in the Struggle for Life," pp. 787, 788, 789, 790, 792–93.

195. Ibid., p. 800.

196. Indeed, Rob Steinfeld observes that it is truly amazing that anyone managed to penetrate Hohfeld's dense prose enough to figure out a use for the system.

197. See Cook, "Boycotts of 'Non-Union' Materials."

198. See Cook, "The Injunction in the Railway Strike," p. 167.

199. See Cook, "Boycotts of 'Non-Union' Materials," p. 540, quoting *Vegelahn v. Guntner*, 167 Mass. 92, 107, 44 N.E. 1077, 1081 (1897).

200. Cook, "The Injunction in the Railway Strike," pp. 169–70.

201. Cook, "The Privileges of Labor Unions in the Struggle for Life," p. 800. See also Cook, "Boycotts of 'Non-Union' Materials," p. 542.

202. Cook, "Boycotts of 'Non-Union' Materials," pp. 539, 542.

203. See Twining, *Karl Llewellyn and the Realist Movement*, p. 393 n. 51 (Karl Llewellyn's assertion that only Cook of the Realists may have been directly influenced).

204. Pound's personal relationship with Cook while at the Nebraska Department of American History and Jurisprudence seems to have been quite straightforwardly that of a junior to senior colleague. Pound clearly moved Cook's career forward. See, for example, Cook to Pound, 5/25/10 (thanking Pound for recommending him as Pound's replacement at Chicago), RPP. Cook even bought Pound's house when he moved to Chicago and Mrs. Pound financed the mortgage. See Cook to Pound, 6/24/10, 6/30/10, RPP. Associates at the Hopkins Institute clearly remember that Cook simply refused to respond to Pound's attack on Realism in his famous piece, "The Call for a Realist Jurisprudence." See George Jaffin to Schlegel, 10/19/81. When the Institute was closed, Cook looked to Pound for help finding a job (Cook to Pound, 6/23/32, RPP), and Pound tried his best to find Cook a place at Harvard (Pound to Cook, 6/25/32 [possibility of replacing Frankfurter who had been nominated for a judgeship], 11/25/32, 2/10/33, RPP).

Yet the matter is substantially more complicated than this, as can be seen from the fact that the two were not junior and senior colleagues but effective contemporaries, born three years apart. Moreover, on certain subjects Cook regularly attacked Pound — most notably Pound's emphasis on the "traditional and known techniques of the Common Law." See, for example, Cook, "Research in Law," p. 313.

At one point in writing this book, I put much effort in trying to understand the relationship of these two men but gave up in disorder. My reason on one side should be obvious; the Cook papers are terribly fragmentary. On the other side, though the Pound papers are massive, we still have no good biography. The first, Sayre, *The Life of Roscoe Pound*, is thoroughly inadequate, and the second, Wigdor, *Roscoe Pound*, while better, is too focused on Pound as a philosopher, a role in which he is thoroughly uninteresting. Laura Kalman's work on Realism has begun to flesh out a reasonable portrait; see Kalman, *Legal Realism at Yale*, pp. 45–46, 56–62, 111, 185, 215. Still, her work is no substitute for a complete biography of Pound that would try to place him in the world of the twentieth-century law professor. Until such is available, questions like this one will be difficult to answer other than with a good guess and a shrug.

205. Hohfeld to Pound, passim, RPP.

206. See Cook, "The Cleveland Criminal Survey."

207. Corbin, "The Law and the Judges," pp. 235, 249–50, 249.

208. "Social Mores, Legal Analysis, and the Journal."

209. See Cook, "Boycotts of 'Non-Union' Materials," pp. 540 nn. 5 and 6, 541 nn. 8 and 9; Cook, "The Privileges of Labor Unions in the Struggle for Life," pp. 783 n. 8, 784 nn. 15 and 16, 799 n. 54. See also Cook, "Book Review" (Holmes, *Collected Legal Papers*). Only Hohfeld got his share of citation, though by no means an adequate share. Corbin is mentioned once (Cook, "The Privileges of Labor Unions in the Struggle for Life," p. 784 n. 16a); Pound never.

210. Holmes, "Privilege, Malice and Intent," p. 8.

211. 167 Mass. 92, 107, 44 N.E. 1077, 1081 (1896).

212. See Williston, "Is the Right of an Assignee of a Chose in Action Legal or Equitable?," pp. 106, 107, 108.

213. Cook, "Book Review" (Frey, *The Labor Injunction*), p. 199.

214. Foundation for Research in Legal History, *A History of the School of Law, Columbia University*, p. 262.

215. I have speculated endlessly, some would say fruitlessly, on this subject. My best explanation follows in the text. Nevertheless, I recognize that I have no answers to questions like, "Why 1922 rather than 1920 or 1928; after all Dewey had been saying these things for some time?" or "Why Dewey and not Morris Cohen, Dewey's great adversary?" Indeed to emphasize that Cook and Moore were "available to" Dewey's thought (as David Matza spoke of juveniles and delinquency) seems to me to obscure more than it illuminates for neither was particularly disquiet at this time and looking for this kind of trouble. Perhaps like Matza's delinquents any kind of trouble would have done the job. Still the fact seems not accidental in hindsight, whatever can be said about foresight.

216. WWC contains the notes of both Dewey's lecture and some of Pound's delivered at the same time. These are the only notes preserved in the papers and at least Cook's widow thought them significant. The notes are extremely difficult to read but not unintelligible and seem reasonably thorough.

217. Common citations were Hall, *Cases on Constitutional Law* (a colleague from Chicago); Pound, *Introduction to the Philosophy of Law*; Holmes, "The Path of the Law"; Isaacs, "The Law and the Facts" (Isaacs was a law professor with a Ph.D. in philosophy who cited Dewey regularly); Drake, "The Sociological Interpretation of Law" (an article in the same issue of the *Michigan Law Review* as another of Isaac's); and Lepaulle, "The Function of Comparative Law." For the most part, Dewey seems to have grabbed a few recent law reviews and run to the lectern.

218. Inductive logic seems to have been good for nothing.

219. Wigmore and Kocourek, *Rational Basis of Legal Institutions*, pp. xx–xxvii.

220. Moore, "Rational Basis of Legal Institutions," pp. 609, 609–10, 612–14, 615, 617.

221. This article is reprinted in Cook, *The Logical and Legal Bases of the Conflict of Laws*; all citations are to this edition.

222. Dewey, *Human Nature and Conduct.*

223. Cook, *The Logical and Legal Bases of the Conflict of Laws*, pp. 3–4.

224. Ibid., p. 4.

225. Dewey, *Essays in Experimental Logic.*

226. Cook, *The Logical and Legal Bases of the Conflict of Laws*, pp. 6, 8.

227. Cook, "The Powers of Courts of Equity," pp. 230, 232.

228. Cook, *The Logical and Legal Bases of the Conflict of Laws*, pp. 9, 20, 26, 29–31, 43, 43–44.

229. The only reference to Dewey is to *Human Nature and Conduct*; the entire tenor of the piece is anthropological.

230. See, for example, Cook, "The Alienability of Choses in Action."

231. See Cook, *The Logical and Legal Bases of the Conflict of Laws*, p. 42.

232. See, for example, Cook, "The Powers of the Courts of Equity" (attacking Langdell and Ames).

233. Cook, *The Logical and Legal Bases of the Conflict of Laws*, p. 29.

234. "Underhill Moore," p. 204.

235. The details of Moore's unhappiness are set forth in ibid., pp. 204–10.

236. Ibid., pp. 211–12.

237. Moore to H. T. Manning, 4/3/28; Frederick J. E. Woodbridge to Moore, 4/29/27 (detailing grants to Moore), UMY.

238. See, for example, Moore to W. L. Trumble (Barclay's Bank), 6/20/27, UMY.

239. See Moore to Young B. Smith, 12/24/27 (recounting use of funds), UMY. Some of the questionnaire research was published as Klaus, "Identification of the Holder and Tender Receipt on the Counter-Presentation of Checks"; see p. 299 and n. 64. Samuel Klaus, a 1927 graduate of Columbia, was one of Moore's research assistants during the academic years 1926–28. See Moore to Hugh Satterlee, 11/26/27, UMY.

240. Moore and Shamos, "Interest on the Balances of Checking Accounts." Abraham Shamos, a 1927 graduate of Columbia, was another of Moore's research assistants. Apparently Shamos did library research while Samuel Klaus did "field" research, a differentiation of function that Moore kept for many years. The library assistant did all of Moore's personal accounts as well as prepared semiannual balance sheets and income statements! See Moore to Shamos, 6/22/27; Moore to David L. Daggett, 4/21/36 (describing job of assistant), UMY.

241. See "Underhill Moore," pp. 212–13.

242. Moore and Hope, "An Institutional Approach to the Law of Commercial Banking."

243. And for some time. "The 'law' governing a particular state of facts which happens to-day is the rule which will to-morrow be applied to the state of facts by the . . . officers engaged in administering justice." Underhill Moore, Answers of Underhill Moore to Questionnaire, n.d. [fall 1923], UMY.

244. Moore and Hope, "An Institutional Approach to the Law of Commercial Banking," p. 703.

245. See Oliphant, "A Return to Stare Decisis."

246. See Llewellyn, *The Bramble Bush.*

247. Moore and Hope, "An Institutional Approach to the Law of Commercial Banking," pp. 703, 704, 705.

248. Discussion of the question dates back at least to Plato. In the narrower commercial context, Anglo-American lawyers think of the opinions of Lord Mansfield as

the starting point of the discussion. See, for example, Ewart, "What Is the Law Merchant?"

249. Moore and Hope, "An Institutional Approach to the Law of Commercial Banking," pp. 706–7, 707.

250. Ibid., pp. 708, 707–9, 711–19, 719.

251. Moore justified his method with the slightly disingenuous observation that it was necessary because the facts in recorded cases "are a small, and very probably non-representative, sample of all behavior" and the cases, "distinguished by dissimilarity rather than similarity one to another." As a result, Moore asserted, legal categories are broad so as to include as many cases as possible and thus "inadequate for classification." Ibid., p. 705. Truth of the matter is, I suspect, that Moore also quite plainly loved the arcane terminology he had invented.

252. Ibid., pp. 711–12, 714–15.

253. Moore's notion of an institutional relation, "frequently following — frequently preceding" (ibid., p. 707), though intended to describe only habitual behavior, in fact implied causality as well. In so doing it raised the possibility that his attempt to establish a causal relation between customary behavior and legal decisions validating conduct in accordance with that behavior might either founder because the assumed underlying causality was absent or succeed, but only because of a spurious correlation with some element in the institutional behavior.

254. See, for example, ibid., p. 715. "The second comparison of the second deviational transaction with its first comparable sequence is made by substituting for the prior terms of the transaction the correlative terms of the comparable sequence." Translation: If we assume a less troublesome circumstance, it may highlight the bank's error.

255. This was especially true in evaluating the degree of deviation between the transaction and a sequence where the factors to be evaluated quite obviously overlapped as well as were loaded in the direction of banker opinion. However, it was also true with respect to the way that the method of deriving comparable entities led away from the transaction in question. Ultimately Moore did not fully understand his own observation about the singularity of litigated phenomena.

256. Moore sent out dozens of reprints of the article. Most went unacknowledged. Of those that were acknowledged, none were accompanied by anything more elaborate than President Butler's objection to the behaviorist psychology in the piece and his prediction that Moore would in time get over it. Butler to Moore, 1/15/29, UMY. Others such as C. J. Keyser, a Columbia philosopher of science, and Alfred L. Kroeber, the anthropologist, were not even this helpful.

257. On Moore's move to Yale, see "Underhill Moore," pp. 213–14, 218.

258. For a discussion of these studies, see Chapter 3.

259. Cook, *Cases and Other Authorities on Equity*.

260. See, for example, American Law Institute, *Proceedings*, 3:225–29, 260–65.

261. See Cook to Frank J. Goodnow (President, Johns Hopkins University), 5/1/26, WWC, and Chapter 4. Also during these years Cook was very much tied up with the decline in health of his first wife, who died of cancer in 1927. See Cook to Pound, 5/31/25, RPP.

262. Cook, "Scientific Method and the Law," pp. 303, 304, 305, 306.

263. Ibid., pp. 306, 306–7, 307, 308.

264. Ibid., pp. 308, 308–9.

265. Ibid., p. 309.

266. For an account of the activities of Cook summarized in this paragraph, see Chapter 4.

267. In Baltimore, Cook lived in an area so fancy that it published its own glossy-paper news magazine, a sedate local gossip column. See, for example, "Interest in Law Institute Grows," *The Roland Park Company's Magazine*, 1/30, p. 11, WWC.

268. Moore summered in Dorset, Vermont; Cook, in a now lost summer colony with the improbable name of Hollywood, New York. For a wonderful portrait of Cook "at home," see Fisher, *Old Hollywood*, pp. 32–35.

269. For Moore's shyness, see "Underhill Moore," pp. 309–10. For Cook's shyness, I rely on interviews with Leon Green, 6/19/75, and Willard Wirtz, 10/29/79, and on a long correspondence with George Jaffin who was a research associate at the Hopkins Institute, though in fact none of these individuals make this point directly. Clark, "Walter Wheeler Cook," pp. 341–42, agrees with this characterization.

270. See, for example, Cook, *The Logical and Legal Bases of the Conflict of Laws*, p. 46.

271. Ibid., pp. 45–46. This may not be a dumb assumption in a field that was essentially about nothing socially concrete. A rule in the field that was not effective would be hard to identify for lack of a readily available referend in terms of human behavior.

272. Cook, "Scientific Method and the Law," pp. 308, 309.

273. See, for example, Twining, *Karl Llewellyn and the Realist Movement*, p. 37; Carey, "Walter Wheeler Cook," p. 346.

274. See generally Schlegel, "Between the Harvard of the Founders and the American Legal Realists."

275. See generally ibid.

276. See Foundation for Research in Legal History, *A History of the School of Law, Columbia University*, pp. 263–64.

277. Interview with Willard Wirtz, 10/29/79.

278. Clark, "Walter Wheeler Cook," p. 342; Carey, "Walter Wheeler Cook," p. 347. Interview with Willard Wirtz, 10/29/79.

279. Fisher, *Old Hollywood*, pp. 32–35.

280. See Cook to Stone, 2/18/19, WWC.

281. See "Underhill Moore," p. 230 n. 215.

282. Clark, "Walter Wheeler Cook"; interview with Willard Wirtz, 10/29/79; Foundation for Research in Legal History, *A History of the School of Law, Columbia University*, p. 484 n. 24.

283. See, for example, "Underhill Moore," pp. 308, 315.

284. See, for example, Clark, "Walter Wheeler Cook"; Carey, "Walter Wheeler Cook"; Interview with Willard Wirtz, 10/29/79. Yntema, "Walter Wheeler Cook," p. 348, disagrees.

285. Cook and Hinton, *Cases on Pleading at Common Law*.

286. Cook, "Improvement of Legal Education and of Standards for Admission to the Bar." This was hardly Cook's idea alone. For the full story, see Stevens, *Law School*.

287. Cook to Pound, 3/27/12, RPP.

288. See AALS, *Handbook and Proceedings, 1920*, p. 64; AALS, *Handbook and Proceedings, 1921*, p. 29.

289. AALS, *Handbook and Proceedings, 1921*, pp. 115–19.

290. Moore to Stone, 6/30/16, UMC.

291. Ultimately he would even play the role of providing support for the young teachers sent to the Midwest as he had been. See Homer F. Carey (Kansas) to Moore, 2/6/29; Moore to Carey, 2/13/29; Carey to Moore, 5/11/30; Moore to Carey, 5/14/30; Carey to Moore, 9/?/31; Moore to Carey, 9/30/31, UMY.

292. Moore to Stone, 5/1/16, UMC.

293. See Moore to Frederick C. Hicks (Columbia law librarian), 6/30/16, 7/11/16 (must not miss a single advance sheet), UMC.

294. See Moore to Max Radin (University of California, Berkeley), 10/27/19 (I am a year behind), UMC.

295. After 1921, he attended only one meeting; see "Underhill Moore," p. 300 n. 646.

296. See Moore to Robert L. Hale, 11/30/18, UMC.

297. See Harold Kellock (classmate) to Moore, 6/20/20, UMC.

298. See, for example, William F. Ogburn to Moore, 7/20/20 (visit to summer home), UMC.

299. See An Inquiry into Business and Production (unpublished study), spring 1920?; Kellock to Moore, 5/20/20, UMC.

300. Moore, "Theft of Incomplete Negotiable Instrument and Negotiation to Holder in Due Course"; Moore, "The Right of the Remitter of a Bill or Note." Moore also published two book reviews at this time, one mildly humorous, Moore, "Book Review" (review of Baty, Loan and Hire), and the other quite serious, Moore and Cook, "Book Review" (review of E. Lorenzen, The Conflict of Laws Relating to Bills and Notes).

301. Smith and Moore, Cases and Materials on the Law of Bills and Notes (1922).

302. M. Cohen, "Book Review," p. 892. On Cohen, see Hollinger, Morris R. Cohen and the Scientific Ideal.

303. Powell to Moore, 6/20/24, UMY. Cohen may well have had Moore in mind as having written one of "the notices of this book [that] have been rather unjust in failing to take account of what the editors actually set out to do" — namely, create "a new type of text for students of law, occupying an intermediate position between the ordinary casebooks and treatises on the general theory of law." M. Cohen, "Book Review," p. 892. But, if so, it is curious that many of their specific complaints were identical. Compare ibid., pp. 893 ("many of the selections seem to me perfectly valueless," "[p]roperty is discussed as if it were just one simple thing existing by itself"), 894 ("the overpowering impression which the reading of this book makes . . . is the awful amount of nonsense written by worthy people on serious and momentous subjects"), with Moore, "Rational Basis of Legal Institutions," pp. 616 ("the selection and arrangement of the material under the heads of property and succession are all that would be expected from a treatment of the institution of property as a single problem to be settled a priori"), 617 ("Upon opening the volume, we thought we sensed a spirit of weariness in Mr. Justice Holmes' Introduction; upon closing the book, our confidence is strengthened that this impression was correct"). Indeed they identified similar good points, too. Compare Cohen, "Book Review," p. 894 (Pound, McMurray, and Charmont), with Moore, "Rational Basis of Legal Institutions," pp. 616, 617 (Pound, Bosanquet, Charmont, and Parsons). It would not have been un-likely for Cohen to have attacked an individual with whom he was in basic agreement. See generally Hollinger, Morris R. Cohen and the Scientific Ideal, pp. 69–70.

304. Thayer, "The Teaching of English Law at Universities," pp. 173, 183.

305. See Ames, "The Vocation of the Law Professor."

306. See, for example, Swan, "Reconstruction of the Legal Profession," pp. 792–94 (a peculiarly mundane example).

307. See, for example, Ames, "The Vocation of the Law Professor," p. 369.

308. See generally Foundation for Research in Legal History, *A History of the School of Law, Columbia University*, pp. 85, 91, 96–98, 110–15, 126–28, 148, 167–68, 210–11.

309. See "Underhill Moore," p. 229 n. 200.

310. Ibid., p. 236.

311. See Moore, "Rational Basis of Legal Institutions," pp. 613–14. Each of the books cited is a general introductory work, occasionally a textbook even, written with one exception (William McDougall) by people at, or associated with, Columbia University in the years on either side of World War I. Each is the kind of book a technical specialist might suggest to an interested but green colleague in response to the lunchtime observation, "That's very interesting; I'd like to read some more about these problems" — the kind of introduction one unlettered in social science could usefully have acquired immediately after becoming seriously interested in it. One of the authors is known to have been a personal friend of Moore — William F. Ogburn; the rest were individuals whom a prominent new faculty member less than forty years old and hired at a quite extraordinary salary would have met at the faculty club of what was still a relatively small university.

312. My understanding of the reception of the "scientific ideal" into American academic thought has been immeasurably aided by many discussions with David Hollinger. He should not, however, be tarred with responsibility for what I have done to his essential insight into American thought around the turn of the century.

313. For a general understanding of Yale in the period, see Pierson, *Yale: The University College*. Kelley, *Yale: A History* pp. 376–86, indirectly demonstrates how the college still dominated Yale at this time, even though the university had already produced several notable scholars, when he notes how much effort had to be put into improving graduate and professional education. Veysey, *The Emergence of the American University*, provides further support.

314. Robert Gordon reminds me that Hohfeld had a place in his system for legislative jurisprudence. "The science of legislation" (see Lieberman, *The Province of Legislation Determined*) probably fuses Hohfeld's legislative and teleological categories.

315. Cook always quotes but never cites this phrase. I finally tired of looking for this needle in Pound's haystack. The idea can be found in such sources as Pound, *The Spirit of the Common Law*; Pound, "Theory of the Judicial Decision"; Pound, "Problems of the Law." My guess is that Cook had *heard* Pound use the phrase.

316. Cook, "Scientific Method and the Law," p. 308.

317. Pound and Frankfurter, *Criminal Justice in Cleveland*.

318. Cook, "The Cleveland Criminal Survey," p. 22.

319. Cook, "The American Law Institute," pp. 87, 88–89, 89.

320. Hohfeld, "A Vital School of Jurisprudence and Law," pp. 99–100.

321. Though eventually the need for expert fact finders would disappear and well-trained lawyers would do. See Chapter 4. As late as 1927 Cook still saw the need for outside experts. See Cook, "Scientific Method and the Law," p. 309.

322. See "Underhill Moore," p. 238.

323. Moore to Cassius J. Keyser (Columbia, Department of Mathematics), 2/6/24, UMC.

324. Moore to James Harvey Robinson, 1/13/34, UMY.

325. See "Underhill Moore," p. 238.

326. The conspicuous exception to this generalization is Roscoe Pound who in *The Spirit of the Common Law* adopted an explicitly causal approach to legal history, but utilized a notion of causation (i.e., what precedes causes what follows) so simple-minded as to only emphasize its similarity with Langdellian lawyer's history of doctrine and its distance from a social history of law such as Robinson, or more obviously his friend Charles Beard, might have written. See, for example, Beard, *An Economic Interpretation of the Constitution of the United States.*

327. See "Underhill Moore," p. 241.

328. See, for example, Clark, "Walter Wheeler Cook," p. 343; Carey, "Walter Wheeler Cook," p. 345; Yntema, "Walter Wheeler Cook," pp. 348–49.

329. Interview with Willard Wirtz, 10/29/79.

330. Cook, *The Logical and Legal Basis of the Conflict of Laws*, p. 47.

331. Ibid., p. ix.

332. Moore, "Rational Basis of Legal Institutions," p. 612.

333. See Foundation for Research in Legal History, *A History of the School of Law, Columbia University*, p. 251.

Chapter 2

1. 208 U.S. 412 (1908).

2. See Maxwell, *Lincoln's Fifth Wheel.*

3. See Davis, *American Heroine.*

4. See *The Autobiography of Florence Kelley.*

5. See McCraw, *Prophets of Regulation.*

6. Mason, *Brandeis: A Free Man's Life*; Strum, *Louis D. Brandeis*, pp. 94–113.

7. Wigdor, *Roscoe Pound*, pp. 194–98.

8. Pusey, *Charles Evans Hughes.*

9. Ibid. On Deming, who was one of the founders of the good-government National Municipal League, see "Horace E. Deming."

10. Pound, "The Scope and Purpose of Sociological Jurisprudence."

11. Pound and Frankfurter, *Criminal Justice in Cleveland.*

12. Kalman, *Legal Realism at Yale*, pp. 102–4.

13. Corbin preferred a policy of hiring good recent graduates of Yale.

14. Kalman, *Legal Realism at Yale*, p. 104.

15. On Clark, see Schick, *Learned Hand's Court*, pp. 29–32. See generally Petruck, *Judge Charles Edward Clark.*

16. See Ashmore, *Unseasonable Truths*, pp. 466–91. See also Dzuback, *Robert M. Hutchins*; McArthur, "A Gamble on Youth."

17. Minutes of the Faculty of the Yale Law School, 2/25/26 (hereinafter cited as "Yale Minutes"). An updated, untitled copy of the proposal is in RMH. The quotation is from the opening of that document.

18. A Program of Research in the Administration of the Law, App. A, at 1, 2, 3, n.d. [summer 1926?], RMH. This document is a proposal directed to the General Education Board, a Rockefeller philanthropy, for a grant of approximately $125,000 for a five-year pilot program.

19. In each field they proposed studies of the rules in force and the actual operation of the rules, and comparative studies of both. Ibid., pp. 2–4. The funds sought were for four half-time faculty salaries, a research assistant for each, and library acquisi-

tions. Ibid., p. 6. From the salaries mentioned and the interests noted, it is apparent that the participants were to be Hutchins, Clark, Leon A. Tulin, and a faculty member not then hired. Although empirical work was contemplated, p. 1, no funds were requested for such work.

20. The occasion of their formulation was a train ride by Hutchins and Clark in December 1925. Clark had complained about the school and indicated his desire to leave. Hutchins chided him about leaving without first trying to change anything. Clark agreed and they thereupon drew up plans for honors courses, the Institute of Procedure, and limitations on enrollment. "We stood absolutely alone on all these matters and were opposed at every step more or less actively by the Dean." Hutchins to Samuel H. Fisher (member of Yale Corporation), 2/24/27, SHF.

21. See Llewellyn to Hutchins, 5/6/26, RMH. See also Hutchins to Llewellyn, 5/17/26; Hutchins to Llewellyn, 5/21/26, RMH.

22. A Program of Research in the Administration of the Law, App. A, pp. 1–2, n.d. [summer 1926?], RMH.

23. Pound, "The Causes of Popular Dissatisfaction with the Administration of Justice."

24. The proposition that the reform of procedural law (together with the simplification of substantive law) is law reform must be counted as one of the stranger notions of the bar. Intoned with monotonous regularity in its Poundian mirror image — the administration of justice has brought disrespect upon the law — the proposition is notable for the fact that evidence in its support, beyond the existence of dissatisfaction (also assumed) and the assertion that the procedural deficiencies of interest to the speaker are its cause, is virtually always lacking. Equally notable is the fact that such dissatisfaction with the administration of justice as there may be is always seen as "popular" and not professional. Marc Galanter has brought to my attention an excellent example of this confusion of popular and professional dissatisfaction: the conference called by Mr. Chief Justice Burger to commemorate the seventieth anniversary of Pound's address. See 70 F.R.D. 79 (1976).

Although I have no difficulty in saying that this misidentification has allowed slightly left-of-center lawyers to make their work simpler while supporting both "reform" and the economic and political "status quo" (see Auerbach, *Unequal Justice*), the lineage and function of this notion about what constitutes "law reform" is unimportant here. What is important at this point is that the notion was available to Hutchins and Clark and that they took it and used it, but in a different way than it had been used in the past.

25. A Program of Research in the Administration of the Law, App. A 3, n.d. [summer 1926?], RMH.

26. Hutchins repeatedly stressed this point. Interview with Robert M. Hutchins, 6/20/75.

27. Ibid.

28. Tracing the intellectual roots of Realist thought is made difficult because the Realists did not usually identify the sources of their ideas. Where such identification is made, as in Llewellyn, "The Effect of Legal Institutions upon Economics," the citations tend to be general and to lump together uncritically rather disparate thinkers, as in Llewellyn's list of "Summer, Holmes, Veblen, Commons and Pound."

29. Yale Minutes, 3/11/26.

30. "Yale Experience," pp. 470–71.

31. Yale Minutes, 5/31/27. The new faculty members were Leon Green and Walter F. Dodd.

32. For an explanation of the original methodology of the Cleveland Crime Survey, see Bettman and Burns, *Prosecution*. Little is known about this singular example of Pound's sociological jurisprudence in action. Pound's biographer tells just enough to suggest that the topic needs exploration. See Wigdor, *Roscoe Pound*, pp. 242–45. Frankfurter's biographer barely mentions the project. Lash, "A Brahmin of the Law."

33. *Report of the School of Law, 1926–27* (Robert M. Hutchins), pp. 118–19.

34. Ibid., p. 119.

35. Clark, "Fact Research in Law Administration." Clark milked his study for all it was worth; he also published what was substantially the same article as Clark, "Some of the Facts of Law Administration in Connecticut"; Clark, "New Types of Legal Research"; Clark, "Methods of Legal Reform"; Clark and King, "Statistical Method in Legal Research." A preliminary version appeared as Clark, "An Experiment in Studying the Business of Courts of a State."

36. Clark and Shulman, *Law Administration in Connecticut*, pp. 4, 206. However, it is not clear that sampling techniques would even have been known to Clark or anyone he might have talked with about the design of the study. Stepan, "History of the Uses of Modern Sampling Procedures," suggests that although isolated examples of what might be called sampling occurred in studies as early as 1914, modern techniques were not generally used in the United States until after 1932 when they were disseminated to the academic community as a part of the New Deal social programs.

37. Clark, "Fact Research in Law Administration," pp. 211, 218–19, 213.

38. Ibid., pp. 224–27. The data also showed that verdicts in jury trials were more often favorable to defendants than was the case in bench trials and that verdicts in jury trials were more likely to be appealed.

39. Ibid., pp. 227–30, 230–33, 212.

40. Ibid., p. 233. Clark's research assistants collected data that led to two more articles. Clark and O'Connell, "The Working of the Hartford Small Claims Court" (survey of cases filed and dispositions), and Clark, "Should Pleadings Be Filed Promptly?" (comparison of timeliness of filing responsive pleading in Connecticut and Massachusetts). Harris, "Joinder of Parties and Causes" (objections to joinder), and Harris, "Is the Jury Vanishing?" (comparison of use of jury in Connecticut, Massachusetts, and New York; very difficult interpretive problem), use figures developed in this initial research of Clark.

41. *Report of the School of Law, 1927–28* (Robert M. Hutchins), p. 116.

42. Clark and Shulman, *Law Administration in Connecticut*, p. 4. Some work was done in Massachusetts: Clark, "Should Pleadings Be Filed Promptly?"; New York: Harris, "Joinder of Parties and Causes"; Ohio: Clark and Shulman, *Law Administration in Connecticut*, p. 5 n. 20; and West Virginia: Arnold, "The Collection of Judicial Statistics in West Virginia."

43. Hoover, "Inaugural Address," pp. 2, 4.

44. Act of Mar. 4, 1929, Pub. L. No. 1034, 45 Stat. 1607, 1613.

45. Other members of the commission were Newton D. Baker, a former Secretary of War; William S. Kenyon, Paul J. McCormick, and William I. Grubb, all federal judges; Kenneth Mackintosh, Judge of the Washington Supreme Court; and Henry W. Anderson, Monte M. Lemann, and Frank J. Lorsch, all prominent attorneys.

46. Yale Minutes, 3/21/29. American Law Institute, *Study: Criminal Cases*, p. 21;

Hutchins to Henry Stimson, 3/18/29, CCB. Connecticut Senator Hiram Bingham set up the meetings that included presentations to Chief Justice Taft, Justice Stone, Attorney General William D. Mitchell, and Idaho Senator William E. Borah. From an undated, untitled copy of the "budget" for the project that can be found in the CCB, it can be inferred that the proposal contemplated use of the major university law schools as centers for the decentralized collection of data. Eighty percent of the budget was for the employment of an army of fieldworkers. See also Clark to Frederick C. Hicks, 1/14/40 (Hoover thought the whole problem was delay; Taft endorsed the project), CCL.

47. Wickersham to Clark, 11/21/29, CCB. The intermediaries apparently were Felix Frankfurter and his friend Max Lowenthal, the Commission's secretary, who were trying to outflank Frankfurter's colleague and Commission member, Roscoe Pound, who proposed to do the work himself. See Clark to Frankfurter, 11/30/29; Frankfurter to Clark, 12/2/29 (reporting Wickersham's enthusiasm for the plan); Clark to Frankfurter, 12/18/29 ("your distinguished colleague and leader had been willing to conduct the whole investigation"; Clark "understood" the intention of Frankfurter and Lowenthal "to guard against the very contingency which has happened"), CCB. But see Hutchins to Clark, 12/18/29 (speculating that Attorney General Mitchell had given the papers from the original Hutchins-Clark presentation to Wickersham, and by inference suggesting that Frankfurter was claiming credit where none was due), RMH.

48. William I. Grubb, District Court Judge in Alabama and a Yale grad, and Monte M. Lemann, a prominent New Orleans attorney and law school classmate and friend of Frankfurter.

49. Clark to Wickersham, 12/30/29 (meetings with Orrin K. McMurray, Dean at University of California, Berkeley, Professor Edmund Morgan, Owen J. Roberts, then in practice in Philadelphia, later Justice of the United States Supreme Court, and Lemann), CCB. Frankfurter was also present, though not an official advisor. Grubb to Clark, 12/24/29, CCB. The other member of the advisory committee was Robert M. Hutchins. American Law Institute, *Study: Criminal Cases*, p. 20.

50. Wickersham to Clark, 1/9/30, CCB.

51. Ibid.; Grubb to Clark, 12/24/29, CCB.

52. Clark to Lowenthal, 3/2/30; Clark to Charles H. Willard (Lowenthal's assistant), 3/25/30, CCB.

53. Clark and Shulman, *Law Administration in Connecticut*, p. 6; American Law Institute, *Study: Criminal Cases*, p. 22. Samenow was a 1929 graduate of the Law School. He had previously published some of his research for Clark as Clark and Samenow, "The Summary Judgment."

54. Douglas and Clark, Interim Report of the Committee on the Study of Law Administration in the Federal Courts, 5/11/30, p. 3, CCB. Pretesting was begun in Connecticut, moved to the Southern District of New York, and thereafter continued in Louisiana, Ohio, and West Virginia. The member of the advisory committee most regularly consulted was Edmund Morgan, a former colleague of Clark's at Yale. See, for example, Clark to Morgan, 2/18/30, CCB.

55. Douglas and Clark, Interim Report of the Committee on the Study of Law Administration in the Federal Courts, 1/11/30, p. 3, CCB. This form, based on that used in the Connecticut courts study, was pretested only in the Southern District of New York.

56. See, for example, Clark to Herschel Arant (Dean, Ohio State), 5/11/30 (Arant was a Law School graduate who had taught at Yale 1920–22, just after Clark had begun teaching); Clark to Rufus Harris (Dean, Tulane), 5/11/30 (Harris was a former student, LL.B. 1923, and graduate student, J.D. 1924, at Yale), CCB. After running out of friends and former students, Clark filled in to fit the need for a cross section of district courts.

57. Douglas and Clark, Interim Report of the Committee on the Study of Law Administration in the Federal Courts, 5/11/30, p. 1 ("While public hysteria and professional criticism will not be motivating causes in the study, much of the subject matter of these will be dealt with"), CCB.

58. Clark and Douglas did manage to find the time in late summer 1930 to attend a Conference on Legal Research sponsored by the Social Science Research Council and organized by Henry M. Bates, Dean at Michigan. The conference was designed to explore the existing pattern of research, principle lines of future development, available personnel, and potential for social science contributions. Lynd, Tentative Agenda for Social Science Research Council Conference on Legal Research, Hanover [New Hampshire], 8/29–9/2/30, SSRC. Other participants included Karl N. Llewellyn from Columbia, Felix Frankfurter and Joseph H. Beale(!) from Harvard, and Hessel F. Yntema of the Institute of Law at Johns Hopkins. See also Clark to Bates, 10/8/30 (good conference; group should be expanded); Bates to Clark, 10/23/30 (rather keep group small, adding perhaps Northwestern and Ohio. Beale should not be included next time; "regrettable incident" brought him this time); Clark to Bates, 10/27/30 (Frankfurter "interesting and stimulating" but too "chauvinistic" to be a good "conference or committee man"), CCB. "Next time" turned out to be never. Commenting on the conference twenty-five years later, Llewellyn suggested that Harvard and Michigan "found themselves unready for research competition . . . and . . . effectively killed off the [Social Science Research] Council's interest in aiding any law school at all in any research looking toward integration of the disciplines." Llewellyn, "On What Makes Legal Research Worthwhile," p. 401. Frankfurter and Pound had attended a similar conference of the Council in 1926, this time on criminal studies. Karl, *Charles E. Merriam*, p. 135.

59. In the process Clark learned, much to his annoyance, that the Columbia faculty was jealous of all the publicity Yale was deriving from running the study and that, as the price for its assistance, wanted to share the limelight, if ever so slightly, by being represented on the advisory committee. See Clark to Wickersham, 10/6/30 (Columbia representative to be Harold Medina who "conducts the best bar cramming course in New York City"); Wickersham to Clark, 10/10/30; Clark to Medina, 10/16/30; Clark to Bates, 11/21/31 (Bates and Thurman Arnold to join advisory committee to cover sellout to Columbia), CCB. I suspect some of the jealousy was also attributable to the fact that Harvard was already represented on the committee.

Schools participating were those of the advisory committee members, California, Columbia, Harvard, Michigan, and Yale; the pretesting sites, Ohio, Tulane, and West Virginia; and Chicago, Colorado (Dean James Grafton Rodgers was a graduate of Yale College and a prominent candidate for the Yale deanship in 1926; Yale Minutes, 1/1/27), Kansas (Professor Thomas Atkinson, J.S.D. 1926, had been a Clark student and teaching fellow while at Yale), and North Carolina (Professor Charles McCormick had taught summer school at Yale and was offered, but declined, a regular appointment thereafter; Yale Minutes, 5/5/27).

60. Clark to Grubb, 1/1/31, CCB.

61. Clark to Lowenthal, 9/10/30, CCB. National Commission, *Progress Report*, p. iv.

62. Even before Clark was hired by the Commission, he was cautioned that funding was precarious (Grubb to Clark, 10/24/29); soon thereafter, he was urged to get foundation financing (Lowenthal to Clark, 3/27/30); and even after the Commission was refunded he was warned that disputes between Congress and Hoover over the scope of the problem to be investigated threatened its continued existence (Lowenthal to Clark, 9/5/30, CCB).

63. Clark to Grubb, 1/3/31; Clark to Wickersham, 1/6/31, CCB.

64. National Commission, *Report on the Enforcement of the Prohibition Laws of the United States*, p. 83.

65. Claire Wilcox (Commission Research Director) to Clark, 1/8/31, CCB.

66. See, for example, Clark to Grubb, 1/3/31; Lemann to Clark, 1/14/31, CCB.

67. Clark to Wickersham, 3/31/31, CCB.

68. Clark to Wickersham, 3/31/31, 4/1/31; Wickersham to Clark, 4/14/31 (reporting contacts with Rockefeller Foundation), CCB.

69. Most notably Dorothy Swaine Thomas; see my discussion in the next section.

70. Clark to Lemann, 10/25/30; Clark to Wickersham, 4/31/31, CCB.

71. Clark to Claire Wilcox, 5/1/31, CCB.

72. Douglas, Arnold, and Clark, Progress Report on the Study of the Business of the Federal Courts (draft), n.d., p. 3, CCB.

73. National Commission, *Progress Report*, pp. 18, 22–23, 28–29, 32, 58.

74. As distinguished from contemporary federal criminal procedure in which, by the addition of lawyers for indigents and the creation of several new constitutional defenses and sentencing guidelines, the legal system seems to have kept the same ultimate results but lengthened the time for disposition.

75. Douglas, Arnold, and Clark, Progress Report on the Study of the Business of the Federal Courts, n.d., p. 4, CCB.

76. National Commission, *Progress Report*, p. 19. The inference was correct. See John A. Danaher (U.S. Attorney for Connecticut) to Clark, 6/10/31, CCB.

77. Owen Roberts to Clark, 5/16/31, CCB.

78. Wickersham to Clark, 5/27/31, CCB. On Pound's objection, see Clark to Alfred Bettman (who originated statistical technique for the Cleveland Crime Survey), 2/9/33; Learned Hand to Clark, 2/15/33 ("You know what a curious person Pound is, and how little you can tell what attitude he is going to take"), CCB.

79. Clark to Wickersham, 5/29/31, CCB. The principal material deleted is quoted in the text at n. 75.

80. National Commission, *Progress Report*, p. 18.

81. See Wickersham to Rockefeller Foundation, 4/13/31; Wickersham to Clark, 5/12/31; Clark to Wickersham, 5/13/31; Clark to Rockefeller Foundation, 5/14/31; Wickersham to Rockefeller Foundation, 5/15/31; Wickersham to Clark, 5/26/31, CCB; National Commission, *Progress Report*, p. iv.

82. Clark to Charles Seymour (Provost, Yale), 9/22/31 (very valuable but unfair to encourage about permanent position), JRA; Clark to Wickersham, 10/2/31, CCB. Samenow was described to me as "brilliant, tactless and intolerant of lesser minds." Interview with David Kammerman (friend, assistant on both Connecticut and federal courts studies), 6/20/75.

Samenow may well have sensed the way in which he was an outsider. A 1932 picture of the faculty shows him defiantly seated with his arms crossed and his fashionable white bucks, the only shoes of that kind in the picture, prominently displayed. He was absolutely essential to the functioning of both courts studies. See, for example, Douglas to Clark, 3/21/31, CCB. For an example of his technical expertise, see Samenow, "Judicial Statistics in General."

83. Douglas, *Go East, Young Man*, pp. 163–64. Why Douglas did not go to Chicago is difficult to say. Hutchins claimed not to know. Interview with Robert M. Hutchins, 6/20/75. Douglas formally told Hutchins that he had "a number of things" that he had to spend the next year "tying up and completing." Douglas to Hutchins, 6/10/31, RMH. Clark speculated that Douglas was unhappy that Hutchins seemed to be delegating to his dean of the social sciences everything about the proposed research project "in the field of finance" — the main attraction for Douglas — and that in general Douglas seemed concerned about Hutchins's ability to deliver on his promises. Clark to Angell, 5/23/31, JRA. The visiting professorship was a way for Douglas to finesse the issue of his concern about Hutchins's promises. Local scuttlebutt had it that Douglas was upset that Hutchins could not deliver the $25,000 salary he had promised. Interview with David Kammerman, 6/2/75. While it is clear that Hutchins could not pay that salary (Douglas to Hutchins, 4/15/32, RMH), the $20,000 per year salary he could deliver was substantially above the best Clark could offer (Clark to Angell, 2/18/32, JRA). Thus money cannot have been a great factor. I suspect that although Douglas talked as if things at Yale were not going well (Douglas to Hutchins, 4/15/32, RMH), Yale looked more attractive than Chicago where the Law School would not support his work, especially since by the time Douglas really had to decide, he had made the contacts with the Harvard Business School that were to absorb him for the next few years. Douglas, *Go East, Young Man*, pp. 172–73.

84. Clark to Wickersham, 10/2/31; Wickersham to E. E. Day (Rockefeller Foundation), 10/6/31; Clark to Day, 10/31/31, CCB.

85. Norma S. Thompson (Rockefeller Foundation) to Wickersham, 11/13/31; Clark to William Draper Lewis (Director, American Law Institute), 1/6/33, CCB.

86. Clark to Wickersham, 6/2/32, 9/20/32; Douglas to Clark, 10/20/32; Clark to Douglas, 12/6/32, CCB.

87. See Lewis to Clark, 9/15/32; Clark to Lewis, 9/19/32; Lewis to Clark, 9/23/32; Clark to Lewis, 9/27/32, 10/21/32, CCB. Clark was worried that since he could not get agreement on the Progress Report from the eleven-member Wickersham Commission it would be impossible to get agreement from the larger American Law Institute council, much less the entire membership of that organization. See Clark to Learned Hand, 2/4/33, Hand to Clark, 2/15/33; Lewis to Clark, 3/1/33; Clark to Lewis, 3/2/33, 3/10/33, CCB.

88. Clark to Lewis, 9/21/33, CCB. Samenow went briefly into practice and then did a study for Herman Oliphant, by then General Counsel of the Treasury Department, on the customs court in New York City. Samenow, *Report of Protest Litigation*. The report lists Clark and Fleming James, Jr., as sponsors of the study as well as a committee of the New York Law Society, a survival from Oliphant's work while at the Institute of Law at Johns Hopkins. See Chapter 4. See James and Stockman, "Work of the New York Law Society." After completing the study, Samenow went to Washington, first to the United States Housing Authority and then to the Rural Electrification Administration as a special assistant to the Administrator until his retirement years later in 1968. He died in 1974. Interview with David Kammerman, 6/2/75; interview with Mrs. Charles U. Samenow, 6/2/75.

89. American Law Institute, *Study: Criminal Cases*, p. 22.

90. See Wickersham to Clark, 10/1/34, CCB.

91. Clark, "Diversity of Citizenship Jurisdiction of the Federal Courts," pp. 500, 501–2, 503.

92. Wickersham to Clark, 7/17/33 (responding to Clark's article), CCB.

93. Clark to Wickersham, 10/4/34, CCB. This time Wickersham backed down and deleted the offending comments. Wickersham to Clark, 10/5/34, CCB.

94. See Clark, "Fact Research in Law Administration"; Clark to Frankfurter, 1/13/30; Clark to Wickersham, 2/4/30; Clark to William F. Berry (successor to Lowenthal as Commission secretary), 12/4/30 (use of secondary data); Clark to Grubb, 1/3/31, CCB.

95. See, for example, Clark to Douglas, 10/26/32, CCB.

96. See, for example, Clark to Bates, 10/18/30, CCB.

97. Clark to Filmer S. C. Northrup, 1/10/48, CCL.

98. Clark and Shulman, *Law Administration in Connecticut*, pp. 42–51, 78, 2.

99. Clark, "Fact Research on Law Administration," pp. 230–33, 212.

100. *Report of the School of Law, 1926–27* (Robert M. Hutchins), p. 119.

101. National Commission, *Progress Report*, p. 4.

102. American Law Institute, *Study: Civil Cases*.

103. Clark and Shulman, *Law Administration in Connecticut*, p. 201.

104. Ibid., pp. 200–201 (almost elegiac in tone), is sufficient proof for this assertion if any is needed. Regarding the early enthusiasm for the courts studies, Clark there noted, "There developed an ambition and pretension about the objectives and values of this kind of study" such that "it came to be believed that from the trial court records statistical data could be collected on all phases of judicial administration and all manner of sociological problems in litigation, and that the statistical data would be the open sesame to solutions." He continued, "The authors and workers on this project never regarded the study with such excessive optimism or gave utterance to claims more extensive than shrewd as to results." Exactly twenty pages later in the book (p. 221) comes the following quotation from the first major article on the study, Clark, "Fact Research in Law Administration," p. 233: "It is felt that the limits of possible investigation of this kind are only set by the capacities of the investigators. Thus it may be possible eventually to go behind the court records and to trace somewhat the potential law suits which never come into court." Experience had dimmed memories too.

105. Interview with Fleming James, Jr., 6/11/75. See Gressley, "Introduction"; Arnold to Pound, 1/23/31; Arnold to Wilson Clough, 3/17/31 (recounting offer from Roscoe Pound of a post at Harvard to head another study of trial courts) in Gressley, *Voltaire and the Cowboy*, pp. 27, 176–80. On Arnold, see Arnold, *Fair Fights and Foul* (autobiography); Kearney, *Thurman Arnold, Social Critic*; Ayer, "In Quest of Efficiency."

106. Arnold helped draft the Progress Report and worked on redrafts of both Samenow's criminal report and the civil report. Progress Report on the Study of the Business of the Federal Courts, 4/30/31 (draft); Clark to Lewis, 10/21/32; Edson R. Sunderland (University of Michigan) to Clark, 6/20/33, CCB. Before coming to Yale, while dean at West Virginia, Arnold did some work for the expanded Connecticut courts study and supervised local pretesting of the criminal forms for the federal courts study. See Arnold, "The Collection of Judicial Statistics in West Virginia," pp. 186–87; Arnold, "Review of the Work of the College of Law," pp. 322–23, 324.

107. Most importantly a seminar, begun in fall 1932 — "The Judicial Process from the Point of View of Social Psychology" — that he gave with George Dession, Jerome Frank, and Edward S. Robinson, a professor in the Yale psychology department. The seminar, known locally as "The Cave of the Winds" (interview with Fleming James, Jr., 6/11/75), was unusually successful. Its products included Arnold, *The Symbols of Government*, and Robinson, *Law and the Lawyers*.

108. See Clark to Sam Bass Warner, 1/25/33; Clark to Edmund Morgan, 2/6/33; Clark to Edson R. Sunderland, 2/17/33; Clark to Arnold, 7/14/33 (draft of proposed law review symposium, Arnold to begin with "indictment of mass statistics"), CCB. See Clark and Shulman, *Law Administration in Connecticut*, p. 200 ("Many persons became interested — some genuinely, others momentarily").

Questions about the genuineness of Arnold's commitment to the courts studies have been raised, for example, by Fleming James, Jr. (interview, 6/11/75). Arnold was an incredible opportunist, and there seems to have been some opportunism in his move to Yale. However, an alternative explanation fits the facts of Arnold's participation in the courts studies at least as well as does one that stresses his opportunism. A quick review of his biography suggests that Arnold's main intellectual characteristic was possession of the attention span of a two-year-old. Once he left practice he changed interests every two or three years. Ultimately, however, he returned to practice, for only there did problems change fast enough. Thus, I rather credit Arnold's profession of interest in the courts studies, at least at the outset.

109. See, for example, Grubb to Clark, 2/18/33; Edwin Sutherland (University of Chicago sociologist and author of the study of the federal courts) to Clark, 1/17/33, CCB. From some came backhanded consolation. Edson R. Sunderland to Clark, 2/21/33 ("If it had been known in advance to what extent statistical methods would lead to important affirmative conclusions, a study of that scope would never have been undertaken"), CCB.

110. Hand to Clark, 2/3/33 (I sit "silent before the authority of statisticians, those modern magicians, who would enslave us all, except for their own benign internecine warfare"), CCB.

111. Lewis to Clark, 3/1/33, CCB.

112. Roberts to Clark, 1/20/33; Thomas E. Atkinson to Clark, 1/25/33 ("dry" Kansas had "wet" judges), CCB.

113. Lemann to Clark, 2/13/33 (question whether the report as a whole adds enough to existing information to justify the money and work); 2/16/33, CCB.

114. Warner to Clark, 1/25/33, CCB; see Warner, *Crime and Criminal Statistics in Boston*; Warner, *Survey of Criminal Statistics in the United States*.

115. Morgan to Clark, 1/24/33, CCB.

116. Frankfurter to Clark, 4/3/33, CCB.

117. Clark identifies Hart's authorship in Clark to Max Lowenthal, 9/19/33, CCB. The Hart memo was untitled and undated. It began with the objection that "on almost no point have we" concrete factual, statistical information "in the sense of data establishing beyond peradventure a conclusion," as well as that the number of districts surveyed and the time period covered were limited. Hart objected as well to the failure to disaggregate cases by type when examining time between commencement of prosecution and disposition. These criticisms are well beside the mark. Establishing anything "beyond peradventure" with the kind of data in question is virtually impossible. The defect in sampling is not the number of districts nor the number of years but the weak scientific basis for the sample chosen, and the figures for anything

but the shortest durations are so small that disaggregation would have robbed them of what little significance they had. Perhaps Hart knew no better. If so, then comments like "One wonders why when detailed study was made of so many trivial matters, conclusions as important as this one [duration by type of case] were left to guessing" or "Many times one gains the strong feeling that things have simply been counted indiscriminately . . . as if all facts were free and equal" were simply out of line. Twenty-five years later Clark was still haunted by Hart's last assertion, which a careful reading of the report in the light of the accepted reform proposals of the day would dispel. See Clark to Filmer S. C. Northrup, 1/10/48, CCL.

118. Clark to Warner, 1/25/33, CCB. Challenged, Warner backed down with an admission that it took much time to complete his own study that was almost exclusively of secondary data. Warner to Clark, 2/3/33, CCB.

119. Clark to Monte Lemann, 2/?/33, CCB.

120. Morgan to Clark, 5/1/33, CCB. This is, of course, the modern argument against plea bargaining; it might have been met had anyone thought to interview prosecutors and defense attorneys.

121. Clark to Morgan, 5/2/33, CCB. Why Clark took Morgan seriously after Morgan had admitted that he had "no burning enthusiasm" for the study as he was "not born an artist" and that appointment to Clark's advisory committee "did not light the necessary fire" within him, "perhaps because there was no ignitable material," is not clear. Morgan to Clark, 2/4/33, CCB. Perhaps Clark valued the apparent, if not actual, disinterest.

122. American Law Institute, *Study: Criminal Cases*, pp. 109, 115 (detailed table 7), 59–67, 71, 81–83, 104–5.

123. American Law Institute, *Study: Criminal Cases*, p. 13. This recommendation supported one recently aired: Miller, "Compromise of Criminal Cases." At least one of Clark's readers opposed the idea; see Orrin K. McMurray to Clark, 6/19/33, CCB.

124. See Smith and Ehrmann, "The Criminal Courts." Smith is Reginald Heber Smith who wrote *Justice and the Poor.*

125. Frankfurter, "Preface," p. vi.

126. American Law Institute, *Study: Civil Cases*, p. 115.

127. Compare ibid., pp. 65–69, 86–92, with Clark, "Fact Research in Law Administration," pp. 218–19.

128. American Law Institute, *Study: Civil Cases*, p. 66.

129. See, for example, Lemann to Clark, 12/6/33 (interesting and useful; regrets that time and money limited scope); Hand to Clark, 10/3/33 ("I do not now see what advantage will be got out of this extremely careful and meritorious collection"), CCB. Friendly people said the usual friendly things. See Thomas E. Atkinson to Clark, 9/21/33 (excellent); Grubb to Clark, 9/15/33 ("fine work"); Lowenthal to Clark, 9/9/33 ("thoroughly worthwhile job"; now try an observational study); Edwin H. Sutherland to Clark, 9/25/33, CCB.

130. Frankfurter to Clark, 9/20/33, CCB.

131. Lemann to Clark, 12/6/33; Warner to Clark, 9/9/33, CCB.

132. Clark to Edson R. Sunderland, 9/29/33, CCB. The article is Clark, "Diversity of Citizenship Jurisdiction of the Federal Courts."

133. Thus it is no accident that the initial piece on the Connecticut courts study is entitled "Fact Research in Law Administration."

134. It would be a mistake to see law reform and social science as somehow "competing" for Clark's soul. They were not in any real sense competing at all. First,

they shared the same slightly left-of-center politics and a view of reform related to that politics. Second, the social scientists largely lacked an agreed model of the way the world to be inquired into was structured. What took its place was a rather virulent positivism. If a metaphoric description of their claims on Clark's attention is needed, the best is "divergent."

135. For example, although the federal courts study managed to dispel the myth of the congestion of the criminal courts, when reporting on civil cases in Connecticut the problem of congestion, especially in negligence actions, reappeared, though it was evidenced only by moderate delay in disposition and that delay was greater for contract than for negligence actions. Compare Clark and Shulman, *Law Administration in Connecticut*, pp. 35, 168–70, with ibid., pp. 37, 39 (table XV). Similarly, Clark's evaluation of the jury (ibid., p. 79) went far beyond his data (ibid., pp. 59–78), particularly with respect to the use of Clark's pet procedural device, the summary judgment. Here, as I suspect is often the case, Clark's academic interests and commitments hobbled his understanding in ways that his collection of everyday views of criminal law did not hobble his understanding of criminal proceedings in the federal courts.

It is wonderfully ironic, as Fred Konefsky has pointed out to me, that Clark's search for a better technique of fact finding to support activist reform led him to a tradition that, through its own primary concerns with being scientific, acted as a drag on the very activism that led Clark to seek it out.

136. Further evidence of this proposition, if any be needed, can be found in Edmund Morgan's review of the Connecticut courts study, which began with the observation that the "results can hardly be called startling or even of prime importance" and finished with the assertion that, as there was no "interpretation" of the data, the "chief contribution" of the book was as an "exposition of a method of investigation," which showed its "deficiencies and excellencies." Morgan, "Book Review."

137. See "Yale Experience," pp. 482–88, 545–56. For an interesting portrait of the Dean of Yale's Medical School, Milton C. Winternitz, see Cheever, *Treetops*, pp. 16–61.

138. Formally both would seem to have been more at home intellectually in the Department of Economics, Sociology, and Government. Unfortunately, that department would have no part of the Institute or its personnel, despite the fact that one of the department's members had been put on the Institute's executive committee in order to foster departmental cooperation. So they were assigned to the Law School. Interview with Robert M. Hutchins, 6/20/75; Charles Seymour (Provost) to Angell, 3/15/28, JRA. The department was the private preserve of the shade of William Graham Sumner and run by his protégé A. G. Keller, both of whom thought empirical social research of a quantifiable nature was somehow anathema. See Oberschall, "The Institutionalization of American Sociology." Compare the interview with Mark May (Director of the Institute), 6/9/75 ("Hutchins would have taken a two bit whore").

139. Interview with Dorothy Swaine Thomas, 6/3/75; interview with Emma Corstvet Llewellyn, 8/19/75.

140. Emma Corstvet remembers keeping statistics about the effect of weather on telephone calls and the effect of colors on male callers. Emma Corstvet Llewellyn to Schlegel, 10/20/75.

141. On the use of statistics in social science, see Bannister, *Sociology and Scientism*; Hinkle and Hinkle, *The Development of Modern Sociology*, pp. 22–28; Ober-

schall, "The Institutionalization of American Sociology," p. 187 (seemingly over-drawn); Lazarsfeld, "An Episode in the History of Social Research," pp. 251–52 (recounting his introduction in America of the notion of spurious correlation in 1933); Stepan, "History of the Uses of Modern Sampling Procedures." See also Ober-schall, *Empirical Social Research in Germany* (no tradition of such research before World War I).

142. Thomas's reputation was based largely on her Ph.D. dissertation, a statistical inquiry into the social consequences of business cycles, "Social Aspects of the Business Cycle," that was done under Arthur L. Bowley, a pioneer English statistician, but also based on her subsequent attempt to establish techniques for increasing the reliability of observations of human behavior. Interview with Donald Slesinger, 8/8/75; inter-view with Dorothy Swaine Thomas, 6/3/75; Thomas, "Contribution to the Herman Wold Festschrift"; *Washington Post*, 5/5/77, sec. C, at 6, col. 1 (obituary). In 1927, after taking short appointments with the New York Federal Reserve Bank as a statisti-cian, the Social Science Research Council as a postdoctoral fellow, and the Laura Spellman Rockefeller Memorial working for W. I. Thomas, she went to Columbia Teachers College. Her work there resulted in publication of Swaine [Thomas], *Some New Techniques for Studying Social Behavior*.

143. Interview with Emma Corstvet Llewellyn, 8/19/75. While an undergraduate, Corstvet took courses from Commons and Tawney and worked for the Wisconsin Industrial Commission. As a result of both experiences she became interested in the causes of poverty, a subject she pursued in graduate school. In between her two stints of what she termed "desultory" graduate study, she worked in Wisconsin and then tried Paris for a while. After returning from London, she worked for the Laura Spellman Rockefeller Memorial, first as a translator and later in criminological stud-ies. From there, in late 1927, she went to Peking with a job as a teacher in a school that had closed by the time she arrived. In order to remain in China she worked on a newspaper until 1929, when, after another stay in Paris, she returned to the United States.

144. Institute of Human Relations, Executive Committee, Minutes, 6/11/29 (she will map out "existing statistical data" and preview "methodological difficulties" in studies), JRA. Her report, Thomas, A Survey of Some Materials Relevant to the Development of a Social Science Program, 9/15/29, JRA, acknowledged the "tremen-dous value" of "path-finding studies, depending on the analysis of behavior records, life histories, etc.," but strongly pushed the use of statistical methods, especially new ones designed to get "fundamental quantitative data on behavior and social milieu."

145. Clark had a bit of trouble securing faculty approval for the appointment because Thomas was female. See Clark to Hutchins, 10/4/29, RMH.

146. Douglas's investigations have been briefly chronicled once before. Hopkirk, "The Influence of Legal Realism on William O. Douglas."

147. On Douglas's move from Columbia to Yale, see Douglas, *Go East, Young Man*, pp. 161–63, an account that reflects a certain amount of license in its composi-tion while it quite accurately captures the flavor of events. For example, Douglas suggests that he was offered a job at Yale the morning after he first met Hutchins, that his proposed salary at Chicago was to be $25,000, and that he was offered the deanship of the Yale Law School in 1937. Ibid., pp. 163, 164, 281. All are possible but none are likely. The first is doubtful; see Yale Minutes, 5/10/28, 5/18/28, 5/31/28; Hutchins to Angell, 5/24/28, JRA. The second is equally so; see my comments in n. 83. The third is even more doubtful since the deanship wasn't open at the time, as

Clark was reappointed to a second five-year term in spring 1934, and the faculty minutes contain no evidence of any such offers having been made. On the other hand, Douglas's stories about the intoxicated Thurman Arnold or a rather stuffy Charles Clark dealing with a student caught with a girl in his room, whether accurate or not, capture their subjects beautifully. Douglas, *Go East, Young Man*, pp. 167, 171.

148. Douglas, "Professor Douglas' Address," pp. 48, 49.

149. Ibid., p. 50. Douglas gave no more evidence for the assertion that "the whole system" had at times been "under suspicion and disrespect" than Hutchins and Clark had given two years before, or the auto accident investigators would give three years later.

150. Ibid., p. 50.

151. Underhill Moore, Douglas, and Douglas's friend Carrol Shanks, acting as the Committee on the Business Unit, had suggested that a group consisting of "a statistician, an accountant, several specialists in business, and a number in law" do general research on the subject of business associations, a course that was apparently to include bankruptcy. Currie, "The Materials of Law Study," p. 23.

152. Memo from Clark to Executive Committee of Institute of Human Relations, 10/?/29, attached as appendix 3 to Minutes of Executive Committee, Institute of Human Relations, 10/7/29, IHR.

153. Plummer and Ritter, *Credit Extension and Causes of Failure among Philadelphia Grocers*, p. ii. Earlier a study had been begun in Louisville. See U.S. Department of Commerce, *Credit Extensions and Business Failures*. Paul O. Ritter, one of the joint authors of this study, had worked on the study for credit as one of Douglas's research assistants during spring 1929, the last semester of his third year of law school. Ritter to Schlegel, 6/5/77.

154. Plummer and Ritter, *Credit Extension and Causes of Failure among Philadelphia Grocers*, p. 1.

155. Ritter to Schlegel, 6/5/77.

156. Plummer and Ritter, *Credit Extension and Causes of Failure among Philadelphia Grocers*, pp. 1, 10.

157. Donovan, "Report of Counsel to Petitioners." The investigation is briefly recounted in Martin, *Causes and Conflicts*, pp. 226–27.

158. Donovan, "Report of Counsel to Petitioners," pp. 79–81.

159. Ibid., pp. 64–65 (order of Judge Thatcher, 3/23/29).

160. Ibid., pp. 180, 64–65, 79–81.

161. "Testimony of William O. Douglas." I am indebted to Mr. Al Borner, librarian at Donovan, Leisure, Newton, and Irvine, New York, New York, for supplying me with a copy of this testimony.

Paul O. Ritter, Douglas's assistant, did a field study of banks and trust companies acting as receivers in bankruptcy proceedings for the investigation. Ritter to Schlegel, 6/5/77.

162. "Testimony of William O. Douglas," pp. 28, 33–36, 38–39, 48–49, 52–54, 59–63.

163. Clark, Douglas, and Thomas, "The Business Failures Project," p. 1014.

164. Douglas and Weir, "Equity Receiverships."

165. Minutes of the Executive Committee, Institute of Human Relations, 10/7/29, IHR. How early the contemporary world of university research funding does appear!

166. Douglas and Weir, "Equity Receiverships," p. 1.

167. Ibid., p. 2.

168. Ibid., p. 3.

169. I detect here the influence of Dorothy Thomas. The tone of the entire report is the same as that of the earlier Philadelphia study, but no conclusions are drawn. Douglas had met Thomas in early summer 1929 (Donald Slesinger to Angell, 6/?/29, IHR); she worked part-time at Yale during fall 1929.

170. Douglas and Weir, "Equity Receiverships," pp. 12–25.

171. Provisions allowing the reorganization of a corporation in bankruptcy were not added to the Bankruptcy Act until 1934. Act of June 7, 1934, Pub. L. No. 296, 48 Stat. 911.

172. Douglas and Weir, "Equity Receiverships," pp. 4–8. Douglas did hazard one observation that went beyond the suggestions based on his data. Speaking of the decision to reorganize or to liquidate, he stated:

> Another factor would be the effect of immediate liquidation on employees as well as on creditors and stockholders. To be sure the employees do not have an investment in the business in the legal or popular sense. Yet their association with the business has given them a prospective income from the business as measured by the labor turnover which is as certain as the bondholders' prospective interest or the stockholders' prospect of dividends.

Ibid., pp. 8–9. That idea has yet to find explicit recognition in the bankruptcy law.

173. Clark, Douglas, and Thomas, "The Business Failures Project," pp. 1015, 1016.

174. Interview with Dorothy Swaine Thomas, 6/3/75.

175. Clark, Douglas, and Thomas, "The Business Failures Project," pp. 1019, 1019–20, 1021–24. The article reads as if she were the major author.

176. Thomas, "Some Aspects of Socio-Legal Research at Yale," p. 217. Dorothy Thomas did not remember what those problems had been (interview with Dorothy Swaine Thomas, 6/3/75); nor did Paul O. Ritter or Saul Richard Gamer, two of Douglas's assistants. Persistent rumors suggesting that the questionnaire was outrageous, for example, that it included questions on the toilet training of bankrupts, are false, as an examination of copies of the questionnaire in JRA shows. I suspect that efforts to begin to develop physical and psychiatric examinations of bankrupts and to measure their intelligence (see Douglas and Thomas, "The Business Failures Project II," p. 1036) made the two investigators too "hot" for Judge Clark to handle.

177. Douglas and Thomas, "The Business Failures Project II," p. 1035. When the study was completed Douglas had collected 91 personal interviews, 359 responses to the court's letter, and 90 to the investigator's letter.

178. Ibid., pp. 1035, 1053, 1037–42, 1042.

179. Ultimately the Department of Commerce published the substantive results of the Newark study and gave Douglas due credit. U.S. Department of Commerce, *Causes of Business Failures and Bankruptcies of Individuals in New Jersey in 1929–30*, p. iv. This study of nearly 500 cases concluded that businesses generally failed because of poor business practices, although bankrupt dishonesty and outside speculation were again prominently featured. Ibid., pp. 1–2. The study of 125 individual bankruptcies disclosed that one-fourth of the petitions were filed to discharge large judgments, particularly in auto accident cases. Ibid., p. 2. Although more complete than the Philadelphia study, the report shows that Dorothy Thomas made no impact on the Department of Commerce.

180. Douglas and Thomas, "The Business Failures Project II," p. 1050 n. 3.

181. Douglas, "Some Functional Aspects of Bankruptcy," p. 329 n. 1.

182. Douglas and Thomas, "The Business Failures Project II," p. 1054.

183. Ibid., p. 1035.

184. Douglas, "Some Functional Aspects of Bankruptcy"; Douglas and Marshall, "A Factual Study of Bankruptcy Administration."

185. Hoover's message is excerpted in *Strengthening of Procedure in the Judicial System*, which is largely a reprint of the report of Thatcher's investigation.

186. Douglas, "Some Functional Aspects of Bankruptcy," pp. 335, 336–60 (examples).

187. Douglas and Marshall, "A Factual Study of Bankruptcy Administration," pp. 25–26, 36–37 (examples).

188. Douglas, "Some Functional Aspects of Bankruptcy," pp. 332–34, 360–64; Douglas and Marshall, "A Factual Study of Bankruptcy Administration," pp. 30–31, 35–37.

189. Douglas, "Some Functional Aspects of Bankruptcy," pp. 363–64; Douglas and Marshall, "A Factual Study of Bankruptcy," pp. 58–59.

190. See Douglas, "Some Functional Aspects of Bankruptcy," pp. 343–52; Douglas and Marshall, "A Factual Study of Bankruptcy Administration," p. 37. The articles together suggest that the ability to condition discharge in cases of speculation and gambling does not lead to a decline in those kinds of behavior, for Douglas's American bankrupts seemed to engage in less objectionable behavior than the more carefully regulated English bankrupts.

191. See *Strengthening of Procedure in the Judicial System*, pp. 4, 45 (thanking Yale Law School and William O. Douglas). Thatcher advocated conditional and suspended discharges in a provision tied directly to the objectionable actions by bankrupts that Douglas had isolated, compulsory examination of bankrupts, and compulsory hearings on discharge applications. Less related to the Newark and Boston studies were proposals to limit creditors' control in the selection of the trustee, to validate and facilitate certain kinds of assignments for the benefit of creditors, and to provide for amortization of the debts of wage earners.

A proposal to establish a mechanism for corporate reorganizations outside the traditional equity receivership was obviously related to the study of equity receiverships in Connecticut. Throughout the report there were references to the data gathered by Douglas in Newark and Boston. See, for example, ibid., pp. 101, 157. In one sense Douglas's articles on the Boston study were presented in support of Thatcher's proposed reforms since they were published after Thatcher's report was issued, though they do not mention that report.

192. Douglas and Thomas, "The Business Failures Project II," p. 1035.

193. Douglas to Hutchins, 4/15/32, 2/2/33, RMH.

194. One related study was made at a later date, though not by Douglas. See Corstvet, "Inadequate Bookkeeping As a Factor in Business Failure."

195. The Department of Commerce ultimately published results of the Boston Study. Sadd and Williams, *Causes of Commercial Bankruptcies*; Sadd and Williams, *Causes of Bankruptcies among Consumers* (most frequent causes of bankruptcies are "extravagance" and "evasion" of judgment debts, including those on foreclosed real estate). Douglas used some of the Newark and Boston results in "Wage Earner Bankruptcies," an article parallel in its use of the data to Douglas, "Some Functional Aspects of Bankruptcy," and Douglas and Marshall, "A Factual Study of Bankruptcy Administration."

196. The following articles, related to the business failures project, were done by students of Douglas at Yale. Gamer, "On Comparing 'Friendly Adjustment' and Bankruptcy" (using New Jersey data); Furth, "The Critical Period before Bankruptcy" (using New Jersey and Boston data to suggest that most bankrupts delay filing until well past the time of bankruptcy and in the interim dissipate their assets; includes interesting speculations on the reasons for variations in data). Douglas was the only one at Yale who managed to generate such student participation in the research enterprise as is so common in contemporary social science, although Clark did something similar when publishing the early data from the Connecticut courts study.

197. Yale Minutes, 2/21/29. Douglas and Leon Green had suggested the desirability of such a study the previous fall.

198. Ballantine was a name partner in with Root, Clark, Buckner & Ballantine, later Dewey, Ballantine, Palmer, Bushby & Wood, now Dewey Ballantine.

199. Committee to Study Compensation, *Report*, p. 2. In addition to Ballantine the New York bar was represented by Henry W. Taft; Philadelphia, by Henry S. Drinker, Jr., and William A. Schnader.

200. Yale Minutes, 2/21/29.

201. Walter F. Dodd (a member of the Committee) to Barry C. Smith (Commonwealth Foundation), 6/1/29, CCB. Dodd was studying workmen's compensation for the Commonwealth Foundation; see "Yale Experience," p. 491.

202. The balance of the executive committee was Ballantine, Joseph P. Chamberlain and Noel T. Dowling, both of the Columbia Law School's faculty, and William Draper Lewis, Executive Director of the American Law Institute. During the progress of the study Dowling resigned, apparently concerned with the potential for conflict of interest since he was doing a study of the constitutionality of the legislation proposed by the Committee.

203. The committee began its study in June 1929. Committee to Study Compensation, *Report*, p. 2. At that time its objective was to suggest the desirability of adopting a compensation system. Dodd to Smith, 6/1/29, CCB. By December the Committee was already beginning to make decisions about the scope of compensation plan. Committee to Study Compensation for Automobile Accidents, Minutes of Executive Committee, 12/13/29, CCB.

204. Committee to Study Compensation, *Report*, pp. 3–5.

205. Ibid., p. 282.

206. Ibid., pp. 8–9. Studies were also made in New York City, Muncie and Terre Haute, Indiana, and San Francisco and San Mateo County, California.

207. Interview with Emma Corstvet Llewellyn, 8/19/75.

208. Ibid.; Corstvet to Clark, 6/23/30, CCB.

209. Committee to Study Compensation, *Report*, p. 256.

210. Corstvet to Clark, 5/19/30, CCB.

211. Committee to Study Compensation, *Report*, p. 257.

212. Ibid., pp. 76–90.

213. Compare ibid., p. 80, with ibid., p. 85. The results are more clearly set out in Corstvet, "The Uncompensated Accident and Its Consequences," p. 470.

214. Committee to Study Compensation, *Report*, pp. 55–62.

215. Clark to Shippen Lewis, 10/17/30, CCB.

216. Corstvet to Clark, 10/28/30; Thomas to Shippen Lewis, 10/28/30, CCB. Dorothy Thomas acted as a statistical advisor for the Committee. Committee to Study Compensation, *Report*, p. 3.

217. Shippen Lewis to Clark, 11/6/30, CCB.

218. Committee to Study Compensation, *Report*, pp. 261, 273–75.

219. Clark to Shippen Lewis, 3/8/30, CCB. (Three-quarters of the entire bulk of the book would be devoted to presenting facts without much in the way of interpretation.)

220. Shippen Lewis to the Executive Committee, 2/28/30; Shippen Lewis to Clark, 3/10/30, CCB.

221. Committee to Study Compensation for Automobile Accidents, Minutes of the Executive Committee, 3/6/31, CCB.

222. Shippen Lewis to the Executive Committee, 4/13/30, 10/14/30, CCB. The rather quick decline in the Committee's financial fortunes and the tone of the entire enterprise are shown by the nature of and change in the physical format of the official record of its operations. In December 1929, its meetings were run from a printed agenda, complete with draft resolutions; its minutes were also printed. While the nature of the agenda and minutes remained the same, by May 1930 both were being typed.

223. Curiously, Clark had indirectly warned Lewis about the problem that actually arose. Shippen Lewis to Clark, 1/17/30 (we want to study "hardship cases"); Clark to Shippen Lewis, 1/18/30 (going to be hard to decide what those are), CCB. Lewis nonetheless went ahead and used the term without further defining it.

224. Committee to Study Compensation for Automobile Accidents, Agenda, 2/18/31, CCB. Costs ranged from $.85 per reported case in Indiana to $2.50 in Philadelphia, $4.00 in New York, and $5.50 in Connecticut.

225. Ibid.

226. Clark to Shippen Lewis, 10/15/31, CCB.

227. Shippen Lewis to Clark, 10/16/31, CCB.

228. Committee to Study Compensation for Automobile Accidents, Minutes, 12/21/31, CCB. Clark did not bother to attend, although up until this time he had attended regularly.

229. Clark to Filmer S. C. Northrup, 1/10/48 ("even up to the House of Lords"), CCL.

230. Clark to Fleming James, Jr., 8/28/59, CCL.

231. Clark to Corstvet, 10/15/31 (quoting Dorothy Thomas); Clark to Corstvet, 3/3/31 (start of IHR study), CCB. For details about this study, see Neely, "A Study of Error in the Interview," pp. 119–40.

232. One of the fieldworkers on the initial study did manage to use the data from both to enrich a Ph.D. thesis that was otherwise drawn from secondary sources. See Neely, "A Study of Error in the Interview." Several years later Emma Corstvet took the Committee's results and turned them into a more poignant and effective plea for a compensation scheme than the Committee had ever managed to make. See Corstvet, "The Uncompensated Accident and Its Consequences."

233. Thomas to Angell, 11/25/30, JRA.

234. Interview with Dorothy Swaine Thomas, 6/3/75.

235. About the time Dorothy Thomas came to Yale she met the Gunnar Myrdals and began a long term study of population migration and business cycles in Sweden. Interview with Dorothy Swaine Thomas, 6/3/75. This work was a continuation of her Ph.D. thesis work on the same subject done with data on Britain, and the beginning of the major work of a career largely devoted to population studies. Thus, in retrospect, her work at Yale and at Columbia before that was really a detour from

what proved to be her major interest. Indeed, in an autobiographical essay, Thomas, "Contribution to the Herman Wold Festschrift," she does not even mention her connection with the Law School.

236. Thomas to Clark, 3/9/33 ("I'll be glad to participate in other seminars, particularly those of Underhill Moore"), UMY.

237. Interview with Emma Corstvet Llewellyn, 8/19/75. The study was first published as Corstvet, "Adequacy of Accounting Records in a Money Economy," p. 273. ("The author owes much to Prof. W. O. Douglas . . . for his direction of this study." But as she remembers it, Douglas left everything to her that was "in the least bit technical." Interview with Emma Corstvet Llewellyn, 8/19/75.) This study only looked at going concerns. The data examined in the first article were then compared with data from the Boston bankrupts in Corstvet, "Inadequate Bookkeeping as a Factor in Business Failure." This article earned her the right to attend the annual banquet of the Yale Law Journal, apparently the first female not a faculty member ever to come other than as a guest. Interview with Emma Corstvet Llewellyn, 8/19/75.

238. Douglas and Thomas, "The Business Failures Project II," p. 1035.

239. Corstvet, "Inadequate Bookkeeping As a Factor in Business Failure," pp. 1207–8.

240. Interview with Emma Corstvet Llewellyn, 8/19/75. One interlude was her work for Clark on a study of lawyer's practices and the legal needs of lower-middle-income clients. See "Yale Experience," pp. 522–81.

241. Interview with Emma Corstvet Llewellyn, 8/19/75.

242. See Bannister, Sociology and Scientism.

243. Interview with Emma Corstvet Llewellyn, 8/19/75.

244. See generally Haskell, The Emergence of Professional Social Science.

245. Emma Corstvet Llewellyn to Schlegel, 10/20/75.

246. This was exactly the same attitude Clark faced in dealing with his Harvard critics who participated in progressive law reform.

247. Two of the most enchanting days I have ever spent were spent interviewing Dorothy Swaine Thomas and Emma Corstvet Llewellyn. The grace, charm, and wit of each plainly captivated me and have surely influenced my view of events at Yale in a way that the generally, though by no means universally, less interesting lawyer interviewees were simply unable to do. Robert Gordon has suggested, quite accurately, I think, that one of these influences is an observable preference in this section for the rather "hard-edged" method that both women were working with in the 1920s and 1930s. But whatever the source, the preference is defensible. Lawyers are quite used to, and comfortable with, "soft" methods; it is very easy to drift from soft methods into the kind of armchair theorizing, really the reifying of one's biases, that is much of legal policy analysis today. Although hard methods have their own problems, most notably the rigid constriction of the sphere of the knowable to that of the countable, given the acknowledged methodological biases of lawyers these problems are preferable to the risk that soft science will turn into no science at all.

248. Act of Mar. 3, 1933, Pub. L. No. 72-420, 47 Stat. 1467.

249. See Douglas, "Wage Earner Bankruptcies."

250. Douglas to Hutchins, 3/1/32 (change of mind; Sturges is "a hot shot in every way" interested in something more than "professional education"), RMH.

251. See Gilmore, "The Storrs Lectures: The Age of Anxiety," pp. 1035–36.

252. See Sturges and Cooper, "Credit Administration and Wage Earner Bank-

ruptcies" (review of secondary literature). This article and the one by Douglas are part of a symposium on the subject that includes two superb pieces of empirical research: Fortas, "Wage Assignments in Chicago"; Nehemkis, "The Boston Poor Debtor Court." Each piece credits Douglas as its inspiration. Whatever one may say about Douglas's own empirical work, he inspired a great amount of very good work by others. That is a significant achievement all by itself. Tangentially related to all of this is Douglas and Frank, "Landlord's Claims in Reorganizations."

253. Douglas, "Wage Earner Bankruptcies," pp. 595, 626–42. This time Douglas did a much better job of presenting the results of the Boston and Newark studies of wage earner bankruptcies than in either of his previous two articles. Nevertheless, the article is still not about the studies; it is an argument using materials from the studies to "prove" that wage earner bankruptcies should be left to state control since the incidence of various kinds of credit problems varied from state to state.

One can exaggerate the effect of the exigencies of the campaign for bankruptcy reform on Douglas's "withdrawal" from empirical legal research. Douglas stopped doing empirical research not simply because the social scientists' concerns over the quality of their product were irrelevant to his need for facts to fuel reform. Just as was the case with Dorothy Thomas, he changed activities in part because ones other than those he was then engaged in seemed more interesting at the time. For Douglas at this time the major other activity was a growing association with several faculty members at the Harvard Business School, an association that eventually resulted in creating the short-lived Yale-Harvard/law-business four-year joint degree. See Douglas, *Go East, Young Man* pp. 172–73. The association with Harvard dated back to 1930. Yale Minutes, 3/27/30 (Moore trip), 5/29/30 (attempt to bring visitor). The first Harvard visitor came in spring 1932 to help in one of Douglas's courses. Yale Minutes, 5/21/31. The law-business program was begun in the fall of 1933. *Report of the School of Law, 1933–34* (Charles E. Clark), pp. 17–18.

254. Interview with Dorothy Swaine Thomas, 6/3/75.

255. Thus, three years later Corstvet tried to do research with Clark (see "Yale Experience," pp. 558–67), who had so fervently defended the "value" of the "detailed work" she had done for the auto compensation study (Clark to Shippen Lewis, 10/15/31, CCB). This collaboration produced a wonderful little article, Clark and Corstvet, "The Lawyer and the Public." Both she and Thomas tried to work with Underhill Moore who was more single-mindedly devoted to scientific method and who more fully accepted the lengthened reform horizon of academic social science than any of his colleagues. See Chapter 3.

256. See "Yale Experience," pp. 558–69.

257. See Douglas, *Go East, Young Man*, pp. 172–73; Kalman, *Legal Realism at Yale*, pp. 136, 273 n. 164; Stevens, *Law School*, pp. 485–86; "Yale Experience," p. 307 nn. 679–80.

258. See U.S. Securities and Exchange Commission, *Report on the Study . . . of Protective and Reorganization Committees*.

259. And surely the fact that Walton H. Hamilton, the one regular full-time faculty member whom everyone at Yale identified as a social scientist, was actively opposed to empirical legal research (interview with Dorothy Swaine Thomas, 6/3/75) meant that such weight as the views of Thomas and Corstvet would otherwise have been given was seriously diminished.

260. Robert Gordon has supplied the unusually apt adjective.

261. Interview with Dorothy Swaine Thomas, 6/3/75.

262. Clark's interest brought forth a study of lawyer's practices and the legal needs of lower-middle-income clients. See "Yale Experience," pp. 558–67. Douglas too would lead one more "empirical" research project before moving to the Securities and Exchange Commission — the mammoth study of the activities of investors' protective committees in corporate reorganizations — a study more in tune with his rough notion of causation. See U.S. Securities and Exchange Commission, *Report on the Study . . . of Protective and Reorganization Committees.* This study was under way by spring 1933. See Douglas to Hutchins, 3/27/33, RMH; *Report of the School of Law, 1933–34* (Charles E. Clark), p. 28.

263. Dorothy Thomas said that foundation funds were not particularly difficult to obtain during the Great Depression. Interview with Dorothy Swaine Thomas, 6/3/75. Although she ought to have known, I can find no one who agrees with her. And even if she were correct, the Law School thought funds were hard to obtain. See *Report of the School of Law, 1931–32* (Charles E. Clark), p. 20.

264. Yale was very badly hit by the Depression. Clark to Hutchins, 3/15/33 ("rumor" that Yale is in worse shape than elsewhere in country), RMH.

265. See "Yale Experience," pp. 545–56.

266. Ibid., pp. 558–67.

Chapter 3

1. Moore to Alexander M. Kidd (University of California, Berkeley, visitor at Columbia 1926–28), 5/15/29, UMY.

2. Moore to Eugene V. Rostow, 3/19/41, UMY.

3. Curiously Hope seems to have done very limited work at Hopkins. See Chapter 4.

4. See Moore and Sussman, "The Connecticut Studies."

5. See Moore, Diary Written during the Cruise from New York to Gibralter on the Schooner Yacht Black Eagle, Aug. 7–Sept. 4, 1929, UMY.

6. Moore's first faculty meeting was November 4, 1929.

7. Moore and Sussman, "Debiting of Direct Discounts: II. The Institutional Method," pp. 564–65.

8. The uninitiated may find the following helpful in unraveling this truly obscure bit of late nineteenth-century and early twentieth-century banking practice.

A customer — individual, partnership, or corporation — with a regular commercial relationship with a bank might try to borrow money from that bank by presenting the bank with the customer's own note, payable to the bank at some future time. If the bank was willing to make the loan, it would accept the note and deposit or "credit" the face value of the note less the interest due under its terms to the customer's account. This process was called discounting, paying the discounted present value of the note. When the note by its terms came due for payment, the bank might seek payment of the face value of the note, thus recouping the interest on the actual amount of funds lent, by withdrawing funds from or "debiting" the customer's account and so (involuntarily) paying the note. If the customer had sufficient funds in the account to pay both the note and all checks outstanding at the time, usually several days later, that the customer received notice of the debit, no harm would be done through this high-handed practice. If the customer did not have sufficient funds to cover all of these obligations, then one or more of the customer's checks would be dishonored by the bank or "bounce," in the modern slang. By suing the bank for wrongful dishonor, the customer possibly was attempting to assert its right to determine the order in which it would pay its debts; in defending, the bank was asserting its right to be paid first. The question is thus ultimately one of the legion of squabbles between creditors, each trying to avoid getting caught in a bankruptcy.

9. Moore and Sussman, "Debiting of Direct Discounts: I. Legal Method," pp. 381–85.

10. Moore and Sussman, "The Connecticut Studies," pp. 752–53.

11. See Moore and Sussman, "Debiting Direct Discounts: II. The Institutional Method," p. 571; Moore and Sussman, "The Connecticut Studies," pp. 754–55.

12. Compare Moore and Sussman, "The Connecticut Studies," pp. 753–54, with ibid., p. 755 (especially questions 22 and 26).

13. Ibid., p. 755 (e.g., the practice of paying interest on the balance in checking accounts).

14. Ibid., pp. 766–67.

15. Sussman visited nineteen (12 percent) of the commercial banks in the state, "each chosen because of its proximity to New Haven and because of the likelihood that it would allow the study to be made." Ibid., p. 766.

16. See ibid., pp. 773–74.

17. See Clark to Moore, 5/17/29 (recounting conversation with Hutchins), UMY. See "Underhill Moore," p. 221 n. 81.

18. Clark to Moore, 3/13/30 (expense money); Moore to Clark, 11/5/31 (Moore's understanding), UMY.

19. Moore and Sussman, "The South Carolina and Pennsylvania Studies," p. 942.

20. Moore to Clark, 3/12/30, UMY. The Connecticut study was finished in March 1930 when the Pennsylvania study was begun.

21. Clark to Moore, 3/13/30, UMY.

22. Moore to Angell, 5/19/30, JRA.

23. Angell to Moore, 5/20/30, JRA.

24. Moore and Sussman, "The South Carolina and Pennsylvania Studies," pp. 942–43.

25. Compare Moore and Sussman, "The Connecticut Studies," pp. 753–55, with Moore and Sussman, "The South Carolina and Pennsylvania Studies," p. 943.

26. Moore and Sussman, "The South Carolina and Pennsylvania Studies," p. 947, report the results in tabular form.

27. Compare Moore and Sussman, "The South Carolina and Pennsylvania Studies," p. 947, with Moore and Sussman, "The Connecticut Studies," pp. 773–74.

28. Moore and Sussman, "The South Carolina and Pennsylvania Studies," pp. 947, 952–53.

29. Ibid., pp. 928–29.

30. More importantly from Professor E. C. Coker of Yale whose brother taught in South Carolina. Gilbert Sussman to Schlegel, 10/1/76 (taped interview).

31. Sussman to Moore, 8/12/30, UMY.

32. Moore and Sussman, "The South Carolina and Pennsylvania Studies," pp. 929, 930–31, 937, 941.

33. Moore and Sussman, "Debiting of Direct Discounts: VI. Decisions," p. 1219 n. 1, directly acknowledges "her skeptical, pointed and invaluable criticism."

34. Interview with Thomas, 6/3/75. Compare Sussman to Schlegel, 10/1/76 (taped interview).

35. Interview with Dorothy Swaine Thomas, 6/3/75.

36. See Clark to Moore, 11/18/30, UMY.

37. Moore and Sussman, "The New York Study," pp. 1055–56, 1055, 1063, 1063–64. See ibid., pp. 1057–63, where the questionnaire is reproduced in detail. Of course, such a change came at some cost—the loss of the sense that behavior is a matter of more or less.

38. Ibid. Table III following p. 1068 reports the results.

39. See Moore to Llewellyn, 4/4/31, 4/11/31, UMY. The relevant articles are Llewellyn, "A Realistic Jurisprudence: The Next Step"; Pound, "The Call for a Realist Jurisprudence"; Llewellyn, "Some Realism about Realism." This part of the controversy is thoroughly summarized in Twining, *Karl Llewellyn and the Realist Movement*, pp. 70–83. Moore thought Llewellyn had blown the matter entirely out of perspective. "I don't see why you are so excited. Personally I am not interested in whether or not there be a school of realists and if there be what Pound's views about the school are." Moore to Llewellyn, 4/4/31, UMY. An earlier part of the controversy is chronicled in Chapter 4.

40. Moore and Sussman, "Debiting of Direct Discounts: VI. Decisions," pp. 1249, 1249–50.

41. A list of the recipients entitled "Debiting Direct Discounts" is in UMY.

42. As an example of Moore's rapidly growing statistical sophistication, he had acquired a decent layman's understanding of the concept of spurious correlation (see Moore and Sussman, "Debiting of Direct Discounts: VI. Decisions," p. 1219)—this at the time when the concept was only first being introduced in the United States. See Lazarsfeld, "An Episode in the History of Social Research," pp. 293–94 (recounting his introduction of the notion of spurious correlation in 1933).

43. Llewellyn to Moore, 7/27/31, UMY. See also Moore to Llewellyn, 7/28/31 (earlier article was "perfectly clear"); Llewellyn to Moore, 7/31/31 ("Perfectly clear to whom?"), UMY.

44. Moore, Memorandum In Re Continuation and More Extensive Prosecution of Work in "Commercial Bank Credit," n.d. [4/31?], UMY.

45. It should be noted that the proposal was based on a different theory of validation than that underlying the debiting study. It is impossible to determine whether Moore understood the significance of this shift from the natural experiment to the cumulation of individual instances, especially since his later banking research shows a shift first to the new theory and then back to the old, for Moore nowhere even notes the fact of these shifts, much less discusses them.

46. Interview with Dorothy Swaine Thomas, 6/3/75.

47. Moore to Llewellyn, 7/28/31, UMY.

48. See Moore to Angell, 4/1/31; Angell to Moore, 4/13/31, UMY. See also Angell to Moore, 4/8/31, JRA.

49. See Moore to Mark A. May (Executive Secretary of the Institute), 5/31/31, UMY.

50. Contract between West Publishing Co. and Underhill Moore, 7/13/31, UMY. Sussman did most of the work on this project. Sussman to Schlegel, 10/1/76 (taped interview).

51. See Moore to Edgar Furniss (Director of the Institute), 2/19/32 (recounting research and enclosing copy of resulting report), UMY.

52. See Clark to Moore, 11/6/31 (reporting decision), UMY.

53. Moore and Sussman, "The Current Account and Set-Offs between an Insolvent Bank and Its Customer."

54. Moore and Sussman, "The Lawyer's Law." The occasion for writing this piece

is unclear. Even Moore's coauthor cannot remember it. Sussman to Schlegel, 7/28/77. Despite the total absence of helpful footnotes to the ideas Moore expressed, one can see in the piece at least three possible occasions. First, the emphasis on prediction is reminiscent of the Realist Controversy. Second, the long central section on the logic of proof in multicausal analysis suggests things Moore might have learned at the methodology seminar that Dorothy Thomas gave at the Law School. Third, the final section on interdisciplinary research seems a logical part of discussions at the time of the Institute's first reorganization; see "Yale Experience," pp. 553–57, 558–60.

55. Moore and Sussman, "The Lawyer's Law," pp. 566, 570–71, 569.

56. See Ray Westerfield (Yale, Department of Political Economy) to Moore, 3/8/32 (pointing out error), UMY.

57. Moore and Sussman, "The Lawyer's Law," pp. 571, 575.

58. Oliphant to Moore, 3/2/32, UMY. Jerome Frank had taken a position on the almost total unpredictability of judicial decisions in *Law and the Modern Mind* such as to preclude effectively the possibility of serious empirical work; Jerome Michael and Mortimer Adler had concluded that there was no scientific knowledge in criminology despite the mountain of research, in their book, *Crime, Law and Social Science*. For some reason Michael and Adler were very interested in Moore's reaction to their book. See Corstvet to Moore, 7/17/33, UMY.

59. Angell to Moore, 3/15/33, UMY. Angell had published *A Research in Family Law* with Columbia Law School Professor Albert C. Jacobs, the pioneer attempt to merge social science data and family law. His piece, "The Value of Sociology to Law," is a good statement of his skeptical position.

60. As a result of Moore's acquaintance with a German anthropologist, Moore and Sussman, "The Lawyer's Law," was translated into German as Moore, Sussman, and Brand, "Das Gesetz des Juristen." Moore to Richard Thurnwalt, 7/18/32, UMY.

61. Moore, Sussman, and Brand, "Stop Payment II."

62. Again a word of explanation to diminish the darkness.

The payee of a check may present that check to the bank on which it is drawn for payment — the receipt of cash — or may ask that it be certified, that the bank attest to the fact that the account in question has funds sufficient to pay the instrument. Certifying a check makes the bank liable for its payment, as it is not liable for an uncertified check or else it could never refuse to pay and thus a depositor could never "bounce" a check. The holder of a certified check thus has a valuable obligation, the bank's, which that holder may use as security for a loan elsewhere or more likely to obtain goods on credit. To make sure that it is not held liable on the same instrument twice, when certifying a check the bank reduces the customer's balance by the amount of the check. When the customer who issued the check discovers the inadequacy of the goods purchased from or the services rendered by the rascal who had the check certified, the customer attempts to stop payment. The case is thus all but identical to that where a customer has stopped payment on an uncertified check after the bank has paid it. What is being worked out in the case is how, if at all, the establishment of branch banks, a new thing in the 1920s, changes existing law, which held (and holds) that the stop payment has to come to the bank's attention before the payment (or certification).

63. Moore, Sussman, and Brand, "Stop Payment II," pp. 1205–10, describes the method of the study in detail. See Moore and Sussman, "The New York Study," pp. 1055–66.

64. Moore, Sussman, and Brand, "Stop Payment II," p. 1209.

65. Moore, Sussman, and Corstvet, "Uncollected Checks II."

66. Moore, Sussman, and Corstvet, "Drawing against Uncollected Checks I," pp. 1–2. The cases were decided the same month.

67. Moore, Sussman, and Corstvet, "Uncollected Checks II," p. 262.

68. See Moore to Sussman, 12/11/35, UMY.

69. Moore, Sussman, and Corstvet, "Uncollected Checks II," p. 262.

70. Moore to Furniss, 3/1/33, UMY.

71. Moore, Sussman, and Brand, "Stop Payment II," pp. 1214–17, 1223, 1203, 1231, 1234–35.

72. Moore to Furniss, 3/1/33, UMY.

73. Ibid.

74. See Angell to Moore, 5/23/33, UMY.

75. Moore to Angell, 6/10/33, UMY. A year or so later Moore described his problem as caused by "the difficulty of utilizing . . . methods which were identical with those pursued in the two preceding studies, . . . the great amount of time and labor necessary to execute it and . . . many difficulties inherent in the field work." Moore, Report of Work Done by Underhill Moore and Associates in Connection with the Institute of Human Relations, n.d. [fall 1934?], UMY.

76. Moore to Angell, 6/10/33, UMY.

77. Moore, Sussman, and Corstvet, "Uncollected Check II," pp. 281–84.

78. As were his explanations for the shift in his activities at Columbia during the twenties. See "Underhill Moore," pp. 218–19, 311.

79. A problem he solved in the uncompleted study of drawing on uncollected checks.

80. See Moore and Sussman, "The Connecticut Studies," pp. 753, 767; Moore and Sussman, "The South Carolina and Pennsylvania Studies," pp. 930–31, 944; Moore and Sussman, "The New York Study," p. 1063.

81. Most obviously in the distinctions between median, modal, and average frequency of the various time intervals.

82. See Chapter 2.

83. Interview with Dorothy Swaine Thomas, 6/3/75; interview with Emma Corstvet Llewellyn, 8/19/75. The relationship between Thomas and Moore was quite definitely that of junior specialist to senior colleague. A full year after she had arrived at Yale she still referred to him as "Mr. Moore"; see Thomas to Moore, 9/3/31, UMY. The more puckish Corstvet quickly solved the relational problem by calling Moore "Honored Professor"; see Corstvet to Moore, 7/17/33, 8/16/33, UMY. Even when giving up her connection with the Law School, Thomas indicated her continuing interest in working with Moore. See Thomas to Clark, 3/9/33 ("I'll be glad to . . . participate in . . . seminars, particularly those of Underhill Moore"; the handwritten note on the blind carbon to Moore said, "I'm at your service, as always"), UMY.

84. Moore and Sussman, "The Lawyer's Law," p. 576.

85. See Thomas to Moore, n.d. [spring 1932?], (plans for seminar), UMY.

86. Several of these undated, untitled, handwritten lists are found in UMY, starting in fall 1930 and continuing to fall 1932. The lists become increasingly technical in nature and ultimately focus on statistical technique.

87. Interview with Emma Corstvet Llewellyn, 8/19/75.

88. See, for example, Corstvet to Moore, 8/16/33, UMY.

89. Moore to Furniss, 2/19/32, UMY.

90. Furniss to Moore, 2/26/32, UMY.

91. Another indication of Moore's growing identification with an academic social science can be seen by examining the list of individuals who received reprints of his early articles. The debiting study went mainly to law professors and social scientists associated with Columbia or the Institute. Two years later only 20 percent of the mailing went to law professors: almost the entire balance went to the social scientists, but not just to acquaintances at Yale. Included on the list were Petirim Sorokin, F. Stuart Chapin, Stuart Rice, Abraham Flexner, Robert Lowie, Bronislaw Malinowski and five other faculty members at the London School of Economics, and Robert E. Park and five of his colleagues in the Department of Sociology at the University of Chicago. This list shows well Moore's wish to gain assistance for his research from anywhere he could, for it lumps together quantifiers and quantification opponents in reckless profusion.

92. For this concept, I must again thank Robert Gordon.

93. The "Stop Payment" study is an exception, as were, of course, the entire projected twenty-five case studies.

94. See Moore, Sussman, and Corstvet, "Uncollected Checks II," pp. 288–92.

95. See Moore, Report of Work Done by Underhill Moore and Associates in Connection with the Institute of Human Behavior, n.d. [fall 1934?], UMY.

96. See, for example, Moore and Sussman, "The Lawyer's Law," pp. 572–74. Compare Moore and Hope, "An Institutional Approach to the Law of Commercial Banking," p. 705.

97. Corstvet to Moore, 8/16/33, UMY.

98. Northrup, "Underhill Moore's Legal Science," suggests that, in shifting from his commercial banking studies to the parking and traffic studies, Moore was influenced (1) by Ehrlich's advocacy of a "deductively formulated," experimentally verified scientific theory (ibid., p. 198); and (2) by an experience of the lack of trustworthiness of even the limited intuitive judgments he allowed himself, in the banking studies (ibid., p. 204). While Moore surely knew the work of Ehrlich—at the very least he attended the 1914 AALS meeting at which a paper was read on Ehrlich's work (see Page, "Professor Ehrlich's Czernowitz Seminar of Living Law")—there is no other evidence to support this half of Northrup's thesis and, indeed, Ehrlich's work did not become generally available in English until 1936, after Moore had made his switch in subject matter. When Ehrlich's *Fundamental Principles of the Sociology of Law* appeared, Moore agreed to review this book for the *Yale Law Journal* (see Eugene V. Rostow to Moore, n.d. [summer 1937?], UMY) but never completed the task. The second half of the thesis fits well with the interpretation presented here, especially the Corstvet paraphrase of Moore's thoughts on the necessity of running risks in adopting a more strictly behaviorist method. However, Northrup's evidence for Moore's conclusion, Moore and Sussman, "Debiting of Direct Discounts: VI. Decisions," p. 1231 n. 35, is rather weak given that Moore had a chance to terminate his banking research when he completed the debiting studies, but instead worked to refine further his methodology.

99. See "Underhill Moore," p. 265.

100. Moore to Furniss, 3/1/33, UMY.

101. Moore to Furniss, 5/25/34, UMY.

102. Moore, Report of Work Done by Underhill Moore and Associates in Connection with the Institute of Human Relations, n.d. [fall 1934?], p. 7, UMY.

103. See Moore to Furniss, 5/26/34, UMY.

104. Moore and Callahan, "Law and Learning Theory," pp. 88–94, 92, 127–28.

105. Moore to Agatha Bowley (family friend), 12/18/34, UMY. In this letter Moore states that he was able to get the New Haven Parking Authority to make and repeal ordinances in order to advance these two studies. Emma Corstvet concurs that this was the case. See Emma Corstvet Llewellyn to Schlegel, 2/80.

106. Moore and Callahan, "Law and Learning Theory," pp. 110–11, 111, 92, 128–30.

107. In one case the normal pattern was through the circle. Here the results conformed to the commonsense hypothesis; only introduction of the stanchions moved all of the traffic out of the area of the circle, although the painted circle moved about three-quarters. In the second, two-thirds of the traffic normally passed on the correct edge of the circle. Painting the circle on the street moved almost all of the traffic out of the circle, but perversely adding the stanchions moved it even farther over. In the third case, the circle was designed to shift the traffic pattern completely around the circle. Only the stanchions accomplished that result; the painted circle functioned generally in the intended manner but hardly decisively. Ibid., pp. 128–30.

108. Compare Moore to Mark A. May (by this time Director of the Institute), 6/15/35 (reporting work during 1934–35), UMY.

109. Moore, Report of Work Done by Underhill Moore and Associates in Connection with the Institute of Human Relations, n.d. [fall 1934?], UMY.

110. I have been asked numerous times by numerous individuals what the Realists meant when they spoke of law as a means of "social control" and where they got the concept. As to the former question, the concept was anything but precise. It referred generally to the proposition that law could be used to control, presumably "antisocial," behavior. I denote no sophistication in either the formulation or the use of this idea. As to the latter question, none of the Realists cites a source. The obvious one is Ross, *Social Control*; Franz Boas is another possibility. But to seek source as if tracing the bloodlines of a horse or who taught a particular pianist's piano teacher is to misunderstand this and similar intellectual material. Ideas in conversation were drawn on and used because they were useful in solving problems, just as Dewey asserted was usually the case. Origin was less important than usefulness.

111. Moore, Report of Work Done by Underhill Moore and Associates in Connection with the Institute of Human Relations, n.d. [fall 1934?], p. 3, UMY.

112. Ibid., p. 6. Moore described his hypothesis as: "difference between the frequency distribution among the various classes of relevant overt behavior before and after the enactment of a statute or ordinance regulating the overt behavior classified is a function (a) of the number of classes, (b) of the distribution of the frequencies among the classes as disclosed by observation before the enactment of the statute or ordinance, and (c) of the formal similarity of the model in the statute or ordinance to the models which describe the classes." Ibid., p. 7.

113. Ibid.

114. Moore to May, 6/15/35, UMY. One parking study was simultaneously undertaken—this time on two different blocks, judged to be comparable, one with a parking limit and the other without. This study discovered that virtually no one parking in either block was remaining longer than the durational limitation, hardly a helpful investigation. Moore and Callahan, "Law and Learning Theory," p. 92.

115. Ibid., pp. 88–94. Two periods of observation, each four days in duration extending over the change in regulation at the end of a month and limited to daylight hours, were undertaken. Observers were hidden in a second floor bay window overlooking the street and parkers were shadowed to learn their destination.

116. Ibid., pp. 88–94.

117. Corstvet to Moore, 6/23/36 (summarizing work done that year), UMY. For this task she had the assistance of William L. Dennis, a Yale undergraduate who was working for Moore as part of his scholarship, and three statisticians associated with the Institute. See Corstvet to Moore, 7/27/36, UMY. Corstvet, Memo on Discussions of Parking Studies — Status As of Fall, 1936, n.d. [summer 1936?] (copy in possession of the author courtesy of Emma Corstvet Llewellyn).

118. Corstvet, Memo on Discussions of Parking Studies — Status As of Fall, 1936, n.d. [summer 1936?].

119. Ibid. The problems she identified were the small size of the sample and the fact that, even when unregulated, nearly two-thirds of the parking on both sides of the street was for less than the shorter permissible duration.

120. Ibid.

121. Interview with Emma Corstvet Llewellyn, 6/19/75. She had married Karl Llewellyn in 1933. Two years later the sudden illness of her father-in-law made it necessary for her to move to New York. The extended commute forced her to cut her work week to three days, but that too proved unsatisfactory, so reluctantly she chose to stop working for Moore.

122. Moore first tried to hire one of the other sociologists at the Institute who lived with Thomas and Corstvet, but she declined even though pressured by Mark A. May to accept. Moore to Ruth Arrington, 1/30/36 ("I am looking for a person who is sufficiently interested and sympathetic with the kind of work . . . [Corstvet and I] have been doing to carry it on, or, better even, to develop it"); Arrington to Moore, 2/3/36; May to Moore, 4/8/36, UMY. Then Moore tried one of the statisticians who had helped Corstvet, but with no success either. See May to Moore, 5/18/36, UMY.

123. Callahan, who was from Ohio, eventually returned to teach at its Law School.

124. Moore to May, 5/26/36, UMY.

125. See "Underhill Moore," pp. 271–72.

126. Ibid., pp. 272–73.

127. Interview with Mark A. May, 6/9/75. Compare May, "A Retrospective View of the Institute of Human Relations at Yale," pp. 148–50.

128. See "Underhill Moore," pp. 273–74.

129. Moore to Angell, 5/18/36 (I have agreed to pay $1,000 of Callahan's salary during next 18 mos.), JRA. Moore to Charles Seymour (Provost), 5/18/36, UMY.

130. Moore to Charles J. Tilden, 11/5/36, UMY.

131. See "Underhill Moore," p. 274.

132. See ibid., p. 275.

133. In the first of these efforts, Moore again sent his observers out to check parking in the area where the prohibition of parking and unlimited parking shifted sides each month. But this time, instead of eight days of observation, he kept his observers in the field for six weeks, eight hours per day, again hidden in a bay window and again shadowing parkers. The second observation was again of an area where parking restrictions were lifted early each evening, but this time the study was moved a block away. For seven weeks observers in a second-floor window of city hall watched parkers for one hour before the restriction was lifted and for one hour after. Moore and Callahan, "Law and Learning Theory," pp. 88–94.

The results of the first study were substantially the same as in the earlier study. Compare ibid., pp. 100–102, with ibid., pp. 102–4. But the second one showed a substantially different and more marked effect from the parking limitation than had the earlier study. Compare ibid., pp. 104–6, with ibid., pp. 106–7. This result in part confirmed Corstvet's feeling that there had been something wrong with that study.

134. As Moore recognized. See ibid., pp. 91–92.

135. See ibid., p. 93. Moore to Corstvet, 12/10/36; Moore to Agatha Bowley, 4/9/38, UMY.

136. Moore and Callahan, "Law and Learning Theory," pp. 88–94.

137. Ibid., p. 117.

138. Ibid., pp. 116–17. For one part of the study only parkers who had stayed fifty minutes beyond the posted time were tagged; for another, all those who had stayed fifteen minutes. Ibid., p. 117.

139. William L. Dennis (research assistant) to Moore, 8/5/37, UMY. See also Dennis to Moore, 8/12/37, 8/17/37, UMY.

140. See Moore and Callahan, "Law and Learning Theory," pp. 117–26.

141. Ibid., p. 90.

142. See "Underhill Moore," p. 277.

143. Moore, Report of the Work Done by Underhill Moore and Associates in Connection with the Institute of Human Relations, n.d. [fall 1934?], p. 6, UMY.

144. Moore, A Quantitative Investigation of Human Behavior, 11/25/36, p. 1 (application to Penrose Fund), UMY.

145. Moore, Memorandum Re an Investigation of the Effect of Statutes and Ordinances and Their Administration, 2/27/37, p. 6 (grant application), JRA, RMH.

146. See Moore to Roswell P. Angier (Yale, Department of Psychology), 6/27/38, UMY.

147. See "Underhill Moore," pp. 278–79.

148. Ibid., p. 279.

149. Moore to May, 4/19/40, UMY.

150. Kocourek to Moore, 5/31/40, UMY.

151. Kocourek, Untitled Memorandum, n.d., accompanying Kocourek to Moore, 5/31/40, UMY. The recipients of the letter who declined were Mortimer Adler, Thurman Arnold, Louis D. Brandeis, Felix Frankfurter, Learned Hand, and Joseph C. Hutcheson, Jr. Kocourek also planned to include pieces representing the views of James Barr Ames, James Collidge Carter, Benjamin N. Cardozo, John Chipman Gray, and Oliver Wendell Holmes, Jr., though this part of the plan was never completed.

152. Moore to Kocourek, 6/17/40, UMY.

153. Moore to Kocourek, 1/16/41, UMY.

154. At this time in his life Moore considered himself a logical positivist. See Moore to Pekelis, 3/29/43, UMY. Others thought so too. See Kocourek to Moore, 6/23/41, UMY. Whether this is true or whether he was following the operationalism of Bridgman (see *The Logic of Modern Physics*) is of no particular importance.

155. Moore and Callahan, "Underhill Moore," pp. 203, 204, 206–7.

156. Ibid., pp. 205, 207–10, 210–11, 211, 211–15.

157. Ibid., pp. 216, 216–17.

158. Ibid., p. 221. Moore explained his thesis as follows:

In life situations in which an individual is being conditioned to give a reinforced response to a sign, the learned responses of others to that sign are part of the stimulus situation. [Also] . . . the degree of pain or reward by which the response of the individual is reinforced varies with the relative frequency of failures to successes in the responses of those others. Accordingly there is a relation, throughout the learning periods in which responses to a large number of signs are learned, between the relative frequency of failures to successes in the behavior of others and the degree of pain or reward by which the response of the individual is conditioned. Since this behavior of others is present to the senses of the individual during the learning process and since the degree of pain or reward varies with it, the behavior of others becomes a part of the sign and differing ratios of failures to successes become parts of different signs to which different responses are learned because differing degrees of pain or reward have been applied in the process of teaching those responses. (Ibid., pp. 221–22)

159. Ibid., pp. 223–25.

160. See, for example, Bowman, "Book Review"; Prosser, "Book Review"; Rose, "Book Review."

161. Reiblich, "Book Review," p. 345; Rottschaefer, "Book Review," p. 772; Laughlin, "Book Review," p. 77.

162. Lucey, "Book Review," p. 801 ("another loud 'toot! toot!,' for social institutions, with dynamic behaviorism supplying the steam"); Hanft, "Book Review," p. 125 ("The principal accomplishment seems to have been to state some fairly simple matters in the other-worldly language of behaviorist psychology"); Bullington, "Book Review," p. 645 ("obfuscating jargon contrived by the sociologists to bolster their scientific pretensions . . . ends with some meaningless mathematical formulae"); Hutcheson, "Book Review," pp. 525–26 ("too long has devoted himself to too much about too little and too little about too much until he has come to know everything about nothing and nothing about everything"). See also Smith, "Book Review," p. 47 ("there is such a thing as getting so scientific that one forgets what he's scientific about"). Moore said he liked this review. See Moore to Smith, 10/12/42, UMY.

163. Husserl, "Book Review," p. 894; Sharp, "Book Review," p. 592; Cairns, "Book Review," pp. 341–42; Cohen, "Book Review," p. 177.

164. Cairns, "Book Review," p. 342.

165. Husserl, "Book Review," p. 894.

166. Rostow to Moore, 4/11/41, UMY.

167. May to Moore, 3/7/41, UMY.

168. Hull to Moore, 3/17/41, UMY.

169. See "Underhill Moore," p. 285.

170. May to Moore, 10/6/42 ("come back after the war is over"); Moore to May, 10/12/42 (enclosing keys), UMY.

171. See Ashbel Gulliver (new dean) to Moore, 4/28/42; Furniss to Moore, 5/6/42, UMY.

172. *Report of the School of Law, 1942–43* (Ashbel Gulliver), p. 14. Part of the reason was lack of money due to reduced enrollments, part to dissatisfaction with Callahan's teaching. See Gulliver to Moore, 5/7/43, UMY. The university was also attempting, to enforce a general policy against reappointments; see Gulliver to Board of Permanent Officers, 5/4/43, UMY. Nevertheless Moore was bitter over the decision. See Moore to Gulliver, 10/16/43, UMY.

173. Moore and Callahan, "Law and Learning Theory," p. 2. Moore hypothesized reasons for this failure as

in great part the result of their harboring, more or less unconsciously, one or more of the following presuppositions. The first of these is that the effect of a rule of law or of its administration is so different from the effect of all other devices affecting behavior that it is to be accounted for by a particular theory, applicable to law alone, and that the effect of law, cannot be accounted for by a general theory of behavior which accounts for the effect of devices other than law. The second presupposition is that a proposition of law, or its administration, is the single and only cause of "its" effect; that is to say, that the behavior which follows the enactment of a law or its enforcement is a dependent variable, the value of which depends alone upon the law or its enforcement and upon no other variable. The presence of either one or both of the first two of these presuppositions so successfully insulates the investigator from contact with the theories and methods of disciplines investigating human behavior that the investigator either withdraws, in limine, from the prospect of unrewarded effort, or undertakes statistical surveys of this and that somehow connected with law and its administration. The third presupposition is either that complete conformity on the part of substantially all the persons whose behavior is prescribed or proscribed by the proposition follows the issuing of the rule, or that, if all do not completely conform, the number or percentage of persons conforming and the degree of conformity are known. Entertaining it leads natural-law and analytical jurists to restrict the study of law to dialectic; historical jurists to the art of writing either the history of a literature of legal propositions or the history of a larger fragment of culture; sociological jurists to speculation upon the more remote consequences of propositions of law, speculation upon the effect of the supposedly known but in fact unknown quantity and degree of conformity to the proposition upon behavior which is not prescribed or proscribed in the proposition; and "realists" to random behavior.

174. Ibid., pp. 5–8.

175. Ibid., pp. 9, 15 (graphs 11–20), 29, 34–39, 37.

176. Ibid., pp. 27–28, 39, 42, 57–60.

177. Ibid., pp. 68–70.

178. Ibid., p. 61, citing Hull, *Principles of Behavior*; Miller and Dollard, *Social Learning and Imitation*.

179. Moore and Callahan, "Law and Learning Theory," pp. 61–63, 61, 63.

180. Ibid., pp. 64–65, 65–66, 66–67, 67–68, 69–70.

181. Ibid., pp. 77, 83, 85, 72–74, 72, 73–74, 74–75, 75, 76.

182. Ibid., pp. 77–78. Note particularly, Moore emphasized that the learned response to the durational limit was not to park at all, and not to park for a shorter time.

183. Ibid., pp. 80, 80–81, 81.

184. Ibid., p. 83. There was no public announcement of the tagging program and the tags were not noticeable to one driving by. Thus the only people affected by the program were those actually tagged.

185. Ibid., pp. 86–87.

186. Rostow to Moore, n.d., UMY. The other three readers were John Dollard, Mark May, and Henry Margenau (Yale, Department of Physics). See Moore to Callahan, n.d. [fall 1943?], UMY.

187. Moore to May, 12/11/43, UMY.

188. Hull, "Moore and Callahan's 'Law and Learning Theory,'" pp. 337, 331.

189. Ibid., pp. 333–34. Hull argued that an ordinance had an effect only in reducing the frequency of parking that was more than 2.3 times the duration specified in the ordinance.

190. Ibid., p. 334. Wondering why "if the parkers took a chance on such an extensive violation of the ordinance, they should be influenced by it at all," Hull suggested an explanation based on "the general practice in American culture for the authorities practically to wink at small violations, but to punish gross violations with increasing certainty and severity." Ibid., pp. 335–36.

191. Yntema, "'Law and Learning Theory' through the Looking Glass of Legal Theory," pp. 340–41, 344–45, 345.

192. Moore to *American Journal of Sociology*, 12/28/41; Moore to *American Sociological Review*, 12/28/41; Moore to Association for Symbolic Logic, 12/28/41; Moore to *Journal of the American Statistical Association*, 12/28/41, UMY.

193. Moore to Barnes & Noble, Co., 12/28/41, UMY.

194. Moore to Angell, 12/19/36, UMY. See also Moore to Frank, 1/5/34 ("I should put the beginning student in an office and give the law professors a generation to get something to put in the curriculum"), UMY.

195. Though he had retired six years earlier, Angell was prominently thanked for his help when "Law and Learning Theory" was published. Moore and Callahan, "Law and Learning Theory," p. 1 n.

196. See "Yale Experience," pp. 482–88, 573–75, for an estimate of Hutchins's part in the formation of the Institute.

197. Also Edgar Furniss who provided Moore with consistent encouragement. See, for example, Furniss to Moore, 2/26/32, 3/4/33, 3/10/37, UMY.

198. Donald Slesinger, Director of the Institute during its first year, should probably also be included. Interview with Donald Slesinger, 7/8/75.

199. See Bannister, *Sociology and Scientism*. In addition, I draw my conclusions here from casual conversations with their students, from scraps in the available works on the professionalization of the social science disciplines (see "Yale Experience," p. 460 n. 4; Ross, *Origins of American Social Science*), from exposure to two of these men, Hull and May, as they appear in the Moore papers, and from an interview with Mark A. May, 6/9/75. Obviously this research needs amplification; I doubt, however, whether I am the one to do it. For an example of research standards in operation in law, see Huger Jervey to Stacy May (Washington lawyer later with the Rockefeller Foundation), 2/20/25 (patronizing response to paper entitled "The Economic Foundations of Legalism" to which are attached handwritten notes from Herman Oliphant and Karl N. Llewellyn), UMY.

200. Fred Konefsky suggested to me that the potential bad name may have been the problem for May, Hull, and the others. He supplied an example that beautifully captures the entire difficulty. Said he, "It's as if A. James Casner had gone to the Littauer School with a project to count fee simples. They laughed after he left the room!"

201. Interview with Dorothy Swaine Thomas, 6/3/75.

202. See "Yale Experience," pp. 527–29, 543–44.

203. See *Yale Daily News*, 5/9/31, p. 5.

204. May to Angell, 11/17/32, UMY.

205. From the acknowledgments at the beginning of Moore and Callahan, "Law and Learning Theory," p. 1 n, and my interview with Jane Moore, 5/19/76, I suspect that Hull's associate John Dollard ought to be included here also.

206. See, for example, Hull to Moore, 10/19/31, 2/13/35 (arranging appearance at Moore's seminar), 11/11/36, UMY.

207. Hull to Institute Staff, 11/30/35; Moore to Hull, 12/7/35 (sorry I missed);

Hull to Moore, 12/9/35 ("I am sure most of the meetings will have no interest for you"), UMY. The seminar was to be "an attempt to integrate the major concepts and principles of the conditioned reaction with those of psychoanalysis." Hull, Notice of Informal Seminar, 1/20/36 (copy in possession of the author courtesy of Emma Corstvet Llewellyn).

208. Hull to May, 12/3/35, 12/18/35; Hull to Moore, 12/18/35, UMY.

209. May to Moore, 1/29/36; Moore to May, 2/5/36, UMY.

210. May to Moore, 2/3/39, UMY.

211. May to Moore, 4/12/40 ($3,000 for 1940–41), 7/1/43 ($600 for Callahan's salary for summer), UMY.

212. May to Moore, 3/7/41, UMY.

213. Hull to Moore, 3/7/41, UMY.

214. May, "Foreword," pp. v, vi.

215. Clark, "Underhill Moore," p. 191; interview with Dorothy Swaine Thomas, 6/3/75.

216. Foundation for Research in Legal History, *A History of the School of Law, Columbia University*, p. 251. This story is clearly apocryphal; Moore's annotations of American negotiable instruments cases survive in UMY.

217. Clark, "Underhill Moore," p. 191; Llewellyn, "On What Makes Legal Research Worthwhile," p. 401. This story is likely untrue except in Clark's version, which omits the season of the year. Work near the Taft Hotel was primarily done in December and January; indeed, only three days of observation were conducted other than in late fall or winter. I detect Thurman Arnold's authorship in this story.

218. Moore to John A. Hanna, 1/14/32, UMY.

219. Hanna to Moore, 1/8/32, UMY.

220. Dorothy Thomas had agreed to give a paper at the Round Table on Jurisprudence and Legal History chaired by Edwin Patterson, Moore's former colleague and companion on the ferry back and forth to their Englewood, New Jersey, homes. Patterson, who claimed to be "genuinely loyal to the movement for fact finding research as an aid to change in, or understanding of, law," had asked Moore to lead discussion of Thomas's paper. Patterson to Moore, 10/15/31, UMY. When Moore wanted to present a paper of his own, Patterson agreed, but with the warning to use a "minimum of novel terminology"; Patterson to Moore, 10/29/31, UMY. Moore's paper, "The Data for the Study of Law and Environment," has not survived. From the evidence provided by a critique of it by Dorothy Thomas (Thomas to Moore, 12/25/31, UMY), it appears to have been a bridge between the Moore and Hope, "Institutional Approach," and Moore and Sussman, "The Lawyer's Law." Compare Moore to Furniss, 3/1/33, UMY. This was Moore's only appearance at an AALS meeting after 1920.

221. Moore to Hanna, 1/14/32, UMY.

222. The sociology department was adamantly opposed to the statistical studies in general and the Institute in particular, largely because it was still controlled by the shade of William Graham Sumner. Interview with Robert M. Hutchins, 6/20/75; interview with Dorothy Swaine Thomas, 6/3/75.

223. Not that either discipline was at the time particularly empirically oriented anyway.

224. See "Underhill Moore," p. 321.

225. Sussman stayed five years, far longer than he had planned. He liked working for Moore and Moore quite obviously liked him. See Moore to Sussman, 12/2/35

("Your loving, hating, admiring and contemptuous friend"), UMY. That fact made staying easier, as did the lack of good alternatives caused by the Depression and exacerbated by prejudice against Jews seeking professional jobs. But, once Sussman made up his mind to leave, he seems to have expressed no regrets at having given up empirical research for the practice of law. Sussman to Schlegel, 10/1/76 (taped interview). Callahan was probably equally trapped by the Depression for he was not much taken with the parking study. Interview with Emma Corstvet Llewellyn, 10/19/75. He likewise never did any other empirical work.

226. Grant Gilmore to Schlegel, 9/19/76; Friedrich Kessler to Schlegel, 2/10/77. Compare Moore to G. H. Robinson, 7/11/30 (comments about a planned casebook; "your book should deal for the most part with the minute problems arising today. The general principles of today are . . . general descriptions of the way in which the minute problems of yesterday were settled"), UMY.

227. Moore and Callahan, "Law and Learning Theory," p. 3.

228. Grant Gilmore to Schlegel, 9/19/76.

229. Malinowski was a personal friend. Interview with Jane Moore, 5/19/76. The two men taught a seminar together in 1940–41.

230. See Moore to Timasheff, 10/3/39, UMY. Moore unsuccessfully tried to bring Timasheff to Yale to join the seminar with Malinowski. See Moore to Gulliver, 11/11/39; Moore to Furniss, 1/16/40, UMY.

231. See Moore, Diary Written during the Cruise from New York to Gibralter on the Schooner Yacht Black Eagle, Aug. 7–Sept. 4, 1929, UMY.

232. Gilmore to Schlegel, 9/19/76. Compare Llewellyn, "On What Makes Legal Research Worthwhile," pp. 400, 403.

233. Douglas, "Underhill Moore," p. 188 ("I was not one to ridicule it. There were many who did").

Chapter 4

1. See Twining, *Karl Llewellyn and the Realist Movement*, pp. 52–54; Foundation for Research in Legal History, *A History of the School of Law, Columbia University*, pp. 303–4; "Underhill Moore," pp. 212–13.

2. "Underhill Moore," pp. 213, 213–14, 213.

3. See Edmund E. Day (Director, Social Sciences Division, Rockefeller Foundation) to Raymond B. Fosdick (Trustee, Rockefeller Foundation), 2/26/30, ROC.

4. "Yale Experience," p. 522.

5. Oliphant to Frank J. Goodnow (President, Hopkins), 6/1/28, HOP.

6. Oliphant to Moore, 5/25/28, UMY.

7. "Underhill Moore," p. 214.

8. Hutchins to Moore, 5/21/28, UMY. See also "Yale Experience," pp. 486–88.

9. Oliphant to Moore, 6/8/28, UMY.

10. Moore to Homer F. Carey, 7/11/28, UMY.

11. *See* Oliphant to Moore, 6/15/28 (replying to Moore's arguments), UMY.

12. See "Underhill Moore," p. 218.

13. Ames to Max Mason (President, Rockefeller Foundation), 4/1/30 (emphasis in original), ROC.

14. Ibid., appendix II, pp. 1–2, 4, 5.

15. Marshall was Dean of the College of Commerce at Chicago from 1909 to 1924. Cook taught at the Law School from 1910 to 1916. Oliphant received his J.D. at

Chicago in 1914. Thereafter in 1914–15 he was an instructor and in 1915–16, an assistant professor of commercial law, in the College of Commerce before becoming an assistant professor at the Law School in fall 1916. See AALS, *Directory of Teachers at Member Schools, 1922*, p. 29 (only source where Oliphant's early career and tie to Marshall are made clear).

16. See "Underhill Moore," p. 211.

17. Moore declined in early June 1928. See Moore to Oliphant, 6/15/28, UMY. Yntema was hired in late June. See Yntema to Goodnow, 6/25/28, HOP.

18. See "Yale Experience," pp. 483–87.

19. See Ames to Mason, 4/1/30, appendix II, p. 5, ROC.

20. Oliphant, *Summary of Studies on Legal Education*, pp. 20–21.

21. French, *A History of the Johns Hopkins University*, pp. 198, 243, 396.

22. Kent, *The Story of Alex. Brown & Sons*, pp. 152, 153, 155, 156, 160, 163, 167–70. See also "B. Howell Griswold."

23. Griswold to James M. Landis (newly dean at Harvard), 9/28/37, BHG. See also Griswold, Personal Narrative of the Founding of the Institute of Law, 1930, p. 25 ("Always there was a lingering thought in . . . [my] mind: Is it the right side or the bright side that wins?"), BHG.

24. Griswold, Personal Narrative, pp. 26–27, BHG.

25. Morawetz, *The Law of Private Corporations*.

26. "Victor Morawetz."

27. Griswold, Personal Narrative, p. 27, BHG.

28. Griswold quotes Buttrick as saying that "he would not cross the street to form a new law school but would jump across the table" for Griswold's school. Ibid., p. 28.

29. See Griswold to Buttrick, 2/16/24 (recounting conversation), ROC.

30. See A School of Jurisprudence at the Johns Hopkins University, n.d. [spring 1924], accompanying Rose, Interview on Thursday, May 15, 1924, with Mr. B. Howell Griswold, ROC. I ascribe authorship to Willoughby because of the similarities of this document and Proposed School of Jurisprudence at the Johns Hopkins University, n.d., WWC, which bears Cook's inscription "Willoughby" and date "Oct. 11, 1924." The latter document is referred to as "Willoughby's plan for the School of Jurisprudence" in Griswold to Abraham Flexner (Director, General Education Board), 12/23/24, and accompanies Griswold to Buttrick, 12/14/24, ROC.

31. See Griswold to Buttrick, 6/28/24, ROC.

32. Buttrick to Griswold, 7/1/24, ROC.

33. Beardsly Ruml, Director of the Memorial, took a good deal of convincing before he saw any merit in the proposal. See Griswold, Personal Narrative, p. 29, BHG; Griswold to Ruml, 11/10/24, ROC. Yet, after being convinced, his Board decided it was uninterested. Griswold, Personal Narrative, p. 29, BHG.

34. Griswold, Personal Narrative, p. 29, BHG. Flexner knew of the project beforehand. See Griswold to Flexner, 12/23/24, ROC.

35. Flexner to Goodnow (President, Hopkins), 4/6/25, ROC.

36. Griswold, Personal Narrative, p. 29, BHG.

37. Flexner to Griswold, 12/26/24, ROC.

38. Griswold, Personal Narrative, p. 30, BHG.

39. See A School of Jurisprudence at the Johns Hopkins University, n.d. [spring 1924], accompanying Rose, Interview on Thursday, May 15, 1924, with Mr. B. Howell Griswold; Griswold to Ruml, 11/10/24, ROC; Proposed School of Jurisprudence at the Johns Hopkins University, n.d., WWC.

40. Proposed School of Jurisprudence at the Johns Hopkins University, n.d., pp. 1, 2, WWC.

41. Ibid., pp. 2–6.

42. Griswold to Ruml, 11/10/24, ROC.

43. Griswold, Personal Narrative, p. 30, BHG. Griswold had approached Morawetz for support for a law school at the time of the 1910 fund drive. See Ira Remsen (President), B. Brent Keyser (President, Board of Trustees), and Griswold to Morawetz, 10/17/10, HOP.

44. In addition he sensibly had no faith in plans but only in people. Being a cautious corporate type he wanted to move very slowly in assembling a faculty by trying out each proposed member for a while. See Griswold, Personal Narrative, p. 30, BHG; Morawetz to Flexner, 9/15/25, ROC.

45. Morawetz to Cook, 4/28/25, WWC.

46. Victor Morawetz was a classic conservative of Kolkoesque proclivities; he seems to have advocated change as a means of fighting off socialism or worse. See generally Morawetz, "The Supreme Court and the Anti-Trust Act."

> A decision following the supposed authority of the *Sugar Trust* case and holding that the Anti-Trust Act does not prevent the effective monopolization of interstate trade or commerce by combining or vesting in a corporation the plants and businesses of practically all manufacturers and sellers of an article of interstate commerce surely would not be accepted by the people of the United States as a final solution of the trust problem. Such a decision probably would result in an imperative popular demand for legislation of a socialistic character and possibly it might lead to an amendment of the Constitution. Governmental regulation of corporations and trusts as to their organization and their methods of conducting business, while leaving them the fruits of monopoly, would not be accepted as sufficient. The demand would be that those who have monopolized a branch of trade or commerce shall be deprived of the fruits of monopoly, either by governmental regulation of the prices of commodities, or by exercise of the taxing power of the government. The evils and dangers that would result from such legislation cannot be overestimated. Therefore, those who are interested in our great industrial combinations or trusts should consider carefully the question whether such a decision would place them ultimately in a better or in a worse position than a decision requiring, as above suggested, the restoration of reasonably competitive conditions. (Ibid., pp. 707–8)

47. See Cook to Morawetz, 12/10/24, WWC. I have not spent an enormous amount of time digging through the debates over the first restatement of the conflict of laws. However, from my reading I gain the sense that the opponents of Beale's draft supported the local law theory for two different, ultimately antagonistic reasons. Liberals like Cook objected to Beale's notion of "vested rights," which, once established, were to be enforced forever and everywhere, because of the resonance of this concept with, and explicit tie to, a reactionary Supreme Court's use of vested rights theory in constitutional law. See, for example, Yntema, "The Hornbook Method and the Conflict of Laws." Conservatives like Morawetz favored local law because it kept the ALI narrowly circumscribed in its task rather than dangerously fiddling with law reform and because local, positive law once known could always be drafted around, a task that was not so easy when vested rights might pop up at unexpected times and in unexpected places at the whim of the Supreme Court.

48. Cook to Morawetz, 12/10/24, WWC.

49. Morawetz to Flexner, 9/15/25, ROC. Curiously, Morawetz was not sure Cook was the "best man to head" the school.

50. Ibid. This is a letter seeking references on Max Radin, a professor at the University of California, Berkeley, Law School, who Victor Morawetz also thought might be a "good man."

51. Stone to Cook, 3/16/26 ("The rules of constitutional law stated in some of these sections are really quite beyond belief"; "judges will never use it and . . . the whole performance will not reflect any credit on the Institute"), WWC.

52. Lorenzen was so displeased with Beale's draft that he resigned from Beale's board of advisors. Lorenzen to William Draper Lewis (ALI Executive Director), 3/3/26, WWC.

53. Goodnow to Cook, 3/24/26, HOP. This letter suggests that Cook may have talked with Goodnow and Willoughby even before Willoughby and Griswold went to see Rockefeller. Goodnow suggested "somewhat different methods of instruction might be adopted with a good deal of emphasis upon the research of legal problems."

54. Cook to Goodnow, 3/29/26, HOP.

55. See Cook to Goodnow, 4/15/26, HOP.

56. Cook to Leon C. Marshall, 4/26/26, WWC. Exactly how Cook came to know Marshall is unclear; I assume that it was through Oliphant while the two were at Chicago. It is interesting that Cook is writing to Marshall about Hopkins less than two weeks after the Columbia curriculum study that was to bring Marshall to that Law School was authorized by the faculty. See "Underhill Moore," p. 210 n. 76. Something had been up for a while.

57. Griswold to Cook, 4/21/26, WWC.

58. See Cook to Goodnow, 5/1/26, HOP.

59. Ibid.; Cook to Griswold, 5/3/26, WWC.

60. Cook to Goodnow, 5/1/26, HOP.

61. Griswold to Cook, 5/6/26 ("I am willing to go bond for you at any time"), WWC.

62. Goodnow to Cook, 5/5/26, WWC.

63. Cook to Goodnow, 5/6/26, WWC.

64. Cook to Thomas W. Swan (Dean, Yale Law School), 5/7/26, WWC.

65. See Cook to Griswold, 5/6/26; Griswold to Cook, 5/5/26; Goodnow to Cook, 5/5/26, WWC. See also Cook to Marshall, 4/26/26, WWC.

66. See Griswold to Cook, 7/4/26 ("Flexner spoke highly of you — said you were on the right track"), WWC.

67. Cook to Goodnow, 4/16/26, HOP.

68. Cook, Suggested Program for a School of Jurisprudence at the Johns Hopkins University, 4/26, pp. 1, 8, WWC.

69. Ibid., p. 9. Marshall was a great supporter of the practice of placing professional training after two years of liberal arts work. See Marshall, "The American Collegiate School of Business." Cook may have got the idea from him, but such plans were hardly novel at this time when ABA accreditation standards only required two years of college. See Stevens, *Law School*, p. 115.

70. Cook, Suggested Program for a School of Jurisprudence at the Johns Hopkins University, 4/26, pp. 9, 3, 7, 8, 3, 4, 4–5, WWC. This functional scheme was one that Cook, Marshall, and Oliphant had "so often discussed"; Cook to Marshall, 4/26/26, WWC. Indeed, it was the one that Oliphant had been pushing at Columbia for three

years and that would dominate the great Columbia curriculum study soon to begin. See "Underhill Moore," pp. 207, 211. It divided all the world into domestic relations, business relations (including labor), and political relations (including law administration, i.e., pleading, practice, evidence, and criminal law and criminology). Cook, Suggested Program for a School of Jurisprudence at the Johns Hopkins University, 4/26, p. 4, WWC.

71. Ibid., pp. 9, 11 (small classes, last of four years "largely research," $3 million endowment adequate for the "formative years").

72. Griswold, who had earlier found having a connection with a professional law school a handicap that would draw faculty from research to teaching (Griswold to Ruml, 11/10/24, ROC), only noted he rejected the idea of providing better vocational training as an objective. Griswold to Cook, 4/21/26, WWC.

73. Griswold to Cook, 4/21/26, WWC. The details of Cook's plan were kept from Morawetz for a time. See Cook to Goodnow, 5/1/26, HOP.

74. The proposed school outlined in the concluding nine paragraphs was presented verbatim to the Rockefeller Foundation by Cook the same spring.

75. Goodnow to Morawetz, 3/9/27, HOP.

76. A piece on equity, quite obviously a knock-off from his recently published three-volume casebook on the subject (Cook, *Cases and Other Authorities on Equity*), did make it into print: "The Present Status of the 'Lack of Mutuality' Rule." It was an article like much of Cook's recent legal work, a big chunk of doctrinal analysis, rigorous, indeed unrelenting, sandwiched between an encomium to the scientific method and a similar, if slightly defensive, peroration on the same subject. This version was notable first, for its assertion of adherence to a behavioristic psychology (ibid., p. 898 n. 5), an assertion not particularly supported anywhere in the body of the work; second, for its emphasis on scientific method in law as consisting of the effort to "formulate general statements which will summarize as accurately as possible . . . past phenomena and also serve as an aid in forecasting future phenomena," namely the conduct of "judges and similar officials" from records "found in the law reports" (ibid., p. 898); third, for its recognition that the desires of "the dominant elements in the community" might possibly have something to do with what legal rules get adopted (ibid., p. 910); and fourth, for the feeling that it was essential to make clear that just because he denied "that rules and principles of law pre-exist as ready made premises for deductive syllogisms" did not mean that there were "no rules and principles of law" (ibid., p. 913), a reflection of a bashing he had taken at an ALI meeting two years before (Scott, "Remarks") and could not forget over fifteen years later. See Cook, *The Logical and Legal Basis of the Conflict of Laws*, p. 47. After this fight Cook resigned from his post as an advisor to Beale on the Restatement of the Conflict of Laws (Cook to William Draper Lewis, 3/3/26, WWC), and though he regularly attended Institute meetings never again spoke on the conflict of laws.

77. French, *A History of the Johns Hopkins University*, pp. 197, 358-59.

78. See Griswold to Cook, 7/4/26, WWC.

79. See Cook to Morawetz, 2/12/27, WWC. The phrase was Griswold's but the idea was Cook's.

80. Griswold to Cook, 2/7/27, WWC.

81. Cook to Morawetz, 2/12/27, WWC.

82. The source of the example was Oliphant, "The Theory of Money in the Law of Commercial Instruments."

83. Cook placed this admission in the back of his revised plan. See [Cook], Sugges-

tions for a School of Jurisprudence, p. 10, n.d. [5/27], enclosed with Cook to Rose, 5/6/27, ROC.

84. [Cook], Suggestions for a School of Jurisprudence, n.d. [5/27], pp. 3, 3–4, 12–13, enclosed with Cook to Rose, 5/6/27, ROC.

85. See, for example, Cook to Griswold, 1/3/27 (men we want may soon be committed elsewhere; I may have to face choice of leaving), WWC.

86. See, for example, Cook to Oliver Wendell Holmes, Jr., 3/22/27, WWC. The document was a version of Cook's article, "Scientific Method and the Law," that left out all discussion of scientific method and left in all of the general outline of the proposed "University School of Jurisprudence." Among the recipients were Justices Holmes and Stone, Judges Cardozo, R. A. Burch of Kansas, Carroll T. Bond of Maryland, and Robert von Moschzisker of Pennsylvania, the presidents of Chicago, Dartmouth, Yale, and the Carnegie Institution, practitioners like Frederick Coudert and Elihu Root, and William Draper Lewis, president of the American Law Institute.

87. See, for example, Harlan Fiske Stone to Cook, 4/5/27 ("immense benefit"); R. A. Burch (Supreme Court of Kansas) to Cook, 4/4/27 ("feasible," "time is ripe"); Carroll T. Bond (Chief Judge, Maryland Court of Appeals) to Cook, 5/25/27 ("Count me as voting now for the school as planned"); Robert von Moschzisker to Cook, 4/5/27; Ernest M. Hopkins (President, Dartmouth College) to Cook, 4/28/27 ("no project more immensely worthwhile or more significant to the rational development of civilization"); John C. Merriam (President, Carnegie Institute of Washington) to Cook, 4/17/27; Frederick R. Coudert to Cook, 5/4/27 ("the time is ripe"), WWC.

88. Cardozo thought that students should first go through "the usual law school courses" to gain "knowledge of the traditional technique involved in the judicial process" (Cardozo to Cook, 4/8/27), and only after receiving a "fuller statement" of the plan was he "quite enthusiastically in favor" (Cardozo to Cook, 4/13/27, WWC).

89. Frederick C. Woodward to Cook, 4/22/27, WWC.

90. Angell to Cook, 6/29/27, WWC. Cook tried to dodge this criticism. See Cook to Angell, 7/1/27 ("need to know how to use the results as far as they exist"), WWC.

91. Root to Cook, 4/20/27, WWC.

92. Cook to Rose, 5/6/27, ROC.

93. Rose, [Memo of meeting with] Doctor W. W. Cook, 5/14/27, ROC.

94. Cook to Rose, 5/19/27, ROC.

95. Rose to Cook, 5/23/27, ROC.

96. Report of the Wednesday Evening Session, Hanover Conference, Social Science Research Council, 8/24/27, WWC. Cook had by this time evolved a standard talk; this is but an otherwise uninteresting example. Another is Cook, "Research in Law," part of another symposium on research.

Cook's talk began with his usual, Dewey-inspired attack on Aristotelian logic. Cohen, in reply, rambled much but denied "that it is possible to construct a non-Aristotelian logic" and asserted that "[t]he laws of mathematics and of formal logic are the laws of all things whatsoever, without qualification." Report of the Wednesday Evening Session, Hanover Conference, Social Science Research Council, 8/24/27, pp. 209, 210, WWC. This hopefully neo-Kantian, but possibly extreme realist, position was ignored by an audience that nevertheless applauded when Cohen suggested that it was a crowded court system that was keeping the courts from "getting the information they desire" and so allowing them to make bad decisions. Ibid., pp. 212–13. On the whole the level of discussion suggests that either the Conference was a dud or that Prohibition was being flagrantly violated.

97. See Cook to Oliver Wendell Holmes, Jr., 9/23/27, WWC.

98. Cook, Suggestions for a School of Jurisprudence of the Johns Hopkins University, 10/27, WWC. This iteration of the project differed only in deleting references to training practitioners that were to be found in earlier drafts, a peculiar change in the light of Wickliff Rose's observation about the sterility of a school devoted to research alone.

99. Griswold, Personal Narrative, pp. 31–32, BHG.

100. See Cook to Goodnow, 12/22/27, HOP. By the right kind of individuals Cook surely meant Oliphant.

101. Though Hopkins was willing to keep Cook on for another year at $15,000, according to an unsigned memorandum, 4/10/28, IOL.

102. See Griswold to Barry C. Smith (Commonwealth Fund), 5/22/28, BHG.

103. Griswold, Personal Narrative, p. 33, BHG.

104. Joseph S. Ames (Acting President, Johns Hopkins) to Willard, 5/29/28, IOL.

105. "Underhill Moore," p. 214.

106. Ames to Griswold, 6/13/28, IOL.

107. The group included Edwin Baetjer, a Baltimore lawyer, and Theodore Marburg, a Baltimore philanthropist, from the trustees and John W. Garrett, grandson of the founder of the Baltimore and Ohio Railway, and Jacob Epstein from Baltimore. The underwriting was said to be for a period of three years. Kent, "Johns Hopkins Grapples with the Law," p. 29.

108. Memorandum Designed to Open the Discussion, 4/15/29, LCM (probably a group project building on Yntema, Memorandum of Points to Be Discussed, 4/13/24, LCM). See also Edmund E. Day (Director, Social Sciences Division, Rockefeller Foundation) to Raymond B. Fosdick (Trustee, Rockefeller Foundation), 2/26/30, ROC.

109. Cook to Ames, 6/19/28, WWC. He later strenuously argued something quite different.

110. Ames to Cook, 7/10/28, WWC.

111. Ames to Marshall, 6/14/28, IOL.

112. Griswold, Personal Narrative, p. 33, BHG.

113. Cook to Ames, 6/19/28, WWC.

114. Ibid.

115. *Baltimore Sun*, 7/22/28. The most complete reproduction of the press release is "The Johns Hopkins Institute of Law."

116. "The Human Effects of Law," p. 531.

117. In thus validating Hurst's ideas, I do not wish to suggest that I agree with Hurst as to where drift and default dominate. Indeed, I find that much of what is labeled drift and default has a certain "tilt" as Morty Horwitz used to say. But stochastic motion, even in a particular direction, is something different than human intention and should be recognized as such more often than is now the case, or so it seems to me.

118. For example, in 1922 the school had only 715 undergraduates. French, *A History of the Johns Hopkins University*, p. 194.

119. Stone to Cook, 4/13/27, WWC.

120. See Cook to Griswold, 5/3/26 (Morawetz "told me how he in his own thinking had to get rid of what Ames and Langdell of Harvard had taught him"), WWC.

121. See, for example, Cook, "Research in Law," pp. 313, 314; Cook "Scientific Method and Law," p. 304.

122. Cook to Morawetz, 2/12/27, WWC.

123. See, for example, ibid.

124. See Rose, Interview, 5/15/24, with Mr. B. Howell Griswold, n.d., ROC; Cook, Suggested Program for a School of Jurisprudence at the Johns Hopkins University, 4/26, p. 12 (adds only the need for a "workshop," which would, given the small student body, not include "large lecture rooms" or space for "duplicate sets of law reports"), WWC; [Cook], Suggestions for a School of Jurisprudence, n.d. [5/27], p. 12 (adds funds for "publication of the researches of faculty and students"), ROC.

125. See Holt, *Historical Scholarship in the United States.*

126. Cook to Ames, 6/19/28, WWC.

127. Eight on a full, two-course-per-semester load; sixteen on a one-course load of the kind that would allow for as much research as Cook always said should be done. The figures never made any sense in any case. Given then current capitalization rates, Cook was talking of current income of $150,000, which at $15,000 per faculty member would pay for a faculty of no more than ten in an unheated building with no secretaries or librarians. At best tuition would heat the building.

128. Whatever the official rules as to which of the four was in charge, all archival sources suggest that the impetus to do anything came from Leon Marshall. Indeed it is his records that make it even vaguely possible to chronicle the Institute's activities. Unfortunately these records give out in the summer of 1930 when he turned the post of "faculty secretary" to Oliphant and so a sense of the daily activities of the faculty is difficult to construct thereafter.

129. Marshall, Memorandum on Next Steps, 10/3/28, LCM.

130. Marshall, Memo Three to the Originating Group, 10/9/28, LCM.

131. Marshall, An Approach to the Financial Situation, 10/15/28 (emphasis in original), LCM.

132. Marshall, Memo Three to the Originating Group, 10/9/28, LCM.

133. Marshall, Memo Four to Members of Originating Group, 10/10/28, LCM.

134. Marshall, Memo, 10/10/28, LCM.

135. Marshall, Memo Two to the Originating Group, 10/8/28; Marshall, Memo concerning the Origination of Research Projects, n.d. [late 10/28], LCM.

136. Who pushed pure research. See Yntema, An Approach to the Financial Situation, 10/17/28, IOL.

137. Marshall, Memorandum on Next Steps, 10/3/28, LCM.

138. Marion J. Harron, Justice for the Poor, 10/22/28, LCM. Harron was a graduate of the University of California, Berkeley, Law School. She eventually became a judge of the United States Tax Court. See "In Memoriam Marion Janet Harron." She likely became acquainted with Oliphant when she worked for the National Industrial Conference Board doing a survey of New York labor laws.

139. A clear knock-off from his work on a labor injunction case. See *Interborough Rapid Transit Company v. William Green et al., Brief for Defendants.*

140. Oliphant, A Beginning List of Problems to Suggest Strategic Points of Attack, n.d. [late 10/28], LCM. Though some of the problems are rather silly or implausibly grandiose, on the whole the list is still a viable one today.

141. Marshall, Lest We Forget Accounting, n.d. [late 10/28], LCM.

142. Cook, List of Projects for Conference Statement, n.d. [12/28]; Cook, Proposal for a Study of the Defense of Persons Accused of Crime, n.d. [12/28], LCM.

143. See Harron, An Analysis of Legal Administration, n.d. [11/28]; Harron, The Desirability of Establishing a Bureau of Judicial Statistics in the Institute for the Study of Law, 11/9/28, LCM.

144. The list included economists like John Commons, T. N. Carver, J. Lawrence Laughlin, and I. L. Sharfman, as well as sociologists like W. I. Thomas and philosophers like Morris Cohen, a few judges, and some law professors. See Suggestions for the Institute, n.d. [late 11/28] (compiling replies), LCM.

145. The exception was James Bonbright, who emphasized the importance of nonjudicial decision makers and the necessity to keep to "simple social problems" and who opined that in fact the Institute would do just what the staff was interested in doing. As to problems with judicial decisions he observed, "When I talk with the younger men at Columbia and Yale who are imbued with the social science theory of legal decisions, I find that their understanding of the problem is confined almost entirely to a mere enthusiasm for the newer idea. They lack woefully a technique for putting this newer idea into practice." Ibid.

146. See Harron, A Preliminary Survey of the Field to be Surveyed in a "Survey of Legal Research in the United States," 12/21/28, LCM.

147. See Marshall, Attempt at Complete Statement of Task of the Institute, n.d. [early 12/28], LCM. Yntema is noted as the author of the appendix on library facilities; Cook, of A Study of Method and Techniques Used in Scientific Investigation, with Special Reference to Social Science.

148. Oliphant, *Summary of Studies in Legal Education*.

149. Oliphant, Considerations Preliminary to Next Steps, 12/2/28, LCM.

150. He emphasized the study of what the members of "the governing group" of a society "*do*" as opposed to what they "*say*" and that the two conditioning factors of outstanding importance in "the study of law-in-action aimed at improvement" are the "facts" of the dispute or question and "the entire procedural machine" in which the decision maker operates. Ibid.

151. See, for example, Cook to Pound, 2/18/29, enclosing the Institute for the Study of Law, Johns Hopkins University, An Immediate Program 8–9, n.d. [early spring 1929], RPP. The document distributed was marked as a "confidential proof." A slightly shorter version exists, which curiously is similarly marked. Institute for the Study of Law, Johns Hopkins University, An Immediate Program [1929], IOL. Ultimately a further revised version was published as Johns Hopkins University, *The Institute for the Study of Law: 1929–30*. No revisions were made in the substance of the faculty's plan but only in the foreword, which was completely reorganized to increase its effectiveness and to make explicit the analogy to the founding of the Medical School at Hopkins.

152. Institute for the Study of Law, Johns Hopkins University, *An Immediate Program*, pp. 14, 18, 21–23, 26, 26–27, IOL.

153. Ibid., p. 32 (emphasis in the original).

154. I have been asked where the idea that there are "basic functions of law" comes from. As was the case with the concept of "social control," there are no clues left behind by anyone as to who introduced the idea at Hopkins and from where it was taken. In one sense the source is obvious; it is Marshall's project to envision a "functional society" and so to study "business organization and management and/or control in relation to such a society." Marshall, Tentative Statement Re Budget and Activities 1929–30, 1/3/29, LCM. And that project had its roots in the "functional" curriculum of the University of Chicago's College of Commerce that he sold to Oliphant for the Columbia Law School. But that answer only poses the question of where Marshall got the idea for his system. Likely that was in the "functional" psychology of Dewey and Angell in vogue at the University of Chicago, which was designed, in part,

to escape the older "faculty" psychology. However, such speculation seems to me to miss the point of the inclusion of this idea in what may be best seen as a list of ideas. Though a paradigm different from the law reform paradigm that Clark and Douglas lived in, and surely a more capacious one at that, it was barely, if at all, noticed as different from the other items on the list. It was in the air, floated by, and someone grabbed it. Ideas have meaning as they are used; unused they are meaningless, evidence here from the obvious proposition that no one at the Institute had a single coherent idea of what the group as a whole might do.

155. Institute for the Study of Law, Johns Hopkins University, *An Immediate Program*, p. 33, IOL.

156. See ibid., pp. 33–35. The Institute "must not now (and, so far as we can see, should never) commit itself to maintaining an orthodox professional school for the training of practitioners." Ibid., pp. 33–34. How far one could see unorthodox schools was left to Cook's imagination.

157. Ibid., pp. 37, 35, 36–37, 38–40, 40–41, 42, 42–44, 44–46.

158. Nor did the budget statement for the entire enterprise, essentially the one detailed by Leon Marshall four months earlier, help. Compare ibid., pp. 83–85, with Marshall, Memo Four to Members of Organizing Group, 10/8/28, LCM.

159. The fifth current project was the collection of histories of typical pieces of litigation, work that became the Survey of Litigation in New York detailed subsequently.

160. Not surprisingly neither Oliphant or Marshall ever published on this subject while or after leaving Hopkins.

161. Such a project would follow the line of research pioneered by Thomas and Znaniecki, *The Polish Peasant in Europe and America*, but to do so would have been to swim against the social science current of the day, which was turning to "hard" method.

162. A good portion of the surviving records of the Institute of Law consists of the files of this fundraising campaign. They are a monument to the proposition that pretty booklets do not make a successful campaign. On the founder and his attachment to pretty books, see "John Price Jones."

163. See Minutes of Institute of Law, 2/1/29 (Twentieth Century Fund), 2/19/19 (Littauer Fund), LCM.

164. Of the academics, few had much of interest to say. James Beard found it "a refreshing contrast to many sterile projects for 'research.' " Beard to Cook, 4/12/29, LCM. Frankfurter was "happy that the group was not tempted to seek 'practical' and quick results." Frankfurter to Cook, 3/1/29, LCM. Joseph Beale, Cook's continuing intellectual adversary, found the document "exceedingly interesting," "hopeful as well as helpful." Beale to Cook, 3/5/29, LCM. Cautions were only heard in terms of the project being overly ambitious, Ernest Freund to Cook, 2/25/29; Edmund Morgan to Cook, 2/21/29, LCM. One individual sought to complain that it was a doubtful practice for anyone other than those actually "preparing members of the bar" to produce teaching materials. C. K. Burdick (Dean, Cornell) to Cook, 4/17/29, LCM.

165. *Authoritative Views on the Need for the Institute of Law at Johns Hopkins University*, IOL, ROC.

166. Goodnow to Cook, 1/16/29, HOP.

167. George H. Jaffin (Yntema's research assistant at the Institute) to Schlegel, 11/28/80.

168. See Yntema, Organization of Administrative Work of Institute for the Study of Law, 4/8/29, LCM.

169. Marshall, Tentative Statement Re Budget and Activities 1929–30, 1/3/29, LCM.

170. Oliphant, Tentative Statement In Re Activities and Budget 1929–30, 1/26/29, LCM.

171. Marshall, Tentative Statement Re Budget and Activities 1929–30, 1/3/29, LCM.

172. Yntema, On the Budget for 1929–30, n.d. [early 2/29], LCM.

173. Oliphant, Tentative Statement In Re Activities and Budget 1929–30, 1/26/29. LCM.

174. Cook, In Re Budget 1929–30, 1/30/29, LCM.

175. Oliphant, Tentative Statement In Re Activities and Budget 1929–30, 1/26/29, LCM.

176. At this time Oliphant was still living in New York. See Yntema, Memo to Drs. Cook and Marshall, 5/15/29, LCM.

177. Minutes of the Institute of Law, 1/21/29, LCM.

178. Oliphant, Tentative Statement In Re Activities and Budget 1929–30, LCM.

179. Institute for the Study of Law, Johns Hopkins University, *An Immediate Program*, p. 59. The request probably came in December 1928. See *Baltimore Sun*, 3/12/29.

180. See [Cook?], Comments on the Proposed Budget for 1929–1930, n.d. [spring 1929], LCM.

181. Jaffin to Schlegel, 10/17/80.

182. Jaffin, Proposal for a Study of the Problem of Conformity by Federal Courts to the Rules of Law and Principles of Public Policy Developed by State Courts, n.d. [2/29 or 3/29], LCM. This proposal, unlike those of his employers, was well thought out, carefully presented, and well written, just what a junior colleague would need to gain the attention of a bunch of busy law professors.

183. Oliphant, Proposal for Study of the Employment Agency Business, n.d. [10/28], LCM. See Oliphant, "A Decision in the Light of Fact." The case was *Ribnik v. McBride*, 277 U.S. 350 (1928). Oliphant's approach was to attempt to disprove the factual assertion made by Mr. Justice Sutherland in the course of his opinion that the business of an employment agency does not differ from that of numerous other business brokers.

184. Cook, Estimate of Cost of Conducting Study of the Defense of Poor Persons Accused of Crime, 3/20/29, LCM. See also Cook, The Defense of Poor Persons Accused of Crime, 3/20/29, LCM.

185. Flexner was in fact fired. See Wheatley, *The Politics of Philanthropy*, pp. 161–66.

186. Griswold, Personal Narrative, p. 30, BHG.

187. [Cook?], Memorandum Designed to Open Discussion, 4/15/29, LCM.

188. George Vincent, Memorandum of an Interview, 5/13/29, ROC. Hopkins was asking for a total of nearly $25 million, mostly for law and humanities and to change the school to a wholly graduate basis.

189. Goodnow emphasized that the proposals to establish a wholly graduate institution and to expand work in the humanities were really part of the same enterprise and that "the Institute of Law" was a second step in the development of specialized work at a very high level, the Medical School being the first of such undertakings. Willard emphasized that "the chief stress" of the University "for the time being" was to be the Institute and not on the so-called "Philosophical Faculty" — the humanities

and social and natural sciences — and noted that past talks with the Foundation and General Education Board had led the University to "hope that . . . substantial gifts would be forthcoming" on the basis of the "interest and sympathetic attitude of the officers." Ibid.

190. Ibid.

191. George E. Vincent to Goodnow, 5/21/29, ROC.

192. The phrase comes from Oliphant, "Bare Bones" Budget for Next Year, 5/18/29, LCM.

193. Institute of Law, Proposed Budget for 1929–30, n.d. [ca. 5/20/29] (prepared by Cook), LCM. Of this only $3,000 was for research expenses other than library.

194. Institute of Law, Budget for 1929–30, n.d. [ca. 5/29/29], LCM.

195. Cook, Minimum Budget for 1929–30, 5/20/29, LCM.

196. Oliphant, "Bare Bones" Budget for Next Year, 5/18/29, LCM.

197. Yntema, Schedule of Work in Comparative Law, Possible and Probable, 5/20/29, LCM.

198. Marshall, Comment on LCM's Budget Needs for Next Year, 5/17/29, LCM. Curiously Marshall did not mention possible work on the survey of litigation in Ohio, though at the same time he announced that $5,000 had been secured for a study that was to survey activities in the courts of common pleas in three selected years, two historical and one contemporary, and envisioned further specialized studies of items such as workmen's compensation, small claims, domestic relations, and criminal justice, among other things. See Marshall, Possible Study in Trends in Litigation in Ohio, 5/17/29, LCM.

199. Oliphant, Fund Raising, 5/18/29, LCM.

200. There is nothing in the minutes of the Institute to show that Oliphant's idea was even discussed.

201. On planning see, for example, Marshall, Informal Memo concerning Accounting and Law, 5/17/29 (plan to hire someone to do the project); Marshall, Proposal to Study Risk and Insurance Covenants in Long Term Leases, 5/17/29; on administration see, for example, Report of Faculty of Law, n.d. [early 6/29]; Minutes of the Institute of Law, 5/20/29 (offer of office to Willoughby; efforts to form National Advisory Committee), LCM.

202. Oliphant, "Mutuality of Obligation in Bilateral Contracts," was his chance to do battle with Sam Williston as Cook had done. See Williston, "The Effect of One Void Promise in a Bilateral Agreement." It was a bit of case law research designed to undermine an argument from principle. He also got into print: Oliphant, "The Future of Legal Education" (publication of a document from 1923 on the functional curriculum; see "Underhill Moore," p. 207); Oliphant, "A Sample of the New Type of Law Examinations" (long true-false examination in contracts); Oliphant and Carey, "The Present Status of the Hitchman Case."

203. See Cook, "Scientific Study and the Administration of Justice" (speech touting the Institute and listing possible projects).

204. Harron, Current Research in Law for the Academic Year, 1928–1929. It was followed by Iddings, Current Research in Law for the Academic Year 1929–1930. The books still repay browsing.

205. The representativeness was not undermined by the refusal of the likes of Felix Frankfurter to cooperate. See Frankfurter to Oliphant, 5/20/29 ("deeply sympathetic with what is afoot in your Institute" but "a perfectly fruitless endeavor, if not mischievous"), FFP.

206. Jaffin to Schlegel, 11/28/80.

207. Rueff, *From the Physical to the Social Sciences.*
One wonders what the crew at Hopkins might have thought of Rueff's later career. In 1931, as a member of the staff of the French Embassy in London, he publicly argued that British unemployment was caused by British unemployment insurance, so that if the British would abolish the dole they would begin to solve their economic problems and escape the Great Depression. During the late 1950s and 1960s, as an economic advisor to De Gaulle, he championed the French return to the gold standard and regularly castigated the United States for not following suit. See Grant, *Money of the Mind*, pp. 272–78.

208. Oliphant and Hewitt, "Introduction," pp. ix, x, xv, xvi, xvii–xix, xx, xxi.

209. Ibid., pp. xxi, xxi–xxii, xxii, xxiii, xxii, xxiii, xxiv.

210. Ibid., pp. xxv, xxv–xxvi, xxvi, xxviii.

211. Though the key assertion that both logical methods were in fact disguised applications of estimates of practicality was either unsupported or unintentionally supported.

212. Langdell, *A Selection of Cases on the Law of Contracts*, p. vii.

213. Veblen, *Higher Learning in America*, p. 211.

214. See Oliphant and Hewitt, "Introduction," p. xxi.

215. This notion is ubiquitous to the Institute's materials starting with Cook's first plan. Cook, Suggested Program for a School of Jurisprudence at Johns Hopkins University, n.d. [4/26], WWC.

216. Cook, "Scientific Study and the Administration of Justice," p. 148.

217. French, *A History of the Johns Hopkins University*, pp. 197, 411, 407–11.

218. Ames to Trevor Arnett (President, General Education Board, a Rockefeller philanthropy), 7/11/29, ROC.

219. Jaffin to Schlegel, 11/28/80. For a copy of Jaffin's questionnaire, see Survey of Concurrent Jurisdiction of the Federal and State Courts, n.d., accompanying Yntema to Frankfurter, 10/18/29, FFP.

220. See Survey of Concurrent Jurisdiction of the Federal and State Courts, n.d., FFP. A copy of the cover letter, but not the questionnaire, is in Yntema to Pound, 10/18/29/, RPP.

221. See, for example, Yntema to Pound, 10/18/29 ("persons of experience who are thoroughly familiar not only with the technical aspects of the administration of justice in the federal courts, but also with its broader implications"), RPP.

222. Yntema to Frankfurter, 11/14/29, FFP.

223. See Oliphant, A Study of Litigation, 4/15/29, LCM.

224. Oliphant to Ames, 11/23/29, HOP. See Survey of Litigation, Questionnaire for Commercial Contract and Negligence Cases, Draft No. 3, n.d. [5/23/29] (an early version of this questionnaire), LCM.

225. See C. C. Burlingham (prominent New York lawyer) to Frankfurter, 12/2/29 (enclosing copy), FFP.

226. Herman Oliphant, A Study of Litigation, 4/15/29, pp. 1–2, 2, LCM.

227. Survey of Litigation, Questionnaire for Commercial Contract and Negligence Cases, Draft No. 3, n.d. [5/23/29], LCM.

228. Oliphant, A Study of Litigation, 4/15/29, p. 2, LCM.

229. Oliphant saw the jury as a source of cost, delay, and uncertainty; suspected that pleading reform, trial court capriciousness in dealing with motions, and perjury contributed to all three and yet was open-minded enough to suggest that the notion

that litigation was uncertain was "a preconception like some of our opinions about women." Ibid., p. 8.

230. Grounds for Yntema's involvement are unclear.

231. Institute of Law, *A Study of Administration of Justice in Ohio: Statement of the Immediate Program*, p. 1. This is Bulletin No. 1 in a series issued by the study. The authors are listed as the Judicial Council of Ohio, the Ohio State Bar Association, and the Institute of Law of the Johns Hopkins University, though internal evidence suggests that the author was Yntema.

232. Jaffin to Schlegel, 11/28/80.

233. A copy of a revision of this form is in Institute of Law, *Report of the Committee of Direction, July 1, 1930: Interim Statement of the Study of Judicial Administration in Ohio*, Ohio Bulletin No. 4. (The actual authors are Yntema and Marshall.)

234. Institute of Law, *A Study of Administration of Justice in Ohio: Statement of the Immediate Program*, Ohio Bulletin No. 1, pp. 2-3.

235. Ibid., p. 4. This study was chosen because it lent itself "to objective statistical methods" since it was "important to make truly objective studies and not merely to engage in exchange of opinions and reiteration of prejudices." Ibid., pp. 4-5.

236. Ibid., pp. 5, 6-7.

237. *Baltimore Sun*, 12/2/29.

238. Yntema, Plans for a Survey of the Judicial System of Maryland, 12/9/29, LCM.

239. Yntema envisioned a rather grand enterprise. Cook would focus his studies of pleading and practice and small claims litigation in Maryland; Yntema and Jaffin would work on the diversity jurisdiction there; and Oliphant, if he thought it "advisable to do so from the point of view of his larger enterprise," would duplicate the survey of litigation. Ibid. Having found a group of young lawyers with whom to work, Oliphant agreed as to the plausibility of extending the survey. Oliphant, Survey of Litigation, n.d. [winter 1930], LCM.

240. Yntema, Study of the Judicial System of Maryland, 1/8/30, LCM.

241. Cook, Study of the Judicial System of Maryland, 1/18/30, LCM. It is a revision of Yntema's earlier memorandum. He initially estimated that the job would take three years and cost $100,000.

242. See *Baltimore Sun*, 3/10/30.

243. Jaffin to Schlegel, 11/28/80.

244. Institute of Law, *Study of the Judicial System of Maryland: Statement of the Immediate Program*, pp. 5, 6. (This is Bulletin No. 1 in a series issued about the study. The authors are listed as the Judicial Council of Maryland and the Institute of Law of the Johns Hopkins University, but internal evidence suggests it was written by Yntema.)

245. Ibid., p. 5, said to be "already" underway in the People's Court of Baltimore City. This last study was begun the previous fall by one of Cook's research assistants, Robert Birdzell, who was "without previous experience in research" but was being given the project in part "to make a beginning in the training of personnel in" "the field [of] procedural law." Cook to Ames, 11/22/29, HOP.

246. See *New York Times*, 3/9/30.

247. Including C. C. Burlingham, Emery Buckner, and Henry W. Taft.

248. Report of the Faculty of the Institute of Law, 11/3/30, LCM; Oliphant, *Study of Civil Justice in New York*, New York Bulletin No. 1, p. iii.

249. Oliphant, Memorandum Re: Budget for Survey of Litigation, 5/19/30, LCM.

250. Program, Conference on Studies in the Administration of Justice, 5/7/30, LCM. For the conference, Marshall wrote a paper on "The Present Status of Judicial Statistics"; it was later published as Marshall, *Judicial Statistics*, Ohio Bulletin No. 2. (Marshall is listed as the author of this document in Report of the Faculty of the Institute of Law, 9/32, LCM, although the author stated on the document is the same as in Bulletin No. 1.) Yntema wrote one on "the theoretical and practical problems involved in securing adequate data as to judicial administration"; it was later published as Yntema, *Facts and the Administration of Justice*, Ohio Bulletin No. 3. (Again Yntema is listed as the author in Report of the Faculty of the Institute of Law, 9/32, LCM. The author stated on the document is the same as in Bulletin No. 1.) The two together prepared a brief statement explaining the scope of the Ohio and Maryland studies. Marshall and Yntema, *Outline Statement Concerning State-Wide Studies of Judicial Administration*. (This unnumbered bulletin is said to be by Marshall and Yntema in an end paper advertisement in Gehlke, *Criminal Actions in the Common Pleas Courts of Ohio*.)

251. The paper, "The Contribution of the Practicing Lawyer to a Realistic Study of the Administration of Justice," was never printed. I have not been able to locate a copy.

252. Frankfurter to Oliphant, 4/20/29, FFP.

253. Frankfurter to Yntema, 11/27/29, FFP. This date is clearly erroneous and is likely the date this copy was retyped for circulation by Frankfurter. The likely date is 11/7/29 as shown by Yntema's reply. Frankfurter's narrow objection was to the use of a questionnaire at the outset of the study rather than after a "field survey" of what "the court records would reveal in the light of the law and practice governing federal and state actions, respectively, in the same jurisdiction." Jaffin's questionnaire would yield not an "objective" but a "subjective" examination, and thus would fail to indicate what doubtless his preferred procedure would find — "the disparity between the factors that really operate and those that people assume are operating in diversity litigation."

254. Frankfurter to Yntema, 11/17/29, FFP. This pronouncement was in reply to Yntema's assertion that much of the information sought, that is lawyer's reasons for choosing one court over another, was not to be found in court records and that a study of court records was to be undertaken as well. Yntema to Frankfurter, 11/14/29, FFP. Yntema's further, sensible response that "varying methods" are "of varying degrees of merit for varying purposes, none of them wholly good or wholly invalid, each to be used where it is effective for given purposes" (Yntema to Frankfurter, 12/4/29, FFP), only brought the return assertion that the "specific inquiry, the specific stages of the inquiry, the specific objectives of the inquiry and the specific question of adaptation of means to . . . specific ends" meant that Jaffin's questionnaire, which focused on the problem as one of "judicial administration" without focusing on "the exploration of the authoritative distinctive data concerning the distinctive elements" of the diversity jurisdiction, was inadequate to the subject. Frankfurter to Yntema, 12/10/29, FFP.

255. See Frankfurter to C. C. Burlingham, 12/21/29 ("I have now examined Greenbaum's questionnaire"), FFP, sent after Burlingham had communicated "Prof. Frankfurter's . . . opinions" to Greenbaum. See Greenbaum to Burlingham, 12/11/29, FFP.

256. See Frankfurter to Burlingham, 12/5/29, FFP. Frankfurter asserted that starting with court records would make for "objective truth," "open up problems in the concrete instead of speculating upon problems in the abstract," and would "restrict

considerably the hit or miss quality of replies to questionnaires." Burlingham duti-
fully transmitted Frankfurter's comments. See Greenbaum to Burlingham, 12/11/29,
FFP. Greenbaum replied that, while he understood and agreed with the objections to
Yntema's questionnaire, those objections were inapplicable to his own because his
group had "carefully considered the possibility of getting our information from court
records and . . . come to the conclusion that these records would not furnish adequate
data to form the basis for a real, intensive study." Ibid. Frankfurter, of course, stuck to
his guns. He emphasized that even if the data were only available through lawyers,
given "the time, attention and thought which lawyers will give to such questionnaires" court records ought to be exhausted first and then lawyers consulted for "the
exploration of difficulties already revealed by objective data." Frankfurter to Burlingham, 12/21/29, FFP.

257. Frankfurter to Burlingham, 12/21/29, FFP. These were rather harsh words for
a study that simply wanted to know in detail how long litigation took and how much
it cost, as well as a bit less than helpful since Greenbaum was seeking an endorsement
that just might have increased the willingness of lawyers to take the time to reply
carefully. It was also more than a bit off point since the major weakness of the study
was not the inaccuracy of the replies, but their representativeness with respect to
litigation as a whole, since the replies would constitute neither a census nor a sample,
matters that Clark at least vaguely understood when he declined Oliphant's request
for a letter of support for the study. See Clark to Oliphant, 1/14/30, FFP.

258. Asked to endorse Oliphant's research, Clark hesitated, based on the lessons
that Dorothy Thomas had already taught at Yale, to "honestly appear to sponsor the
movement to an extent beyond what my beliefs really are." See Clark to Oliphant,
1/14/30, FFP. His careful suggestion of ways to get the information that Oliphant and
Greenbaum wanted and his apparently honest willingness to see if "better results can
be obtained" than he had suggested would be the case were, in their own way, helpful.
Ibid. Still, Clark's action in sending a blind copy of the letter to Frankfurter (ibid.)
suggests less than the best will toward the project. See also Clark to Frankfurter,
12/19/29 ("I have had reports recently of *their* activities in Ohio") (emphasis supplied), FFP. Frankfurter's action in immediately sending Clark's letter on to Burlingham (Frankfurter to Burlingham, 1/15/30, FFP) was no better spirited. At the
same time, in Clark's partial defense, if not Frankfurter's, it should be noted that at the
time there simply were no known statistical techniques for dealing with the random
responses that one gets from questionnaires, and that even today there is great difficulty in learning anything from a questionnaire that is not sent to a real universe of
potential respondents but only to self-selected subgroup such as Oliphant and Greenbaum seemed to be contemplating. The general level of support for the work at
Hopkins in the academic legal community can be seen in the comment by Sam Bass
Warner, a Harvard faculty member, that Clark's work on the first draft of the ALI
criminal study was "no better than a good Johns Hopkins report." Warner to Clark,
1/25/33, CCB. It was truly the unkindest cut of all.

259. For example, Frankfurter chose to share his correspondence over Jaffin's
questionnaire with C. C. Burlingham (see Burlingham to Frankfurter, 12/5/29, FFP),
who was a member of the Institute's advisory committee and the President of the
Association of the Bar of the City of New York. At that time Frankfurter knew that
Oliphant and Greenbaum were seeking the Association's endorsement for their study.
Frankfurter did the same thing with Charles P. Howland, member of the Hopkins
Trustees. See Howland to Frankfurter, 12/30/29 (returning letters), FFP.

260. Frankfurter, "Preface," pp. vi–viii.

261. Marshall and Yntema, *Outline Statement concerning State-Wide Studies of Judicial Administration*, pp. 1–2. "The development of methods for obtaining dependable data and perfecting of techniques of investigation" rather than "undertaking a series of specific detailed studies of special topics" was to be the Institute's task because of "the inadequacy of the means available for obtaining and interpreting the necessary data and because the specific studies to be effective needed to be integrated with fairly comprehensive studies of the whole system of the administration of justice."

262. See ibid., pp. 4, 5–9.

263. Marshall, *Judicial Statistics*, Ohio Bulletin No. 2, pp. 6, 9, 11.

264. Yntema, *Facts and the Administration of Justice*, Ohio Bulletin No. 3, p. 3. This decision had been criticized privately by Clark (see Clark to Wickersham, 2/4/30, CCB, and Thomas, Interview with Dorothy Swaine Thomas, 6/3/75), because of the inability of the researchers to control the activities of their clerks, or, as he put it, "the primary personnel for securing information as to the work of the courts." Here Yntema chose simply to canvass the available alternatives — project fieldworkers, attorneys, parties, and court officials — and list the strengths and limitations of each. He asserted that "there is no unique type of personnel from which alone adequate scientific results can be anticipated," but rather "the problem is a highly practical one of securing the necessary information from those who can furnish it most accurately and with the greatest economy in time and money." Yntema, *Facts and the Administration of Justice*, Ohio Bulletin No. 3, p. 8. This, he concluded was the clerks, at least at the present time.

265. Yntema, *Facts and the Administration of Justice*, Ohio Bulletin No. 3, pp. 9, 10.

266. Ibid., p. 13. He then asserted that this seeming contradiction presented "no difficulty . . . since the lawsuit or controversy furnishes the most convenient integer for the purpose" of social analysis. Ibid. Within the lawsuit the problem was simply that of describing the parties ("age, race, sex, marital status, occupation, residence, income") and the transaction ("place, time, form, type, amount involved . . ."). The legal process, he asserted, could be described similarly. All well and good, except that the choice to use court clerks as data collectors meant that they could "be expected to report only upon matters as to which they are in a position to obtain information without undue expenditure of effort." This practical limitation meant the "exclusion" of nonlegal material with the result that the asserted primary aspect of the studies, "the portion of the analysis . . . directed to the actual effects of law, [was] scarcely represented." Ibid., pp. 14, 19, 21.

267. Ibid., p. 21.

268. Ibid.

269. Institute of Law, *Report of the Committee of Direction, July 1, 1930. Interim Statement*, Ohio Bulletin No. 4, where six months of civil cases were to be analyzed.

270. Ibid., pp. 6–7.

271. Marshall and Yntema, *Outline Statement concerning State-Wide Studies of Judicial Administration*, p. 9.

272. Ibid., pp. 10–11. Of this list only two were ever completed and published, the cost study and the appellate court study. The others including studies of the municipal courts of Cleveland, Columbus, and Cincinnati; of the court systems in two rural counties; of the Courts of Appeals and Supreme Court and of the history of court organization in the state never saw print.

273. Jaffin to Schlegel, 11/28/80.

274. See Oliphant, Memorandum Re: Budget for Survey of Litigation, 5/19/30, LCM.

275. Institute of Law, *State Wide Studies in Judicial Administration: A Report of Progress*, Ohio Bulletin No. 2 and Maryland Bulletin No. 5, pp. 4–5. These documents are identical except for their title pages. Ohio was now collecting, in addition to the common-pleas cases previously mentioned, divorce cases, criminal cases, appeals, both in the Ohio Supreme Court and the Court of Appeals, municipal court cases in three cities, and other inferior courts in one county. The Maryland study began collecting similar data about civil, criminal, and divorce cases and municipal court cases as well, though all fewer in numbers, reflecting the fact that Maryland was smaller in population than Ohio. Special studies of the cost of litigation in Maryland, the small-claims court in Baltimore, and the Maryland Public Service Commission were also arranged.

276. Interview with Paul F. Douglass, 10/10/80.

277. Institute of Law, *State Wide Studies in Judicial Administration: A Report of Progress*, Ohio Bulletin No. 2 and Maryland Bulletin No. 5, pp. 8–10.

278. Oliphant, *Study of Civil Justice in New York*, New York Bulletin No. 1, pp. 3, 21–22, 26–27, 31–33.

279. Ames to Marshall, 7/22/31, HOP.

280. The exceptions were the Ohio Supreme Court study, where one year of old cases was to be half the selection, and the Maryland divorce study, where all the cases were old.

281. It was, it should be said, a quite impressive list. Ohio alone expected 10,000 divorce actions; 40,000 civil, nondivorce actions in the Court of Common Pleas; 9,000 criminal cases in the Court of Common Pleas; 1,300 Supreme Court cases; 3,000 intermediate appellate court cases; 17,000 cases from justice of the peace and similar courts in one county, and 25,000 municipal court cases. "Report of the Faculty of the Institute of Law, 1930–31," p. 222.

282. *State Wide Studies in Judicial Administration: A Report of Progress*, Ohio Bulletin No. 5 and Maryland Bulletin No. 2.

283. Oliphant, *Study of Civil Justice in New York*, New York Bulletin No. 1, pp. iii, 10–11 n. 4, 31–33.

284. Ibid., pp. 1, 2–3.

285. Ibid., pp. 4–5. These data were rather interesting in that it showed that in the most inferior court (Municipal Court) a greater percentage of cases was disposed of in relatively brief times (73 percent in the first year) than in the next most inferior court (City Court) (34 percent in the first year). In both courts, however, there was a steady decrease in the percentage of cases disposed of as the duration of the action increased. However, in the least inferior court (Supreme Court) the percentage of cases disposed of increased until it peaked at two and a half years and then declined. Possibly, just possibly, the more complicated cases were taking longer.

286. Ibid., pp. 6, 10, 11.

287. Ibid., p. 12.

288. And that the "dominant questions" in such accident litigation as requires trial "relate to jury trials, perjury, expert testimony and contributory negligence."

289. Ibid., pp. 12–13 (emphasis in original). Where this last point came from is nowhere apparent.

290. Ibid., p. 13.

291. For example, negligence cases proceed all the way to the point of trial because the defense lawyer was the first person with authority to offer a substantial settlement on behalf of the insurance company. Ibid., p. 22.

292. Ibid., pp. 16–17, 17, 19.

293. Ibid., pp. 19, 20.

294. In malicious moments I wish to have forced and then observed the long-term interaction of Oliphant and Dorothy Thomas.

295. Ibid., p. 11.

296. See Oliphant, Agenda of Faculty Meeting, January 17, 1930, LCM. They did deal with mighty minuscule questions. See Minutes of the Institute of Law, 1/13/30 (approval of stenographic assistance for Roswell Magill *if* he comes for a visit), LCM. Regular faculty meetings still took place, and at least Oliphant thought the group was too occupied with administration and too little with research problems.

297. See Cook to Ames, 11/22/29 (tone of real irritation at the tasks), HOP.

298. See Donald Hammond, Final Report on the Campaign for the Institute of Law at the Johns Hopkins University, 6/7/30, IOL.

299. Ibid.

300. See Minutes of the Institute of Law, 1/2/30, LCM. The University, of course, saw Marshall, as it saw Cook, as the Director of the Institute. The difference over the name as well as the fetish over group faculty meetings clearly reflects Cook's experiences with Stone at Columbia and everyone else's experiences with Smith's appointment there. The Institute was to be a *community* of scholars, Institute for the Study of Law, Johns Hopkins University, An Immediate Program [1929], p. 34, IOL, though, of course, in the modern university it was a community of administrators.

301. See Oliphant, More Eye Wash, n.d. [11/29] (annotation by Marshall), LCM.

302. Oliphant, Predraft of a Memorandum, 12/16/29, LCM. See also Oliphant, The Institute of Law from a Number of Points of View, 2/15/30 (more formal, more general, and less personalized; clearly states scientific method as a separate area of study, placating Cook), LCM.

303. See Statement of the Present Status of the Institute of Law, the Johns Hopkins University, 3/32, appendix A, IOL. Neither the Illinois lectures nor the one at the New School survives. The lecture at Brookings was published as Cook, "The Possibilities of Social Study as a Science." Although the article relies heavily on a then recent book, Lewis, *The Mind and the World Order*, it shows essentially no advance on Cook's earlier thinking, emphasizing that statements of fact are always predictions as to what will happen if the speaker were to act with respect to the fact in question, though the points are put with a growing sophistication.

304. Cook, "Jurisdiction of Sovereign States and the Conflict of Laws."

305. See Cook to Ames, 11/22/29, HOP. This study, which began by collecting form contracts from all over the country and which was to finish with an examination of "the actual usages and practices in the commercial community" (*Washington Post*, 11/28/29), was designed to see whether the existing law of chattel mortgages, security taken in goods already owned by the debtor, and that of conditional sales, security taken in goods newly purchased by the debtor, could be combined in one body, a question that was ripe for field study since one state had created a natural experiment by abolishing the distinction. Cook to Ames, 11/22/29, HOP.

306. Marshall to Ames, 11/21/29, IOL.

307. See Marshall to Ames, 10/1/29 (motion pictures, aeronautical industries), HOP.

308. See Hammond to Marshall, 6/4/30, HOP.

309. Marshall to Pound, 12/23/29, IOL.

3 10. His sole significant publication was a brief paper on the divorce study given at the American Statistical Association. Marshall, "A Statistico-Legal Study of the Divorce Problem."

311. See Oliphant and Carey, "The Present Status of the Hitchman Case." He continued his interest in the yellow dog contract issue that he had acquired doing pro bono work while still at Columbia. See *Interborough Rapid Transit Company v. William Green et al., Brief for Defendants*. Oliphant was cocounsel with Robert F. Wagner, Joseph Crater, Simon Rifkind, Nathan Perlman, and Samuel Mezansky. He apparently organized the entire effort and was personally responsible for putting together the social and economic background that was presented in the brief. See Oliphant, "Preface," p. (3).

312. Oliphant, "The New Legal Education," p. 494.

313. Oliphant, The Need for Research in Legislation, 12/7/29, LCM.

314. Oliphant to Ames, 11/23/29, HOP.

315. See Financial Statement, 11/15/29, 12/15/29, LCM.

316. Yntema, Suggestions as to the Development of Work in Comparative Law, 2/13/30, LCM. Strangely he proposed to start a project on "double" taxation of interstate corporations. Yntema to Ames, 11/21/29, IOL.

3 17. Yntema, "The Purview of Research in the Administration of Justice."

318. Yntema and Jaffin, "Preliminary Analysis of Concurrent Jurisdiction."

319. Yntema, "The Purview of Research in the Administration of Justice," pp. 348, 341, 343.

320. See Frankfurter, "Distribution of Judicial Power between United States and State Courts," p. 523.

321. Yntema and Jaffin, "Preliminary Analysis of Concurrent Jurisdiction," pp. 879–81, 889.

322. The ability to take dichotomous variables and check the operation of each in a split sample where only one is operable and in a homogeneous sample where both are operable had the kind of elegance that made Harry Kalven talk about baseball!

323. Here Yntema ought to have had support from Cohen and others on the proposition that these reasons, while not determinative, were at least a factor in the choice of forum. Of course, no such support was forthcoming—for the dispute in these quarters was not really about method but about the centrality of rules to our understanding of law.

324. Ibid., pp. 914, 915.

325. The disproportionate percentage of appellate opinions in diversity cases suggested that diversity cases might be taking up a disproportionate amount of available time.

326. Pound, "The Call for a Realist Jurisprudence," p. 701.

327. Yntema and Jaffin, "Preliminary Analysis of Concurrent Jurisdiction," p. 917.

328. Twining, *Karl Llewellyn and the Realist Movement*, p. 70. See also Hull, "Some Realism about the Llewellyn-Pound Exchange over Realism."

329. Adler, "Legal Certainty."

330. Llewellyn, "Legal Illusion."

331. Adler, "Legal Certainty," pp. 91, 92, 97, 103.

332. Frank to Adler, 1/12/31, WWC.

333. See Felix Cohen (book review editor, *Columbia Law Review*, and son of Morris Cohen) to Oliphant, 11/8/30, WWC.

334. Cook, "Legal Logic."

335. Cook noted that he disagreed with this part of Frank's argument. Ibid., p. 108 n. 28.

336. Ibid., pp. 112–13, 113–14.

337. Frank to Cook, 10/11/30, WWC.

338. Frank to Cook, 1/12/31, WWC.

339. Holmes, Jr., to Cook, 2/3/31, WWC.

340. Dewey to Cook, 2/5/31, WWC.

341. Cook to Dewey, 2/7/31, WWC.

342. Cohen to Cook, 1/29/31, WWC.

343. Cook to Cohen, 2/2/31, WWC.

344. A position that at different times both Cook and Oliphant had taken. See Cook, "Scientific Method and the Law," p. 308; Cook, "Scientific Study and the Administration of Justice," p. 160; Cook, "The Legal Method"; Oliphant, "A Return to Stare Decisis," pp. 72, 160.

345. Cohen, "Justice Holmes and the Nature of Law."

346. Cook, "Book Review" (Cohen, *Reason and Nature*). Frank tried to help with the review (Frank to Cook, 4/8/31, WWC), but acted too late.

347. Cook, "Book Review" (Cohen, *Reason and Nature*), pp. 726, 727. And finally he expressed a bit of bewilderment that Cohen's present positions seemed to contradict positions he had taken earlier. Ibid., pp. 727–28.

348. Yntema, "Mr. Justice Holmes' View of Legal Science."

349. Yntema, "The Rational Basis of Legal Science," pp. 933, 935, 942, 955, 953.

350. See Llewellyn, "Some Realism about Realism."

351. Both may have sensed that the Institute might fold, in which case, in seeking a new job, Pound's support might prove valuable. George Jaffin recalled that by spring 1931 the faculty had made it reasonably clear to the research assistants that the Institute was in deep financial difficulty. See Jaffin to Schlegel, 11/28/80.

352. Ibid.

353. Jaffin, "Theorems in Anglo-American Labor Law," p. 1133. The article appeared in an issue honoring Brandeis. Jaffin sent copies to his two heroes — Holmes and Brandeis. Holmes replied expressing the hope that the attack would not harm Jaffin's academic career. Jaffin to Schlegel, 11/28/80. Being Jewish and poor and it being the Depression, Jaffin, of course, had no academic career to harm.

354. See Edmund E. Day (Director, Social Sciences Division, Rockefeller Foundation) to Raymond B. Fosdick (Trustee, Rockefeller Foundation), 2/26/30 (recounting events), ROC.

355. For a brief biography see "Edwin Baetjer." He was soon to become Chairman of the Board of Dun & Bradstreet.

356. Hammond, Final Report on the Campaign for the Institute of Law at the Johns Hopkins University, 6/7/30, pp. 30–31, IOL.

357. See Hammond to Marshall, 6/4/30, IOL. This approach was not wholly scholarly, as it was assumed that Brandeis's appointment would open access to Rosenwald and Filene money.

358. Cardozo to Ames, 6/24/30, IOL.

359. See Alexander du Pont to Ames, 10/21/29 (declining); Irénée du Pont to

Ames, 10/23/29; Ames to Lammont du Pont, 5/28/30; Ames to T. Coleman du Pont, 6/4/30; T. Coleman du Pont to Ames, 6/10/30 (declining), IOL. See also Ames to Andrew W. Mellon, 4/7/30 (requesting meeting to explain project), IOL.

360. See, for example, Oliphant, Memo on Associates, 10/16/29; Yntema, Institute Memorandum to Mr. Baetjer, 4/25/30, LCM.

361. Irénée du Pont to Ames, 10/22/29, IOL.

362. Ames to Irénée du Pont, 11/25/29, IOL.

363. Compare Institute of Law, *The Story of the Institute of Law* (fall; pure endowment sought: "vastly improved social control should grow out of a synthesis of the social sciences"; ibid., p. 10) with Institute of Law, *Law as a Social Instrument* (late spring; endowment for faculty and staff, memorials for research groups or special studies; purpose is "to study laws in operation and to determine by investigation and study their effect upon our social structure and the individuals who comprise it"; ibid., p. 11).

364. See Griswold to Baetjer, 6/19/30, BHG.

365. See, for example, Marshall, A Sample Minimum Set-Up for the Effective Study of the Economic and Legal Aspects of Labor Relations, 11/5/29 (40–50 K per year); Cook, Tentative Draft of General Document for Mr. Baetjer to Accompany the Sample Minimum Set Ups for Different Fields, 11/15/29 (curiously "law administration" not in list of fields, rather penciled in later); Oliphant, A Sample Minimum Set Up for an Effective Study of Policies and Techniques of Legislation, 11/22/29 (52–57 K per year); Cook, A Sample Minimum Set Up for the Effective Study of Criminal Law and Criminology, 11/29/29 (50 K per year), LCM. None of these budgets ever got used in fundraising material, after Yntema, acting in Marshall's absence, noticed how the total sums requested amounted to more than that necessary for the still unsecured endowment and were in any case likely to be viewed as extravagant in most circles outside the largest foundations. Yntema, Memorandum concerning Institute Finances, 4/7/30, LCM.

366. See Institute of Law, *The Story of the Institute of Law*; Institute of Law, *Authoritative Views on the Need for the Institute of Law*; Institute of Law, *Law as a Social Instrument*, IOL.

367. Walker, "Fitting Law to Life"; Kent, "Johns Hopkins Grapples with the Law"; Johnson, "How Does the Law Work?"

368. See *Baltimore Sun*, 3/4/30.

369. Ames to Max Mason (President, Rockefeller Foundation), 4/1/30, ROC.

370. See Hammond, Final Report on the Campaign for the Institute of Law at Johns Hopkins University, 6/7/30, p. 30, IOL.

371. Yntema, Institute Memorandum to Mr. Baetjer, 4/25/30, LCM, which, as Yntema put it, had found that, "The experience of the past two years indicates that to secure a sufficient endowment will probably be a long-time undertaking."

372. Oliphant, Memorandum Re: Budget for Survey of Litigation, 5/19/30, LCM.

373. Marshall, Comments on the Proposed Budget, n.d. [5/19/30], accompanying Marshall to Ames, 5/19/30 (tendering budget), LCM.

374. Marshall to Ames, 5/19/30, LCM. The increase was apportioned as follows: $20,000 for Oliphant, half of it for research workers that he now found necessary because of the "mechanical part" of reporting cases from large companies and large law firms and to recruit lawyers in smaller practices (see Oliphant, Memorandum Re: Budget for Survey of Litigation, 5/19/30, LCM); $10,000 for Maryland; $15,000 for Ohio; $5,000 to expand work into Louisiana; and $25,000 to establish a central

statistical unit for the entire enterprise, all justified on the ground of the need "to maintain our grip on this field. . . . Any sign of faltering . . . this next year . . . would not only handicap us in further research . . . , but would also seriously restrict our chances for securing funds." Marshall to Ames, 5/19/30, LCM.

375. Marshall, Thoughts, n.d. [4/30], LCM.

376. By going after endowment in large sums and forming the always proposed group of contributing associates.

377. Ibid. (emphasis in original).

378. Tentative Agenda for Social Service Research Council Conference on Legal Research, Hanover (N.H.), 8/29–9/2/30, SSRC. Henry Bates, Joseph Beale, Clark, Frankfurter, and Llewellyn were there. In defense of the faculty it was well known that the council had little, if any, money to give away. Marshall, Actions of Social Science Research Council, 4/6/29, LCM.

379. See French, *A History of the Johns Hopkins University*, pp. 375, 413–14. Yale was in no better shape. See "Underhill Moore," p. 272.

380. See Griswold to Ames, 6/21/30, enclosing Frances P. Garvan to Griswold, 6/20/30, IOL.

381. Ames to Willard, 10/9/30, IOL.

382. If for no other reason that Baetjer had pledged $100,000 to the Institute, the second largest pledge in hand.

383. See Marshall to Ames, 10/29/30, HOP.

384. Max Mason to Ames, 12/8/30, ROC.

385. Edmund E. Day to Marshall, 12/10/30, ROC.

386. See Budget, Study of Judicial Administration in Ohio, 10/8/30 ($135,000 pledged, three largest pledges total only $25,000), IOL.

387. See, for example, Baetjer to Ames, 6/2/30 (recognizes that approach is not working; slogs on), IOL.

388. See Marshall, Thoughts, n.d. [spring 1930], LCM.

389. See Hammond to Ames, 10/29/30, HOP.

390. Hammond to Ames, 11/5/30, HOP.

391. See Marshall to Willard, 11/19/30, HOP; Hammond to Ames, 11/25/30; Ames to David E. Finley (U.S. Treasury official), 3/16/31, IOL. Ames to Marshall, 3/22/31, HOP.

392. See Ames to Joseph C. France, 2/11/31, IOL.

393. See Ames to Marshall, 7/22/31, HOP.

394. Oliphant to Ames, 8/11/31, HOP.

395. If only partially; see subsequent discussion on the Institute's relationship to the Faculty of Philosophy.

396. Ames to Marshall, 11/22/31, HOP.

397. See Cook to Pound, 2/8/33, RPP (however, this letter dates the event as January 1933); Frederick Keppel (President, Carnegie Foundation), Memo, FPK and Professor Marshall, 5/6/32 (quoting Marshall), CAR. Both documents assert that Hopkins had just lost $700,000 in assets. However, it is unlikely that either Cook or Marshall had accurate information and in any event the time of the railway's demise is relatively unimportant, for it can only have been part of the problem. At then current capitalization rates, a $700,000 default would have meant a loss of only $35,000 in income and the problem was clearly more extreme than that. French, *A History of the Johns Hopkins University*, pp. 413–14, indicates that in 1928–29, before the market crash, Hopkins ran a deficit of nearly $30,000; that in 1929–30 it was nearly

$90,000; and that thereafter it grew steadily reaching over $180,000 in 1934–35. My guess is that by 1931–32 Hopkins was facing a deficit of at least $180,000 and probably more, if nothing were done to cut costs.

Cutting back on the Institute was part of cost containment.

398. It might have removed more from the budget to the extent that other items, such as the need for a central statistical unit, could be obliviated as well.

399. Statement of the Present Status of the Institute of Law, the Johns Hopkins University, 3/32, Financial Statement, p. 1, IOL. Considering how important the Institute's financial, situation was from the beginning, it is hard to get an accurate, consistent picture of it in detail. I have pieced together the following round numbers from the indicated sources:

	1928–29	1929–30	1930–31
Budget[a]	?	107,000	171,000
Direct expenditures	54,000[b]	114,000	170,000[c]
Fundraising expenses[d]	28,000	54,000	0
Receipts[c]	61,000	85,000	73,000
Deficit[c]	21,000	83,000	97,000

[a]Marshall to Ames, 5/19/30, LCM.

[b]Budget, 2/28/30, BHG.

[c]Statement of the Present Status of Institute of Law, the Johns Hopkins University, 3/32, Financial Statement, p. 1, IOL.

[d]Budget, 3/29/32–6/30/31, BHG. (This document is misdated and covers 3/29/32–6/30/32. It lists total fundraising costs as $82,000. I have done the necessary allocation and subtraction.)

Even my reconstruction makes sense only if Oliphant was on the Columbia payroll for all of the first year while at work on the write-up of the Columbia curriculum study, since the expenditures for 1928–29 are less than the total salaries for the four faculty, and there were research assistants and typists around from the beginning. And at least Griswold objected to charging the Institute any of the fundraising expenses since the fundraiser raised next to nothing for the Institute. See Griswold to Isaiah Bowman (Ames successor as President), 1/6/37, BHG. Having looked at the work of the fundraiser, I doubt whether it raised much for the general university either. Much of what it had done was little more than good advertising copy editing; for example, Cook's research assistant assembled the materials on possible individual and foundation donors for the fundraiser! See Cook to Ames, 11/22/29, HOP.

400. Ames to Oliphant, 9/14/31, HOP.

401. Jaffin to Schlegel, 11/28/80.

402. Ames to Edmund E. Day, 9/19/31 ("I believe that through the efforts of . . . [leading members of the New York bar] an additional $5,000 can be raised"); Norma S. Thompson (Secretary, Rockefeller Foundation) to Ames, 10/9/31 (notice of grant), ROC.

403. As leading a member of the New York bar as one could find.

404. See Cravath to Russell C. Leffingwell (member of the Foundation's Executive Committee), 10/30/31; Frederick P. Keppel to Oliphant, 10/15/31 (notice of grant), CAR.

405. S. Page Nelson (Secretary to Trustees) to Baetjer, 10/27/31, HOP.

406. See Baetjer to Fred W. Allen (other subcommittee member), 12/3/31 (work to be completed by July 1932), BHG.

407. Oliphant, Survey of Litigation in New York, Studies to Appear during the Academic Year 1931–32, n.d. [12/3/31]; Cook, Study of the Judicial System of Maryland, n.d. [12/3/31], HOP. No similar document exists for Ohio, Marshall having reported the material to Baetjer already. Oliphant noted that all the coding and punching of his case data were done and that similar work on the lawyers' reports was going on. Survey of Litigation in New York, Studies to Appear during the Academic Year 1931–32, n.d. [12/3/31], HOP. He projected that seven studies — three on calendar practice, one each on English pretrial practice, on the costs of litigation, on workmen's compensation, and on methodological problems — would be published during the year. Cook reported that "a very large number of the [civil] cases filed during . . . [the study] period are not yet closed"; indeed less than half of his data was in. Study of Judicial System of Maryland, n.d. [12/3/31], HOP. Criminal cases were similarly far behind and the small claims study had run into sampling problems. Only the divorce study was likely to appear and perhaps one on the public costs of litigation and another on the Public Service Commission. Marshall had collected all or nearly all of his data but almost none had been coded, much less punched, run, and analyzed. Baetjer to Fred W. Allen, 12/3/31, BHG.

408. See Cook and Oliphant to Willard, 12/24/31, WWC.

409. At least four drafts, only one dated, exist in IOL. At first Ames provided for a budget of up to $75,000, the actual amount to be limited to the funds in hand in summer of 1932. Ames, Memo ("The expenses of the Institute of Law . . ."), 12/31/31, IOL. If a smaller sum was raised it would support first Marshall, whose salary was "guaranteed for one more year," and then Yntema, because the University was "obligated" to continue the Ohio study "for one year after the present." Ames was to act as director and if funds for years beyond 1932–33 became available "all questions . . . [as to the] form of organization, the salaries of its staff, personnel, etc." were to be opened for discussion. This proposal was slowly transformed into one making Marshall the Director and letting the faculty "free to establish new connections if this present situation seems to them attended with too great risks." Ames, Memo ("The expenses of the Institute of Law . . ."), n.d. [after 12/31/31], IOL.

410. Ames, Memo ("Because of its conviction"), n.d. [after 12/31/31], IOL.

411. See Cook to Willard, 1/7/32, WWC and HOP.

412. Cook and Oliphant to Willard, 12/24/31, WWC and HOP. This letter was written before Ames's recommendations were known but after it had been learned that the Trustees had even discussed closing the Institute.

413. See Hollander to Ames, n.d. [early 2/32], IOL.

414. See Ames to Newton Baker, 3/10/32, IOL.

415. See Academic Council to Board of Trustees, 2/17/32, IOL. This document and similar ones from the four faculties of the University were never given to the Trustees because Willard asked that they be withheld and assured the relevant groups that he shared their opinion and that opinion would be followed by the Trustees. See Memo ("(1) The persons here present"), n.d. [late 1/32] (recounting earlier events), JHH.

416. See, for example, Department of Political Economy to Ames, 1/15/32, IOL.

417. French, *A History of the Johns Hopkins University*, p. 414.

418. See George G. Vincent, Memorandum of an Interview, 5/13/29, ROC.

419. Department of Political Science to Ames, 3/10/32, IOL.

420. Cook to Willard, 1/16/32, WWC.

421. Ames to Newton Baker (Trustee), 3/10/32 (emphasis added), IOL.

422. See Ames to Willard, 3/16/32, IOL.

423. See Ames to Pound, 3/3/32, RPP.

424. Statement of the Present Status of the Institute of Law, the Johns Hopkins University, 3/32, p. 1, IOL.

425. "Approximately twenty-five graduates of law schools have been trained as research assistants," "[v]arious critical articles and lectures" have served "to expose and subject to analysis the theoretical ideas underlying the work of the Institute," and "an imposing amount of data as to the contemporary administration of justice" have been "accumulated" leading to "the stimulation" of the collection of "judicial statistics," though "one or two years" would be necessary "for a reasonably representative report to be made on the data already in hand" (ibid., pp. 3, 4, 6).

426. Ibid., p. 7.

427. See Statement of the Present Status of the Institute of Law, the Johns Hopkins University, 3/32, Financial Statement, p. 4, IOL.

428. Resolution of Board of Trustees, the Johns Hopkins University, 3/24/32, IOL.

429. See Ames to Griswold, 3/30/32, HOP.

430. See Cook to Ames, 7/6/32, IOL.

431. See Marshall to Guy Moffett (Spellman Fund), 3/29/32 (attempt to save grant application by Ohio and Maryland judicial councils that might seem to be dependent on continuation of Institute), HOP.

432. Excerpt from Mr. M.'s [Max Mason] Diary, 2/3/32, ROC.

433. Minutes of the Rockefeller Foundation, 4/13/32, ROC.

434. Marshall, A Confidential Analysis: The Present Situation and Future Possibilities of the Institute of Law, 4/2/32, pp. 1, 2, 3, HOP.

435. Ibid., pp. 4–5. He clearly preferred the third or fourth alternatives, believing, contrary to what he had said earlier in the report, that "[t]here are a few individuals (whose names should not be put on paper)" who would contribute, and that the "Associates" program could raise $25,000 to $30,000 per year. There was some real pie in the sky as well; small grants might come from foundations and a "modest" guarantee of $30,000 per year for five years would help.

436. Resolution Passed by the Executive Committee of the Board of Trustees, 5/2/32, IOL. The other two members were C. C. Burlingham and Walter S. Gifford (President, American Telephone & Telegraph).

437. See FPK and Professor Marshall, 5/6/32, CAR; Interview, Professor L. C. Marshall et al., 5/6/32, ROC; Marshall to Ames, 5/10/32, HOP.

438. See Hammond to C. C. Burlingham, 7/21/32, IOL.

439. See Marshall, Main Features of a Practical Plan to Maintain and Develop the Institute of Law, n.d. [5/32]; Marshall, Significant Steps in the Planning of the Next Six Months, n.d. [5/32], IOL. These documents were clearly for the meeting with the committee.

440. [Marshall?], The Institute of Law—It's Status and Future, 7/21/32, IOL. This document was sent to Burlingham and Gifford. See Hammond to Walter S. Gifford, 7/21/32, IOL.

441. Cook, Oliphant, and Yntema to Ames, 5/16/32, HOP. Yntema transmitted the letter to the Trustees, Ames, and all the deans. See Ames to Yntema, 5/18/32, IOL.

442. See Cook to Pound, 6/23/32, RPP. Pound suggested that since Frankfurter had been nominated to the Massachusetts Supreme Court his spot on the faculty would

open up and, with some shifting, that would open the professorship in legislation. Pound to Cook, 6/25/32, RPP. Cook was interested (see Cook to Pound, 6/28/32, RPP), but, of course, nothing came of it as Frankfurter turned down the position. See Cook to Pound, 9/1/32, RPP. Pound, however, remained optimistic that something would turn up.

443. See Yntema to Pound, 1/12/32, RPP.

444. See Oliphant to Ames, 5/23/32 (progress), 6/15/32 (success), HOP. For a statement of the later work of this group, see James and Stockman, "The Work of the New York Law Society."

445. See Marshall to Ames, 10/15/33, HOP.

446. That task began with efforts to get the Departments of Justice and Commerce to accept the classification as the basis for the FBI's collection of police reports and the Bureau of Prisons' survey of incarcerations and then of convincing the Census Bureau to do the same in collecting reports on criminal prosecutions. Marshall to Ames, 12/1/32, HOP. Institute of Law, *A Standard Classification of Offenses for Criminal Statistics*, Ohio Bulletin No. 10, is a report to the two departments from an ad hoc committee of which Marshall was chairman. At the same time there was the matter of convincing the states to do the same, a question of working with the various state judicial councils, the National Conference of Judicial Councils, the American Bar Association's Section on the Judiciary, and the Commissioners on Uniform State Laws, which was working on a Uniform Criminal Statistics Act. See Marshall to Ames, 9/28/32, HOP; Marshall, Hotchkiss, Gehlke, *Judicial Criminal Statistics*, Ohio Bulletin No. 11, is a report prepared for the Conference and the Section for a joint meeting held in fall 1932. And, of course, this effort eventually led into that of standardizing statistics in civil cases. See Marshall to Ames, 1/14/33 (reporting meetings at the Department of Justice), HOP.

447. See Marshall to Ames, 12/1/32 (by end of year only 10,000 of 30,000 civil actions will have been run; have separated out studies of municipal courts in Cleveland, Cincinnati, and Columbus), HOP.

448. See Ames to Willard, 11/17/32, IOL.

449. See Marshall to Ames, 11/15/32, HOP.

450. This is peculiar because his budget of $20,000 had room for only "one person of professorial rank . . . plus a couple of research assistants." He spoke of pushing the development of judicial statistics and court organization, of including a few research associates and "a few *really* able, and preferably eminent, persons *not* in the academic world" who would affiliate "without stipend" and "be productive of scholarly pieces of work," and of using the fundraising plan focused around the "Associates in law" scheme he and the faculty had pushed earlier. Ibid.

451. Ames to Willard, 11/17/32, IOL.

452. Report of Meeting Held at the Home of Dr. Ames, January 23, 1/24/33, HOP. For terms of the opposition, see Memo ("(1) The persons here present"), n.d. [late 1/33]; Arthur O. Lovejoy to Ames, 1/24/33 (Institute "parasitic" on the University; Philosophical Faculty "gravely imperiled"), JHH. The drum beat from all sides was the same: the cost of the Institute is sapping the *real* University. In defense of this position it should be noted that to cope with declining resources the university had stopped filling vacant professorships, stopped promotions, and froze, then cut, all salaries. Still the odor of pushing an unwelcome soul out of a life boat is overwhelming.

453. See Ames to Marshall, 2/7/33, HOP; Ames to Cook, 2/7/33, WWC; Ames to Yntema, 2/7/33, IOL.

454. See Hollander et al. to Ames, 2/15/33 (killing the Institute "a great service to Johns Hopkins"); Ames to Hollander, 2/15/33 (aw shucks, but "the faculties of the University are really *the* University"), JHH.

455. Ames to Cook, 2/7/33, WWC.

456. Cook to Ames, 2/8/33, WWC. Due to lack of funds for research assistants and stenographers, the Maryland study was not likely to get past processing the civil data by late spring. Thus no writing would be done. [Cook?], Status of the Maryland Study, n.d. [2/33], WWC.

457. Cook to Willard, 2/8/33; Cook to Griswold, 2/8/33, WWC.

458. See Griswold to Isaiah Bowman, 1/6/37 (Institute "strangled in one room"; "result was brought about by prejudice"; considered resigning from Board of Trustees), BHG.

459. Willard to Cook, 2/10/33, HOP.

460. H. W. Tyler (General Secretary, AAUP) to Ames, 2/16/33, IOL.

461. Cook to Tyler, 2/27/33, WWC.

462. Lovejoy to Tyler, 2/20/33, WWC.

463. Cook to Tyler, 2/27/33, WWC. See also Lovejoy to Tyler, 3/4/33 (but conversations with Trustees were unofficial and "virtually all" Hopkins faculty share my views); Cook to Tyler, 3/9/33 (Trustees official representatives of University; younger men support me), WWC. Cook also took the trouble to send the Chairman of the Association's Committee on Tenure and Privileges an eight-page summary of the events. See Cook to S. A. Mitchell, 4/29/33, enclosing Cook, "The Institute of Law was formed . . . ," n.d., WWC. In the memo Cook argued that what Lovejoy took to be a "resignation" the previous May was in fact nothing of the kind but rather was "intended as no more than a suggestion that it was probably desirable at that time . . . to decide, and make public the decision, to close the Institute's work on June 30, 1933, leaving open the problem of the University's obligations to the professors in case other positions were not available."

464. See Ames to Marshall, 3/40/33, HOP; Pollack, "Memorial of Herman Oliphant," p. 435.

465. See "Walter Wheeler Cook."

466. Cook, "The Institute of Law was formed . . . ," 4/29/33, WWC. See also Oliphant to Griswold, 4/18/33, BHG.

467. See Pound to Cook, 2/10/33, RPP. The post at Harvard evaporated because Frankfurter wished to bring Henry Hart into the public law group. Pound to Cook, 11/25/32, RPP.

468. See Frank to Cook, 12/29/32 (enclosing Jerome N. Frank to Clair B. Hughes [President, Michigan Alumni Association], 12/8/32), WWC; Pound to Cook, 3/7/33, RPP.

469. Oliphant to Griswold, 3/27/33; Yntema to Griswold, 4/5/34, BHG.

470. Cook, "The Institute of Law was formed . . . ," 4/29/33, WWC.

471. See Ames to Frederick P. Keppel, 2/8/33, CAR; Ames to Max Mason, 2/8/33, HOP. See also Willard to Nicolas Murray Butler (President, Columbia University), 4/20/30, ROC.

472. See Ames to Willard, 2/13/33, HOP.

473. Ames to Willard, 6/2/33, HOP.

474. Two on divorce litigation (May, *Divorce Law in Maryland*, Maryland Bulletin No. 4; Marshall and May, *The Divorce Court: Maryland*), one on the Public Service Commission (Burke, *The Public Service Commission of Maryland*), and another by

Marshall himself on criminal litigation (Marshall, *Maryland Trial Court Criminal Statistics, 1930*, Maryland Bulletin No. 3).

475. Calendar practice was published before Oliphant's assistant left (Oliphant and Hope, *A Study of Day Calendars*, New York Bulletin No. 2) and the study of the public costs of justice as well (Chase and Klaus, *Expenditures of Public Funds in the Administration of Civil Justice in New York City*, New York Bulletin No. 3). Greenbaum finished his study of English pretrial practice (Greenbaum and Reade, *Kings Bench Masters and English Interlocutory Practice*).

476. In the first of the two years, it published two pieces on criminal litigation (Hotchkiss and Gehlke, *Uniform Classifications for Judicial Criminal Statistics*; Marshall, *Comparative Judicial Criminal Statistics: Ohio and Maryland*), one on divorce (May, *Divorce Law in Ohio*, Ohio Bulletin No. 6), one on appellate litigation (Harris, *Draft of Legislation to Provide a Simplified Method of Appellate Review*, Ohio Bulletin No. 9), and two on minor trial courts (Douglass, *The Justice of the Peace Courts of Hamilton County, Ohio*; Yntema, *Draft of a Uniform Municipal Court Act for the State of Ohio*, Ohio Bulletin No. 7); and a bit of history (Amer, *The Development of the Judicial System of Ohio from 1787–1932*, Ohio Bulletin No. 8). In the second, it published studies of receiverships (Billig, *Equity Receiverships in the Common Pleas Court of Franklin County, Ohio*), waiver of jury trial (Martin, *The Waiver of Jury Trial in Criminal Cases in Ohio*), another on appeals (Harris, *Appellate Courts and Appellate Procedure in Ohio*), the public cost of justice (Marshall and Reticker, *The Expenditure of Public Money for the Administration of Justice in Ohio*), inferior courts (Douglass, *The Mayors' Courts of Hamilton County*), and more on divorce (Marshall and May, *The Divorce Court: Ohio*).

477. See "Report of the Faculty of the Institute of Law, 1931–32," pp. 199 (Maryland), 199–200 (Ohio), IOL; Oliphant to E. E. Day, 6/23/32 (New York), ROC.

478. Three were on judicial statistics. Marshall, *Comparative Criminal Statistics: Six States*; Marshall, *The Improvement of Divorce Statistics in Ohio*, Ohio Bulletin No. 12; Marshall, *Judicial Criminal Statistics in Maryland, 1931: Courts of General Criminal Jurisdiction*, Maryland Bulletin No. 5. See also Marshall, "Judicial Statistics in the United States," and Marshall, Hotchkiss, and Gehlke, *Judicial Criminal Statistics*, Ohio Bulletin No. 11.

479. Marshall to Frederick, 5/15/33, CAR.

480. Marshall, *Unlocking the Treasuries of the Trial Courts*.

481. Marshall to Keppel, 5/15/33, CAR.

482. Marshall, *Unlocking the Treasuries of the Trial Courts*, p. 12 n. 16. He received a good deal of support and encouragement from others. See Marshall to Ames, 6/8/33, HOP. Support for the project was sought from the Carnegie Foundation (Marshall to Keppel, 5/15/33, CAR), though eventually none appeared (Keppel to Marshall, 10/30/33, CAR).

483. Cook, "Substance and Procedure."

484. Cook, "The Legal Method"; Cook, "Statewide Studies in the Administration of Justice." He moved the grand scientific method project along some by producing a set of teaching materials; see "Report of the Faculty of the Institute of Law, 1931–32," p. 195, LCM; Cook to Pound, 6/23/32, RPP. These materials were prepared for use in the Northwestern Law School summer session of 1932.

485. With Adler he had completed a draft of their seminal book Michael and Adler, *The Nature of Judicial Proof*. See Michael to Cook, 11/28/31 (tendering manuscript); Cook to Michael, 12/3/31 (demurring; "Mr. Adler and I belong to different schools

of logic"); Michael to Cook, 12/16/31 (don't understand your problem; simply use "principles of implication, equivalence and contradiction"); Cook to Michael, 12/18/31 (fine, but I am interested in "actual processes of right thinking" that include "formal logic"; I object to severing the connection "between the forms of validity and the attainment of validated knowledge"); Michael to Cook, 12/21/31 (not understanding, or perhaps understanding too well: but from your conflicts work, I thought you were interested in "formal analysis"); Cook to Michael, n.d. [12/31] (I am interested in formal analysis, but only as "an integral part of the broader field"), WWC. He also staged a radio dialogue on law with Llewellyn and Frank. Llewellyn, Cook, and Frank, *How the Law Functions.*

486. Yntema, "The Jurisdiction of the Federal Courts in Controversies between Citizens of Different States."

487. Yntema, "The Implications of Legal Science."

488. Oliphant, "Parallels in the Development of Legal and Medical Education."

489. Oliphant, "The Public and the Law" (remember law can only reduce crime somewhat, increase in civil litigation is a function of new technology and shift to credit economy).

490. Oliphant, "Facts, Opinions, and Value-Judgments," p. 127.

491. Ibid., pp. 127, 128, 129, 130.

492. Ibid., pp. 131, 132, 133.

493. Ibid., pp. 134, 135, 136.

494. Ibid., pp. 137, 138–39, 137.

495. See Oliphant to Ames, 2/9/33, HOP.

496. See Cook to Carroll T. Bond, 2/9/33, WWC.

497. Cook to Pound, 2/8/33, RPP.

498. See Marshall to David H. Stevens (Rockefeller Foundation), 2/9/33, ROC; Frederick Keppel to Marshall, 5/22/33 (about position at Duke), CAR.

499. Marshall to Ames, 5/26/33, HOP.

500. Ames to Marshall, 6/14/33, HOP.

501. Ibid.

502. Ibid. This position did not sit well with Cook. See Cook to Joseph N. Ulman (Chief Judge, Baltimore Superior Court), 6/30/33, IOL.

503. See Ames to Marshall, 6/14/33, HOP.

504. See Marshall to Ames, 10/17/33, HOP.

505. Blackburn, *The Administration of Justice in Franklin County, Ohio*; Gehlke, *Criminal Actions in the Common Pleas Courts of Ohio.*

506. "Leon C. Marshall."

507. Yntema to Griswold, 4/5/34, BHG.

508. See Cook to Pound, 10/9/33; Pound to Cook, 10/21/33, RPP.

509. Cook to Pound, 1/16/34, RPP. Cook served as general secretary from fall 1933 till fall 1935.

510. See Yntema, "Walter Wheeler Cook," p. 353.

511. See Griswold to Isaiah Bowman, 1/6/37; Griswold to James B. Landis, 9/28/37, BHG.

512. See Ames, Dear ——: ("In accordance with action . . ."), n.d., [spring 1933], IOL.

513. See P. Stewart Macaulay (Secretary of the University) to Isaiah Bowman, 3/14/39, IOL; Minutes of the Board of Trustees, 6/8/39, HOP. Marshall concurred in this action. See Isaiah Bowman to Newton D. Baker, 5/1/39, HOP.

514. Frederick Keppel to Marshall, 10/30/33, CAR.

515. Griswold to Isaiah Bowman, 1/6/37, BHG.

516. Llewellyn, "On What Makes Legal Research Worthwhile," pp. 400–401.

517. Yntema, "The Rational Basis of Legal Science," p. 951.

518. Lazerson, "In the Halls of Justice the Only Justice Is in the Halls."

519. Oliphant, *Study of Civil Justice in New York*, New York Bulletin No. 1.

520. Marshall, *Maryland Trial Court Criminal Statistics, 1930*, Maryland Bulletin No. 3.

521. Bettman et al., *Ohio Criminal Statistics, 1931*.

522. It is difficult to assess the contribution of each to the project. My guess is that Marshall and his faithful assistants Elva Marquard and Ruth Reticker did the statistical work; May, the rest.

523. See Ulmann et al. (Advisory Committee), "Foreword," p. 14.

524. Marshall and May, *The Divorce Court: Maryland*, pp. 208–9. Though, of course, both numbers were small. Only 5 percent of the separation cases went through contested hearings; in divorce cases, the figure was 2 percent.

525. Ibid., pp. 214, 220–21, 222, 312–15, 173–75, 167–198. A few additional interesting results appeared upon careful analysis. The data documented the tendency of divorce to bulk large in the early years of marriage and strongly suggested that the old adage that childlessness is a cause of divorce was unlikely to be true since divorce often came before any but rabbits could have successfully bred. And the careful reader would have noticed the existence of a rather small specialist divorce bar, in Baltimore at least. Ibid., pp. 60–65, 29. The Ohio data took the same general outline, though curiously even fewer actions were formally contested. See Marshall and May, *The Divorce Court: Ohio*, pp. 243–45. Unfortunately, the resulting volume was somewhat drier, in part due to the lack of the wonderful transcripts in Maryland that were used with great effectiveness.

526. Gehlke, *Criminal Actions in the Common Pleas Courts of Ohio*, pp. 33, 53, 33–54, 236, 162, 88, 80–81.

527. And the actual results of the criminal court studies that pushed the statistical project forward were on the whole enlightening, though they show the same sense of being overwhelmed by the detailed variations that other, narrower studies exhibit. Significant differences between Ohio and Maryland with respect to the incidence of trial and of nonjury trial and with respect to the use of incarceration in sentencing were disclosed. Marshall, *Comparative Judicial Criminal Statistics: Ohio and Maryland*, pp. 25–35. The relative dominance of the prosecutor; the uniform disappearance, except in cases involving violence, of trial as a method of determining guilt; the difficulty of proving guilt in embezzlement and fraud cases as opposed to other kinds of property crimes; and the refusal to use incarceration as a penalty in cases involving offenses against families and children are all striking when even broader data are considered. Marshall, *Comparative Judicial Criminal Statistics: Six States, 1931*, pp. 31–33, 42, 48–49, 56–57. Thus, on the whole, the work was good and useful, though here of course, bewilderment at local variation again bulked large (see, e.g., ibid., p. 31) and, in its own way, was debilitating to effective presentation.

528. Burke, *The Public Service Commission of Maryland*.

529. Douglass, *The Justice of the Peace Courts of Hamilton County, Ohio*. See also Douglass, *The Mayors' Courts of Hamilton County, Ohio* (not as good but a similar minor criminal jurisdiction).

530. Only Burke, *The Public Service Commission of Maryland*, is an exception; it dealt with a single tribunal.

531. Marshall and May, *The Divorce Court: Maryland*, pp. 57, 266, 306.

532. Marshall and May, *The Divorce Court: Ohio*, p. 21.

533. Douglass, *The Justice of the Peace Courts in Hamilton County Ohio*, p. 52.

534. Not surprisingly the recommendations appended to the study would, if enacted, have eliminated most of the variation. Ibid., pp. 113-15.

535. Gehlke, *Criminal Actions in the Common Pleas Courts of Ohio*, pp. 3-8.

536. Gehlke knew generally about this problem but was limited to working only with crude measures of unreliability such as differences between means, median, and quartiles.

537. Blackburn, *The Administration of Criminal Justice in Franklin County, Ohio*, clearly does not measure up to the rest of the work, modeled as it is on the earlier crime surveys. The same is true of Martin, *The Waiver of Jury Trial in Criminal Cases in Ohio*, though here the problem is not the antique nature of the technique but the failure to exploit a very rich data source — answers to open-ended questionnaires — in the search for a recognized statistical relationship between support for the waiver, an open question at that time, and other attitudes about criminal justice. Billig, *Equity Receiverships in the Common Pleas Court of Franklin County, Ohio*, is a very good piece of research, marred, I think, by a lack of sympathy for the problems it is exploring and a clear preference for the federal forum as more cost-effective to creditors. Its picture of a receivership bar full of vultures is quite devastating. Marshall and Reticker, *The Expenditure of Public Money for the Administration of Justice in Ohio, 1930*, is a monument to the public cost accountant's art, though it makes an elementary mistake by first following governmental conventions and expensing capital projects and then estimating capital costs for capital projects already completed. It is a matter of taste whether one prefers its extensive presentation of detailed methodology or the financial statement form of Chase and Klaus, *Expenditures of Public Funds in the Administration of Civil Justice in New York City*.

538. See Cook, Law and Reason, n.d. [1934], WWC.

Cook made one more attempt to set forth his views on science and law; see Cook, "Walter Wheeler Cook," in Kocourek's *My Philosophy of Law*. This piece is no more satisfactory than the earlier efforts when it makes the same arguments as before, this time in the name of "scientific empiricism," "the Unified Science movement," and Dewey's ideas about ethical questions as empirical. It is a sad, defensive, and angry work, which suggests that Cook's last years were not intellectually rewarding.

539. See Chapter 5.

540. Robert Gordon kindly forced me to see this.

541. See E. E. Day to Raymond B. Fosdick, 2/26/30, ROC.

542. See Wheatley, *The Politics of Philanthropy*, pp. 162-63, 161-62. All of the confusion that Griswold felt over which Rockefeller entity to speak to was a reflection of the coming change.

543. The former quotation is from Beardsly Ruml, the latter from Steven C. Wheatley. Both are found in Wheatley, *The Politics of Philanthropy*, pp. 161, 162. The discussion so far in the paragraph summarizes Wheatley's sensible argument.

544. See Rose, Memo of a meeting with Doctor W. W. Cook, 5/14/27, ROC.

545. See French, *A History of the Johns Hopkins University*, pp. 190-91, and generally, for the contrast in tone between the description of the Ames and Goodnow presidencies. French was a part of the Philosophical Faculty's "party."

546. Fred Konefsky made this point to me.

547. See "Jacob Harry Hollander."

548. See "Arthur O. Lovejoy."

549. Griswold blamed Donald Hammond, the professional fundraiser who was ultimately attached to the President's staff, for the animosity to the Institute and for, in effect, duping Ames. See Griswold to Isaiah Bowman, 1/6/37, BHG. I can find no evidence to support or disprove this assertion and have thus chosen to ignore it, though my hunch is that it is incorrect. Griswold was more accurate when at the time of the 1932 trustees' meeting he squarely blamed Ames's hostility to the Institute for much of its internal problems. Griswold to Willard, 3/16/32, BHG.

550. See [Ames], "Foreword," n.d. [1930–31] ("It is now about six years . . ."), IOL.

551. Clearly Ames would not have kept Cook whose summer school teaching obviously rankled him and thus led to the inclusion of the clause in prohibiting work for outside remuneration in the reorganization plan. See Cook to Ames, 6/6/32 (request to teach during the academic year at Howard Law School where the father of his first wife was once University President), HOP; no such request exists for teaching at Northwestern for, of course, Cook would have felt that his summers were his own to do with as he pleased.

552. French, *A History of the Johns Hopkins University*, p. 416.

553. Ames to Hollander, 2/15/32 (emphasis in original), JHH.

554. Griswold to Ames, 3/31/32, BHG.

555. The history of that business (Kent, *The Story of Alex, Brown & Sons*, pp. 172, 174) peculiarly slights this effort with the observation that many public banks failed but few private ones and that, "[l]ike the rest of the investment banking community, Alex, Brown & Sons suffered severely in the early 1930's from the depreciation of assets and the loss of operating revenue."

556. Statement of the Present Status of the Institute of Law, the Johns Hopkins University, 3/32, IOL.

557. Minutes of Staff Conference, 11/28/30, ROC. The speaker was Edmund E. Day. Marshall saw this too. See Marshall, Thoughts, n.d. [3/30], LCM.

558. Cook to Hutchins, 11/16/29, WWC; Oliphant to Angell, 6/7/29, HOP.

559. George H. Jaffin saw Pound as the main sniper at Harvard and emphasized his Realist article as evidence. Jaffin to Schlegel, 11/28/30. That is possible, though I tend to doubt it since Cook and Yntema were both friends of Pound.

560. See Newton Baker to Ames, 9/20/29 (Cook deeply philosophical but impractical), IOL.

561. See Griswold to Willard, 5/30/30, IOL.

562. See Marshall, Memorandum to Mr. W. W. Cook, 11/13/29, LCM.

Chapter 5

1. See *Conference on the Aims and Methods of Legal Research*; Abe Fortas to Bernard Berelson (Director, Behavioral Science Division, Ford Foundation), 2/17/55 (work on the jury study "the type of collaborative research to which we aspired at the Yale Law School . . . but which we did not attain"), FRD.

2. See, for example, Cavers, "Comment."

3. But see Beutel, *Some Potentialities of Experimental Jurisprudence*, pp. 105–14.

4. See, for example, Berelson to H. Rowan Gaither (Associate Director, Ford Foun-

dation), Memo, Law and The Behavioral Sciences, 5/19/52 (interesting because when it speaks of earlier empirical research it refers to "Yale in the Robinson-Arnold era," a misconstruction that allowed for the observation that there was "an orientation upon teaching and general formulation and relatively little emphasis upon actual field work and research"); Dyke Brown (Associate Director, Ford Foundation) to Gaither and Berelson, 4/18/52 (recounting comments at visits to major law schools), FRD (grant 52-151).

5. For a revealing account of Hoover's policies as Secretary of Commerce, see Rothbard, "Essay."

6. See, for example, President's Committee on Social Trends, *Recent Social Trends*, discussed extensively in Karl, "Presidential Planning and Social Science Research."

7. See Haber, *Efficiency and Uplift*.

8. See generally Boorstin, *The Americans: The Democratic Experience*, pp. 165–244.

9. For a recounting of this process of specialist separation in a single discipline, see Furner, *Advocacy and Objectivity* (economics); for more general accounts, see Haskell, *The Emergence of Professional Social Science*; Ross, *The Origins of American Social Science*. See also Bernard and Bernard, *Origins of American Sociology*; Buck, *The Social Sciences at Harvard*.

10. Yale's Department of Economics, Sociology, and Government is a good example of the halfway stage in the fragmentation of the social sciences. Psychology did not split off from philosophy at Yale until 1927.

11. See Bannister, *Sociology and Scientism*. Interview with Dorothy Swaine Thomas, 6/3/75.

12. Social Science Research Council, *Methods in Social Science, a Case Book*, is a good example of such a work.

13. On a medical education, see Stevens, *American Medicine and the Public Interest*; on legal education, Stevens, *Law School*.

14. See Wheatley, *The Politics of Philanthropy*; Lagemann, *The Politics of Knowledge*.

15. See *A History of Columbia College on Morningside*; Kelley, *Yale: A History* (1974); French, *A History of the Johns Hopkins University*. See generally Veysey, *The Emergence of the American University*.

16. On the history of the American Law Institute, see Hull, "Restatement and Reform"; Goodrich and Wolkin, *The Story of the American Law Institute*. These authors would, however, rather strongly disagree with my characterization of the ALI program. Brown, *Lawyers, Law Schools and the Public Service*, p. 243 n. 1, is some support for my position.

17. "Yale Experience," pp. 558–67.

18. Then to scrounging for free assistants from the government.

19. Interview with Jane Moore, 5/19/76. The records of the Institute bear this out. See Moore to May, 5/10/37 (over $3,000 spent to date), IHR. See also Moore to Angell, 5/18/36, JRA.

20. Yale did likewise though with less brutal effect. See "Yale Experience," p. 573.

21. See ibid., pp. 477–96, 499, 573–74.

22. See, for example, Arnold, Smith, and Thomas, Memo, 11/27/31, UMY. The suggestions included evidence studies, studies of the relationship between taxation and saving, and studies of state Blue Sky laws.

23. "Yale Experience," pp. 558–67.

24. The participants in the Law School's periodic exodus to Washington included Arnold, Clark, George Dession, Douglas, Fortas, Walton Hamilton, Howard Marshall, Harry Schulman, and Sturges. Some, like Fortas and Marshall, never returned to Yale; others worked anywhere from just a summer to a year in Washington.

25. For an explanation of why this was the case, see Schlegel and Trubek, "Charles E. Clark and the Reform of Legal Education."

26. The growth of the committee system can be seen only by patiently reviewing the minutes of the Law School's *weekly* faculty meetings for the period of Clark's deanship, a job that reminds one how trivial one's own faculty politics must be.

27. See, for example, Clark to Wickersham, 10/2/31; Clark to Sam Bass Warner, 1/25/33, CCB. For examples of similar efforts with respect to the bar survey, see Clark to Llewellyn, 3/4/36; Clark to Corstvet, 6/8/37, CCB.

28. See Schick, *Learned Hand's Court*, p. 242 (although Schick emphasizes Clark's quarrelsomeness); Douglas, *Go East, Young Man*, pp. 170–71; interview with Dorothy Swaine Thomas, 6/3/75. Compare Rodell, "For Charles E. Clark"; Rostow, "Judge Charles E. Clark."

29. Moore and Clark fought repeatedly. See, for example, Thomas W. Farnam to Angell, 4/20/36 (detailing attempts to mediate a fight between the two over research assistants; "This will be my last effort to get these two contrary characters together"), JRA. Moore believed that Clark's "temperament" resulted in "leadership and administration" that was "morale-destroying." Moore to Corbin, 4/28/39, UMY. Clark, on the other hand, was more charitable, at least in public. See Clark, "Underhill Moore." I doubt that the two men could ever have gotten along, but their relationship was not helped by the fact that Moore's salary was greater than Clark's (see Clark to Charles Seymour [Provost], 2/10/34, JRA) and that Moore bought the house next door which was larger and up the hill. See Clark, "Memories of My Father," pp. 161–62.

30. Jack Hyman contributed this felicitous description of this aspect of Clark's style of leadership.

31. For a look at these ideas, see Schlegel and Trubek, "Charles E. Clark and the Reform of Legal Education."

32. Clark to Filmer S. C. Northrup, 1/10/48, CCL. See also Clark to Ruth Field, n.d. (written in response to Simpson and Field, "Law and the Social Sciences"), CCL.

33. See Leon Green to Schlegel, 6/4/75, not that the observation really needs any support.

34. Put another way, Clark was not faced with a problem of "wet tinder" such that his job as dean might have been described as lighting fires. Clark's faculty was more like late summer chaparral. The danger of brush fires was always present and the major problem was that, like most brush fires, the faculty burned very hot but not for very long — other than Corbin and Moore, few men on Clark's faculty were known for their sustained scholarship. But compare Angell to Clark, 11/17/31 ("The moment you appear to falter, or lose heart, your colleagues will instantly be unfavorably affected"), JRA.

35. See Foundation for Research in Legal History, *A History of the School of Law, Columbia University*, p. 250; "Underhill Moore," p. 308.

36. See, for example, Moore to Ruth Arrington, 1/30/36; Moore to Eugene V. Rostow, 2/27/36, UMY. Friedrich Kessler to Schlegel, 2/10/77; Sussman to Schlegel, 10/1/76 (taped interview). Clark, "Underhill Moore," pp. 189, 191.

37. Interview with Jane Moore, 5/19/76, wholly born out throughout the Moore Papers.

38. Douglas, "Underhill Moore," p. 188.

39. Sturges to Moore, 3/29/39, UMY.

40. Gilmore to Schlegel, 9/19/76; Kessler to Schlegel, 2/10/77. Compare Moore to G. H. Robinson, 7/11/30, UMY. (In comments about a planned casebook, Moore noted that "your book should deal for the most part with the minute problems arising today. The general principles of today are ... general descriptions of the way in which the minute problems of yesterday were settled.")

41. Gilmore to Schlegel, 9/10/76; Kessler to Schlegel, 2/10/77.

42. "Underhill Moore," pp. 310-11.

43. Moore to Eugene V. Rostow, 3/19/41, UMY.

44. "Underhill Moore," pp. 310-11.

45. Donald Slesinger provided this description of the activities of all of the Realists at Yale. Interview, 7/8/75. It fits Moore's work better than that of anyone else.

46. See n. 29. Compare James William Moore to Clark, 11/11/41 (suggesting that Underhill Moore led the forces opposing Clark's teaching of procedure at Yale to fill in for J. W. Moore who had taken a year's leave of absence to teach at Texas), CCL; Moore to Corbin, 4/28/39 (referring to a deanship candidate as having a temperament such that "his leadership and administration would be afflicted with the same morale-destroying defects which have marred Judge Clark's deanship"), UMY. Sussman to Schlegel, 10/1/76 (taped interview).

47. Interview with Jane Moore, 5/19/76; interview with Emma Corstvet Llewellyn, 8/19/75. See, for example, Arnold to Moore, 10/21/36, UMY.

48. See Moore to Corbin, 4/28/39, UMY.

49. The other alternatives were mostly out of the question. Edwin Borchard seems to have been a bit of an outcast at Yale and was extremely jealous of Moore's special arrangements for research assistance. See Clark to Thomas W. Farnam, 4/27/36, JRA. Walton Hamilton opposed empirical research generally. Interview with Dorothy Swaine Thomas, 6/3/75. Roscoe Turner Steffen, "a man of great resentments," was embittered by the arrival of Moore and Douglas to teach in what he considered to be his field. Interview with Fleming James, Jr., 6/11/75. William Reynolds Vance, whom Moore had known at least since 1912, actively disliked Moore's work. See Vance to E. C. Coker, 10/28/31; Coker to Moore, 11/5/31, UMY. Ernest G. Lorenzen, who had been a colleague at Wisconsin, seems to have kept to himself. And that left Wesley A. Sturges, who, although a former student, seems not to have been a good friend. I have been unable to learn why.

50. See "Underhill Moore," pp. 313-14.

51. The key to recognizing this friendship is address. Corbin was the only faculty member Moore addressed by his first name.

52. "Yale Experience," pp. 492-93, 503.

53. Allan Axelrod to Schlegel, 10/12/76.

54. See Moore to Charles J. Tilden (Yale, Department of Engineering), 11/5/36, UMY.

55. Here and in the following pages my interpretation of Moore's career differs markedly from Northrup, "Underhill Moore's Legal Science," which locates the causes for the decline of Moore's research in certain problems with the nature of scientific proof, particularly, with respect to social science. I do not see such considerations in Moore's research; that may well be my blindness, I admit.

56. Interview with Dorothy Swaine Thomas, 6/3/75; interview with Emma Corstvet Llewellyn, 8/19/75. Which is not to say that Moore was capable of doing the

direct manipulation of his own data unaided; he was not. Sussman to Schlegel, 10/1/76 (taped interview).

57. The introduction to Moore and Hope, "An Institutional Approach to the Law of Commercial Banking," pp. 703–5, is a comment on the debate over the adequacy of the traditional system for the classification of legal materials that developed during the curriculum reform debate at Columbia. Moore and Sussman, "Legal Method"; Moore, Sussman, and Brand, "Legal and Institutional Methods Applied to Orders to Stop Payment of Checks: I. Legal Method"; Moore, Sussman, and Corstvet, "Drawing against Uncollected Checks: I," are, taken together, a series of demonstrations of the inadequacy of lawyerly intuitive analysis, traditional doctrinal analysis, and introspective sociological jurisprudence, respectively, to provide answers to legal questions that Moore's institutional method could answer. See Moore, Sussman, and Corstvet, "Drawing against Uncollected Checks: I," p. 3. See also Moore and Sussman, "Legal and Institutional Methods Applied to the Debiting of Direct Discounts: II. Institutional Method," pp. 555–60 (comment on preceding article). Moore and Sussman, "The Lawyer's Law," can also be seen as a part of this attempt to contribute, for it states his own theories. His other attempts, Moore to Cohen, 3/16/31; Moore, Report of Work Done by Underhill Moore and Associates in Connection with the Institute of Human Relations, fall 1934, UMY; Moore and Callahan, "Underhill Moore," pp. 203–5; Moore and Callahan, "Law and Learning Theory," p. 2, are more like bits of guerrilla warfare, but still are aimed at the debates of the time. And there is a none too subtle comment on a jurisprudential issue in the traffic circle study where Moore had the circle in place before the relevant ordinance was adopted and removed while the ordinance was still in effect. This little ploy still infuriated Llewellyn twenty years later. See Llewellyn, "On What Makes Legal Research Worthwhile," p. 400. See "Underhill Moore," p. 285 n. 562.

Unfortunately in his dabblings in jurisprudence Moore's literal-mindedness again led him astray. He took at face value the proposition that the debate was about legal method. His was, so he thought, demonstratively the best, for it was truly scientific. He seems never to have understood that the manifest content of the debate masked a deeper dispute about control of the legal system and thus the degree that its rules reflected all relevant interests. This blindness on his part is nevertheless puzzling because he quite firmly believed in a rather general way in the notion that law is a reflection of class interests. See Moore to Oswald Garrison Villard, 5/10/27, UMY.

Mr. Ernst's position is the result of his harboring a very common preconception. He thinks of the governing group existing in a particular geographical area as consisting of all or most of the people in the area. He thinks that the interests of the governing group are the interests of the inhabitants, and that the ethics of both should be the same. If he abandoned his preconception and were more realistic, he would see the government as only one among a number of groups, such as the United States Steel Corporation, the American Federation of Labor, and the Rockefeller Foundation. Further, he would note that the governing group is much smaller in number than he supposes. He would not expect the interests and ethics of the governing group to be the same as those of the other inhabitants, but would rather expect them to be class interests and class ethics. Consequently he would not be surprised in a case like the Sacco-Vanzetti case, to find many members of the governing group, including the courts, sharing the feelings of the prosecutor, one of their fellow members. Nor would he urge, by argument, the governing group to restrict its power by changing its rules. (Ibid. [said of Ernst, "Deception according to Law"])

This letter was printed as a reply from "A Professor of Law whose name must be withheld," in *Nation* 124 (June 8, 1927): 630.

58. Much less could Moore have known that it would be thirty-five years before the development of a statistical technique powerful enough to readily handle his data, even in simplified form. See James Meeker, The Impact of Law on Behavior: A Re-analysis of Moore and Callahan (unpublished student work). He surely would have been pleased to learn that reprocessing his data with modern techniques of log-linear analysis demonstrates that, after the length of the durational regulation, the next most influential factor in determining parking behavior is a cultural aspect of legitimacy — the appropriateness of the particular regulation in the place where it is imposed.

59. Ames to Willard, 6/2/33, HOP.

60. See Griswold to Isaiah Bowman, 1/6/37, BHG.

61. Frank to Clair B. Hughes (President, Michigan Law Alumni Association), 12/8/32, WWC.

62. Joseph N. Ulman (Chief Judge, Baltimore Superior Court) to Griswold, 7/3/33, IOL.

63. He, like Moore, may also have been very shy. I am less sure of this though.

64. Interview with Willard Wirtz, 10/29/79; Mary C. Hall (daughter) to Schlegel, 10/30/81; Clark, "Walter Wheeler Cook," p. 342; Foundation for Research in Legal History, *A History of the School of Law, Columbia University*, p. 484 n. 24.

65. Over fifteen years after the event Cook still could complain that Austin W. Scott had once accused Cook of not believing in the possibility of making generalizations (Cook, *The Logical and Legal Bases of the Conflict of Laws*, p. 47). Similarly he could not resist having at a simple nobody who said that Cook's work would not mean much of a change in the results of cases (ibid., p. 186); and his dispute with Arthur O. Lovejoy carried on through an intermediary (see Cook to H. W. Tyler [General Secretary, AAUP], 2/17/33, 3/9/33, refusing to "engage" in a controversy but making "two brief statements," WWC) can only be described as petulant.

66. For example, both Hohfeld and Dewey drop out of the panoply of citation almost as soon as their contributions are acknowledged.

67. Although he did virtually no independent work on the Maryland study in the list of projected publications, he is listed as lead author in each. See "Report of the Faculty of the Institute of Law, 1931–32," p. 200.

68. Interview with Wallard Wirtz, 10/29/79; Clark, "Underhill Moore."

69. I gather this from talking with Willard Wirtz, reading Clark's obituary, and from an interview with Leon Green, 6/19/75. However, none of these sources say this, and Green and Wirtz might even deny it.

70. Jaffin to Schlegel, 11/28/80.

71. Cook's daughter denied that his moves were driven by his desire for a higher salary; Mary C. Hall to Schlegel, 10/30/91. The search for a better place can be seen in Cook to Stone, 2/18/19, WWC; Cook to Moore, 3/24/19, UMC. My guess is that the two motives fit rather well together.

72. Cook to Pound, 6/23/32, RPP.

73. See Cook to Stone, 2/18/19, WWC.

74. Marshall to Griswold, 7/14/33, IOL.

75. Cook to S. A. Mitchell, n.d. (marked "not sent"), WWC.

76. See Memorandum of Interview, held May 13, 1929 at 61 Broadway etc., ROC. Interview with George H. Jaffin, 5/25/81.

77. Jaffin to Schlegel, 11/28/80.

78. See Hammond, Final Report on the Campaign for the Institute of Law at the Johns Hopkins University, 6/7/30, IOL.

79. Jaffin to Schlegel, 11/28/80. See also Cook, Memo, 3/20/29 (budget for his project on indigent criminal defendants showing need to hire principal investigator), LCM.

80. Interview with Paul Douglass, 10/10/80.

81. See generally Chapter 4.

82. See, for example, Ames to Marshall, 5/26/33, HOP.

83. See, for example, Marshall and Yntema, *Outline Statement concerning State-Wide Studies of Judicial Administration*, p. 2.

84. See, for example, Marshall, *Judicial Statistics*; Marshall, *Judicial Criminal Statistics in Maryland*; Marshall, Hotchkiss, and Gehlke, *Judicial Criminal Statistics*.

85. See Marshall to Ames, 9/28/32 ("Mr. May's participation in . . . [the divorce study] has been competent and helpful"), HOP.

86. See, for example, Marshall to David Stevens, 2/9/33, ROC.

87. David Stevens to Marshall, 2/14/33 (quoting Marshall), ROC.

88. Interview with Jane Moore, 5/18/76.

89. Interviews with George H. Jaffin, 1/10/81, 5/25/81, support this characterization.

90. See Oliphant, Considerations Preliminary to Next Steps, 12/2/28; Oliphant, Predraft of a Memorandum, 12/16/29, LCM.

91. Interview with George H. Jaffin, 5/25/81; Jaffin to Schlegel, 11/28/80.

92. In this he reminds me most of Thurman Arnold, who also finished his career in a Washington practice.

93. Yntema to Frankfurter, 11/27/29 (misdated, actually 11/7/29), FFP.

94. My colleague, Wade J. Newhouse, once a student at Michigan, provided me with a vivid depiction of Yntema's teaching style.

95. Interview with George H. Jaffin, 5/25/81; Jaffin to Schlegel, 11/28/80.

96. This is apparent from his markings on Oliphant, Considerations Preliminary to Next Steps, 12/2/28, LCM.

97. Jaffin to Schlegel, 10/19/81, asserts that it was obvious that Marshall needed a lawyer to help with the Ohio study. That is probably true but does not explain why that lawyer was Yntema. Perhaps it was just the well-known phenomenon of senior partners levying on their juniors.

98. See Schlegel and Trubek, "Charles E. Clark and the Reform of Legal Education."

99. William O. Douglas may or may not fit the pattern.

100. The same seems to me to be true of a number of recent academic fads — sociobiology comes first to mind. The limiting case would surely be the law and economics scholarship of the present era. Posner and the founders of law and economics were classic malcontents, though of a different political persuasion. Would such economics scholarship have fed the Realists' malcontent had it "just happened" along? That seems doubtful, and not just because of the conservative politics of the law and economic malcontents. By focusing on the rules of law, law and economics fits with the law professor's professional self-image in ways that social science does not. It thus does not feed the malcontent in the way social science did and thus was not as difficult for the legal academy to absorb. But here I anticipate my argument.

101. These materials have a long history. They were begun while Cook was at Yale in the 1920s. See Cook, "Modern Movements in Legal Education" (describing some of the contents). The first mimeographed edition I have found is Cook, *Readings on Legal Method* (1931), which Cook used when teaching his course in the political science department at Hopkins and at the Northwestern Law School summer session that year. An outline of an earlier edition exists — Cook, "Readings on Jurisprudence and the Philosophy of Law (1927)," WWC — as does a complete, later edition, Cook, *Readings on Legal Method* (1940). All editions consist of a selection of cases plus excerpts from articles or books by Holmes, Gray, Beale, Dewey, Cardozo, Pound, and other lesser known writers. Cases clearly dominate the materials. Actual materials by scientific writers were treated as "collateral" readings. By today's standards, the materials are unexceptionable. When first presented, Pound, Beale, and William Draper Lewis all found them unsuitable for law students but good for prospective law teachers; see Pound, Beale, and Lewis, "Comments," pp. 51, 54, 55.

102. All of interest analysis in its many variants is right there in the articles for anyone to pick up. The genius of David Cavers, Brainerd Currie, and others was to do the picking and work it out.

103. The second of these two points — the creation of new premises — was constantly troublesome because in law the debate was focused around the syllogism. Thus, all the confusion in the jurisprudential literature between perceiving the facts differently or changing the category — that is, altering the minor or major premise — could have been avoided if everyone had given up on the syllogism and looked at thought as Dewey wanted them to, as a process without the three Aristotelian parts.

104. Llewellyn, *The Common Law Tradition*, pp. 509–10.

105. See Dewey to Cook, 2/5/31, WWC. In this favorable comment on Cook's piece about *Law and the Modern Mind*, Dewey nowhere mentions this problem with the piece, though he catches two modest errors in Cook's discussion.

106. This understanding still is reflected in the practitioner's distinction between the law that the schools are to teach and the practice that is not law that one learns outside of law school.

107. Thus it was Holmes's suggestion, not Freund's, that first mucked up the boundary between law and political science. Law had always seen itself from the inside whereas political science had looked at law from the outside.

108. Any doubt that this was Cook's understanding should be eliminated by looking at who was hired at the Institute. Cook and Oliphant wanted Moore to join them. Not only was he a big name, he wanted to do empirical research; Yntema really did not. Only on a generalized notion that anything could be done scientifically could one substitute Yntema, a scholar in historical and comparative law, for a confirmed empiricist.

109. These are most fully set out in Pound, *Jurisprudence*, 3:8–9. The original formulation is Pound, *Introduction to American Law*, and Pound, *Introduction to the Philosophy of Law*.

110. The classic citation is Kolko, *The Triumph of Conservatism*.

111. See Auerbach, *Unequal Justice*, for the whole, sad story.

112. Douglas to Hutchins, 4/7/34, RMH.

113. Oliphant's introduction was surely what was generally read. Interview with Paul H. Douglass, 10/10/80; interview with George H. Jaffin, 5/25/81.

114. Oliphant and Hope, *A Study of Day Calendars*.

115. See *Report of the Commission on the Administration of Justice in New York*

State. The Commission thanked Oliphant for his help (ibid., p. 8), used his data (ibid., pp. at 88, 640), cited his work (ibid., pp. 345–46, 383, 385, 696–97, 714, 798, 808) and that of his assistants (ibid., pp. 694, 791), and included a study started by an Institute research associate (ibid., p. 963).

116. For the history of this organization, see Harley, "Concerning the American Judicature Society"; Belknap, *To Improve Justice.*

117. I know of no history of this movement, which is the ancestor to all judicial administration work.

118. Yntema, *Draft of a Uniform Municipal Court Act of the State of Ohio.*

119. Harris, *Draft of Legislation to Provide a Simplified Method of Appellate Review.* Both this and Yntema's draft indicate that they were "Prepared with the assistance of a committee of the Judicial Council of Ohio and a committee of the Ohio State Bar Association."

120. There was a difference between the constituency for law reform and that for judicial administration. At least if Paul Douglass's experience is any guide, the judicial administrators were not as openly hostile to research results that were contrary to their needs as were the law reformers, although here Douglass's choice to mouth the correct platitudes in his recommendations, even though those recommendations were contrary to the tenor of the rest of his book, suggests that there may have been limits even with this group.

121. See "Underhill Moore," pp. 253–54, 317 n. 733.

122. See, for example, Moore to Friedrich Kessler, 1/13/42 (remarking that he was "not much interested in the description and analysis of literature" in response to receiving a reprint of Kessler, "Theoretic Basis of Law"); Moore to Frank, 1/5/34 (doubt as to "whether a law school has . . . anything substantial to offer to a student of law"), UMY.

123. See Schlegel and Trubek, "Charles E. Clark and the Reform of Legal Education." It is an interesting exercise in what might have been to contrast the law school envisioned by Moore and possibly Clark with the one envisioned by Cook. In his heart of hearts Cook really wanted Hopkins to set up a law school that would duplicate at least part of Hohfeld's Vital School. It would be a school where law was taught scientifically rather than where legal science was taught, the law school that Columbia never got because Oliphant was not the dean and that Yale was denied, first, by Hohfeld's death and, then, by the legacy of Swan's appointments, Ernest Lorenzen, Edmund Morgan, Edward S. Thurston, William R. Vance. All were a drag on the school. See "Yale Experience," pp. 464–65. It was a novel idea and to this date untried; one could fuse Hohfeld's school of law and his school of jurisprudence and turn out better practitioners. Indeed, it is arguable that this is the same school that Oliphant wanted at Columbia, but that somehow got lost in the press for a school devoted to research. If so, Twinings's distinction between the scientists and the prudents at Columbia is quite overdrawn. I doubt that what a fly on the wall would tell about those two years at Columbia is the same story that Sam Howard, Currie, and Twining have told.

124. See Purcell, *The Crisis of Democratic Theory.*

125. There was a deeper problem here than I have averted to in the text. Though everyone tossed around the slogan, "the law on the books and the law in action," it was never clear what the referend for either was. Pound used cases like *Ives v. South Buffalo Ry.,* 201 N.Y. 271, 94 N.E. 431 (1911), the workman's compensation case, when talking about the problem. The law on the books, due process and freedom of

contract, was fine on the books but in action it kept society from dealing with the problem of industrial accidents. Thus, on Pound's usage the gap is between formal statement and concomitant justification of a rule and the actual circumstances to which that rule is applied. This was not the gap, the space where official action undermines the purposes of case law or legislation, that the Hopkins crew talked of and that I have spoken of in the text. Exactly how the shift from Pound's meaning came about is not clear, but by the time that the Hopkins Institute was formed, the law in action had become the pattern of official action and the gap to be closed, that between act and intent. The importance of the difference is brought firmly to mind by recognizing that Pound's gap cannot be closed. The only thing that can happen is for the courts to realize the gap and so apply the rules in a way that will comport with modern conditions. Pound's slogan is thus not a sociological one but an urging that a different result be had in a case.

126. And not all of it because it was completely unknown. The work of Ehrlich, probably the most narrowly relevant, had been presented at an AALS meeting that both Cook and Moore attended, and Llewellyn knew Weber's work in the original German, though probably not until his trip to lecture in Germany in 1928-29.

127. See Karl, *Charles E. Merriam and the Study of Politics.*

128. Karl, "Presidential Planning and Social Science Research," chronicles Ogburn's work on one of the earliest presidential social science advisory studies. Moore, a friend from Columbia, reacted to it with the observation that the work was "a piece of high class journalism" and wanted to know why Ogburn had bothered to do it. Moore to Ogburn, 9/1/33, UMY.

129. Though I can see reasons to doubt it.

130. Here it is amusing to note the similarity between the reaction of Vance and Lorenzen at Yale, or Dickinson and Fuller, Adler and Cohen, to the Realist's empiricism and that of contemporary legal establishment to critical legal studies. See Carrington, "Of Time and the River"; Johnson, "Do You Sincerely Want to Be Radical?"; and Schwartz, "With Gun and Camera through Darkest CLS-Land." In both cases it is one group of insiders objecting to the adoption of an outsider's perspective by another group of insiders. Here Carrington's solution, that those with the outsider perspective on law should voluntarily leave the legal academy, is predictable — extrude the foreign body — as is the alternative solution, treat CLS, like feminist criticism of law or critical race theory, as if all three were just a few of many possible perspectives on law — recharacterize the opposition and so domesticate it. Whatever the approach, the objective is the same; law must be seen as an insider would.

131. Friedrich Kessler to Schlegel, 2/10/77.

132. Kessler was another of Moore's projects. Although Kessler resisted getting into the "sociology of law" (Moore to Mark A. May, 10/10/34), Moore worked to get money for him to stay at Yale (Moore to Stacy May, 4/19/35), and tried hard to get him a summer school teaching job away from Yale (see, e.g., Moore to Charles K. Burdick, 12/18/35, UMY). The two men did a little joint teaching, even tried to write an article together; however, Kessler's "lack of sympathy" with Moore's approach led to "a mild estrangement" (Kessler to Schlegel, 3/10/77). That estrangement suggests another side to Moore. He was not charitable in intellectual matters. Several years later when thanking Kessler for a copy of his article "Theoretic Basis of Law," Moore could not resist simultaneously remarking that he was "not much interested in the description and analysis of literature." Moore to Kessler, 1/13/42, UMY.

133. Interview with Robert M. Hutchins, 6/20/75.

134. Kessler to Schlegel, 2/10/77, quite directly admits this ambivalence. Gilmore to Schlegel, 9/19/76, does not, but shows it. See also Clark, "Underhill Moore," p. 191.

135. Clark, "Underhill Moore," p. 191; interview with Dorothy Swaine Thomas, 6/3/75.

136. Clark, "Underhill Moore," p. 191.

137. Lasswell and McDougal, "Legal Education and Public Policy."

138. Press Release, Committee on Public Administration, Social Science Research Council, n.d. [ca. 6/42], accompanying Committee on Research in Judicial Administration, *Research in Judicial Administration*. The work is notable for how little credit is given to the Hopkins studies in chapters written by Charles U. Samenow, Clark's assistant on the procedure research.

139. See Ashmore, *Unseasonable Truths*, pp. 302–4.

140. Levi, Chicago Law School Proposal of March 28, 1951, pp. 1, 2, 3, FRD (grant 52-151).

141. Dyke Brown to H. Rowan Gaither, 5/1/51, FRD (grant 52-151).

142. See Hutchins's note "not now" written on Gaither to Hutchins, 6/1/51, FRD (grant 52-151).

143. Although the Foundation wanted no part of Levi's clinic or law revision group (Bernard Berelson, Memo, Research Program in the Behavioral Sciences and the Law, 1/23/52, FRD (grant 52-151), first makes this clear), Levi tried hard to keep those pieces in his proposal. See Levi, Research on Behavioral Sciences and the Law, 3/6/52; Brown to Gaither and Berelson, 4/18/52 (reporting conversation), FRD (grant 52-151).

144. Levi, Research on Behavioral Sciences and the Law, p. 1, 3/6/52, FRD (grant 52-151).

145. The terminology echoes Llewellyn, "Law and the Social Sciences." Llewellyn began teaching at Chicago in the fall of 1951.

146. Levi, Research on Behavioral Sciences and the Law, pp. 2–3, 3/6/52, FRD (grant 52-151).

147. Brown to Gaither and Berelson, 4/18/52 (Chicago ahead but "not so obviously so" as to rule out others); Berelson to Gaither, 5/19/52 (concentrate resources at Chicago); Berelson to Brown, 4/26/52 (same—however, Berelson tried to save the law revision aspects of the proposal), FRD (grant 52-151). It seems likely that Gaither sent Brown to look at other law schools because of Berelson's connection to Levi and Hutchins as a former faculty member at the University of Chicago.

148. Levi, Research on Law and the Behavioral Sciences, 6/10/52, p. 16, FRD (grant 52-151). Undaunted by Ford's lack of interest, however, Levi maintained the importance of access to the clinic and law revision group to gain "empirical and even experimental data" and to "anchor . . . projects to definite remedial changes" and "provide a clear common focus of attention" respectively. Ibid., pp. 4, 3–4. The grant application eliminated funding for the legal clinic and the law revision group.

149. Ibid., p. 1.

150. Ibid., pp. 1, 2, 16. Part of the $400,000 was to work with an advisory committee in planning a "more detailed program."

151. Ibid., pp. 1, 3.

152. Ibid., p. 2.

153. The Docket, Section 1, p. 2 (prepared for board meeting 7/15–7/16/52), FRD (grant 52-151). The staff's recommendation emphasized that: "The program should

result in increased understanding of certain legal problems, the development of methods by which lawyers and behavioral scientists can cooperate on such problems, the development of a group of trained people for work in this field and the application of behavioral science knowledge in the process of law revision."

154. Adopted after starting and then giving up on research on obscenity. See [Levi?], Law and Behavioral Science Program, University of Chicago, 12/21/54, pp. 10–11 (the program's first report to the Foundation as well as an application for further funding); Law and Behavioral Science Program at the University of Chicago, Interim Report to the Ford Foundation, 10/30/58, pp. 10–11, FRD.

155. Law and Behavioral Science Program at the University of Chicago, Interim Report to the Ford Foundation, 10/30/58, p. 10, FRD.

156. Milton Katz (consultant, originally an Associate Director of the Foundation) to William McPeak (Vice-President, behavioral sciences programs), 3/8/55, FRD.

157. See [Levi?], Law and Behavioral Science Program, University of Chicago, 12/21/54, p. 2, FRD. The other principal faculty member was Ernest A. Haggard, Mentschikoff's collaborator on the arbitration project.

158. Ibid., p. 5.

159. Real jury deliberations were also listened to with rather disastrous results; see n. 173.

160. [Levi?], Law and Behavioral Science Program, University of Chicago, 12/21/54, pp. 5–6, FRD.

161. Ibid., p. 8.

162. Ibid., pp. 1, 19, 14, 4.

163. Judge Herbert L. Goodrich (former law school dean and longtime ALI stalwart); Carl Hoveland (psychologist from Yale) and Milton Katz of the Harvard Law School.

164. Goodrich to Berelson, 2/21/55 ("very much impressed"); Berelson, Memo to the File, 2/21/55 (Goodrich calls the project "a dandy," "a beaut"); Hoveland to McPeak and Berelson, 2/28/55 ("ideal situation for social science research"); Berelson, Memo to the File, 2/24/55 (Hoveland says this is a "good project," "set up could not be duplicated elsewhere"); Katz to McPeak, 3/8/55 ("much meat" to project), FRD.

165. Goodrich to Berelson, 2/21/55 ("gives promise of being valuable in the future"); Berelson, Memo to the File, 2/21/55 (Goodrich began skeptical but convinced "good stuff"); Hoveland to McPeak and Berelson, 2/28/55 ("a natural for good research"); Berelson, Memo to the File, 2/24/55 (Hoveland says a "gold mine" because of simpler situation than jury study); Katz to McPeak, 3/8/55 ("less impressive," "some meat and some promise"), FRD.

166. Goodrich to Berelson, 2/21/55 ("Well done" but "do not care so much for it"); Berelson, Memo to the File, 2/21/55 (Goodrich "more skeptical," project "less desirable" but "still worth doing"); Hoveland to McPeak and Berelson, 2/28/55 ("most marginal," "extremely difficult" area to work in); Berelson, Memo to the File, 2/24/55 (Hoveland says "by a good deal the least impressive," "relatively simpleminded approach to a very complex problem"); Katz to McPeak, 3/8/55 ("much less convincing"), FRD.

167. Goodrich to Berelson, 2/21/55, FRD.

168. Joseph McDaniel, Jr. (Secretary of Foundation) to Lawrence Kempton (University of Chicago Chancellor), 7/19/55, FRD. The grant was, however, conditioned on Levi's remaining at the University and continuing to direct the Program.

169. See Law and Behavioral Science Program at the University of Chicago Law School, Interim Report to the Ford Foundation, 10/30/58, pp. 5–6 ("The obstacles were of a technical nature and raised central questions as to whether, through the interview or questionnaire method . . . , a meaningful picture of community attitudes could be obtained where the key reference was to questions as complicated and subtle as those involved in the federal tax structure"), FRD. The project's tombstone is Blum and Kalven, "The Art of Opinion Research." About the same time a small project on interstate inheritance was begun.

170. Law and Behavioral Science Program at the University of Chicago, Interim Report to the Ford Foundation, 10/30/58, pp. 1, 6–7, FRD.

171. Law and Behavioral Science Program at the University of Chicago Law School, Second Interim Report to the Ford Foundation, 3/9/60, p. 8, FRD. Among the more notable are Kalven, "The Jury, the Law and the Personal Injury Damage Award"; Zeisel, "The New York Expert Testimony Project"; Strodtbeck, James, and Hawkins, "Social Status in Jury Deliberations"; Broeder, "The Function of the Jury."

172. See Law and Behavioral Science Project of the University of Chicago Law School, Interim Report to the Ford Foundation, 10/30/58, pp. 10–11; Law and Behavioral Science Project of the University of Chicago Law School, Second Interim Report to the Ford Foundation, 3/9/60, p. 9; Law and Behavioral Science Project of the University of Chicago Law School, Third Interim Report to the Ford Foundation, 11/10/61, p. 9; Law and Behavioral Science Program at the University of Chicago Law School, Fourth Interim Report to the Ford Foundation, 9/19/62, p. 3, FRD. See also Kalven, "Report on the Jury Project." Two were to be on the experimental jury trials; one each, on the posttrial juror interviews, the judge-jury difference study for criminal cases, the similar study for civil cases, and the jury and the defense of insanity; and two collections of essays, one on the public image and reputation of the jury and the other on differences among individual jurors.

173. Note ought to be made of the most infamous product of the jury study, 18 U.S.C. 1508, prohibiting eavesdropping on jury deliberations. The project had surreptitiously, but with permission of court and counsel, taped the deliberations of six juries. In McCarthyite America the righteous were outraged. Senate hearings were held for two days and legislation ultimately resulted. The story is well chronicled in the *New York Times*, 10/6/55, p. 15, col. 3; 10/7/55, p. 51, col. 3; 10/8/55, p. 37, col. 1; 10/13/55, p. 1., col. 1; 10/14/55, p. 1, col. 4.

174. Law and Behavioral Science Program at the University of Chicago Law School, Interim Report to the Ford Foundation, 10/30/58, p. 7, FRD.

175. Ibid. One on decision making in commercial arbitration, another on a survey of decision making in trade associations, a third on decision making in the New York Stock Exchange, and a fourth on "the interrelation of exchanges and trade associations in terms of their function in the market place, the impact of differing functions and different commodities on the type of law-government machinery which has occurred."

176. Jones, "Three Centuries of Commercial Arbitration in New York"; Jones, "An Inquiry into the History of the Adjudication of Mechantile Disputes in Great Britain and the United States"; Jones, "History of Commercial Arbitration in England and the United States."

177. Mentschikoff, "Commercial Arbitration"; Smith, "Commercial Arbitration at the American Arbitration Association." Hal Muir Smith was a research fellow in 1955–56. Years later came the first substantive report. Haggard and Mentschikoff, "Responsible Decision-Making in Dispute Settlement."

178. See Law and Behavioral Science Program at the University of Chicago Law School, Second Interim Report to the Ford Foundation, 3/9/60, FRD.

179. See [Levi?], A Further Note on the Impact on Legal Education, 2/15/55, FRD. In 1958 Harry Kalven observed that the Program "had little impact on regular law students—or even on non-participating faculty once [the projects] were underway. Work in progress proved not to be even an interesting topic for lunch conversations." "There wasn't even much interchange among those working on the various research projects going on . . . simultaneously." Cavers, Walter E. Meyer Research Institute of Law (Draft 1), n.d. [ca. 1980], ch. III, p. 17, DCP.

180. See Levi, Chicago Law School Proposal of March 28, 1951, p. 1, FRD (grant 52-151).

181. Though it might have through the proposed study of "the youthful offender."

182. I know; I was part of that first class organized by Frank Zimring, then a student, and Alexander Aikman, a recent graduate then working at the Center. Zeisel was both captivating and insightful. He had given a seminar for the fellows in 1958–59. See Law and Behavioral Science Program at the University of Chicago Law School, Second Interim Report to the Ford Foundation, 3/9/60, p. 5, FRD.

183. Blum and Kalven, "The Art of Opinion Research."

184. The twenty-two individuals were run through varyingly conceived seminars designed to acquaint them with law and social science generally and the program at the Law School in particular and then left to work on their own research projects. A complete list of the fellows can be found in Law and Behavioral Science Program at the University of Chicago Law School, Third Interim Report to the Ford Foundation, 11/10/61, pp. 2–4, FRD. This document also details the varying seminar arrangements.

185. The Law and Behavioral Science Program at the University of Chicago, Second Interim Report to the Ford Foundation, 3/9/60, p. 5, FRD.

186. Philip Selznick, Erwin O. Smigel, Fred Kort, Harry Ball, David Matza, and John Schmidhauser.

187. Law and Behavioral Science Program at the University of Chicago, Second Interim Report to the Ford Foundation, 3/9/60, p. 5, FRD.

188. The application to the Ford Foundation to include these costs of the study in the grant, Research on Court Congestion and Judicial Administration, 8/5/57, FRD, is too sober in style to have been written by Herman Oliphant, but tracks his concerns uncannily. The law reform impetus is obvious; the project began as a collaboration with the New York Temporary Commission on the Courts (ibid., p. 4).

189. See Levi to McPeak, 12/13/61 (citing Mentschikoff and Katzenbach, Unification of International Private Law, and noting that "much of this material came from the Arbitration Project"), FRD.

190. Interview with David Cavers, 2/26/86.

191. Cavers, Walter E. Meyer Research Institute of Law (Draft 1), n.d. [ca. 1980], ch. II, p. 1 n. 1, DCP.

192. Ibid., p. 3.

193. Ibid., pp. 5–6. The dean at New York University understandably voiced opposition to Rostow's suggestion, since his school would have been cut out, and Harry Jones representing Columbia, suggested that the foundation established seek out "neglected" areas for research and bring in other law schools and other disciplines.

194. Cavers, Walter E. Meyer Research Institute of Law (Draft 1), n.d. [ca. 1980],

ch. III, p. 1, DCP. Some division of funds, if not that proposed by Cavers, was favored by each law school representative.

195. Ibid., pp. 2–3.

196. Ibid., pp. 7–10, 12–13, 16–19. Harry Kalven, another consultant, asserted that collaboration between lawyers and social scientists was possible but urged that projects be keep small. Ibid., pp. 18, 20.

197. Ibid., pp. 19–21. The decedent's nephews still opposed any limit to the four named schools.

198. Cavers, Walter E. Meyer Research Institute of Law (Draft 1), n.d. [ca. 1980], ch. IV, pp. 4–5, DCP. Ralph S. Brown of Yale was named Director.

199. Ibid., pp. 5–6.

200. Cavers, Walter E. Meyer Research Institute of law (Draft 1), n.d. [ca. 1980], ch. VI, p. 14 (forty-one in the first year and a half and forty-eight in the following two years), DCP.

201. See Cavers, "Report of the President" (1962–64), p. 8.

202. Cavers, Walter E. Meyer Research Institute of Law (Draft 1), n.d. [ca. 1980], ch. VI, pp. 1, 2–5, 14 (for this two-year period there were ninety-four applications), DCP.

203. See *St. Louis Southwestern Ry. Co. v. Loeb*, 318 S.W. 2d 246 (1959). The issue was whether certain noncumulative preferred shares were participating; the decision that they were not greatly increased the value of the common shares that were the substance of the bequest.

204. Cavers, Walter E. Meyer Research Institute of Law (Draft 1), n.d. [ca. 1980], ch. VI, pp. 14, 8–11, DCP.

205. Cavers, Walter E. Meyer Research Institute of law (Draft 1), n.d. [ca. 1980], ch. VII, pp. 1, 2–3, DCP.

206. Ibid., pp. 14–16.

207. See Walter E. Meyer Research Institute of Law, *Law for a Changing America* (conference papers and summary of proceedings), DCP.

208. Cavers, Walter E. Meyer Research Institute of Law (Draft 1), n.d. [ca. 1980], ch. VIII, p. 13, DCP.

209. Ibid., pp. 16–22.

210. Cavers, Walter E. Meyer Research Institute of Law (Draft 2), n.d. [ca. 1984], ch. II, pp. 20–21, 22, DCP. A program related to paralegal services proved just as disappointing. Ibid., p. 22.

211. Ibid., pp. 21, 22–24, 24, 26–27. The final product of the grant to the Social Science Research Council was Lipson and Wheeler, *Law and the Social Sciences*, which contains a useful history of law and social sciences research in the United States.

212. Cavers, Walter E. Meyer Research Institute of Law (Draft 1), n.d. [ca. 1980], ch. VII, p. 18, DCP.

213. Cavers, Walter E. Meyer Research Institute of Law (Draft 1), pp. 28, 31, n.d. [ca. 1980], DCP.

214. Ackerman, *The Uncertain Search for Environmental Quality*.

215. Conard, *Auto Accident Costs and Payments*.

216. Handler, *The Lawyer and His Community*.

217. Keeton and O'Connell, *Basic Protection for the Traffic Victim*.

218. Kuh, *Foolish Figleaves?*.

219. Macaulay, *Law and the Balance of Power*.

220. Rosenberg, *The Pretrial Conference and Effective Justice*.

221. Rosenberg and Sovern, "Delay and the Dynamics of Personal Injury Litigation."

222. "Interrogations in New Haven."

223. "Standardless Sentencing."

224. In 1988 Robert Ellickson was named Walter E. Meyer Professor at Yale; this is not a research professorship, however.

225. To this point my discussion draws on an unpublished history of Russell Sage written by Stanford Wheeler that he has kindly provided me with.

226. Russell Sage Foundation, *Annual Report, 1960–1961*, pp. 16, 17, 16. The application for the grant was submitted by three law professors, Edward Barrett, Jr., Frank C. Newman, then dean, and Yosal Rogat, and the Center's director, Philip Selznick.

227. Ibid., pp. 17–18. Willard Hurst was the coapplicant on this grant. Both the Rockefeller and Ford Foundations also supported this program, Russell Sage Foundation, *Annual Report, 1961–1962*, p. 51. The sociologists were expected to work with Frank J. Remmington, whose interest was primarily in criminal justice and corrections.

228. Russell Sage Foundation, *Annual Report, 1962–1963*, pp. 17–18. See University of Wisconsin, Proposal to the Russell Sage Foundation: Sociology and Law, 4/10/63 (in possession of the author courtesy of Stewart Macaulay). The original grant was for $40,000 (Russell Sage Foundation, *Annual Report, 1960–1961*, p. 78); to that grant was added first $12,000 (Russell Sage Foundation, *Annual Report, 1961–1962*, p. 74); then $210,000 (Russell Sage Foundation, *Annual Report, 1962–1963*, p. 80); next $100,000 (Russell Sage Foundation, *Annual Report, 1964–1965*, pp. 86–87); and finally $245,000 (Russell Sage Foundation, *Annual Report, 1965–1966*, pp. 88–89).

229. Russell Sage Foundation, *Annual Report, 1963–1964*, pp. 15–16. The original grant was for $210,000. Ibid., p. 72. That was later increased. See Russell Sage Foundation, *Annual Report, 1966–1967*, pp. 92–93. This was originally a collaboration between two social scientists, Victor Rosenblum and Richard D. Schwartz, and a law professor, John E. Coons.

230. Ibid., p. 17: $40,000 over two years, starting in 1963.

231. Russell Sage Foundation, *Annual Report, 1963–1964*, p. 17: $300,000 over five years, starting in 1964. The original grant was for $105,000. Ibid., p. 72. That was later increased by $15,000 (Russell Sage Foundation, *Annual Report, 1964–1965*, pp. 86–87) and then by $185,000 (Russell Sage Foundation, *Annual Report, 1965–1966*, pp. 88–89). The Foundation joined with the Walter E. Meyer Foundation to support the SSMILE, Social Science Methods in Legal Education, summer workshops held at Denver. See Russell Sage Foundation, *Annual Report, 1967–1968*, pp. 34, 92–93 ($25,000); Russell Sage Foundation, *Annual Report, 1968–1969*, pp. 86–87 ($47,000); Russell Sage Foundation, *Annual Report, 1969–1970*, pp. 92–93 ($96,000). I sense that this seminar for law professors was not very effective in increasing interest in the field, but I may be wrong.

232. Russell Sage Foundation, *Annual Report, 1967–1968*, pp. 43–44, 108–9. The grant was for $250,000 over five years, starting in 1967.

233. Ibid., pp. 44–46, 96–97. The grant was for $115,000 over three years, starting in 1967. The program was directed by Marvin Wolfgang and Anthony Amsterdam.

234. Russell Sage Foundation, *Annual Report, 1971–1972*, pp. 28–29. The grant was for nearly $60,000 over three years, starting in 1972.

235. Russell Sage Foundation, *Annual Report, 1963–1964*, pp. 18–19. For a few years predoctoral students were also included in the program.

236. The cost estimate comes from Final Report of the Committee to Review the Program in Law and Social Science of the Russell Sage Foundation, p. 3 (1976) (in possession of the author).

237. Russell Sage Foundation, *Annual Report, 1967–1968*, pp. 40–41, 108–9. The original grant was for $205,000. That was later increased. See Russell Sage Foundation, *Annual Report, 1970–1971*, p. 102.

238. Final Report of the Committee to Review the Program in Law and Social Science of the Russell Sage Foundation, p. 16 (1976) (in possession of the author).

239. Ibid., pp. 10, 11–12.

240. Harry Kalven pointed this out in the 1960s when he noted that the jury project had not rubbed off on his colleagues; see Cavers, Walter E. Meyer Research Institute of Law (Draft 1), n.d. [ca. 1980], ch. III, pp. 17–18, DCP. Whether the appearance on the law faculty of Frank Zimring, now Director of the Earl Warren Institute at the Law School, will change things remains to be seen. See Zimring, *The Earl Warren Legal Institute: A Prologue and a Proposal*.

241. The list includes Lawrence Friedman, Joel Grossman, Joel Handler, Jack Ladinsky, Stewart Macaulay, and Robert Rabin.

242. Friedman, *Contract Law in America*; Friedman and Krier, "A New Lease on Life"; Friedman, *Government and Slum Housing*; Friedman and Macaulay, *Law and the Behavioral Sciences*; Grossman, *Lawyers and Judges*; Grossman, "Social Backgrounds and Judicial Decisions"; Grossman, "Dissenting Blocks on the Warren Court"; Handler, *The Lawyer and His Community*; Handler and Hollingsworth, *The Administration of Social Services in AFDC*; Handler and Hollingsworth, *Stigma, Privacy and Other Attitudes of Welfare Recipients*; Handler and Hollingsworth, *Work and Aid to Families with Dependent Children*; Handler, *Coercion in the Caseworker Relationship*; Handler, *Justice for the Welfare Recipient*; Ladinsky, "Careers of Lawyers, Law Practice and Legal Institutions"; Ladinsky, "Higher Education and Work Achievement among Lawyers"; Macaulay, *Law and the Balance of Power*; Macaulay, "Non-Contractual Relations in Business"; Rabin, "Do You Believe in a Supreme Being?"; Rabin, "Some Thoughts on Tort Law from a Sociopolitical Perspective"; Rabin, "Implementation of the Cost of Living Adjustment for AFDC Recipients."

243. Among the students in the program were Theodore Becker, William Clune, Shari Diamond, C. Thomas Dienes, Janet Gilboy, James Levine, Mark McDonald, Joseph Sanders, Stephen Sugarman, and Francis Kahn Zemans.

244. Among the recipients are Carl Baar, William Chambliss, William Clune, Thomas Y. Davies, Gary Dubin, Joel Grossman, Jerrold Gubman, Craig W. Haney, Morton J. Horwitz, Robert Kagan, Samuel Krislov, Stanley I. Kutler, Richard Lempert, Sanford I. Levinson, Wallace Loh, Leon Mayhew, A. Mitchell Polinsky, John Robertson, Lawrence Rosen, H. Lawrence Ross, Austin Sarat, Robert B. Stevens, Neil J. Vidmar, James E. Wallace, and Stephen Wasby. The conclusion about shift in interests toward law and social science comes from Final Report of the Committee to Review the Program in Law and Social Science of the Russell Sage Foundation, p. 5 (1976) (in possession of the author).

245. Ibid., p. 17.

246. Carlin, *Lawyers' Ethics.*

247. Getman, Goldberg, and Herman, *Union Representation Elections.*

248. Heinz and Laumann, *The Social Structure of the Bar.*

249. Ianni and Ianni, *A Family Business.*

250. Johnson, *Justice and Reform.*

251. Ruebhausen, "Foreword," p. 2.

252. My guess is that much is. In the late 1960s the upcoming retirements of Donald Young, the Foundation's President, and Leonard S. Cottrell seem to have set the Law and Social Science program into a tail spin, but I simply do not know enough about the internal workings of the organization to be sure I am correct.

253. Stanford was funded after support for all but Berkeley had been terminated.

254. Russell Sage Foundation, *Annual Report, 1964–1965*, pp. 49–50, 82–83 ($55,000); Russell Sage Foundation, *Annual Report, 1967–1968*, pp. 56, 198–99 ($30,000). The journal began as a mimeographed newsletter of the three-month-old Law and Society Association. See Harry V. Ball to Dear Fellow Member, 11/13/64, enclosing Law and Society Association, *Newsletter*, 11/64 (marked "Vol. o, No. 1"). Leonard S. Cottrell, Jr., of the Foundation was a member of the Ad Hoc Committee of Organization. Of the fourteen other members, eight were Sage grantees: Harry V. Ball (chair), Robert B. Yeggee (counsel), Richard D. Schwartz (editor), Robert R. Alford, Allen H. Barton, Sheldon L. Messinger, Philip Selznick, and Jerome Skolnick. In less than two years, the *Review*'s first issue was announced and the six-page newsletter has grown to forty pages, including both notes and comments and a bit of empirical research; Alford and Messinger, "The Prospects of a Law and Society Association." (Documents in the possession of the author courtesy of Stewart Macaulay.) The *Law and Society Review* appeared in fall 1966.

255. See Russell Sage Foundation, *Annual Report, 1968–1969*, p. 64.

256. Felice Levine kindly provided me with this thumbnail history of the NSF program.

257. Macaulay, "Law and the Behavioral Sciences: Is There Any There There?"

258. Robert Gordon has argued to me that Cook's science of law is not a theory but only a slogan, so that while this theory might have sold in law schools, it would not have sold to the social scientists. I suppose that this observation is correct, at least as we have come to understand what theory is. Still, the question I wish to address is not what the social scientists thought or might think, but what the law professors interested in empirical research might have used to build their own enterprise. I have earlier examined the strengths and weakness of Cook's theory. For the law professors this slogan, if that is what it was, ought to have been good enough. At least it was substantially less threatening than the theory implicit in Moore's work.

259. The American Bar Foundation is only a modest *per contra*. A look at its annual reports would identify how close it is to the profession's reform agenda. Moreover, only recently has it developed scholars with a strong enough personal research agenda to have escaped being "just staff" and never has anyone other than the director been a "big name" such as were three of four of the founders of the Institute.

260. There is no history of this program; however, for a good sense of its flavor see Trubek and Galanter, "Scholars in Self-Estrangement."

261. This program was supported by both Sage and Walter Meyer. There is little published work on it. See Wheeler, "Social Science Methodology in Legal Education."

262. See Schlegel, "Between the Harvard of the Founders and the American Legal Realists."

263. See Sugarman, "The Legal Boundaries of Liberty," p. 107.

264. See Schlegel, "Between the Harvard of the Founders and the American Legal Realists"; Schlegel, "Langdell's Legacy."

265. See Beale, in Pound, Beale, and Lewis, "Comments," p. 53. ("Now there is the teaching of law, and there is the teaching of other sciences.")

266. Gray, *Select Cases and Other Authorities on the Law of Property.*

267. Thayer, *Cases on Constitutional Law.*

268. See Schlegel, "Langdell's Legacy"; Schlegel, "American Legal Theory and American Legal Education."

269. See "Underhill Moore," pp. 291–92, 305.

270. There is a wonderful ambivalence to the story of Moore working on sections of the Negotiable Instruments Law. If one had broken completely free of the old professional identity then why parse the NIL? Moore could no longer publish the old stuff, but, in the absence of anything else, the old five-finger exercises were still something to do.

271. Stewart Macaulay and Joel Handler are the major names that come to mind.

272. Llewellyn, "On What Makes Legal Research Worthwhile," pp. 400–403.

Ackerman, Bruce A. *The Uncertain Search for Environmental Quality*. New York: Free Press, 1974.

Adler, Mortimer. "Legal Certainty." *Columbia Law Review* 31 (January 1931): 91–115.

Amer, Francis J. *The Development of the Judicial System of Ohio from 1787– 1932*. Study of Judicial Administration in Ohio, Bulletin No. 8. Baltimore: Johns Hopkins Press, 1932.

American Law Institute. *Proceedings*. Vol. 3. Philadelphia: American Law Institute, 1925.

———. *A Study of the Business of the Federal Courts*. 2 vols. Vol. 1, *Criminal Cases*. Vol. 2, *Civil Cases*. Philadelphia: American Law Institute, 1934.

Ames, James Barr. "The Vocation of the Law Professor." In *Lectures on Legal History*, pp. 354–69. Cambridge: Harvard University Press, 1913.

Angell, Robert C. "The Value of Sociology to Law." *Michigan Law Review* 31 (February 1933): 512–25.

Angell, Robert C., and Albert C. Jacobs, eds. *A Research in Family Law*. New York: Robert C. Angell and Albert C. Jacobs, 1930.

Arnold, Thurman Wesley. "The Collection of Judicial Statistics in West Virginia." *West Virginia Law Quarterly* 36 (February 1930): 184–90.

———. *Fair Fights and Foul: A Dissenting Lawyer's Life*. New York: Harcourt, Brace & World, 1965.

———. "Review of the Work of the College of Law." *West Virginia Law Quarterly* 36 (June 1930): 319–29.

———. *The Symbols of Government*. New Haven: Yale University Press, 1935.

Ashmore, Harry S. *Unseasonable Truths: The Life of Robert Maynard Hutchins*. Boston: Little, Brown, 1989.

Association of American Law Schools. *Directory of Teachers at Member Schools, 1922*. St. Paul: West Publishing, 1922.

———. *Handbook and Proceedings, 1925*. Association of American Law Schools, 1925.

———. *Handbook and Proceedings, 1921*. Association of American Law Schools, 1921.

———. *Handbook and Proceedings, 1920*. Association of American Law Schools, 1920.

———. *Handbook and Proceedings, 1914*. Association of American Law Schools, 1914.

———. *Handbook and Proceedings, 1910*. Association of American Law Schools, 1910.

Auerbach, Jerold S. *Unequal Justice: Lawyers and Social Change in Modern America.* New York: Oxford University Press, 1976.

Ayer, Douglas. "In Quest of Efficiency: The Ideological Journey of Thurman Arnold in the Interwar Period." *Stanford Law Review* 23 (June 1971): 1049–86.

"Baetjer, Edwin." In *The National Cyclopaedia of American Biography,* 34:299. New York: James T. White, 1948.

Baldwin, Simeon E. "The Constitutional Questions Incident to the Acquisition and Government by the United States of Island Territory." *Harvard Law Review* 12 (January 1899): 393–416.

Bannister, Robert C. *Sociology and Scientism: The American Quest for Objectivity, 1880–1940.* Chapel Hill: University of North Carolina Press, 1987.

Bates, Henry. "Address of the President." In Association of American Law Schools, *Handbook and Proceedings,* 1914, pp. 29–46. Association of American Law Schools, 1914.

Beale, Joseph. "The Necessity for a Study of Legal System." In Association of American Law Schools, *Handbook and Proceedings,* 1914, pp. 31–45. Association of American Law Schools, 1914.

Beard, Charles Austin. *An Economic Interpretation of the Constitution of the United States.* New York: Macmillan, 1913.

Belknap, Michael. *To Improve the Administration of Justice: A History of the American Judicature Society.* Chicago: American Judicature Society, 1992.

Bernard, Luther Lee, and Jessie Shirley Bernard. *Origins of American Sociology.* New York: Russell & Russell, 1965.

Bettman, Alfred, W. C. Jamison, Leon Marshall, and R. E. Miles. *Ohio Criminal Statistics, 1931.* Baltimore: Johns Hopkins Press, 1932.

Bettman Alfred, and Howard Fletcher Burns. *Prosecution.* Cleveland: Cleveland Foundation, 1921.

Beutel, Frederick Keating. *Some Potentialities of Experimental Jurisprudence As a New Branch of Social Science.* Lincoln: University of Nebraska Press, 1957.

Billig, Thomas Clifford. *Equity Receiverships in the Common Pleas Court of Franklin County, Ohio, in the Years 1927 and 1928.* Baltimore: Johns Hopkins Press, 1932.

Bingham, Joseph W. "What Is the Law?" *Michigan Law Review* 11 (November 1912): 1–25; 11 (December 1912): 109–21.

Blackburn, William J. *The Administration of Criminal Justice in Franklin County, Ohio.* Baltimore: Johns Hopkins Press, 1935.

Blum, Walter, and Harry Kalven. "The Art of Opinion Research." *University of Chicago Law Review* 24 (Autumn 1956): 1–63.

Bodenheimer, Edgar. *Jurisprudence: The Philosophy and Method of the Law.* Cambridge: Harvard University Press, 1962.

Boorstin, Daniel J. *The Americans: The Democratic Experience.* New York: Random House, 1973.

Bowman, Harold M. "Book Review." *Boston University Law Review* 22 (June 1942): 487–93. (Review of *My Philosophy of Law: Credos of Sixteen American Scholars,* by the Julius Rosenthal Foundation, 1942.)

Bridgman, P. W. *The Logic of Modern Physics.* New York: Macmillan, 1928.

Broeder, Dale W. "The Function of the Jury." *University of Chicago Law Review* 21 (Spring 1954): 386–424.

Brown, Esther Lucile. *Lawyers, Law Schools and the Public Service.* New York: Russell Sage Foundation, 1948.

Bryce, James. *The American Commonwealth.* 2d ed., rev. New York: Macmillan, 1889.

Buck, Paul Herman. *The Social Sciences at Harvard, 1860–1920.* Cambridge: Harvard University Press, 1965.

Bullington, John P. "Book Review." *Texas Law Review* 20 (May 1942): 644–45. (Review of *My Philosophy of Law: Credos of Sixteen American Scholars,* by the Julius Rosenthal Foundation, 1942.)

Burke, Henry Gershon. *The Public Service Commission of Maryland.* Baltimore: Johns Hopkins Press, 1932.

Cairns, Huntington. "Book Review." *Iowa Law Review* 27 (January 1942): 337–43. (Review of *My Philosophy of Law: Credos of Sixteen American Scholars,* by the Julius Rosenthal Foundation, 1942.)

Calabresi, Guido. *The Costs of Accidents: A Legal and Economic Analysis.* New Haven: Yale University Press, 1970.

Cardozo, Benjamin N. *The Nature of the Judicial Process.* New Haven: Yale University Press, 1919.

Carey, Homer F. "Walter Wheeler Cook." *Illinois Law Review* 38 (1944): 344–47.

Carlin, Jerome E. *Lawyers' Ethics: A Survey of the New York City Bar.* New York: Russell Sage Foundation, 1966.

Carrington, Paul. "Of Time and the River." *Journal of Legal Education* 34 (1984): 222–28.

Cavers, David F. "Comment." In *Conference of Aims and Methods of Legal Research,* edited by Alfred F. Conard, pp. 21–23. Ann Arbor: University of Michigan Law School, 1955.

———. "Report of the President." In *Walter E. Meyer Institute of Law, Report for the Period July 1, 1962–June 30, 1964,* pp. 7–11. New Haven: Walter E. Meyer Institute, 1964.

Chase, Anthony. "The Birth of the Modern Law School." *American Journal of Legal History* 23 (1979): 329–48.

Chase, Stuart, and Ida Klaus. *Expenditures of Public Funds in the Administration of Civil Justice in New York City.* Study of Judicial Administration in New York, Bulletin No. 3. Baltimore: Johns Hopkins Press, 1932.

Cheever, Susan. *Treetops: A Family Memoir.* New York: Bantam Books, 1991.

Clark, Charles Edward. "Diversity of Citizenship Jurisdiction of the Federal Courts." *American Bar Association Journal* 19 (September 1933): 498–503.

———. "An Experiment in Studying the Business of Courts of a State." *American Bar Association Journal* 14 (June 1928): 318–19.

———. "Fact Research in Law Administration." *Connecticut Bar Journal* 2 (1928): 211–33.

———. "Methods of Legal Reform." *West Virginia Law Quarterly* 36 (December 1929): 106–18.

———. "New Types of Legal Research." *New York State Bar Association Bulletin* 1 (November 1929): 394–404.

———. "Should Pleadings Be Filed Promptly?" *Connecticut Bar Journal* 3 (1929): 69–79.

———. "Some of the Facts of Law Administration in Connecticut." *Connecticut Bar Journal* 3 (May 1929): 161–69.

——. "Underhill Moore." *Yale Law Journal* 59 (January 1950): 189–213.

——. "Walter Wheeler Cook." *Illinois Law Review* 38 (1944): 341–44.

Clark, Charles Edward, and Emma Corstvet. "The Lawyer and the Public: An A.A.L.S. Survey." *Yale Law Journal* 47 (June 1938): 1272–93.

Clark, Charles Edward, and Elwin A. King. "Statistical Method in Legal Research." *Yale Scientific Magazine* 5 (1930): 15–22.

Clark, Charles Edward, and Richard D. O'Connell. "The Working of the Hartford Small Claims Court." *Connecticut Bar Journal* 3 (1929): 123–29.

Clark, Charles Edward, and Charles U. Samenow. "The Summary Judgment." *Yale Law Journal* 38 (February 1929): 423–72.

Clark, Charles Edward, and Harry Shulman. *Law Administration in Connecticut*. New Haven: Yale University Press, 1927.

Clark, Elias. "Memories of My Father." In *Judge Charles E. Clark*, edited by Peninah Petruck, pp. 153–63. New York: Oceana Publications, 1991.

Clark, William, William O. Douglas, and Dorothy S. Thomas. "The Business Failures Project: A Problem in Methodology." *Yale Law Journal* 39 (May 1930): 1013–24.

Cohen, Benjamin. "Professor Underhill Moore and His Influence on the Growth of the Law School." *Bulletin of the Alumni Association of the Law School of Columbia University* 2 (1929): 3.

Cohen, Felix S. "Book Review." *Tulane Law Review* 18 (October 1942): 172–78. (Review of *My Philosophy of Law: Credos of Sixteen American Scholars*, by the Julius Rosenthal Foundation, 1942.)

Cohen, Morris Raphael. "Book Review." *Yale Law Journal* 33 (June 1924): 892–94. (Review of *Rational Basis of Legal Institutions*, by John Henry Wigmore and Albert Kocourek, 1924.)

——. "Justice Holmes and the Nature of Law." *Columbia Law Review* 31 (March 1931): 352–67.

——. *Reason and Nature*. New York: Harcourt, Brace & World, 1931.

Committee on Research in Judicial Administration. *Research in Judicial Administration: An Outline of Suggested Research Topics*. Washington, D.C.: Social Science Research Council, 1942.

Committee to Study Compensation for Automobile Accidents. *Report to the Columbia University Council for Research in the Social Sciences*. Philadelphia: Press of International Printing, 1932.

Conard, Alfred Fletcher. *Auto Accident Costs and Payments: Studies in the Economics of Injury Reparation*. Ann Arbor: University of Michigan Press, 1964.

Cook, Walter Wheeler. "Agency by Estoppel." *Columbia Law Review* 5 (January 1905): 36–47.

——. "The Alienability of Choses in Action." *Harvard Law Review* 29 (June 1916): 816–37.

——. "The Alienability of Choses in Action: A Reply to Professor Williston." *Harvard Law Review* 30 (March 1917): 449–85.

——. "The American Law Institute." *New Republic* 34 (1923): 87–89.

——. "The Associated Press Case." *Yale Law Journal* 28 (February 1918): 387–91.

——. "Book Review." *Columbia Law Review* 23 (February 1923): 198–99. (Review of *The Labor Injunction*, by John P. Frey, 1923.)

——. "Book Review." *Columbia Law Review* 31 (April 1931): 725–28. (Review of *Reason and Nature*, by Morris R. Cohen, 1924.)

——. "Book Review." *Yale Law Journal* 30 (May 1921): 775–76. (Review of *Collected Legal Papers of Oliver Wendell Holmes*, edited by Harold Laski, 1920.)

——. "Boycotts of 'Non-Union' Materials." *Yale Law Journal* 27 (February 1918): 539–42.

——. *Cases and Other Authorities on Equity.* St. Paul: West Publishing, 1923.

——. "The Cleveland Criminal Survey." *New Republic* 32 (August 30, 1922): 22–23.

——. "The Conclusiveness of State Judgments under the Full Faith and Credit Clause." *Yale Law Journal* 28 (April 1919): 579–83.

——. "Conversion by Innocent Agents." *Yale Law Journal* 28 (December 1918): 175–78.

——. "Estoppel by Misrepresentation and the Recording Acts." *Yale Law Journal* 28 (May 1919): 685–90.

——. "Full Faith and Credit to Judgments of Other States." *Yale Law Journal* 28 (January 1919): 264–68.

——. "Hohfeld's Contributions to the Science of Law." *Yale Law Journal* 28 (June 1919): 721–38.

——. "How May the United States Govern the Philippine Islands?" *Political Science Quarterly* 16 (March 1901): 68–78.

——. "Improvement of Legal Education and of Standards for Admission to the Bar." *American Law School Review* 4 (December 1917): 338–45.

——. "The Injunction in the Railway Strike." *Yale Law Journal* 32 (December 1922): 166–71.

——. "The Jurisdiction of Sovereign States and the Conflict of Laws." *Columbia Law Review* 31 (March 1931): 368–84.

——. "Legal Logic." *Columbia Law Review* 31 (January 1931): 108–15.

——. "The Legal Method." In *Proceedings of the Fifth Conference of Teachers of International Law, Washington D.C. April 26–27, 1933*, pp. 50–57. Washington, D.C.: Carnegie Endowment for International Peace, 1933.

——. *The Logical and Legal Basis of the Conflict of Laws.* Cambridge: Harvard University Press, 1942.

——. "Modern Movements in Legal Education." In Association of American Law Schools, *Handbook and Proceedings, 1928*, pp. 40–46. Association of American Law Schools, 1928.

——. "The Place of Equity in Our Legal System." *American Law School Review* 3 (Fall 1912): 173–78.

——. "The Possibilities of Social Study As a Science." In *Essays on Research in the Social Sciences*, edited by the Brookings Institute, pp. 27–48. New York: Kennilcat Press, 1931.

——. "The Powers of Congress under the Full Faith and Credit Clause." *Yale Law Journal* 28 (March 1919): 421–49.

——. "The Powers of Courts of Equity." *Columbia Law Review* 15 (January 1915): 37–54; 15 (February 1915): 106–41; 15 (March 1915): 228–52.

——. "The Present Status of the 'Lack of Mutuality' Rule." *Yale Law Journal* 36 (May 1927): 897–913.

——. "The Privileges of Labor Unions in the Struggle for Life." *Yale Law Journal* 27 (April 1918): 779–801.

——. *Readings on Legal Method.* Chicago: Northwestern University, 1940.

——. *Readings on Legal Method.* Baltimore: Johns Hopkins Press, 1931.

——. "Recognition of 'Massachusetts Rights' by New York Courts." *Yale Law Journal* 28 (November 1918): 67–71.

——. "Research in Law." *Science* 65 (April 1927): 311–14.

——. "Scientific Method and the Law." *American Bar Association Journal* 13 (June 1927): 303–9.

——. "Scientific Study and the Administration of Justice." *Maryland State Bar Association Bulletin* (1929): 144–61.

——. "Specific Intent in the Acquisition of Domicile." *Columbia Law Review* 20 (January 1920): 87–88.

——. "Statewide Studies in the Administration of Justice." *Indiana Law Journal* 7 (November 1931): 112–23.

——. "'Substance and Procedure' in the Conflict of Laws." *Yale Law Journal* 42 (January 1933): 333–58.

——. "Walter Wheeler Cook." In *My Philosophy of Law: Credos of Sixteen American Scholars*, edited by the Julius Rosenthal Foundation, pp. 49–66. Boston: Boston Law Book, 1941.

——. "What Constitutes an 'Injury' to 'Real Property'?" *Yale Law Journal* 28 (December 1918): 171–74.

——. "What Is the Police Power?" *Columbia Law Review* 7 (May 1907): 322–36.

"Cook, Walter Wheeler." In *Dictionary of American Biography, Supplement 3*, pp. 185–87. New York: Charles Scribner's Sons, 1973.

Cook, Walter Wheeler, and Edward Wilcox Hinton. *Cases on Pleading at Common Law*. Chicago: Callaghan, 1923.

Corbin, Arthur L. "The Law and the Judges." *Yale Review* 3 (January 1914): 234–50.

Corstvet, Emma. "Adequacy of Accounting Records in a Money Economy." *Accounting Review* 10 (September 1935): 273–86.

——. "Inadequate Bookkeeping As a Factor in Business Failure." *Yale Law Journal* 45 (May 1936): 1201–22.

——. "The Uncompensated Accident and Its Consequences." *Law and Contemporary Problems* 3 (October 1936): 466–75.

Currie, Brainerd. "The Materials of Law Study." *Journal of Legal Education* 8 (September 1955): 1–78.

Curti, Merle Eugene, and Vernon Roseo Christensen. *The University of Wisconsin: A History, 1848–1925*. Madison: University of Wisconsin Press, 1949.

Davis, Allen Freeman. *American Heroine: The Life and Legend of Jane Addams*. New York: Oxford University Press, 1973.

Davis, Kenneth Culp. *Discretionary Justice: A Preliminary Inquiry*. Baton Rouge: Louisiana State University Press, 1969.

"Deming, Horace E." In *The National Cyclopaedia of American Biography*, 33:424. New York: James T. White, 1947.

Dewey, John. *Essays in Experimental Logic*. Chicago: University of Chicago Press, 1916.

——. *How We Think*. Boston: D. C. Heath, 1910.

——. *Human Nature and Conduct*. New York: H. Holt, 1922.

Dicey, Albert Venn. *Can English Law Be Taught in the Universities?* London: Macmillan, 1883.

Dickinson, John. "Legal Rules: Their Application and Elaboration." *University of Pennsylvania Law Review* 79 (June 1931): 1052–96.

———. "Legal Rules: Their Function in the Process of Decision." *University of Pennsylvania Law Review* 79 (May 1931): 833–68.

Donovan, William J. "Report of Counsel to Petitioners Filed in *In Re* an Inquiry into the Administration of Bankrupt Estates, No. 501 (S.D.N.Y., March 22, 1930)." In House Committee on the Judiciary, 71st Congress, 3d Session, *Administration of Bankrupt Estates*, pp. 1–245. Washington, D.C.: Government Printing Office, 1931.

Douglas, William O. *Go East, Young Man.* New York: Random House, 1974.

———. "Professor Douglas' Address." *Journal of the National Association of Referees in Bankruptcy* 3 (January 1929): 48–50.

———. "Some Functional Aspects of Bankruptcy." *Yale Law Journal* 41 (January 1932): 329–64.

———. "Underhill Moore." *Yale Law Journal* 59 (January 1950): 187–88.

———. "Wage Earner Bankruptcies — State vs. Federal Control." *Yale Law Journal* 42 (February 1933): 591–642.

Douglas, William O., and Jerome Frank. "Landlord's Claims in Reorganizations." *Yale Law Journal* 42 (May 1933): 1003–50.

Douglas, William O., and J. Howard Marshall. "A Factual Study of Bankruptcy Administration and Some Suggestions." *Columbia Law Review* 32 (January 1932): 25–59.

Douglas, William O., and Dorothy S. Thomas. "The Business Failures Project: II. An Analysis of Methods of Investigation." *Yale Law Journal* 40 (May 1931): 1034–54.

Douglas, William O., and John H. Weir. "Equity Receiverships in the United States District Court for Connecticut: 1920–29." *Connecticut Bar Journal* 4 (1930): 1–30.

Douglass, Paul F. *The Justice of the Peace Courts of Hamilton County, Ohio.* Baltimore: Johns Hopkins Press, 1932.

———. *The Mayors' Courts of Hamilton County, Ohio.* Baltimore: Johns Hopkins Press, 1933.

Drake, Joseph H. "The Sociological Interpretation of Law." *Michigan Law Review* 16 (June 1918): 599–616.

Duxbury, Neil. "In the Twilight of Legal Realism: Fred Rodell and the Limits of Legal Critique." *Oxford Journal of Legal Studies* 11 (1991): 354–95.

———. "Jerome Frank and the Legacy of Realism." *Journal of Law and Society* 18 (1991): 175–205.

———. "Robert Hale and the Economy of Force." *Modern Law Review* 53 (1990): 421–44.

———. "Some Radicalism about Realism: Thurman Arnold and the Politics of Modern Jurisprudence." *Oxford Journal of Legal Studies* 10 (1990): 11–41.

Dzuback, Mary Ann. *Robert M. Hutchins: Portrait of an Educator.* Chicago: University of Chicago Press, 1991.

Ehrlich, Eugen. *Fundamental Principles of the Sociology of Law.* New York: Arno Press, 1975.

Eliot, Charles W. "Langdell and the Law School." *Harvard Law Review* 33 (February 1920): 518–25.

Ellsworth, Frank L. *Law on the Midway.* Chicago: Law School of the University of Chicago, 1977.

Ernst, Morris. "Deception according to Law." *Nation* 124 (June 1, 1927): 602–3.

Ewart, John Skirving. *The Principles of Estoppel by Misrepresentation.* Chicago: Callaghan, 1900.

——. "What Is the Law Merchant?" *Columbia Law Review* 3 (March 1903): 135–54.

Fisher, Lewis. *Old Hollywood: The Story of the Jordan Club, 1890–1980.* Edited by Paul Jamieson. New York: St. Lawrence County Historical Association, 1980.

Fisher, William W., III. "The Development of Modern Legal Theory and Judicial Interpretation of the Bill of Rights." In *The Culture of Rights: The Bill of Rights in Philosophy, Politics and Law, 1791–1991,* edited by Michael J. Lacey and Knud Haakonssen, pp. 266–365. Cambridge: Cambridge University Press, 1991.

Fortas, Abe. "Wage Assignments in Chicago-State Street Furniture Co. v. Armour & Co." *Yale Law Journal* 42 (February 1933): 526–60.

Foundation for Research in Legal History. *A History of the School of Law, Columbia University.* New York: Foundation for Research in Legal History, Columbia University Press, 1955.

Frank, Jerome. *Law and the Modern Mind.* Gloucester: Peter Smith, 1930.

Frankfurter, Felix. "Distribution of Judicial Power between United States and State Courts." *Cornell Law Quarterly* 13 (June 1928): 499–530.

——. Preface to *Criminal Justice in Cleveland,* edited by Roscoe Pound and Felix Frankfurter, pp. v–ix. Cleveland: Cleveland Foundation, 1922.

Fratcher, William F. *The Law Barn: A Brief History of the School of Law, University of Missouri-Columbia.* Columbia: School of Law, University of Missouri at Columbia, 1978.

French, John Calvin. *A History of the University Founded by Johns Hopkins.* Baltimore: Johns Hopkins Press, 1946.

Freund, Ernst. *The Police Power, Public Policy and Constitutional Rights.* Chicago: Callaghan, 1904.

Friedman, Lawrence M. *Contract Law in America: A Social and Economic Case Study.* Madison: University of Wisconsin Press, 1965.

——. *Government and Slum Housing: A Century of Frustration.* Chicago: Rand McNally, 1968.

Friedman, Lawrence M., and James E. Krier. "A New Lease on Life: Section 23 Housing and the Poor." *University of Pennsylvania Law Review* 116 (February 1968): 611–47.

Friedman, Lawrence M., and Stewart Macaulay. *Law and the Behavioral Sciences.* Indianapolis: Bobbs-Merrill, 1969.

Friedmann, Wolfgang. *Legal Theory.* New York: Columbia University Press, 1967.

Fuller, Lon. "American Legal Realism." *University of Pennsylvania Law Review* 82 (March 1934): 429–62.

Furner, Mary O. *Advocacy and Objectivity: A Crisis in the Professionalization of American Social Science, 1865–1905.* Lexington: University Press of Kentucky, 1975.

Furth, Joseph Herbert. "The Critical Period before Bankruptcy." *Yale Law Journal* 41 (April 1932): 853–63.

Gamer, Saul Richard. "On Comparing 'Friendly Adjustment' and Bankruptcy." *Cornell Law Quarterly* 16 (December 1930): 35–73.

Garlan, Edwin N. *Legal Realism and Justice.* New York: Columbia University Press, 1941.

Gehlke, Charles. *Criminal Actions in the Common Pleas Courts of Ohio*. Baltimore: Johns Hopkins Press, 1935.

Gellhorn, Walter. *Ombudsmen and Others: Citizens' Protectors in Nine Countries*. Cambridge: Harvard University Press, 1966.

Getman, Julius, Stephen B. Goldberg, and Jeanne B. Herman. *Union Representation Elections: Law and Reality*. New York: Russell Sage Foundation, 1976.

Gilmore, Grant. *Ages of American Law*. New Haven: Yale University Press, 1977.

———. "Legal Realism: Its Cause and Cure." *Yale Law Journal* 70 (June 1961): 1037–48.

———. "The Storrs Lectures: The Age of Anxiety." *Yale Law Journal* (April 1976): 1022–44.

Goodrich, Herbert Funk, and Paul A. Wolkin. *The Story of the American Law Institute, 1923–1961*. St. Paul: American Law Institute Publishers, 1961.

Goodspeed, Thomas. *A History of the University of Chicago*. Chicago: University of Chicago Press, 1916.

Grant, James. *Money of the Mind: Borrowing and Lending in America from the Civil War to Michael Milken*. New York: Farrar, Straus, Giroux, 1992.

Gray, John Chipman. *Select Cases and Other Authorities on the Law of Property*. 6 vols. Cambridge: C. W. Sever, 1888–92.

Green, Leon A. *Judge and Jury*. Kansas City: Vernon Law Book Company, 1930.

Greenbaum, Edward S., and L. I. Reade. *The Kings Bench Masters and English Interlocutory Practice*. Baltimore: Johns Hopkins Press, 1932.

Gressley, Gene M., ed. *Voltaire and the Cowboy: The Letters of Thurman Arnold*. Boulder: Colorado Associated University Press, 1977.

Grey, Thomas C. "Langdell's Orthodoxy." *University of Pittsburgh Law Review* 45 (Fall 1983): 1–53.

Griffin, Clifford S. *The University of Kansas: A History*. Lawrence: University Press of Kansas, 1974.

"Griswold, B. Howell." In *The National Cyclopaedia of American Biography*, 41:70–71. New York: James T. White, 1956.

Grossman, Joel B. "Dissenting Blocks on the Warren Court." *Journal of Political Economy* 30 (November 1968): 1068–90.

———. *Lawyers and Judges: The ABA and the Politics of Judicial Selection*. New York: J. Wiley, 1965.

———. "Social Backgrounds and Judicial Decisions." *Journal of Politics* 29 (May 1967): 334–51.

Haber, Samuel. *Efficiency and Uplift: Scientific Management in the Progressive Era, 1890–1920*. Chicago: University of Chicago Press, 1964.

Haggard, Ernest A., and Soia Mentschikoff. "Responsible Decision-Making in Dispute Settlement." In *Law, Justice, and the Individual in Society: Psychological and Legal Issues*, edited by June Louin Tapp and Felice J. Levine, pp. 277–94. New York: Holt Rinehart and Winston, 1977.

Hall, James Parker. "Communication." *American Law School Review* 2 (Fall 1910): 476–77.

———. *Illustrative Cases on Constitutional Law*. St. Paul: West Publishing, 1914.

Handler, Joel F. *Coercion in the Caseworker Relationship: A Comparative Overview*. Madison: Institute for Research on Poverty, University of Wisconsin, 1968.

———. *Justice for the Welfare Recipient: Fair Hearings in AFDC: The Wisconsin Ex-*

perience. Madison: Institute for Research on Poverty, University of Wisconsin, 1968.

———. *The Lawyer and His Community: The Practicing Bar in a Middle-Sized City.* Madison: University of Wisconsin Press, 1967.

Handler, Joel F., and Ellen Jane Hollingsworth. *The Administration of Social Services in AFDC: The Views of Welfare Recipients.* Madison: Institute for Research on Poverty, University of Wisconsin, 1969.

———. *Stigma, Privacy and Other Attitudes of Welfare Recipients.* Madison: Institute for Research on Poverty, University of Wisconsin, 1969.

———. *Work and the Aid to Families with Dependent Children.* Madison: Institute for Research on Poverty, University of Wisconsin, 1969.

Hanft, Frank. "Book Review." *North Carolina Law Review* 20 (December 1941): 123–26. (Review of *My Philosophy of Law: Credos of Sixteen American Scholars,* by the Julius Rosenthal Foundation, 1942.)

Harley, Herbert. "Concerning the American Judicature Society." *Journal of the American Judicature Society* 20 (1936): 9–18.

Harris, Silas Adelbert. *Appellate Courts and Appellate Procedure in Ohio.* Baltimore: Johns Hopkins Press, 1933.

———. *Draft of Legislation to Provide a Simplified Method of Appellate Review.* Study of Judicial Administration in Ohio, Bulletin No. 9. Baltimore: Johns Hopkins Press, 1932.

———. "Is the Jury Vanishing?" *Connecticut Bar Journal* 4 (1930): 73–94.

———. "Joinder of Parties and Causes." *West Virginia Law Quarterly* 36 (February 1930): 192–99.

Harron, Marion. *Current Research in Law for the Academic Year 1929–1930: Based on a Survey Made by the Institute of Law.* Baltimore: Johns Hopkins Press, 1930.

Hart, H. L. A. *The Concept of Law.* Oxford: Clarendon Press, 1961.

Haskell, Thomas L. *The Emergence of Professional Social Science: The American Social Science Association and the Nineteenth-Century Crisis of Authority.* Urbana: University of Illinois Press, 1977.

Heinz, John P., and Edward O. Laumann. *The Social Structure of the Bar.* New York: Russell Sage Foundation, 1982.

Herbst, Jurgen. *The German Historical School in American Scholarship: A Study in the Transfer of Culture.* Ithaca: Cornell University Press, 1965.

Hinkle, Roscoe, Jr., and Gisela J. Hinkle. *The Development of Modern Sociology: Its Nature and Growth in the United States.* New York: Random House, 1954.

A History of Columbia College on Morningside. New York: Columbia University Press, 1954.

Hohfeld, Wesley Newcomb. "Fundamental Legal Conceptions As Applied in Judicial Reasoning." *Yale Law Journal* 26 (June 1917): 711–70.

———. *Fundamental Legal Conceptions As Applied in Judicial Reasoning and Other Legal Essays.* Edited by Walter Wheeler Cook. New Haven: Yale University Press, 1923.

———. "The Individual Liability of Stockholders and the Conflict of Laws." *Columbia Law Review* 9 (June 1909): 492–522; 10 (April 1910): 283–326; 10 (June 1910): 520–49.

———. "Nature of Stockholders' Individual Liability for Corporation Debts." *Columbia Law Review* 9 (April 1909): 285–320.

———. "The Relations between Equity and Law." *Michigan Law Review* 11 (June 1913): 537–71.

———. "Some Fundamental Legal Conceptions As Applied in Judicial Reasoning." *Yale Law Journal* 23 (November 1913): 16–59.

———. "A Vital School of Jurisprudence and Law: Have Universities Awakened to the Enlarged Opportunities and Responsibilities of the Present Day?." In Association of American Law Schools, *Handbook and Proceedings, 1914*, pp. 76–139. Association of American Law Schools, 1914.

"Hollander, Jacob Harry." In *Dictionary of American Biography, Supplement 2*, pp. 310–12. New York: Charles Scribner's Sons, 1958.

Hollinger, David A. *Morris R. Cohen and the Scientific Ideal.* Cambridge: MIT Press, 1975.

Holmes, Oliver Wendell. *The Common Law.* Boston: Little, Brown, 1881.

———. "The Path of the Law." *Harvard Law Review* 10 (March 1897): 457–78.

———. "Privilege, Malice and Intent." *Harvard Law Review* 8 (April 1894): 1–14.

Holt, W. Stull, ed. *Historical Scholarship in the United States, 1876–1901: As Revealed in the Correspondence of Herbert Baxter Adams.* Baltimore: Johns Hopkins Press, 1938.

Hoover, Herbert. "Inaugural Address." In *Public Papers of the President of the United States: Herbert H. Hoover, 1929.* Washington, D.C.: Government Printing Office, 1974.

Hopkirk, John W. "The Influence of Legal Realism on William O. Douglas." In *Essays on the American Constitution*, edited by Gottfried Dietz, pp. 59–76. Englewood Cliffs, N.J.: Prentice-Hall, 1964.

Horwitz, Morton J. *The Transformation of American Law, 1870–1960: The Crisis of Legal Orthodoxy.* New York: Oxford University Press, 1992.

Hotchkiss, Willis L., and Charles E. Gehlke. *Uniform Classifications for Judicial Criminal Statistics with Particular Reference to Classification of Dispositions.* Baltimore: Johns Hopkins Press, 1931.

Hoxie, R. Gordon. *A History of the Faculty of Political Science, Columbia University.* New York: Columbia University Press, 1955.

Hull, Clark L. "Moore and Callahan's 'Law and Learning Theory': A Psychologist's Impressions." *Yale Law Journal* 53 (March 1944): 330–47.

———. *Principles of Behavior: An Introduction to Behavior Theory.* New York: Appleton-Century, 1943.

"Hull, Clark Leonard." In *The National Cyclopaedia of American Biography*, 21:69–70. New York: James T. White, 1956.

Hull, N. E. H. "Restatement and Reform: A New Perspective on the Origins of the American Law Institute." *Wisconsin Law Review* 1990 (Spring 1990): 55–96.

———. "Some Realism about the Llewellyn-Pound Exchange over Realism." *Wisconsin Law Review* 1987 (1987): 921–69.

"The Human Effects of Law." *American Bar Association Journal* 14 (October 1928): 530–31.

Hurst, James Willard. *The Growth of American Law: The Law Makers.* Boston: Little, Brown, 1950.

Husserl, Gerhart. "Book Review." *Columbia Law Review* 42 (May 1942): 894–99. (Review of *My Philosophy of Law: Credos of Sixteen American Scholars*, by the Julius Rosenthal Foundation, 1942.)

Hutcheson, Joseph C., Jr. "Book Review." *Yale Law Journal* 51 (January 1942):

523–26. (Review of *My Philosophy of Law: Credos of Sixteen American Scholars*, by the Julius Rosenthal Foundation, 1942.)

Ianni, Francis A. J., and Elizabeth Reuss-Ianni. *A Family Business: Kinship and Social Control in Organized Crime*. New York: Russell Sage Foundation, 1972.

Iddings, Elizabeth. *Current Research in Law for the Academic Year 1929–30*. Baltimore: Johns Hopkins Press, 1930.

"In Memoriam Marion Janet Harron." *United States Tax Court Reports*, April 1, *1972–September 30, 1972*, pp. v–vii.

Institute of Law. *Authoritative Views on the Need for the Institute of Law*. Baltimore: Johns Hopkins Press, 1930.

——. *Law As a Social Instrument*. Baltimore: Johns Hopkins Press, 1930.

——. *Report of the Committee of Direction, July 1, 1930. Interim Statement of the Study of Judicial Administration in Ohio*. Study of Judicial Administration in Ohio, Bulletin No. 4. Baltimore: Johns Hopkins Press, 1930.

——. "Report of the Faculty of the Institute of Law, 1930–31." In *Annual Report of the President, Johns Hopkins University*, pp. 220–25. Baltimore: Johns Hopkins Press, 1931.

——. *A Standard Classification of Offenses for Criminal Statistics*. Study of Judicial Administration in Ohio, Bulletin No. 10. Baltimore: Johns Hopkins Press, 1932.

——. *State Wide Studies in Judicial Administration: A Report of Progress*. Study of Judicial Administration in Maryland, Bulletin No. 2. Baltimore: Johns Hopkins Press, 1931.

——. *State Wide Studies in Judicial Administration: A Report of Progress*. Study of Judicial Administration in Ohio, Bulletin No. 5. Baltimore: Johns Hopkins Press, 1931.

——. *The Story of the Institute of Law*. Baltimore: Johns Hopkins Press, 1929.

——. *A Study of Administration of Justice in Ohio: Statement of the Immediate Program*. Study of Judicial Administration in Ohio, Bulletin No. 1. Baltimore: Johns Hopkins Press, 1929.

——. *Study of the Judicial System of Maryland: Statement of the Immediate Program*. Study of Judicial Administration in Maryland, Bulletin No. 1. Baltimore: Johns Hopkins Press, 1930.

Interborough Rapid Transit v. William Green et al., Brief for Defendants. New York: Workers Education Bureau Press, 1928.

"Interrogations in New Haven." *Yale Law Journal* 76 (July 1967): 1519–1648.

Isaacs, Nathan. "The Law and the Facts." *Columbia Law Review* 22 (January 1922): 1–13.

Jaffin, George H. "Theorems in Anglo-American Labor Law." *Columbia Law Review* 31 (November 1931): 1104–33.

James, Fleming, Jr., and Abram H. Stockman. "The Work of the New York Law Society." *Georgetown Law Journal* 27 (April 1939): 680–98.

"The Johns Hopkins Institute of Law." *American Law School Review* 6 (December 1928): 336–38.

Johns Hopkins University. *The Institute for the Study of Law, 1929–30*. Baltimore: Johns Hopkins University, 1929.

Johnson, Earl. *Justice and Reform: The Formative Years of the OEO Legal Services Program*. New York: Russell Sage Foundation, 1974.

Johnson, Gerald W. "How Does the Law Work?" *World's Work* 59 (December 1930): 63–65.

Johnson, Philip E. "Do You Sincerely Want to Be Radical?" *Stanford Law Review* 36 (1984): 247–92.

Johnson, William R. *Schooled Lawyers: A Study in the Clash of Professional Cultures.* New York: New York University Press, 1978.

"Jones, John Price." In *Dictionary of American Biography, Supplement* 7, p. 401. New York: Charles Scribner's Sons, 1981.

Jones, William. "History of Commercial Arbitration in England and the United States." *International Trade Arbitration* (1958): 127–36.

———. "An Inquiry into the History of the Adjudication of Mechantile Disputes in Great Britain and the United States." *University of Chicago Law Review* 25 (Spring 1958): 445–64.

———. "Three Centuries of Commercial Arbitration in New York: A Brief Survey." *Washington University Law Quarterly* 1956 (April 1956): 193–221.

Kalman, Laura. *Legal Realism at Yale, 1927–1960.* Chapel Hill: University of North Carolina Press, 1986.

Kalven, Harry, Jr. "The Jury, the Law and the Personal Injury Damage Award." *Ohio State Law Journal* 19 (Spring 1958): 158–78.

———. "A Report on the Jury Project of the University of Chicago Law School." *Insurance Counsel Journal* 24 (October 1957): 368–81.

Kalven, Harry, Jr., and Hans Zeisel. *The American Jury.* Boston: Little, Brown, 1966.

Karl, Barry Dean. *Charles E. Merriam and the Study of Politics.* Chicago: University Of Chicago Press, 1974.

———. "Presidential Planning and Social Science Research: Mr. Hoover's Experts." *Perspectives in American History* 3 (1969): 347–409.

Kearney, Edward N. *Thurman Arnold, Social Critic: The Satirical Challenge to Orthodoxy.* Albuquerque: University of New Mexico Press, 1970.

Keener, William A. "The Methods of Legal Education." *Yale Law Journal* 1 (March 1892): 143–49.

Keeton, Robert E., and Jeffrey O'Connell. *Basic Protection for the Traffic Victim: A Blueprint for Reforming Automobile Insurance.* Boston: Little, Brown, 1965.

Kelley, Brooks Mather. *Yale: A History.* New Haven: Yale University Press, 1974.

Kelley, Florence. *The Autobiography of Florence Kelley: Notes on Sixty Years.* Edited by K. Sklar. Chicago: C. H. Kerr Publications, 1986.

Kennedy, Duncan. "Toward an Historical Understanding of Legal Consciousness: The Case of Classical Legal Thought in America, 1850–1940." *Research Law and Sociology* 3 (1980): 3–24.

Kennedy, Walter B. "Realism, What Next?" *Fordham Law Review* 7 (May 1938): 203–15; 8 (January 1939): 45–78.

Kent, Frank R. "Johns Hopkins Grapples with the Law." *Scribner's Magazine* 87 (May 1930): 26–32.

———. *The Story of Alex. Brown & Sons, 1800–1975.* Baltimore: Barton-Gillet, 1975.

Kessler, Friedrich. "Theoretic Basis of Law." *University of Chicago Law Review* 9 (December 1941): 98–112.

Kirkwood, Marion Rice, and William B. Owens. *A Brief History of the Stanford Law School, 1894–1946.* Palo Alto, Calif.: Stanford Law School, 1961.

Klaus, Samuel. "Identification of the Holder and Tender of Receipt on the Counter-Presentation of Checks." *Minnesota Law Review* 13 (March 1929): 281–324.

Kolko, Gabriel. *The Triumph of Conservatism: A Re-Interpretation of American History, 1900–1916*. New York: Free Press of Glencoe, 1963.

Kuh, Richard H. *Foolish Figleaves? Pornography in and out of Court*. New York: Macmillan, 1967.

Ladinsky, Jack. "Careers of Lawyers, Law Practice and Legal Institutions." *American Sociological Review* 28 (February 1963): 47–54.

———. "Higher Education and Work Achievement among Lawyers." *Sociological Quarterly* 8 (1967): 222–32.

Lagemann, Ellen Condliffe. *The Politics of Knowledge: The Carnegie Corporation, Philanthropy and Public Policy*. Middletown, Conn.: Wesleyan University Press, 1989.

Langdell, Christopher Colombus. "A Brief Survey of Equity Jurisdiction." *Harvard Law Review* 1 (May 1887): 55–72; 2 (January 1889): 241–67; 3 (January 1890): 237–62; 4 (October 1890): 99–127; 5 (October 1891): 101–38; 10 (May 1896): 71–97.

———. *A Brief Survey of the Equity Jurisdiction*. Cambridge: Harvard Law Review, 1905.

———. "Harvard Celebration Speech." *Law Quarterly Review* 3 (1887): 123–25.

———. Preface to *A Selection of Cases on Contracts*, pp. vii–ix. Boston: Little, Brown, 1879.

———. *A Selection of Cases on the Law of Contracts*. Boston: Little, Brown, 1871.

———. "The Status of Our New Territories." *Harvard Law Review* 12 (January 1899): 365–92.

Larson, Magali Sarfatti. *The Rise of Professionalism: A Sociological Analysis*. Berkeley: University of California Press, 1977.

Lash, Joseph P. "A Brahmin of the Law: A Biographical Essay." In *From the Diaries of Felix Frankfurter*, edited by Joseph P. Lash, pp. 3–98. New York: W. W. Norton, 1975.

Lasswell, Harold Dwight, and Myres Smith McDougal. "Legal Education and Public Policy." *Yale Law Journal* 52 (March 1943): 203–95.

Laughlin, Charles V. "My Philosophy of Law: A Synthesis." *Washington and Lee Law Review* 3 (Fall 1941): 61–80.

Lazarsfeld, Paul F. "An Episode in the History of Social Research: A Memoir." *Perspectives in American History* 2 (1968): 270–337.

Lazerson, Mark H. "In the Halls of Justice the Only Justice Is in the Halls." In The *Politics of Informal Justice*. Vol. 1, *The American Experience*, edited by Richard L. Abel, pp. 119–66. New York: Academic Press, 1982.

Lepaulle, Pierre. "The Function of Comparative Law." *Harvard Law Review* 35 (May 1922): 838–58.

Lewis, Charles Irving. *The Mind and the World Order: Outline of a Theory of Knowledge*. New York: Dover, 1929.

Lewis, William Draper. "The Law Teaching Branch of the Profession." In Association of American Law Schools, *Handbook and Proceedings, 1924*, pp. 65–75. Association of American Law Schools, 1924.

Lieberman, David. *The Province of Legislation Determined: Legal Theory in Eighteenth-Century Britain*. New York: Cambridge University Press, 1989.

Lipson, Leon, and Stanton Wheeler, eds. *Law and the Social Sciences*. New York: Russell Sage Foundation, 1986.

Llewellyn, Karl N. *The Bramble Bush*. New York: Oceana Publications, 1930.

——. *The Common Law Tradition: Deciding Appeals*. Boston: Little, Brown, 1960.

——. "The Effect of Legal Institutions upon Economics." *American Economic Review* 15 (December 1925): 665–83.

——. "Law and the Social Sciences — Especially Sociology." *Harvard Law Review* 62 (June 1949): 1286–1305.

——. "Legal Illusion." *Columbia Law Review* 31 (January 1931): 82–90.

——. "On What Makes Legal Research Worthwhile." *Journal of Legal Education* 8 (1956): 399–421.

——. "A Realistic Jurisprudence: The Next Step." *Columbia Law Review* 30 (April 1930): 431–65.

——. "Some Realism about Realism: Responding to Dean Pound." *Harvard Law Review* 44 (June 1931): 1222–56.

——. "Wesley Newcomb Hohfeld — Teacher." *Yale Law Journal* 28 (June 1919): 795–98.

Llewellyn, Karl, Walter Wheeler Cook, and Jerome Frank. *How the Law Functions*. Chicago: University of Chicago Press, 1933.

"Lovejoy, Arthur O." In *Dictionary of American Biography, Supplement 7*, pp. 480–83. New York: Charles Scribner's Sons, 1981.

Lucey, Francis E. "Book Review." *Georgetown Law Review* 30 (June 1942): 800–802. (Review of *My Philosophy of Law: Credos of Sixteen American Scholars*, by the Julius Rosenthal Foundation, 1942.)

——. "Natural Law and Justice." *Georgetown Law Journal* 30 (April 1942): 493–533.

Macaulay, Stewart. *Law and the Balance of Power: The Automobile Manufacturers and Their Dealers*. New York: Russell Sage Foundation, 1966.

——. "Law and the Behavioral Sciences: Is There Any There There?" *Law and Policy* 6 (April 1984): 149–87.

——. "Non-Contractual Relations in Business: A Preliminary Study." *American Sociological Review* 28 (February 1963): 55–63.

Marshall, Leon Carroll. "The Collegiate School of Business." In *Higher Education in America*, edited by R. Kent, pp. 3–36. New York: Ginn, 1930.

——. *Comparative Criminal Statistics: Six States, 1931*. Baltimore: Johns Hopkins Press, 1932.

——. *Comparative Judicial Criminal Statistics: Ohio and Maryland*. Baltimore: Johns Hopkins Press, 1932.

——. *The Improvement of Divorce Statistics in Ohio*. Study of Judicial Administration in Ohio, Bulletin No. 12. Baltimore: Johns Hopkins Press, 1933.

——. *Judicial Criminal Statistics in Maryland, 1931: Courts of General Criminal Jurisdiction*. Study of Judicial Administration in Maryland, Bulletin No. 5. Baltimore: Johns Hopkins Press, 1932.

——. *Judicial Statistics*. Study of Judicial Administration in Ohio, Bulletin No. 2. Baltimore: Johns Hopkins Press, 1930.

——. "Judicial Statistics in the United States." *Annals of the American Academy of Political and Social Science* 167 (May 1933): 135–42.

——. *Maryland Trial Court Criminal Statistics, 1930*. Study of Judicial Administration in Maryland, Bulletin No. 3. Baltimore: Johns Hopkins Press, 1931.

——. "A Statistico-Legal Study of the Divorce Problem." *Journal of the American Statistical Association* 26 (March 1931): Supplement 96-106.

——. *Unlocking the Treasuries of the Trial Courts.* Baltimore: Johns Hopkins Press, 1933.

"Marshall, Leon C." In *The National Cyclopaedia of American Biography*, Curr. Vol. F, p. 154. New York: James T. White, 1942.

Marshall, Leon Carroll, Willis L. Hotchkiss, and Charles E. Gehlke. *Judicial Criminal Statistics.* Study of Judicial Administration in Ohio, Bulletin No. 11. Baltimore: Johns Hopkins Press, 1932.

Marshall, Leon Carroll, and Geoffrey May. *The Divorce Court.* 2 vols. Vol. 1, *Study of the Judicial System of Maryland.* Vol. 2, *Study of the Judicial System of Ohio.* Baltimore: Johns Hopkins Press, 1932–33.

Marshall, Leon Carroll, and Ruth Reticker. *The Expenditure of Public Money for the Administration of Justice in Ohio, 1930.* Baltimore: Johns Hopkins Press, 1933.

Marshall, Leon Carroll, and Hessel Yntema. *Outline Statement concerning State-Wide Studies of Judicial Administration.* Baltimore: Johns Hopkins Press, 1930.

Martin, George Whitney. *Causes and Conflicts: The Centennial History of the Association of the Bar of the City of New York, 1870–1970.* Boston: Houghton, Mifflin, 1970.

Martin, Kenneth J. *The Waiver of Jury Trial in Criminal Cases in Ohio.* Baltimore: Johns Hopkins Press, 1933.

Mason, Alpheus T. *Brandeis: A Free Man's Life.* New York: Viking Press, 1946.

Maxwell, William Quentin. *Lincoln's Fifth Wheel: The Political History of the United States Sanitary Commission.* New York: Longmans, Green, 1956.

May, Geoffrey. *Divorce Law in Maryland.* Study of Judicial Administration in Maryland, Bulletin No. 4. Baltimore: Johns Hopkins Press, 1932.

——. *Divorce Law in Ohio.* Study of Judicial Administration in Ohio, Ohio Bulletin No. 6. Baltimore: Johns Hopkins Press, 1932.

May, Mark A. Foreword to *Law and Learning Theory: A Study in Legal Control*, by Underhill Moore and Charles C. Callahan, pp. v–vi. New Haven: Yale Law Journal, 1943.

——. "A Retrospective View of the Institute of Human Relations at Yale." *Behavior Science Notes* 6 (1971): 141–72.

McArthur, Benjamin. "A Gamble on Youth: Robert M. Hutchins, the University of Chicago and the Politics of Presidential Selection." *History of Education Quarterly* 30 (Summer 1990): 161–86.

McCraw, Thomas K. *Prophets of Regulation: Charles Francis Adams, Louis D. Brandeis, James M. Landis, Alfred E. Kahn.* Cambridge: Belknap Press of Harvard University, 1984.

McDougal, Myres S. "Fuller v. The American Legal Realists: An Intervention." *Yale Law Journal* 50 (March 1941): 827–40.

Mechem, Philip. "The Jurisprudence of Despair." *Iowa Law Review* 21 (May 1936): 669–92.

Mensch, Elizabeth. "A History of Mainstream Legal Thought." In *The Politics of Law: A Progressive Critique*, edited by David Kairys, pp. 11–37. New York: Pantheon Books, 1989.

Mentschikoff, Soia. "Commercial Arbitration." *Columbia Law Review* 61 (May 1961): 846–69.

Michael, Jerome, and Mortimer J. Adler. *Crime, Law and Social Science.* New York: Harcourt, Brace, 1933.

——. *The Nature of Judicial Proof: An Inquiry into the Logical, Legal and Empirical Aspects of the Law of Evidence.* New York: Ad Press, 1931.

Miller, Justin. "The Compromise of Criminal Cases." *Southern California Law Review* 1 (November 1927): 1–31.

Miller, Neal E., and John Dollard. *Social Learning and Imitation.* New Haven: Yale University Press, 1941.

Moore, Underhill. "Book Review." *Columbia Law Review* 19 (March 1919): 87–88. (Review of Loan and Hire, by T. Baty).

——. "Book Review." *Illinois Law Review* 4 (March 1910): 607–8. (Review of *Cases on Damages*, by Floyd R. Meecham and Barry Gilbert.)

——. *Illustrative Cases of the Law of Bills and Notes.* 4th ed. St. Paul: West Publishing, 1914.

——. "Negotiable Instruments." In *American Law and Procedure*, vol. 7, edited by James Parker Hall, pp. 1–159. Chicago: LaSalle Extension University, 1912.

——. "Rational Basis of Legal Institutions." *Columbia Law Review* 23 (November 1923): 609–17.

——. "The Right of the Remitter of a Bill or Note." *Columbia Law Review* 20 (November 1920): 749–65.

——. "Significance of the Term 'Contract' in Article I, Section 10 of the Constitution." *Kansas Lawyer* 14 (1907): 1–7.

——. "Theft of Incomplete Negotiable Instrument and Negotiation to Holder in Due Course." *Columbia Law Review* 17 (1920): 617–21.

Moore, Underhill, and Charles C. Callahan. "Law and Learning Theory: A Study in Legal Control." *Yale Law Journal* 53 (December 1943): 1–136.

——. "Underhill Moore." In *My Philosophy of Law: Credos of Sixteen American Scholars*, edited by the Julius Rosenthal Foundation, pp. 201–25. Boston: Boston Law Book, 1941.

Moore, Underhill, and Walter Wheeler Cook. "Book Review." *Columbia Law Review* 20 (March 1920): 365–68. (Review of *The Conflict of Laws Relating to Bills and Notes*, by Ernest G. Lorenzen.)

Moore, Underhill, and Theodore S. Hope, Jr. "An Institutional Approach to the Law of Commercial Banking." *Yale Law Journal* 38 (April 1929): 703–19.

Moore, Underhill, and Abraham Shamos. "Interest on the Balances of Checking Accounts." *Columbia Law Review* 27 (June 1927): 633–49.

Moore, Underhill, and Gilbert Sussman. "The Current Account and Set-Offs between an Insolvent Bank and Its Customer." *Yale Law Journal* 41 (June 1932): 1109–33.

——. "The Lawyer's Law." *Yale Law Journal* 41 (February 1932): 566–76.

——. "Legal and Institutional Methods Applied to the Debiting of Direct Discounts: I. Legal Method: Banker's Set-Off." *Yale Law Journal* 40 (February 1931): 381–400.

——. "Legal and Institutional Methods Applied to the Debiting of Direct Discounts: II. Institutional Method." *Yale Law Journal* 40 (March 1931): 555–75.

——. "Legal and Institutional Methods Applied to the Debiting of Direct Discounts: III. The Connecticut Studies." *Yale Law Journal* 40 (March 1931): 752–78.

——. "Legal and Institutional Methods Applied to the Debiting of Direct Discounts: IV. The South Carolina and Pennsylvania Studies." *Yale Law Journal* 40 (April 1931): 928–53.

——. "Legal and Institutional Methods Applied to the Debiting of Direct Discounts: V. The New York Study." *Yale Law Journal* (May 1931): 1055–73.

——. "Legal and Institutional Methods Applied to the Debiting of Direct Discounts: VI. The Decisions, the Institutions, and the Degrees of Deviation." *Yale Law Journal* 40 (June 1931): 1219–50.

Moore, Underhill, Gilbert Sussman, and C. E. Brand. "Das Gesetz des Juristen." *Sociologus* 8 (1932): 385–400.

——. "Legal and Institutional Methods Applied to Orders to Stop Payment of Checks: II. Institutional Method." *Yale Law Journal* 42 (June 1933): 1198–1235.

Moore, Underhill, Gilbert Sussman, and Emma Corstvet. "Drawing against Uncollected Checks: I." *Yale Law Journal* 45 (November 1935): 1–38.

——. "Drawing against Uncollected Checks: II." *Yale Law Journal* 45 (December 1935): 260–92.

Morawetz, Victor. "The Supreme Court and the Anti-Trust Act." *Columbia Law Review* 10 (December 1910): 687–768.

——. *A Treatise on the Law of Private Corporations Other Than Charitable.* Boston: Little, Brown, 1882.

"Morawetz, Victor." In *Dictionary of American Biography, Supplement* 2, pp. 470–71. New York: Charles Scribner's Sons, 1958.

Morgan, E. M. "Book Review." *Harvard Law Review* 51 (April 1938): 1133–34. (Review of *A Study of Law Administration in Connecticut*, by Charles E. Clark and Harry Schulman, 1937.)

National Commission on Law Observance and Enforcement. *Progress Report on the Study of the Federal Courts.* Washington, D.C.: Government Printing Office, 1931.

——. *Report on the Enforcement of the Prohibition Laws of the United States.* Washington, D.C.: Government Printing Office, 1931.

Neely, Twila Emma. "A Study of Error in the Interview." Ph.D. dissertation, Columbia University, 1932.

Nehemkis, Peter R., Jr. "The Boston Poor Debtor Court: A Study in Collection Procedure." *Yale Law Journal* 42 (February 1933): 561–90.

"New History Professor." *Scarlet and Cream* 2 (May 24, 1901): 12.

Northrup, F. S. C. "Underhill Moore's Legal Science: Its Nature and Significance." *Yale Law Journal* 59 (January 1950): 196–213.

Norton, Charles Phelps. *Handbook of the Law of Bills and Notes.* 4th ed. With an appendix by Underhill Moore and Harold M. Wilkie. St. Paul: West Publishing, 1914.

"Notes and Personals." *American Law School Review* 3 (November 1914): 577–92.

"Notes and Personals." *American Law School Review* 3 (Fall 1912): 577–92.

"Notes and Personals." *American Law School Review* 2 (Fall 1908): 237–49.

"Notes and Personals." *American Law School Review* 1 (Fall 1904): 238–42.

Oberschall, Anthony. *Empirical Social Research in Germany, 1848–1914.* New York: Basic Books, 1965.

——. "The Institutionalization of American Sociology." In *The Establishment of Empirical Sociology: Studies in Continuity, Discontinuity, and Institutionalization*, edited by Anthony Oberschall, pp. 187–251. New York: Harper & Row, 1972.

Oliphant, Herman. "A Decision in the Light of Fact." *American Labor Legislation Review* 19 (1929): 95–96.

——. "Facts, Opinions, and Value-Judgments." *Texas Law Review* 10 (February 1932): 127–39.

——. "The Future of Legal Education." *American Law School Review* 6 (December 1928): 329–36.

——. "Mutuality of Obligation in Bilateral Contracts." *Columbia Law Review* 28 (December 1928): 997–1013.

——. "The New Legal Education." *Nation* 131 (September 1930): 493–95.

——. "Parallels in the Development of Legal and Medical Education." *Annals of the American Academy of Political and Social Science* 167 (May 1933): 156–64.

——. Preface to *Interborough Rapid Transit Company v. William Green et al., Brief for Defendants*, pp. 1–3. New York: Workers Education Bureau Press, 1928.

——. "The Public and the Law: The Three Major Criticisms of the Law and Their Validity." *American Bar Association Journal* 18 (December 1932): 787–93; 19 (January 1933): 46–50.

——. "A Return to Stare Decisis." *American Bar Association Journal* 14 (February 1928): 71–76, 107.

——. "A Sample of the New Type of Law Examinations." *American Law School Review* 6 (May 1929): 490–98.

——. *Study of Civil Justice in New York*. Study of Judicial Administration in New York, Bulletin No. 1. Baltimore: Johns Hopkins Press, 1931.

——. *Summary of Studies on Legal Education*. New York: Columbia University School of Law, 1928.

——. "The Theory of Money in the Law of Commercial Instruments." *Yale Law Journal* 29 (April 1920): 606–24.

Oliphant, Herman, and Homer F. Carey. "The Present Status of the Hitchman Case." *Columbia Law Review* 29 (April 1929): 441–60.

Oliphant, Herman, and Abram Hewitt. Introduction to *From the Physical to the Social Sciences: Introduction to a Study of Economic and Ethical Theory*, by Jacques Rueff, translated by Herman Green, pp. ix–xxxii. Baltimore: Johns Hopkins Press, 1929.

Oliphant, Herman, and Theodore S. Hope. *A Study of Day Calendars*. Study of Judicial Administration in New York, Bulletin No. 2. Baltimore: Johns Hopkins Press, 1932.

Page, William. "Professor Ehrlich's Czernowitz Seminar of Living Law." In Association of American Law Schools, *Handbook and Proceedings, 1914*, pp. 46–75. Association of American Law Schools, 1914.

Pattee, William S. "The College of Law." In *Forty Years of the University of Minnesota*, edited by E. Bird Johnson, pp. 141–51. Minneapolis: General Alumni Association, 1910.

Patterson, Edwin W. *Jurisprudence: Men and Ideas of the Law*. Brooklyn: Foundation Press, 1953.

Petruck, Peninah, ed. *Judge Charles Edward Clark*. New York: Oceana Publications, 1991.

Phelps, Edward J. "The Methods of Legal Education." *Yale Law Journal* 1 (March 1892): 139–61.

Pierson, George Wilson. *Yale: The University College, 1921–1937*. New Haven: Yale University Press, 1955.

Plummer, W. C., and Paul O. Ritter. *Credit Extension and Causes of Failure among*

Philadelphia Grocers. United States Department of Commerce, Trade Information Bulletin No. 700. Washington, D.C.: Government Printing Office, 1930.

Pollack, Franklin S. "Memorial of Herman Oliphant." In *The Association of the Bar of the City of New York, 1939,* pp. 432–36. New York: L. Middleditch, 1939.

Pomeroy, John Norton, Jr. "John Norton Pomeroy." In *Great American Lawyers,* vol. 8, edited by William Draper Lewis, pp. 89–133. Philadelphia: John C. Winston, 1909.

Pound, Roscoe. "The Call for a Realist Jurisprudence." *Harvard Law Review* 44 (March 1931): 697–711.

——. "The Causes of Popular Dissatisfaction with the Administration of Justice." In *Report of the American Bar Association, 1906,* pp. 400–417. Philadelphia: American Bar Association, 1906.

——. "The Decadence of Equity." *Columbia Law Review* 5 (January 1905): 20–35.

——. *An Introduction to American Law.* Cambridge: Dunster House, 1924.

——. *An Introduction to the Philosophy of Law.* New Haven: Yale University Press, 1954.

——. *Jurisprudence.* St. Paul: West Publishing, 1959.

——. "The Problems of the Law." *American Bar Association Journal* 12 (February 1926): 81–87.

——. "The Scope and Purpose of Sociological Jurisprudence." *Harvard Law Review* 24 (June 1911): 591–619; 25 (December 1911): 140–68; 25 (April 1912): 489–516.

——. "Some Comments on Law Teachers and Law Teaching." *Journal of Legal Education* 3 (Summer 1951): 519–32.

——. *The Spirit of the Common Law.* Boston: Marshall Jones, 1921.

——. "The Theory of the Judicial Decision." *Harvard Law Review* 36 (April 1923): 641–62.

Pound, Roscoe, and Felix Frankfurter, eds. *Criminal Justice in Cleveland.* Cleveland: Cleveland Foundation, 1922.

Pound, Roscoe, Joseph Beale, and William Draper Lewis. "Comments." In Association of American Law Schools, *Handbook and Proceedings, 1928,* pp. 51–56. Association of American Law Schools, 1928.

Prosser, William L. "Book Review." *Cornell Law Quarterly* 27 (February 1942): 292–95. (Review of *My Philosophy of Law: Credos of Sixteen American Scholars,* by the Julius Rosenthal Foundation, 1942.)

Purcell, Edward A., Jr. *The Crisis of Democratic Theory: Scientific Naturalism and the Problem of Value.* Lexington: University Press of Kentucky, 1973.

Pusey, Merlo, Jr. *Charles Evans Hughes.* New York: Macmillan, 1951.

Rabin, Robert L. "Do You Believe in a Supreme Being?" *Wisconsin Law Review* 1967 (1967): 642–84.

——. "Implementation of the Cost of Living Adjustment for AFDC Recipients." *University of Pennsylvania Law Review* 118 (July 1970): 1143–66.

——. "Some Thoughts on Tort Law from a Sociopolitical Perspective." *Wisconsin Law Review* 1969 (1969): 51–81.

Reiblich, G. Kenneth. "Book Review." *Maryland Law Review* 26 (June 1942): 340–48. (Review of *My Philosophy of Law: Credos of Sixteen American Scholars,* by the Julius Rosenthal Foundation, 1942.)

Reimann, Mathias W. "Holmes' *Common Law* and German Legal Science." In *The*

Legacy of Oliver Wendell Holmes Jr., edited by Robert W. Gordon, pp. 72–114. Stanford: Stanford University Press, 1992.

Report of the Commission on the Administration of Justice in New York State. Albany: J. B. Lyon, 1934.

"Report of the Faculty of the Institute of Law, 1931–32." In *Annual Report of the President, Johns Hopkins University*, pp. 195–202. Baltimore: Johns Hopkins Press, 1932.

"Report of the Faculty of the Institute of Law, 1929–30." In *Annual Report of the President, Johns Hopkins University*, pp. 192–98. Baltimore: Johns Hopkins Press, 1929.

"Report of the Faculty of the Institute of Law, 1928–29." In *Annual Report of the President, Johns Hopkins University*, pp. 190–93. Baltimore: Johns Hopkins Press, 1929.

Report of the School of Law to the President and Fellows of Yale University, 1942–43. New Haven: Yale University Press, 1943.

Report of the School of Law to the President and Fellows of Yale University, 1933–34. New Haven: Yale University Press, 1934.

Report of the School of Law to the President and Fellows of Yale University, 1931–32. New Haven: Yale University Press, 1932.

Report of the School of Law to the President and Fellows of Yale University, 1927–28. New Haven: Yale University Press, 1928.

Report of the School of Law to the President and Fellows of Yale University, 1926–27. New Haven: Yale University Press, 1927.

Reubehausen, Oscar. Foreword to Russell Sage Foundation, *Annual Report, 1975–76*, pp. 1–3. New York: Russell Sage Foundation, 1976.

Reuschlein, Harold Gill. *Jurisprudence: Its American Prophets: A Survey of Taught Jurisprudence*. Indianapolis: Bobbs-Merrill, 1951.

Risk, Richard. "John Skirving Ewart: The Legal Thought." *University of Toronto Law Journal* 37 (1987): 335–57.

Roalfe, William R. *John Henry Wigmore: Scholar and Reformer*. Evanston, Ill.: Northwestern University Press, 1977.

Robinson, Edward Stevens. *Law and the Lawyers*. New York: Macmillan, 1935.

Rodell, Fred. "For Charles E. Clark: A Brief and Belated but Fond Farewell." *Columbia Law Review* 65 (December 1965): 1323–30.

Rose, William H. "Book Review." *Ohio State University Law Journal* 8 (June 1942): 353–56. (Review of *My Philosophy of Law: Credos of Sixteen American Scholars*, by the Julius Rosenthal Foundation, 1942.)

Rosenberg, Maurice. *The Pretrial Conference and Effective Justice: A Controlled Test in Personal Injury Litigation*. With a preface by Tom C. Clark. New York: Columbia University Press, 1964.

Rosenberg, Maurice, and Michael I. Sovern. "Delay and the Dynamics of Personal Injury Litigation." *Columbia Law Review* 59 (December 1959): 1115–70.

Rosenthal, Douglas E. *Lawyer and Client: Who's in Charge?* New York: Russell Sage Foundation, 1974.

Ross, Dorothy. *The Origins of American Social Science*. Cambridge: Cambridge University Press, 1991.

Ross, Edward A. *Social Control*. Cleveland: Press of Case Western Reserve University, 1969.

Ross, H. Laurence. *Settled Out of Court: The Social Process of Insurance Claims Adjustments.* Chicago: Aldine Publishing, 1970.

Rostow, Eugene V. "Judge Charles E. Clark." *Yale Law Journal* 73 (November 1963): 1–2.

Rothbard, Murray N. "Essay." In *Herbert Hoover and the Crisis of American Capitalism,* pp. 35–58. Cambridge, Mass.: Schenkman Publishing, 1973.

Rottschaefer, Henry. "Book Review." *Minnesota Law Review* 26 (May 1942): 771–72. (Review of *My Philosophy of Law: Credos of Sixteen American Scholars,* by the Julius Rosenthal Foundation, 1942.)

Rueff, Jacques. *From the Physical to the Social Sciences: Introduction to a Study of Economic and Ethical Theory.* Translated by Herman Green with an introduction by Herman Oliphant and Abram Hewitt. Baltimore: Johns Hopkins Press, 1929.

Rumble, Wilfrid E., Jr. *American Legal Realism: Skepticism, Reform, and the Judicial Process.* Ithaca: Cornell University Press, 1968.

Russell Sage Foundation. *Annual Report, 1971–1972.* New York: Russell Sage Foundation, 1972.

———. *Annual Report, 1969–1970.* New York: Russell Sage Foundation, 1970.

———. *Annual Report, 1968–1969.* New York: Russell Sage Foundation, 1969.

———. *Annual Report, 1967–1968.* New York: Russell Sage Foundation, 1968.

———. *Annual Report, 1966–1967.* New York: Russell Sage Foundation, 1967.

———. *Annual Report, 1965–1966.* New York: Russell Sage Foundation, 1966.

———. *Annual Report, 1964–1965.* New York: Russell Sage Foundation, 1965.

———. *Annual Report, 1962–1963.* New York: Russell Sage Foundation, 1963.

———. *Annual Report, 1961–1962.* New York: Russell Sage Foundation. 1962.

———. *Annual Report, 1960–1961.* New York: Russell Sage Foundation, 1961.

Sadd, Victor, and Robert Williams. *Causes of Bankruptcies among Consumers.* United States Department of Commerce, Domestic Commerce Series No. 82. Washington, D.C.: Government Printing Office, 1933.

———. *Causes of Commercial Bankruptcies.* United States Department of Commerce, Domestic Commerce Series No. 69. Washington, D.C.: Government Printing Office, 1932.

Samenow, Charles U. "Judicial Statistics in General." In *Practical Applications of the Punched Card Method in Colleges and Universities,* edited by George Walter Bachne, pp. 319–26. New York: Columbia University Press, 1935.

———. *Report of Protest Litigation.* New York: New York Customs District, 1938.

Sayre, Paul Lombard. *The Life of Roscoe Pound.* Iowa City: College of Law Committee, State University of Iowa, 1948.

Schick, Marvin. *Learned Hand's Court.* Baltimore: Johns Hopkins Press, 1970.

Schlegel, John Henry. "American Legal Theory and American Legal Education: A Snake Swallowing Its Tail." In *Critical Legal Thought: An American-German Debate,* edited by Christian Juerges and David M. Trubek, pp. 49–79. Baden-Baden, Germany: Nomos Verlagsgesellschaft, 1991.

———. "Between the Harvard of the Founders and the American Legal Realists: The Professionalization of the American Law Professor." *Journal of Legal Education* 35 (September 1985): 311–25.

———. "Langdell's Legacy or, The Case of the Empty Envelope." *Stanford Law Review* 36 (July 1984): 1517–33.

———. "A Tasty Tidbit." *Buffalo Law Review* 41 (Fall 1993): 1045–70.

——. "The Ten Thousand Dollar Question." *Stanford Law Review* 41 (January 1989): 435–67.

Schlegel, John Henry, and David M. Trubek. "Charles E. Clark and the Reform of Legal Education." In *Judge Charles Edward Clark*, edited by Peninah Petruck, pp. 81–114. New York: Oceana Publications, 1991.

Schofield, Henry. *Constitutional Law and Equity*. Foreword by John Henry Wigmore. Boston: Chipman Law Publishing, 1921.

——. "Discussion." *American Law School Review* 3 (Fall 1912): 178–82.

Schwartz, Louis B. "With Gun and Camera through Darkest CLS-Land." *Stanford Law Review* 36 (1984): 413–64.

Scott, Austin W. "Remarks." *Proceedings of American Law Institute* 3 (1925): 229–31.

Seavey, Warren A. "The Association of American Law Schools in Retrospect." *Journal of Legal Education* 3 (Winter 1950): 153–73.

Sharp, Malcolm. "Book Review." *Illinois Law Review* 36 (1942): 591–93. (Review of *My Philosophy of Law: Credos of Sixteen American Scholars*, by the Julius Rosenthal Foundation, 1942.)

Simon, Rita James. *The Jury and the Defense of Insanity*. Boston: Little, Brown, 1967.

Singer, Joseph William. "Legal Realism Now." *California Law Review* 76 (March 1988): 465–544.

——. "The Legal Rights Debate in Analytical Jurisprudence from Bentham to Hohfeld." *Wisconsin Law Review* 1982 (1982): 975–1059.

Skolnick, Jerome H. *Justice without Trial: Law Enforcement in Democratic Society*. New York: Wiley, 1966.

Smith, Hal M. "Commercial Arbitration at the American Arbitration Association." *Arbitration Journal* 11 (1956): 3–20.

Smith, Howard Leslie, and Underhill Moore. *Cases and Materials on the Law of Bills and Notes*. 3d ed. St. Paul: West Publishing, 1932.

——. *Cases and Materials on the Law of Bills and Notes, Selected from Decisions of English and American Courts*. 2d ed. St. Paul: West Publishing, 1922.

——. *Cases and Materials on the Law of Bills and Notes, Selected from Decisions of English and American Courts*. St. Paul: West Publishing, 1910.

Smith, Reginald Heber. *Justice and the Poor*. New York: Scribner's Sons, 1919.

Smith, Reginald Heber, and Herbert B. Ehrmann. "The Criminal Courts." In *Criminal Justice in Cleveland*, edited by Roscoe Pound and Felix Frankfurter, pp. 229–374. Cleveland: Cleveland Foundation, 1922.

Smith, T. V. "Our Mistress, the Law." *Ethics* 53 (1942): 46–55.

"Social Mores, Legal Analysis, and the Journal." *Yale Law Journal* 29 (November 1919): 83–85.

Social Science Research Council. Committee on Scientific Method in the Social Sciences. *Methods in Social Science, a Case Book*, edited by Stuart A. Rice. Chicago: University of Chicago Press, 1931.

Speciale, Marcia. "Langdell's Concept of Law as Science: The Beginning of Anti-Formalism in American Legal Theory." *Vermont Law Review* (Spring 1980): 1–37.

"Standardless Sentencing." *Stanford Law Review* 21 (June 1969): 1297–1497.

Stepan, Frederick F. "History of the Uses of Modern Sampling Procedures." *American Statistical Association Journal* 43 (1948): 12–39.

Stephens, Frank F. *A History of the University of Missouri*. Columbia: University of Missouri Press, 1962.

Stevens, Robert. *Law School: Legal Education in America from the 1850s to the 1980s*. Chapel Hill: University of North Carolina Press, 1983.

———. "Two Cheers for 1870: The American Law School." *Perspectives in American History* 5 (1971): 405–548.

Stevens, Rosemary. *American Medicine and the Public Interest*. New Haven: Yale University Press, 1971.

Strengthening of Procedure in the Judicial System. Senate Document Number 65, 72d Congress, 1st Session. Washington, D.C.: Government Printing Office, 1932.

Strodtbeck, Fred L., Rita M. James, and Charles Hawkins. "Social Status in Jury Deliberations." *American Sociological Review* 22 (December 1957): 713–19.

Strum, Phillipa. *Louis D. Brandeis: Justice for the People*. Cambridge: Harvard University Press, 1981.

Sturges, Wesley A., and Don E. Cooper. "Credit Administration and Wage Earner Bankruptcies." *Yale Law Journal* 42 (February 1933): 487–525.

Sugarman, David. "The Legal Boundaries of Liberty." *Modern Law Review* 46 (January 1983): 102–11.

Sutherland, Arthur E. *The Law at Harvard: A History of Ideas and Men, 1817–1967*. Cambridge: Belknap Press of Harvard University, 1967.

Swan, Thomas W. "Reconstruction of the Legal Profession." *Yale Law Journal* 28 (June 1919): 784–94.

Thayer, James Bradley. *Cases on Constitutional Law, with Notes*. Cambridge: C. W. Sever, 1895.

———. "Our New Possessions." *Harvard Law Review* 12 (February 1899): 464–85.

———. "The Teaching of English Law at Universities." *Harvard Law Review* 9 (October 1895): 169–84.

Thomas, Dorothy Swaine. "Contribution to the Herman Wold Festschrift." In *Scientists at Work: Festschrift in Honour of Herman Wold*, edited by Tore Dalenuis, Georg Karlson, and Sten Malmquist, pp. 216–27. Stockholm: Almgvist and Wiksell, 1970.

———. "Social Aspects of the Business Cycle." Ph.D. dissertation, University of London, 1925.

———. "Some Aspects of Socio-Legal Research at Yale." *American Journal of Sociology* 37 (September 1931): 213–21.

———. *Some New Techniques for Studying Social Behavior*. New York: Teacher's College, Columbia University, 1929.

Thomas, William I., and Florian Znaniecki. *The Polish Peasant in Europe and America*. New York: Dover, 1958.

Trubek, David M., and Marc Galanter. "Scholars in Self-Estrangement: Some Reflections on the Crisis in Law and Development Studies in the United States." *Wisconsin Law Review* 1974 (1974): 1062–1102.

Twining, William L. *Karl Llewellyn and the Realist Movement*. London: Weidenfeld and Nicolson, 1973.

———. "Talk about Realism." *New York University Law Review* 60 (June 1985): 329–84.

Ulmann et al. Foreword to *The Divorce Court*. Vol. 1, *Study of the Judicial Systems of Maryland*, by Leon C. Marshall and Geoffrey May, pp. 11–15. Baltimore: Johns Hopkins Press, 1932.

United States Department of Commerce. *Causes of Business Failures and Bank-ruptcies of Individuals in New Jersey in 1929–30*. Domestic Commerce Series No. 54. Washington, D.C.: Government Printing Office, 1931.

——. *Credit Extensions and Business Failures*. Domestic Commerce Series No. 627. Washington, D.C.: Government Printing Office, 1929.

United States Securities and Exchange Commission. *Report on the Study and Investigation of the Work, Activities, Personnel and Functions of Protective and Reorganization Committees*. Washington, D.C.: Government Printing Office, 1936–40.

University of Missouri. *Announcements of the Department of Law, University of Missouri, 1905–06*. Columbia: University of Missouri Press, 1906.

——. *Announcements of the Department of Law, University of Missouri, 1904–05*. Columbia: University of Missouri Press, 1904.

University of Nebraska. *1869–1919, Semi-Centennial Anniversary Book*. Lincoln: University of Nebraska Press, 1919.

——. *Catalog for the Year 1903–04 and Announcements for the Year 1904–05*. Lincoln: University of Nebraska Press, 1903.

——. *Catalog for the Year 1901–02 and Announcements for the Year 1902–03*. Lincoln: University of Nebraska Press, 1902.

——. *Catalog for the Year 1900–01 and Announcements for the Year 1901–02*. Lincoln: University of Nebraska Press, 1901.

Veblen, Thorstein. *Higher Learning in America: A Memorandum on the Conduct of Universities by Business Men*. New York: B. W. Huebsch, 1918.

Verdun-Jones, Simon. "Cook, Oliphant and Yntema." *Dalhousie Law Journal* 5 (January 1979): 3–44.

——. "The Jurisprudence of Jerome N. Frank: A Study in American Legal Realism." *Sydney Law Review* 7 (September 1974): 180–210.

——. "The Jurisprudence of Karl Llewellyn." *Dalhousie Law Journal* 1 (October 1974): 441–81.

——. "Jurisprudence Washed with Cynical Acid: Thurman Arnold and the Psychological Bases of Scientific Jurisprudence." *Dalhousie Law Journal* 3 (October 1976): 470–509.

——. "The Voice Crying in the Wilderness." *International Journal of Law and Psychiatry* 1 (1978): 375–94.

Veysey, Lawrence R. *The Emergence of the American University*. Chicago: University of Chicago Press, 1965.

Walker, Mabel L. "Fitting Law to Life." *Survey* 64 (June 1930): 230, 253, 256.

Warner, Sam Bass. *Crime and Criminal Statistics in Boston*. Cambridge: Harvard University Press, 1934.

——. *Survey of Criminal Statistics in the United States*. Washington, D.C.: Government Printing Office, 1931.

Warren, Charles. *History of the Harvard Law School and of Early Legal Conditions in America*. New York: Lewis Publishing, 1908.

——. *The Supreme Court in United States History*. Boston: Little, Brown, 1926.

Wheatley, Steven Charles. *The Politics of Philanthropy: Abraham Flexner and Medical Education*. Madison: University of Wisconsin Press, 1988.

Wheeler, Stanton. "Social Science Methodology in Legal Education." In Association of American Law Schools, *Handbook and Proceedings, 1969*, pp. 127–30. Washington, D.C.: Association of American Law Schools, 1969.

Whitney, Edward B. "Another Philippine Constitutional Question: Delegation of Legislative Power to the President." *Columbia Law Review* 1 (January 1901): 33–49.

"Whitney, Edward B." In *Who's Who in New York City and State*, p. 1371. New York: L. R. Hamersly, 1909.

Wigdor, David. *Roscoe Pound: Philosopher of Law*. Westport, Conn.: Greenwood Press, 1974.

Wigmore, John Henry, and Albert Kocourek, eds. *Rational Basis of Legal Institutions*. With an introduction by Oliver Wendell Holmes. New York: A. W. Kelley, 1969.

Williston, Samuel. "The Effect of One Void Promise in a Bilateral Agreement." *Columbia Law Review* 25 (November 1925): 857–69.

———. "Is the Right of an Assignee of a Chose in Action Legal or Equitable?" *Harvard Law Review* 30 (December 1916): 98–108.

———. "The Word 'Equitable' and Its Application to the Assignment of Choses in Action." *Harvard Law Review* 31 (April 1918): 822–33.

Yntema, Hessel E. *Draft of a Uniform Municipal Court Act for the State of Ohio*. Study of Judicial Administration in Ohio, Bulletin No. 7. Baltimore: Johns Hopkins Press, 1932.

———. *Facts and the Administration of Justice*. Study of Judicial Administration in Ohio, Bulletin No. 3. Baltimore: Johns Hopkins Press, 1930.

———. "The Hornbook Method and the Conflict of Laws." *Yale Law Journal* 37 (February 1928): 468–83.

———. "The Implications of Legal Science." *New York University Law Quarterly Review* 10 (March 1933): 279–310.

———. "The Jurisdiction of the Federal Courts in Controversies between Citizens of Different States." *American Bar Association Journal* 19 (February 1933): 71–76; 19 (March 1933): 149–54.

———. " 'Law and Learning Theory' through the Looking Glass of Legal Theory." *Yale Law Journal* 53 (March 1944): 338–47.

———. "Mr. Justice Holmes' View of Legal Science." *Yale Law Journal* 40 (March 1931): 696–703.

———. "The Purview of Research in the Administration of Justice." *Iowa Law Review* 16 (April 1931): 337–60.

———. "The Rational Basis of Legal Science." *Columbia Law Review* 31 (June 1931): 925–55.

———. "Walter Wheeler Cook." *Illinois Law Review* 38 (1944): 347–54.

Yntema, Hessel E., and George H. Jaffin. "Preliminary Analysis of Concurrent Jurisdiction." *University of Pennsylvania Law Review* 79 (May 1931): 869–919.

Zeisel, Hans. "The New York Expert Testimony Project: Some Reflections on Legal Experiments." *Stanford Law Review* 8 (July 1956): 730–48.

Zeisel, Hans, Harry Kalven, Jr., and Bernard Bucholz. *Delay in the Court*. Boston: Little, Brown, 1959.

Zimring, Franklin E. *The Earl Warren Legal Institute: A Prologue and a Proposal*. Berkeley: School of Law, University of California, 1985.

Abbott, Nathan, 26, 277 (n. 17), 278 (n. 21), 284 (n. 155)
Ackerman, Bruce, 247
Adams, Charles Francis, 81
Adams, Henry, 235
Adams, Herbert Baxter, 159
Adams v. Lindsell, 31
Addams, Jane, 81
Adler, Mortimer, 19, 122, 184, 185, 186, 198, 226, 227, 263, 320 (n. 151)
Aikman, Alexander B., 370 (n. 182)
Alexander Brown & Sons, 150, 357 (n. 555)
American Arbitration Association, 241
American Association of University Professors, 194, 199, 209, 354 (n. 509)
American Bar Association, 72, 84
American Bar Association Journal, 90, 158
American Bar Foundation, 244, 247, 374 (n. 259)
American Judicature Society, 84, 231
American Law and Procedure Series, 282 (n. 103)
American Law Institute, 77, 83, 84, 90, 94, 152, 162, 174, 178, 199, 212, 256, 329 (n. 76); Cook on, 77
American Law Institute, Study of the Business of the Federal Courts. *See* Federal Courts, Study of the Business of
American Legal Realism, 1–10, 25; causes of disappearance, 2; current understandings of, 2; membership in the movement, 2; and empirical legal research, 2, 8–10, 25, 211–38, 252, 253–56; as jurisprudence, 2–8, 273

(n. 6); in broad context, 8; two stories about, 15–21; service in the New Deal, 19, 359 (n. 24); case law analysis, 25, 255–56; as a form of malcontentedness, 224, 363 (n. 100); and historical scholarship, 235. *See also* Empirical legal research
American Settlement House Association, 81
American Sociological Society, 133
American University, 199
Ames, James Barr, 25, 42, 44, 45, 46, 48, 65, 276 (n. 13); on professional role, 27, 36–37, 73, 74–75, 320 (n. 152)
Ames, Joseph S., 148, 157, 158, 171, 187, 188, 189, 192, 194, 200, 206, 208, 219, 221, 235, 263; position in disputes about the Institute, 190–91, 193, 195, 198–99, 208, 219, 357 (nn. 549, 551)
Analytical jurisprudence, 24, 40, 42–44, 46–50, 53–57
Andrews, E. Benjamin, 29
Angell, James R., 39, 98, 110, 117, 120, 121, 124, 141, 142, 156, 209, 263, 333 (n. 154)
Angell, Robert C., 122
Aristotelian logic. *See* Syllogistic reasoning
Arnold, Thurman, 5, 19, 20, 94, 113, 217, 235, 263, 301 (n. 107), 320 (n. 151), 324 (n. 217), 359 (n. 24); *Symbols of Government*, 19; work on federal courts study, 88, 93, 300 (n. 106), 301 (n. 108)
Association of American Law Schools, 24, 39, 40, 45, 72, 73, 74, 83, 144, 247, 252, 275 (n. 4), 317 (n. 98)

Association of the Bar of the City of
New York, 178
Atcheson, Topeka and Santa Fe Rail-
road, 150
Atkinson, Thomas E., 94
Austin, John, 43, 49
Auto accidents, study of compensation
for, 99, 105–9, 110–11, 309 (n. 224)

Baetjer, Edwin, 187, 188, 189, 199,
263, 345 (n. 355), 347 (n. 382)
Baker, Newton D., 209
Ballantine, Arthur, 105, 229, 263
Baltimore Sun, 157
Banking studies, 115–24; on debiting
direct discounts, 116–20, 124–25,
312 (n. 8); methodology underlying,
116, 120, 126–28, 129–30; on stop
payments, 122, 123–24, 125, 315
(n. 62); on uncollected checks, 122–
23, 124, 125, 126–27, 130; reasons
for termination of, 124–28
Bankruptcy law reform, 9, 104, 105,
307 (nn. 190, 191)
Barton, Alan, 240
Bates, Henry, 45, 46, 297 (n. 58), 347
(n. 378)
Beale, Joseph, 45, 46, 66, 79, 263, 297
(n. 58), 334 (n. 164), 347 (n. 378);
on the conflict of laws, 64, 152, 227,
327 (n. 47), 328 (n. 52), 329 (n. 76)
Beard, Charles E., 50, 235, 293
(n. 326), 334 (n. 164)
Behaviorism, 125, 127, 329 (n. 76).
See also Logical positivism; Opera-
tionalism
Behaviorist psychology, 63
Bentham, Jeremy, 49, 83
Berle, A. A., 7, 20
Berry, Chuck, 79
Bigelow, Harry, 281 (n. 97)
Birdzell, Robert, 338 (n. 245)
Blum, Walter, 240, 263
Boas, Franz, 50, 318 (n. 110)
Bodenheimer, Karl, 4
Bohlen, Francis, 7
Bonbright, James, 7, 16
Bond, Carroll T., 166, 167, 174, 198,
199, 330 (n. 86)

Borchard, Edwin, 360 (n. 49)
Brandeis, Louis D., 20, 55, 81, 187,
320 (n. 151), 345 (nn. 353, 357)
Brandt, C. E., 122
Brookings Institute, 181–82, 199
Brown, Ralph S., 371 (n. 198)
Brown University, 29
Budapest String Quartet, 222
Burdick, Francis M., 276 (n. 17)
Burdick, William L., 30
Burgess, Ernest, 110
Burgess, John W., 279 (n. 35)
Burlingham, Charles C., 209, 229, 340
(n. 259)
Business failures project, 99–105, 107,
109, 228, 306 (n. 179); work with
Department of Commerce, 100, 105;
equity receiverships, 101, 102, 306
(n. 172); work in Newark, 102–3,
306 (nn. 178, 179), 311 (n. 253);
work in Boston, 103–4, 311 (n. 253)
Butler, Nicholas Murray, 15–16, 17,
147, 156, 221, 263, 289 (n. 256);
criticism of legal education, 15
Butler, Pierce, 188
Buttrick, Wallace, 151, 263

Calabrisi, Guido, 247
California, University of, Berkeley:
Russell Sage grant to Center for the
Study of Law and Society, 248, 249,
372 (n. 226); Jurisprudence and
Social Policy Program, 249; Law
School, 249; program in Law, Soci-
ety, and Criminal Justice, 249;
School of Criminology, 249
Callahan, Charles E., 131, 133, 134,
136, 264, 319 (n. 123), 321 (n. 172),
324 (n. 225)
Cardozo, Benjamin N., 20, 61, 170,
174, 187, 320 (n. 151), 330 (nn. 86,
88)
Carey, Homer, 71
Carlin, Jerome, 250
Carnegie, Andrew, 150
Carnegie Foundation, 190, 199, 229
Carter, James Coolidge, 320 (n. 151)
Case method of legal education, 25, 26,
30

"Cave of the Winds, The," 19, 301 (n. 107)

Cavers, David F., 244, 245, 246, 264, 364 (n. 102)

Center for Studies in Criminal Justice, 243

Chapin, F. Stuart, 110, 317 (n. 91)

Chicago, University of, 76, 142, 238; College of Commerce, 15, 16, 182, 222, 325 (n. 15), 333 (n. 154)

Chicago, University of, Law School, 15–17, 23, 33, 35, 38, 39, 51, 67, 195, 239; Jury Project, 10, 240, 240–41, 243, 369 (n. 172); summer session, 40, 281 (n. 99); commercial arbitration project, 239–40, 241, 243, 369 (n. 175); income tax project, 240, 242, 243; absence of empirical work after Ford money ran out, 255; recording jury deliberations, 369 (n. 173). See also Law and Behavioral Science Program

Clark, Charles E., 1, 5, 9, 17, 19, 21, 71, 80, 82, 112, 118, 159, 164, 165, 172, 198, 203, 209, 213, 214, 219, 224, 226, 228, 229, 238, 257, 259, 264, 297 (n. 58), 299 (n. 88), 311 (n. 255), 347 (n. 378), 359 (n. 24); later career, 20, 113; Connecticut courts study, 83, 84, 173, 201, 206, 209, 214, 234, 295 (n. 38), 300 (nn. 104, 106), 303 (n. 135); Institute of Procedure, 83, 293 (nn. 18, 19), 294 (n. 20); federal courts study, 85–91, 172, 201, 202, 209, 214, 234, 295 (n. 46), 296 (nn. 47, 48, 49, 54), 298 (n. 62), 301 (n. 117), 302 (n. 121), 303 (n. 135); conflict between commitment to empirical research and values of progressive law reform, 91–98, 111, 114, 141, 144, 229–30, 302 (n. 134), 303 (n. 135); auto accidents study, 106–9, 111, 214, 230, 309 (n. 224); study of the legal needs of the public, 113, 311 (n. 255), 312 (n. 262); relationship with Moore, 117, 131, 215, 217, 359 (n. 29), 360 (n. 46); work as dean, 117, 214, 215, 216, 359

(n. 34); antagonism toward the Institute of Law, 175, 209, 340 (n. 258); personality and style, 214–16, 218, 224; vision of legal education, 232, 365 (n. 123). See also Connecticut courts study; Federal courts study

Clark, William, 101, 102

Clarke, John H., 55

Classical legal thought, 7, 8, 9, 20, 30–35, 36–37, 42–43, 43–44, 46–50, 73, 79; modified by Cook and Hohfeld, 40–41, 42, 46–50; further modified by Cook, 59–62, 65–67, 76–78, 226–27, 253, 364 (n. 107)

Cleveland Crime Survey, 76, 82, 84, 91, 95, 175, 202, 295 (n. 32); Cook on, 76–77

Cohen, Felix, 20

Cohen, Morris R., 6, 7, 19, 20, 74, 156, 185–86, 186, 198, 226, 227, 264, 291 (n. 303), 330 (n. 96)

Colonial service, 26–27, 35–37, 75; implausibility of the ideal, 26, 277 (n. 20), 278 (n. 21), 279 (n. 31)

Columbia University, 50, 106, 120, 212; faculty of School of Political Science, 28, 75, 282 (n. 123)

Columbia University Law School, 6, 15–17, 23, 25, 26, 28, 50, 52, 53, 57, 67, 81, 83, 99, 106, 110, 114, 140, 166, 222, 224, 239, 244, 278 (n. 21), 279 (n. 31), 297 (n. 59), 365 (n. 123); deanship fight in 1923, 16, 23; curriculum study, 16–17, 62, 99, 149, 160, 161, 305 (n. 151), 328 (nn. 56, 70); deanship fight in 1928, 17, 62, 99, 115, 147, 157, 216; Special Conferences in Jurisprudence, 23–25; Columbia Law Review, 58; Russell Sage grants, 249; author of school's history identified, 275 (ch. 1, n. 2)

Commercial arbitration project. See Chicago, University of, Law School: commercial arbitration project

Commercial banking, 9, 62, 64, 145. See also Banking studies

Commission on the Administration of Justice in New York State, 230–31

Committee to Study Compensation for Automobile Accidents, The, 105, 108, 109, 110–11, 309 (nn. 222, 224); executive committee membership, 106, 308 (n. 202)

Commons, John, 38, 63, 304 (n. 143)

Comstock, Ada, 86

Conard, Alfred, 247

Conflict of laws, 40, 53, 60–61, 64, 67, 152–53, 182, 204, 225, 227, 327 (n. 47), 328 (n. 52), 329 (n. 76), 364 (n. 102)

Connecticut courts study, 83, 84, 87, 91, 99, 173, 201, 206, 209, 214, 234, 295 (n. 38), 300 (nn. 104, 106), 303 (n. 135); early work, 85–86; later results, 92–93, 97

Constitutional law, 32–35, 37, 54–55, 218, 335 (n. 183), 344 (n. 311)

Contract law: agency in, 30–32, 36; assignment of rights, 48–49

Cook, Walter Wheeler, 5, 6, 8–9, 10, 11, 15, 17, 17–18, 20, 23, 27, 42, 43, 44, 50, 51, 52, 56, 68, 80, 115, 140, 146, 148, 149, 161, 169, 170, 171, 181, 184, 185, 186, 190, 200, 205, 206, 209, 220, 221, 222, 223, 228, 230, 252, 253, 255, 256, 257, 259, 264, 278 (n. 21), 328 (n. 56), 329 (n. 76), 353 (n. 485), 366 (n. 126); lectures at Columbia in 1922, 23–25; at Columbia, 23–25, 53, 57, 67, 224; response to Dewey's lectures, 24–25, 59–61, 69–70, 76–77, 77, 78, 79, 253, 254, 257, 287 (n. 215); family background, 27–28; background in science, 28; courses taught, 28, 35, 280 (n. 56); education at Columbia, 28, 71, 153; at Nebraska, 28–29, 35, 72; at Missouri, 30, 35, 38; "Agency by Estoppel," 30–32; on governance of the Philippine territories, 32–33, 43; on the police power, 33–35, 47, 227; professional identity, 35, 36–38, 40, 41, 72–73, 75–78, 79–80, 253–54, 255, 256; salary, 35, 53, 57, 71, 153, 155, 191, 192, 362 (n. 71); relationship with Pound, 35, 56, 186, 193,

195, 280 (n. 78), 288 (n. 204), 345 (n. 351), 357 (n. 559); at Wisconsin, 38, 39, 67; at Chicago, 38, 67; and Hohfeld, 40, 42, 51, 52–53, 68, 76, 77, 80, 253; "The Place of Equity in the Legal System," 40–41; on equity, 40–41, 46–47, 64, 329 (n. 76); "The Powers of Courts of Equity," 46–47, 60, 283 (nn. 128, 130, 131, 134); assignment of rights, 48–49, 283 (nn. 138, 140), 284 (n. 141); at Yale, 50–51, 57, 64, 67, 68, 75–76, 153; on conflict of laws, 53, 60–61, 64, 67, 152–53, 182, 196, 204, 225, 227, 327 (n. 47), 329 (n. 76), 364 (n. 102); on labor law, 54–56; "The Logical and Legal Bases of the Conflict of Laws," 59–61, 61–62; on legal (scientific) method, 60, 61–62, 64, 65–66, 67, 69–70, 76–77, 77, 78, 153, 164, 170, 181–82, 196, 198, 205, 224–29, 232, 233, 238, 252, 254, 255, 257, 329 (n. 76), 330 (n. 96), 356 (n. 538), 364 (nn. 101, 108), 374 (n. 258); at Johns Hopkins, 64, 71, 146, 153–58, 159, 328 (n. 49), 328 (n. 53), 330 (n. 86); "Scientific Method and the Law," 65–67, 154; plans for the Hopkins's school, 66–67, 153, 54, 156, 158; lack of interest in empirical research projects, 67, 164, 220, 226, 230; similarity of background to Moore's, 67–68; personality and style, 68, 71–72, 79, 219–20, 223, 224, 287 (n. 209), 290 (n. 267), 357 (n. 551), 362 (nn. 65, 66, 67); differences from Moore, 68, 72–80; lack of practice experience, 70; at Northwestern, 71, 79, 199; casebook on common law pleading, 72; on empirical inquiry, 76–78, 159; project on installment sales, 148, 149, 182, 206, 343 (n. 305); founding of the Institute of Law, 152–58; terms of appointment at Hopkins, 157, 191, 194–95; limits of Cook's ideas about scientific method in law, 158–59, 224–29, 255, 256; initial research plans, 165,

165–66, 166, 167; serves as Institute's secretary, 165, 181; Study of the Judicial System of Maryland, 174, 194, 198, 200, 223; participates in the Realist Controversy, 184–86; and closing of the Institute, 191, 194, 194–95, 195, 352 (n. 463); resigns from the Institute, 193; search for a new job, 193, 195, 345 (n. 351), 350 (n. 442), 352 (n. 467); second marriage, 195; later career, 198–99, 354 (n. 509); first wife's sickness and death, 289 (n. 261); as a behaviorist, 329 (n. 76); vision of legal education, 365 (n. 123)

Cook, William W., 209

Corbin, Arthur, 6, 17, 50–51, 56–57, 82, 217, 237, 256, 264, 284 (n. 155), 287 (n. 209)

Cornell Law School, 277 (n. 17)

Corstvet (Llewellyn), Emma, 9, 98–99, 109, 111, 130, 131, 133, 142, 145, 232, 264, 303 (n. 140), 304 (n. 143), 309 (n. 232), 310 (nn. 237, 247); early career, 98, 99, 304 (n. 143); works with Clark, 107–8, 311 (n. 255); later career, 109–10, 319 (n. 121); as a social scientist, 112, 113, 230, 238; works for Moore, 122–24, 124, 125, 126, 127, 128–30, 131, 217, 316 (n. 83); ideas for projects, 161

Corwin, Edward, S., 20

Cottrell, Leonard S., 248, 374 (n. 252), 374 (n. 254)

Council on Law-Related Studies, 246–47, 247, 248

Cravath, Paul D., 190, 229

Critical legal studies, 7, 366 (n. 130)

Cromwell, William Nelson, 189

Cultural understandings of law, 59, 63, 126–27, 134–35, 145, 219, 288 (n. 248)

Currie, Brainerd, 364 (n. 102), 365 (n. 123)

Davis, Kenneth Culp, 247

Dawson, John, 7

DeCapriles, Miguel, 245

Deming, Horace E., 81, 279 (n. 36)

Dennis, William L., 319 (n. 117)

Denver, University of, Law School, 249, 250

Depression, the, 10, 213, 216, 312 (n. 263)

Dession, George, 301 (n. 107), 359 (n. 24)

Dewey, John, 8–9, 10, 24–25, 39, 50, 57, 60, 61, 78, 81, 145, 169, 185, 198, 208, 209, 227, 264, 333 (n. 154), 362 (n. 66), 364 (n. 101); lectures at Columbia Law School, 24–25, 57–58, 68–69, 77, 78, 225, 231–32, 287 (nn. 217, 218)

Dicey, Albert Venn, 37

Dickens, Charles, 83

Dickinson, John, 3, 6, 19, 226, 227

Dissatisfaction with legal education, 159, 224, 365 (n. 123)

Diversity jurisdiction, 91; studied at the Institute of Law, 148, 166, 167, 172, 175, 177, 182, 183–84, 196, 344 (n. 325)

Divorce law, 174, 177, 202, 203–4

Dollard, John, 323 (n. 205)

Donovan, William J., 100, 101, 104

Douglas, William O., 5, 9, 17, 18, 19, 20, 80, 90, 143, 144, 147, 214, 215, 216, 217, 218, 219, 226, 228, 229, 237, 264, 297 (n. 58), 299 (n. 83), 305 (n. 151), 311 (n. 253), 359 (n. 24); later career, 20, 113; federal courts study, 87–89, 93; business failures project, 99–105, 215, 228, 306 (nn. 169, 172), 307 (n. 191), 311 (n. 253); testimony in Southern District of New York, 100–101; and progressive law reform, 111, 111–12, 114, 141, 229–30, 307 (n. 191); study of bondholder protection committees, 113; student work inspired by, 308 (n. 196), 310 (n. 252)

Douglass, Paul, 365 (n. 120)

Du Pont family, 187, 189

Eddington, Arthur S., 146

Ehrlich, Eugen, 235, 317 (n. 98), 366 (n. 126)

Ely, Richard T., 38

Empirical legal research, 8, 9, 10, 19, 224; after World War II, 10–11; usage defined, 21; Moore on, 59, 75, 125–26, 127, 134, 205, 206, 227, 231–34, 236, 237, 238, 254; Cook on, 60, 61, 64, 65–66, 67, 69–70, 76–77, 77, 78, 153, 158, 164, 170, 181–82, 196, 198, 205, 224–29, 232, 233, 238, 252, 254, 255, 257, 330 (n. 96), 356 (n. 538), 364 (nn. 101, 108), 374 (n. 258); Clark and Hutchins on, 83, 84–85; Connecticut courts study, 84–85, 96; federal courts study, 86–91; Clark's understanding of, 91–92, 96–98; problem of routine nature of inquiry, 92–93; and business failures project, 99–105; funding of, 114, 131, 213, 298 (n. 62), 312 (n. 263); by Moore, 115–41; reaction of most law professors to, 120, 144–45, 146, 175, 183, 198, 200, 204, 206, 209, 211, 234, 237–38, 324 (n. 220), 339 (nn. 253, 254, 256), 340 (nn. 257, 258, 259), 366 (n. 126); at Hopkins, 160–99; Oliphant on, 168–71, 196–98, 205, 227; Yntema on, 182–83, 186, 196, 205; reasons for expecting that it might prosper, 211–12; the Depression as a reason for its decline, 213, 312 (n. 263); personalities as a reason for its decline, 213–24; nature of the research enterprise as a reason for its decline, 224–38; similarity of results at both Hopkins and Yale, 233; and professional identity, 252–56. See also, Moore, W. Underhill: funding of his parking research

Empirical social science, 69, 110–11, 112, 168–70, 230

Equity, 40–42, 44, 46–47

Equity receiverships, 101, 102

Evolution, 56, 65

Faris, Elsworth, 110

Farm Credit Administration, 195

Federal Bureau of Investigation, 231

Federal Courts, Study of the Business of, 85–91, 172, 201, 202, 209, 214, 234, 295 (n. 46), 296 (nn. 47, 48, 49, 54), 298 (n. 62), 301 (n. 117), 302 (n. 121), 303 (n. 135); findings, 95, 96

Federal Rules of Civil Procedure, 113, 218

Field Code, 84

Flexner, Abraham, 151, 152, 153, 154, 156, 166, 206, 206–7, 264, 317 (n. 91)

Ford Foundation, 239, 242, 243, 244, 246, 247, 367 (n. 143)

Formalism, 24, 276 (n. 11). *See also* Classical legal thought; Legal science

Fortas, Abe, 19, 359 (n. 24)

Frank, Jerome N., 5, 19, 20, 122, 170, 185, 186, 195, 219, 235, 260, 264, 301 (n. 107), 353 (n. 485); *Law and the Modern Mind*, 18, 184–85

Frankfurter, Felix, 7, 8, 20, 183, 229, 265, 297 (n. 58), 320 (n. 151), 347 (n. 378), 350 (n. 442), 352 (n. 467); and federal courts study, 94, 96, 296 (n. 47); and Cleveland Crime Survey, 95–96; antagonism toward the Institute of Law, 175, 183, 198, 209, 339 (nn. 253, 254, 256), 340 (nn. 257, 259)

Freund, Ernst, 33–35, 36, 37, 39, 47, 265, 275 (n. 4), 334 (n. 164), 364 (n. 107)

Friedmann, Wolfgang, 4

Fuller, Lon, 3, 6, 7, 20, 226, 227

"Functional" curriculum, 15–16, 176, 328 (n. 70), 333 (n. 154)

Functions of law, basic, 333 (n. 154)

Funding for empirical legal research (1920s and 1930s), 114, 141, 213, 312 (n. 263)

Furniss, Edgar, 323 (n. 197)

Fustel de Coulanges, Numa Denis, 235

Galanter, Marc, 294 (n. 24)

Garlan, Edwin N., 3

Garrison, Lloyd K., 104

Gehlke, Charles E., 202, 356 (n. 536)

Gellhorn, Walter, 247

General Education Board, 151, 156, 293 (n. 18), 335 (n. 189)

German scholarship, ideal of, 27, 46, 256

Getman, Julius, 250

Giddings, Frank, 75, 110

Gilmore, Eugene, 281 (n. 93)

Gilmore, Grant, 256, 276 (n. 11)

Goebel, Julius, 275 (ch. 1, n. 2)

Goodnow, Frank J., 153, 155, 162, 166, 171, 207, 208, 265, 279 (n. 35), 328 (n. 53), 335 (n. 189)

Gordon, Robert W., 282 (n. 123), 292 (n. 314), 310 (n. 247), 311 (n. 260), 317 (n. 92), 356 (n. 540), 374 (n. 258)

Gray, John Chipman, 20, 27, 253

Great Curriculum Debate. See Columbia University Law School: curriculum study

Green, Leon, 18, 79, 265

Greenbaum, Edward S., 165, 172, 174, 177, 180, 222, 229, 265

Griswold, B. Howell, 162, 166, 188, 207, 265; founding of the Institute, 150–52, 153, 154, 155, 157, 200, 206, 208, 328 (n. 53); closing of the Institute, 191, 194, 199, 208, 209, 357 (nn. 549, 555)

Grubb, W. I., 296 (n. 48)

Haggard, Ernest A., 368 (n. 157)

Hale, Robert L., 16, 20, 265

Hall, James Parker, 39

Hamilton, Walton H., 19, 20, 218, 265, 311 (n. 259), 359 (n. 24), 360 (n. 49)

Hammond, Donald, 187, 357 (n. 549)

Hand, Learned, 90, 93, 96, 320 (n. 151)

Handler, Joel, 247

Harley, Herbert M., 231

Harper, William Rainey, 38

Harris, Silas, 231

Hart, Henry, 94, 301 (n. 117), 352 (n. 467)

Harvard Law School, 25, 26, 36, 39, 52, 93, 94, 96, 166, 175, 195, 199, 201, 239, 244, 276 (n. 12), 279

(n. 31), 297 (n. 59), 352 (n. 467); endowment drive, 16, 17; Harvard Law Review, 58; Russell Sage grant to, 249, 250. See also Walter E. Meyer Research Institute of Law

Hebrew University, 244

Heinz, John, 250

Hillary rules, 84

Hitchman Coal and Coke v. Mitchell, 54–55, 55

Hohfeld, Wesley N., 6, 8, 24, 40, 42, 43, 44, 50–51, 53, 55, 68, 265, 287 (n. 209), 362 (n. 66), 365 (n. 123); "Relations between Law and Equity," 42, 47, 52; "A Vital School of Law and Jurisprudence," 43, 45–46, 51–52, 53, 74–75, 76, 77, 80, 154, 158, 282 (n. 123), 292 (n. 314), 365 (n. 123); "Fundamental Legal Conceptions," 43, 46–47, 48–49, 52, 54–55, 73, 182, 228, 256, 283 (nn. 128, 140), 284 (n. 141), 288 (n. 196); death, 52

Hollander, Jacob Harry, 191, 208, 265

Hollinger, David, 292 (n. 312)

Holmes, Oliver Wendell, Jr., 20, 31, 49, 55, 57, 61, 62, 185, 186, 227, 232, 320 (n. 151), 330 (n. 86), 345 (n. 353), 364 (n. 107)

Hoover, Herbert, 86, 87, 90, 104, 211, 214

Hope, Theodore S., 115, 143, 265

Horwitz, Morton J., 7, 8

Howard, Samuel F., 275 (ch. 1, n. 2), 365 (n. 123)

Howland, Charles P., 209, 340 (n. 259)

Huberich, Charles H., 275 (n. 4)

Hughes, Charles Evans, 81

Hull, Clark, 120, 136, 140, 143, 144, 146, 217, 219, 265, 322 (n. 189)

Hurst, Willard, 158; advice to the Meyer Trustees, 244–45, 248, 251

Hutchins, Robert M., 90, 106, 209, 229, 237, 238, 239, 299 (n. 83); at Yale, 17, 18, 19, 82, 83, 84, 85, 98, 105, 115, 116, 117, 142, 147, 148, 206, 265, 293 (n. 18), 294 (n. 20); personality and style, 214

Hyman, Jacob D., 359 (n. 30)

Illinois, University of, Law School, 181
Inanni, Elizabeth Reuss, 250
Inanni, Francis A. J., 250
Institute of Human Relations. *See* Yale University: Institute of Human Relations
Institute of Law, 10, 18, 19, 65–66, 94, 115, 140, 226, 227, 238, 255; founding, 147–48, 150–60, 328 (nn. 56, 70), 330 (n. 86), 332 (n. 127); installment sales project, 148, 149, 343 (n. 305); study of diversity jurisdiction, 148, 166, 167, 172, 175, 177, 182, 183–84, 196, 344 (n. 325); relationship with the Rockefeller philanthropies, 148–49, 151, 156, 166–67, 167, 168, 187, 188, 189, 190, 192, 206–7, 209, 220; necessity of developing a program for, 149; need for support from Johns Hopkins, 149; need for support from the general university community, 149, 209; fundraising, 150–51, 156, 157, 160, 166–67, 187–89, 345 (n. 357), 346 (n. 365), 347 (n. 382); plans for research, 154, 158, 164, 167, 171; terms of faculty appointments, 157; governance of, 157, 165, 192, 343 (n. 300); finances of, 157, 187–89, 189–90, 192, 199, 199–200, 213, 332 (n. 127), 348 (n. 399); limits inherent in the faculty's education and training, 159, 164; budgets of, 159–60, 165, 167, 188, 190, 200, 346 (n. 374), 348 (n. 399); style of administration at, 160, 181, 222, 343 (n. 296); creating a program for, 160–62, 239; survey of legal research, 161, 168, 175, 182; slogans at the root of the program, 161–62, 205–6; initial program, 162–64; faculty's lack of known interest in empirical research projects proposed and bias toward library research, 164; initial projects, 164, 167, 171–72; Conference on Studies in the Administration of Justice, 174–76; law school hostility toward, 175, 183, 198, 209, 340 (n. 258);

and progressive law reform, 178–81, 222, 223, 229, 230–31; plan for associates, 187; closing of, 190–95, 349 (n. 415), 350 (n. 435), 351 (nn. 450, 452); Hopkins' faculty hostility toward, 191, 193–94, 207–8, 351 (n. 452); publications of, 192, 195, 200–205; reasons for demise of, 199–209; evaluation of work product of, 200–205; results of the disorder of program, 206–9; personality and style of faculty as cause of decline, 219–24; ultimate failure to develop a program, 222–23. *See also* Diversity jurisdiction; Johns Hopkins University; Study of Civil Justice in New York; Study of the Judicial System of Maryland; Study of the Judicial System of Ohio
Institutional basis of social life, 59, 63
Intellectual history, 4–5, 11–13, 259–61, 318 (n. 110), 353 (n. 154)

Jacobs, Albert C., 315 (n. 59)
Jaffe, Louis, 7
Jaffin, George M., 190, 266, 345 (n. 353), 357 (n. 559); work on study of the diversity jurisdiction, 166, 167, 172, 173, 177, 178, 182, 186; work on the Study of the Judicial System of Ohio, 173, 177, 178; work on the Study of the Judicial System of Maryland, 174, 177, 178
James, Fleming, Jr., 299 (n. 88)
Jervey, Huger W., 16, 17, 266
John Price Jones Corporation, 164, 187
Johns Hopkins University, 10, 18, 64, 146, 150–51, 156, 157, 158, 159–60, 164, 165, 166, 167, 171, 187, 188, 192, 193, 199, 206, 207, 212, 220, 223, 238, 331 (n. 118), 335 (nn. 188, 189); Philosophical Faculty, 10, 156, 171, 191, 194, 206, 207–9, 213, 223, 335 (n. 189), 351 (n. 452), 356 (n. 545); Department of Political Science, 151, 191; Medical School, 152, 155, 157, 191, 207; financial position in the Depression, 188, 189–90, 191, 199–200, 347 (n. 397).

Faculty Academic Council, 191, 349 (n. 415), 356 (n. 545). *See* Institute of Law

Johnson, Earl, 250

Judicial administration, 165, 173, 231, 238, 365 (n. 120). *See also* Judicial statistics

Judicial decision making, 3–4, 5–6, 18–19, 62–63, 65–66, 121–22, 168–70, 184–86, 232–33, 321 (n. 173), 329 (n. 76), 361 (n. 57), 364 (n. 103)

Judicial legislation, 55

Judicial statistics, 175, 176, 177, 193, 204; leads into project on criminal statistics, 193. *See also* Judicial administration

Jural relations, 24, 48–49

Jurisprudence and Social Policy Program of University of California, Berkeley, Law School, 249

Jury Project. *See* Chicago, University of, Law School: Jury Project

Kalman, Laura, 7, 8, 286 (n. 204)

Kalven, Harry, 240, 251, 255, 266, 371 (n. 196), 373 (n. 240)

Kansas, University of, 29; Law School, 30, 38, 39

Keener, William, 25–26

Keeton, Robert E., 247

Keller, A. G., 76, 303 (n. 138)

Kelley, Florence, 81

Kennedy, Duncan, 273 (n. 34)

Kennedy, Walter B., 3

Kessler, Friedrich, 145, 237, 366 (n. 132)

Keyser, C. J., 289 (n. 256)

Klaus, Samuel, 288 (n. 240)

Kocourek, Albert, 58, 133, 266

Konefsky, Fred, 12, 222, 303 (n. 135), 323 (n. 200), 357 (n. 546)

Kroeber, Alfred L., 289 (n. 256)

Kuh, Richard, 247

Kurland, Philip B., 240

Labor law, 54–56, 182

LaFollette, Robert M., 38

Landis, James, 7, 20

Langdell, Christopher Columbus, 20, 32, 36, 45, 62, 65, 146, 170, 224, 235, 252, 275 (nn. 11, 12, 13); teaching law from cases, 25, 26, 50, 253, 275 (n. 13); on equity, 42, 44, 47

La Salle Extension University, 282 (n. 103)

Lasswell, Harold D., 110, 238

Laumann, Edward O., 250

Laura Spellman Rockefeller Memorial Foundation, 86, 151

Law and Behavioral Science Program, 238–44; initial program application, 239; first funded application, 239–40, 367 (n. 143); directors of Jury Project listed, 240; Jury Project, 240, 240–41, 243, 369 (n. 172), 369 (nn. 173, 175); commercial arbitration project, 240, 241, 243, 369 (n. 175); funding, 240, 242; income tax project, 240, 242, 243; second program application, 241–42, 243, 368 (n. 168); major publications, 242; work with Temporary Commission on the Courts in New York, 242, 244; evaluation, 242–44; *The American Jury*, 243; fellowship program, 243–44, 370 (n. 186)

Law and custom. *See* Cultural understandings of law

Law and economics, 363 (n. 100)

Law and Society Association, 251, 251–52; early history tied to Russell Sage Foundation, 374 (n. 254)

Law and Society Review, 251

Law-in-action, 160, 162, 181, 229, 233, 234, 333 (n. 150), 365 (n. 125). *See also* Pound, Roscoe: sociological jurisprudence (interest analysis)

Law professors, 11, 12; teaching loads of, 28, 30, 35, 280 (nn. 55, 56), 281 (nn. 91, 96)

Law schools: resources of early schools, 27; admissions standards, 30

Lawson, John D., 30

Legal education, history of, 11

Legal history, 235, 293 (n. 326)

Legal method. *See* Adler, Mortimer; Classical legal thought; Cohen,

Morris R.; Cook, Walter Wheeler:
  on legal (scientific) method; Legal
  science
Legal process, 8
Legal profession: attitude toward
  empirical legal research, 212–13
Legal scholarship: at small midwestern
  schools, 30
Legal science, 1, 8, 9, 30–35, 36–37,
  42–43, 43–45, 50, 73, 78, 146,
  226–27, 232, 253, 364 (n. 107)
Lemann, Monte, 94, 96, 266, 296
  (n. 48)
Levi, Edward H., 239, 240, 241, 244,
  266, 367 (n. 143), 368 (n. 168)
Levine, Felice, 374 (n. 256)
Lewis, Shippen, 105, 106, 107, 108,
  109, 266
Lewis, William Draper, 94, 266, 330
  (n. 86)
Llewellyn, Karl N., 2–3, 4, 5, 16, 18,
  19, 20, 21, 52, 62, 69, 83, 110, 119,
  170, 184, 186, 225, 226, 255, 256,
  266, 347 (n. 378), 353 (n. 485), 366
  (n. 126); significance of being left
  behind at Columbia, 6; *The Bramble
  Bush*, 18; response to Moore's
  research, 120, 146, 211, 237;
  response to Hopkins' research, 200,
  204, 206, 211, 234; at Chicago, 239
Logic: Dewey on, 58
Logical positivism (Vienna Circle), 134,
  136, 205, 320 (n. 154). *See also*
  Behaviorism
Lorenzen, Ernest, 153, 237, 255, 328
  (n. 52), 360 (n. 49), 365 (n. 123)
Lovejoy, Arthur O., 191, 194, 208,
  266, 352 (n. 463), 362 (n. 65)
Lowenthal, Max, 296 (n. 47)
Lowie, Robert, 317 (n. 91)
Lucey, Francis E., 3

Macaulay, Stewart, 248
McDougal, Myres S., 238, 245
Mach, Ernst, 60
Maine, Henry, 235
Maitland, Frederic W., 42, 44
Malinowski, Bronislaw, 145, 317
  (n. 91), 325 (n. 229)

Marshall, Carrington T., 165
Marshall, J. Howard, 359 (n. 24)
Marshall, Leon C., 10, 16, 18, 67,
  149, 157, 159, 188, 193, 199, 200,
  208, 221, 222, 223, 238, 266, 325
  (n. 15), 328 (nn. 56, 69); work on
  Study of the Judicial System of Ohio,
  149, 165, 173, 177, 178, 182, 192,
  193, 199, 201, 202, 222–23, 223; at
  the Institute of Law, 160, 161, 182,
  189, 325 (n. 15), 328 (n. 70); administrative style, 160, 181, 192–93,
  198, 220–21, 223, 332 (n. 128);
  writes early fundraising material,
  160–61; interest in management
  problems in large business organizations, 161, 164, 184, 206, 222; interest in preparing teaching materials,
  164; initial research plans, 165, 167,
  206; and judicial administration,
  165, 173, 204, 231, 238; work on
  the Study of the Judicial System of
  Maryland, 174; defends the Institute's program, 175–76; serves as
  Institute's secretary, 177, 178; serves
  as Institute's director, 190, 192, 192–
  93, 221, 223; publications, 195–96,
  201, 202; later career, 199; on Cook,
  220; personality and style, 220–21
Maryland Public Service Commission,
  203
Mason, Max, 149, 223, 266
Matza, David, 287 (n. 215)
May, Geoffrey, 202
May, Mark A., 318 (n. 108)
Mead, George Herbert, 39
Mechem, Philip, 3
Medina, Harold, 297 (n. 59)
Meecham, Floyd, 281 (n. 97)
Mellon, Andrew, 189, 190, 200
Meltzer, Bernard, 240
Mentschikoff, Soia, 240, 243, 266, 368
  (n. 157)
Merriam, Charles E., 39, 110, 237
Merton, Robert K., 238
Michael, Jerome, 122, 196, 353
  (n. 485)
Michigan, University of, Law School,
  195, 199

Mill, J. S., 58, 65
Missouri, University of, 29; Law
 School, 30, 35, 38, 39
Mitchell, Wesley C., 50, 75, 110
Modern Legal Philosophy Series,
 23–24, 58
Momsen, Theodor, 235
Moore, John Bassett, 279 (n. 35)
Moore, Thomas S., 28
Moore, W. Underhill, 5, 6, 8–9, 9–10,
 11, 15, 16, 17, 18, 19, 20, 25, 27,
 36, 50, 57, 68, 71, 76, 78, 109, 110,
 113, 114, 147–48, 157, 209, 224,
 227, 234, 252, 253, 255, 257, 259,
 267, 276 (n. 11), 278 (n. 21), 364
 (n. 108), 366 (n. 126); at Columbia,
 23, 50, 53, 62, 67, 68, 72, 73–74,
 75, 78, 114, 115, 147–48, 305
 (n. 151); reaction to Dewey's lectures
 (review of Wigmore, *Rational Basis
 of Legal Institutions*), 25, 58–59, 61,
 62, 74, 77, 80, 121, 134, 145, 219,
 287 (n. 215), 292 (n. 311); family
 background, 28; practice experience,
 28, 68, 70; education at Columbia,
 28, 72, 144; at Kansas, 30, 38, 72,
 281 (n. 88); professional identity as
 law professor, 36–37, 72, 73, 73–75,
 79; at Chicago, 38, 39, 50, 67, 72,
 73; at Wisconsin, 38, 39, 67, 72, 73;
 at Dewey's 1922 lectures, 57, 58, 69;
 "institutional method," 59, 63–64,
 115, 118, 119–20, 120–21, 143, 289
 (nn. 251, 253, 255, 256); views on
 empirical social science, 59, 75, 124–
 26, 127, 134–36, 205, 206, 227,
 231–34, 236, 237, 238, 254; views
 on other kinds of legal theory or
 legal scholarship, 59, 121–22, 134,
 137, 321 (n. 173), 361 (n. 57); and
 anthropology, 59, 126–27, 134–35,
 145, 219; and psychology, 59, 134–
 35, 138–39, 145; early attempts at
 empirical work, 62; at Yale, 64, 72,
 115, 142, 143–44, 144, 145, 146,
 217–18, 237–38; banking studies,
 64, 115–24, 124, 126–27, 232, 234,
 235; parking and traffic studies, 64,
 128–41, 232, 234, 235, 238, 318

(n. 105), 319 (n. 133); similarity of
 background to Cook's, 67–68; personality and style, 68, 72, 78, 80,
 145, 216–19, 224, 290 (nn. 268,
 269); differences from Cook, 68, 72–
 80; methodology of studies, 115–16,
 120–21, 126–28, 128, 129–30, 130,
 131–32, 134–36, 137, 314 (n. 45);
 relationship with Clark, 117, 131,
 215, 217, 359 (n. 29), 360 (n. 46);
 and Institute of Human Relations,
 119, 121, 128, 131, 142–44, 145,
 213, 214, 217, 218; "The Lawyer's
 Law," 121–22, 125, 314 (n. 54);
 methodological sophistication,
 124–25, 126, 219, 314 (n. 45), 360
 (n. 56); reasons for terminating
 banking studies, 124–28, 317
 (n. 98); view of self as adhering to
 behaviorism, etc., 125, 127, 134,
 136, 320 (n. 154); relationship with
 Thomas and Corstvet, 125–26, 217,
 316 (n. 83); professional identity as
 social scientist, 127–28, 142, 144–
 46, 218–19, 254, 317 (n. 91), 375
 (n. 270); funding of his parking
 research, 131, 132, 133, 141, 145,
 200, 213; *My Philosophy of Law*,
 133–36, 144, 217; responses to *My
 Philosophy of Law*, 136; "Law and
 Learning Theory," 137–40, 254;
 social scientists reaction to, 142–44,
 322 (n. 189), 323 (nn. 197, 205);
 adverse views of his work in the law
 schools, 144–45, 146, 237–38, 324
 (n. 220); defects in his understanding
 of his research, 218–19; courses
 taught, 280 (n. 55), 281 (nn. 92, 96);
 research assistants, 288 (n. 240), 319
 (n. 117); and recipients of reprints of
 banking articles, 317 (n. 91); vision
 of legal education, 365 (n. 123)
Morawetz, Victor, 150, 152, 153,
 154, 155, 156, 158, 159, 267, 327
 (nn. 46, 47), 328 (n. 49), 329 (n. 73)
Morgan, Edmund M., Jr., 94, 234,
 267, 302 (n. 121), 303 (n. 136), 365
 (n. 123)
Morgan, J. P., 150

Morgenthau, Henry, 195, 199
Morris, Norval, 243
Muller v. Oregon, 81

Narrative theory, 13
Nation, 81
National Commission on Law
    Observance and Enforcement. *See*
    Wickersham Commission
National Crime Commission, 84
National Bureau of Economic
    Research, 221
National Institutes of Health, 248
National Recovery Administration, 199
National Science Foundation, 251, 255,
    256
Nebraska, University of, 29, 279
    (n. 44); American History and
    Jurisprudence, Department of, 28,
    35, 280 (n. 75); Law School, 35, 39
Nelles, Walter, 235
Newhouse, Wade J., 363 (n. 94)
New Republic, 76, 81
New School for Social Research, 181,
    284 (n. 148)
New York Chamber of Commerce, 178
New York Industrial Commission, 81
New York Law Society, 193, 198, 299
    (n. 88)
New York Stock Exchange, 241
New York University Law School, 244,
    245
Non-Euclidian geometry, 65
Northrup, F. S. C., 317 (n. 98)
Northwestern University Law School,
    39, 41, 193, 199, 277 (n. 17); Rus-
    sell Sage grants to, 249, 250, 372
    (n. 229); graduates of the J.D.-Ph.D.
    program, 373 (n. 243)

O'Connell, Jeffrey, 247
Ogburn, William F., 50, 110, 237
Ohio Bar Association, 173
Ohlin, Lloyd E., 249
Oliphant, Herman, 5, 6, 10, 18, 19, 20,
    57, 62, 67, 78, 115, 122, 148, 149,
    156, 168, 171, 176, 181, 184, 185,
    186, 188, 190, 191, 192, 193, 195,
    206, 209, 222, 223, 226, 227, 228,

229, 267, 299 (n. 88), 325 (n. 15),
    328 (nn. 56, 70), 344 (n. 311),
    365 (n. 123); at Columbia, 15–16,
    17, 23, 147, 161; functional curricu-
    lum, 15–16, 176, 328 (n. 70), 333
    (n. 154); founding of the Institute of
    Law, 67, 147–48, 157, 328 (n. 70),
    364 (n. 108); community of scholars
    ideal, 147, 149, 158, 343 (n. 300);
    work on Study of Civil Justice in
    New York, 149, 165, 172, 173, 174,
    175, 177, 178–81, 188, 189, 190,
    192, 193, 198, 201, 222, 228, 230–
    31, 337 (n. 229); lists of projects,
    161, 167–68, 182, 221, 222; at the
    Institute of Law, 161, 182, 196; cri-
    tique of Institute's program, 161–
    62, 167, 181, 205, 221, 222, 333
    (n. 150); interest in preparing teach-
    ing materials, 164, 165, 167; trade
    regulation, 164, 165, 167; initial
    research plans, 165, 166, 167; pref-
    ace to *From the Physical to the Social
    Sciences*, 168–70, 230; on empirical
    legal research, 170–71, 171, 196–98,
    205, 222, 227; and progressive law
    reform, 178–81, 222, 223, 229,
    230–31; explains the Study of Civil
    Justice in New York, 178–81, 228;
    labor law, 182, 344 (n. 311); serves
    as Institute's secretary, 189; resigns
    from the Institute, 193, 195; later
    career, 195, 199; personality and
    style, 221–22, 223, 224
Operationalism, 134, 136, 205, 320
    (n. 154). *See also* Behaviorism; Logi-
    cal positivism
Order of the Coif, 72–73
Oregon, University of, 29

Park, Robert E., 110, 317 (n. 91)
Parking studies, 64, 128–41, 232, 234,
    235, 238; origin, 128; traffic circle
    study, 128–29, methodology under-
    lying, 129, 129–30, 130, 131–32,
    134–36, 137, 318 (n. 105); results,
    129, 132; tagging study, 132
Parsons, Talcott, 238
Patterson, Edwin W., 4, 324 (n. 220)

Pennsylvania, University of, Law School, 249, 372 (n. 233)
Philippines, 32–33, 37, 43
Pitney, Mahlon, 54, 55
Poincare, Henri, 60
Policy analysis, 256
Pomeroy, John Norton, 25
Pound, Roscoe, 2–3, 6, 7, 8, 18, 20, 24, 35, 40, 41, 52, 56, 68, 81, 83, 86, 89, 119, 184, 186, 188, 195, 198, 226, 267, 275 (n. 4), 280 (n. 78), 284 (n. 155), 293 (n. 326), 297 (n. 58), 350 (n. 442), 357 (n. 559); sociological jurisprudence (interest analysis), 5, 24, 53–54, 56, 76, 77, 82, 162, 186, 229, 233, 234, 256, 295 (n. 32), 365 (n. 125); relationship with Cook, 35, 56, 186, 193, 195, 280 (n. 78), 288 (n. 204), 345 (n. 351); in Department of American History and Jurisprudence at Nebraska, 35, 280 (n. 75)
Powell, Thomas Reed, 15, 23, 74, 267
Pragmatic logic. See Cook, Walter Wheeler: on legal (scientific) method; Dewey, John: lectures at Columbia Law School
Pragmatism, 24, 205
Prediction of judicial decisions, 61, 62–63, 121–22
Professional identity, 11, 79, 252–56
Professionalization, 70–71
Professionalization in law teaching, 26–27, 36–37, 252–54; support for, 26, 36; nature of professional role or vocation, 26–27, 36–37, 44–46, 74–75, 79, 278 (n. 28), 279 (n. 31); and appropriate scholarship, 226–28, 254–56; change in role, 256
Professionalization in social science, 37, 142–43, 323 (n. 199)
Progressive law reform: and the Yale courts studies, 9, 92–93, 93–98, 229–30, 303 (n. 136); conflict with the values of the emerging social sciences, 9, 93–98, 110–14; and the auto accidents study, 9, 110–11; and the business failures project, 9, 111, 111–12, 141, 229–30, 307 (n. 191);

projects, 81, 82, 244; as a style of politics, 81–82, 114, 141, 158, 206, 212, 226, 238, 365 (n. 120); intellectual elements of the style, 83, 84, 97; and the Study of Civil Justice in New York, 178–81, 222, 223, 229, 230–31; role in legal scholarship, 229–31
Progressivism, 20, 234
Prohibition, 86, 88
Psychological understandings of law, 59, 134–35, 138–39, 145, 219
Purcell, Edward, 5–6, 7, 8

Realism. See American Legal Realism
Realist Controversy, 2–3, 18–19, 92, 119, 184–86, 314 (n. 39)
Research funding. See Funding for empirical research (1920s and 1930s)
Reuschlein, Harold G., 4
Rice, Stuart, 317 (n. 91)
Richards, Harry S., 26, 39
Ritter, Paul O., 305 (n. 153)
Roberts, Owen, 94
Robinson, Edward S., 235, 267, 301 (n. 107); Law and the Lawyers, 19
Robinson, James Harvey, 50, 78, 145, 235, 293 (n. 326)
Rockefeller Foundation, 90, 106, 108, 148, 149, 166–67, 167, 168, 187, 188, 189, 190, 192, 206–7, 209, 220, 335 (nn. 188, 189)
Rodell, Fred, 218, 267
Rodgers, Henry Wade, 50, 51
Roosevelt, Franklin D., 174, 230
Root, Elihu, 156, 158, 267, 330 (n. 86)
Rose, Wickliff, 151, 156, 267
Rosenberg, Maurice, 248
Rosenblum, Victor, 250
Rosenthal, Douglas, 250
Ross, Edward A., 38, 318 (n. 110)
Ross, H. Lawrence, 248
Rostow, Eugene, 136, 140, 244, 245, 246, 267
Rueff, Jacques, 168, 196, 337 (n. 207)
Rumble, Wilfred E., Jr., 5, 7, 8
Russell Sage Foundation, 10, 202, 248–51, 252, 255; funds dispensed, 248, 249; law school grants, 248–49, 249–50; and history of Law and

Social Science program, 248–49, 250–51, 374 (n. 252); grants made in tandem with Meyer Institute, 249; fellowship program, 249, 250; research grants program, 249, 250; evaluation, 249–51; creation of Law and Society Association, 251, 374 (n. 254); program as foundation for Law and Social Science program of the Nation Science Foundation, 251; SSMILE, 252; recipients of fellowships, 373 (n. 244)

Samenow, Charles U., 87, 88, 89, 90, 93, 159, 268, 296 (n. 53), 298 (n. 82), 299 (n. 88), 367 (n. 138)
Schofield, Henry W., 41, 44, 268, 282 (n. 110)
Scientific management, 212
Scientific method. See Cook, Walter Wheeler: on legal (scientific) method; Moore, W. Underhill: views on empirical social science; Oliphant, Herman: on empirical legal research; Yntema, Hessel: on empirical legal research
Scott, Austin W., 362 (n. 65)
Seavey, Warren, 7
Shamos, Abraham, 288 (n. 240)
Shanks, Carrol, 305 (n. 151)
Sharp, F. C., 38
Shils, Edward, 240
Shulman, Harry, 359 (n. 24)
Simon, Rita James, 243, 268
Skolnik, Jerome, 248
Slessinger, Donald, 323 (n. 198)
Small, Albion, 110
Smith, Howard L., 281 (n. 93)
Smith, Monroe, 279 (n. 35)
Smith, Young B., 16, 17, 99, 147, 221, 268
Social control, 129–30, 160, 161, 233, 234, 318 (n. 110)
Social policy, 53–54, 256
Social Science Research Council, 100, 156, 188, 238, 297 (n. 58), 347 (n. 378); Social Science and Law Committee, 247
Social sciences, development of, 1, 9,

16, 82, 91, 110, 113, 125, 212, 237, 334 (n. 154), 356 (n. 536), 358 (n. 10); and conflict with values of progressive law reform, 93–98, 110–14; Moore's exposure to method in the, 124–26; and development of statistical technique, 295 (n. 36), 303 (n. 140), 314 (n. 42), 340 (n. 258)
Social survey, 82
Sociological jurisprudence. See Law-in-action; Pound, Roscoe: sociological jurisprudence (interest analysis)
Sorokin, Petirim, 317 (n. 91)
Southern District of New York, United States District Court for the, 100; bankruptcy scandal in, 100–101
Spencer, Herbert, 236
SSMILE (Social Science Methods in Legal Education), 252
Stanford Law School, 40, 41, 46, 53, 276 (n. 17); Russell Sage grant to, 249
Statistics, interest in, 212, 303 (n. 140)
Steffen, Roscoe Turner, 360 (n. 49)
Steinfeld, Robert, 286 (n. 196)
Stevens, Robert, 6
Stone, Harlan F., 15–16, 23, 50, 62, 152, 153, 158, 268, 330 (n. 86)
Story, Joseph, 61
Strodtbeck, Fred, 240
Strong, Frank R., 29
Study of Civil Justice in New York, 10, 67, 148, 149, 172, 174, 175, 188, 189, 190, 193, 206; origins, 165; early work on, 172–73, 174; studies contemplated, 177, 349 (n. 407); data collected for, 178, 349 (n. 407); explained by Oliphant, 178–81, 337 (n. 229), 342 (n. 285); moves to New York Law Society, 193, 198; publications, 195, 201
Study of the Judicial System of Maryland, 10, 67, 148, 149, 174, 178, 189, 192, 194, 198, 199, 200, 220; studies contemplated, 174, 177, 342 (n. 275); early work on, 174, 177, 349 (n. 407); origin, 174, 338 (nn. 239, 241); structure, 176, 177; publications, 195, 201, 202, 203,

204, 362 (n. 67); results, 200–201, 202–3, 203–4; on divorce law, 201, 202, 203

Study of the Judicial System of Ohio, 10, 67, 148, 149, 172, 178, 182, 189, 192, 193, 198, 199, 200, 231; origins, 165, 222–23, 223, 336 (n. 198); early work on, 173, 175, 177; data collected, 173, 177, 193, 342 (n. 281); structure, 176, 177; studies contemplated, 177, 241 (n. 272), 342 (n. 275); publications, 195, 199, 201, 202–3, 203, 203–4, 204, 355 (nn. 524, 525, 527), 356 (n. 537); results, 200–201, 202; on divorce law, 203–4

Sturges, Wesley, 5, 19, 20, 112, 216, 218, 268, 359 (n. 24), 360 (n. 49)

Sumner, William Graham, 50, 76, 236, 303 (n. 138), 324 (n. 222)

Sunshine Commission, 81

Sussman, Gilbert, 115, 116, 117, 118, 119, 120, 268, 324 (n. 225)

Swan, Thomas W., 17, 51, 82, 268, 365 (n. 123)

Syllogistic reasoning, 61, 68–69; in law, 65, 65–66, 184, 185, 186, 329 (n. 76), 364 (n. 103). See also Adler, Mortimer; Classical legal thought; Cohen, Morris R.; Cook, Walter Wheeler: on legal (scientific) method; Legal science

Temporary Commission on the Courts in New York, 242

Thatcher, Thomas D., 100, 101, 103, 105, 307 (n. 191)

Thayer, James Bradley, 32, 235, 253; on professional role, 27, 73, 74, 75

Theory and practice, 364 (n. 106)

Thomas, Dorothy Swaine, 9, 98–99, 107, 109, 110, 111, 173, 198, 268, 304 (n. 142); early career, 98, 310 (n. 247), works with Douglas, 102–5, 143, 215, 306 (n. 169); later career, 110, 309 (n. 235); as a social scientist, 112, 113, 113–14, 230, 238; works with Moore, 118, 120,

125, 126, 127, 143, 217, 316 (n. 83), 324 (n. 220)

Thomas, William I., 38, 304 (n. 142)

Thorndike, E. L., 50, 75, 110

Thurston, Edward S., 365 (n. 123)

Timasheff, Nicholas S., 145, 325 (n. 230)

Trade regulation, 164, 165, 167

Traffic studies. See Parking studies

Tulin, Leon A., 293 (n. 19)

Turner, Frederick Jackson, 38

Twining, William, 6, 8, 365 (n. 123)

Underhill, Abraham, 28

United States Bureau of the Census, 231

United States Department of Commerce, 100, 101, 104, 211, 221, 306 (n. 179), 307 (n. 195)

United States Department of the Treasury, 199

United States Sanitary Commission, 81

United States Steel Corporation, 150

Universities: conditions at in early twentieth century, 29, 276 (n. 12); development in the twenties and thirties, 213, 237; limited interest in empirical legal research, 236–37

University law school, the ideal of the, 74–75, 84

Vance, William Reynolds, 237, 255, 360 (n. 49), 365 (n. 123)

Van Hise, Charles R., 38

Veblen, Thorstein, 38, 50, 63, 74, 78, 145, 170, 209, 284 (n. 148)

Vegelahn v. Guntner, 57

Vincent, George E., 206, 268

Vinogradoff, Paul, 235

Walter E. Meyer Research Institute of Law, 10, 244–48, 248, 249, 251, 252, 255; origins, 244; initial program, 244–45, 370 (nn. 193, 194), 371 (nn. 196, 198); program refocused, 245; grants made, 245, 246, 247, 247–48; finances, 245–46, 247; grants to law schools, 246; program refocused again, 246–47; Council on

Law-Related Studies, 246–47, 247, 248; evaluation of, 247–48; grants made in tandem with Russell Sage Foundation, 249

Warner, Sam Bass, 94, 96, 268, 340 (n. 258)

Weber, Max, 235, 236, 238, 366 (n. 126)

Wheeler, Stanton, 249, 372 (n. 225)

Wickersham, George, 86, 89–90, 90, 90–91, 96, 209, 213, 226, 229, 268

Wickersham Commission, 9, 86, 87, 88, 182, 214, 231, 296 (n. 47), 298 (n. 62); membership, 86, 295 (n. 45)

Wigmore, John Henry, 26, 27, 39, 40, 58, 62, 133, 256, 269, 275 (n. 4), 276 (n. 17)

Willard, Daniel, 155, 157, 158, 166, 188, 190, 191, 193, 194, 207, 208, 269, 335 (n. 189), 349 (n. 415)

Williston, Samuel, 27, 40, 48–49, 53, 79, 256, 269, 283 (nn. 138, 140), 284 (n. 141)

Willoughby, W. W., 151–52, 153, 154, 159, 191, 195, 208, 269, 328 (n. 53)

Winternitz, Milton C., 303 (n. 137)

Wisconsin, University of, 38, 76; Law School, 26, 39, 67, 248, 255; Russell Sage grants to Law School, 248–49, 249–50, 251, 372 (n. 227); Department of Sociology, 250

Yale University, 50, 75–76, 82, 106, 120, 131, 144, 146, 149, 156, 206, 212, 292 (n. 313), 303 (n. 138); Institute of Human Relations, 10, 98, 101, 109, 114, 115, 119, 121, 128, 131, 136, 142–44, 145, 148, 149, 213, 214; impact of the Depression on, 131

Yale University Law School, 6, 7, 17, 23, 50–51, 52, 53, 64, 67, 82–83, 83, 109, 115, 133, 136, 142, 144, 153, 154, 166, 214, 216, 217, 218, 226, 230, 239, 244, 246, 248, 257, 297 (n. 59), 365 (n. 123); *Yale Law Journal*, 26, 51, 53, 56, 140, 310 (n. 237); fundraising for the "Yale School of Law and Jurisprudence," 51–52; Yale-Harvard law and business joint degree program, 113, 299 (n. 83), 311 (n. 253); Russell Sage grants to, 249, 250

Yntema, Hessel, 10, 18, 149, 157, 159, 174, 181, 184, 186, 188, 193, 195, 198, 222, 245, 252, 269, 297 (n. 58), 345 (n. 351), 346 (n. 365), 357 (n. 559), 364 (n. 108); comments on "Law and Learning Theory," 140; on empirical legal research, 140, 182–83, 196, 198, 205; at Institute of Law, 161, 182; interest in preparing teaching materials, 164; initial research plans, 165, 167; work on Jaffin's diversity jurisdiction research, 167, 172, 196, 205; work on Study of Judicial System of Ohio, 173, 196, 223, 231, 363 (n. 97); defends the Institute's program, 175, 176, 186; defends the study of the diversity jurisdiction, 183–84; participates in the Realist Controversy, 184, 186; serves and Institute's secretary, 192; resigns from the Institute, 193; later career, 198, 199; on findings of Institute's research program, 200–201; advice to the Meyer Trustees, 245

Zeisel, Hans, 240, 243, 255, 269, 370 (n. 182)

Zimring, Frank, 370 (n. 182), 373 (n. 240)